Eastern and Western Perspectives on Therapy and Healing

Dr. Monalisa Nayak

notionpress
.com
INDIA • SINGAPORE • MALAYSIA

ISBN 979-8-89699-651-4

Contents

Western Perspectives

Preface

Psychology has experienced rapid development in the last few decades by research, technological advancement, and human behavior understanding. A rise in mental health problems dominating our lives has a need for new approaches toward therapy. The book Emerging Psychotherapies in the Field of Psychology explores innovative and transformative therapies that are building the future of psychological care.

It's on these observations, having experienced life as a student, a practitioner, and just being interested in psychology that inspired this book. Of course, classic therapies like psychoanalysis, cognitive-behavioral therapy, or humanism are essential. Still, the more innovative models are continually moving beyond and providing novel, effective strategies for recovery. Consider the possibilities in mindfulness-based therapies, neurofeedback, virtual reality exposure therapy-these, of course, just open a door. Still, though, an accessible repository for consolidation and discussion of these therapies was needed-an objective I try to address in this book.

Each chapter represents a distinct approach, with a discussion of its theoretical underpinnings, practical applications, case studies, and populations served. There has been an effort to take complex ideas and present them in an accessible way, making this resource suitable for students, professionals, and anyone interested in the dynamic evolution of psychology.

This book is intended for students of psychology, aspiring therapists, and other mental health professionals seeking broader horizons. It can also be a good resource for researchers who would like to explore some innovative therapeutic techniques.

I would like to thank all the mentors, teachers, students and peers who have impacted my perception of psychology. Their guidance inspires me to remain curious and committed to learning in this ever-growing field.

I hope this book inspires readers to be innovative while honoring the roots of psychotherapy. Emerging therapies open up new horizons in the rapidly evolving landscape of mental health care to support healing, growth, and transformation.

Acknowledgements

I am deeply grateful to my father, Kishore Chandra Nayak, whose wisdom and unwavering support have guided me throughout this journey. To my mother, Anusuya Nayak, whose nurturing care and strength have always been my foundation. This book is a reflection of your love, guidance, and encouragement. Thank you for being my pillars.

Eastern Perspectives

Chapter 1

Acupuncture in Psychotherapy - Eastern Wisdom meets Western Healing

Nayama Mahmood School of Liberal Studies (SLS), CMR University, Bangalore

Introduction

Acupuncture is increasingly becoming popular in the general population due to its use in treatment of various health disorders since it is a safe and tolerable non-medication therapy. Now there are more protocols being adapted in psychotherapy practice where acupressure works in tapping stimulation of acupuncture points. This method is based on the hypothesis that tapping generates activating and deactivating signals, which influence the brain regions involved by the focus of attention from the client in real-time. This implies that therapists can quickly induce cognitive and neurological changes through change of the word and imagery in the tapping process. However, this method has both positive and negative views because of its several criticisms. Most psychotherapists manage to incorporate acupoint stimulation techniques in their already used psychological theories and practices.

Historical Overview

Acupuncture is one of the ancient Chinese medical practices that have been in practice for more than 2,000 years. The term "acupuncture" is derived from two Latin terms: *acus* meaning "needle or sharp point" and *punctura* meaning "to pierce." It is the process of inserting fine, thread-like needles into specific points on the body for medicinal purposes. With the insertion of the needle into the skin, in traditional acupuncture it is manipulated manually through up-and-down and rotational movements, which is commonly referred to as "manual needling," to reopen the body's energy channels or meridians which lead to the resumption of the flow of blocked *Qi* (vital energy) on its natural course. Its roots stem from traditionally naturalistic theories conformed with the philosophies of Confucianism and Taoism. The works from this classic view the human body as a mini-universe, and these physicians consider their responsibility to preserve the inner equilibrium of the human body along with harmony with the outer world as part of the duty. The revival in the 20th century is mostly attributed to George Soulié de Morant, French diplomat to China between 1901 and 1917, who brought this theory into European medicine. His translations and teachings popularized terms in acupuncture such as "meridian" and "energy," helping to acculturate it as a part of Western medical practice. Clinical acupuncture in Europe has co-evolved with biomedical science since the 1950s, influencing its current use.

Increasingly, acupuncture has been applied in the field of psychology as a complementary treatment, bringing benefits towards various mental health conditions. In 1970, psychologist Roger Callahan invented the art of psychotherapy and acupuncture point stimulation by developing Thought Field Therapy (TFT). Over time, modified versions of Callahan's original techniques appeared under the umbrella term "energy psychology," but the most practiced forms are within the techniques of Emotional Freedom Techniques (EFT).

Fundamentals and Practice

The history of TCM is long and started over 2,000 years ago. The two central theories that underlie it are *yin-yang* and the five elements, which explain all the changes and phenomena in the universe and even in human nature as well. This theory states that the universe constitutes the whole consisting of a duality between two principles, *yin* and *yang*, both form a delicate balance, which should be maintained in harmony - inside the body and on earth. The Five Phases ("*Wu Xing*") (Wood, Fire, Earth, Metal, and Water) all interact with each other in physiological and pathological ways. Pathological syndromes are more likely to appear when the balance among the Five Phases is disrupted. Two other important theories would be *Qi* and Meridians. *Qi*, or Chi, refers to the vital life force or energy flowing through the body. It is believed that the smooth flow of *Qi* is important for physical and mental health. The blockage or lack of balance causes an illness. There are 12 main meridian pathways through which *Qi* flows to all parts of the body. Each associated with organs and functions. Acupuncture focuses on these meridians to restore normal flow of *Qi*.

Acupuncture is administered to diagnose and treat medical conditions according to the theories of *Yin* and *Yang* based on the idea that everything must be in balance with these opposing forces. Practitioners manage the flow of *Qi* along meridians, which are believed to cause pain and illness due to blockages. It works by disrupting the blocked flow of *Qi* by manipulating the specific points, or acupoints, eliminating or alleviating symptoms like pain, tension, and disorders of the digestive system, maintaining or re-establishing equilibrium.

Additionally, the Five Elements Theory provides a foundation for evaluating imbalances in terms of the elements (Wood, Fire, Earth, Metal, Water), and the practitioner may lead the patient toward restoration of disrupted balance. Acupuncture includes combining all these theories and treating both the physical and emotional and spiritual conditions. Depression, anxiety, and mania belong to psychopathological syndromes characterized by mood disturbances. Disruption of "*shen*" and imbalance between "*yin*" and "*yang*" are closely related to these diseases. A patient with depression usually suffers from excess "*yin*, while someone with mania shows an excess of "*yang*." By rebalancing the "*yin*" and "*yang*", patients may be helped to recover from these diseases.

Acupuncture Mechanism

Acupuncture is based on various styles, including Japanese, Korean hand acupuncture, Leamington Five-Elements, French energetic, and Chinese TCM styles. Specialized techniques are aimed at specific body areas, including hand-foot, auricular, and scalp acupuncture. It also contains modern methods, like electricity and lasers, which serve as alternatives to traditional needles.

From the perspective of modern science, acupuncture has been reported to affect the autonomic nervous system to create relaxation and reduce tension. This can also enhance blood flow and reduce inflammation that it may help in enhancing faster recovery as well as diminish pain.

Acupuncture involves stimulation of specific body points leading to activation of the nervous system, thereby creating a cascade of neurobiological effects. Insertion of needles at acupoints results in the release of neurotransmitters such as endorphins and serotonin, which mitigate pain and improve mood.

Psychophysiology of Stress and Trauma: How Psychological Stress Manifests in the Body

Herbert and Cohen (1993) stated that such stress hormones can damage the body's organs, disable mental ability, and weaken one's immune system. Since the condition of being stressed becomes chronic, there is an increased likelihood that the response of the mind stays in this type, leading to a significantly increased allostatic load. Hence, it will become a state in which both body and brain will stay "tired" and remain unable to work up enough energy for repairing. Once stress and anxiety develop into the state of a disorder, they can interfere with normal areas of bodily function. The chronic and devastating nature of depression, of course, complicates the prognosis of many chronic diseases and makes the situation of disease and disability worse.

Acupuncture in Mental Health

Results indicate that acupuncture treatments affect the production of serotonin, which acts as a neurotransmitter in regulating mood. At specific points it maintains the body's natural emotional balance and can also increase serotonin levels, thereby helping alleviate depression symptoms. Research suggests that acupuncture can stimulate serotonin production; therefore, an improvement in mood and overall well-being is anticipated. It could significantly alleviate depressive symptoms by affecting serotonin and dopamine pathways in the brain. It concluded sometimes its effects were comparable to pharmacological antidepressants.

Research on acupuncture has shown it to soothe the nervous system and minimize the effects of anxiety, thereby helping in the management of stress through control of the autonomic nervous system. This regulation ensures a balance between sympathetic (fight or flight) and parasympathetic (rest and digest) responses, thus bringing about feelings of relief from tension and from worry. Regarding trauma and PTSD, acupuncture facilitates recovery through the modulation of the body's stress response as well as the healing of emotions. It helps to release stored trauma and brings emotional regulation and balance to the often-compromised nervous system through trauma. It is also useful in dealing with insomnia and other sleeping disorders by activating certain points that regulate the body's internal clock, where the body tends to sleep more deeply and restoratively yet decreases the under-*lying* causes such as stress and anxiety. For those emotionally dysregulated, acupuncture will harmonize the flow of energy in the body. And from here, one expects to come across emotional stability, less mood swings, and is rescued from problems such as irritability or apathy that can usually be symptoms of other mental health disorders.

Common Acupuncture Points for Psychological Well-being

HT7 (Shen Men)

Shen Men or Heart 7, located at the wrist crease, is on the ulnar side just next to the depression due to the tendon of the flexor carpi ulnaris muscle. It is an important acupuncture point regarding the matter of emotional control and is frequently used for the calming of spirit, as in psychological imbalance. It is particularly useful in the treatment of anxiety, insomnia, and other emotional disturbances because several clinical studies have demonstrated that HT7 stimulation drastically reduces symptoms of anxiety.

Third Eye Point (Yintang)

The Yintang point lies at the midline between the eyebrows, just above the nose. The main reason why the point of Yintang is widely administered for stress, tension, and anxiety is due to its relaxing action on the nervous system. It also facilitates good sleeping quality. The tranquilizing action that it has on the mind aids in treating disorders like insomnia and headache caused by stress.

An Mian

Located just behind the ear, the An Mian is primarily used to enhance sleep as an adjunct in the management of insomnia. Quieting the nervous system, with its benefits helping to decrease anxiety, and treating a myriad of disorders related to stress, studies have proven that the stimulation of the An Mian significantly increases the quality of sleep in patients suffering from insomnia, thus its utility as an adjunct treatment.

DU20 (Baihui)

DU20, Baihui, is located at the vertex of the head, here ear line crosses midline of the head. It is employed commonly in several acupuncture therapies to increase energy and activate spirits when depression and mental fatigue are prevalent. The acupoint also helps to alleviate mental restlessness and headaches along with psychological and physiological anxiety and stress. This point is said to stimulate the improvement of mood and cognitive clarity, especially among those patients with cognitive impairment or mood disorders.

Pericardium 6 (PC6)

PC6 is also known as Neiguan. It is found on the forearm, primarily three finger-widths above the wrist crease between the tendons of the palmaris longus and flexor carpi radialis. It is very famous for its soothing effects to humans. This point is very effective against anxiety, palpitations, and emotional discomfort. It is also very effective in cases of nausea or other digestive issues where such individuals are inflicted by stress or anxiety. Studies show that stimulation of PC6 provided stress decreases and overall mental well-being.

Liver 3 (LV3)

LV3, or Taichong, is located on the dorsum of the foot, in the depression between the first and second toes. This point is famous for its capacity to soothe emotions and relieve stress. It is very beneficial to use LV3 for anger, irritability, and emotional tension-a very common symptom of Liver *Qi* stagnation. LV3 is also known to be somewhat effective at reducing anxiety and depression.

Psychotherapy and Acupuncture: Synergistic Approaches

Acupuncture therapy is integrated with psychotherapy, which fosters a synergistic treatment approach that amplifies the patient's mental health treatment. The direction of this trend seems to be an extension of the tendency in the healthcare industry toward integrative healthcare, which uses multiple modalities of treatment to accomplish its work. This recognizes that mind and body are not compartmentalized entities. One pragmatic approach is the combination of acupuncture with Cognitive Behavioral Therapy, in which the somatic effects of acupuncture may enhance cognitive alterations that in turn help patients change their thinking and behavior more systematically. This combined treatment promotes further cognitive restructuring while enhancing relaxation and emotional equilibrium.

Another interesting interface is that which has been provided by Mindfulness-Based Stress Reduction (MBSR) interventions. Acupuncture can serve as an adjunctive procedure to the mindfulness practice by achieving improved relaxation, reduction of anxiety, and enhancement of one's self-awareness.

This trauma-informed acupuncture had proved to be an effective strategy in support of a variety of trauma therapies, including Eye Movement Desensitization and Reprocessing (EMDR) and Somatic Experiencing.

Psychodynamic Approaches can be undertaken in conjunction with acupuncture, and the treatment of emotional issues can be achieved by revealing deeper emotions through the practice. This way, the patient opens and lets the suppressed emotions go, and self-awareness is heighted among the patients, thus being able to tackle a higher-level work emotionally in a safe environment. Together, these are the integrative approaches that indicate the potential integration of acupuncture with psychotherapy can offer more holistic and effective treatments for mental disorders.

Mechanism of Actions: Neuroscience and Acupuncture

Acupuncture has drawn much attention in terms of its multiple mechanisms, and it is also important for its use in the nervous system. From this point of view, one necessary mechanism involves the stimulation of the vagal nerve that has paramount influence in the regulation of the autonomic nervous system. It is advisable to enhance vagal tone as acupuncture would increase parasympathetic responses (relaxation and digestion) while inhibiting sympathetic ones (fight or flight reactions). This regulation is associated with decreases in stress, improves emotional regulation, and an overall state of calmness; this is the reason why acupuncture is valuable for the management of anxiety and stress disorders. Apart from the effects on the nervous system itself, another aspect of the positive impact perhaps is about neuroplasticity. It is especially important in psychological trauma, wherein acupuncture might facilitate recovery through the adaptive capacity of the brain. It may stimulate the release of certain neurotrophic factors, which induce neuronal growth and repair through the activation of specific acupuncture points. Consequently, this can enhance cognitive and emotional recovery in trauma victims.

Lastly, it modulates the effects of neurotransmitters, such as serotonin and dopamine, in turn involved in mood regulation. The biochemical pathways will balance out due to the intervention of acupuncture, which will manage symptom expression of a depressed or anxious individual by carr*ying* a holistic approach towards their mental health treatment.

Future Directions in Acupuncture for Mental Health

Advanced research innovations are shifting new explorations on how to apply acupuncture in mental health care: recent studies have focused attention on how acupuncture affects psychological states, especially on neurobiological mechanisms through which it has been proposed to treat depression, anxiety, and PTSD. Advanced imaging such as with fMRI and PET scans can be used to define the activity of brain areas following acupuncture, which will eventually unlock the door to understanding its effects on mood-regulation-related brain areas and in the regions involved in stress response and emotional processing. Long-term benefits of acupuncture therapy as an adjunctive therapy for mental health, thus opening a window into establishing evidence-based protocols for clinical practice, are of great importance.

Additionally, the practice of acupuncture is also developing by embracing modern technology through electro-acupuncture and laser acupuncture. Electro-acupuncture has improved the therapeutic outcomes of traditional acupuncture, most importantly in mood disorders, by appl*ying* electrical currents to the needles. Such a procedure facilitates modulation of neurotransmitters such as serotonin and dopamine more than was achieved in traditional acupuncture, hence giving extra advantages in dealing with anxiety and depression. Another example is low-level laser acupuncture, where the same rationale as in traditional acupuncture is applied but without using needles and instead uses low-level lasers. This is a non-invasive modality that may help certain patients who have needle phobias. These technologies make acupuncture more versatile and accessible in mental health care.

Case Studies

Case Study 1

A study by Assouline et al. (2022) involved a group of people with PTSD, each carrying a different story of trauma, but all struggling with symptoms that hadn't improved much despite previous treatments. Among these individuals were veterans, accident survivors, and others who had faced deeply distressing events. They shared similar symptoms: restless anxiety, vivid flashbacks that felt as if they were reliving the trauma, and a hyper-alertness that made it hard to feel safe. Many also dealt with chronic inflammation, a physical burden that only added to their emotional load.

How Acupuncture and Therapy Worked Together

The approach here was both structured and sensitive. The sessions began by gently guiding patients into recalling their traumatic memories with the support of a therapist. This memory retrieval stage was vital but challenging; it brought past pain to the surface but allowed patients to confront their memories safely. During this phase, the therapist closely monitored each patient's reactions, providing reassurance and grounding them when needed. The goal was to trigger the memories in a controlled setting so that they could be addressed without overwhelming the patient.

After memory retrieval, patients moved into acupuncture sessions. The acupuncture points selected were chosen to specifically help with stress responses, targeting areas that could influence the nervous system and help reduce inflammation. Many PTSD sufferers experience a heightened state of alertness, as though their nervous system is constantly on high alert. Acupuncture was used here to calm these heightened responses, allowing patients to relax more deeply than they might otherwise.

The Outcomes: How Acupuncture Helped Patients Feel and Heal

The results were encouraging. Physiologically, the acupuncture sessions had a calming effect, helping patients feel more settled and less physically tense. Some patients shared how they felt an unexpected calmness after their sessions, as if the constant buzzing of anxiety had softened. For some, this calm allowed them to reflect on their memories without the usual rush of distress. With reduced inflammation and a more balanced nervous system, many patients found they were better able to manage their PTSD symptoms. The flashbacks became less intense, and anxiety levels dropped.

Mentally, the combination of acupuncture and memory retrieval helped reinforce the gains from therapy. The relaxed state allowed them to process the emotional weight of their memories in a way they hadn't before. Over time, patients noticed a change in how they related to their memories—they felt more empowered and less controlled by the trauma. The acupuncture seemed to help their body "absorb" the work they were doing in therapy, making it possible for them to integrate these gains into their lives more fully.

Conclusion and Implications: A New Path to Healing

This case study underscores the potential of combining acupuncture with traditional trauma therapy for PTSD. Trauma affects both mind and body, and this approach recognized that healing needs to address both aspects. Acupuncture's ability to support the nervous system and reduce inflammation offered these patients a unique source of relief, complementing the cognitive gains they made in therapy. This method offers hope for future treatment approaches that aim to address the whole person, helping individuals with PTSD find pathways toward both psychological and physical recovery.

Case Study 2

In 2019, Armour et al. (2019b) conducted a meta-analysis to explore how acupuncture might help people with Major Depressive Disorder (MDD), especially when used alongside traditional antidepressant treatments. Depression can be incredibly complex and challenging, affecting not only how people feel emotionally but also their physical well-being. This analysis reviewed nearly 30 studies, involving over 2,200 people with MDD, who were experiencing different levels of depression. They found that adding acupuncture to regular antidepressant treatment could boost the effectiveness of the treatment, offering hope and support to those dealing with depression.

Study Sample and Approach: Who Were the Participants?

The study reviewed trials involving people from different backgrounds, age groups, and cultures, all diagnosed with MDD. These participants had been using standard antidepressant medications, but some of them also received acupuncture treatments during their course of therapy. The acupuncture sessions were typically held once to three times a week over several weeks, giving each participant a chance to experience its potential benefits in a structured and supportive way.

The researchers used widely recognized measures to track symptoms, like the Hamilton Depression Rating Scale (HAM-D) and Beck Depression Inventory (BDI). These scales helped gauge how participants were feeling before and after treatments, tracking changes in their symptoms and mood.

Findings: How Acupuncture Helped People Feel and Heal

The results showed that acupuncture had a meaningful impact, improving both physical and emotional symptoms in ways that added to the effects of antidepressants. The treatment seemed to help the body and mind respond more fully, enhancing recovery in three significant ways:

Acupuncture seems to help people with depression by working on both body and mind. First, it activates the vagal nerve, which helps calm the body's stress response, bringing relief from the constant tension many people with depression feel. It also boosts endorphins, the body's natural mood lifters and pain relievers, creating moments of lightness and reducing physical symptoms like fatigue and aches. Finally, acupuncture may help balance key brain chemicals like serotonin and dopamine, supporting the effects of antidepressants and promoting a more stable mood. Together, these effects offer a unique, holistic way of addressing both emotional and physical sides of depression.

Real-Life Outcomes: What Patients Experienced

The people receiving both acupuncture and antidepressants generally reported feeling better than those on medication alone. They noticed:

Participants who received acupuncture alongside antidepressants found meaningful relief from their depression symptoms. They reported feeling less burdened by hopelessness, fatigue, and low motivation depression felt lighter and more manageable. Acupuncture's calming effects helped them feel more balanced and grounded emotionally, providing a steady sense of calm. Additionally, acupuncture seemed to ease some side effects of their medications, such as stomach discomfort and fatigue, which made it easier for them to stick with their treatment. Altogether, acupuncture offered support that helped both body and mind, making the journey through depression a bit gentler.

A Comprehensive Approach to Depression Treatment

This meta-analysis supports the idea that acupuncture can be an effective addition to traditional depression treatment, addressing both the emotional and physical layers of depression. By combining antidepressant medication with acupuncture, people can benefit from a more holistic approach to recovery—one that engages both body and mind. It's a hopeful step forward, suggesting that therapies like acupuncture might help support resilience and healing in ways that feel both natural and deeply rooted in the body's own systems.

References

Han, J. (2014). Acupuncture. In *Springer eBooks* (pp. 123–136). https://doi.org/10.1007/978-1-4939-1821-8_10

Helms, J. M. (1998). An overview of medical acupuncture. *PubMed*, *4*(3), 35–45. https://pubmed.ncbi.nlm.nih.gov/9581320

Haddad, N. E., & Palesh, O. (2014). Acupuncture in the treatment of Cancer-Related Psychological Symptoms. *Integrative Cancer Therapies*, *13*(5), 371–385. https://doi.org/10.1177/1534735413520181

APA PsycNet. (n.d.). https://psycnet.apa.org/buy/2022-61876-001

Feinstein, D. (2012). AcuPoint Stimulation in Treating Psychological Disorders: Evidence of Efficacy. *Review of General Psychology*, *16*(4), 364–380. https://doi.org/10.1037/a0028602

Callahan, R. (1997). Thought Field Therapy: The case of Mary. *Traumatology an International Journal*, *3*(1). https://doi.org/10.1177/153476569700300105

Mayer, M. (2009). *Energy Psychology: Self-Healing Practices for Bodymind Health*. https://www.amazon.com/Energy-Psychology-Self-Healing-Practices-Bodymind/dp/1556437242

MacPherson, H., Richmond, S., Bland, M., Brealey, S., Gabe, R., Hopton, A., Keding, A., Lansdown, H., Perren, S., Sculpher, M., Spackman, E., Torgerson, D., & Watt, I. (2013). Acupuncture and Counselling for depression in Primary Care: a randomised controlled trial. *PLoS Medicine*, *10*(9), e1001518. https://doi.org/10.1371/journal.pmed.1001518

Armour, M., Smith, C., Wang, L., Naidoo, D., *Yang*, G., MacPherson, H., Lee, M., & Hay, P. (2019). Acupuncture for Depression: A Systematic Review and Meta-Analysis. *Journal of Clinical Medicine*, *8*(8), 1140. https://doi.org/10.3390/jcm8081140

Lao, L., Xu, L., & Xu, S. (2012). Traditional Chinese medicine. In *Pediatric oncology* (pp. 125–135). https://doi.org/10.1007/978-3-642-04201-0_9

Freeman, L.W.; Lawlis, G.F. *Mosby's Complementary & Alternative Medicine*; Mosby: Mosby, MO, USA, 2004. [Google Scholar]

Matos, L. C., Machado, J. P., Monteiro, F. J., & Greten, H. J. (2021). Understanding Traditional Chinese Medicine Therapeutics: An Overview of the basics and clinical applications. *Healthcare*, *9*(3), 257. https://doi.org/10.3390/healthcare9030257

Zhang, Z., Chen, H., Yip, K., Ng, R., & Wong, V. T. (2009). The effectiveness and safety of acupuncture therapy in depressive disorders: Systematic review and meta-analysis. *Journal of Affective Disorders*, *124*(1–2), 9–21. https://doi.org/10.1016/j.jad.2009.07.005

Chan, Y., Lo, W., *Yang*, S., Chen, Y., & Lin, J. (2015). The benefit of combined acupuncture and antidepressant medication for depression: A systematic review and meta-analysis. *Journal of Affective Disorders*, *176*, 106–117. https://doi.org/10.1016/j.jad.2015.01.048

Lin, M., Wu, H., Hsieh, Y., Su, C., Shih, Y., Lin, C., & Wu, J. (2012). Evaluation of the Effect of Laser Acupuncture and Cupping with Ryodoraku and Visual Analog Scale on Low Back Pain. *Evidence-based Complementary and Alternative Medicine*, *2012*, 1–7. https://doi.org/10.1155/2012/521612

Sancier, K. M. (1994). THE EFFECT OF *QI*GONG ON THERAPEUTIC BALANCING MEASURED BY ELECTROACUPUNCTURE ACCORDING TO VOLL (EAV): a PRELIMINARY STUDY. *Acupuncture & Electro-Therapeutics Research*, *19*(2), 119–127. https://doi.org/10.3727/036012994816357295

Lin, L., Li, H., *Yang*, J., Hao, X., Yan, S., Wang, L., Yu, F., Shi, G., & Liu, C. (2021). Acupuncture for Psychological Disorders Caused by Chronic Pain: a review and future directions. *Frontiers in Neuroscience, 14*. https://doi.org/10.3389/fnins.2020.626497

Samuels, N., Gropp, C., Singer, S. R., & Oberbaum, M. (2008). Acupuncture for Psychiatric Illness: A Literature review. *Behavioral Medicine, 34*(2), 55–64. https://doi.org/10.3200/bmed.34.2.55-64

July-August 1993 - Volume 55 - Issue 4: Psychosomatic Medicine. (n.d.). https://journals.lww.com/psychosomaticmedicine/toc/1993/07000

Tan, Y., Duan, R., & Wen, C. (2024). Efficacy of acupuncture for depression: a systematic review and meta-analysis. *Frontiers in Neuroscience, 18*. https://doi.org/10.3389/fnins.2024.1347651

Yang, X., *Yang*, N., Huang, F., Ren, S., & Li, Z. (2021). Effectiveness of acupuncture on anxiety disorder: a systematic review and meta-analysis of randomised controlled trials. *Annals of General Psychiatry, 20*(1). https://doi.org/10.1186/s12991-021-00327-5

Ding, N., Li, L., Song, K., Huang, A., & Zhang, H. (2020). Efficacy and safety of acupuncture in treating post-traumatic stress disorder. *Medicine, 99*(26), e20700. https://doi.org/10.1097/md.0000000000020700

Hu, H., Li, Z., Cheng, Y., & Gao, H. (2022). The Efficacy and Safety of Acupuncture for Depression-Related Insomnia: Protocol for a Systematic Review and Meta-Analysis. *Journal of Pain Research, Volume 15*, 1939–1947. https://doi.org/10.2147/jpr.s370476

Dong, B., Chen, Z., *Yin*, X., Li, D., Ma, J., *Yin*, P., Cao, Y., Lao, L., & Xu, S. (2017). The Efficacy of Acupuncture for Treating Depression-Related Insomnia Compared with a Control Group: A Systematic Review and Meta-Analysis. *BioMed Research International, 2017*, 1–11. https://doi.org/10.1155/2017/9614810

Cox, R. C., & Olatunji, B. O. (2015). A systematic review of sleep disturbance in anxiety and related disorders. *Journal of Anxiety Disorders, 37*, 104–129. https://doi.org/10.1016/j.janxdis.2015.12.001

Hollifield, M., Sinclair-Lian, N., Warner, T. D., & Hammerschlag, R. (2007). Acupuncture for posttraumatic stress disorder. *The Journal of Nervous and Mental Disease, 195*(6), 504–513. https://doi.org/10.1097/nmd.0b013e31803044f8

Ho, F. Y., Choi, W., Yeung, W., Lam, H., Lau, W., & Chung, K. (2021). The efficacy of integrated cognitive behavioral therapy (CBT) and acupressure versus CBT for insomnia: a three-arm pilot randomized controlled trial. *Sleep Medicine, 87*, 158–167. https://doi.org/10.1016/j.sleep.2021.08.024

Mackey, S., Gilam, G., Darnall, B., Goldin, P., Kong, J., Law, C., Heirich, M., Karayannis, N., Kao, M., Tian, L., Manber, R., & Gross, J. (2022). Mindfulness-Based stress reduction, cognitive behavioral therapy, and acupuncture in chronic low back pain: protocol for two linked randomized controlled trials. *JMIR Research Protocols, 11*(9), e37823. https://doi.org/10.2196/37823

Mattar, S., & Frewen, P. A. (2020). Introduction to the special issue: Complementary medicine and integrative health approaches to trauma therapy and recovery. *Psychological Trauma Theory Research Practice and Policy, 12*(8), 821–824. https://doi.org/10.1037/tra0000994

Winnegge, K. A. (n.d.). *When East meets West*: an exploratory study of how Reiki is integrated into psychodynamic practice. Smith ScholarWorks. https://scholarworks.smith.edu/theses/1030?utm_source=scholarworks.smith.edu%2Ftheses%2F1030&utm_medium=PDF&utm_campaign=PDFCoverPages

Li, Q., Shi, G., Xu, Q., Wang, J., Liu, C., & Wang, L. (2013). Acupuncture effect and central autonomic regulation. *Evidence-based Complementary and Alternative Medicine, 2013*, 1–6. https://doi.org/10.1155/2013/267959

Liu, K., Jiang, J., & Lu, S. (2021). Effect characteristics and mechanism of acupuncture in autonomic nerve regulation. *Acupuncture Research, 46*(4), 335–341. https://doi.org/10.13702/j.1000-0607.200665

Yin, T., Ma, P., Tian, Z., Xie, K., He, Z., Sun, R., & Zeng, F. (2020). Machine Learning in Neuroimaging: A New approach to understand Acupuncture for Neuroplasticity. *Neural Plasticity, 2020*, 1–14. https://doi.org/10.1155/2020/8871712

Mayer, D. J. (2000). Biological mechanisms of acupuncture. *Progress in Brain Research*, 457–477. https://doi.org/10.1016/s0079-6123(08)62157-3

Arvidsdotter, T., Marklund, B., & Taft, C. (2013). Effects of an integrative treatment, therapeutic acupuncture and conventional treatment in alleviating psychological distress in primary care patients - a pragmatic randomized controlled trial. *BMC Complementary and Alternative Medicine, 13*(1). https://doi.org/10.1186/1472-6882-13-308

Maizes, V., Rakel, D., & Niemiec, C. (2009). Integrative Medicine and Patient-Centered care. *EXPLORE, 5*(5), 277–289. https://doi.org/10.1016/j.explore.2009.06.008

Coates, D., Coppleson, D., & Travaglia, J. (2021). Factors supporting the implementation of integrated care between physical and mental health services: an integrative review. *Journal of Interprofessional Care, 36*(2), 245–258. https://doi.org/10.1080/13561820.2020.1862771

Chen, A. H., Murphy, E. J., & Yee, H. F. (2013). EReferral — a new model for integrated care. *New England Journal of Medicine, 368*(26), 2450–2453. https://doi.org/10.1056/nejmp1215594

Ernst, E. (2009). Ethics of complementary medicine: practical issues. *British Journal of General Practice, 59*(564), 517–519. https://doi.org/10.3399/bjgp09x453404

Maizes, V., & Horwitz, R. (2004). Ethics, Education, and Integrative medicine. *The AMA Journal of Ethic, 6*(11). https://doi.org/10.1001/virtualmentor.2004.6.11.oped1-0411

Langevin, H. M., Wayne, P. M., MacPherson, H., Schnyer, R., Milley, R. M., Napadow, V., Lao, L., Park, J., Harris, R. E., Cohen, M., Sherman, K. J., Haramati, A., & Hammerschlag, R. (2010). Paradoxes in acupuncture Research: Strategies for moving forward. *Evidence-based Complementary and Alternative Medicine, 2011*, 1–11. https://doi.org/10.1155/2011/180805

Zhang, Z., Chen, H., Yip, K., Ng, R., & Wong, V. T. (2009). The effectiveness and safety of acupuncture therapy in depressive disorders: Systematic review and meta-analysis. *Journal of Affective Disorders, 124*(1–2), 9–21. https://doi.org/10.1016/j.jad.2009.07.005

Napadow, V., Ahn, A., Longhurst, J., Lao, L., Stener-Victorin, E., Harris, R., & Langevin, H. M. (2008). The Status and Future of Acupuncture Mechanism Research. *The Journal of Alternative and Complementary Medicine, 14*(7), 861–869. https://doi.org/10.1089/acm.2008.sar-3

Assouline, A., Mendelsohn, A., & Reshef, A. (2022). Memory-directed acupuncture as a neuromodulatory treatment for PTSD: Theory, clinical model and case studies. *Translational Psychiatry, 12*(1). https://doi.org/10.1038/s41398-022-01876-3

Armour, M., Smith, C., Wang, L., Naidoo, D., Yang, G., MacPherson, H., Lee, M., & Hay, P. (2019). Acupuncture for Depression: A Systematic Review and Meta-Analysis. *Journal of Clinical Medicine, 8*(8), 1140. https://doi.org/10.3390/jcm8081140

Chapter 2

Chakra Healing

Saloni Vishnoi School of Liberal Studies (SLS), CMR University, Bangalore

Introduction

Chakra healing is a holistic practice that involves balancing and aligning the body's energy centers, known as chakras, to promote emotional, physical, and spiritual well-being. The word "chakra" comes from the Sanskrit term meaning "wheel" or "disk," referring to the spinning vortices of energy believed to govern various aspects of the human experience. Each chakra is associated with specific emotions, behaviors, and physiological functions, and any blockage or imbalance in these energy centers can lead to mental, emotional, or physical health issues. Chakra healing techniques, such as meditation, breathwork, sound therapy, and visualization, are designed to unblock and restore the flow of energy, enhancing psychological resilience and inner harmony.

The concept of chakras has its origins in Indian philosophy, primarily rooted in ancient Vedic texts and later elaborated in Tantric traditions. In the Upanishads, an essential part of the Vedic literature, the chakras were first described in connection with the body's subtle energies. Tantric practices further explored the idea of chakras as part of Kundalini yoga, emphasizing the awakening of latent energy and spiritual consciousness. These traditions underscore the belief that health is not merely the absence of disease but the alignment of mind, body, and spirit through energy harmony.

In recent years, chakra healing has gained significant relevance as a complementary tool in mental health care, especially alongside traditional psychotherapy, and counselling. Mental health practitioners increasingly incorporate chakra-based practices—such as meditation, breathwork, and energy healing—into their therapeutic frameworks to address emotional imbalances and stress-related issues. Though scientific validation is still limited, anecdotal reports from therapists and clients suggest that chakra work provides significant mental health benefits.

Chakras

The chakra system consists of seven key energy centers thought to influence physical, emotional, and spiritual well-being. These chakras are aligned along the spine, stretching from the base to the top of the head. Each chakra is associated with distinct elements of human experience, such as emotions, instincts, personal strength, and spiritual insight.

Root Chakra (Muladhara) – Stability and Survival

The Root Chakra, situated at the base of the spine, is associated with feelings of safety, security, and stability. It symbolizes our foundation and connection to the physical realm. When balanced, it fosters a sense of grounding, confidence, and resilience in handling daily challenges. However, blockages in this chakra can manifest as anxiety, fear, or insecurity, alongside physical symptoms like fatigue or lower body discomfort, including joint pain. Grounding techniques, mindful walking, and yoga poses such as Mountain Pose or Warrior Pose are beneficial for restoring balance and stability to this energy center.

Sacral Chakra (Swadhisthana) – Emotions and Creativity

The Sacral Chakra lies just below the navel and governs emotional well-being, relationships, creativity, and pleasure. It influences how people experience and express emotions, particularly joy and intimacy. A balanced sacral chakra allows for healthy emotional expression and creativity, while blockages may lead to emotional instability, addictive behaviours, or difficulty in forming meaningful relationships. Physical symptoms can include menstrual problems or lower abdominal discomfort. Engaging in creative activities, practicing dance or movement therapy, and using aromatherapy can promote balance in this chakra.

Solar Plexus Chakra (Manipura) – Confidence and Willpower

The Solar Plexus Chakra is located above the navel and is considered the center of personal power, confidence, and motivation. It controls willpower, self-discipline, and the ability to take decisive actions. A balanced solar plexus chakra fosters high self-esteem and the courage to pursue personal goals. Imbalances can lead to low self-worth, procrastination, or controlling behaviors. Physically, symptoms may manifest as digestive issues or stress-related disorders. Techniques such as core-strengthening exercises, affirmations, and mindfulness practices help activate this chakra.

Heart Chakra (Anahata) – Love and Compassion

The Heart Chakra, found in the center of the chest, serves as a bridge between the lower chakras associated with physical needs and the upper chakras connected to spiritual awareness. It governs love, compassion, empathy, and forgiveness.

When balanced, individuals experience relationships, emotional openness, and self-acceptance. Blockages may result in isolation, emotional numbness, or unresolved grief.

Throat Chakra (Vishuddha) – Communication

The Throat Chakra, situated in the throat area, is responsible for communication, self-expression, and staying true to oneself. It helps individuals convey thoughts and emotions clearly and fosters the ability to listen and understand others. When in balance, the throat chakra allows people to express their truth confidently. Blockages can lead to fear of speaking, difficulty expressing emotions, or social anxiety. Physical symptoms might include sore throats or thyroid imbalances. Practices such as chanting, journaling, or working with affirmations focused on self-expression can support the healing of this chakra.

Third Eye Chakra (Ajna) – Intuition and Insight

The Third Eye Chakra, located between the eyebrows, is linked to intuition, insight, and heightened perception. It oversees inner wisdom, creativity, and mental clarity. When balanced, this chakra supports clear decision-making, sharp focus, and confidence in one's instincts. Blockages may lead to confusion, overthinking, or a feeling of detachment from reality, often accompanied by physical symptoms like headaches or vision problems. Practices such as meditation, visualization, and keeping a dream journal can help activate and harmonize the third eye chakra.

Crown Chakra (Sahasrara) – Spiritual Connection

The Crown Chakra, positioned at the top of the head, symbolizes spiritual connection, enlightenment, and unity with the universe. It is associated with higher consciousness and a sense of life purpose. When balanced, this chakra promotes spiritual growth, inner harmony, and a feeling of interconnectedness. Blockages can result in existential anxiety, depression, or a sense of disconnection from the world.

Physical Manifestations of Emotional Blockages

Blocked chakras can also lead to psychosomatic symptoms—physical ailments that arise from emotional disturbances. Examples include:

- Root Chakra: Chronic fatigue, joint pain, and digestive issues
- Heart Chakra: Tightness in the chest, palpitations, or respiratory problems
- Third Eye Chakra: Headaches, vision problems, and insomnia

These physical symptoms highlight how emotional imbalances can take a toll on the body, reinforcing the importance of addressing both the mind and body in healing practices.

Chakra Healing Techniques for Mental Health

Meditation and Visualization

Meditation plays a central role in chakra healing by helping individuals become more aware of their emotional and energetic states. Through focused meditation on specific chakras, people can visualize healing light or colors associated with the energy centers. For example, visualizing a red light at the root chakra fosters grounding and emotional security, while a green glow around the heart chakra encourages love and compassion. These meditative practices reduce stress by slowing down racing thoughts and promoting mindfulness, thereby improving self-awareness and emotional resilience. Regular meditation has also been shown to reduce symptoms of anxiety and depression, making it an effective complementary tool in psychotherapy.

Yoga and Breathwork (Pranayama)

Yoga integrates body, mind, and spirit, making it a powerful practice for balancing the chakras. Specific yoga postures, known as *asanas*, are designed to stimulate different energy centers. For instance, *tree pose* strengthens the root chakra by promoting stability, while *camel pose* opens the heart chakra to foster emotional release and empathy. Breathwork, or *pranayama*, further enhances the therapeutic benefits of yoga by regulating the nervous system. Techniques such as alternate nostril breathing (Nadi Shodhana) or deep belly breathing activate the parasympathetic nervous system, calming the mind and improving emotional regulation. Yoga and pranayama help people develop focus, reduce stress, and gain mental clarity, making them effective in managing psychological conditions like anxiety and trauma.

Sound Therapy (Mantras)

Sound vibrations play a significant role in chakra healing through the repetition of mantras and sacred sounds. Each chakra resonates with a specific frequency, and chanting its corresponding sound can help clear blockages. For example, the sound "LAM" is associated with the root chakra, while "YAM" corresponds to the heart chakra. The universal mantra "OM" is widely used to cultivate.

Yoga and Breathwork (Pranayama)

Yoga integrates body, mind, and spirit, making it a powerful practice for balancing the chakras. Specific yoga postures, known as *asanas*, are designed to stimulate different energy centers. For instance, *tree pose* strengthens the root chakra by promoting stability, while *camel pose* opens the heart chakra to foster emotional release and empathy. Breathwork, or *pranayama*, further enhances the therapeutic benefits of yoga by regulating the nervous system. Techniques such as alternate nostril breathing (Nadi Shodhana) or deep belly breathing activate the parasympathetic nervous system, calming the mind and improving emotional regulation. Yoga and pranayama help people develop focus, reduce stress, and gain mental clarity, making them effective in managing psychological conditions like anxiety and trauma.

Sound Therapy (Mantras)

Sound vibrations play a significant role in chakra healing through the repetition of mantras and sacred sounds. Each chakra resonates with a specific frequency, and chanting its corresponding sound can help clear blockages. For example, the sound "LAM" is associated with the root chakra, while "YAM" corresponds to the heart chakra. The universal mantra "OM" is widely used to cultivate inner peace by aligning all chakras, helping individuals feel grounded and connected to the present moment. Sound therapy also calms the mind by regulating brain waves, leading to relaxation and emotional balance. Chanting mantras, singing bowls, and tuning forks are commonly used in therapy settings to help people manage stress, anxiety, and emotional disturbances.

Crystal Therapy and Aromatherapy

Crystal therapy involves placing specific gemstones on or near the chakras to enhance energy flow and support emotional healing. For instance, red jasper and black tourmaline are used for grounding and balancing the root chakra, while rose quartz helps open the heart chakra to love and compassion. Crystals are believed to interact with the body's energy field, amplifying intentions and promoting healing on an emotional level.

Challenges of Chakra Healing

Lack of Scientific Validation:

Chakra healing is rooted in spiritual and metaphysical beliefs rather than empirical science, which makes it difficult to validate within conventional medical frameworks. This absence of scientific evidence leads to skepticism among healthcare professionals, limiting its acceptance in mainstream mental health care. Despite anecdotal evidence of its benefits, more rigorous studies are needed to assess chakra healing's effectiveness, mechanisms, and applications.

Inconsistent Standards and Practices:

Chakra healing practices vary significantly depending on the healer's background, spiritual beliefs, and training, leading to inconsistencies. There is no universally accepted standard for chakra healing, which results in varied experiences and outcomes for individuals. This lack of standardization can lead to misunderstandings or ineffective treatment when chakra healing is practiced in a generalized or superficial manner.

Difficulty in Measuring Efficacy:

Chakra healing operates primarily on a subjective, energetic level, making it difficult to quantify results using traditional mental health metrics. Concepts like "energy balance" and "emotional release" are challenging to measure objectively. This limitation poses a barrier for therapists and clients who prefer to track treatment progress through tangible, evidence-based outcomes.

Potential for Psychological Discomfort:

For individuals with complex or severe mental health conditions, chakra healing can occasionally lead to psychological distress. For example, intense focus on opening specific chakras, such as the heart chakra, can bring buried emotions to the surface, which may be overwhelming without adequate support.

Cultural Misinterpretation and Appropriation:

Originating from ancient Indian and Eastern spiritual traditions, chakra healing practices can sometimes be oversimplified or misrepresented in Western contexts. This reduction of chakra healing to a commercialized or superficial practice can dilute its cultural significance, leading to misunderstandings and ineffective application. Misinterpretation of these practices also runs the risk of alienating those who seek authentic chakra healing experiences.

Case Studies

Case 01: Meditation and Visualization: Healing Trauma and Anxiety

In one case, a 40-year-old woman with chronic anxiety due to childhood trauma engaged in guided chakra meditation. Her therapist led her through visualizing a red glow around her root chakra to restore feelings of safety and stability. Over 12 weeks, she reported significant reductions in anxiety levels, better sleep, and fewer panic attacks. The patient also gained a deeper connection with her emotions, allowing her to identify triggers and respond with mindfulness rather than fear.

Visualization helped her anchor herself in the present moment, alleviating the sense of insecurity that had dominated her life.

Case 02: Yoga and Pranayama: Overcoming Depression

A 35-year-old man battling depression found little relief through medication alone and began practicing yoga and pranayama as part of an integrative mental health program. His yoga instructor focused on poses that opened the heart chakra, such as *camel pose* and *cobra pose*, encouraging emotional release and self-compassion. Complementing this with breathing exercises like Nadi Shodhana (alternate nostril breathing) helped the patient regulate his emotions. After several months of practice, he experienced noticeable improvements in his mood, better emotional regulation, and a greater sense of inner peace. The patient also reported reduced dependency on medication and reconnected with his family, fostering healthier relationships.

Case 03: Sound Therapy: Reducing Overthinking and Enhancing Focus

A young woman in her early 20s struggled with chronic overthinking and indecisiveness, impairing her academic performance. She sought help through chakra sound therapy and began working with a therapist using singing bowls and mantras focused on the third eye chakra. Weekly sessions included chanting the sound "OM" to calm her racing mind, accompanied by focused listening to vibrations from the bowls. Over eight weeks, she reported increased clarity, fewer intrusive thoughts, and improved concentration. Her academic performance improved, and she felt more connected to her intuition, making better decisions with confidence.

Reflection

Reflecting on this chapter, I have gained a nuanced appreciation of how chakra healing can impact mental and emotional health, bridging ancient Eastern philosophies with modern therapeutic practices. This journey through chakra healing has highlighted how interconnected our mental and physical health truly are, and how addressing imbalances within these energy centres can facilitate emotional release, self-discovery, and a sense of grounding. Concepts like visualizing colours to balance chakras, using crystal and sound therapy to facilitate emotional regulation, and the powerful effects of yoga and breathwork for energy alignment emphasize the holistic approach that chakra healing embodies.

This chapter has also illuminated the challenges faced in integrating chakra healing into mainstream practices, where scientific validation is often prioritized. The need for further empirical research becomes clear, as it would strengthen the credibility of chakra healing within conventional mental health care. Equally important is the reminder of cultural respect, where ancient practices must be preserved and honoured rather than diluted or commercialized. This chapter has reinforced the potential chakra healing holds as a supportive practice in mental health, encouraging a more open, balanced approach to healing those values both modern evidence-based practices and ancient wisdom.

References

Anand, A., & Srivastava, M. (2021). *Eastern body, western mind: Exploring the integration of eastern chakra healing in modern psychology*. Mind-Body Research Institute.

Bradshaw, G., & Rojas, T. (2020). Understanding energy work: A qualitative analysis of chakra healing practices. *Journal of Holistic Mental Health, 28*(2), 113-130.

Chatterjee, S. (2019). *The healing power of chakras: A holistic approach to balancing energy and emotion*. Lotus Press.

Frawley, D. (2018). *Yoga and the sacred fire: Self-realization and planetary transformation*. Lotus Press.

Khalsa, S., & Kaplan, H. (2017). Mindfulness, meditation, and energy flow: An integrative approach to reducing stress through chakra healing. *Global Journal of Wellness Practices, 12*(4), 150-165.

Northrup, C. (2020). *Women's bodies, women's wisdom: Creating physical and emotional health and healing*. Bantam Books.

Singh, V., & Sharma, P. (2022). The role of breathwork and mantra in emotional healing. *International Journal of Spiritual Psychology, 14*(3), 207-218.

Srinivasan, S. (2019). *Crystals and chakras: Ancient tools for modern healing*. Balboa Press.

Tiwari, R. (2018). Cultural misinterpretation in alternative therapies: Challenges in integrating chakra healing in Western practices. *Journal of Cross-Cultural Health, 9*(1), 45-62.

van der Kolk, B. (2015). *The body keeps the score: Brain, mind, and body in the healing of trauma*. Viking.

Chapter 3

Ecotherapy - Mind Over Mud

Swathi M School Of Liberal Studies, CMR University, Bangalore

Introduction

The disconnection from nature is undeniable in a world increasingly dominated by technology and urban sprawl. As humans have drifted away from their natural roots, mental health challenges such as anxiety, depression, and stress have surged. Enter eco-therapy, a practice rooted (pun intended) in reconnecting with the great outdoors to foster emotional and psychological healing.

Eco-therapy, also known as nature therapy, taps into humans' inherent bond with the environment. From hiking in forests to gardening, this therapeutic approach leverages nature's calming and restorative properties to enhance well-being.

Tracing the Roots of Eco therapy: An Overview

Eco-therapy, also known as nature therapy or green therapy, has deep historical roots that can be traced back to ancient practices and philosophies. The concept of utilizing nature for healing and well-being is not a modern invention but rather a continuation of age-old traditions that recognize the interconnectedness between humans and the natural world.

In many indigenous cultures, nature has long been revered as a source of healing and spiritual connection. Traditional healing practices often incorporate elements of the natural environment, such as plants, water, and animals. These practices illustrate a holistic approach to health that emphasizes balance between mind, body, and nature.

The formal recognition of nature's therapeutic benefits gained momentum in the late 19th and early 20th centuries. During this period, the "nature cure" movement emerged in Europe, advocating for the use of outdoor activities and natural remedies to improve physical and mental health. This movement was largely a response to industrialization and urbanization, which led to increasing rates of mental health issues and physical ailments. Advocates such as Swiss physician Henry Lindlahr promoted the idea that exposure to fresh air, sunlight, and natural landscapes could significantly enhance well-being.

The formalization of eco-therapy continued in the mid-20th century as psychological theories began to evolve. Pioneering psychologists like Carl Jung recognized the importance of nature in personal development and healing.

Modern Resurgence of Eco-Therapy

The late 20th and early 21st centuries witnessed a significant resurgence of interest in eco-therapy, driven by growing concerns over mental health crises and the effects of urbanization. As society has become more aware of the mental health benefits associated with spending time in nature, eco-therapy has gained popularity as a complementary therapeutic approach.

This modern resurgence has been bolstered by a wealth of research demonstrating the psychological benefits of nature exposure. Studies have shown that spending time outdoors can reduce symptoms of anxiety and depression, enhance mood, and improve overall well-being. The work of researchers like Howard Frumkin and Stephen Kaplan has helped to solidify the theoretical foundations of eco-therapy, linking it to established psychological principles and emphasizing its benefits for mental health.

In recent years, various forms of eco-therapy have emerged, including wilderness therapy, horticultural therapy, and animal-assisted therapy. These practices cater to diverse populations, from at-risk youth to individuals experiencing chronic stress, providing accessible and effective means of healing through nature.

The increasing recognition of eco-therapy within mental health circles highlights its potential to address not only individual psychological issues but also broader societal concerns related to mental health and well-being. As the field continues to evolve, eco-therapy stands as a testament to the enduring bond between humans and the environment, inviting individuals to reclaim their mental health through the transformative power of nature.

Theoretical Framework: Nature's Influence on Mental Health

The theoretical framework for eco-therapy is built upon several key psychological theories and concepts that underscore the profound impact of nature on human well-being.

Biophilia Hypothesis

The biophilia hypothesis, introduced by biologist Edward O. Wilson, in the 1980s, proposed that humans have an inherent connection to nature and living organisms.

This connection is rooted in our evolutionary history, as early humans relied on nature for survival. Exposure to natural environments evokes feelings of comfort and rejuvenation, contributing to psychological well-being. This concept serves as a foundational principle for eco-therapy, highlighting the therapeutic benefits of reconnecting with nature.

Attention Restoration Theory (ART)

Attention Restoration Theory, developed by psychologists Stephen Kaplan and Rachel Kaplan, proposes that natural environments facilitate recovery from mental fatigue and enhance cognitive functioning. According to ART, modern life demands sustained attention, leading to mental exhaustion. Natural settings provide an opportunity for "soft fascination," allowing individuals to restore their attention capacity. This restoration is crucial for improving mental clarity and reducing symptoms of stress and anxiety.

Stress Reduction Theory (SRT)

Stress Reduction Theory, formulated by environmental psychologist Roger Ulrich, suggests that exposure to nature can significantly reduce stress and promote relaxation. Natural environments evoke positive emotions and physiological responses, such as lowered heart rate and decreased cortisol levels. By providing a tranquil setting, eco-therapy facilitates emotional regulation and resilience, offering individuals a powerful tool for managing stress and enhancing overall mental health.

Ecopsychology

Ecopsychology explores the relationship between human beings and the natural environment, positing that disconnection from nature contributes to psychological distress. It emphasizes that reconnecting with the natural world can promote healing and well-being. This field recognizes the necessity of understanding environmental issues as integral to psychological health, aligning closely with the principles of eco-therapy.

Nature-Based Mindfulness

Nature-based mindfulness practices integrate mindfulness techniques with outdoor experiences, enhancing emotional regulation and reducing anxiety. Engaging in mindfulness while immersed in natural settings encourages individuals to focus on their surroundings, fostering a sense of presence and connection that enhances the therapeutic effects of eco-therapy.

The Stress-Buffering Hypothesis

The Stress-Buffering Hypothesis given by Sheldon Cohen and Thomas Ashby Wills suggests that social support can mitigate the effects of stress on health. In eco-therapy, engaging in nature-based activities with others enhances social support, providing a dual benefit of nature's restorative qualities and positive social interaction. This combination fosters resilience and effective coping mechanisms.

Benefits of Eco-Therapy: Reconnecting with Nature for Mental Well-Being

Reduction of Stress and Anxiety

One of the most significant benefits of eco-therapy is its ability to reduce stress and anxiety levels. Research has demonstrated that exposure to natural environments can reduce cortisol levels, which are linked to stress.

Spending time in nature can evoke feelings of calmness and relaxation, providing a respite from the pressures of daily life. Activities such as forest bathing or nature walks allow individuals to engage their senses and promote mindfulness, which can further alleviate anxiety symptoms.

Improved Mood and Emotional Regulation

Eco-therapy has a profound impact on mood enhancement. Exposure to natural settings is linked to increased feelings of happiness and well-being. Engaging in eco-therapy activities can lead to the release of endorphins, the body's natural mood lifters. Additionally, individuals often report a greater sense of emotional stability and improved coping mechanisms when regularly participating in nature-based therapy.

Enhanced Cognitive Functioning

Nature has a restorative effect on cognitive functioning, which can be particularly beneficial for individuals experiencing mental fatigue or attention difficulties. The Attention Restoration Theory suggests that being in natural environments allows the brain to recover from mental overload. Eco-therapy can improve focus, creativity, and problem-solving skills, making it a valuable tool for enhancing overall cognitive performance.

Increased Physical Activity

Many forms of eco-therapy involve physical activity, whether through hiking, gardening, or other outdoor exercises. This increased physical activity not only promotes physical health but also contributes to improved mental health. Regular exercise is known to release endorphins and serotonin, further enhancing mood, and reducing symptoms of depression.

Strengthened Connection to Nature

Participating in eco-therapy fosters a deeper connection to the natural world, promoting environmental stewardship and a sense of responsibility toward the earth. This connection can lead to greater appreciation for the environment and increased motivation to engage in sustainable practices. By understanding their role within the ecosystem, individuals may experience a sense of purpose and belonging.

Improved Social Connections

Eco-therapy often involves group activities, such as nature retreats or community gardening, which can enhance social connections and reduce feelings of isolation. Building relationships with others who share a passion for nature can foster a supportive community, providing individuals with a sense of belonging and mutual understanding.

Holistic Healing

Eco-therapy embraces a holistic approach to mental health, recognizing the interconnectedness of the mind, body, and environment. By addressing psychological, emotional, and physical aspects of well-being, eco-therapy promotes comprehensive healing. Participants often find that engaging with nature facilitates personal growth, self-discovery, and a deeper understanding of themselves.

Limitations of Eco-Therapy: Understanding the Challenges of Nature-Based Healing

Accessibility and Availability

One of the primary limitations of eco-therapy is the accessibility of natural environments. Not everyone has easy access to parks, forests, or other natural settings, particularly those living in urban areas. This geographical barrier can hinder individuals from fully engaging in eco-therapy practices. Additionally, the availability of trained eco-therapy professionals may vary, making it challenging for some to find suitable programs or guidance.

Individual Differences

Eco-therapy may not be equally effective for everyone. Individual differences, such as personal preferences, past experiences with nature, and specific mental health conditions, can influence how someone responds to eco-therapy. For example, individuals with anxiety disorders may initially feel overwhelmed in open or unfamiliar natural settings. Personalizing eco-therapy approaches to accommodate individual needs is crucial for ensuring positive outcomes.

Environmental Factors

Weather and environmental conditions can significantly impact the feasibility and effectiveness of eco-therapy. Extreme weather conditions, such as heavy rain, extreme heat, or cold temperatures, can limit outdoor activities and make participation in eco-therapy challenging. Additionally, individuals with specific allergies or sensitivities may find it difficult to engage in nature-based activities comfortably.

Lack of Standardization

The field of eco-therapy is still developing, leading to a lack of standardization in practices and methodologies. This variability can create confusion regarding the effectiveness and application of eco-therapy techniques. Without a clear framework or guidelines, individuals and practitioners may struggle to determine the most suitable approaches for their specific needs.

Limited Research

Although the interest in eco-therapy is growing, the body of empirical research supporting its effectiveness is still limited compared to more traditional therapeutic modalities. More rigorous studies are needed to validate the claims surrounding eco-therapy's benefits and to better understand its mechanisms of action. The lack of comprehensive research can make it challenging for practitioners to justify eco-therapy as a primary treatment option for mental health issues.

Potential for Nature-Related Anxiety

While nature is generally considered beneficial for mental health, some individuals may experience nature-related anxiety, particularly in unfamiliar environments. This anxiety can stem from fears of wildlife, getting lost, or feeling vulnerable in natural settings. Eco-therapy practitioners must be mindful of these concerns and provide appropriate support to help individuals feel safe and comfortable during their nature-based experiences.

Cultural Sensitivity

Eco-therapy practices may not resonate with all cultural backgrounds. Different cultures have varying relationships with nature and may prioritize different healing modalities. Practitioners must be culturally sensitive and adaptable, ensuring that eco-therapy approaches align with the values and beliefs of diverse populations.

Applications of Eco-Therapy

Green Spaces in Urban Planning:

Eco-therapy has inspired city planners to incorporate more parks, rooftop gardens, and green belts within urban areas. These green spaces offer city dwellers easy access to nature, reducing stress and promoting well-being.

Nature-Based Counseling Sessions:

Therapists have started to conduct sessions outdoors in parks, forests, or other natural settings. This approach can help clients feel less constrained and more connected to nature, enhancing openness and therapeutic outcomes.

Wilderness Therapy Programs:

Popular among young adults and teens, these programs integrate outdoor adventure activities (hiking, camping, etc.) with therapeutic techniques to improve mental health. Research shows positive impacts on self-esteem, resilience, and emotional regulation.

Horticultural Therapy:

Gardening as a therapeutic activity is used in mental health settings, rehabilitation centers, and even prisons. Studies have shown that engaging with plants helps reduce anxiety, encourages mindfulness, and fosters a sense of responsibility.

Animal-Assisted Eco-Therapy:

Combining eco-therapy with animal-assisted interventions (like working with therapy animals in natural environments) helps clients gain social support, self-compassion, and relaxation, especially effective for PTSD and depression.

School-Based Eco-Therapy Programs:

Schools integrate eco-therapy activities like gardening, nature walks, and outdoor learning sessions. These programs are beneficial for children's emotional regulation, concentration, and social skills development.

Digital Eco-Therapy:

For those unable to access natural settings physically, virtual reality (VR) applications simulate nature environments. Studies suggest VR-based nature experiences can significantly reduce stress and induce calm, especially for hospitalized patients.

Findings on Eco-Therapy's Effectiveness

- **Reduced Anxiety and Depression:** Multiple studies have shown that eco-therapy effectively reduces symptoms of anxiety and depression by promoting relaxation, grounding, and a sense of purpose.
- **Enhanced Resilience and Coping Skills:** Engaging in eco-therapy helps people develop better coping mechanisms. Exposure to nature teaches resilience, as individuals face unpredictable elements in outdoor settings, building their mental and emotional strength.
- **Improvement in PTSD Symptoms:** Veterans and trauma survivors have reported significant improvements in PTSD symptoms following wilderness and animal-assisted eco-therapy, with nature offering a safe space for processing trauma.
- **Positive Impact on Physical Health:** Beyond mental health, eco-therapy has shown positive impacts on physical well-being by lowering blood pressure, reducing cortisol levels, and improving immune function, indicating that nature therapy benefits both mind and body.
- **Increased Social Connections:** Group-based eco-therapy, such as community gardening or nature retreats, fosters social interaction and reduces feelings of isolation, which can be therapeutic for people struggling with loneliness or social anxiety.
- **Boost in Cognitive Functioning:** Studies have observed improvements in attention, memory, and problem-solving abilities in participants engaged in eco-therapy, especially helpful for ADHD and neurocognitive disorders.
- **Mindfulness and Emotional Regulation:** Nature facilitates mindfulness and emotional regulation by grounding individuals in the present moment. Forest bathing, for instance, emphasizes slow, mindful walks that help regulate emotions and reduce stress.

Future Directions of Eco-Therapy: Expanding Horizons in Nature-Based Healing

Increased Research and Evidence-Based Practices

One of the most crucial future directions for eco-therapy is the expansion of empirical research. Conducting rigorous studies to validate the effectiveness of eco-therapy interventions will enhance credibility and acceptance in the mental health field. Researchers should focus on exploring various populations, mental health conditions, and settings to identify the most effective approaches. This evidence-based research will contribute to a stronger theoretical foundation and inform best practices in eco-therapy.

Integration with Traditional Therapeutic Approaches

Eco-therapy can benefit from being integrated into traditional therapeutic frameworks, such as cognitive-behavioral therapy (CBT) or mindfulness-based therapies. By combining eco-therapy with established modalities, practitioners can create more holistic and personalized treatment plans that leverage the strengths of both approaches. This integration can enhance the therapeutic process, providing clients with diverse tools for managing their mental health.

Technological Innovations in Eco-Therapy

The advancement of technology offers exciting opportunities for eco-therapy. Virtual reality (VR) and augmented reality (AR) can simulate natural environments, making nature-based experiences accessible to those who may have difficulty engaging with the outdoors. Additionally, mobile applications can facilitate mindfulness practices, nature-based journaling, and guided outdoor activities, helping individuals connect with nature in a variety of settings. Embracing technology can broaden the reach of eco-therapy and make it more adaptable to individual needs.

Emphasis on Environmental Sustainability

As awareness of environmental issues grows, eco-therapy can play a pivotal role in fostering a connection between mental health and environmental sustainability. Practitioners can encourage clients to engage in environmental stewardship activities, such as community gardening, conservation projects, or eco-volunteering. This dual focus on personal well-being and ecological health can empower individuals to take an active role in caring for the planet while enhancing their mental health.

Community-Based Eco-Therapy Programs

Expanding eco-therapy into community settings can increase accessibility and promote social connection. Community-based programs can offer group activities, workshops, and nature retreats that encourage collaboration and support among participants. These initiatives can strengthen social networks, reduce isolation, and foster a sense of belonging while providing valuable therapeutic experiences in nature.

Cultural Adaptation and Inclusivity

As eco-therapy continues to develop, it is essential to ensure that it is culturally sensitive and inclusive. Practitioners should consider diverse cultural perspectives on nature and healing, adapting eco-therapy approaches to resonate with various communities. Engaging with local cultures can enhance the relevance and effectiveness of eco-therapy, making it a more inclusive practice for individuals from all backgrounds.

Case Studies and Evidence

Case Study 1

Jesse, a 37-year-old woman from Ontario, Canada, was diagnosed with Lyme disease, which led to significant cognitive impairments, including brain fog and memory issues. After seeking conventional treatments like antibiotics and consulting various specialists, Jesse found herself unable to work for over a year due to persistent symptoms. Frustrated with the lack of progress, Jesse turned to the Nature-Based Regenerative Healing model in hopes of finding a new path to recovery.

Methodology:

The NBRH Model: The NBRH model, a comprehensive eco therapeutic approach, was customized for Jesse's specific needs. It consists of six phases, including Brain Processing, Barometric Adaptation, and the Regenerative Now Bubble phase, all of which emphasize the healing potential of nature.

- ***Daily Nature Walks:*** Incremental walking in natural settings played a key role in Jesse's treatment. As she increased the distance and time spent in nature, her cognitive and emotional resilience grew.
- ***Memory Work and Affirmations:*** Jesse incorporated memorizing poetry and daily affirmations into her walks. This helped rewire her brain, reducing anxiety and fostering cognitive improvement.
- ***Barometric Adaptation:*** This phase involved monitoring environmental and psychological factors that influenced Jesse's healing process, ensuring they were conducive to recovery.
- ***Altered States of Mind:*** Through repetition, disciplined focus, and gradual progress, Jesse achieved altered states of mind, essential for her cognitive healing.

The model emphasized the importance of living in the present moment and using nature's influence to promote mental clarity and emotional well-being.

Results

Jesse's progress was notable. After eight counseling sessions, she experienced a drastic improvement in her general activity levels, mood, and life enjoyment. Key measurable outcomes included:

- **Improvement in Symptom Severity:** Jesse's symptoms, particularly brain fog and cognitive dysfunction, improved significantly. Her mood scores dropped from 8-9 to 3, indicating a more stable emotional state.
- **Neurological Assessment:** In July, Jesse's memory had improved to the point where she no longer needed to retake her driving test.
- **Return to Work:** By November, Jesse returned to work part-time, and by January, she was working full-time again. She described herself as feeling like a "different person," with only minor lingering symptoms.

Case Study 2:

Introduction

Ecotherapy has emerged as a potential intervention to address both mental and physical health challenges, integrating nature-based activities into therapeutic practice. This article by Hinde, Bojke, and Coventry (2021) explores the cost-effectiveness of ecotherapy as a healthcare intervention. The study aims to evaluate whether ecotherapy provides a financially viable alternative to more conventional treatments, such as medication or traditional therapy while offering measurable health benefits.

Case Study Overview

The study examines the outcomes of various ecotherapy programs offered across different healthcare settings in the UK. The programs, which include activities such as guided nature walks, community gardening, and outdoor group therapy sessions, were analyzed for their impact on patients with mental health conditions such as depression, anxiety, and stress.

Methodology: Cost-Effectiveness Evaluation

- **Program Costs:** The researchers collected data on the costs of implementing ecotherapy programs, including resources for training eco therapists, maintenance of nature spaces, and materials for therapeutic activities.

- **Health Outcomes:** Patient-reported outcomes were used to evaluate the improvement in mental and physical health after participating in the ecotherapy programs. These outcomes were measured using standardized tools for assessing anxiety, depression, and overall well-being.
- **Cost-Utility Analysis:** The study applied a cost-utility analysis, comparing the cost of ecotherapy to the health benefits gained (measured in quality-adjusted life years, or QALYs). This method allowed the authors to assess whether the cost per QALY gained through ecotherapy was within an acceptable threshold for healthcare interventions.

Results

- **Health Improvement:** Patients who participated in ecotherapy programs reported significant improvements in their mental health, with reductions in anxiety and depressive symptoms. Additionally, they noted enhanced physical activity and social connectedness, contributing to an overall improvement in well-being.
- **Cost Savings:** Ecotherapy was found to be a cost-effective intervention compared to traditional treatments. The study demonstrated that ecotherapy programs cost less per QALY gained than the standard threshold typically used to assess healthcare interventions in the UK.
- **Sustainability:** The long-term sustainability of ecotherapy was highlighted, as nature-based interventions do not rely heavily on expensive medical resources or ongoing drug treatments, making them an affordable option for healthcare systems in the long run.

Discussion

The findings suggest that ecotherapy could be a viable alternative to traditional mental health treatments, especially in community and outpatient settings. The low cost of implementation, combined with the substantial mental health benefits observed in patients, supports the integration of ecotherapy into broader healthcare strategies. However, the article also notes that further research is needed to assess the scalability of ecotherapy programs and their effectiveness across diverse populations.

Conclusion

The study concludes that ecotherapy is not only beneficial for mental and physical health but also a cost-effective intervention for healthcare systems. By "separating the wood from the trees," this research highlights the importance of investing in nature-based therapies as a sustainable and affordable approach to healthcare.

Case study 3

Introduction

This pilot study by Matise and Price-Howard (2020) investigates the use of ecotherapy as a therapeutic modality for individuals with trauma-related stress disorders, particularly post-traumatic stress disorder (PTSD). With growing interest in alternative therapies, ecotherapy offers a nature-based approach to help trauma survivors manage stress and regain emotional balance.

Case Study Overview

The pilot study focused on a small group of participants diagnosed with PTSD, many of whom experienced severe symptoms such as flashbacks, hypervigilance, and social withdrawal. Traditional therapies had only provided partial relief for their trauma-related symptoms, leading to the exploration of ecotherapy as a complementary treatment.

Methodology: Ecotherapy Intervention

- **Participant Selection:** The study included participants with diverse trauma backgrounds, such as veterans and survivors of abuse, to evaluate ecotherapy's efficacy across different types of traumas.
- **Therapeutic Activities:** Participants engaged in structured nature-based activities, including forest bathing, mindful walking in natural settings, and grounding exercises using natural elements like water and soil. Group discussions in natural environments allowed for emotional expression and peer support.
- **Duration:** The pilot study ran for eight weeks, with participants attending regular ecotherapy sessions facilitated by trained eco therapists.
- **Measurement Tools:** To assess changes in trauma symptoms, researchers used standardized scales like the PTSD Checklist (PCL-5) and the Depression, Anxiety, and Stress Scale (DASS-21) before and after the intervention.

Results

- **Reduction in PTSD Symptoms:** Most participants experienced a noticeable reduction in PTSD symptoms by the end of the eight-week program. Flashbacks and hypervigilance were particularly reduced, as were general anxiety and depressive symptoms.
- **Increased Emotional Regulation:** Participants reported better emotional regulation, which they attributed to the calming effects of nature and the opportunity to process traumatic memories in a less clinical, more holistic setting.
- **Enhanced Connection to Nature:** Several participants described feeling more grounded and connected to nature, which helped foster a sense of peace and safety that had been difficult to achieve in traditional indoor therapy settings.
- **Social Support and Engagement:** The group format allowed participants to build social connections, alleviating the sense of isolation commonly associated with trauma. The shared experience of nature enhanced feelings of trust and solidarity among participants.

The pilot study demonstrated the potential benefits of ecotherapy for individuals with trauma-related stress disorders, particularly for those who did not respond fully to conventional therapies. Nature-based interventions offer a unique therapeutic environment that supports healing through multisensory experiences and mindfulness. By removing participants from clinical settings, ecotherapy provided a space where trauma survivors could engage with their emotions in a non-threatening way.

Conclusion

While this was a pilot study with a limited sample size, the findings suggest that ecotherapy may be an effective modality for reducing PTSD symptoms and improving emotional well-being. The study highlights the need for further research with larger populations to explore the full potential of ecotherapy in trauma treatment. Nonetheless, the success seen in this initial trial offers promise for integrating ecotherapy into holistic trauma recovery programs.

Reflective Experience

Working on this eco-therapy paper has been a transformative journey, challenging me to bridge the relationship between mental health and the natural environment in new and profound ways. As I delved into the research, I realized that eco-therapy is much more than a therapeutic trend; it's a response to a growing disconnection from nature that so many of us experience, especially in urban and modern lifestyles.

Initially, I approached the topic with curiosity, hoping to understand how eco-therapy techniques, like forest bathing and horticultural therapy, could complement traditional therapeutic methods. However, as I gathered findings, I began to see eco-therapy as a philosophy of reconnection. Each case study, research finding, and theory unfolded the deep impact that natural environments have on reducing stress, fostering emotional regulation, and even enhancing physical health.

The applications of eco-therapy truly stood out to me. Discovering how urban planning, digital nature experiences, and animal-assisted interventions can all be adapted to meet diverse needs opened my eyes to eco-therapy's versatility. I reflected on how powerful it could be for populations that might otherwise have limited access to natural spaces—patients in hospitals, urban communities, and individuals with limited mobility, to name a few. This insight inspired me to think about eco-therapy not only as a mental health intervention but also as a social movement that could reshape how we view our environment and our place within it.

Throughout this process, I encountered several challenges. The literature often presented eco-therapy in broad strokes, which made it challenging to find concrete, empirical evidence for some areas. This limitation reminded me of the importance of advocating for more robust research in emerging therapeutic fields, particularly those rooted in alternative approaches like eco-therapy.

In reflecting on my own values, this paper reinforced my belief in the holistic treatment of mental health. I felt a personal connection to eco-therapy's grounding practices and even considered how I might integrate similar principles into my daily life—whether by spending more time outdoors or encouraging those around me to do the same. This exploration helped me appreciate the potential eco-therapy has not just for clinical application, but for everyday mental wellness.

In summary, this eco-therapy paper has not only deepened my understanding of an emerging therapeutic approach but has also expanded my perspective on mental health. It has been both an academic endeavor and a personal journey, one that has enriched my commitment to exploring diverse, meaningful pathways in clinical psychology.

Conclusion

The theoretical framework for eco-therapy highlights the significance of nature in psychological healing. By grounding eco-therapy practices in established psychological theories, practitioners can effectively utilize the restorative power of nature to enhance mental well-being and promote resilience in individuals facing various mental health challenges.

The benefits of eco-therapy are extensive and multifaceted, providing individuals with powerful tools for enhancing mental and emotional well-being. From reducing stress and improving mood to fostering connections with nature and others, eco-therapy offers a holistic pathway to healing. As individuals increasingly seek alternative and complementary approaches to mental health care, eco-therapy stands out as an effective and transformative practice that reconnects people with the healing power of the natural world.

While eco-therapy presents a promising approach to enhancing mental health, it is crucial to acknowledge its limitations and challenges. Accessibility, individual differences, environmental factors, and a lack of standardization all pose potential barriers to effective implementation. By understanding these limitations, practitioners and participants can work together to tailor eco-therapy experiences, ensuring they are beneficial and inclusive for everyone involved.

The future of eco-therapy holds exciting possibilities for enhancing mental health and fostering a deeper connection to the natural world. By prioritizing research, integrating traditional therapies, embracing technology, and promoting environmental sustainability, eco-therapy can continue to evolve and meet the diverse needs of individuals and communities. As this field grows, it has the potential to transform the landscape of mental health care, emphasizing the profound healing power of nature.

References

Bowler, D. E., Buyung-Ali, L., Knight, T. M., & Pullin, A. S. (2010). A systematic review of evidence for the added benefits to health of exposure to natural environments. BMC Public Health, 10, 456. https://doi.org/10.1186/1471-2458-10-456

Kellert, S. R., & Wilson, E. O. (1993). The Biophilia Hypothesis. Island Press.

Kaplan, S. (1995). The restorative benefits of nature: Toward an integrative framework. *Journal of Environmental Psychology, 15*(3), 169-182. https://doi.org/10.1016/0272-4944(95)90001-2

Roger S. Ulrich,View Through a Window May Influence Recovery from Surgery.*Science*224,420-421(1984). DOI:10.1126/science.6143402

Berry, G. The well-evidenced benefits of ecotherapy.

Maller, C., Townsend, M., St Leger, L., & Henderson-Wilson, C. (2010). Healthy parks, healthy people: The health benefits of contact with nature in a park context. *BMC Public Health, 10*, 456. https://doi.org/10.1186/1471-2458-10-456

Puk, T. (2021). Nature-based regenerative healing: A case-study of interpersonal ecotherapy. European Journal of Ecopsychology, 7(1), 19-40.

Joschko, L., Palsdottir, A. M., Grahn, P., & Hinse, M. (2023).

Rueff, M., & Reese, G. (2023). Depression and anxiety: A systematic review on comparing ecotherapy with cognitive behavioral therapy. Journal of Environmental Psychology, 102097.

Matise, M., & Price-Howard, K. (2020). A pilot study utilizing ecotherapy as a therapeutic modality for persons with trauma-related stress disorders. The Practitioner Scholar: Journal of the International Trauma Training Institute, 2, 26-46.

Hinde, S., Bojke, L., & Coventry, P. (2021). The cost effectiveness of ecotherapy as a healthcare intervention, separating the wood from the trees. International journal of environmental research and public health, 18(21), 11599.

Chapter 4

Exploring the Efficacy of Herbal Remedies as Adjuncts in Psychotherapy

Nikita Priyanka Dsa, Dr Monalisa Nayak School of Liberal Studies (SLS), CMR University, Bangalore

Introduction

Psychotherapy is one of the most important therapeutic interventions for anxiety, depression, and stress-related psychopathology. However, the recent evidence indicates that holistic interventions including herbal treatments might enhance psychotherapy outcomes. This is somewhat like a larger trend in healthcare, which moves toward the biopsychosocial model, which considers the influence of both physiological as well as psychological factors along with social elements for a treatment plan.

Herbal Remedies and Their Uses in Psychotherapy

St. John's Wort (Hypericum perforatum):

Psychological Use:

It has been used traditionally in the treatment of minor to moderate depression. Due to its supposed effects on neurotransmitters like serotonin, dopamine, and norepinephrine, it has provided some degree of mood stabilization.

Clinical Evidence:

Meta-analyses demonstrate that St. John's Wort is at least equivalent to SSRIs in symptom reduction for mild-to-moderate depression, while it is less reliably effective for the severe form. Lower dropout rates from therapy are also associated with use of St. John's Wort, which may be due to enhanced mood stability.

Pregnancy Considerations:

St. John's Wort may cause serotonin syndrome when used concomitantly with SSRIs and interacts with many drugs including antidepressants.

Valerian Root (Valeriana officinalis):

Psychological Application:

The valerian root has been used to alleviate anxiety and insomnia; hence, it is recognized for its anxiolytic and sedative effects.

Clinical Evidence:

Valerian root could modestly improve the quality of sleep. Thus, this indirectly supports psychotherapy because cognitive function and emotional resilience would be improved. It could possibly reduce symptoms of anxiety as well, thereby aiding patients in dealing with stressors during treatment.

Kava (Piper methysticum):

Psychological Use:

Kava has been used for many centuries in the Polynesian societies for its sedative and anxiolytic properties and is often prescribed today for generalized anxiety disorder as well as social anxiety.

Clinical Research:

There are several controlled clinical studies documenting the efficacy of kava for reducing anxiety. Its anxiolytic nature makes it an ancillary therapy in psychotherapies that demand patients confront stimuli that cause fear, as in exposure therapies.

Ginkgo Biloba:

Psychological Use:

Ginkgo biloba has been used traditionally as a memory enhancer and cognitive functioning booster where it is primarily useful in the treatment of cognitive impairment, ADHD, and mood disorder treatment.

Clinical Evidence:

There is much evidence regarding the enhancing effect of Ginkgo on memory, but the stimulating impact on mood balance is entirely ambiguous. However, there is some indication that Ginkgo has an ameliorative effect on mood in older adults and even enhances cognitive focus, which will help the patient to be more attentive in therapy.

Ashwagandha (Withania somnifera):

Psychological Use:

Ashwagandha has been categorized as an adaptogen, therefore a substance that might help the body adapt and recover from stress. It has been shown in multiple studies to diminish symptoms of anxiety and depression, thus it is useful as an adjunct in stress-related disorders.

Clinical Evidence:

There exist studies indicating that ashwagandha decreases cortisol, meaning it helps regulate the body's response to stress. This may interact with other psychosocial therapies like CBT, as this would assist patients in gaining better control of emotional response.

Mechanisms of Action: How Herb Medications May Potentiate Psychotherapy

Herb medications interact with the neurochemical pathways in the human body, which may serve to enhance the objectives of psychotherapy:

Modification of Neurotransmitter Activity:

Many herbs work directly on neurotransmitters and thereby modify mood. For example, St. John's Wort elevates serotonin levels; such an action can increase therapeutic benefit in mood-disordered patients.

Reducing Physiological Symptoms:

Anxiolytic drugs like valerian and kava may also decrease the somatic symptoms of anxiety and thus promote more effective therapy.

These include herbs like ginkgo biloba, which are known to increase cognitive functions and thus improve attention and memory, so a patient may learn more therapeutic tools and concepts.

Stress Response Regulation:

While helping in reducing body's stress response, the adaptogenic nature of ashwagandha can be very useful in therapeutic procedures with stress management cores.

Theoretical Background of Herbal Remedies in Psychotherapy

Herbal remedies have been used for centuries by many cultures in the practice of traditional medicine and have often been used to treat both psychological and bodily afflictions. Psychotherapy draws on grounds theoretically derived from integrative health approaches to life that consider mind and body to be interdependent with each other.

Biopsychosocial Model of Mental Health

The biopsychosocial model provides a conceptual framework that can explain why herbal remedies a part of the mental health therapy should be. The model postulates that mental health disorders have their roots in all the three domains: biological, psychological, and social. Herbal remedies do impact the biological domain through impacts on neurotransmitter levels, hormonal balance, and other physiological mechanisms that constitute the causation of mental health disorders. This will occur only when those biological factors are provided with support, thereby ensuring that psychotherapy has the desired impact on the psychological and social side of the personality - hence a more holistic means of achieving wellness.

Neurobiological Mechanisms of Herbal Compounds

Numerous herbs used in psychiatric therapeutics, including for depression, such as St. John's Wort, valerian root, and ashwagandha, contain neuroactive agents. Such herbs act either by resembling neurotransmitter molecules or by altering neurotransmitter reuptake in systems that include serotonin, dopamine, and gamma-aminobutyric acid (GABA), all of which play significant roles in mood regulation, anxiety, and cognitive functioning.

Complementary and Integrative Medicine (CIM)

Complementary and integrative medicine (CIM) offers a theoretical framework for herbal remedies to be used in psychotherapy. CIM targets the treatment of the whole individual and not just symptoms; CIM places natural products in an ambience of health improvement. Herbs are designed to be adjunctive agents that would improve stress-resistance, emotional regulation, and cognitive abilities and, therefore, meet the goals of psychotherapy. This would thus resonate with psychotherapeutic practices that are based on patient empowerment and holistic approach towards better health, observing and seeing that there was also a great connection between the physical health and psychological one, and vice versa.

Adaptogens and Stress Regulation

Adaptogens, a family of herbs that comprises ashwagandha and rhodiola, are said to help your body adapt to stress by modulating the hypothalamic-pituitary-adrenal (HPA) axis. The HPA axis is central to the body's stress responses, and, therefore, impacts the release of cortisol levels as well as the degree of activation in the autonomic nervous system. Chronic stress dysregulates the system and thus leads to mental health disorders like anxiety and depression. It has been hypothesized that the restorative balance to the HPA axis may provide a means through which adaptogens could reduce stress and promote resilience. This will help patients deal with stress more effectively and, more broadly, more actively participate in therapeutic procedures that focus on emotional regulation.

Mind-Body Connection and Psychoneuroimmunology

Psychoneuroimmunology is the investigation of how psychological factors could influence the nervous system and eventually affect the immune system. Chronic psychological stress has been shown to weaken the immune system. This, in turn, might exacerbate mental health-related conditions. Herbal treatments like ginseng or echinacea, which are immuno-modulators, may strengthen the immune system to promote, by proxy, mental well-being. In psychotherapy, this mind-body approach provides a theoretical foundation for herbal remedies to enhance resilience, provide an adjunct to mood stabilizing actions which alleviate stress-induced immunosuppression and contribute to increased body and mind vitality.

Cultural and Historical Perspective

Herbal remedies have been widely used across cultures throughout history in attempts to treat emotional and psychological distress. The therapeutic application of TCM, Ayurveda, and Indigenous healing systems treat the mind and the body as interconnected entities and make wide use of plants and other natural substances. Herbal remedies in psychotherapy fit into this tradition of understanding and allow practitioners to honor cultural practices while acquiring additional therapeutic tools. This may be of value in culturally sensitive psychotherapy, which involves the acceptance of a patient's cultural background to further strengthen the therapeutic alliance and improve treatment outcomes.

The Placebo Effect and Mindset Enrichment

The placebo effect provides another theoretical model under which belief in a treatment confers some therapeutic benefit. Beliefs patients have regarding the efficacy of herbal remedies may indeed influence their psychological response to treatment through such mechanisms as increasing motivation, self-efficacy, and engagement. In psychotherapy, where change is focused in mindset or behavior, the beliefs a patient has about the value of herbal remedies increase commitment to the goals of treatment and, therefore, maximizes any gains made.

Psychopharmacology of Natural Substances

Several herbal products are included in psychopharmacology and explore the effects of natural substances on mood and cognition. Some of the herbs are anxiolytic, antidepressant, and sedatives in nature, and on account of their mode of activity, produce lesser side effects in some subjects than equivalent pharmacological drugs.

Implementation Procedure of Herbal Remedies in Psychotherapy

Implementation of herbal remedies in psychotherapy is an aware, systematic, client-centered procedure that will aim to integrate the physiological benefits of herbal treatment with psychotherapeutic intervention to improve mental health outcomes, especially in mildly to moderately affected individuals afflicted with anxiety, depression, or stress.

History and Screening Intake:

This is the onset of herbal medication prescription during psychotherapy. This starts with a broadened evaluation of the patient's mental status, overall health, and lifestyle:

Mental Health Survey:

Assess the patient's symptoms of psychologic disorder, history, and medications currently prescribed. Psychotherapists may use standardized assessment tools such as Beck Depression Inventory or GAD-7 to establish symptoms at baseline.

Review of the Complete Medical History:

It is important to understand the whole medical history of a patient, including the allergies, drugs he or she is taking currently and the health conditions he or she suffers from. Herbal remedies may react with prescribed medicines and impact physical health.

Patient Preferences:

Some patients may have preferences for or against use of herbal remedy. It is by engaging such patients in discussions about their interests and beliefs about natural or complementary treatments that will lead to building trust and shared decision-making.

Informed Consent and Education

Since herbal remedies can reflect both positive benefits and side effects, it is essential to obtain informed consent:

Explain the Reason:

You should explain that herbal remedies are used as additives to supplement, not substitute conventional treatment methods. These may reduce symptoms, such as stress or insomnia, which otherwise may disrupt therapy.

Risks and Benefits:

Consider the potential benefits (e.g., reduced anxiety, mood stabilization) along with potential risks: potential interactions with other medications, or even cause toxicity: valerian root is sedating; kava hepatotoxic.

Setting Expectations:

Educate patients that herbal remedies aren't a cure all. Sometimes they can take weeks to appear and should be considered adjunctive not therapeutic.

Choice of Herbs According to Symptoms

Selection of suitable herbal remedies appropriate to the patient's symptoms and therapeutic objectives

For Anxiety and Stress:

The most recommended herbs for anxiolytic and calming effect are valerian root, kava, and ashwagandha. These may be beneficial to patients who experience chronic stress and anxiety since they can help alleviate physiological symptoms that interfere with the effectiveness of therapy.

For Mild to Moderate Depression:

St. John's Wort is often prescribed as it might level out the neurotransmitter serotonin but should be used with reservations in case, they are also under prescription for antidepressants.

To Assist Improvement of Cognitive Function:

Ginkgo biloba might be beneficial to patients who have impaired cognitive function or other forms of mild forgetfulness due to age or conditions like ADHD, where the extracts may enhance concentration and memory, thereby assisting better in facilitating therapy engagement.

For sleep disorders:

Supplements with valerian root and passionflower can be prescribed to sleep disorder patients who experience insomnia or other forms of sleep disorders because these conditions usually accompany mental disorders. Better sleep improves a patient's ability to concentrate and expend energy, with improved emotional balance in their general treatment.

Developing an Integrated Plan of Treatment

After identification of herbal remedies, the next step would be to develop a tailored, integrated plan of treatment:

How each herbal remedy will aid in the pursuit of therapeutic goals:

For example, a goal for the patient who has high anxiety is to use ashwagandha to allow lowering of general stress levels to enable cognitive-behavioral therapy sessions to go more effectively.

Dosage and Administration:

Collaborate with an herbalist or an experienced healthcare provider to determine the correct dosage and preparation: tinctures, teas, and/or capsules. Start with lower dosages to assess tolerance.

Dosage and Administration:

Determine the frequency and duration of how the herbal remedy will be consumed in conjunction with the course of treatment or duration of symptom reduction.

Monitoring and Modifications:

Schedule frequent follow-ups to track the results, adverse effects, and compliance by the patient. Dosage or the herb itself needs to be altered as and when there is some improvement and development of tolerance.

Symptom Management as an Adjunct Therapy

Herbal medicines can also provide relief from symptoms that might otherwise interfere with therapeutic work:

Diminished Physiological Symptoms:

In anxious or stressed patients, herbal interventions, such as valerian root, can reduce symptoms, such as muscle tension and insomnia, so that there is less physiological interference with the ability to work on therapeutic activities.

Enhancement of an Emotional Mood and Resilience:

St. John's Wort may have a mood-stabilizing effect, which can make it easier for patients to participate in psychotherapy, to rehearse skills learned in the session, and to sustain motivation throughout the treatment process.

Improved Cognitive Engagement:

Herbs that improve memory and concentration, such as ginkgo biloba, can potentially improve the ability of patients to retain information and follow up on exercises and homework ordered in physical therapy.

Ongoing Monitoring and Evaluation

Monitor and evaluate the integrative treatment regularly, in terms of its efficacy.

Symptom Monitoring:

The changes in symptoms should be monitored both using subjective and objective scales. These could be a reduction in anxiety or better sleep and stabilized mood. Such would include self-report symptom scales, therapist observations or physiological measures when appropriate.

Side Effect Monitoring:

Side effects are also possible from herbal remedies. For example, kava has been claimed to interfere with liver functions. Thus, periodic monitoring of liver enzymes is suggested.

Therapeutic Engagement:

Assess whether herbal therapies are aiding in the achievement of therapy goals, such as improved focus during sessions, improved emotional regulation, or improved positive mood.

Dose Tapering Process

If therapeutic goals have been met or if side effects occur, herbals may need to be tapered: Taper herbs with psych activities like valerian or St. John's wort gradually.

Reappraisal of Symptoms:

Consider whether improvements in the symptoms are stable when the herbal treatment is tapered down or discontinued. This could help determine if the patient is ready to continue to make gains without adjunctive treatment alone or if some form of adjunctive treatment is still needed.

Encourage Continued Self-Care:

Teach the patient lifestyle activities that might serve as alternatives or supplements to the positive benefits of herbal remedy-exercise, meditation, or dietary modification.

Continuing Education and Support

As a holistic practitioner, you need to continue with patient education and support even after the herbal remedy has been completed:

Empower Patient's Self-Care:

Teach patient on self-regulation skills, such as breathing exercises or mindfulness, that might eventually replace the herb function and empower the patient to later handle their symptoms better.

Follow Up:

See to regular follow-up therapy sessions with a patient to continue monitoring their mental status and ensure that they are on the right track after having been treated.

Therapeutic Techniques of Herbal Therapies in Psychotherapy

Herbal therapies in psychotherapy use specific techniques for their application with common psychotherapy techniques. The techniques aim at symptom relief, mind-body integration, and improving therapeutic engagement.

Symptom-Specific Herbal Protocols

Symptom-specific protocols involve the choice of herbs as targeted remedies for the identified symptom, thereby giving psychotherapy a focused approach in herbal support:

Anxiety and Stress Relief:

These patients are given prescriptions of medicines that include valerian root, ashwagandha, and kava. They act as anxiolytic and sedative agents. They will control the physiological manifestations of anxiety like muscle tension and racing thoughts so that greater focus is made on cognitive-behavioral strategies and other therapeutic interventions.

Mood Stabilizer:

Since St. John's Wort does affect the levels of serotonin and has been used to sometimes enhance mood, it is considered an adjunct for mild to moderate depression. Mood stabilization might enable the patient to go for psychotherapy and to perform cognitive restructuring and do motivation-building exercises.

Sleep Regulation:

Valerian root and passionflower are often used to promote sleep, which can be a lifeline for patients who suffer from insomnia secondary to anxiety or stress. Improved sleep enhances cognitive functioning, emotional regulation, and overall therapeutic engagement.

Therapists can coordinate these protocols with therapy objectives, matching herbal treatment cycles to phases of therapy to provide symptom reduction that can be linked to specific therapeutic activities.

Adaptogenic Support with Stress Management:

Adaptogenic herbs regulate the impact of stress on the body by modulating the HPA axis, thereby lowering cortisol levels while serving to influence resilience. The most used adaptogen in psychotherapy is ashwagandha for patients with chronic stress or burnout; other adaptogens used include Rhodiola and holy basil.

Adaptogens could be used early in treatment as some of the earliest treatment components, building some physiological resilience to stress that could better prepare patients to respond appropriately to the entrance of most stressors. Ashwagandha is just one example that reduces physiological responses to stress and so supports therapies like DBT and MBSR.

Improved Mindfulness and Emotional Control:

Patients who are taught mindfulness can be helped with these adaptogens because herbs generally tend to suppress stress responses, thus making it easier for a patient to reach the state of calmness and concentration needed in proper mindfulness practice.

Psychoeducational Herbal Counselling

Psycho-educational herbal counselling makes the patient, or a client better informed about the benefits, mechanism, and safe usage of herbal remedies. Information delivery and involving the patient helps enhance empowerment, adherence to the treatment process, and self-management skills.

Empowering Patients:

Educating a patient on how herbs work, its side effects, and what might be expected from the herbal remedy helps them make informed choices that may build confidence and motivation for the therapeutic process.

Symptom Monitoring and Self-Management:

The therapists can teach the patients how they can monitor the symptoms and the side effects so that they become empowered to understand how the herbal remedy interplays with their mental and physical states. It, therefore, opens for self-awareness and thereby strengthens the therapeutic gains.

Goal Setting:

Teaching a goal-specific herbal remedy, for instance, using valerian root in sleep hygiene, can make the personal goals of the patient interplay with treatment to ensure that the engagement in or adherence to the therapeutic becomes enhanced.

Mind-Body Therapies:

Herbal supplements are combined with practices such as mindfulness, breathing, or other forms of progressive relaxation and used to soothe patients while helping them master self-regulation techniques.

Teas:

Blending soothing herbal teas like chamomile or lemon balm with mindfulness use may be particularly effective in nurturing relaxation and a gentle ritual to induce self-care. This can be helpful with anxious patients; as they master this soothing ritual, they learn a healthy approach to managing anxiety and stress.

Aromatherapy and Guided Relaxation:

Aromatherapy using essential oils from herbs like lavender, peppermint, or bergamot combines well with guided imagery or progressive muscle relaxation. Lavender has a calming effect that may enhance the relaxing response even more, thereby allowing patients to attain a much deeper level of rest in relaxation exercises.

Mindfulness with Adaptogens:

Patients can use adaptogens such as ashwagandha along with mindfulness meditation to enhance emotional regulation. The physiological support from the adaptogen can facilitate better presence and management of stress response within mindfulness practices.

Phased Herbal Integration with Psychotherapeutic Techniques

The phased integration refers to the adjustment of herbal remedies to suit various stages of psychotherapy. It allows for a tailored support system with herbal elements.

Early stages - Calming and stabilizing:

During the early stages of therapy, soothing herbs, like valerian root, may be initiated to alleviate initial anxiety or stress to have patients more open to rapport-building during therapy and foundational interventions such as psychoeducation.

Middle Phases - Mood Stabilization and Resistance:

The use of herbs like St. John's Wort or Adaptogenic herbs like ashwagandha can be incorporated into more aggressive therapy like exposure therapy or CBT with a goal of mood stabilization as well as developing resistance. Improved mood stabilization and resilience would enable her to better digest issues of a deeper nature.

Later Phases - Cognitive Enhancement and Enablement:

The herbs that enhance cognitive function, like ginkgo biloba, are added in the skill-building phases or may be included during self-reflection and empowerment therapy. The herbs enhancing concentration and clarity of thought would enable the patient to absorb those insights and tools into their lives more easily.

Group-Lifestyle Herbal Interventions

For patients who need lifestyle modifications that improve mental well-being, herbal therapies may be an adjunct to a more general lifestyle intervention:

Herbal Support for Lifestyle Habits:

Therapists may prescribe herbs to support habits of lifestyle change consistent with the goals of therapy. For instance, peppermint tea for digestive aids in patients engaged in healthy eating practices or ashwagandha to help patients building up exercise habits for reducing stress levels.

Dietary and Physical Health Counselling:

The holistic health counsellor can guide the patients who may receive education in herbal supplement support for physical health, such as digestive aids of ginger and ginseng herbs supporting energy and indirectly mental health by keeping the person generally healthy and not anxious over unhealthy situations.

Monitoring and Tapering Techniques

Therapists ensure safe and effective use by using monitoring and tapering techniques, particularly when the herbal remedy was started to assist with short-term goals:

Structured Symptom and Side Effect Logging:

If therapists require patients to track their symptom intensity, dosage of the herbal compound, and any side effects that arise, they can change the herbal treatment in response.

Gradual Tapering to Long-Term Stability:

A patient who enters stability with a combination of therapy and herbal support may be advised by therapists to taper down herbal dosages to see if one can continue steady progress. Gradually tapering helps one find out if the patient maintains symptom relief on his own without herbal support.

Review of Progress:

They help patients reflect on the benefits and challenges of herbal therapy through regular review sessions, to reinforce the skills learned in therapy and encourage autonomy in managing symptoms.

Debriefing and Reflective Therapy

During the latter stages of the treatment, therapists often perform a debriefing session with the intent to enable them to reflect on the herbal therapy as part of their overall treatment course:

Review of Herbal Therapy Effect:

The therapeutic regimes can be conceptualized in terms of how herbal therapy had impacted symptomatic management, emotional strength, and the level of engagement in therapy sessions, providing individuals with insight into what self-care arrangements they prefer.

Empowerment in Self-Management:

The patient is empowered to explore how they can effectively use herbal therapies in the future, as part of lifestyle practices and skills gained through therapy.

This is the closure and moving on stage, which confirms there should be maintained self-care activity, which had been initiated; this will encourage the patients to carry on healthy practices in their lives long after therapy.

Main Advantages of Herbal Remedies in Psychotherapy

- The herbs include valerian root, kava, and ashwagandha that have been proven to relieve anxiety and stress characterized by soothing the nervous system, thus enabling patients to become calmer and more attentive in therapy sessions.
- **Mood stabilization:** Some of the herbs, such as St. John's Wort, balance mood-an attribute useful more for people with mild depression and fortify resilience and emotional stability. Improve sleep quality: herbal sleep inducer such as valerian and passionflower facilitate good sleep quality, which is crucial to cognitive functioning and the regulation of emotions within therapy.
- **Support for Cognitive Function:** Plants such as ginkgo biloba can improve attention and memory, which may be helpful to patients doing concentration or cognitive-based therapeutic activities.

Limitations of herbal therapy

- **Lack of Standardization:** Herbal supplements are quite variable in potency and quality. This lacks consistency to the dependability of such effects and may elicit unforeseen interactions.
- **Safety and Side Effects:** Many herbs interact with psychotropic medications to increase risks for adverse effects. For example, St. John's Wort when used along with SSRIs may cause serotonin syndrome.
- **Lacking in studies is extensive research on long-term effects.** Most research looks at short-term effects, with limited data on long-term safety, especially regarding liver toxicity associated with herbs such as kava.

Recommendations for further research and practice of herbal therapies

- **High-Quality Controlled Studies on Efficacy:** A better and wider clinical trial should be conducted on the efficacy of selected herbs, like valerian, ashwagandha, and St. John's Wort, which are said to treat specific mood disorders, like anxiety, depression, and sleep disorder. It is a controlled group situation that identifies the best herb for specific symptoms or its symptoms in different patients.
- **Evaluating Integrative Approaches:** Studies of the possibility of effective blending of herbal remedies with other therapeutic approaches-such as CBT or mindfulness-based treatment offer insight into how the therapy outcome could be further improved. Developing Patient-Centered Guidelines and warning of safe herbal use can only be realized by providing practical

guidelines by which therapists may educate patients on adequate herbal, quality considerations, potential interactions, and symptom-based, need-based recommendations.

It is in this regard that the biochemical pathways involved with herbs commonly used in mental health treatment might clarify how they influence mood, cognitive processes, and responses to stress, thus improving our understanding of their role in psychotherapy. Promote Culturally Sensitive Practice: Because most herbal therapies are based in traditional cultures, the research may highlight the development of culturally sensitive practice in psychotherapy in support and validation of the use of traditional remedies as part of treatment for patients from diverse cultural backgrounds.

Case Studies

Psychological ailments and their treatment protocols: a case study of Swati traditional healers in Mpumalanga Province, South Africa

Case Study: The Role of Swati Traditional Healers in Managing Mental Health Complaints in Kanyamazane

Background:

This case study explores the treatment approach of a Swati traditional healer (TH) in the Kanyamazane peri-urban township in Mpumalanga Province, South Africa. The healer, referred to as "Gogo Maseko" (a pseudonym), has been practicing in her community for over two decades and is known for her holistic treatment methods addressing various psychological issues. Gogo Maseko is frequently approached by community members for mental health issues, often due to cultural beliefs around bewitchment, ancestral calling, or the breaking of taboos, and she also encounters cases of adjustment disorders, depression, and substance-induced mental illness.

Methods:

The methods of treatment employed by Gogo Maseko combine Swati cultural practices with elements she has adapted through personal experience. Her approach typically involves:

- **Assessment through Divination:** Using bones and other traditional tools, Gogo Maseko assesses the underlying cause of the client's distress, determining if it stems from ancestral issues, bewitchment, or a more general psychological disturbance.
- **Herbal and Ritual-Based Interventions:** For cases attributed to ancestral calling or breaking taboos, she uses herbal remedies and performs rituals that include invoking ancestral spirits or conducting purification ceremonies.
- **Counselling and Social Support:** Gogo Maseko provides counsel, helping clients address feelings of shame or guilt associated with certain conditions. Her practice also extends to guidance on lifestyle changes and social reintegration strategies.

Case Example:

One of Gogo Maseko's clients, a young woman named Zanele, approached her after experiencing symptoms of depression and anxiety believed to stem from a broken taboo. Zanele reported feeling detached, hearing voices, and struggling with insomnia. Through divination, Gogo Maseko concluded that Zanele's symptoms were tied to a "broken ancestral bond." Gogo Maseko performed a ritual to restore this connection and prescribed an herbal mixture for Zanele's physical symptoms. Over the next few weeks, Gogo Maseko also provided Zanele with counselling to address her feelings of isolation and helplessness.

Results:

After a month of treatment, Zanele reported a significant improvement in her mood, decreased anxiety, and fewer auditory hallucinations. She was also reintegrated into her social circle with the support of Gogo Maseko's guidance. Gogo Maseko continues to monitor Zanele's progress and remains available for further counselling if needed.

Conclusion:

This case highlights the culturally embedded methods used by Swati traditional healers like Gogo Maseko to manage mental health issues within their communities. Traditional healers such as Gogo Maseko play a significant role by providing culturally relevant care, addressing both the psychological and social dimensions of mental illness. The integrated approach used by THs has been effective in promoting mental health and bridging gaps in formal mental health services, especially in rural or peri-urban areas with limited access to Western healthcare facilities.

Herbal medicines in the treatment of psychiatric disorders: a systematic review, Jerome Sarris

Case Study: Herbal Medicine in Treating Anxiety and Depression

Background:

This case study examines the application of herbal medicine for managing anxiety and depression in a 35-year-old woman, Maria, who experienced recurring symptoms of both conditions. Maria sought a natural treatment option due to the adverse effects of traditional psychotropic medications. She consulted a licensed naturopath who specializes in psychotherapy and is knowledgeable about the use of evidence-supported herbs like *St John's wort* and *kava*, which have shown effectiveness in treating depression and anxiety, respectively.

Methods:

Maria's treatment plan included:

- **St John's Wort for Depression:** Known for its antidepressant properties, St John's wort (Hypericum perforatum) was administered at a standardized dosage based on clinical evidence. The herb is believed to work by modulating neurotransmitters like serotonin, dopamine, and norepinephrine.
- **Kava for Anxiety:** To address her anxiety, Maria was prescribed a kava extract (*Piper methysticum*), which is known for its anxiolytic effects. Kava has been found to increase levels of GABA, a neurotransmitter that has a calming effect, without causing sedation.

Results:

Over the course of eight weeks, Maria experienced notable improvements. Her depressive symptoms, including low mood and loss of interest in daily activities, significantly decreased with the use of St John's wort. Likewise, her anxiety levels, including physical symptoms like palpitations and racing thoughts, were reduced through the use of kava. Maria did not experience any adverse side effects during this period, though her naturopath closely monitored for potential interactions, especially with St John's wort, which can interact with several pharmaceutical medications.

Conclusion:

This case illustrates the potential effectiveness of certain herbal medicines for managing anxiety and depression, with St John's wort and kava serving as safe, effective alternatives in the absence of strong side effects. The results suggest that herbal treatments may offer a complementary option in managing mild-to-moderate psychiatric symptoms, though caution is required with herbal-pharmaceutical interactions. This case underscores the importance of further research into the clinical efficacy and safety of psychotherapy for various psychiatric conditions, especially for patients seeking alternatives to conventional psychiatric medications.

Use of Alternative Remedies by Psychiatric Patients: Illustrative Vignettes and a Discussion of the Issues

Case Study: Navigating the Use of Alternative Herbal Remedies in Psychiatric Treatment

Background:

This case study highlights the experience of Dr. Chen, a psychiatrist, with a patient, John, a 45-year-old man with generalized anxiety disorder and mild depression. John reported frequent headaches and insomnia, which led him to try alternative therapies, including herbal supplements such as *St. John's wort* for depression and *valerian root* for insomnia. John was initially reluctant to disclose his use of these remedies due to concerns about judgment from healthcare providers.

Clinical Encounter:

During an initial assessment, Dr. Chen took a comprehensive history and asked John about any alternative or complementary therapies he might be using, taking a non-judgmental approach. This encouraged John to disclose his use of herbal supplements. Dr. Chen, aware of potential interactions between St. John's wort and other medications, especially those affecting serotonin levels, carefully explained the risks to John, as he was considering prescribing an SSRI for John's anxiety.

Treatment Plan:

Dr. Chen and John collaborated on a treatment plan that took both John's preferences for natural remedies and his mental health needs into account. Dr. Chen suggested gradually tapering off St. John's wort to avoid serotonin syndrome if they decided to start an SSRI. To address insomnia, Dr. Chen recommended safer sleep hygiene practices and monitored the use of valerian root, discussing potential side effects and reinforcing caution around its sedative properties. They also agreed on regular follow-ups to assess any changes in John's symptoms and to discuss alternative therapies he might consider in the future.

Outcome:

Over the following months, John saw improvement in his anxiety with the SSRI and felt reassured that his herbal remedy use was being taken seriously. By building trust, Dr. Chen helped John feel more comfortable discussing alternative treatments, facilitating an open, transparent therapeutic relationship. As a result, John became more willing to communicate openly about any new supplements or herbal products he encountered.

Conclusion:

This case underscores the importance of non-judgmental inquiry and a balanced, collaborative approach to managing patients who use alternative therapies. As the popularity of herbal remedies continues to grow, mental health professionals must be knowledgeable about common herbs, understand their potential interactions, and be prepared to address patient concerns sensitively. This patient-centered approach fosters trust, enhances treatment adherence, and mitigates potential risks associated with alternative remedies in psychiatric care.

Conclusion

Medicinal herbs are promising adjunctive treatments in psychotherapy, especially in the treatment of symptoms associated with anxiety disorders, depression, and stress. Both clinical studies and systematic reviews confirm the therapeutic activity with some herbal species, including lavender 'Lavandula angustifolia', for nervous anxiety and stress relief in combination with ashwagandha 'Withania somnifera'. However, more rigorous, large-scale research will be needed to confirm these potential therapeutic benefits and help to safely generate well-validated protocols for their use. Adding herbal remedies to the treatment protocol with some conventional psychotherapy approaches might improve treatment outcomes, but the required dosing, drug-drug interactions, and long-term safety have implications requiring caution. Research directions in this area do, however, promise some interesting clinical applications to set in the direction of presenting new avenues in holistic and patient-centered care.

References

Cavanagh, H. M. S., & Wilkinson, J. M. (2002). Lavender essential oil: A review. *Australian Journal of Herbal Medicine, 14*(1), 29-35.

Darbinyan, V., Kteyan, A., Panossian, A., & Wagner, H. (2007). Rhodiola rosea in stress-induced fatigue: A double-blind randomized placebo-controlled trial. *Phytomedicine, 14*(5), 333-339. https://doi.org/10.1016/j.phymed.2006.11.004

Eisenhardt, J., Sarris, J., & Scholey, A. (2015). The effects of Passiflora incarnata on anxiety and sleep: A systematic review of randomized controlled trials. *Journal of Clinical Medicine, 4*(2), 123-134. https://doi.org/10.3390/jcm4020123

Ernst, E. (2004). Kava: A comprehensive review of the literature. *Psychotherapy Research, 18*(7), 547-552. https://doi.org/10.1002/ptr.1561

Gupta, A., Kaur, R., & Gupta, S. (2021). Adaptogens and their role in stress management: A review of current research. *Journal of Integrative Medicine, 19*(3), 219-226. https://doi.org/10.1016/j.joim.2020.10.001

Gupta, L., Saini, V., & Sharma, S. (2021). Ashwagandha (Withania somnifera) in the management of stress and anxiety: A systematic review and meta-analysis. *Journal of Clinical Psychopharmacology, 41*(2), 175-182. https://doi.org/10.1097/JCP.0000000000001421

Hausenblas, H. A., Schoulda, J. A., & Smoliga, J. M. (2013). Saffron (Crocus sativus) as a treatment for major depressive disorder: A systematic review and meta-analysis. *Psychotherapy Research, 27*(3), 345-350. https://doi.org/10.1002/ptr.4915

Houghton, P. J. (2017). Valerian root and its anxiolytic properties: A review of recent studies. *Psychotherapy Research, 31*(6), 879-885. https://doi.org/10.1002/ptr.5806

Pittler, M. H., & Ernst, E. (2003). Kava for anxiety. *Cochrane Database of Systematic Reviews, 2003*(1), CD003383. https://doi.org/10.1002/14651858.CD003383

Schmidt, R. R., Houghton, P. J., & Houghton, R. (2007). The pharmacology of Valerian root: An overview. *Psychotherapy Research, 31*(8), 1131-1139. https://doi.org/10.1002/ptr.5805

Chapter 5

Herbal Medicine

Natasha Suzan Mathew School of Liberal Studies, CMR University, Bangalore

Introduction

The Eastern perspective of psychology in therapy emphasizes a holistic approach that integrates the mind, body, and spirit. Rooted in ancient philosophies and healing practices from regions such as China, India, and Japan, this perspective often highlights the interconnectedness of physical and mental health. In therapy, this approach may include traditional practices such as meditation, mindfulness, energy healing (like Reiki), and yoga, which aim to balance the individual's internal energies. Herbal medicine also plays a significant role, using natural remedies derived from plants to address both psychological and physiological imbalances. The Eastern approach focuses on preventative care, restoring balance, and promoting long-term wellbeing, often integrating these practices alongside or as an alternative to conventional Western methods.

From an Eastern perspective, herbal medicine has long played a crucial role in therapeutic practices, deeply embedded within traditional medical systems such as Traditional Chinese Medicine (TCM) and Ayurveda. These holistic systems view health as a dynamic balance of body, mind, and spirit, emphasizing the interconnectedness of an individual with nature. Herbal remedies are crafted from various plant parts, including roots, leaves, seeds, and flowers, and are selected based on their energetic properties, such as warming or cooling effects, as well as their ability to influence the body's fundamental energies (e.g., qi in TCM or doshas in Ayurveda).

History of Herbal Medicine and its Integration into Modern Sciences

Herbal medicine has a rich history in treating both physical and mental health conditions, deeply rooted in various cultures around the world.

Ancient Beginnings (Pre5000 BCE to 1000 BCE)

Prehistoric Evidence (Around 5000 BCE and earlier)

The use of plants for healing dates to prehistoric times, where early humans learned the medicinal properties of herbs through trial and error. Archaeological evidence shows that Neanderthals in Iraq used herbs like yarrow and chamomile as far back as 60,000 years ago, suggesting an early understanding of medicinal plants.

Sumerian and Ancient Egyptian Use (Around 3000 BCE – 1000 BCE)

Sumerians (circa 3000 BCE): The earliest written records of herbal medicine appear on clay tablets, listing over 250 plants, including poppy, thyme, and mustard.

Ancient Egyptians (circa 1500 BCE): The Ebers Papyrus, an Egyptian medical text, lists over 850 herbal remedies. Herbs like mandrake and myrrh were used for their calming and sedative effects, hinting at early uses for mental disturbances.

Ancient India and Ayurveda (Around 2000 BCE – 1000 BCE)

Ayurveda, one of the world's oldest medical systems, emerged around 2000 BCE in India. The sacred texts, the Vedas, detailed the medicinal uses of herbs like ashwagandha (for stress and anxiety) and brahmi (to enhance mental clarity). Ayurveda emphasizes balancing the body, mind, and spirit, with herbs tailored to treat psychological imbalances.

Traditional Chinese Medicine (TCM) Foundations (Shang Dynasty, 1600 BCE – 1046 BCE)

Early records of TCM practices, such as the use of herbal medicine, appear during the Shang Dynasty. Texts like the Huangdi Neijing (Yellow Emperor's Classic of Internal Medicine) discuss using herbs to balance the body's Qi (energy) and address mental disturbances. By 1000 BCE, herbs like ginseng and Chinese skullcap were commonly prescribed.

Classical Antiquity (1000 BCE – 500 CE)

Ancient Greece and the Hippocratic Tradition (5th Century BCE)

Hippocrates (460–370 BCE), the "Father of Medicine," emphasized the use of plants in healing. He believed in the connection between the body and mind, prescribing herbs like St. John's wort for "melancholia" (an early term for depression).

Dioscorides (40–90 CE): A Greek physician who wrote De Materia Medica, a comprehensive 5volume work detailing the medicinal properties of over 600 plants. Herbs like valerian were used to calm anxiety and promote sleep.

Ancient Rome (1st Century CE)

Galen (129–216 CE), a prominent Roman physician, expanded on Hippocratic principles and emphasized the use of herbs for mental health. Melissa (lemon balm) was used to lift the spirits, while opium poppy extracts were used to treat insomnia and emotional distress.

Traditional Chinese Medicine (Han Dynasty, 206 BCE – 220 CE)

The Shennong Ben Cao Jing (Divine Farmer's Materia Medica), compiled during the Han Dynasty, lists 365 medicinal plants. Suan Zao Ren (Ziziphus seed) was documented as a treatment for insomnia and anxiety, highlighting the integration of herbal therapy for mental health in TCM.

Medieval Period (500 CE – 1500 CE)

Islamic Medicine and the Golden Age (8th – 14th Century)

Islamic scholars like Avicenna (980–1037 CE) contributed to the understanding of herbal medicine through texts such as The Canon of Medicine, which described herbs for emotional and mental health issues, including borage for sadness and rosemary for improving memory.

Mental health treatment in Islamic medicine was holistic, incorporating herbs, diet, and spiritual practices. Hospitals in Baghdad and Persia used herbal gardens to treat patients.

Medieval Europe (11th – 15th Century)

Monastic medicine: Monks preserved and translated ancient Greek and Roman medical texts, growing, and using herbs like lavender and St. John's wort for calming and treating melancholy.

Hildegard of Bingen (1098–1179 CE), a German abbess and healer, wrote extensively about herbal remedies for mental health, such as hyssop for grief and sage for nervousness.

Renaissance and Early Modern Period (1500 – 1800)

The Herbalists of the Renaissance (16th – 17th Century)

Paracelsus (1493–1541): A Swiss physician who emphasized the "Doctrine of Signatures," suggesting that the physical form of a plant indicated its healing properties. He used herbs like valerian for calming and foxglove for heart related emotional issues.

Nicholas Culpeper (1616–1654): An English herbalist who wrote The Complete Herbal (1653), which made herbal knowledge accessible to the general public. He described the use of hops for anxiety and St. John's wort for depression.

Traditional Chinese Medicine Expands (Ming Dynasty, 1368–1644)

The Bencao Gangmu (Compendium of Materia Medica) by Li Shizhen (1578) detailed the properties of over 1,800 substances, including herbs used to treat emotional disturbances. This text became a cornerstone of herbal medicine in China.

19th – 20th Century: Integration and Scientific Validation

19th Century Western Herbalism

Herbal medicine in Europe and the United States became intertwined with homeopathy and naturopathy. Practitioners like Samuel Thomson popularized herbal remedies for nervous disorders, including passionflower and skullcap.

The industrial revolution saw a decline in herbal practices, but interest in traditional medicine persisted in rural areas.

20th Century Revival and Scientific Research

In the 1960s and 1970s, the counterculture movement in the U.S. reignited interest in natural medicine, leading to a resurgence of herbal therapies for mental health.

Scientific studies validated the effects of herbs like kava kava for anxiety and ginkgo biloba for cognitive enhancement, bridging the gap between traditional knowledge and modern medicine.

Modern Developments (21st Century)

Contemporary Use and Global Acceptance

Herbal medicine is now widely accepted and integrated into complementary and alternative medicine (CAM). The World Health Organization (WHO) has recognized the importance of traditional medicine, including herbal treatments, for mental health.

Today, herbs like ashwagandha and CBD (cannabidiol) are popular for stress relief and anxiety, with growing scientific evidence supporting their use.

Herbal medicine's journey from ancient rituals to modern science highlights a deep cultural and empirical understanding of plant-based healing. The consistent use of certain herbs, like St. John's wort for depression or ginseng for energy, underscores the enduring legacy of herbal medicine in promoting mental wellbeing. Each era built upon the previous one, blending traditional wisdom with emerging scientific insights to improve therapeutic approaches.

Benefits of Herbal Medicine

Balance and Holistic Healing

YinYang Theory (TCM):

Herbal medicine is used to balance yin (passive, cooling energy) and yang (active, warming energy) in the body, promoting overall harmony. An imbalance between these forces is thought to cause illness.

Five Elements Theory (TCM):

The Five Elements Wood, Fire, Earth, Metal, and Water are associated with different organs and emotional states. Herbs are chosen to balance these elements and restore organ function, thus affecting both physical and emotional wellbeing.

Ayurvedic Doshas:

Ayurveda divides people into three primary doshas (Vata, Pitta, and Kapha), representing bodymind types. Herbal treatments are tailored to balance these doshas, aiming to prevent illness and promote vitality.

Natural and Sustainable Healing

Herbs are seen as natural and gentle on the body compared to synthetic pharmaceuticals. They are believed to work in harmony with the body's processes, minimizing side effects and supporting the body's natural healing mechanisms.

Eastern medicine often emphasizes the importance of sustainable use of herbs, incorporating respect for nature in gathering and using herbal resources.

Prevention and Longevity

Preventative Care:

Herbal medicine in Eastern traditions places a significant emphasis on preventing disease rather than merely treating symptoms. Herbs are often used daily to maintain health, strengthen immunity, and delay the aging process.

Tonic Herbs (TCM):

Adaptogens, such as ginseng and astragalus, are believed to enhance the body's resilience to stress, boost energy, and slow down aging.

Personalized Treatment

Both TCM and Ayurveda view each patient as unique. Herbal formulas are custommade to address the specific root causes of a patient's ailments. For instance, two people with the same illness may receive different herbal treatments based on their individual constitution and life circumstances.

Integration of Mind-Body-Spirit

Emotional Healing:

In TCM, emotions are linked to physical health. For example, herbs that nourish the liver (like milk thistle) are thought to soothe anger, while herbs that strengthen the heart (such as hawthorn) may support joy and relieve sadness.

Spiritual Wellbeing (Ayurveda):

Certain herbs are used to cleanse energy pathways, calm the mind, and promote spiritual awareness. Ashwagandha, for example, is used to reduce anxiety and promote mental clarity, while holy basil (tulsi) is considered sacred and beneficial for spiritual balance.

Detoxification and Cleansing

Herbal medicines are often used to cleanse and detoxify the body. For example, TCM uses herbs like dandelion root and chrysanthemum to support liver detoxification, while Ayurveda uses herbs like triphala to promote healthy digestion and elimination of toxins.

Detoxification is not just physical; it also encompasses emotional and mental purification.

Support for Chronic Conditions

Many chronic illnesses, such as arthritis, diabetes, and digestive disorders, are treated with longterm herbal remedies to support the body's healing processes. The emphasis is on strengthening the immune system, improving energy flow (Qi in TCM), and reducing inflammation.

Herbs like turmeric (used in Ayurveda) have powerful antiinflammatory and antioxidant properties, which help manage chronic pain and inflammation.

Energetic and Medicinal Properties

Herbs are categorized based on their energetic properties, such as warming, cooling, moistening, or drying effects. This classification helps in selecting the right herbs to balance the patient's current energetic state.

In Ayurveda, herbs are also selected based on their taste (sweet, sour, salty, bitter, pungent, astringent), which is believed to influence the mind and body differently.

Use of Medicinal Mushrooms (TCM)

Medicinal mushrooms like reishi, cordyceps, and lion's mane are commonly used to boost immune function, enhance mental clarity, and reduce stress. They are valued for their adaptogenic and longevity promoting properties.

Synergistic Formulations

Herbs are often combined into complex formulas, where each herb enhances the effectiveness of the others. This synergy is believed to create a more balanced and effective treatment.

Common Herbal Medicines and Their Uses

- **Ginseng (Ren Shen):** Boosts energy, strengthens the immune system, and helps with mental clarity.
- **Turmeric (Haldi):** Reduces inflammation, promotes digestion, and supports liver function.
- **Licorice Root (Gan Cao):** Harmonizes other herbs in formulations, soothes sore throats, and reduces digestive discomfort.
- **Ashwagandh:** Reduces stress, improves sleep, and supports adrenal function.
- **Holy Basil (Tulsi):** Reduces anxiety, purifies the blood, and supports respiratory health.

Key Philosophies and Practices

Herbal medicine, deeply ingrained in Eastern medical traditions, has been practiced for thousands of years, evolving through extensive knowledge passed down from generation to generation. Below is a detailed exploration of how herbal medicine has been used in therapy from an Eastern perspective, focusing on key philosophies and practices.

Traditional Chinese Medicine (TCM)

Philosophical Foundation:

TCM is based on the concepts of Qi (vital energy), the balance of Yin and Yang, and the Five Elements (Wood, Fire, Earth, Metal, Water), which govern bodily functions and the natural world. Illness is believed to result from imbalances or disruptions in these systems.

Key Herbs and Formulas:

- **Ginseng (Ren Shen):** Known for boosting energy and strengthening the body's resistance to stress.
- **Gingko Biloba (Yin Xing):** Used to improve blood circulation and cognitive function.
- **Rehmannia (Shu Di Huang):** Commonly used for nourishing blood and treating conditions like anemia and hormonal imbalances.
- **Licorice Root (Gan Cao):** Harmonizes formulas, soothes digestive complaints, and balances hormone levels.

***Therapeutic Approach*:**

Practitioners carefully diagnose imbalances through a variety of methods, such as tongue and pulse diagnosis, and then prescribe herbal formulations tailored to the individual. Herbs are combined in precise formulas to create synergy and minimize side effects.

Ayurvedic Medicine (India)

Philosophical Foundation:

Ayurveda is based on the principles of the Doshas (Vata, Pitta, and Kapha), which are energies that govern physiological and psychological processes. Health is maintained by balancing these doshas through diet, lifestyle, and herbal therapy.

Key Herbs and Formulas:

- **Ashwagandha:** A powerful adaptogen that helps reduce stress, boost immunity, and promote mental clarity.
- **Turmeric (Curcumin):** Celebrated for its anti-inflammatory and antioxidant properties.
- **Neem:** Known for purifying the blood, detoxifying the body, and treating skin ailments.
- **Holy Basil (Tulsi)**: Used for respiratory conditions, stress relief, and boosting the immune system.

***Therapeutic Approach*:**

Ayurveda emphasizes personalized care, where herbal remedies are integrated into a broader lifestyle plan that includes dietary adjustments, meditation, yoga, and detoxification practices like Panchakarma. Herbs are chosen to complement the individual's constitution and current imbalance.

Traditional Korean Medicine (TKM)

Philosophical Foundation:

Like TCM, TKM uses concepts of Qi, Yin and Yang balance, and the Five Elements, but it has unique interpretations and applications, influenced by Korean history and culture.

Key Herbs and Formulas:

- **Red Ginseng:** Widely used for enhancing stamina, boosting the immune system, and improving cognitive function.
- **Angelica Root (Dang Gui):** Known as a "female tonic," it is used to regulate menstruation and improve circulation.
- **Schisandra Berries (Omija):** Used to enhance vitality, improve lung function, and protect the liver.
- **Mugwort (Ssuk):** Applied for digestive and reproductive health, and also in moxibustion therapy.

***Therapeutic Approach*:**

TKM uses herbal prescriptions in conjunction with therapies such as acupuncture, Chuna manual therapy (similar to chiropractic care), and moxibustion (burning herbs over specific acupoints).

Japanese Kampo Medicine

Philosophical Foundation:

Kampo, adopted from TCM, was adapted to Japanese culture and includes a more systematic categorization of herbal formulas. Kampo practitioners place a strong emphasis on understanding the "pattern" of disease rather than just symptoms.

Key Herbs and Formulas:

- **ShakuyakuKanzoTo**: A combination of peony root and licorice, used to relieve muscle pain and cramps.
- **Kampo Formulas (e.g., Maoto):** Commonly used for conditions like the common cold, they are precise mixtures of herbs adjusted to the patient's condition.

Therapeutic Approach:

Kampo utilizes comprehensive physical examinations, especially abdominal palpation, to diagnose and customize treatments. Herbal medicine in Kampo is widely integrated into modern medical practice in Japan, with herbs used alongside conventional treatments.

Southeast Asian Herbal Traditions

Thai Herbal Medicine:

Influenced by Ayurveda, TCM, and indigenous practices, it focuses on herbs like Plai (a type of ginger) for inflammation and Kaffir Lime for respiratory and digestive health.

Indonesian Jamu:

A traditional system using a variety of local herbs and spices, like Turmeric and Tamarind, to maintain health and treat ailments. Jamu is often consumed as a tonic drink.

Common Themes in Eastern Herbal Therapy

- *Holistic Approach:* Emphasizes treating the whole person (mind, body, and spirit) rather than just the symptoms.
- *Preventative Medicine:* Focuses on maintaining health and preventing disease through daily use of herbal tonics and lifestyle adjustments.
- *Customized Treatments:* Herbal prescriptions are highly individualized, considering the patient's unique constitution, environment, and emotional state.

This deep historical and cultural heritage of herbal medicine remains a cornerstone of therapy in many parts of Asia, respected for its emphasis on balance, natural healing, and harmony with the environment.

Theoretical Background

Traditional Chinese Medicine (TCM) Perspective

Concept of Qi (Vital Energy):

In TCM, the body is believed to be governed by a vital energy called Qi, which flows through pathways called meridians. The proper flow and balance of Qi are crucial for health. Herbal medicine is used to regulate, harmonize, and boost Qi.

Yin and Yang Theory:

Health in TCM is about maintaining balance between Yin (cooling, nourishing energy) and Yang (warming, activating energy). Herbs are classified based on their ability to either nourish Yin, strengthen Yang, or restore equilibrium between the two forces.

Five Elements Theory:

The human body and its functions are associated with five elements: Wood, Fire, Earth, Metal, and Water. Each element corresponds to specific organs and bodily systems. Herbal treatments are designed to bring harmony among these elements, using herbs that correspond to organ imbalances.

Herb Classification and Functions:

Herbs are categorized based on their properties (e.g., warming, cooling, moistening, drying), tastes (bitter, sweet, sour, salty, pungent), and effects on organs or systems. For instance, ginseng is known for its Qi tonifying properties, while mint is used to clear heat and promote the smooth flow of energy.

Ayurvedic Medicine Perspective (India)

Dosha Theory:

Ayurveda describes three primary energies or doshas - Vata (air and ether), Pitta (fire and water), and Kapha (earth and water). Each person has a unique constitution determined by these dosha, and health is about keeping them in balance. Herbs are used to correct dosha imbalances.

Herbal Classification by Properties and Actions:

Herbs in Ayurveda are categorized according to their Rasa (taste), Guna (quality), Virya (potency), Vipaka (postdigestive effect), and Prabhava (special effect). For instance, turmeric is widely used for its antiinflammatory and digestive properties, while ashwagandha is an adaptogen that supports stress relief.

- **Holistic Healing:** Ayurveda emphasizes that herbs should be used in conjunction with diet, lifestyle changes, and spiritual practices. This holistic approach ensures that treatment not only addresses physical symptoms but also mental and spiritual wellbeing.
- **Preparation Methods:** Herbal remedies are often prepared as teas, powders, pastes, oils, or capsules, with specific methods tailored to enhance the therapeutic effects of each herb.

Traditional Korean Medicine (TKM)

Influence of YinYang and Five Elements:

Like TCM, TKM also relies on YinYang theory and the Five Elements to explain the interconnectedness of the body's organs and systems. Herbal remedies are used to balance these elements and ensure smooth energy flow.

Sasang Constitution Medicine:

A unique feature of TKM is Sasang constitutional medicine, which categorizes individuals into four types based on their physiological and psychological traits. Herbal prescriptions are tailored to each person's constitution to maximize therapeutic outcomes.

Focus on Preventative Medicine:

Herbal medicine in TKM emphasizes prevention and maintaining health. Ginseng, for example, is a wellknown herb used to boost immunity and energy levels.

Traditional Japanese Medicine (Kampo)

Adoption and Adaptation from TCM:

Kampo medicine has its roots in TCM but has evolved uniquely in Japan. It emphasizes the use of herbal formulas (called Kampo) that are prescribed based on detailed symptom analysis and body constitution rather than focusing on individual herbs.

Holistic Diagnostic Approach:

Diagnosis considers the patient's overall physical, emotional, and environmental state. Practitioners often use tongue and pulse diagnosis to determine the underlying issues before recommending herbal remedies.

Standardized Formulas:

Unlike TCM, Kampo uses more standardized herbal combinations that are welldocumented and studied. Common Kampo formulas include Shosaikoto (for liver issues and boosting immunity) and Rikkunshito (for digestive problems).

Philosophical Foundations

Holistic Health Philosophy:

Eastern herbal medicine emphasizes the interconnection between mind, body, and spirit. Illness is seen as a manifestation of imbalance within these realms, and treatment aims to restore harmony.

Nature as Healer:

The Eastern perspective views nature as a powerful source of healing. Plants are seen as life forces imbued with energy that can be harnessed to promote wellness. This philosophy encourages a deep respect for nature and sustainable use of herbal resources.

Preventive and Personalized Medicine:

Rather than treating disease symptoms in isolation, Eastern herbal therapy aims to prevent illness through dietary, lifestyle, and herbal interventions personalized to an individual's constitution and environment.

Applications of Herbal Medicine

Traditional Chinese Medicine (TCM)

In TCM, herbal medicine is used in conjunction with acupuncture, dietary therapy, and qigong. Herbs are categorized according to their properties (hot, cold, neutral), their tastes (bitter, sweet, sour, salty, pungent), and their meridian effects (which organ systems they influence). The goal is to restore balance in the body's Qi (vital energy) and to harmonize the Yin and Yang.

Adaptogens: Herbs like Ginseng and Astragalus are used to increase vitality, enhance immune function, and reduce stress.

Detoxification: Gua Lou and Pu Gong Ying are used for purging heat and clearing toxins from the body, promoting liver and skin health.

Circulatory Health: Dang Gui (Angelica Sinensis) is considered beneficial for blood circulation and is often used in cases of anemia or blood deficiencies.

Digestive Health: Chen Pi (dried tangerine peel) and Shen Ling Bai Zhu San are commonly used to support the digestive system by enhancing the digestive Qi and promoting the flow of the stomach and spleen.

Respiratory Health: Chuan Bei Mu and Herba Ephedra are used for clearing lung heat and relieving cough.

Ayurveda

Ayurvedic medicine, originating from India, is built on the concept of balancing the body's three doshas (Vata, Pitta, and Kapha). Herbal therapy is a key element in achieving this balance, along with diet, yoga, and meditation. Herbs in Ayurveda are also classified based on their properties (Rasa taste, Virya potency, and Vipaka postdigestive effect).

Anti Inflammatory: Turmeric (Curcuma longa), a wellknown Ayurvedic herb, is used for its antiinflammatory properties and is often prescribed for conditions like arthritis or skin diseases.

Digestive Health: Triphala, a blend of three fruits (Amalaki, Bibhitaki, and Haritaki), is one of the most widely used remedies for digestion, constipation, and detoxification.

Detoxification and Liver Health: Milk Thistle (Silybum marianum) and Guduchi (Tinospora cordifolia) are used for their liver detoxifying and regenerative properties.

Stress Relief and Mental Health: Ashwagandha (Withania somnifera) is a potent adaptogen used to manage stress, anxiety, and improve overall vitality.

Cardiovascular Health: Arjuna (Terminalia arjuna) is traditionally used to strengthen the heart, improve circulation, and reduce blood pressure.

Unani Medicine

Originating in the GrecoArabic tradition, Unani medicine incorporates various herbal remedies to restore balance and health. Similar to Ayurveda and TCM, Unani is based on the balance of the four humors (blood, phlegm, yellow bile, and black bile).

Digestive Health: Herbs like Fennel and Coriander are used to regulate digestion, improve appetite, and alleviate bloating and indigestion.

Liver and Kidney Support: Chicory and Bitter Melon are used for cleansing the liver and kidneys and are considered important for detoxification.

Respiratory Health: Licorice Root (Glycyrrhiza glabra) is used in Unani medicine to soothe sore throats and coughs, and Eucalyptus is used for respiratory congestion.

Traditional Korean Medicine (TKM)

Similar to TCM, Korean herbal medicine uses a holistic approach, considering the body's physical, emotional, and spiritual states. Korean herbs are used for their healing properties and often involve combinations of herbs.

Qi Restoration: Ginseng and Angelica Sinensis are used to replenish Qi and blood, enhancing energy and stamina.

Pain and Inflammation: Turmeric and Ginger are commonly used to reduce inflammation, manage pain, and enhance circulation.

Southeast Asian Herbal Medicine

In countries such as Thailand, Vietnam, and Indonesia, herbal medicine is integrated into both daily life and traditional healing. Many herbs used in Southeast Asia have similar uses to those in TCM and Ayurveda but may be adapted to local practices.

Herbal Poultices: A mix of local herbs such as Lemongrass and Turmeric is used in poultices applied to the body to reduce pain, inflammation, and muscular tension.

Tonic and Immunity: Papaya leaves are used in traditional medicine for their purported antimalarial and immunity boosting properties.

Digestive Health: Kaffir lime leaves and Ginger are often consumed to ease digestive discomfort.

Tibetan Medicine

Tibetan medicine blends aspects of Ayurveda, TCM, and indigenous healing traditions. It uses herbs in combination with meditation and rituals to promote health and longevity.

Detoxification: Herbs like Cordyceps and Yarshagumba (often used for enhancing energy and vitality) are seen as powerful tonics.

Joint Health: Salvia and Himalayan plants like Moringa are used for their antiinflammatory properties to alleviate joint pain and stiffness

Applications in Therapy

- **Chronic Illness:** Herbs like Ginseng, Ashwagandha, and Licorice Root are commonly used in the management of chronic conditions like arthritis, diabetes, and hypertension.
- **Mental Health:** Herbs such as Lavender (from European influence), Ashwagandha, and Bacopa Monnieri are used in the treatment of stress, depression, and anxiety. Adaptogenic herbs are popular for improving mental clarity and reducing anxiety.
- **Pain Management:** Herbal applications for pain relief include Turmeric, Ginger, Boswellia, and Capsaicin, which are used topically or internally to alleviate musculoskeletal pain, headaches, and inflammation.
- **Detoxification:** Many of the herbs used in Eastern medicine help detoxify the body by supporting the liver, kidneys, and digestive systems, such as Milk Thistle, Triphala, and Dandelion Root.
- **Antiaging:** Herbs like Ginseng, Goji Berries, and Schisandra are used in Eastern medicine for their antioxidant properties, supporting longevity and improving overall vitality.

Contemporary Practices in Herbal Medicine for Mental Health

Integration with Western Medicine

In the contemporary world, Eastern herbal medicine is increasingly integrated with Western approaches to mental health. Research is ongoing into the efficacy of herbs such as Ginkgo Biloba (for cognitive disorders) and St. John's Wort (for depression). Practitioners in the West often combine these herbs with psychotherapy, pharmaceuticals, or lifestyle changes.

Modern Applications

Stress and Anxiety: Herbs like Ashwagandha and Rhodiola are popular in modern formulations to combat stress, particularly in highpaced urban environments.

Cognitive Enhancement: Adaptogens and nootropic herbs such as Bacopa Monnieri (Brahmi) and Ginkgo Biloba are used to enhance memory, focus, and cognitive performance, particularly in aging populations.

Insomnia and Sleep Disorders: Herbs such as Valerian, Jujube, and Passionflower are commonly prescribed to improve sleep and reduce insomnia without the side effects associated with pharmaceutical sleep aids.

Steps and Processes in Herbal Therapy

Diagnosis and Evaluation

Eastern Medicine emphasizes the importance of diagnosing the root cause of an illness, not just its symptoms. Several diagnostic techniques are used, including:

- ***Pulse Diagnosis (in TCM):*** Different pulses are interpreted to assess the flow of Qi (energy) and the condition of various organs.
- ***Tongue Diagnosis (in TCM):*** The appearance, color, coating, and shape of the tongue are observed for signs of imbalance in the body.
- ***Observing the Body and Skin:*** In both Ayurveda and TCM, looking at the skin's complexion, body posture, and signs of aging helps to determine the body's constitution (dosha in Ayurveda) and the state of health.
- ***Interviews & History:*** In both Ayurvedic and Chinese traditions, health history, lifestyle, and emotional state are also crucial in diagnosis. For example, Ayurveda looks at a person's dosha (Vata, Pitta, and Kapha) to understand their unique constitution and any imbalances.

Identifying Imbalances

Herbal therapy in Eastern systems is aimed at addressing imbalances in the body's internal environment. These imbalances can be seen in the following ways:

- ***TCM:*** The focus is on the balance of Yin and Yang and the smooth flow of Qi through meridians (energy pathways). Herbs are selected to either tonify or disperse energies based on the diagnosed condition.
- ***Ayurveda:*** The focus is on the three doshas (Vata, Pitta, Kapha), and herbs are chosen to either balance excess or deficiency in any of these doshas.
- ***Energy and Elements:*** In both systems, the elements (wood, fire, earth, metal, water in TCM and the five elements in Ayurveda) are considered for determining herbal treatments.

Herb Selection

Herbal remedies are chosen based on their properties, functions, and interactions within the body, considering:

- ***The Nature of the Herb:*** Herbs may be warming or cooling, moistening, or drying, and tonifying or dispersing. The selection will depend on whether the patient has a deficiency of heat or cold, moisture or dryness, or excess or depletion of vital energy.
- ***Herb Potency:*** Potency can be determined by the herb's ability to influence the body's constitution and energy. For example, tonic herbs might be used for strengthening and nourishing, while stimulants might be chosen for clearing stagnation.
- ***Herb Synergy:*** In Eastern herbal therapies, formulations often consist of a combination of several herbs that work together to balance each other, enhance therapeutic effects, and reduce side effects.

Preparation of Herbs

The way herbs are prepared plays a crucial role in their efficacy. Common methods include:

- ***Decoctions (TCM):*** Herbs are boiled in water to extract their medicinal properties. This method is used for harder and denser herbs (roots, barks).
- ***Infusions (TCM & Ayurveda):*** Herbs are steeped in hot water. This method is typically used for leaves and flowers.
- ***Powders and Pastes (Ayurveda):*** Ground herbs are often made into powders, or pastes mixed with liquids like ghee, honey, or oil.
- ***Tinctures (both systems):*** Alcohol Based extracts of herbs, which are potent and can be taken in small doses.
- ***Essential Oils (Ayurveda):*** These may be extracted and used in aromatherapy or for topical application.

Herbal Formulation and Customization

- ***Blending Herbs:*** Formulations are often customized based on individual needs. For example, in TCM, a formula might include several herbs, each with different properties (to nourish, clear, or balance).
- ***Ayurvedic Chyawanprash or Lehyams:*** These are complex formulations containing a wide range of herbs and are used for rejuvenation, digestion, and immunity.
- ***Adjusting Dosages:*** The dosage depends on the severity of the imbalance, the patient's constitution, and the overall therapeutic plan.

Administration of Herbs

Herbs can be administered in different forms, including:

- ***Internal Consumption:*** As teas, pills, powders, decoctions, or capsules.
- ***External Use:*** For topical applications such as poultices, oils, or balms. Ayurvedic oil massages (Abhyanga) or Chinese herbal compresses might be used for specific conditions like muscle pain or joint issues.
- ***Aromatherapy:*** Essential oils are inhaled to address respiratory issues or enhance mental clarity.

Lifestyle and Dietary Considerations

In both Ayurveda and TCM, herbal treatments are often paired with specific lifestyle and dietary recommendations to enhance the effects of the therapy. These may include:

- ***Dietary Modifications:*** In Ayurveda, for example, people are advised to follow a diet based on their dosha (Vata, Pitta, Kapha) to maintain balance.
- ***Exercise and Breathing:*** Practices such as Tai Chi, Qigong (in TCM), or yoga (in Ayurveda) can help maintain energy flow and balance within the body.
- ***Mental and Emotional Balance:*** Emotional health and stress management techniques like meditation, mindfulness, and acupuncture are often integrated into herbal therapy.

Continuous Monitoring and Adjustment

- ***Followup Assessments:*** Regular followup consultations help assess the effectiveness of the herbal treatment and make necessary adjustments.
- ***Adjustment of Herb Formulas:*** The herbal formula is modified according to the patient's progress, changes in their condition, or shifting imbalances.
- ***Seasonal Adjustments:*** In both systems, herbal remedies might be adjusted according to the changing seasons to maintain harmony with nature. For example, more cooling herbs might be used in summer, while warming herbs are employed in winter.

Integration with Other Therapies

Eastern herbal medicine is rarely used in isolation but as part of a holistic therapy plan that can include:

- ***Acupuncture (in TCM):*** Used alongside herbs to restore the smooth flow of Qi and enhance the healing process.
- ***Massage (in Ayurveda):*** Techniques like Abhyanga are used to improve circulation and support the body's detoxification process.
- ***Meditation and Breathwork:*** These are integral to both Ayurveda and TCM to calm the mind and balance the body's energy.

Herbal medicine in Eastern therapy is a deeply integrative approach, combining the knowledge of herbal properties, individual constitution, and environmental influences. It is about understanding the patient's unique needs and finding the appropriate herbs, treatments, and lifestyle changes that restore balance and vitality.

In the Eastern perspective, herbal medicine is viewed as a holistic approach, where the goal is to bring harmony between the body, mind, and spirit. It emphasizes the importance of balance, particularly the flow of energy (Qi in Chinese medicine) or the balance of the five elements (wood, fire, earth, metal, water). Herbs are used to address underlying imbalances rather than just symptoms. For example, adaptogenic herbs like ginseng are often used to help the body cope with stress and enhance vitality, while ginger or turmeric may be used to improve circulation and reduce inflammation, promoting overall health. Eastern herbal remedies frequently work in synergy, meaning a combination of herbs is tailored to suit an individual's unique constitution and current health condition. Many remedies are believed to not only treat physical ailments but also promote emotional wellbeing. This perspective integrates diet, lifestyle changes, and mindfulness practices, aiming to treat the whole person body, mind, and spirit thus enhancing the body's natural healing ability. Herbal therapies are considered gentle, yet powerful tools in this broader therapeutic approach, often seen to connect deeply with nature's wisdom.

Case Studies

Case Study 1

Patient Background:

A 42-year-old female presented to a Traditional Chinese Medicine (TCM) clinic with symptoms of chronic anxiety, depression, and insomnia. She had been experiencing these issues for several years and had previously been prescribed antidepressants, which provided minimal relief and caused side effects like fatigue and weight gain.

TCM Diagnosis:

The patient's symptoms were diagnosed as "Liver Qi Stagnation with Spleen Qi Deficiency" in TCM terms, which translates to emotional imbalances (anxiety and depression) linked to poor energy flow and digestive weakness.

Herbal Treatment:

The practitioner prescribed a combination of the following herbs:

- **Xiao Yao San (Free and Easy Wanderer):** A well-known formula in TCM that helps move stagnant liver qi and strengthens the spleen.
- **He Huan Pi (Albizia bark):** Known for its calming effects, it is often used to treat emotional issues such as anxiety, depression, and insomnia.
- **Ren Shen (Ginseng):** To replenish the body's energy and nourish the mind.

Outcome:

After 6 weeks of treatment, the patient reported a significant reduction in anxiety and depressive symptoms, improved sleep quality, and an overall sense of emotional wellbeing. The patient continued the herbal regimen for another 3 months, with ongoing improvements.

Discussion:

This case illustrates how TCM's holistic approach focusing not just on the mind but also on the body's energy flow can be effective in treating mental health conditions. Herbal combinations like Xiao Yao San are commonly prescribed for stress related disorders, and the effectiveness can be greater when combined with acupuncture and dietary adjustments.

Case Study 2

Patient Background:

A 35-year-old male presented with chronic insomnia. Despite trying various sleep medications, he had trouble falling asleep, waking up multiple times during the night, and experiencing restless sleep. The insomnia was attributed to work stress, poor eating habits, and excessive screen time before bed.

TCM Diagnosis:

The diagnosis was "Heart Blood Deficiency with Liver Qi Stagnation." In TCM, the heart is considered the "house of the mind," and its health is crucial for restful sleep. The liver's role in the smooth flow of Qi is essential for mental calmness and restful sleep.

Herbal Treatment:

The practitioner prescribed:

- **Suan Zao Ren (Zizyphus seed):** A calming herb used to treat insomnia, anxiety, and restlessness.
- **Bai Zi Ren (Platycladus seed):** Known for nourishing the heart and calming the mind.
- **He Huan Pi (Albizia bark):** To reduce stress and promote relaxation.

Outcome:

After 4 weeks, the patient reported a marked improvement in sleep quality, with fewer night awakenings and the ability to fall asleep faster. Over a period of 3 months, the patient was able to achieve consistent restful sleep without the need for over the counter or prescription medications.

Discussion:

This case emphasizes the role of TCM in treating insomnia through restoring balance to both the mind and body. In contrast to pharmaceutical solutions, TCM herbs such as Suan Zao Ren work by nourishing the heart and calming the mind, supporting the body's natural sleep cycles.

Conclusion

These case studies demonstrate how herbal medicine from Eastern traditions like TCM and Ayurveda can be effective in treating a variety of physical and mental health conditions. The key advantage of these therapies is their holistic approach, treating the person rather than just focusing on isolated symptoms. By restoring balance to the body's energies, herbs can often offer longterm relief, especially when combined with lifestyle changes, dietary adjustments, and mindbody practices like meditation or yoga. However, it's important to note that these treatments should be approached under the guidance of a trained practitioner, as herbal medicine requires careful formulation and monitoring.

References

Bachmeier, B. E., Killian, P. H., & Pfeffer, U. (2010). Markers and mechanisms of efficacy in herbal medicines. *Frontiers in Pharmacology*. Retrieved from https://www.frontiersin.org/articles/10.3389/fphar.2010.00024/full

Fries, A. M. (2019). Traditional versus modern medicine: Evolution of herbal use in clinical settings. *Journal of Ethnopharmacology*. Retrieved from https://www.frontiersin.org/articles/10.3389/fphar.2019.00089/full

Garrard, J., Harms, S., & Eberly, L. (2003). Evaluation of herbal remedies for depression and anxiety. *Advances in Psychiatric Treatment*. Retrieved from https://www.cambridge.org/core/journals/advances-in-psychiatric-treatment/article/herbal-remedies-for-depression-and-anxiety/96A0738CF28BE1791F81CFB3CA60E704

Li, X., Yuan, W., & Bachmeier, B. (2016). Clinical benefits of herbal medicines for mental health disorders. *Pharmacology Reports*. Retrieved from https://www.mdpi.com/1420-3049/22/8/1329

National Institutes of Health. (2020). Efficacy of herbal medicines in mental health treatments: Current trends. *Nutrients*, 12(11). Retrieved from https://www.mdpi.com/2072-6643/12/11/3421

American Psychiatric Association. (2022). The role of herbal medicine in psychiatric treatment. *American Journal of Psychiatry*. Retrieved from https://www.apa.org/pubs/journals

Wright, C. (2005). Clinical comparisons: Herbal versus synthetic drugs for anxiety. *Journal of Psychopharmacology*. Retrieved from https://www.cambridge.org/core/journals/journal-of-psychopharmacology/article/clinical-benefits-herbal-versus-synthetic-drugs/123

Schisandra, R., & Ginseng, P. (2022). Gut-brain interactions of medicinal plants. *Nutrients*, 14(10). Retrieved from https://doi.org/10.3390/nu14102111

Gupta, A., & Mehta, K. (2021). The psychophysiological benefits of herbal teas. *Complementary Therapies in Medicine*, 27. Retrieved from https://www.journals.elsevier.com/complementary-therapies-in-medicine

Yuan, H., Ma, Q., Ye, L., & Piao, G. (2016). The traditional medicine and modern treatment perspectives. *Pharmacognosy Review*. Retrieved from https://academic.oup.com

Chapter 6

Ho'oponopono

Patra Raja Sulochana School of Liberal Studies (SLS), CMR University, Bangalore

Introduction

Definition of Ho'oponopono

According to Thakurdas, Ho'oponopono is an age-old Hawaiian technique for reducing tension, resolving disputes, and removing energy from both individuals and surroundings. In her article, she discusses transformative wisdom and its modern psychological and spiritual applications.

Ho'oponopono is a profound healing method that promotes the Universal Law of the Interconnection of Life. It is a powerful method that may address today's difficult problems.

Ho'oponopono is a complex and culturally rich healing method based on Hawaiian traditions that takes a holistic approach to both personal and collective well-being. It draws on core cultural values like reconciliation, forgiveness, and harmony. The phrase "Ho'oponopono" is derived from two Hawaiian language elements: "Ho'o," a prefix meaning "to make" or "to cause," and "Pono," which has numerous levels of meaning such as "rightness," "balance," "goodness," and "harmony." When repeated, "Pono" highlights the need of getting things twice right, representing the restoration of perfect harmony in relationships and inside oneself.

In cooperation with other traditional healing practitioners and community leaders, elderly veteran ho'oponopono practitioners have formally sponsored programs to teach and guide a new generation of students with an interest in becoming ho'oponopono practitioners in the traditions of their ancestors since the 1970s.

Early Hawaiians recognized that physical health and emotional well-being were intertwined and required for optimal overall health. This idea, known as 'mauli ola', or the breath of life, encompasses the physical, spiritual, mental, and emotional well-being of an individual, family, and community (Oshiro, 2015). Early practitioners called for treating an individual's physical ailments often compelled the sick person to undertake ho'oponopono with his or her family if the treatment was not effective (Gutmanis, 2013).

Ho'oponopono, a family-based healing tradition, is passed down and taught by community elders. Many modern-day ho'oponopono traditions primarily draw from Mary Kawena Pukui's approach, which she learnt from her family in Ka'u, Hawai'i Island (Handy and Pukui, 1972).

Ho'oponopono as a Healing Technique

The primary goal of Ho'oponopono is to address not just problems with others, but also problems within oneself. Healing one's relationship with oneself is viewed as necessary for healing relationships with others.

Forgiveness is crucial to the healing process. Ho'oponopono says that forgiving oneself and others creates a route to recovery. Forgiveness is viewed as a spiritual and emotional cleaning that dissolves bad energy such as guilt, resentment, and rage.

Ho'oponopono, like many Eastern ideas on psychotherapy, emphasizes the significance of balance, wholeness, and community. According to this perspective, societal harmony and family dynamics are closely linked to mental and emotional well-being rather than being seen as distinct from an individual. Healing, therefore, is a social process rather than an independent one.

Healing through Confession, Prayer, Repentance, and Forgiveness

According to the Hawaiian dictionary, Ho'oponopono means "to be healed through confession, prayer, repentance, discussion, and forgiveness." This treatment method takes a holistic approach, viewing the person with sickness as a member of the family rather than a separate entity. It serves as a conflict settlement procedure, also known as "setting things right" or "keeping things in order."

The fundamental goal of this practice is to work through issues with oneself and others. Healing is viewed as a sequential process, with forgiveness serving as the necessary first step toward well-being. The process begins when the mind is ready to address, heal, and let go, and then progresses to healing the body.

According to traditional Hawaiian culture, Ho'oponopono is a methodical healing procedure. In addition to settling conflicts, the approach deals with personal imbalances that could be evident in relationships within the family or community. Hawaiian belief holds that illness is frequently caused by conflict in relationships or the environment rather than being just a bodily or mental problem that an individual experiences.

Ho'oponopono and Modern Techniques

This study investigates the origins and components of ho'oponopono, a traditional Native Hawaiian conflict resolution method, as well as modern restorative justice (RJ) techniques. Ho'oponopono, a traditional restorative therapy, has been practiced by Native Hawaiians for centuries and is led by a recognized practitioner known as a "haku". A practicing haku ho'oponopono who also instructs others in the art is Kaulukukui. A haku is a revered community healer or leader who is quite common to be an elderly family member (Pukui & Elbert, 1986; Handy & Pukui, 1972). Kaulukukui is a retired social worker and the chair of the state-wide ho'oponopono elders council for the Hawai'i state.

Modern RJ methods, which originated in the 1970s, are democratic, non-adversarial, and spiritual to the extent that participants bring them to the group. Both methods engage family members until harmony is restored and changes are implemented. Indigenous cultures may have different presumptions regarding their conflict resolution techniques since their traditional worldviews differ greatly from Western perspectives (Pukui, Haertig & Lee, 1972; Yantzi, 1998).

The concept of "huna" was developed by a Westerner and is now popularly regarded as a Hawaiian concept, even though it is not. Both procedures are similar in that they bring people together in groups to talk about how misbehavior has affected them and how to mend broken connections.

Process or Steps of Ho'oponopono

There are several essential elements in the Ho'oponopono technique that promote emotional healing and reconciliation. Every phase is intended to confront and settle emotional disputes, bring about equilibrium, and encourage forgiveness.

Preparation

The process starts with a time of preparation. As they mentally and emotionally get ready for the practice, participants consider the current problems. Setting healing intentions and remaining receptive to the process are part of this phase. To ground participants and make sure they are prepared to participate completely in the exercise, the preparation phase is essential. A Hawaiian kahuna and contemporary advocate of Ho'oponopono, Morrnah Simeona, claims that this stage aids in establishing the proper frame of mind for the healing process.

Invocation

Invoking a higher power or spiritual guidance is the first step for participants. Because it helps create a sacred environment for the procedure, this phase is crucial to traditional Ho'oponopono. Participants are reminded of the greater purpose and support that are at their disposal by requesting spiritual assistance. This invocation typically entails a prayer or meditation to establish a connection with the divine, though it might differ depending on personal beliefs and cultural contexts (Makua, 1997).

Confession and Repentance

People own up to their mistakes and accept responsibility for their deeds. They acknowledge the harm done and show sincere regret. Taking responsibility for one's actions and the effects they have had on other people is the goal of this phase. Releasing guilt and shame, which frequently stand in the way of emotional recovery, requires confession and repentance. According to research by James (2008), admitting guilt can greatly lessen sentiments of unforgiveness.

Forgiveness

Participants show their desire to forgive and seek forgiveness. This reciprocal interaction is essential for healing and letting go of unpleasant feelings. Anger, resentment, and other bad emotions can be resolved by both giving and receiving forgiveness. Forgiveness is a transforming process that brings harmony and balance back to relationships and communities, as noted by Kaulukukui and Walker (2021).

Gratitude and Love

Expressing love and gratitude is the last phase. "Thank you" and "I love you" are repeated by participants to reaffirm pleasant feelings and bring peace back. This phase fosters sentiments of gratitude and love while strengthening the healing process. According to Kuman (2022), showing love and gratitude has quantifiable positive effects on mental and emotional health, improving general wellbeing.

Benefits of Ho'oponopono

Emotional Healing

An effective technique for assisting people in letting go of unpleasant feelings like guilt, resentment, and anger is ho'oponopono. People can experience emotional release and enhance their mental health and peace of mind by admitting their feelings and asking for forgiveness. According to research by James (2008), those who practiced Ho'oponopono had a significant decrease in unforgiveness, which is directly related to emotional recovery. This approach promotes inner serenity and aids people in letting go of old hurts.

Spiritual Growth

Ho'oponopono helps people connect with their higher selves, which promote introspection and spiritual growth. By frequently saying "I'm sorry," "Please forgive me," "Thank you," and "I love you," practitioners develop a sense of balance and harmony within themselves. Ho'oponopono's spiritual component is essential to its traditional practice, according to Kuman (2022), who highlights the importance of love and good intentions in fostering harmony and advancing general wellbeing.

Enhanced Mental Health

Ho'oponopono can significantly improve mental health when included into therapeutic techniques. It promotes trauma recovery, lessens anxiety and depressive symptoms, and improves psychological health in general. According to Kuman's (2022) research, Ho'oponopono practice influences heart and brain waves, fostering a calm and coherent state that improves mental health outcomes. Ho'oponopono's holistic approach tackles many facets of mental health and offers a thorough method of recovery.

Stress Reduction

The Ho'oponopono words can be repeated as a meditative technique that efficiently lowers anxiety and stress. People can better handle stress by engaging in this repetitive, peaceful practice, which fosters a feeling of calm and center. When combined with acts of love and gratitude, the practice of asking for and giving forgiveness can calm the mind and lessen the physical reactions linked to stress.

Improved Relationships

Ho'oponopono improves relationships by encouraging forgiveness and reconciliation. In order to rebuild trust and enhance communication within families and communities, the technique promotes candid conversation, forgiveness, and teamwork in resolving disputes. Integrating Ho'oponopono into restorative justice programs improves the process by attending to people's emotional and spiritual needs, which foster cooperation and togetherness, claim Kaulukukui and Walker (2021).

Applications of Ho'oponopono

Personal Healing

Individuals employ ho'oponopono to deal with emotional suffering and personal difficulties. People can relieve bad feelings and foster inner peace by repeating the words "I'm sorry," "Please forgive me," "Thank you," and "I love you." This exercise promotes introspection and accountability, which promotes mental health and emotional recovery.

Spiritual Practices

Ho'oponopono is a common part of many people's spiritual practices. It is consistent with a few spiritual practices and beliefs that emphasize personal development, forgiveness, and healing. Invoking a higher power or spiritual guidance is part of the practice, which increases the healing process' efficacy.

Mental health Counseling

Ho'oponopono is included in mental health counseling by therapists and counselors to assist clients in overcoming trauma, guilt, and resentment. It supports emotional healing and general psychological well-being by giving clients a safe place to explore their emotions, face previous traumas, and ask for forgiveness.

Family and Relationship Therapy

Conflicts within families and relationships are frequently resolved using family and relationship therapy. Family harmony is restored, and open communication and forgiveness are encouraged by ho'oponopono. Families can restore trust and reinforce their ties by confronting problems head-on and working toward reconciliation.

Community and Organizational Settings

In community and organizational settings, Ho'oponopono helps resolve conflicts and foster collaboration. It encourages open communication, respect for one another, and cooperative problem-solving in both community and professional contexts by promoting a sense of shared accountability and solidarity.

Case Studies

Case Study 1

Marissa is nineteen. She shares a home in Honolulu as a single-family with her parents, sister Kaylyn, 16year old, and paternal grandmother. For the past two years after graduating from high school, Marissa has been employed full-time at a hardware store. She also attends a part-time community college. Kaylyn, Marissa's younger sister, shares a bedroom with her. Recently, Kaylyn has been wearing Marissa's new outfits without asking permission. Kaylyn borrowed Marissa's new shirt two months ago.

When Marissa returned home from work and discovered Kaylyn wearing her clothing, the sisters argued, escalating into a shouting scene. The sisters were arguing in the garage when their mother entered and attempted to ease the situation by yelling at them to stop. Kaylyn was knocked unconscious after being struck in the head by Marissa's push. Marissa and the family were questioned, "How was Kaylyn injured?" when the ambulance arrived.

The ambulance driver stated she had to call the police when she told them what had happened. That day, Marissa was taken into custody for assaulting a relative. Kaylyn spent two days in the hospital after suffering a concussion, but she recovered well, with the exception of intermittent headaches that the doctor feels will go away with time. Marissa regrets the harm she caused to her sister. Kaylyn feels shame over her sister's potential criminal record and the need to fulfill necessary commitments.

Although Kaylyn did not report her sister, any crimes against members of the home must be punished under Hawaii state law. Marissa enters a guilty plea to assaulting a family member. Anecdotal evidence suggests that families' involvement in hoʻoponopono motivates them to participate more actively in local cultural events. This culturally grounded chance for long-term development offers families a special chance to recover and develop.

Hoʻoponopono applied to the Case study

A hoʻoponopono practitioner is recommended to do family sessions in Marissa's family's house because they are a Part-Hawaiian family. The practitioner examines the family's spiritual preferences, such as their father's belief in ancestral methods and their mother's attendance at Christian churches. The practitioner must respect each family member's fundamental spiritual convictions. The family is encouraged to use their strengths, emotional, psychological, and spiritual resources to work out their differences in the session's opening prayer.

The prayer enumerates the problems that need to be fixed and reminds them of the mindset that is required to right the wrongs. Additionally, the prayer calls on family members to cooperate as a single unit, emphasizing open communication, deference, and attentive listening. By using this method, family members may listen more viscerally, which fosters harmony.

To make amends and forgive one another, impacted family members might share their opinions about a situation through the Hawaiian custom known as haku. This procedure, called hoʻoponopono, aids the family in removing the tangles that have caused discord. In order to highlight significant values and actions, the haku also integrates customs of respecting elders, cultural viewpoints on personal accountability, and traditional storytelling.

In addition, it examines sorrow and loss as well as family relationships through the prism of colonization and historical trauma. To strengthen the community, the haku also stresses the significance of producing morally upright adults. Families may decide to continue hoʻoponopono for multiple sessions to acquire new communication skills after the session concludes with a prayer.

Case Study 2

Lani, a 45-year-old mother, suffered the terrible loss of her teenage son, Koa, through a car accident. Koa was a bright young man who was dearly loved by his family and neighborhood. Even though the disaster was beyond her capability, Lani felt a strong sense of remorse and self-blame. She felt she could have done anything to prevent it, such as keeping a closer eye on him or offering better advice. Self-blame overwhelmed her life, resulting in sadness, social isolation, and terrible insomnia. Lani was introduced to Ho'oponopono, a traditional Hawaiian healing practice that focuses on restoring harmony within and between people. Lani set out on a path of self-discovery and self-reconciliation, led by a recognized haku practitioner from her community.

Lani's Healing Process Using Ho'oponopono

Every step of Ho'oponopono was critical to Lani's emotional restoration and acceptance.

- **Preparation Phase: Reflecting on the Root of Pain**

  Lani and her haku practitioner talked about her guilt and the source of her grief during the first few sessions. They spent time studying the precise occurrences and experiences that prompted her self-blame, which helped Lani recognize herself and mentally prepare for the delicate process of forgiving. The haku gently encouraged her to be willing to embrace healing and reminded her that this was a path of self-forgiveness.

- **Invocation: Creating a Sacred Space**

  At each session, the haku led Lani in a customary invocation, which included requesting spiritual guidance and ancestral support. They recited a short prayer, praying for clarity, healing, and forgiveness. This phase was critical in establishing a safe, sacred atmosphere in which Lani felt spiritually encouraged and prepared to face her pain.

- **Confession and Repentance: Acknowledging Regrets**

  Lani was encouraged at this stage to express her regrets freely, including specific events or behaviors related to Koa's injury. She expressed her grief when she realized she "should have known better." This revelation enabled Lani to confront her thoughts honestly and bring everything to the surface that had previously been suppressed due to tearing remorse.

  Lani constantly remarked, "I'm sorry, Koa," expressing her emotions of responsibility, no matter how absurd. This act of confession allowed her to express her sorrows and was the first step toward releasing her self-judgment.

- **Forgiveness: Letting Go of Self-Blame**

  Lani found forgiveness to be a turning point in her life. Her practitioner assisted her in expressing the words "Please forgive me," not only to her son's memory, but also to herself. Lani struggled at first, as forgiving herself seemed difficult and contradictory given her immense guilt.

  However, with continued practice, she learned to see forgiveness as a technique of releasing herself from pain, rather than explaining or excusing the terrible event. She gradually felt a sense of relief, as if she was accepting that she had done her best as a mother, even if she couldn't have prevented the accident. This stage enabled her to accept her humanity and let go of the unreasonable standards she had set for herself.

- **Gratitude and Love: Rebuilding Positive Connections**

  Lani spent the final sessions expressing gratitude for the happy times she had with Koa. The haku advised her to say "Thank you" and "I love you" to reframe her relationship with his memories. Instead of equating Koa's memory with sadness and grief, Lani decided to enjoy his life and the joy he offered her. This stage assisted Lani in replacing feelings of guilt with love and respect, reconnecting with her son's spirit in a way that valued both their relationship and her current life.

Outcome and Transformation

The Ho'oponopono sessions supported Lani in transforming her feelings of despair and remorse into acceptance and peace. She no longer saw herself as "at fault" but as a caring mother who had done her best. Throughout the process, she discovered that she could remember her son with love instead of suffering, and this shift in perspective inspired her to reconnect with her family and friends.

Lani's healing also inspired her to make positive contributions to her community. She started volunteering at a youth center, providing support and guidance to teenagers. Lani thought that by assisting others, she was honoring her son's memory and adding purpose to her path. Her therapeutic experience with Ho'oponopono not only provided her personal serenity, but it also revived her sense of purpose.

Challenges

Resisting Forgiveness

This healing process, Ho'oponopono- or more simply, forgiveness and reconciliation-culture, can be very therapeutic at the same time, but never so simple. One of the biggest difficulties that people face is in their tolerance. People especially after having gone through heavy trauma may find it near to impossible to move out of anger and resentment in life. It is completely common when the definition is, forgive, holding a cup of bitterness or believing to forgive someone means forgetting our ordeal.

Ego Resistance

Ego resistance is the most significant factor in making it hard to practice Ho'oponopono. The practice calls for us to take full responsibility for everything that happens in our lives, including other people's actions. If we have been conditioned to blame other people for our actions, then this may feel awkward. When we accept responsibility for circumstances that we could not have controlled, self-blame or guilt easily creeps in. Since our egos frequently oppose the notion that we are responsible for any of the difficulties we encounter, adopting the practice completely might be challenging.

Misunderstanding

Another issue relates to the very misunderstanding of the technique itself. Ho'oponopono is not the mere repetition of the phrase "I'm sorry" or "Please forgive me" without real meaning, but an acknowledgment of your responsibility for everything in your life and actually living these words. If one doesn't really get this, then it may appear like a ritual that doesn't create change at all and, indeed, will hamper its power. Additionally, individuals with diverse backgrounds will find it difficult to comprehend the actual meaning of Ho'oponopono because of its foreign cultural setting.

Emotional Releases

Emotional discharges can also be difficult to deal with. Ho'oponopono challenges us to face our suffering, which for many involves bringing up long-suppressed feelings. This can unleash emotions or traumas that have been suppressed for years, and sometimes those feelings are too strong to handle. The emotional cost can be high, especially when there appears to be much healing to do.

Expectation of quick results

Another problem is the demand for instant results. Healing is a slow process, yet people often want changes to happen immediately. Because ho'oponopono works on a subtle level, it is easy to get frustrated when results take time to manifest. Doubt and frustration may result from the improvements' initial smallness, incrementalism, or difficulty.

Forgiving others

Forgiveness is another difficulty that many people encounter. Forgiving ourselves is one thing; forgiving others, especially when they have hurt us greatly, is sometimes considerably more difficult. It might be challenging to take responsibility for everything in our life when we believe that someone else has harmed us, yet Ho'oponopono encourages us to do so. If the conflict persists, this struggle becomes much more difficult since forgiveness seems impossible, and the sorrow isn't really healed.

Lack of support

There is usually a lack of support as well. Ho'oponopono is often practiced in isolation, which can be alienating, especially when the rest of those in your life do not understand or are unsupportive of your healing process. There may come a time when you may become confused or unclear as to whether you are doing it correctly. A group or someone to share your experiences with would help you feel more grounded and encouraging.

Confusing responsibility with self-blame

Another barrier will be mistaking accountability with self-blame. Acceptance of responsibility for your emotional responses and your healing process does not have to mean that you blame yourself for everything that has gone wrong in life. Ho'oponopono encourages embracing your emotions without being owned by guilt or shame, but one can easily separate responsibility with self-blame. Yet there could be the danger of misinterpreting the practice as one way to justify cruelty or to disregard limits.

Skepticism

For most, skepticism can be an obstacle. With spiritual practices, people tend to be naturally skeptical about those that seem too easy or too good to be true. They wonder if uttering a few sentences can, in fact, heal one deeply. It is hard to commit when you don't trust the process.

External stressors

Practice can be more challenging when faced with real-life obstacles. Maintaining attention on the practice can be more difficult when faced with outside distractions like work or family matters. Sometimes the inner calm that Ho'oponopono aims to provide is overshadowed by the stress of everyday life, which results in dissatisfaction when it appears like nothing is changing.

Similarly, sometimes you are not emotionally set up for the monumental efforts forgiveness demands, and by trying to impose forgiveness, you make the whole act harder than it ought to be.

Ho'oponopono is a path that requires emotional strength, wisdom, and patience, even if it does bring potent healing. Responsibility, facing pain, and forgiving ourselves and others form part of the discipline. Though the difficulties are real, they are part of the process. Patience, self-compassion, and a willingness to remain open will help people benefit from this practice.

Conclusion

Ho'oponopono is a profound, culturally significant healing practice that promotes emotional, spiritual, and interpersonal harmony through forgiveness and reconciliation. It is an effective method for resolving both personal and social disputes since it emphasizes holistic and community-based treatment. As seen in the case study, Ho'oponopono offers families a disciplined and polite way to face and mend interpersonal conflicts.

The advantages of the practice, such as decreased stress, improved relationships, and improved mental health, emphasize its continuing significance. Integrating Ho'oponopono concepts into modern therapeutic and restorative frameworks demonstrates their adaptability, especially in culturally diverse settings. Its emphasis on forgiveness, accountability, and harmony is consistent with restorative justice objectives, making it a successful strategy for promoting community resilience and individual well-being.

References

Christianto, Victor & Smarandache, Florentin. (2020). A Review on how an Ancient Forgiveness Way Called Ho'oponopono Can Boost Human Health and Immune System.

Chun, K. H., & Wendt, L. D. (2013). Cultural implications of Ho'oponopono: A Hawaiian approach to conflict resolution and emotional healing. *Conflict Resolution Quarterly, 30*(3), 199-215. https://doi.org/10.1002/crq.21056

Gutmanis, J. (2013). Hawaiian perspectives on healing and medicine: The role of Ho'oponopono in emotional and physical health. *Journal of Hawaiian Cultural Medicine*, 11(2), 89-101.

Handy, E. S. C., & Pukui, M. K. (1972). Family dynamics and social healing: Traditional Hawaiian approaches. *Journal of Polynesian Studies*, 6(3), 23-35.

Ho'oponopono. (n.d.). Google Books. https://books.google.co.in/books?hl=en&lr=&id=4M_OPDXgWEIC&oi=fnd&pg=PA2&dq=Ho%27oponopono&ots=DIdfvskzlS&sig=1GrOj6wu-lwZCpRCpBbZjCY_jqI&redir_esc=y#v=onepage&q=Ho'oponopono&f=false

James, J. (2008). The psychological impact of forgiveness in Ho'oponopono practice. *Journal of Pacific Psychological Studies*, 14(1), 45-56.

Makua, H. (1997). Cultural practices in healing: Ho'oponopono as a framework for spiritual well-being. *Hawaiian Cultural Studies Journal*, 15(4), 70-85.

Kamaka, M. L., & Paloma, D. S. (2020). Ho'oponopono: A Native Hawaiian Healing Practice. *American Journal of Health Studies*, 35(4), 278–288. This paper explains Ho'oponopono as a culturally based practice and its role in contemporary health care

Kaulukukui, M. & Walker, L. (2021). Comparison of Native Hawaiian Traditional Hoʻoponopono and Modern Restorative Justice Practices, Comparative Restorative Justice. Ed. T. Gavrielides: New York: Springer, 305-323.

Krägeloh, C. U. (2019). *A Systematic Review of Studies Using the Modern Ho'oponopono Protocol. International Journal of Mental Health and Addiction*, 17(3), 676–693. This academic article reviews the psychological and therapeutic applications of Ho'oponopono in modern contexts.

Kuman, T. (2022). Spiritual and emotional outcomes of Ho'oponopono practice: A quantitative analysis. *Journal of Alternative Therapies and Integrative Health*, 28(3), 33-47.

Oshiro, M. (2015). Mauli ola and the role of spiritual and communal well-being in Hawaiian wellness. *Journal of Indigenous Health and Wellness*, 10(3), 22-30.

Paglinawan, R. K., Paglinawan, L. K. K., & Kamehameha Schools. (2012). Living Hawaiian Rituals: Lua, Hoʻoponopono, and Social Work. In University of Hawaiÿi at Mänoa, *Living Hawaiian Rituals: Lua, HoʻOponopono, and Social Work.*

Paglinawan, R. (2005). Hawaiian solutions to community issues: Integrating Ho'oponopono in family therapy. *Journal of Indigenous Conflict Resolution*, 19(2), 67-80.

Patten, T. H. (1994). Ho'oponopono: A Cross Cultural Model For Organizational Development And Change. *The International Journal Of Organizational Analysis*, *2*(3), 252–263. Https://Doi.Org/10.1108/Eb028811

Pukui, M. K., Haertig, E. W., & Lee, C. A. (1972). *Nānā I Ke Kumu (Look to the Source)*. This book offers an in-depth look at Hawaiian cultural practices, including Ho'oponopono, and how it has been traditionally used in conflict resolution and healing.

Pukui, M. K. (1983). *Hawaiian Dictionary: Hawaiian-English, English-Hawaiian*. University of Hawaii Press. This dictionary provides the meanings of "Ho'o," "Pono," and related terms. Pukui, M. K., Haertig, E. W., & Lee, C. A. (1972). *Nana I Ke Kumu (Look to the source)*. Hui Hanai.

Pukui, M. K., Haertig, E. W., & Lee, C. A. (1972). Reconciliation and forgiveness in Hawaiian culture: Ho'oponopono's role in family healing. *Polynesian Family and Cultural Studies Review*, 10(1), 112-127.

Sharma, M., & Rush, A. R. (2020). The effects of mindfulness and emotional processing on psychological outcomes: A case study approach. *Journal of Clinical Psychology, 76*(8), 1442-1455. https://doi.org/10.1002/jclp.22968

Thakurdas, A. (2008). Ho'oponopono: Universal Healing Method for Mankind. *Transforming Wisdom Journal.*

Vitale, Joe & Len, Ihaleakala. (2011). Zero Limits: The Secret Hawaiian System for Wealth, Health, Peace, and More. 10.1002/9781118258118.

Chapter 7

Kouksundo - A Unique Mind-Body Practice

Riashree Talukdar School of Liberal Studies (SLS), CMR University, Bangalore

Introduction

Kouksundo is an ancient Korean practice that harmonizes the mind, body, and spirit through a combination of deep breathing, meditation, and slow, flowing movements. Originating from the Taoist traditions of ancient Korea, it is deeply rooted in the belief that energy, or "ki," flows through the body and can be cultivated and directed to promote health, longevity, and spiritual growth. Kouksundo, places a strong emphasis on balance, self-awareness, and the development of inner serenity.

To maximize the flow of energy through the body's meridians, Kouksundo primarily focuses on posture and breathing control. In addition to better physical and mental health, practitioners frequently report feeling more centered, grounded, and at ease. Eventually, Kouksundo hopes to create a connection with nature as well as a sense of interior balance.

In the present era, Kouksundo has become more well-known outside of Korea, as practitioners from other nations seek its advantages for lowering stress and enhancing mental and physical health. With an emphasis on how non-invasive, mindful procedures can promote well-being, Kouksundo has gained international attention due to the growing interest in holistic approaches to health. People looking for a well-rounded approach to health welcome it, and it is frequently included into wellness initiatives and utilized in therapeutic contexts.

It combines traditional knowledge with modern demands to provide a unique route to physical wellness and awareness. In keeping with its core values of harmony, flow, and balance between the mind, body, and spirit, Kouksundo has continued to develop while adjusting to contemporary living.

History of Kouksundo

The origins of Kouksundo can be found more than 9,700 years ago, long before Korea was a single country, during the period of ancient Korean shamanism and Taoist rituals. According to legend, the teachings of the "Sindo," Or "the way of the mountain gods," which refers to the energy work done by ancient Korean sages who lived in nature, far from civilization, to improve their physical and spiritual well-being, was where Kouksundo had its start. These practitioners felt that they could develop a deeper connection to the universal energy that permeates all living things by training the body and mind via movement, breathing, and meditation.

The traditional Korean mind-body practice of Kouksundo, sometimes spelled "Guksundo," places a strong emphasis on energy cultivation, meditation, and overall health. This age-old practice, which has its origins in Korean history and culture, integrates physical exercises, breathing exercises, and meditation to encourage balance among the body, mind, and spirit. Although it is comparable to other Eastern techniques such as yoga, tai chi, and qigong, its philosophy and methodology are different.

Kouksundo became increasingly codified as Korea changed dynasties, particularly during the Three Kingdoms era (57 BC–668 AD). Kouksundo was systematized into a more systematic practice that included philosophical lessons on balance, duality, and the significance of harmony between humans and nature because of the impact of Taoism and Buddhism during this time.

During the Joseon Dynasty (1392–1897), Kouksundo declined under the strong influence of Confucianism. To avoid punishment, many Kouksundo practitioners withdrew farther into isolated regions, and the state-sponsored emphasis on Confucian principles eclipsed other spiritual traditions. On the other hand, the custom persisted in certain remote areas and was handed down through the generations.

Kouksundo saw a renaissance in the 20th century, especially following the Korean War (1950–1953). Rapid modernization in South Korea sparked a renewed interest in customs that might offer equilibrium in a world growing more fast-paced and industrialized. As Kouksundo practice moved from the highlands into cities, it became more accessible to the general people.

Since then, kouksundo has developed into a well-known mind-body technique in Korea and beyond. Kouksundo has evolved to accommodate the demands of contemporary practitioners, emphasizing stress reduction, physical well-being, and mental clarity while preserving its spiritual elements.

Core Practices and Techniques

To circulate and enhance "ki," Kouksundo practitioners employ a variety of breathing exercises, postures, and motions. The idea of "Dan-jeon" (or "Dantian" in Chinese), an energy point in the lower belly, is fundamental to Kouksundo. To develop and store energy in this area, practitioners concentrate on controlled breathing.

Kouksundo's techniques include:

Danjeon Breathing: The goal of this deep, abdominal breathing technique is to increase attention and internal energy.

Meditation Movements: These slow, intentional movements, which are like those in Qigong and Tai Chi, are intended to promote the flow of energy and enhance circulation.

Postures and Stances: Standing meditation is one position that is used to increase mental clarity and physical endurance.

Steps or Process of Kouksundo

Preparation and Warm-Up

Objective: To prepare the body and mind for the practice by loosening muscles and calming the mind.

Gentle Stretches: To relieve physical stress and improve blood flow to muscles and joints, practitioners start with a series of gentle stretches. In addition to preventing injuries, this step gets the body ready for the next motions.

Mindful Posture: Practitioners concentrate on anchoring themselves while standing or sitting in a solid, comfortable stance. The goal is to alleviate any mental strain and encourage a calm and concentrated state of mind.

Dan-Jeon Breathing (Abdominal Breathing)

Objective: To cultivate energy (Qi) by practicing deep, diaphragmatic breathing from the lower abdomen. Breath Focus: In Eastern techniques, the Dan-Jeon, a point approximately two inches below the navel, is thought to represent the body's energy core. This is where practitioners focus their attention.

Inhaling: They draw the breath down to the Dan-Jeon by taking a slow, deep breath through the nose, which causes the abdomen to swell. By stimulating the parasympathetic nervous system, this breathing technique aids in relaxing.

Exhaling: As the breath is expelled, the abdomen can softly contract thanks to the calm, steady exhale. With every exhalation, practitioners focus on releasing any tension in their bodies or minds.

Rhythmic Breathing: Over time, practitioners can increase their body awareness by using this regulated, rhythmic breathing to build energy (Qi) in the Dan-Jeon.

Movement Sequences (Physical Postures)

Objective: To open energy channels, improve flexibility, and promote circulation through specific movements and poses.

Deliberate, Slow Motions: Kouksundo motions are often flowing, soft, and slow, with each movement in time with the breath. This procedure aids in balancing and activating the body's energy flow.

Energy Cultivation: Exercises are intended to flow Qi through the body's meridians, or energy pathways, improving circulation and encouraging Yin and Yang energy balance.

Body Alignment: Maintaining proper posture and alignment is crucial since it keeps the body attentive and calm. The goal of mindful movement is for practitioners to be conscious of each position and how it affects their bodily and emotional states.

Movement Examples: Some examples of movements are bending, twisting, and mild stretching. Because they encourage flexibility, strength, and balance, poses like standing with your arms lifted or gradually transferring your weight between your legs are popular.

Meditation and Mindfulness

Objective: To focus the mind, achieve inner calm, and cultivate a sense of unity between body and mind.

Breath Awareness: Practitioners stay aware of each inhalation and exhalation while maintaining their attention on their breathing. This concentration deepens the state of calm and prevents the mind from straying.

Visualization: Practitioners are occasionally instructed to see the Qi flowing through their body, nourishing every bodily part as well as the mind. This imagery enhances the meditative state and supports the energy flow.

Body Awareness: To be present and connected to their bodily state, practitioners are urged to keep an awareness of how each body part feels. A deeper comprehension of one's own body and mind is fostered by this focused awareness.

Closing and Centering

Objective: To conclude the session by rebalancing energy and grounding oneself.

Gentle Cooling-Down Movements: To help the body release any tension that may have remained, practitioners may conclude with a few additional slow motions or gentle stretches.

Centering: Practitioners place their hands over the lower belly and feel the warmth of their energy core while refocusing on the Dan-Jeon. To allow their energy to settle in the Dan-Jeon, which represents the containment and balancing of Qi within the body, they might take a few last breaths.

Gratitude and Reflection: It is common for practitioners to pause and recognize any changes in their emotional, mental, or bodily states. As they complete the practice, this contemplation strengthens their sense of serenity, clarity, and groundedness.

Applications of Kouksundo

Kouksundo, with its integrated approach to mind-body harmony, has applications across a variety of fields, benefiting individuals in different life stages and settings. Its core elements of deep breathing, gentle physical postures, and mindfulness have made it a valuable tool In healthcare, corporate wellness, educational institutions, elder care, and personal wellness practices.

In healthcare, Kouksundo serves as an effective complementary therapy for patients facing chronic conditions, stress-related ailments, and mental health challenges. Its emphasis on mindful breathing and slow movements supports physical rehabilitation by improving circulation, flexibility, and relaxation, especially for those with chronic pain or limited mobility. In psycho-oncology, for example, Kouksundo has been Introduced as a holistic practice to help cancer patients cope with the physical and emotional demands of treatment. Patients undergoing chemotherapy have reported improvements in energy levels, emotional resilience, and a sense of control, highlighting Kouksundo's potential as an empowering adjunct to traditional care.

Within corporate settings, Kouksundo is increasingly adopted as part of workplace wellness programs aimed at reducing stress and promoting mental clarity among employees. In high-stress environments, such as finance or tech industries, corporate wellness initiatives that include Kouksundo help employees manage workplace pressures, improve focus, and maintain emotional balance. By integrating Kouksundo into weekly routines, companies have seen positive outcomes in employee well-being, including higher job satisfaction, enhanced productivity, and lower burnout rates.

Educational institutions have also found value in Kouksundo, especially in promoting emotional regulation and mental resilience among adolescents. Schools that incorporate Kouksundo into their mindfulness curricula see students benefitting from improved emotional self-control, reduced anxiety, and better academic performance. This practice helps adolescents cultivate a calm and focused mind, equipping them with effective stress-management skills that support both academic and personal growth.

Kouksundo also has significant applications in elderly care, where it helps address both physical and mental health challenges common in aging populations. Its gentle movements and breathing exercises are suitable for older adults, improving balance, mobility, and respiratory health. Additionally, practicing Kouksundo in group settings fosters a sense of community, reducing loneliness and promoting mental clarity and emotional well-being in retirement communities. Studies have shown that elderly individuals practicing Kouksundo experience a decrease in fall rates, improvements in mood, and a stronger sense of social connection.

Overall, the applications of Kouksundo extend across multiple domains, affirming its relevance in contemporary society as a practice that fosters resilience, mental clarity, physical vitality, and a deeper connection to self.

Benefits of Kouksundo

Physical Health Benefits

Kouksundo enhances physical health by improving bodily functions and boosting overall vitality. The slow, controlled movements and deep breathing exercises contribute to these specific physical benefits:

Improved Respiratory Health:

The breathing techniques practiced in Kouksundo are designed to increase lung capacity and improve oxygen intake. Deep, rhythmic breathing encourages the diaphragm to move more efficiently, helping the lungs function at their best and leading to better overall respiratory health.

Cardiovascular Health:

Slow, steady breathing can help lower blood pressure and improve circulation, reducing the strain on the heart. These effects promote cardiovascular health, which can lead to a lower risk of heart disease and other related conditions.

Enhanced Immune Function:

By regulating the body's energy flow and reducing stress, Kouksundo can support a healthy immune system. Reduced stress helps the body to maintain balanced immune responses, making it more resilient to illnesses.

Increased Flexibility and Joint Health:

The gentle, flowing movements in Kouksundo improve flexibility, strength, and balance. Practicing regularly can enhance joint mobility, reduce stiffness, and relieve tension, which is especially helpful for people with joint pain or arthritis.

Reduction in Physical Tension:

Many physical health issues arise from prolonged muscle tension. Kouksundo promotes relaxation through slow, mindful movements, which can help release muscle tension, reduce pain, and improve body awareness.

Mental Health Benefits

Kouksundo has powerful mental health benefits that stem from the combination of breathing exercises, mindfulness, and meditation.

These benefits include:

Stress Reduction:

The slow breathing and calming movements naturally activate the body's parasympathetic nervous system, which helps reduce stress levels. This relaxation response calms the mind, decreasing feelings of anxiety and promoting mental peace.

Improved Focus and Mental Clarity:

Through mindful breathing and meditation, Kouksundo helps practitioners increase their ability to focus on the present moment. Over time, this practice improves mental clarity and concentration, enabling individuals to focus more effectively in their daily tasks.

Better Emotional Regulation:

Kouksundo fosters self-awareness and mindfulness, helping practitioners recognize and regulate their emotions more effectively. As a result, they can handle challenging or stressful situations with a calmer, more balanced perspective.

Cognitive Flexibility:

Practicing Kouksundo enhances cognitive flexibility, allowing individuals to adapt better to changes, solve problems creatively, and maintain a positive mindset. This adaptability contributes to mental resilience, which is essential for coping with life's challenges.

Spiritual and Emotional Well-Being

Kouksundo is more than a physical or mental practice—it also has deep spiritual benefits. Many practitioners report an increase in emotional balance and a deeper sense of meaning in life, which can be attributed to:

Self-Awareness and Inner Peace:

Kouksundo encourages introspection, allowing practitioners to connect with their inner selves. By cultivating awareness of their body, mind, and breath, practitioners develop a sense of inner peace and stability that is both calming and empowering.

A Deeper Connection with Oneself:

The meditative aspects of Kouksundo encourage a deep connection with the self, fostering self-acceptance and compassion. As individuals become more in tune with their needs and emotions, they often experience greater harmony within themselves and improved relationships with others.

Life Purpose and Meaning:

Kouksundo's emphasis on the balance of body, mind, and spirit often leads practitioners to reflect on their life path and values. This sense of purpose brings a feeling of alignment with one's deeper self and fosters a life lived with greater intention.

Alignment with the Natural Flow of Life:

Kouksundo aligns individuals with the natural rhythms of life, which is an important aspect of Eastern philosophies. Practicing regularly can help people feel more grounded, connected to nature, and in tune with the world around them, encouraging a deeper appreciation of life's cycles and flow.

Challenges of Kouksundo

Difficulty in Mastering Breathing Techniques

Beginners may find it difficult to practice the deep, controlled breathing that is essential to Kouksundo, particularly the Dan-Jeon (lower abdominal) breathing. It could take some time, patience, and effort to learn how to breathe deeply from the abdomen while keeping a steady rhythm because many people are used to shallow breathing. Although it can be first painful and psychologically difficult, mastering this technique is essential to reaping the full advantages of Kouksundo.

Physical and Postural Challenges

For those with limited flexibility or mobility limitations, Kouksundo may be challenging due to its gentle motions and specialized postures. It could take some time to establish the balance and coordination needed for some postures and stretches. It may be uncomfortable for beginners or people with joint problems, especially in the knees or hips. To prevent strain or damage, adjustments could be required, and certain people might require individualized advice.

Maintaining Consistency

For best results, Kouksundo requires frequent, consistent practice, much like any other self-development activity. Maintaining discipline and motivation can be difficult, particularly for people with hectic schedules or those who don't see results right away. Although Kouksundo has cumulative effects that intensify over time, some people may find the requirement for dedication depressing.

Mental Distractions and Mindfulness Challenges

Kouksundo places a strong emphasis on awareness and mindfulness, yet it can be difficult, especially for newcomers, to keep a clear, concentrated mind. It might be challenging for people who are new to meditation to focus and achieve a relaxed state because of mental distractions. If practitioners have trouble focusing on their breath or movements, or if they have trouble quieting their minds, they may become frustrated.

Cultural and Philosophical Learning Curve

Kouksundo is rooted in Eastern philosophy, specifically Taoist and Korean traditions. The concepts of Qi (vital energy), Dan-Jeon (energy centers), and Yin-Yang balance may be unfamiliar to individuals from different cultural backgrounds. Some practitioners may find it challenging to grasp these ideas, and it can take time to internalize and fully appreciate the philosophical aspects that are integral to the practice.

Lack of Access to Qualified Instructors

Kouksundo is less widely known than practices like yoga or tai chi, which means there may be limited access to qualified instructors, especially outside of Korea. Practicing without proper guidance can lead to incorrect techniques, potentially limiting the benefits of Kouksundo and increasing the risk of injury. Learning Kouksundo through online videos or books may be helpful, but many aspects of the practice are best taught in person by a knowledgeable instructor.

Physical Fatigue and Initial Discomfort

For those unaccustomed to any physical or breathing discipline, Kouksundo may initially lead to physical fatigue or mild discomfort. The exercises, though gentle, require focus and endurance, which can be tiring for beginners. Moreover, the deep breathing techniques and prolonged postures can create initial discomfort as the body adjusts.

Patience Required for Results

Kouksundo is a gradual practice, where results appear over time through sustained effort and commitment. Individuals looking for quick physical or mental results may find it challenging to remain patient. The benefits of Kouksundo tend to develop progressively, and those who expect immediate improvements might feel discouraged if they don't experience noticeable changes right away.

Suggestions of Kouksundo

When beginning or deepening a Kouksundo practice, a few key suggestions can help individuals maximize their experience and stay motivated. First, it's recommended to start under the guidance of a qualified instructor, especially for beginners. Learning from someone well-versed in the techniques ensures that each movement and breathing exercise is performed correctly and safely. Moreover, a knowledgeable teacher can introduce practitioners to the deeper philosophies of Kouksundo, helping them understand the connection between breath, movement, and energy flow.

Consistency is essential in Kouksundo. Rather than practicing sporadically, practitioners are encouraged to establish a regular schedule, even if they can only dedicate a short amount of time each session. Practicing for 10–15 minutes daily is often more beneficial than infrequent, lengthy sessions.

Mindfulness is also a central aspect of Kouksundo, and practitioners should focus on being fully present during each session. This means letting go of outside distractions, grounding oneself in each movement, and allowing breathwork to cultivate a state of calm awareness. Kouksundo is not about rushing through exercises but about experiencing each moment and understanding the flow of Qi within the body.

Adaptability is another useful suggestion. Kouksundo should be adjusted to meet the individual's physical condition and comfort level. For instance, someone with physical limitations can modify movements to avoid strain, ensuring the practice remains safe and enjoyable. Being mindful of one's own body signals and adapting accordingly can prevent overexertion and make the practice more accessible to people of all fitness levels and ages.

Case Studies of Kouksundo Practice

Case Study 1: Stress Management in Corporate Employees

Context:

A corporate wellness program in Seoul sought to address the high levels of stress and burnout among employees working in demanding roles. Kouksundo was introduced as part of an experimental wellness initiative to improve mental health and productivity. Fifty employees, ranging from entry-level workers to senior managers, participated in Kouksundo classes twice a week, facilitated by a certified instructor.

Method:

The program included a structured, twice-weekly Kouksundo class over six months. Each session lasted about an hour, incorporating deep breathing exercises, gentle movements, and guided meditation to reduce stress and promote mental clarity. Employees were encouraged to practice mindful breathing and relaxation techniques during breaks as well.

Results:

After six months, employees reported a marked reduction in perceived stress levels. Many described an improved ability to focus and greater emotional resilience when handling work pressures. Several participants noted that their mood and overall sense of well-being had improved, making it easier to manage work challenges without feeling overwhelmed. Quantitative assessments showed an approximate 25% decrease in reported stress, and 60% of participants said they would continue practicing Kouksundo independently.

Implications:

This case demonstrates how integrating Kouksundo into corporate settings can be a valuable strategy for reducing stress, improving productivity, and creating a healthier work environment. The findings suggest that Kouksundo can be a practical, sustainable addition to wellness programs aimed at enhancing employee mental health and resilience.

Case Study 2: Rehabilitation from Chronic Pain

Context:

A 45-year-old patient experiencing chronic back pain due to a spinal injury struggled with limited mobility and dependence on pain medication. Traditional physical therapy alone had not yielded sufficient pain relief, so Kouksundo was added to their rehabilitation plan as a complementary therapy.

Method:

The patient began practicing Kouksundo daily, with sessions tailored to their physical limitations. The routine included gentle movements to improve flexibility, breathwork to manage pain, and meditation to promote mental relaxation. The instructor adjusted postures to avoid strain on the back and emphasized mindful breathing techniques.

Results:

Over one year, the patient's pain levels significantly decreased, allowing them to reduce their reliance on pain medication. Improved flexibility and range of motion were observed, and the patient experienced a renewed sense of autonomy over their body. By the end of the year, they reported an increased quality of life, with greater ease in daily activities and improved mental resilience in managing their condition.

Implications:

This case highlights Kouksundo's potential in chronic pain management, particularly for individuals seeking alternative or complementary therapies to improve mobility and reduce pain medication dependency. The study underscores the importance of personalized practice, especially for patients with physical limitations.

Case Study 3: Kouksundo for Cancer Recovery

Context:

In a psycho-oncology setting, 20 patients undergoing chemotherapy for breast cancer participated in a Kouksundo program alongside their conventional treatments. The program aimed to support physical and emotional recovery and improve patients' overall resilience to treatment side effects.

Method:

Patients practiced Kouksundo three times a week for three months, with a focus on gentle breathing exercises and meditation to alleviate fatigue and emotional stress. Movements were modified to suit participants' physical conditions, especially for those experiencing physical weakness due to chemotherapy.

Results:

After three months, patients reported reduced fatigue and improved emotional well-being. They described feeling more in control of their recovery, attributing the practice to a deeper sense of inner strength and optimism. Family members and healthcare providers also observed enhanced emotional resilience and a positive outlook in patients, which contributed to better engagement in their recovery process.

Implications:

This case suggests that Kouksundo can serve as a supportive practice in oncology settings, particularly to help patients cope with the physical and emotional stress of cancer treatments. The findings indicate that incorporating mind-body practices like Kouksundo may help improve quality of life for cancer patients and support holistic recovery.

Conclusion

Kouksundo offers a unique pathway to holistic health, blending ancient wisdom with modern needs. Its emphasis on deep breathing, energy flow, and mindful movement makes it a versatile practice that can benefit people of all ages and fitness levels. While it faces challenges in terms of accessibility and scientific validation, Kouksundo's potential for improving mental, physical, and spiritual well-being is significant. As interest in mind-body practices continues to grow, Kouksundo has the potential to become a valuable tool for cultivating balance and harmony in an increasingly stressful world.

References

Ahn, J. H. (2018). *Breath and balance: Integrating Kouksundo into modern health practices*. Seoul University Press.

Bae, M. J., & Kim, Y. K. (2020). Therapeutic effects of Kouksundo on stress and mental health. *Journal of Korean Healing Arts*, 12(2), 45-57.

Chang, H. S. (2019). *Kouksundo: Ancient practices for contemporary wellness*. Korea Health Publications.

Choi, D. Y., & Lee, H. J. (2017). Benefits of Kouksundo for respiratory health in aging adults. *Asian Journal of Wellness Studies*, 15(3), 203-215.

Han, J. (2021). The impact of Kouksundo practice on emotional regulation in adolescents. *Journal of Mindfulness in Education**, 9(1), 22-37.

Jeong, S., & Moon, Y. (2016). A comparative study of Kouksundo and Qigong in energy cultivation. *Eastern Wellness Journal*, 8(4), 87-102.

Jung, Y. K. (2022). *Mind-body connections in Kouksundo: A pathway to inner harmony*. New Horizon Press.

Kang, M. J. (2018). Breath-centered meditation in Kouksundo: A qualitative study. *Mind and Body Journal*, 6(1), 54-68.

Kim, C. (2020). *Traditional Korean practices for mental health: Insights from Kouksundo*. East-West Health Publishers.

Kim, D. S., & Park, Y. (2019). Kouksundo and its role in corporate wellness programs. *Journal of Workplace Wellness*, 11(2), 115-130.

Kim, H. J. (2018). *Kouksundo for beginners: A guide to ancient Korean practices*. Seoul Light Press.

Kim, S., & Jung, T. (2021). Exploring Kouksundo as an adjunct therapy for chronic pain. *Journal of Alternative and Complementary Medicine*, 27(3), 151-160.

Ko, B. J. (2019). *The philosophy of Kouksundo: Cultivating energy and balance*. Korean Cultural Press.

Kwon, J., & Han, L. (2017). The physiological effects of Kouksundo breathing techniques. *Journal of Traditional Medicine and Therapy*, 23(1), 49-58.

Lee, C. S. (2020). Kouksundo practice in elderly populations: A case study. *Aging and Wellness*, 10(2), 78-87.

Lee, H. J. (2019). *Healing through breath: The transformative power of Kouksundo.* Earth Heart Publishers.

Lee, J., & Kwon, S. (2018). Kouksundo's impact on cancer recovery and emotional well-being. *Journal of Psycho-Oncology and Wellness*, 4(2), 90-105.

Lim, K. (2016). *Understanding Kouksundo: History, practice, and science*. East Asian Health Institute.

Moon, H. (2017). Kouksundo and mindfulness: A study of self-awareness. *Journal of Mindfulness and Practice*, 14(4), 120-132.

Nam, Y., & Shin, G. (2021). Physical benefits of Kouksundo for aging adults. *Journal of Geriatric Health*, 18(1), 43-58.

Oh, S. J. (2018). Kouksundo breathing and its impact on mental health. *Journal of East Asian Studies*, 9(2), 64-76.

Park, H., & Choi, S. (2019). Incorporating Kouksundo into modern psychotherapy. *Journal of Integrative Mental Health*, 16(1), 58-72.

Park, J. (2021). *Eastern wisdom for modern life: The Kouksundo path*. Harmony Press.

Park, M., & Kim, J. (2020). Kouksundo as a complementary practice in psycho-oncology. *Journal of Complementary Cancer Therapies*, 7(1), 105-115.

Shin, J. (2017). Effects of Kouksundo on quality of life in chronic pain patients. *Journal of Pain Management and Therapy*, 12(3), 213-228.

Song, E. (2019). *Mindfulness and movement: Kouksundo for inner peace*. Asia-Pacific Wellness Books.

Sung, M. H., & Lee, K. (2021). Kouksundo as a stress management tool for corporate employees. *Wellness and Corporate Culture*, 15(2), 89-100.

Woo, H. S. (2018). *The art of balance: Exploring Kouksundo practices*. Mountain River Press.

Yang, C., & Park, T. (2020). Therapeutic applications of Kouksundo in Korean hospitals. *Journal of Complementary Health Practices*, 19(1), 95-108.

Yoo, M. (2017). Kouksundo meditation for mental resilience in adolescents. *Youth Mental Health Review*, 5(3), 33-47.

Yoon, H., & Kwon, D. (2016). Kouksundo's role in respiratory health among adults. *Korean Journal of Wellness*, 13(4), 112-124.

Yoon, S. K. (2019). *Ancient Korean wisdom for today's world: The practice of Kouksundo*, Sunlight Path Publishers.

Chapter 8

Mandala Art Therapy

Prathima Kumari Mourya R. School of Liberal Studies (SLS), CMR University, Bangalore

History of Mandala Art Therapy

Mandala art is a symbolic representation, especially prominent in Hinduism and Buddhism, where it is seen as a metaphor for the universe. The term "mandala" is derived from the Sanskrit word for "circle," signifying completeness and balance. These artworks typically feature intricate, circular patterns that radiate from a central point, symbolizing unity and cosmic harmony. In spiritual traditions, mandalas are used as tools for meditation and self-contemplation, believed to foster mindfulness, focus, and a deeper connection with the universe and the self.

Hinduism (around 1500 BCE)

In Hinduism, mandalas are utilized as meditation aids and are seen as representations of the universe and cosmic order. They frequently take the form of intricate geometric designs, symbolizing various aspects of divinity and the cosmos.

Buddhism (around the 4th century CE)

Mandalas became central to Buddhist art, especially in Tibetan Buddhism. They are employed in meditation, healing, and for focusing spiritual energy. Tibetan sand mandalas, crafted from colored sand, are ceremonially dismantled after completion, symbolizing the transient nature of life.

Jungian Psychology (20th century)

Swiss psychologist Carl Jung introduced the concept of mandalas into Western psychology in the early 1900s. He viewed them as symbols of the "Self" and believed they could be used in therapy to explore the unconscious. Jung noted that his patients often created mandalas spontaneously, which he interpreted as a reflection of their inner psychological state.

Introduction to Mandala Art Therapy

In contemporary times, mandalas have gained widespread popularity not only for their aesthetic appeal but also for their therapeutic properties. They are often utilized in art therapy to help individuals reduce stress, express emotions, and promote inner healing. Mandala designs can vary greatly in complexity, ranging from simple geometric shapes to highly intricate patterns, reflecting the cultural or personal influences of the creator. In the Eastern world, mandalas have long been used as a tool for meditation and healing, particularly in Buddhist and Hindu traditions.

In Tibetan Buddhism, mandalas are often created to aid in mindfulness, mental purification, and emotional healing. The intricate process of creating a sand mandala, which is ritualistically destroyed after completion, symbolizes the impermanence of life and the need to let go of attachments.

More recently, mandala-based art therapy has been applied in clinical settings across Asia and globally. This therapeutic approach helps individuals express their emotions, reduce anxiety, and manage stress. Mandala art therapy has been recognized for its potential in enhancing focus, promoting emotional healing, and fostering a sense of unity between mind and body.

Techniques used in Mandala Art Therapy

Spontaneous Mandala Creation

In this technique, individuals are invited to create mandalas without any prior plan or guidelines. The freedom of drawing without constraints allows clients to access their subconscious and express emotions or thoughts they may not be fully aware of. The process encourages creativity and provides insight into inner psychological and emotional states. This open-ended approach helps bypass mental blocks and engages the unconscious mind. Therapists can interpret the use of space, lines, and colors to gain insights into a client's emotional and mental well-being.

Coloring Pre-Designed Mandalas

Coloring pre-drawn mandalas is another widely used technique in mandala therapy. The focus on symmetrical designs and intricate patterns engages the brain in a calming, meditative activity. The colors chosen can also reveal the client's emotional state. The repetitive nature of coloring fosters relaxation, reduces anxiety, and improves focus. Therapists might guide clients to reflect on their color choices and any emotional associations with them.

Thematic or Guided Mandala Creation

Therapists may provide clients with specific themes or prompts, such as "create a mandala that reflects your present emotions" or "design a mandala that represents your life journey." This structured approach helps clients focus on issues or experiences they need to explore. Guided themes help bring clarity to specific emotions or experiences, allowing individuals to express themselves within a therapeutic framework. Themes can be customized based on therapeutic goals.

Symbolic Representation in Mandalas

This technique involves encouraging clients to embed personal symbols within their mandalas, representing aspects such as relationships, personal challenges, or aspirations. These symbols provide a visual means of expressing complex emotions or life experiences. The inclusion of symbols such as hearts for love or spirals for growth helps clients externalize internal conflicts or desires. Therapists analyze the symbols to understand deeper psychological meanings.

Sand Mandalas

Inspired by Tibetan Buddhist practices, this technique involves creating mandalas with colored sand. The meticulous process promotes concentration and mindfulness. Once completed, the mandala is often ritualistically dismantled to symbolize impermanence and the acceptance of change. This technique is deeply meditative, requiring patience and focus. The destruction of the mandala encourages clients to reflect on the transient nature of life and the importance of letting go.

Layered or Progressive Mandala Creation

In this method, clients work on a mandala over several sessions, adding new layers or expanding the design. This progressive creation symbolizes personal growth or healing over time. The technique allows for a gradual exploration of deep-seated emotions, as each session provides an opportunity to add meaning and new insights. It reflects the therapeutic journey of self-discovery.

Reflective Journaling with Mandalas

After completing a mandala, clients are encouraged to engage in reflective journaling. This process involves writing about the experience, the emotions that surfaced, and the meaning they associate with the shapes, colors, and symbols in their mandala. Writing helps to deepen self-reflection, enabling clients to articulate their emotions and the therapeutic experience. It bridges the gap between visual expression and verbal processing.

Mindfulness and Mandala Creation

This approach emphasizes mindfulness during the creation of the mandala. Clients focus on their breath, body sensations, and the present moment while drawing or coloring the mandala. This helps in reducing stress and increasing awareness. The act of mindful drawing allows clients to stay present, promoting calmness and reducing mental clutter. Therapists might combine this technique with breathing exercises or body scans.

Collaborative or Group Mandalas

In group therapy settings, individuals work together to create a mandala. Each participant contributes to the design, fostering connection, collaboration, and a shared therapeutic experience. This technique encourages teamwork and group cohesion. It also provides individuals with the opportunity to express themselves within a collective framework, offering therapeutic benefits for those dealing with social anxiety or relational issues.

Collage Mandalas

Rather than drawing, clients use images, textures, and colors from magazines or other materials to create a mandala collage. This technique is useful for those who may struggle with drawing but still wish to engage in creative expression. The tactile experience of cutting and arranging materials can provide a different sensory experience, aiding in emotional expression and creativity. It also allows for the exploration of different mediums

Applications of Mandala Art Therapy

Alleviating Stress and Anxiety

Mandala art therapy is frequently employed to help individuals reduce stress and manage anxiety. The structured, repetitive designs of mandalas promote mindfulness and relaxation. By focusing on creating or coloring a mandala, individuals can take their mind off stressful situations and practice being in the moment. Studies have demonstrated that coloring mandalas can significantly lower anxiety levels, especially in individuals suffering from chronic anxiety. This meditative process engages the brain in a calming activity, helping to reduce overall stress levels.

Facilitating Emotional Expression

For people who find it difficult to verbalize their feelings, mandala art therapy offers a visual means of emotional expression. The circular design of mandalas provides a safe and structured space for people to project their inner emotions and experiences, making it especially useful for trauma therapy or emotional regulation. The creation of mandalas helps individuals externalize emotions such as sadness, anger, or fear. This non-verbal mode of expression allows for a deeper exploration of one's feelings, often leading to therapeutic breakthroughs and emotional release.

Encouraging Self-Discovery and Growth

Mandala therapy is a powerful tool for self-exploration and personal growth. The process of creating mandalas enables individuals to reflect on their inner thoughts and aspirations, providing insights into their emotional and psychological state. By exploring the symbols, colors, and patterns that emerge in their mandalas, individuals can gain a better understanding of their subconscious mind. This can be especially helpful during times of life transitions or existential questioning, aiding in personal growth and transformation.

Cognitive and Emotional Integration

Mandala creation activates both the logical and creative sides of the brain, helping to bridge the gap between cognition and emotion. The structured patterns engage the brain's logical functions, while the creative design elements tap into emotional and artistic expression. This balanced brain activation encourages mental coherence and harmony. By engaging both hemispheres of the brain, individuals can process their thoughts and emotions more holistically, promoting mental clarity and emotional stability.

Mindfulness and Meditation

The creation of mandalas serves as a form of active meditation. The intricate designs and repetitive patterns encourage individuals to focus on the present moment, cultivating mindfulness and reducing mind-wandering. This meditative practice can improve attention span, reduce intrusive thoughts, and enhance overall mental well-being. Mandala art therapy is especially beneficial for individuals dealing with depression, anxiety, or post-traumatic stress, as it helps quiet the mind and promote emotional calm.

Healing from Trauma

Mandala art therapy is often used as a therapeutic tool for trauma recovery. Individuals who have experienced trauma may find it difficult to express their pain verbally. Mandalas provide a symbolic way for them to represent their internal struggles and work through unresolved emotions in a controlled environment. Trauma survivors benefit from mandala creation as it provides a safe space to process difficult emotions. This non-verbal approach allows them to engage with their trauma at their own pace, leading to gradual emotional healing and regulation.

Improving Focus and Concentration

For individuals who struggle with attention deficits, such as those with ADHD, mandala therapy helps improve focus and concentration. The detailed nature of mandala creation encourages prolonged attention and cognitive engagement. The act of drawing or coloring a mandala helps enhance concentration and cognitive control. Regular practice can lead to improvements in attention span, making mandala art therapy a useful tool for managing attention disorders.

Group Therapy and Social Connection

Mandala creation is also effective in group therapy settings. Collaborative mandala projects foster communication, cooperation, and social bonding among participants. Group members often share personal insights and experiences during the process, creating a supportive community environment. In group therapy, mandala art serves as a medium for collective healing. The act of creating mandalas together fosters a sense of shared purpose and unity, strengthening connections among participants and enhancing mutual support.

Mental Health Treatment in Clinical Settings

Mandala art therapy is utilized in various clinical settings, such as hospitals, mental health clinics, and rehabilitation centers. Patients dealing with mental health conditions like depression, anxiety, or chronic illness can benefit from the calming and restorative effects of mandala creation. Clinical studies have shown that mandala therapy can improve mental health outcomes by reducing symptoms of anxiety and depression. It also aids in emotional regulation, mood enhancement, and mental clarity, making it a valuable therapeutic tool for mental health professionals.

Spiritual Exploration and Balance

Mandalas have deep spiritual significance, particularly in Eastern traditions such as Buddhism and Hinduism. In therapeutic contexts, mandala creation can help individuals explore their spirituality and achieve greater balance between mind, body, and spirit. By engaging with the sacred geometry of mandalas, individuals can experience deeper self-awareness and spiritual insights. This practice promotes inner peace and helps individuals find a sense of connection to the larger universe, facilitating spiritual healing and growth.

Challenges in Mandala Art therapy

Cultural Sensitivity

Cultural sensitivity is paramount in mandala art therapy because mandalas hold significant spiritual and cultural meaning in traditions like Hinduism and Buddhism. Therapists must be aware of the historical context and cultural implications of mandalas to avoid cultural appropriation. This awareness involves recognizing the sacredness of mandalas in their original settings and ensuring that therapy does not trivialize or distort their meaning. Failing to approach the use of mandalas with respect can lead to misunderstandings, discomfort, or even alienation among clients from those cultural backgrounds. Therefore, therapists need to engage in ongoing education about the cultural roots of mandalas and facilitate discussions about their significance with clients.

Client Resistance

Client resistance to engaging in art therapy, including mandala creation, can be a significant barrier in the therapeutic process. Many individuals may feel intimidated by the idea of creating art, fearing they lack artistic skills or worrying about being judged by others. This apprehension can result in reluctance to participate fully, diminishing the potential benefits of the therapy. To overcome this challenge, therapists must establish a trusting relationship with their clients, encourage exploration without fear of judgment, and normalize the artistic process as a means of self-expression rather than a competition. Building a safe space for creativity is essential to help clients feel comfortable and willing to engage in the therapeutic process.

Emotional Overwhelm

The act of creating mandalas can bring forth strong emotions, particularly for clients dealing with trauma or significant life challenges. While this emotional release is often beneficial, it can also lead to feelings of overwhelm and distress. As clients delve into their emotions while creating art, they may confront unresolved feelings that can trigger anxiety or discomfort. Therapists need to be equipped to manage these emotional responses and provide support during sessions. This requires creating a safe and nurturing environment where clients feel secure enough to express their emotions and process them with guidance. Offering grounding techniques or coping strategies can help clients navigate these intense experiences more effectively.

Individual Differences in Response

Each client may have a unique response to mandala art therapy based on various factors, such as personality traits, past experiences, and emotional states. While some individuals may find significant therapeutic benefits from creating mandalas, others may not experience the same level of engagement or emotional release. This variability highlights the need for therapists to be adaptable and tailor their approaches to meet each client's individual needs. Understanding the reasons behind a client's unique response can lead to more personalized and effective interventions. Therapists must remain open and observant, using feedback to adjust the therapeutic process and ensure it aligns with the client's preferences and emotional readiness.

Limited Training and Expertise

Not all therapists possess specialized training in art therapy or an in-depth understanding of the psychological aspects of mandala creation. This lack of expertise can result in ineffective therapeutic practices, which may undermine the potential benefits of mandala art therapy. Therapists need to have a solid foundation in both art therapy techniques and the principles of psychology to guide clients effectively. Ongoing professional development and training in mandala art therapy can enhance therapists' confidence and competence in implementing this approach. By equipping themselves with the necessary skills and knowledge, therapists can provide clients with meaningful and impactful experiences in their therapeutic journey.

Access to Resources

Access to art supplies and resources can be a significant challenge, particularly in low-income or underserved communities. Limited availability of materials can hinder the implementation of mandala art therapy, as clients may not have the necessary tools to fully engage in the creative process. This challenge requires therapists to be resourceful and innovative, finding alternative materials or utilizing digital platforms for mandala creation. By adapting to available resources and ensuring that clients can still participate in mandala therapy, therapists can help overcome barriers related to access. Additionally, community partnerships or funding sources can be explored to improve the availability of art supplies for those in need.

Time Constraints

Therapeutic sessions are often limited in duration, which can make it challenging for clients to fully engage in the mandala creation process. The intricate nature of mandalas often requires extended periods to achieve a sense of completion and satisfaction. When sessions are time-constrained, clients may feel rushed or unable to explore their creativity adequately. To address this challenge, therapists must consider how to structure sessions to allow enough time for both the creation of mandalas and subsequent reflection on the process. Encouraging clients to continue their work outside of sessions can also help foster a more in-depth engagement with their art, extending the therapeutic benefits beyond the therapy room.

Subjectivity of Interpretation

The interpretation of mandalas can be highly subjective and influenced by personal experiences, cultural backgrounds, and emotional states. This subjectivity can complicate therapeutic discussions, as what a mandala signifies for one person may differ significantly for another. Therapists need to navigate these varying interpretations carefully, encouraging clients to articulate their meanings while providing insights based on psychological principles. Establishing a collaborative dialogue where clients feel comfortable sharing their perspectives fosters a richer understanding of their inner world and enhances the therapeutic process. It is essential for therapists to validate clients' interpretations while guiding them to explore deeper meanings that may emerge through their mandala creations.

Integration with Other Therapeutic Modalities

Mandala art therapy is often integrated with other therapeutic approaches, such as cognitive-behavioral therapy (CBT) or mindfulness practices. However, finding the right balance and integration can pose challenges for therapists. Each modality has its principles and techniques and blending them requires a nuanced understanding of both approaches. Therapists must be mindful of how mandala therapy complements other therapeutic interventions and ensure that the integration is seamless and beneficial for clients. Adequate training in both mandala art therapy and the other modalities used can facilitate effective integration, allowing therapists to provide comprehensive and holistic care.

Case studies related to Mandala Art Therapy

Case Study 1: Integrating Jungian Therapy and Mandala Art Therapy for Depression Treatment

Introduction

This case study explores the treatment of a 27-year-old female diagnosed with depression, employing an integrative approach that combines Jungian therapy with transpersonal art therapy, specifically mandala art therapy. The study highlights the significance of this combined therapeutic approach and its effectiveness in promoting emotional healing and recovery.

Client Background

The client is a 27-year-old female who has been diagnosed with depression. Her symptoms included persistent feelings of sadness, low energy, and difficulties in daily functioning. She sought therapy to address these challenges and improve her overall emotional well-being.

Therapeutic Approach

Jungian Therapy - Jungian therapy focuses on exploring the unconscious mind and utilizing archetypes as tools for personal growth and healing. In this case, the archetype of the Great Mother, represented by the African goddess Iemanjá, was central to the client's therapeutic work. This symbol served as a catalyst for the exploration of her inner emotions and facilitated a deeper understanding of her experiences.

Mandala Art Therapy - Mandala art therapy involves creating and reflecting on mandalas as a means of self-expression and emotional processing. During therapy sessions, the client engaged in mandala creation, which allowed her to visually express her feelings and experiences. The mandala served as a focal point for her healing journey, promoting mindfulness and emotional openness.

Complementary Techniques

In addition to Jungian and mandala art therapy, complementary techniques were integrated into the treatment plan, including:

- **Visualization Practices:** Guided imagery exercises to enhance emotional awareness and relaxation.
- **Energy Therapy:** Techniques aimed at balancing and harmonizing the client's energy.
- **Creativity and the Brain Course:** An educational component that explored the relationship between creativity and mental health.

Conclusion

This case study underscores the therapeutic potential of mandala art therapy, particularly when combined with archetypal imagery and sensory elements within a Jungian framework. The findings suggest that mandala art therapy can be a valuable complementary tool in depression treatment plans, enhancing emotional healing and overall well-being. Further research is warranted to explore the efficacy of this integrative approach in diverse clinical populations.

Case Study 2: Mandala Art Therapy for Reducing Test Anxiety in College Students

Introduction

This case study investigates the effectiveness of mandala art therapy in reducing test anxiety among female undergraduate students. Test anxiety, characterized by cognitive, physiological, and behavioral responses, can adversely affect academic performance and overall mental health. By employing mandala art therapy, this study aimed to explore a creative and non-verbal intervention that promotes emotional expression and mindfulness.

Client Background

The study involved nine female undergraduate students who reported experiencing test anxiety. Test anxiety symptoms included feelings of nervousness, worry about performance, physical tension, and difficulty concentrating during exams. The participants were selected based on their self-reported anxiety levels and willingness to engage in the therapeutic process.

Methodology

Research Design - A quasi-experimental one-group pretest-posttest design was utilized to measure the impact of mandala art therapy on test anxiety. The study involved the following steps:

1. ***Pretest Measurement:*** Participants completed Spielberg's Test Anxiety Inventory to establish baseline anxiety levels.
2. ***Intervention:*** Participants engaged in a six-week mandala drawing intervention, with one session per week. Each session focused on creative expression through drawing mandalas, emphasizing calming and meditative effects.
3. ***Posttest Measurement:*** After the intervention, participants completed the Test Anxiety Inventory again to assess changes in anxiety levels.

Mandala Art Therapy Intervention

The mandala art therapy sessions encouraged emotional expression and mindfulness through creative and repetitive patterns. Participants were guided to create mandalas that reflected their feelings and thoughts related to test anxiety. The therapeutic process aimed to foster a sense of relaxation and focus, providing a safe space for emotional exploration.

Results

Following the six-week intervention, the results indicated that:

- **Reduction in Anxiety:** Seven out of nine participants experienced a significant reduction in test anxiety levels, as measured by the posttest scores.

- **Variability in Responses:** One participant reported an increase in anxiety levels, while another participant's anxiety levels remained unchanged.
- **Improved Emotional Regulation:** Most participants reported enhanced emotional regulation and a greater sense of control over their anxiety related to exams.

Discussion

The findings of this case study suggest that mandala art therapy can be an effective non-verbal therapeutic tool for managing test anxiety among college students. While individual responses to the intervention varied, the overall trend indicated a positive impact on reducing anxiety levels. The creative process of mandala drawing appears to facilitate emotional expression and mindfulness, contributing to improved coping strategies for test-related stress.

Conclusion

This case study highlights the potential of mandala art therapy as a valuable intervention for reducing test anxiety in college students. The results support the idea that creative therapies can enhance emotional well-being and academic performance. Further research is recommended to explore the long-term effects of mandala art therapy and its applicability across diverse student population.

References

Anagarika, G. L. (1974). *The psychological attitude of early Buddhist philosophy: And Its Systematic Representation According to Abhidhamma Tradition.*

Govinda, A. (1961). The psychological attitude of early Buddhist philosophy and its systematic representation according to Abhidhamma tradition.

Art Therapy Association. "Mandala Art Therapy: Benefits and Healing Properties." *Art Therapy Journal*, 2019.

Henderson, P. G. (2012). *Empirical study of the healing nature of artistic expression: Using mandalas with the positive emotions of love and joy.* Texas A&M University.

Fincher, S. F. (1991). Creating mandalas: For insight, healing, and self-expression.

Henderson, P., Rosen, D., & Mascaro, N. (2007). Empirical study on the healing nature of mandalas. *Psychology of Aesthetics, Creativity, and the Arts, 1*(3), 148.

Curry, N. A., & Kasser, T. (2005). Can coloring mandalas reduce anxiety? *Art Therapy, 22*(2), 81-85.

Carneiro, C. (2010). Art Therapy as a complementaray therapy in the treatment of depression: a case study. *Journal of Transpersonal Research, 2*(1), 62-72.

Angellim, C., Satiadarma, M. P., & Subroto, U. (2020). Mandala drawing for reducing test anxiety in college student. *Proceedings of the 2nd Tarumanagara International Conference on the Applications of Social Sciences and Humanities (TICASH 2020).* https://doi.org/10.2991/assehr.k.201209.069

Nasiri, M., Sajadi, S. A., Farsi, Z., & Heidarieh, M. (2024). The effects of mandala coloring and free coloring on mindfulness and the score of posttraumatic stress disorder in veterans. *Holistic Nursing Practice.* https://doi.org/10.1097/hnp.0000000000000680

Curry, N. A., & Kasser, T. (2005). Can coloring mandalas reduce anxiety? *Art Therapy*, *22*(2), 81–85. https://doi.org/10.1080/07421656.2005.10129441

Curry, N. A., & Kasser, T. (2005b). Can coloring mandalas reduce anxiety? *Art Therapy*, *22*(2), 81–85. https://doi.org/10.1080/07421656.2005.10129441

Schnitzer, G., Holttum, S., & Huet, V. (2021). A systematic literature review of the impact of art therapy upon post-traumatic stress disorder. *International Journal of Art Therapy*, *26*(4), 147–160. https://doi.org/10.1080/17454832.2021.1910719

Babouchkina, A., & Robbins, S. J. (2015). Reducing negative mood through mandala Creation: a randomized controlled trial. *Art Therapy*, *32*(1), 34–39. https://doi.org/10.1080/07421656.2015.994428

Henderson, P., Rosen, D., & Mascaro, N. (2007). Empirical study on the healing nature of mandalas. *Psychology of Aesthetics Creativity and the Arts*, *1*(3), 148–154. https://doi.org/10.1037/1931-3896.1.3.148

Malchiodi, C. A. (1998). *The Art Therapy Sourcebook*. McGraw Hill Professional.

Chapter 9

Massage Therapy

Sambhav Kumar School of Liberal Studies (SLS), CMR University, Bangalore

Introduction

Massage is relatively one of the oldest healing traditions. Numerous ancient people including the Ancient Greeks, Egyptians, Chinese and Indians believed in the healing power of massage and treated an array of conditions with it.

Massage therapy is when masses a person's muscles and other soft tissue to improve the persons wellbeing or health. Manual therapy involving the manipulation of muscles, tendons, ligaments, and fascia.

Massage therapy is a general term that refers to a variety of techniques of varying degrees of intensity by means of touch and application of pressure.

Massage therapy is a manual therapy that involves manipulating the body's soft tissues, such as muscles, tendons, and ligaments, to improve health and wellness. It can help with a variety of conditions, including:

- Stress and fatigue
- Pain and anxiety
- Sleep disorders
- High blood pressure
- Diabetes
- Low back pain
- Depression

It can likewise assist with enhanced cancer symptoms (pain, swelling, depression and lack of energy.

History

Ancient Roots

Massage therapy is first documented in writing in China, India, and Egypt. Massage then was virtually exclusive to the ancient form of what's now known as doctors.

Records of the earliest known Chinese text on massage therapy date back to 2700 B.C. It's entitled "The Yellow Emperor's Classic Book of Internal Medicine." Published in English in 1949, it has become a classic in massage training arenas and in many other venues of alternative medicine.

Taken from Egyptian tomb paintings dated around 2500 BC, these manuscripts included references to massage therapy as a common treatment method of the time. Egyptians are responsible for the first Known. The Greeks and Romans were heavily influenced by their studies and traditions.

India is the home of the first recorded traditions of massage therapy, but its practice might have begun as far back as 3000 BC. Practiced by Hindus, Ayurveda — an English language derivative from Sanskrit. It literally means "health science of life" or "life health."

The United States

By the early 20th century, new and rediscovered massage techniques were written about and practiced more and more in the United States. Massage was also used to treat individuals with nerve injury or shell shock from World War I. However, for many years, it was shunned as a treatment mode and considered a luxury that only the rich could afford.

Natural healing in the second half of the 20th century revived interest in massage. More and more states began to regulate, and licensing as well as education emerged among what is considered normal for industry.

Olympic Standards

Because of its advantages for sports, massage truly took off in the United States in the 1980s. Athletes employed massage treatment during the 1984 Summer Olympics in Los Angeles. The Summer Olympics in Atlanta in 1996 provided yet another significant boost. In this year, the US Olympic Team began using massage therapy as a primary treatment. Since then, massage has become more popular in both business and sports.

Types of Massage Therapy

Wellness Massage

This is a whole body or region-based massage conducted by massage therapists at a spa, hotels, and other equivalent establishments with a view of reducing stress levels, promotion of relaxation. Improvement in function, reduction of pain as well as some muscle tenderness not contributed to a diagnosed medical condition. Clients receive this type of massage at will without any prescription, or reference from a hospital.

Clinical Massage

This is a kind of healthcare that rehabilitates patients diagnosed with certain medical conditions that are associated with massage, treats complications of the medical condition, and solves problems that come with surgical issues. Clinical massage takes place in different practice settings, which include hospitals, physical therapy clinics, chiropractic clinics, sports clinics, etc. Clients who receive this kind of massage do so according to prescription and medical directives, and their purpose for receiving massage therapy would be condition related.

Applications of Massage therapy

- **Pain relief:** Massage can help relieve pain and muscle tension.
- **Stress reduction:** Massage can help reduce stress hormones and relieve stress.
- **Improved circulation:** Massage can improve circulation, which can help increase the body's natural repair cells to reach injury sites.
- **Increased flexibility:** Massage can increase the flexibility of muscles by increasing tissue temperature and decreasing scar tissue.
- **Improved recovery:** Massage can help improve recovery from soft tissue injuries.
- **Fibro-myalgia symptoms:** Massage can help improve symptoms of fibromyalgia, a chronic illness that causes muscle and joint pain and fatigue.
- **Infant care:** There is some evidence that massage can help premature infants gain weight.

Massage Therapy and Mental Health

Some of the main conclusions about massage's benefits for mental health were included in a recent review paper (Rapaport et al., 2018). For example, massage appears to influence brain activity in ways that promote relaxation while preserving awareness. The brain's somatic sensory pleasure pathway may also be implicated, according to certain theories.

The hypothalamic-pituitary-adrenal (HPA) axis and neurohormone levels, including the "bonding" hormone oxytocin, appear to benefit from massage as well. Numerous brain structures and functions are comparable to those addressed by conventional mental health therapies.

Rapport and associates (2018) also discuss several research that indicate massage may help lessen anxiety and depressive symptoms. Additionally, it could help with sleep, which is known to be a symptom and a contributing factor in a few mental health conditions.

Although the cost of massage can be prohibitive for many people, this is not a good reason to not consider it seriously as a mental health intervention. After all, many people cannot afford the out-of-pocket expenses of their psychiatric medications or their visits to therapists and prescribers, which is why they have and use health insurance.

Massage Techniques

Effleurage (Stroking)

Hands move rhythmically, flowing constantly over a patient's skin in one way and for the purpose of furthering blood flow within one direction, stretching of tissue, relaxation of client as well as aiding its facilitation of waste by dispersing it. Word comes from French meaning 'skim'. It is always the first and last technique used in a massage session, and it involves stroking movements of the hands sliding over the skin. Effleurage may be applied with varying tempo and pressure according to the stage of the condition and whatever the desired effect of the massage is.

Performing Effleurage

Either use both hands at once or switch between them to cover a large area of the palmar surfaces of the palms and fingers. To promote venous return, pressure is maintained throughout the stroke and is constantly directed toward the heart. The hands should keep light touch and steer clear of the upward stroke's path when making the return stroke. Depending on the technique's goal and the body part being massaged, the motions' location, pace, and direction will change. For instance, the arms and legs may benefit from lengthy, stroking motions, but the neck and back may benefit from a more circular action.

Petrissage (Kneading/Rolling)

Soft tissues like skin or muscle are compressed, lifted, picked, or decompressed before being released After being raised, the skin is pinched, rolled, and compressed. In certain muscle conditions, alternately squeezing and relaxing the tissues might help relieve discomfort and increase local circulation. Petrissage means "to knead" and is taken from a French term. **Percussion/Tapotement Manipulations**

This includes a rhythmic motion on percussion. The exercise involves tapping, pincement, hacking, clapping, beating, pounding, or vibrations, cupping, etc. Carried out through the drape, clothes, or can be administered with bare skin. Always fore-warn the patient; because some of the tapotements produce very noise effects in bare skin, if done. May use shallow or deep and must use different speed and power of impacts. when applied gently it helps in relaxation but when applied vigorously helps in stimulation so vigorous application is more suitable for larger muscular areas like back, hips, thighs, and calves.

Myofascial Release

A manual method for stretching the fascia with the goal of releasing fascia limitations is called myofascial release. Our body's skeletal components, muscles, and organs are all connected by fascia, which is found between the skin and the underlying structure of bone and muscle. Poor posture, stress, trauma, and injuries can all cause fascia to become constricted.

Trigger Point Therapy

To alleviate pain and dysfunction in other areas of the body, trigger point treatment applies pressure on sensitive muscle tissue. Acupuncture needles frequently intersect with trigger points, which are active sites of excitability in the muscles.

Deep Transverse Frictions

Direct application of transverse connective tissue treatment by fingers is known as transverse frictions. Pressure that oscillates is exerted over the tissue fibers. mostly applied to ligament or tendon injuries to aid in the breakdown of painful, thicker scar tissue.

Compression Massage

Deep hyperemia and a softening effect on the tissues are produced by rhythmically compressing the muscles. utilized as a warm-up for deeper, more focused massage therapy in sports massage.

Cross Fiber Massage

Deep transverse friction is applied to specific muscle and connective tissue sites to decrease adhesions and promote strong, flexible repair during the healing process. Alternatively, cross-fibre friction techniques are applied generally to produce a stretching and broadening effect in large muscle groups.

***The sequence used is generally*: -**

- **Effleurage:** Gliding strokes with the palms, thumbs and/or fingertips
- **Petrissage:** Kneading movements with the hands, thumbs and/or fingers
- **Friction:** Circular pressures with the palms of hands, thumbs and/or fingers
- **Vibration:** Oscillatory movements that shake or vibrate the body
- **Percussion:** Brisk hacking or tapping
- **Passive and active movements:** Bending and stretching.

Pros of Massage Therapy

Relaxes muscles

The purpose of massage treatment is to increase lymphatic and blood circulation. It helps you feel calm and relaxed by reducing tension in the tissues that surround your muscles. Increasing blood circulation also helps wounded cells receive more oxygen, which speeds up the healing process.

Lower Blood Pressure

According to one research, within just five minutes, massage treatment helped reduce blood pressure in hypertension individuals. This advantage is thought to be facilitated by the calming effects of massage.

Eases Pain

One popular method of pain management is massage therapy. Pain treatment is one of the primary reasons individuals seek massage therapy. By distributing the fluid accumulation that can lead to muscular tension and inflammation, massage helps reduce discomfort. Additionally, it releases endorphins, which are chemicals with inherent analgesic effects.

Increase Energy levels

Massage treatment breaks up any fluid accumulations in the muscles and improves blood circulation. Consequently, it provides you with more vitality and endurance to face the day. According to studies, cancer patients receiving chemotherapy have reported feeling more energized after receiving massage therapy. Indeed, after receiving their massages, most of them said they felt more energized.

Reduces stress level

It goes without saying that massage treatment is a great way to lower stress levels. According to one study, a single massage session was sufficient to lower mood-related symptoms and cortisol, a hormone generated during stressful situations.

Promotes mental health

Additionally, it has been demonstrated that massage treatment increases dopamine and serotonin, two neurotransmitters that are frequently linked to happiness and pleasure, respectively, and anxiety. For people who have major depressive disorder (MDD), this can assist lower depression levels and elevate your mood.

Reduces Anxiety

Massage treatment has been demonstrated to help lower anxiety levels in addition to depression levels. Indeed, according to a research, massage treatment can reduce anxiety by as much as 68%.

Improves Sleep Quality

Adults' sleep quality has been demonstrated to improve with massage treatment. According to one research, those who experienced chronic pain, worry, or exhaustion found that massage treatment improved the length and quality of their sleep.

Boost Cognitive Function

It has also been demonstrated that massage treatment improves adult cognitive performance. According to research, following just one massage, participants' scores on cognitive function tests improved.

Limitations

Side effects

It is uncommon for massage treatment to have side effects. They may, however, include headaches, nausea, pain in the massaged muscles, bruising or bleeding in some situations, exhaustion, lightheadedness, fainting, mental/emotional discomfort (anxiety), and skin irritation.

Expensive

Depending on the style of massage and the practitioner you choose, massage treatment might be costly. Massage treatment can be very expensive if you don't have insurance, but if you do, it's probable that at least some of the charges will be covered.

Not Always Available

It's not always possible to have massage therapy. It's not as well-known as other therapies like medicine or surgery, despite its growing popularity. You might have to travel far to get therapy if you don't live close to a therapist.

Time Consuming

It might take a lot of time to receive massage therapy. The length of a massage session might range from 30 minutes to two hours, depending on the sort of massage you receive. This might not be the ideal course of action for you if you're pressed for time.

Can be Uncomfortable

Massage treatment can be painful for some people. It may take some getting accustomed to if you're not used to someone touching your body in a particular manner.

Injury

Minor injuries like bruises or torn muscles are possible, though they are uncommon. To prevent any harm, let the therapist know if you are pregnant, have any health issues, or take any medications before to the session.

Effectiveness

Not everyone benefits from massage treatment, even though it has been demonstrated to offer several advantages. After a session, some persons might not notice any improvements in their general health, stress levels, or mood.

Painful

Massage treatment can be too uncomfortable for some people; however this is uncommon. Make sure your therapist is aware of any chronic pain you may be experiencing or low pain threshold so they can modify their therapy.

Not an Immediate cure

You shouldn't expect massage treatment to solve every health issue you have. Don't anticipate immediate results after a single session; it takes time and patience to experience the advantages.

Case Studies

Case study 1- Chronic lower back pain

Objective

To investigate the benefits of massage on persistent low-back pain in a patient with four distinct diagnoses: osteoarthritis, scoliosis, spinal stenosis, and degenerative disc disease. The patient wanted to reduce the quantity of pain medication he took.

Method

A 63-year-old guy with persistent back pain had four massages during a twenty-day period. The Oswestry Low Back Pain Scale was used to track progress as he self-reported his pain levels and interference with everyday activities.

Result

Nine out of ten assessments of self-reported pain and everyday activities showed improvement, except for his capacity to move heavy things, which remained unaltered. The most significant differences were improvements in his walking capacity and discomfort levels. The customer also reported being able to reduce his pain medication and ride his bike for the first time in years.

Conclusion

Massage therapy is a viable treatment for persistent low-back pain in people who may have numerous diseases, any of which might be causing the problem. Further research is recommended to assess the efficacy of massage therapy as a widely available, lower-cost option to more intrusive therapies, as well as a complement to normal medical care, where appropriate.

Case Study 2- Tinnitus

Presenting symptoms

A 58-year-old dentist crashed while waterskiing and landed hard on the right side of his skull. He eventually got bilateral tinnitus. CAT scans, cerebral angiograms, and X-rays taken at

Massachusetts General Hospital's ENT department were all normal. He had problems sleeping since the ringing was worse at night. He was prescribed anxiety medication after three sleep investigations came out normal. A multi-factorial therapy regimen was recommended, which included medication, P-Stim, chiropractic, and acupuncture. He came to 360 NMT to treat any soft tissue causes of his tinnitus.

Evaluation, clinical reasoning & treatment strategizing

Tinnitus is a persistent ringing in the ears that is often related with sleep and cognitive issues. He reported his symptoms as a pulsatile high-pitched shrieking noise that rated 8/10 at worst and 5/10 at best. He had no hearing loss. As a dentist, he sat on the left, thus his upper torso and head were constantly turning to the right. We suspected that this may be a perpetuating element.

Treatment

Tinnitus is tough to treat. Specific head and neck muscles that have been linked to tinnitus include the trapezius, infraspinatus, splenius capitis, semispinalis capitis, sternocleidomastoid, middle scalenes, masseter (particularly the deep head), and temporalis. Dr. William Teachey, a tinnitus expert and 360 NMT collaborator, has stated that 50% of patients will not react to soft-tissue treatments, 25% will respond extremely well, and 25% will get some advantages from soft-tissue treatment. We treated each of the muscles.

Outcomes and Follow-up

During several treatments, we were able to get the patient's symptoms down to a 2/10. He called anything below a 6/10 "livable." The highest results were obtained when paired with trigger point injections from his Otolaryngic specialist. He gets the maximum alleviation from isometric contractions of his neck muscles. This shows that a soft-tissue component is still causing the tinnitus. He continues to undergo therapy to preserve his current outcomes.

Conclusion

Massage treatment provides several advantages, including physical benefits such as reduced muscular discomfort and tension and improved sleep, as well as mental and emotional benefits such as reduced stress and increased happiness.

Massage treatment provides several advantages to the body and, when provided by a certified therapist, poses low danger. Massage, with its preventative and restorative advantages, is a health-promoting treatment for everybody, regardless of present health status.

Massage therapy has benefits for women in labor both physically and emotionally, according to three journals. The journals' findings showed that massage therapy can effectively manage pain during childbirth by reducing stress, anxiety, and labor duration. It also decreases cortisol levels and excessive fetal activity. Massage therapy is easy to apply, has no side effects, and is therefore a good intervention during labor that the group fully supports for pain management during childbirth.

References

Nicholls, D. A. (2021). The role of neurasthenia in the formation of the physiotherapy profession. Physiotherapy Theory and Practice, 37(3), 376–388.

Mak, S., Allen, J., Begashaw, M., Miake-Lye, I., Beroes-Severin, J., De Vries, G., Lawson, E., & Shekelle, P. G. (2024). Use of massage therapy for pain, 2018–2023: A systematic r review. JAMA Network Open, 7(7).

Einstein, A. (2022). Massage techniques, mobilizations, stretches, endangerment sites, and contraindications. In Massage techniques: Principles and practice (p. 136). Elsevier.

Hand on training massage school. (2019, May 10). Petrissage. https://www.youtube.com/watch?v=Pa6R8WcBHBU

Hands on training massage school. (2019, May 10). Tapotement https://www.youtube.com/watch?v=EFbVKdFmD10

Rapaport, M. H., Schettler, P. J., Larson, E. R., Carroll, D., Sharenko, M., Nettles, J., & Kinkead, B. (2018). Massage Therapy for Psychiatric Disorders. Focus (American Psychiatric Publishing), 16(1), 24–31.

Akkerman, M. (2019, May 10). Trigger point explained with animation. https://www.youtube.com/watch?v=sltGyJvbvWw

Müller-Oerlinghausen, B., & Eggart, M. (2020). Touch Research-Quo Vadis? A Plea for High-Quality Clinical Trials. Brain sciences, 11(1), 25.

Kumar, S., Beaton, K., & Hughes, T. (2013). The effectiveness of massage therapy for the treatment of nonspecific low back pain: A systematic review of systematic reviews. International Journal of General Medicine, 6, 733.

National Institutes of Health. (2019, May 9). Massage therapy for health purposes. National Center for Complementary and Integrative Health. https://nccih.nih.gov/health/massage/massageintroduction.htm

Chapter 10

Music therapy

Sera Mary Solaman, Dr Monalisa Nayak School of Liberal Studies (SLS), CMR University, Bangalore

Historical development of music therapy

The music has been used for healing purposes in ancient civilizations cultures like Egypt and Greece and for ritual purposes as well. Pythagoras believed that music has the power to heal and the ability to align the soul, spirit, and body.

In the early 19th century, doctors in Europe began to use music for further treatments and Jean Esquirol, a French physician used music in psychiatric-related treatments Florence Nightingale used music to calm injured soldiers in a war.

After World War First and World War II, the field of therapy began to grow and played for veterans suffering from physical and emotional trauma, and doctors noticed improvements in patients' recovery and morale. This led to the beginning of the establishment of music therapy.

In the United States, music treatment got to be more organized in the mid-20th century. In 1950, the National Affiliation for Music Treatment (NAMT) was shaped, which afterward became the American Music Treatment Affiliation (AMTA) in 1998. These organizations set measures for instruction, clinical preparing, and certification in the field.

Benefits of Music therapy

Reduces Anxiety and Stress:

Music has a calming effect on the mind and body. Listening to relaxing music can lower heart rate and cortisol levels, helping to reduce anxiety and stress. Music therapy sessions often incorporate rhythm, melody, and harmony to create a soothing environment for patients dealing with anxiety disorders.

Improves Mood and Emotional Health:

Music can lift moods and bring about positive emotions. For those struggling with depression, engaging with music can act as a form of expression, helping them to process difficult emotions and reconnect with positive memories.

Enhances Cognitive Skills:

Music therapy can improve memory, attention, and problem-solving skills. It has shown promise in working with individuals with dementia or Alzheimer's disease, helping them retain cognitive functions and reconnect with memories.

Boosts Social and Communication Skills:

In group music therapy sessions, individuals work together to create music, which can foster social interaction, teamwork, and communication. This is especially helpful for children with autism spectrum disorder, as music therapy can help improve verbal and nonverbal communication skills.

Provides Pain Relief:

Studies have shown that listening to music can reduce the perception of pain by releasing endorphins and providing a distraction from physical discomfort. This is helpful for individuals with chronic pain or during post-operative recovery.

Encourages Self-Expression and Creativity:

Music therapy allows people to express feelings they may struggle to articulate in words. Creating music can be a nonverbal outlet for emotions, making it easier for people to process trauma, grief, or anger.

Limitations of Music Therapy

Individual Differences in Response:

Not everyone responds to music therapy in the same way. Personal preferences, cultural background, and individual psychological differences affect how effective music therapy can be for each person.

Limited Evidence for Some Conditions:

While music therapy is proven effective for some mental health issues, such as anxiety and depression, its effectiveness for certain other conditions, like severe autism or schizophrenia, may have limited or mixed evidence.

Dependency on Therapist Skill:

The success of music therapy can be heavily influenced by the therapist's skills and experience. Untrained or inexperienced therapists might not achieve the same outcomes, limiting its effectiveness.

Challenges in Standardization:

Because music therapy often needs to be tailored to each person, it lacks standardization, which makes it challenging to compare results across different studies or cases.

Cost and Accessibility:

Music therapy sessions can be expensive, and there may be limited availability in certain regions, which restricts access to people who could benefit from it.

Not a Standalone Treatment:

Music therapy is often most effective as a complementary therapy alongside other treatments, such as medication or psychotherapy. It may not be effective as the sole treatment for certain conditions.

Misinterpretation of Music's Effects:

In some cases, individuals might misinterpret music therapy as a cure rather than as a therapeutic tool, which can lead to unrealistic expectations.

Time-Intensive Process: Music therapy often requires regular sessions over extended periods to see results, which can be challenging for patients seeking quick solutions.

Criticism and Challenges in Music Therapy

Lack of Standardized Protocols and Training

Challenge: The practice of music therapy can vary widely in approach, with different therapists employing diverse techniques without standardized methods.

Criticism: Critics argue that without clear, standardized protocols, it's hard to ensure consistent outcomes and proper training for practitioners. This can make it difficult for some professionals and patients to take the practice seriously.

Insufficient Scientific Evidence

Challenge: While there are studies suggesting music therapy's positive effects, some argue that more rigorous, large-scale research is needed.

Criticism: Critics believe that anecdotal evidence and small studies are not enough for music therapy to be accepted within mainstream medicine. Lack of strong evidence may also lead to skepticism from medical professionals and insurers, affecting funding and accessibility.

Placebo Effect Concerns

Challenge: Because music is inherently enjoyable for many, critics argue that its effects might be largely due to a placebo effect rather than any inherent therapeutic power.

Criticism: This view suggests that people might feel better simply because they enjoy the music, not because of a structured therapeutic process. This raises questions about music therapy's true efficacy.

Cultural Bias in Music Selection

Challenge: Music therapy often draws on Western music traditions, which may not resonate with people from diverse cultural backgrounds.

Criticism: Without cultural sensitivity in music selection, some individuals may not feel comfortable or connected, which can impact the therapy's effectiveness. This also raises ethical concerns about imposing one cultural perspective on clients.

Ambiguity in Defining Outcomes

Challenge: The benefits of music therapy can be hard to measure objectively. Outcomes such as "improved mood" or "reduced anxiety" are subjective and challenging to quantify.

Criticism: This ambiguity makes it hard to assess music therapy's true impact and to differentiate it from other forms of relaxation or entertainment. Standardized ways to measure outcomes are needed to validate its efficacy.

Professional Recognition and Reimbursement Issues

Challenge: Music therapy struggles for recognition as a legitimate healthcare profession. Many health insurance companies do not cover it as a reimbursable service.

Criticism: Without widespread recognition and reimbursement, music therapists face financial barriers, which limits accessibility for clients who could benefit from the therapy.

Emotional Overwhelm for Some Clients

Challenge: Music has the power to evoke strong emotions, which can sometimes be overwhelming or even distressing, especially for clients with trauma.

Criticism: Without proper training, therapists may unintentionally cause clients distress or discomfort, highlighting the need for careful emotional management and assessment of client readiness.

Music Therapy and Healthcare

Pain Management

Music therapy is widely used in healthcare to alleviate both acute and chronic pain. Research shows that music can influence pain perception, reducing the intensity of pain by diverting attention and promoting relaxation.

Cancer Patients

For patients undergoing cancer treatments such as chemotherapy, music therapy has been found to reduce pain, fatigue, and anxiety. A study published in The Journal of Pain and Symptom Management found that music therapy helped cancer patients manage both pain and emotional distress.

Post-Surgical Recovery

Patients recovering from surgery often experience pain and discomfort. Music therapy can help reduce the need for pain medication post-surgery. In a meta-analysis published in The Lancet, researchers found that patients exposed to music after surgery experienced lower levels of pain and required less analgesia.

Neurological Rehabilitation

Music therapy has shown promising results in neurological rehabilitation for conditions such as stroke, traumatic brain injury (TBI), and Parkinson's disease. Specific music therapy techniques, such as Neurologic Music Therapy (NMT), use rhythm and melody to stimulate neural pathways and promote functional recovery.

Stroke Recovery

Music therapy can help stroke survivors regain motor functions and improve speech through techniques like Rhythmic Auditory Stimulation (RAS), which uses rhythm to assist in gait training. In a study published in Frontiers in Neurology, stroke patients who received music therapy showed significant improvement in walking speed and stride length.

Parkinson's Disease

Patients with Parkinson's disease often experience difficulties with movement, such as freezing of gait and tremors. Music therapy, particularly rhythmic-based interventions, can help improve coordination, balance, and mobility. According to a study in The Journal of Music Therapy, rhythmic music interventions helped improve motor function in patients with Parkinson's disease by facilitating smoother movements.

Mental Health and Emotional Well-being

Music therapy is an effective tool for addressing mental health issues such as anxiety, depression, PTSD, and other emotional disorders.

Anxiety and Depression

Music therapy can reduce symptoms of anxiety and depression by promoting relaxation and encouraging self-expression. A 2020 systematic review in BMC Psychiatry concluded that music therapy had a significant positive effect on people with clinical depression, helping them manage symptoms and improve mood.

PTSD in Veterans

Veterans with PTSD often benefit from music therapy as it provides a non-verbal outlet for processing traumatic memories and emotions. Group music therapy and song writing have been found to help veterans' express feelings that are difficult to verbalize, thereby reducing symptoms of PTSD. Research published in The Arts in Psychotherapy highlighted how music therapy helped veterans improve emotional regulation and cope with trauma.

Cognitive and Developmental Disorders

Music therapy is widely used for individuals with cognitive and developmental disabilities, including autism spectrum disorder (ASD), dementia, and Alzheimer's disease.

Autism Spectrum Disorder (ASD):

Music therapy helps individuals with ASD develop communication and social skills. Structured music activities, such as singing and rhythmic movement, improve non-verbal communication and promote engagement. A study in The Journal of Autism and Developmental Disorders found that music therapy significantly improved social interaction and communication in children with autism.

Dementia and Alzheimer's Disease:

Music therapy is effective in helping individuals with dementia and Alzheimer's disease by stimulating memory and improving mood. Music from the patient's past can evoke memories and improve cognitive function. A 2018 study published in Aging & Mental Health showed that music therapy reduced agitation and improved mood in dementia patients, enhancing their quality of life.

Hospice and Palliative Care

Music therapy is frequently used in hospice and palliative care to provide emotional support and comfort to patients in the final stages of life. Music can help patients cope with physical symptoms like pain and shortness of breath while also offering emotional and spiritual comfort.

Pain and Symptom Management:

In hospice settings, music therapy is used to manage symptoms like pain, fatigue, and nausea. It can also ease feelings of anxiety and depression that often accompany terminal illnesses. A study published in The American Journal of Hospice & Palliative Care found that music therapy reduced symptoms of distress and helped patients achieve a sense of peace at the end of life.

Emotional and Spiritual Support:

Music therapy provides emotional and spiritual support for both patients and their families. It helps patients process emotions, express feelings, and find meaning in their experiences during the final stages of life.

Group Therapy and Community Health

Music therapy is also used in group settings, such as addiction recovery programs, mental health facilities, and community health centers.

Addiction Recovery:

Music therapy helps individuals recovering from substance use disorders by providing a creative outlet for emotional expression and enhancing mindfulness. It also fosters a sense of community in group settings, helping individuals build trust and relationships during recovery. A study in The Journal of Substance Abuse Treatment found that group music therapy improved emotional expression and coping skills in individuals undergoing addiction treatment.

Key Concepts in Music Therapy

Music as a Restorative Tool:

Music is utilized as a implies to accomplish helpful objectives, such as making strides temperament, diminishing uneasiness, upgrading cognitive work, or encouraging physical rehabilitation. The sort of music utilized changes agreeing to the individual's needs, inclinations, and social background.

Dynamic vs. Open Methods:

Active Music Treatment:

Includes clients effectively making or performing music. This can incorporate singing, playing disobedient, composing, or extemporizing music. It energizes self-expression, enthusiastic discharge, and social interaction. Receptive Music Treatment: Clients tune in to live or recorded music chosen by the advisor. This makes a difference in unwinding, passionate handling, and decreasing push. Guided symbolism is some of the time utilized nearby responsive strategies to help clients investigate their considerations and feelings.

Individualized Approach:

Music treatment is profoundly personalized. A specialist tailors' sessions to the interesting needs, objectives, and capacities of each client. The music chosen, whether for tuning in or playing, is based on what will resound most with the person and evoke the craved helpful outcomes.

Helpful Relationship:

The association between the advisor and client plays a vital part in the victory of music treatment. This relationship cultivates believe, security, and openness, permitting clients to investigate feelings and encounters more unreservedly through music.

Neuroscientific Basis:

Music has a coordinate effect on brain action. Thinks about appear that tuning in to and locks in with music can fortify regions of the brain related with memory, dialect, feelings, and engine coordination. Music treatment advances neuroplasticity—the brain's capacity to reorganize and frame unused neural connections—making it particularly compelling in treating brain wounds and neurodegenerative infections like Parkinson's and Alzheimer's.

Psychosocial Benefits:

Music treatment makes a difference in passionate control by giving a non-verbal outlet for expression. It is regularly utilized to decrease side effects of misery, uneasiness, and trauma. It moreover underpins socialization and communication, especially in bunches, where music gets to be a shared encounter, cultivating community and connection.

All-encompassing Approach:

Music treatment considers the entirety person—body, intellect, and soul. It recognizes the interconnecting of mental, enthusiastic, and physical wellbeing, utilizing music to bolster all viewpoints of well-being.

Social Sensitivity:

Music is profoundly tied to culture and character. Music specialists are prepared to be socially delicate and utilize music that adjusts with the client's foundation and inclinations, guaranteeing that the treatment feels significant and strong.

Techniques of Music Therapy

Receptive Listening

Receptive listening is a core technique in music therapy, where clients listen to pre-recorded or live music selected by a therapist to evoke certain emotional, mental, or physiological responses. It differs from active techniques (such as playing instruments or singing) by focusing on the auditory experience alone.

It can help in several ways like Emotional Release and Processing, Stress and Anxiety Reduction, Cognitive and Memory Stimulation, Physical Relaxation, Self-Awareness, and Reflection.

Applications: This technique is commonly used for stress reduction, pain management, and relaxation. It is also effective in palliative care or with patients suffering from anxiety disorders.

Improvisation

Clients are encouraged to create spontaneous music using their voice or instruments. This allows them to express feelings that may be difficult to verbalize.

Applications: Improvisation is useful in promoting emotional expression, communication, and self-exploration. It is particularly helpful for individuals with trauma, non-verbal children, or those with developmental delays.

Instrumental Playing

Clients play instruments either with or without guidance from the therapist. It can be structured (playing specific rhythms or melodies) or unstructured (free play).

Applications: Instrumental playing promotes motor skills, coordination, and self-expression. It is often used in rehabilitation settings for physical therapy, as well as for emotional expression in mental health contexts.

Guided Imagery and Music (GIM)

This technique involves listening to music in a relaxed state while the therapist guides the client through imagery, often focused on personal growth or healing.

Applications: GIM is often used for exploring subconscious emotions, reducing anxiety, and fostering self-awareness. It's effective in trauma therapy, stress management, and personal development.

Songwriting

Clients collaborate with the therapist to write original songs or lyrics that express personal experiences, thoughts, or emotions.

Applications: Songwriting is particularly effective in helping clients process trauma, grief, or life changes. It fosters creativity, self-expression, and a sense of accomplishment.

Lyric Analysis

In lyric analysis, clients and therapists examine the lyrics of pre-existing songs to explore emotions, thoughts, and perspectives. This process can lead to discussions and insights that might not emerge otherwise.

Applications: This technique is effective for helping clients with emotional processing, especially for those dealing with depression, trauma, or relationship issues.

Rhythmic Auditory Stimulation (RAS)

RAS is a neurologic music therapy technique that uses rhythmic patterns to improve motor control and coordination, especially in individuals with motor impairments.

Applications: Primarily used in rehabilitation, particularly with stroke patients, individuals with Parkinson's disease, or those recovering from traumatic brain injuries.

Vocalization and Singing

Singing and vocal exercises are used to promote breathing control, emotional expression, and verbal communication. The act of singing can activate various brain areas and improve respiratory and vocal function.

Applications: This technique is useful for individuals with speech and communication difficulties, such as after a stroke or in those with developmental disorders.

Music-Assisted Relaxation

Music is used to induce relaxation through slow tempos, soothing melodies, or familiar sounds. This can be paired with deep breathing exercises, progressive muscle relaxation, or mindfulness techniques.

Applications: Commonly used in stress reduction, pain management, and for patients in palliative care. It is also effective for reducing anxiety before medical procedures.

Music-Cued Memory Recall

This technique uses music to stimulate memory recall, often by playing songs from the client's past that trigger specific memories or emotions.

Applications: Frequently used with individuals with Alzheimer's or dementia to improve cognitive function, memory recall, and communication.

Benefits of Music Therapy

Reduces Anxiety and Stress:

Music has a calming effect on the mind and body. Listening to relaxing music can lower heart rate and cortisol levels, helping to reduce anxiety and stress. Music therapy sessions often incorporate rhythm, melody, and harmony to create a soothing environment for patients dealing with anxiety disorders.

Improves Mood and Emotional Health:

Music can lift moods and bring about positive emotions. For those struggling with depression, engaging with music can act as a form of expression, helping them to process difficult emotions and reconnect with positive memories.

Enhances Cognitive Skills:

Music therapy can improve memory, attention, and problem-solving skills. In particular, it has shown promise in working with individuals with dementia or Alzheimer's disease, helping them retain cognitive functions and reconnect with memories.

Boosts Social and Communication Skills:

In group music therapy sessions, individuals work together to create music, which can foster social interaction, teamwork, and communication. This is especially helpful for children with autism spectrum disorder, as music therapy can help improve verbal and nonverbal communication skills.

Provides Pain Relief:

Studies have shown that listening to music can reduce the perception of pain by releasing endorphins and providing a distraction from physical discomfort. This is helpful for individuals with chronic pain or during post-operative recovery.

Encourages Self-Expression and Creativity:

Music therapy allows people to express feelings they may struggle to articulate in words. Creating music can be a nonverbal outlet for emotions, making it easier for people to process trauma, grief, or anger.

Aids in Trauma Recovery:

Music therapy can play a valuable role in trauma recovery, particularly for those with PTSD. Creating or listening to music can help individuals regain a sense of safety and control, and it may facilitate processing traumatic memories in a safe environment.

Case studies and Music therapy

Music Therapy with Adolescents Experiencing Trauma

A study focused on adolescent females in a residential treatment program for trauma. Music therapy was used to help the clients express their emotions and manage symptoms of anxiety, depression, and PTSD. Techniques included lyric analysis, songwriting, and improvisation.

Findings: Music therapy allowed the adolescents to externalize their trauma in a non-threatening way, leading to improvements in mood, self-esteem, and emotional regulation.

Music Therapy with Dementia Patients

This study involved older adults diagnosed with Alzheimer's and dementia in a memory care unit. The music therapist used familiar songs from the patients' past to engage memory recall and support cognitive function.

Findings: Patients showed improved recall, decreased agitation, and more social interaction during and after sessions. Familiar music helped reduce confusion and brought a sense of calm to the patients.

Music Therapy for Pain Management in Cancer Patients

A case study at a cancer treatment center used music therapy for patients experiencing chronic pain related to chemotherapy. Techniques included active listening to calm, soothing music, and rhythmic drumming for pain distraction.

Findings: Music therapy significantly reduced the patients' reported pain levels and enhanced their mood, making them more comfortable and relaxed.

Music Therapy for Autism Spectrum Disorder (ASD)

A young boy with ASD received weekly music therapy sessions focusing on social interaction, communication, and emotional expression. Techniques such as drumming and guided improvisation were used to encourage engagement and interaction.

Findings: The therapy helped improve the boy's eye contact, turn-taking, and verbal expression. He became more comfortable communicating through music, which gradually extended to verbal interactions.

References

Aldridge, D., & Jörg Fachner. (2006). Music and altered states : consciousness, transcendence, therapy and addiction. J. Kingsley Publishers

Ansdell, G., & Pavlicevic, M. (2010). Practicing "Gentle Empiricism" – The Nordoff Robbins Research Heritage. Music Thrapy Perspectives, 28(2), 131–139. https://doi.org/10.1093/mtp/28.2.131

Baker, F., & Wigram, T. (2005). Songwriting. Jessica Kingsley Publishers.

Bienenstock, J., Goetzl, E. J., & Blennerhassett, M. G. (2003). Autonomic neuroimmunology. Taylor & Francis.

Bittman BB, Berk LS, Felten DL, Westengard J, Simonton OC, Pappas J, Ninehouser M. Composite effects of group drumming music therapy on modulation of neuroendocrine-immune parameters in normal subjects. Altern Ther Health Med. 2001 Jan;7(1):38-47. PMID: 11191041.

Bradt, J., Dileo, C., & Potvin, N. (2013). Music for stress and anxiety reduction in coronary heart disease patients. Cochrane Library, 2021(9). https://doi.org/10.1002/14651858.cd006577.pub3

Brotons M, Koger SM. The impact of music therapy on language functioning in dementia. J Music Ther. 2000 Fall;37(3):183-95. Doi: 10.1093/jmt/37.3.183. PMID: 10990596.

Bruscia, K. E. (1987). Improvisational Models of Music Therapy. Charles C. Thomas Publisher.

Castelino, A. (2009). The Effect of Single Sessions of Music Therapy on the Level of Anxiety in Older Persons with Psychiatric Disorders: A Pilot Study. https://doi.org/10.26686/wgtn.16967539.v1

Clift SM, Hancox G. The perceived benefits of singing: findings from preliminary surveys of a university college choral society. J R Soc Promot Health. 2001 Dec;121(4):248-56. Doi: 10.1177/146642400112100409. PMID: 11811096.

Falk, S., Lanzilotti, C., & Schön, D. (2017). Tuning Neural Phase Entrainment to Speech. Journal of Cognitive Neuroscience, 29(8), 1378–1389. https://doi.org/10.1162

Friedman, N., Reinkensmeyer, D. J., & Bachman, M. (2013). Universal Access to Participatory Musical Experiences for People with Disabilities. In Lecture notes in computer science (pp. 484–489). https://doi.org/10.1007/978-3-642-39188-0_52

Gfeller, K. (2012). Music Perception of Cochlear Implant Recipients and Implications for Counseling and (Re) habilitation. Perspectives on Hearing and Hearing Disorders Research and Diagnostics, 16(2), 64. https://doi.org/10.1044/hhd16.2.64

Jacobsen, S. L., Pedersen, I. N., & Bonde, L. O. (2019). A Comprehensive Guide to Music Therapy, 2nd Edition: Theory, Clinical Practice, Research and Training. Jessica Kingsley Publisher

Kenny, C. (2015). Performing Theory: Playing in the Music Therapy Discourse. Journal of Music Therapy, 52(4), 457–486. https://doi.org/10.1093/jmt/thv019

Kim, Y. (2004). The Early Beginnings of Nordoff-Robbins Music Therapy. Journal of Music Therapy, 41(4), 321–339. https://doi.org/10.1093/jmt/41.4.321

Magill L. The use of music therapy to address the suffering in advanced cancer pain. J Palliat Care. 2001 Autumn;17(3):167-72. PMID: 11816757.

Postu, A. (2023). Music Therapy. History, Methods and effects. Musicology Papers, 36(2), 78–91. https://doi.org/10.47809/mp.2021.36.02.05

Raglio, A., & Oasi, O. (2015). Music and health: what interventions for what results? Frontiers in Psychology, 6. https://doi.org/10.3389/fpsyg.2015.00230

Silverman, M. J. (2015). Music Therapy in Mental Health for Illness Management and Recovery. Oxford University Press.

Tony Wigram. (2011). British Journal of Music Therapy, 25(2), 66–81. ://doi.org/10.1177/135945751102500207

Tsaqifa, F., & Fitriani, A. (2023). Relationship between intensity of listening to the song Diri by Tulus and Self-Acceptance in the Solo Tulus Friends community. JURNAL SENI MUSIK, 12(2), 217–223. https://doi.org/10.15294/jsm.v12i2.71591

Welch, G. F., Howard, D. M., & Nix, J. (2019). *The Oxford Handbook of Singing*. Oxford Library of Psychology.

Chapter 11

Naikan and Morita Therapy

Riya Satya Rohilla, Ritu School of Liberal Studies (SLS), CMR University, Bangalore

Introduction

Psychotherapies like Naikan and Morita reflect the broader cultural values of Eastern traditions. Naikan, derived from Japanese Buddhism, emphasizes introspection and gratitude as central to healing (Reynolds, 2017). Morita therapy, on the other hand, is grounded in Zen principles of accepting emotions and focusing on purposeful action rather than emotional analysis (Morita, 1928). Both therapies are focused on action and reflection, encouraging patients to find meaning in their experiences and cultivate self-awareness through structured practices.

Historical Background

Eastern psychotherapies, particularly Naikan and Morita Therapy, arose in Japan during the 20th century. These therapies are deeply embedded in Japan's cultural and philosophical traditions, particularly Buddhism and Zen, which emphasize self-reflection, acceptance, and a harmonious way of living. Both therapies were created as responses to emotional and psychological challenges that could not be adequately addressed by Western psychological frameworks alone.

Naikan Therapy was developed by Ishin Yoshimoto in the 1940s. Naikan, meaning "inside looking" or introspection, emerged from Yoshimoto's personal practice of Jōdo Shinshū Buddhism, a sect of Pure Land Buddhism. The therapy encourages individuals to reflect on their relationships with others by focusing on three key questions: "What have I received from others?", "What have I given to others?", and "What troubles or difficulties have I caused others?" (Reynolds, 2017). The primary goal of Naikan is to foster a sense of gratitude and responsibility by helping individuals become more aware of the ways in which they impact the lives of others.

The development of Naikan coincided with post-war Japan's search for meaning, moral integrity, and social cohesion, making it a culturally relevant and powerful psychotherapeutic tool at the time.

Morita Therapy was created earlier, in the 1920s, by Shoma Morita, a Japanese psychiatrist and professor of psychology. Morita originally designed his therapy to treat anxiety disorders, particularly *shinkeishitsu*, or what is now considered to be a form of obsessive-compulsive disorder (OCD). He was heavily influenced by Zen Buddhism, which emphasizes accepting things as they are without trying to control or change them, a concept known as *arugamama* (Morita, 1998).

Morita Therapy's approach contrasts with Western psychotherapies that typically focus on identifying and changing negative thought patterns or analyzing emotions. Instead, Morita believed that emotions could not be directly controlled, and the attempt to do so often exacerbates distress (Suzuki, 2000). His therapy encourages clients to accept their feelings without judgment while focusing on engaging in constructive activities that provide meaning and purpose. Over time, this process helps individuals achieve a sense of mental balance and stability.

Relevance in Modern Psychotherapy

In recent years, Eastern psychotherapies like Naikan and Morita Therapy have gained increasing attention within the global mental health community due to their unique approach to psychological healing, which contrasts with Western therapeutic models. These therapies emphasize introspection, acceptance, and action-oriented approaches rather than focusing on symptom elimination or cognitive restructuring, which are common in Western therapies. As mindfulness and acceptance-based practices continue to rise in popularity, the relevance of these traditional Eastern methods has been increasingly acknowledged in contemporary clinical practice (Levine, 2020).

One reason for this growing interest is the movement toward integrating holistic methods that consider the mind, body, and spirit in therapeutic settings. Western psychotherapies have historically been rooted in scientific rationalism and the medical model of mental health, where symptoms are pathologized, and the goal is often symptom reduction. Eastern approaches, on the other hand, align with the growing field of integrative psychotherapy, where the focus shifts to self-awareness, emotional regulation through acceptance, and aligning actions with one's values (Kirmayer, 2007).

Naikan Therapy is particularly relevant in modern contexts due to its ability to address interpersonal conflicts, guilt, and lack of gratitude. With the rise of individualism in many societies, issues related to disconnection from others, entitlement, and relationship breakdowns have become more prevalent (Reynolds, 2017). Naikan encourages clients to consider their actions in relation to others and to cultivate a sense of gratitude and responsibility. This emphasis on relational healing is particularly useful in addressing family therapy, couple's therapy, and even workplace dynamics (Ishikawa, 2015). Modern-day clinics and rehabilitation centers have reported positive outcomes using Naikan in the treatment of addiction, suggesting that fostering gratitude and reflection on past relationships aids in recovery and long-term sobriety (Kitanishi & Mori, 2016).

Morita Therapy is likewise relevant in addressing contemporary mental health concerns such as anxiety, depression, and obsessional neurosis. With rising rates of anxiety and stress disorders globally, Morita's action-based approach offers a solution that departs from the introspective and cognitive models of Western therapy. Morita believed that emotions, especially anxiety, cannot and should not be directly controlled; instead, individuals must learn to accept these emotions and continue with purposeful action (Morita, 1998). This philosophy aligns with modern mindfulness-based interventions (MBIs) and acceptance and commitment therapy (ACT), both of which teach clients to accept unwanted thoughts and feelings without engaging with or trying to change them (Hayes et al., 2006).

Principles of Morita Therapy

Morita Therapy, developed by Japanese psychiatrist Shoma Morita in the early 20th century, is a unique therapeutic approach grounded in the principles of Zen Buddhism. Its primary focus is on accepting reality as it is (*arugamama*) and engaging in purposeful action despite uncomfortable emotions or thoughts. Unlike Western psychotherapies that emphasize cognitive restructuring or emotional exploration, Morita Therapy encourages individuals to move beyond attempts to control or eliminate emotions and instead focus on accepting them while engaging in constructive, goal-directed activities (Kora, 2015).

The principles of Morita Therapy are organized around the idea that emotions, especially anxiety and distress, are natural responses to life circumstances and should not be treated as pathological. Morita's approach is built on four fundamental principles that guide the therapeutic process:

Acceptance of Feelings

One of the central tenets of Morita Therapy is the idea that emotions, particularly negative ones such as anxiety, fear, or depression, cannot be directly controlled. This principle emphasizes the importance of accepting one's emotional state rather than trying to avoid or change it. Morita believed that emotions are transient and will naturally change over time, making it unnecessary and counterproductive to resist or suppress them (Morita, 1998). This acceptance of feelings aligns with the Buddhist concept of non-attachment, where individuals are encouraged to let go of their desire to control emotions and instead observe them without judgment (Kondo & Kurosawa, 2018).

Focus on Purposeful Action

Another core principle of Morita Therapy is the emphasis on taking purposeful, goal-directed action regardless of one's emotional state. Morita argued that emotional states should not dictate behavior; rather, individuals should engage in meaningful activities even when they feel anxious, depressed, or unmotivated. This action-oriented approach is based on the belief that feelings of accomplishment and satisfaction come from action, not from the elimination of negative emotions (Levine, 2020).

Awareness of the Present Moment (Mindfulness)

Though Morita Therapy does not involve meditation in the same way that some mindfulness-based therapies do, it shares an underlying principle with mindfulness: an emphasis on present-moment awareness. Morita believed that individuals should not get lost in worrying about their future or ruminating on their past emotions but should instead focus on their present experience and the tasks at hand. This present-focused awareness is seen as a way to break the cycle of obsessive thinking and emotional turmoil (Morita, 1998). It helps clients become more engaged in life, promoting a sense of clarity and peace.

Morita Therapy teaches that, by focusing on the present and letting go of emotional attachment to future outcomes, individuals can develop a more grounded and realistic perspective on life's challenges. This aligns with Zen teachings, where the present moment is considered the only moment that truly exists, and clinging to future desires or past grievances is seen as a source of suffering (Suzuki, 2000).

Natural Change in Emotional States

Morita Therapy rests on the principle that emotions, especially negative ones, are naturally impermanent and will change over time. Rather than seeking to immediately eliminate discomfort, individuals are encouraged to trust in the natural ebb and flow of their emotional experiences. This principle is closely related to the Buddhist idea of *impermanence*, which teaches that all things, including emotions, are in constant flux and will pass on their own if left undisturbed (Reynolds, 2017). Morita believed that emotional suffering often stems from the futile attempt to resist this natural process.

In therapy, clients are taught to stop fighting their emotions and instead allow them to rise and fall naturally. This trust in the process is fundamental to the therapeutic journey and is what differentiates Morita Therapy from other modalities that emphasize immediate symptom relief (Kondo & Kurosawa, 2018). By allowing emotions to take their natural course, individuals often find that their anxiety or distress diminishes over time without needing to engage in extensive emotional analysis or cognitive restructuring.

Phases of Morita Therapy

Morita Therapy is often implemented in four distinct phases, each designed to guide clients through the process of acceptance and action:

Rest and Isolation

The therapy begins with a period of complete rest and isolation, typically lasting for a few days. This phase is designed to help the client disconnect from their habitual routines and focus on the body's natural rhythms without external distractions. During this phase, the client is encouraged to simply observe their thoughts and emotions without engaging in any action (Kitanishi & Mori, 2016).

Light Work

After the initial period of rest, clients gradually re-engage with the world through simple, light tasks, such as cleaning or gardening. These tasks are not emotionally or cognitively demanding but allow the client to experience the satisfaction that comes from purposeful action. This phase helps clients shift their focus from internal emotional turmoil to external, goal-directed behavior (Morita, 1998).

Heavier Work and Reflection

As therapy progresses, clients take on more complex tasks and are encouraged to reflect on their emotional states in relation to their actions. The goal of this phase is to teach the client that even in the face of difficult emotions, meaningful action is possible and can lead to a sense of accomplishment and peace (Kondo & Kurosawa, 2018).

Reintegration

The final phase involves reintegrating the client back into their normal routine, with a renewed focus on purposeful living. The client is encouraged to continue applying the principles of Morita Therapy in their daily life by accepting their emotions and focusing on constructive actions (Levine, 2020).

Morita Therapy's emphasis on action over introspection, combined with its acceptance-based approach to emotions, offers a powerful alternative to Western therapeutic models that focus on cognitive change. In modern psychotherapeutic practice, Morita Therapy is especially useful in treating anxiety disorders, depression, and obsessional neurosis, where the struggle to control or avoid negative emotions can perpetuate suffering (Reynolds, 2017).

Principles of Naikan Therapy

Naikan therapy, which originated from the introspective practices of Jōdo Shinshū Buddhism, centers around structured self-reflection with the goal of fostering gratitude, responsibility, and emotional healing. The therapeutic framework of Naikan is built upon three central questions that guide this introspective process:

What have I received from others?

This question encourages the individual to reflect on the support, care, and kindness they have received throughout their lives. By focusing on this aspect, the goal is to shift the individual's attention away from feelings of entitlement or resentment and towards a sense of gratitude. This reflection highlights the often-overlooked generosity that permeates human relationships and can counter feelings of isolation or victimization (Reynolds, 2017).

What have I given to others?

Here, the individual examines their own contributions to the well-being of others. This question prompts honest reflection on how one's actions have impacted the people around them, allowing for a more balanced understanding of personal responsibility. It encourages individuals to move beyond their own needs and self-interest and assess whether they have reciprocated the care they have received (Ishikawa, 2015). The process fosters a deeper awareness of interdependence and mutual support within relationships.

What troubles and difficulties have I caused others?

This question often brings about the most profound emotional realizations. It requires individuals to confront the ways in which their actions, either intentional or unintentional, may have caused pain or difficulty to others. Unlike Western therapeutic models that might emphasize forgiveness of the self, Naikan focuses on cultivating a sense of responsibility for one's actions, prompting the individual to consider how they can make amends or improve their behavior in the future (Kondo & Kurosawa, 2018). This principle encourages individuals to shift from a self-centered perspective to one that is more outwardly focused on others.

Application of Naikan Therapy in Modern Psychotherapy

Clinical Applications of Naikan Therapy

Treatment of Depression and Anxiety

Naikan therapy has been found particularly effective in treating depression and anxiety, especially in individuals who experience feelings of isolation, worthlessness, or guilt. These conditions often arise when individuals focus excessively on their own suffering and fail to appreciate the positive aspects of their relationships or the contributions of others. By encouraging clients to reflect on the kindness they have received from others and the ways they may have contributed to others' difficulties, Naikan shifts the focus away from the self and towards an outward, relational perspective (Kitanishi & Mori, 2016).

Research indicates that many patients undergoing Naikan therapy report a reduction in depressive symptoms and an increase in life satisfaction. This effect is believed to result from the development of gratitude, which is fostered through Naikan's structured introspection (Reynolds, 2017). Gratitude has been shown in various studies to correlate with improved mental health outcomes, particularly in reducing symptoms of depression and enhancing emotional well-being (Wood et al., 2010). Naikan therapy taps into this dynamic by creating a framework for patients to reflect on their positive relationships and life experiences, which in turn counteracts the negative thinking patterns associated with depression and anxiety.

One of the key mechanisms of Naikan's success in treating anxiety is its promotion of acceptance over control. Rather than attempting to eliminate anxious feelings, Naikan encourages individuals to accept their emotions while focusing on their interactions with others. This principle is particularly beneficial for anxiety disorders, where a common issue is the individual's attempt to control or avoid anxious thoughts. Naikan therapy helps to reduce this hyper-control, allowing clients to focus on interpersonal gratitude rather than internal anxiety (Kondo & Kurosawa, 2018).

Addiction Recovery

Naikan therapy has also been applied successfully in addiction treatment programs, especially those focusing on behavioral change and personal accountability. Addictive behaviors are often linked to a deep sense of guilt, shame, or emotional pain, which Naikan addresses by encouraging clients to confront their past actions and take responsibility for their impact on others. By reflecting on how their addiction has affected the people around them, clients often experience a shift in perspective that motivates them to make amends and seek recovery (Ishikawa, 2015).

Naikan therapy has been integrated into addiction recovery programs in Japan and some Western countries as part of a comprehensive approach to rehabilitation. Its focus on self-reflection complements other therapeutic techniques, such as cognitive-behavioral therapy (CBT) or 12-step programs, by fostering a sense of accountability and gratitude, both of which are essential components of long-term recovery (Kitanishi & Mori, 2016). Unlike traditional therapies that focus on the individual's internal emotional struggles, Naikan directs attention toward the social and relational aspects of recovery, which is particularly useful in overcoming the isolation often experienced by individuals struggling with addiction.

Family and Relationship Counseling

Another significant application of Naikan therapy is in the realm of family and relationship counseling. The therapy's focus on interpersonal relationships makes it a valuable tool for helping clients understand and improve their familial and romantic relationships. In this context, Naikan therapy encourages clients to reflect on how they have contributed to the well-being of their loved ones, as well as the difficulties they may have caused (Reynolds, 2017). This process helps individuals develop greater empathy and compassion for others, which can lead to improved communication and deeper emotional connections.

In relationship counseling, Naikan is often used to address issues such as resentment, lack of appreciation, and unresolved conflicts. For example, couples undergoing Naikan therapy are guided through a structured process of introspection where they reflect on what they have received from their partner, what they have given in return, and how they may have contributed to conflicts in the relationship. This structured reflection helps to diffuse tension, foster mutual understanding, and rebuild trust (Levine, 2020). By emphasizing responsibility and gratitude, Naikan therapy can be a powerful tool for healing fractured relationships.

Naikan in Modern Therapeutic Settings

Naikan therapy has been integrated into a variety of therapeutic settings, ranging from clinical psychology to corporate wellness programs. Its adaptability and focus on gratitude make it an appealing complement to more traditional therapeutic approaches in both individual and group therapy contexts. While Naikan's philosophical roots are distinctly Japanese, its application has been increasingly embraced in Western therapeutic practices, particularly as mindfulness-based therapies have gained popularity.

Group Therapy and Retreats

Naikan is frequently conducted in the form of intensive retreats, where participants spend multiple days reflecting on their relationships and experiences. These retreats offer a structured environment in which individuals can focus entirely on introspection without the distractions of daily life. Research has shown that participants often experience profound emotional breakthroughs during these retreats, reporting increased emotional clarity, reduced resentment, and a deeper sense of peace (Kitanishi & Mori, 2016). Naikan retreats are particularly effective in group therapy settings, where individuals can support one another through the reflective process.

Corporate Wellness Programs

In recent years, Naikan therapy has also been incorporated into corporate wellness programs aimed at improving employee well-being and enhancing interpersonal dynamics in the workplace. The therapy's emphasis on gratitude and responsibility aligns well with initiatives designed to foster positive workplace culture and improve mental health among employees. In these settings, Naikan helps employees reflect on their contributions to team success and encourages a greater sense of appreciation for their colleagues (Sugimoto & Green, 2019).

Integration with Other Therapies

Naikan therapy is often used in conjunction with other therapeutic modalities, such as cognitive-behavioral therapy (CBT), mindfulness-based stress reduction (MBSR), and acceptance and commitment therapy (ACT). These combinations allow for a more comprehensive approach to treatment by addressing both the cognitive and emotional aspects of psychological issues. For example, Naikan's focus on gratitude and responsibility complements the cognitive restructuring techniques used in CBT, creating a more balanced therapeutic experience (Reynolds, 2017).

Challenges and Limitations

While Naikan therapy offers many benefits, it is not without its challenges and limitations. One of the primary critiques of Naikan is its potential for intensifying feelings of guilt or shame in individuals who are highly self-critical. Since the therapy focuses on personal responsibility and the ways in which individuals have caused harm to others, it can sometimes exacerbate negative self-judgment in those who are prone to excessive guilt (Kondo & Kurosawa, 2018). For this reason, Naikan therapy may not be appropriate for all clients, particularly those with severe mood disorders or low self-esteem.

Additionally, Naikan therapy's emphasis on self-reflection may not resonate with all cultural contexts. While it has been widely embraced in Japan and certain Western settings, the therapeutic approach may need to be adapted for individuals from cultures that do not place as much value on introspection or personal responsibility (Ishikawa, 2015). Nonetheless, with proper adaptation, Naikan therapy has the potential to be an effective tool for promoting emotional well-being and improving relationships across a wide range of settings.

Case Studies in Naikan Therapy

Case Study 1: Naikan in the Treatment of Depression and Guilt

Patient Profile:

A 45-year-old female patient presented with major depressive disorder. She reported feelings of intense guilt, chronic sadness, and a belief that she was a burden to her family, stemming from a troubled relationship with her aging parents. Her guilt was exacerbated by her perceived failures in fulfilling her caregiving responsibilities.

Therapeutic Process:

Naikan therapy was introduced to help the patient reflect on her relationships with her parents, focusing on three key questions central to Naikan therapy: What have I received from them? What have I given to them? What troubles have I caused them? Through this structured reflection, the patient began to recognize the kindness her parents had shown her throughout her life, despite their strained relationship in recent years. She also acknowledged the efforts she had made in caring for them, which she had previously minimized.

Outcome:

After six weeks of Naikan therapy, the patient reported a significant reduction in depressive symptoms and an improvement in her relationship with her parents. Her feelings of guilt were reframed, and she developed a greater sense of gratitude and peace. The introspective process of Naikan allowed her to focus on the positive aspects of her relationship rather than fixating on perceived failures (Kitanishi & Mori, 2016).

Introduction to Morita Therapy

Morita Therapy, founded by Japanese psychiatrist Shoma Morita in the early 20th century, is a cornerstone of Eastern psychotherapeutic practice. Initially developed for the treatment of shinkeishitsu, a form of anxiety-based neurosis prevalent in Japan, Morita Therapy has expanded into a versatile approach for addressing various psychological conditions such as anxiety, depression, obsessive-compulsive disorder (OCD), and trauma. The therapy is grounded in principles of Zen Buddhism, specifically emphasizing acceptance of emotions, mindfulness, and purposeful action rather than the control or suppression of feelings (Kitanishi & Kondo, 2017). Unlike many Western therapies, which aim to eliminate negative emotions, Morita Therapy teaches individuals to accept these emotions as part of the natural human experience, thereby promoting resilience and adaptation (Morita, 1928/1998).

Philosophical Foundations of Morita Therapy

Morita Therapy draws heavily from Eastern philosophy, particularly the ideas found in Zen Buddhism regarding the nature of suffering and the impermanence of emotional states. One of its key tenets is that emotions, both positive and negative, are transient and should not be overly controlled or judged. This stands in contrast to Western cognitive-behavioral approaches, which often focus on restructuring negative thought patterns to alleviate emotional distress (Levine, 2020). Morita believed that excessive focus on controlling or eliminating feelings leads to further psychological suffering, as it creates an internal conflict where the individual is constantly battling against their emotions.

Instead, Morita Therapy encourages patients to focus on behavior and action—what one does in the face of emotional discomfort. The idea is that emotions cannot be directly controlled, but actions can be. By engaging in purposeful activities and accepting feelings as they come, patients learn to live more fully and function more effectively, regardless of their emotional state (Ishiyama, 1986). This principle is often summarized in Morita's famous dictum: "Give up trying to eliminate symptoms and learn to live with them."

Core Concepts of Morita Therapy

Acceptance of Natural Emotions

A primary aspect of Morita Therapy is the acceptance of natural emotions. Morita posited that emotional distress is part of the human condition, and attempting to eliminate feelings such as anxiety, fear, or sadness often results in more suffering (Kitanishi, 2018). The therapy encourages individuals to acknowledge their emotions without judgment or avoidance, allowing them to coexist with these feelings rather than being overwhelmed by them. This acceptance is rooted in Zen's concept of mindfulness, where awareness of the present moment without attachment or aversion is crucial (Levine, 2020).

Focus on Purposeful Action

Morita Therapy shifts the therapeutic focus from emotional regulation to purposeful action. Instead of trying to change how they feel, patients are guided to focus on what they can control: their actions. In this context, individuals are encouraged to continue with their daily activities, work, and responsibilities, regardless of how they feel internally. This behavioral focus aligns with Japanese cultural values, emphasizing perseverance and diligence, often referred to as ganbatte, or the act of doing one's best despite difficulties (Kitanishi & Kondo, 2017).

Experiential Learning and Nature

Morita Therapy often involves an element of experiential learning, where patients are encouraged to engage with nature as part of their recovery process. This includes practices like gardening, outdoor walks, and other forms of physical labor. Morita believed that being in nature helps individuals reconnect with the rhythms of life and provides a space where they can reflect on their emotions without being consumed by them (Reynolds, 2017). Nature in this context is seen not only as a therapeutic setting but also as a metaphor for the impermanence of emotions—just as seasons change, so too do our feelings.

Four Stages of Morita Therapy

Traditional Morita Therapy is structured into four stages, which guide the patient through a process of acceptance, rest, and gradual re-engagement with life. These stages are:

Stage 1: Isolation and Rest

The first stage involves a period of isolation where the patient is removed from their daily life and responsibilities. This period, typically lasting between five to seven days, allows for emotional and physical rest without distractions. Patients are encouraged to refrain from intellectual activities like reading or writing, creating a space where they can focus solely on their inner emotional state (Ishiyama, 1986).

Stage 2: Light Occupational Therapy

Following the rest period, patients gradually re-engage in simple, repetitive tasks such as cleaning or gardening. These activities are meant to help the patient become aware of their emotional state without being overwhelmed by it. By focusing on external tasks, patients are encouraged to experience their emotions in the background while maintaining a sense of purpose through their actions (Levine, 2020).

Stage 3: Full Occupational Therapy

In this stage, patients take on more complex tasks that require sustained attention and effort. These tasks further the goal of focusing on action over emotion, teaching the patient to manage their emotional state by engaging in meaningful work. This stage also emphasizes the importance of self-discipline and perseverance, key components in Morita's philosophy (Reynolds, 2017).

Stage 4: Reintegration into Daily Life

The final stage involves the patient returning to their normal life, equipped with the skills they have learned in therapy. The focus remains on accepting emotions without judgment and maintaining purposeful actions in the face of distress. Patients are encouraged to apply these principles in their daily routines, relationships, and work, reinforcing the idea that emotional well-being arises not from the absence of distress but from the ability to function effectively despite it (Kitanishi & Kondo, 2017).

Relevance in Modern Psychotherapy

Morita Therapy continues to gain recognition beyond Japan, particularly as mindfulness and acceptance-based approaches grow in popularity in Western psychotherapy. The therapy's focus on action and acceptance offers an alternative to emotion-centric models, making it particularly appealing in contexts where individuals are overwhelmed by the need to control or change their emotions (Reynolds, 2017). Recent studies have shown Morita Therapy's effectiveness in treating a range of disorders, including generalized anxiety disorder, obsessive-compulsive disorder, and mood disorders (Kitanishi, 2018).

Core Principles of Morita Therapy

Morita Therapy, deeply rooted in Eastern philosophy, emphasizes several key principles that distinguish it from other psychotherapeutic methods. These principles form the foundation of Morita's approach to treating psychological distress and guide both the therapeutic process and the patient's recovery journey. The focus on acceptance, purposeful action, and the natural flow of emotions are essential elements that inform the therapy's structure and goals (Kitanishi & Kondo, 2017). Unlike many Western approaches that prioritize the resolution of symptoms, Morita Therapy emphasizes living a full and meaningful life in the presence of discomfort, rather than trying to eliminate it (Morita, 1928/1998).

Acceptance of Natural Emotions

The cornerstone of Morita Therapy is the acceptance of natural emotions without resistance or judgment. In the context of mental health, Morita argued that emotions, including anxiety, fear, or depression, are natural and should be embraced rather than fought against. He believed that emotional suffering is exacerbated by the tendency to control or suppress negative feelings. Therefore, the goal is not to eliminate symptoms but to accept them as part of the human experience (Levine, 2020). This concept parallels Buddhist teachings on non-attachment, where individuals learn to observe their emotional states without becoming overly attached to them.

This principle challenges the Western emphasis on cognitive restructuring, which often seeks to modify distorted thoughts to change emotional responses. Instead, Morita Therapy teaches patients to stop trying to control their emotions, which can lead to greater emotional freedom. Patients are encouraged to acknowledge their emotions and continue with their lives despite experiencing discomfort (Kitanishi, 2018). This approach reflects the understanding that emotions are temporary and will naturally dissipate if left alone, a perspective that aligns with Eastern notions of impermanence (Reynolds, 2017).

For example, in treating anxiety disorders, Morita Therapy does not aim to reduce the anxious feelings directly. Rather, the individual is encouraged to experience the anxiety while continuing to engage in their daily activities. Over time, the anxiety loses its overwhelming power as the patient learns that it does not need to be feared or avoided (Levine, 2020). This principle has been supported by contemporary research on acceptance-based therapies, such as Acceptance and Commitment Therapy (ACT), which also highlight the importance of accepting distressing emotions rather than trying to alter them (Hayes, Strosahl, & Wilson, 1999).

Focus on Purposeful Action

A defining feature of Morita Therapy is its focus on purposeful action rather than emotional or cognitive processes. Morita believed that while individuals cannot directly control their emotions, they can control their actions. Therefore, the therapy emphasizes doing rather than feeling, where patients are encouraged to continue with meaningful tasks and responsibilities even when experiencing emotional turmoil (Ishiyama, 1986). This behavioral focus is central to recovery and aligns with Japanese cultural values that emphasize perseverance and self-discipline.

Patients are taught that the key to overcoming emotional distress is not by avoiding or minimizing feelings but by living a purposeful life despite them. This perspective resonates with the existential philosophy that life gains meaning through purposeful actions, even in the face of suffering. Morita Therapy encourages individuals to perform tasks such as cleaning, working, or gardening, focusing their attention on the present moment and the task at hand (Kitanishi & Kondo, 2017). Over time, the emphasis on purposeful action helps to shift the individual's focus away from their emotional distress and toward their contributions to life.

The Natural Flow of Feelings

Morita Therapy is grounded in the idea that emotions have a natural flow and will change over time if they are allowed to run their course. Just as weather patterns fluctuate, Morita posited that emotions, too, are impermanent and should not be controlled or resisted. This concept draws from Zen Buddhism, which teaches that suffering arises when we cling to pleasant experiences or resist unpleasant ones (Levine, 2020). Morita's therapeutic approach encourages patients to experience their emotions fully and without interference, trusting that these feelings will naturally subside (Kitanishi, 2018).

The acceptance of the natural flow of emotions reflects the Eastern understanding of the cyclical nature of life. In Morita's view, emotions such as anxiety or fear are not pathologies to be cured but natural responses to life's challenges. Rather than treating these emotions as problems to be solved, Morita Therapy encourages patients to see them as part of the ebb and flow of existence. This approach stands in stark contrast to Western models of psychotherapy, which often seek to reduce or eliminate emotional symptoms as quickly as possible (Reynolds, 2017).

Gradual Exposure to Life's Challenges

Morita Therapy also incorporates a gradual, staged approach to re-engaging with life's challenges. This process involves moving from a state of rest and reflection to purposeful action and full participation in daily life. Initially, patients may be removed from their normal routines and placed in a structured environment where they can reflect on their emotional state without external pressures. Over time, they are gradually introduced to light tasks, followed by more complex responsibilities, eventually reintegrating into their daily lives with a new mindset of acceptance and action (Ishiyama, 1986).

This staged process is designed to help individuals build emotional resilience. By gradually increasing the level of challenge, patients learn to tolerate discomfort and uncertainty, developing a more flexible and adaptive approach to life. This method bears some resemblance to exposure therapy, a treatment commonly used in cognitive-behavioral therapy (CBT), where patients are gradually exposed to feared stimuli in a controlled manner, ultimately reducing their emotional reactivity (Levine, 2020). However, unlike exposure therapy, which is aimed at reducing fear, Morita Therapy is focused on teaching patients to live with fear and discomfort without the need for elimination.

Comparison with Naikan Therapy

Morita Therapy's focus on action over reflection provides an interesting contrast to Naikan Therapy, another Eastern approach that emphasizes introspection. While both therapies share the goal of fostering acceptance, Naikan places a greater emphasis on examining one's relationships and past behaviors, encouraging deep reflection and gratitude (Krech, 2001). In contrast, Morita Therapy teaches patients to live in the present moment, focusing on what can be done today rather than reflecting on the past. These differences highlight the diversity within Eastern psychotherapeutic approaches and provide valuable tools for individuals seeking to improve their mental health through either introspection or action.

Relevance in Contemporary Therapy

In recent years, Morita Therapy has gained increasing recognition outside of Japan, particularly as part of the global movement toward mindfulness-based therapies. Its emphasis on acceptance, non-judgmental awareness, and purposeful action resonates with the principles of Acceptance and Commitment Therapy (ACT) and Mindfulness-Based Stress Reduction (MBSR), both of which are widely practiced in the West (Kitanishi & Kondo, 2017). Modern applications of Morita Therapy have shown promise in treating conditions such as generalized anxiety disorder, depression, and obsessive-compulsive disorder (OCD), where acceptance and action-based approaches have proven effective (Kitanishi, 2018).

Application of Morita Therapy in Clinical Practice

Treatment Modalities and Techniques

In clinical practice, Morita Therapy is characterized by several treatment modalities and techniques that focus on facilitating the patient's engagement with life while accepting their emotional states. The therapy is typically structured into four stages:

4. ***Isolation and Rest:*** Initially, patients are often placed in a calming environment where they can reflect on their thoughts and feelings without the usual distractions of daily life. This stage allows for the initial processing of emotions, akin to a period of introspection (Ishiyama, 1986).
5. ***Gradual Engagement:*** Following the rest period, patients are gradually encouraged to engage in simple tasks. This step is crucial for fostering a sense of normalcy and encouraging the practice of mindful action. Patients might begin with low-stress activities, such as cleaning or organizing their space, gradually increasing the complexity of their tasks as their emotional resilience builds (Levine, 2020).

6. ***Purposeful Action:*** This stage emphasizes the importance of acting purposefully in daily life, even when experiencing discomfort. Patients are taught to recognize that they can choose to act regardless of their emotional state, thus reinforcing the therapy's core principle of action over feeling (Kitanishi, 2018).
7. ***Integration and Reflection:*** The final stage involves reflecting on the progress made and integrating the insights gained from therapy into everyday life. Patients learn to carry the skills and mindset cultivated during therapy into their ongoing lives, fostering lasting change (Ishiyama, 1986).

These stages are tailored to everyone's needs, making Morita Therapy a flexible approach that can be adapted based on the patient's unique circumstances.

Clinical Effectiveness

Research has shown that Morita Therapy can be effective in treating various mental health issues, including anxiety disorders, depression, and obsessive-compulsive disorder (OCD). A meta-analysis conducted by Kitanishi (2018) revealed that patients undergoing Morita Therapy reported significant reductions in anxiety and depressive symptoms, as well as improvements in overall well-being.

One of the therapy's strengths is its focus on acceptance and behavioral activation. Studies indicate that integrating these elements can lead to improved emotional regulation and life satisfaction (Crane et al., 2014). Moreover, the therapy's emphasis on engaging in meaningful activities aligns well with findings from positive psychology, which highlights the importance of purpose and engagement in fostering mental health (Seligman, 2011).

Suitability for Diverse Populations

Morita Therapy's principles are suitable for diverse populations, including those who may be hesitant to engage in more traditional Western therapeutic methods. Its emphasis on action and acceptance rather than intellectualizing emotions resonates with individuals who may prefer a more pragmatic approach to therapy. For example, individuals from cultures that value collectivism and interdependence may find Morita Therapy particularly appealing, as it aligns with the cultural understanding of emotional experiences within a social context (Reynolds, 2017).

Additionally, Morita Therapy has shown promise in treating individuals experiencing chronic illness or physical disabilities. In these cases, the therapy encourages patients to engage in life fully despite their limitations, fostering a sense of agency and empowerment (Kitanishi, 2018). This aspect of the therapy is particularly relevant in contexts where chronic pain or illness may lead to feelings of helplessness and despair.

Integration with Other Therapeutic Approaches

Morita Therapy can be effectively integrated with other therapeutic approaches, creating a comprehensive treatment plan that addresses both emotional and behavioral aspects of psychological distress. For instance, combining Morita Therapy with Cognitive Behavioral Therapy (CBT) can enhance treatment outcomes by allowing patients to process their emotions through acceptance while also learning practical strategies for changing maladaptive thought patterns (Hayes et al., 1999).

Furthermore, the rise of mindfulness-based therapies has opened new avenues for incorporating Morita principles into existing treatment modalities. Mindfulness practices, which emphasize acceptance and present-moment awareness, complement the Morita focus on experiencing emotions fully and engaging in purposeful action (Dimidjian et al., 2011). This integration can provide patients with a more rounded therapeutic experience, equipping them with a diverse set of tools for managing their mental health.

Challenges and Limitations of Morita Therapy

Cultural Considerations and Misunderstandings

Morita Therapy originates from Japanese cultural contexts, where acceptance of emotional states and the prioritization of social harmony play significant roles. For practitioners in Western contexts, cultural differences may lead to misunderstandings about the core principles of Morita Therapy. Western therapeutic models often emphasize emotional expression and exploration of feelings, which can contrast sharply with Morita's focus on acceptance and action (Kitanishi, 2018).

For instance, patients accustomed to Western therapies may struggle with the notion of accepting their feelings without attempting to alter them actively. This difference in approach can create resistance to the therapy, making it challenging for clinicians to effectively implement Morita Therapy with patients who are unfamiliar with its principles (Reynolds, 2017). To overcome this, practitioners need to invest time in educating their clients about the underlying philosophies of Morita Therapy, emphasizing the benefits of acceptance as a pathway to action rather than a denial of emotional experience.

Limited Research and Evidence Base

Despite a growing interest in Morita Therapy, there remains a limited body of empirical research specifically validating its effectiveness compared to more widely studied therapeutic modalities like Cognitive Behavioral Therapy (CBT) and Dialectical Behavior Therapy (DBT). While several studies have demonstrated positive outcomes associated with Morita Therapy, the overall evidence base is still emerging (Kitanishi & Kondo, 2017).

The lack of rigorous randomized controlled trials (RCTs) and large-scale studies makes it difficult for practitioners to justify the use of Morita Therapy in clinical settings, especially in evidence-based practice environments. This limitation may deter some mental health professionals from incorporating Morita Therapy into their therapeutic repertoire, despite its potential benefits (Kitanishi, 2018).

Suitability for Diverse Psychological Disorders

While Morita Therapy has shown efficacy in treating anxiety, depression, and stress-related disorders, it may not be suitable for all psychological issues. Patients with severe psychiatric disorders, such as schizophrenia or bipolar disorder, may require more intensive interventions and stabilization before engaging in Morita Therapy (Ishiyama, 1986).

Furthermore, Morita Therapy's focus on action may not be appropriate for individuals experiencing debilitating symptoms that hinder their ability to engage meaningfully in life. For example, someone in a severe depressive episode may find it challenging to participate in purposeful activities, leading to frustration and a sense of failure in therapy (Levine, 2020). Thus, clinicians must carefully assess a patient's readiness and ability to engage in the therapeutic process before implementing Morita Therapy.

Potential for Misapplication

The potential for misapplication of Morita Therapy is another challenge faced by practitioners. Morita Therapy is fundamentally about balancing acceptance and action; however, some clinicians may inadvertently place too much emphasis on the action component, neglecting the essential aspect of accepting one's emotional state (Crane et al., 2014).

For instance, a therapist might pressure a patient to engage in activities before they have fully processed their emotions, which can lead to feelings of invalidation and distress. Such misapplication can diminish the therapeutic alliance and hinder the overall effectiveness of treatment (Kitanishi, 2018). Practitioners need to be mindful of maintaining a balance between encouraging action and fostering emotional acceptance to ensure the therapy is applied effectively.

Integration into Existing Treatment Models

Integrating Morita Therapy into existing treatment models presents challenges. Clinicians trained in Western therapeutic practices may find it difficult to blend Morita principles with familiar modalities like CBT or psychodynamic therapy. This integration requires a comprehensive understanding of both frameworks and the ability to navigate their differences in philosophy and technique (Hayes et al., 1999).

Moreover, differing therapeutic language and terminology can create barriers to integration. For example, while Morita Therapy emphasizes "acceptance," traditional models may focus on "processing emotions" or "working through feelings." Bridging these conceptual gaps requires ongoing training, supervision, and open dialogue among mental health professionals to create cohesive treatment plans that benefit patients (Dimidjian et al., 2011).

Conclusion

In conclusion, while Morita Therapy presents numerous benefits for treating mental health issues, it is important to acknowledge its challenges and limitations. Cultural considerations, a limited research base, suitability for diverse psychological disorders, potential for misapplication, and integration into existing treatment models are crucial aspects that practitioners must navigate. Addressing these challenges through education, training, and awareness will enhance the effective implementation of Morita Therapy and contribute to its growing acceptance in the global mental health community.

Future Directions and Research Opportunities for Morita Therapy

As mental health awareness continues to expand globally, the need for diverse therapeutic approaches, such as Morita Therapy, is becoming increasingly recognized. This section discusses the future directions and research opportunities for Morita Therapy, focusing on enhancing its empirical support, expanding its applications, and fostering cross-cultural adaptation.

Expanding Empirical Research

One of the primary future directions for Morita Therapy involves the need for more robust empirical research. While existing studies have shown promising outcomes, larger-scale randomized controlled trials (RCTs) are necessary to establish the therapy's effectiveness across various populations and mental health conditions (Kitanishi, 2018).

Future research could aim to:

- ***Compare Morita Therapy to Established Treatments:*** Conducting head-to-head trials comparing Morita Therapy with established treatments, such as Cognitive Behavioral Therapy (CBT) and Dialectical Behavior Therapy (DBT), could clarify its relative effectiveness for specific disorders (Crane et al., 2014). Such research would provide invaluable information for clinicians seeking evidence-based treatment options.
- ***Longitudinal Studies:*** Implementing longitudinal studies to assess the long-term effects of Morita Therapy on patients' emotional well-being and daily functioning would contribute to the understanding of its sustained impact over time (Kitanishi & Kondo, 2017).
- ***Mechanisms of Change:*** Investigating the underlying mechanisms that contribute to the effectiveness of Morita Therapy is essential. Understanding how acceptance, action, and the integration of emotional experiences facilitate change can help refine therapeutic approaches and improve treatment outcomes (Levine, 2020).

Broader Applications

As mental health issues become increasingly diverse and complex, the application of Morita Therapy could expand beyond its traditional scope. Future research may explore:

- ***Applications in Chronic Illness Management:*** Investigating the effectiveness of Morita Therapy in treating individuals with chronic illnesses or pain conditions may yield valuable insights. Given its focus on acceptance and purposeful action, Morita Therapy could help individuals navigate the emotional challenges associated with chronic conditions (Ishiyama, 1986).
- ***Integration with Digital Mental Health Platforms:*** With the rise of telehealth and digital mental health interventions, there is an opportunity to adapt Morita Therapy for online platforms. Researching the effectiveness of virtual Morita Therapy sessions could facilitate access to treatment for those unable to attend in-person sessions (Dimidjian et al., 2011).
- ***Application to Non-Clinical Populations:*** Exploring the use of Morita Therapy principles in non-clinical settings, such as educational institutions or workplace wellness programs, could offer a preventive approach to mental health by promoting emotional resilience and well-being (Reynolds, 2017).

Cross-Cultural Adaptation and Training

As Morita Therapy gains popularity outside of Japan, efforts to adapt its principles for diverse cultural contexts are essential. Future research should focus on:

- ***Cultural Sensitivity and Adaptation:*** Developing culturally sensitive adaptations of Morita Therapy to accommodate different belief systems, values, and communication styles will enhance its accessibility and effectiveness (Kitanishi, 2018). For instance, tailoring the therapy's language and examples to resonate with various cultural backgrounds may facilitate better engagement.

- ***Training for Mental Health Professionals:*** Expanding training programs for mental health professionals on Morita Therapy and its application across different cultures will foster a deeper understanding of the therapy's principles and techniques. This training should emphasize the integration of Morita Therapy with other therapeutic modalities to enhance its appeal to practitioners familiar with Western approaches (Hayes et al., 1999).

Collaboration with Interdisciplinary Fields

Future directions for Morita Therapy should also include collaboration with interdisciplinary fields, such as neuroscience, positive psychology, and cultural studies. Researching the intersections between these fields can provide new insights into the benefits of Morita Therapy and help bridge the gap between Eastern and Western therapeutic practices.

- ***Neuroscience Perspectives:*** Investigating how the principles of Morita Therapy impact brain function and emotional regulation through neuroscience research could provide compelling evidence for its effectiveness. Understanding the neurobiological mechanisms involved in acceptance and action may enhance the scientific foundation of Morita Therapy (Dimidjian et al., 2011).
- ***Positive Psychology:*** Aligning Morita Therapy principles with the tenets of positive psychology can facilitate a broader understanding of how acceptance and purposeful action contribute to overall well-being. This alignment can foster new research avenues exploring the impact of Morita Therapy on enhancing life satisfaction and resilience (Seligman, 2011).

Case Study 2: Morita Therapy for Generalized Anxiety Disorder

Background

The case study presented here focuses on a 32-year-old female patient, whom we will refer to as Sarah, diagnosed with Generalized Anxiety Disorder (GAD). Sarah reported experiencing excessive worry about various aspects of her life, including work, relationships, and health. This anxiety significantly interfered with her daily functioning, leading to sleep disturbances, difficulty concentrating, and a pervasive sense of dread. After unsuccessful attempts with cognitive-behavioral therapy (CBT), which focused heavily on challenging negative thoughts, Sarah's therapist recommended Morita Therapy as an alternative approach.

Assessment

Upon initial assessment, Sarah expressed a strong desire to eliminate her anxiety and frequently described her emotions as problematic. Her history revealed a pattern of avoidance behavior, where she would withdraw from social situations and procrastinate tasks to evade feelings of anxiety. This avoidance reinforced her anxiety, creating a cycle that exacerbated her condition. The therapist explained the core principles of Morita Therapy, emphasizing acceptance of feelings rather than attempting to eliminate them, and framed the therapeutic process around taking purposeful action despite anxiety.

Intervention

The treatment plan for Sarah incorporated the following Morita Therapy techniques:

1. **Acceptance**: The therapist guided Sarah in recognizing and accepting her anxiety without judgment. Instead of labeling her anxiety as "bad" or "unwanted," Sarah learned to see it as a natural part of her emotional experience.
2. **Structured Daily Activities**: A key aspect of Morita Therapy is the focus on structured daily activities. Sarah and her therapist collaborated to create a daily schedule that included specific tasks she needed to complete, ranging from work responsibilities to social interactions. This structure aimed to encourage engagement in life despite her feelings of anxiety.
3. **Mindful Observation**: Sarah was instructed to practice mindful observation, which involved paying attention to her anxiety as it arose without attempting to suppress or control it. This practice aimed to reduce the power her anxiety held over her decisions and actions.
4. **Purposeful Action**: The therapist encouraged Sarah to take purposeful actions aligned with her values and responsibilities, regardless of her anxiety levels. For example, she was guided to participate in a social gathering she had been avoiding, focusing on the action itself rather than the accompanying anxiety.
5. **Journaling**: To reflect on her experiences, Sarah was encouraged to maintain a journal documenting her feelings, thoughts, and actions throughout the therapy. This reflective practice helped her identify patterns and recognize her progress over time.

Progress and Outcomes

Over the course of eight sessions, Sarah exhibited significant improvements:

1. **Increased Acceptance**: Sarah gradually learned to accept her anxiety as a normal emotional response rather than a debilitating condition. This shift in perspective diminished the fear associated with her anxiety, allowing her to engage more fully in daily life.
2. **Enhanced Engagement**: The structured daily activities created a sense of accountability and accomplishment. Sarah reported completing tasks she previously avoided, including attending social events and meeting work deadlines. This engagement fostered a sense of control over her life.
3. **Reduction in Anxiety Symptoms**: While Sarah's anxiety did not disappear entirely, she reported a noticeable reduction in the intensity and frequency of her anxious episodes. The ability to observe her anxiety without judgment contributed to a sense of relief, allowing her to function more effectively in her personal and professional life.
4. **Increased Self-Confidence**: Through her successful engagement in activities despite anxiety, Sarah's self-confidence improved. She began to view herself as capable of handling challenging situations, which further motivated her to pursue new opportunities.
5. **Sustained Change**: At the conclusion of therapy, Sarah expressed a commitment to continue applying the principles of Morita Therapy in her daily life. She reported feeling more equipped to manage anxiety as it arose, viewing it as part of her emotional landscape rather than an obstacle to be eliminated.

Conclusion

This case study illustrates how Morita Therapy can be effectively utilized to help individuals like Sarah overcome anxiety through acceptance and structured engagement in life. By focusing on purposeful action and minimizing the struggle against emotions, Morita Therapy facilitated Sarah's journey towards greater emotional resilience and improved mental health. This approach underscores the potential for Morita Therapy to provide valuable therapeutic alternatives for those struggling with anxiety disorders.

Similarities and Differences

Naikan and Morita therapies, while emerging from the same cultural backdrop of Japan, differ significantly in their approaches and goals. Both therapies, however, share a fundamental connection to traditional Japanese philosophies that emphasize harmony, reflection, and the acceptance of life's realities.

Core Values

At their foundation, both Naikan and Morita therapies prioritize the role of self-reflection and acceptance but with nuanced differences in focus. Naikan therapy is rooted in interpersonal reflection—the individual's relationship with others—and emphasizes gratitude, responsibility, and self-awareness. The core value here is the realization of how much one has received from others and how little one has reciprocated. This is reflective of traditional Japanese values that emphasize interdependence and humility (Kawai, 2016). Naikan practitioners believe that by understanding these relationships more deeply, individuals develop a sense of responsibility and emotional resilience (Reynolds, 2017).

In contrast, Morita therapy focuses on acceptance of reality, especially concerning one's emotions and thoughts. Inspired by Zen Buddhism, Morita therapy teaches that emotions like anxiety, fear, and depression are natural parts of life and should not be avoided or suppressed. Instead, individuals are encouraged to accept these feelings and focus on purposeful action in their daily lives (Kitanishi, 2018). The core value of Morita therapy is to embrace discomfort and take action regardless of one's emotional state, which contrasts with Western psychotherapies that often seek to modify or control emotions (Levine, 2020).

Therapeutic Goals

The therapeutic goals of Naikan and Morita therapies are distinct yet complementary in their impact on mental well-being. Naikan therapy's primary aim is self-discovery through introspection. The goal is to help clients understand the ways in which they have interacted with others and reflect on how they can improve their relationships by acknowledging their responsibilities. This deep reflection fosters an emotional transformation rooted in gratitude and connectedness to others (Sugimoto, 2015).

Morita therapy, on the other hand, focuses on action and purpose. The goal is not to change or eliminate emotions but to help clients develop the strength to live purposefully, even in the presence of anxiety, fear, or uncertainty. Clients are guided to engage in constructive activities, such as work or nature-related tasks, that align with their values, thereby helping them overcome emotional paralysis (Kitanishi, 2018).

Thus, while Naikan aims to cultivate emotional insight through reflection, Morita promotes behavioral engagement despite emotional distress. Both therapies ultimately seek to restore mental balance, but Naikan does so by transforming how individuals view their relationships, and Morita achieves this by helping individuals accept emotions and engage in meaningful action.

Therapeutic Techniques

Therapeutic techniques in Naikan and Morita therapies reflect their differing goals and values. Naikan therapy employs structured self-reflective sessions, where clients are encouraged to reflect on three core questions:

1. What have I received from person X?
2. What have I given to person X?
3. What troubles and difficulties have I caused person X?

This structured reflection often takes place over an extended period, sometimes as long as a week, in a retreat-like setting where the client is isolated from distractions. The method fosters deep personal insight, often leading to emotional breakthroughs (Sugimoto, 2015).

Morita therapy, in contrast, involves a structured regimen of activities divided into four stages:

1. Rest, where the client is allowed complete rest to observe their emotions,
2. Light occupational therapy, where the client engages in simple tasks like writing or cleaning,
3. Heavy occupational therapy, involving more challenging physical activities, and
4. Reintegration into daily life, where the client returns to their normal routine with the aim of maintaining their focus on action despite emotional challenges (Levine, 2020).

Both therapies emphasize non-verbal and non-interpretive techniques, relying less on talking and more on personal action or reflection, which stands in stark contrast to Western talk therapies that heavily rely on verbal processing and cognitive restructuring (Kawai, 2016).

Integration with Western Psychotherapy: How Naikan and Morita Have Been Adapted or Integrated into Western Practices

The integration of Naikan and Morita therapies into Western psychotherapeutic practices reflects a growing interest in incorporating Eastern philosophical approaches into the broader field of mental health. These therapies offer a counterbalance to the predominantly cognitive-behavioral and psychoanalytic traditions of Western psychology, bringing a fresh focus on acceptance, reflection, and purposeful action. Both Naikan and Morita therapies have found their way into Western mental health practices, either as stand-alone therapies or as complementary approaches within established therapeutic frameworks. This section will explore how these Eastern therapies have been adapted and how they offer unique insights that resonate with Western therapeutic models.

Acceptance-Based Approaches in Western Therapy

One of the most significant points of integration between Morita therapy and Western psychology has been through the Acceptance and Commitment Therapy (ACT) model, which emphasizes acceptance of thoughts and emotions rather than their suppression or modification (Hayes, 2016). The core of

Morita therapy—teaching clients to accept and coexist with uncomfortable emotions while engaging in purposeful action—has strong parallels with the principles of ACT. In both approaches, the goal is not to eliminate anxiety or distress but to engage in meaningful life activities despite emotional discomfort (Levine, 2020).

Morita's emphasis on "arugamama", or accepting things as they are, without judgment or resistance, aligns closely with ACT's use of mindfulness and acceptance-based strategies. Research has shown that integrating Morita's principles into ACT has been particularly beneficial in treating anxiety disorders and obsessive-compulsive disorder (OCD), where clients often struggle with intrusive thoughts and feelings (Kitanishi, 2018). This integration into the broader ACT framework illustrates how Morita's approach to acceptance has influenced contemporary Western therapeutic practices.

The Use of Naikan in Positive Psychology

Naikan therapy's focus on gratitude, self-reflection, and interpersonal responsibility has also found resonance within the Western positive psychology movement, which emphasizes building strengths and fostering well-being, rather than just addressing pathology. Western therapists have increasingly incorporated gratitude practices derived from Naikan therapy into therapeutic interventions aimed at improving emotional well-being (Emmons & Mishra, 2017).

Naikan's structured reflection process has been adapted into Western therapeutic settings to help clients develop a sense of connectedness and responsibility in their relationships. This approach has proven effective in family therapy, where Naikan-inspired techniques are used to help individuals reflect on their familial roles, promoting forgiveness, gratitude, and improved relational dynamics (Reynolds, 2017). Additionally, gratitude practices based on Naikan have been applied in positive psychology interventions aimed at enhancing life satisfaction and reducing depressive symptoms (Seligman & Csikszentmihalyi, 2014).

Integrating Eastern and Western Therapeutic Techniques

While Naikan and Morita therapies have clear philosophical differences from many Western models, their techniques can be complementary to cognitive-behavioral strategies. Western therapists have found ways to incorporate Naikan's emphasis on reflective introspection and Morita's focus on action despite discomfort into existing therapeutic practices, particularly in mindfulness-based and acceptance-based therapies (Kawakami, 2018).

In mindfulness-based cognitive therapy (MBCT), for example, elements of Morita's teachings—such as observing emotions without trying to change them—are integrated to help clients learn to live with anxiety and distress (Segal et al., 2013). Similarly, Naikan's focus on reflecting on one's actions, gratitude, and the impact of others has been used to complement compassion-focused therapies, which aim to cultivate self-compassion and kindness towards oneself and others (Gilbert, 2015). The structured self-reflection used in Naikan has also been applied in narrative therapy, where clients engage in reflective practices that encourage them to explore their personal histories and relationships more deeply (Muramoto, 2020).

Naikan in Clinical Settings: Use of Naikan Therapy in a Rehabilitation Center for Addiction Recovery

Naikan therapy has increasingly been applied in clinical settings around the world, especially in the context of rehabilitation centers that deal with addiction recovery. As a form of structured self-reflection, Naikan allows individuals struggling with addiction to reflect on their past relationships and life experiences in a way that fosters both gratitude and responsibility. Addiction, often rooted in patterns of avoidance and denial, can benefit from Naikan's reflective practices, which encourage individuals to confront the impact of their actions on others and develop a sense of interpersonal accountability (Sugimoto, 2015).

The Role of Self-Reflection in Addiction Recovery

In rehabilitation centers, the three primary questions of Naikan—"What have I received from others?", "What have I given to others?", and "What troubles or difficulties have I caused to others?"—are used to guide clients through deep self-examination. These questions are particularly powerful for those recovering from addiction because they prompt individuals to reflect on their behavioral patterns, the support they have received from others (often unrecognized), and the harm they may have caused through their addiction (Muramoto, 2020).

By encouraging clients to move away from a victim mentality and toward a perspective of gratitude and personal responsibility, Naikan therapy helps to reframe the narrative that individuals may have about their lives. For example, clients in addiction recovery often focus on their struggles and may harbor resentment toward people they perceive as contributing to their difficulties. Naikan, by shifting the focus to the positive aspects of relationships, helps to break this cycle of negative thinking and self-pity (Reynolds, 2017).

Case Study 3: Use of Naikan Therapy in a Rehabilitation Center for Addiction Recovery

In a rehabilitation center for addiction recovery in Japan, a 43-year-old male with a history of alcohol dependency was introduced to Naikan therapy as part of his treatment. The patient had been struggling with addiction for over a decade and had previously relapsed after multiple attempts at traditional addiction counseling and 12-step programs. His relationships with his family and friends had deteriorated, and he frequently blamed external circumstances for his continued substance abuse.

During the Naikan therapy sessions, the patient was asked to reflect on the three central Naikan questions. Initially, he found it difficult to identify positive aspects of his relationships and focused mainly on the harm others had caused him. However, over the course of a two-week Naikan retreat, where he spent several hours each day in self-reflection, he began to recognize the support he had received from his parents and friends, even during his struggles with addiction (Sugimoto, 2015).

Through this process, the patient developed a profound sense of gratitude toward his parents, particularly his mother, who had continued to support him despite the challenges he had posed to the family. He also came to terms with the trouble he had caused his friends, recognizing that his addiction had strained his relationships and led to isolation. By the end of the retreat, the patient expressed a renewed sense of personal responsibility and motivation to rebuild these damaged relationships.

The outcomes of this Naikan-based intervention were promising. The patient reported a significant reduction in feelings of shame and guilt, as Naikan helped him to re-contextualize these emotions as part of a broader understanding of his relationships. Follow-up interviews six months later indicated that the patient had remained sober and had begun to repair relationships with his family and friends. The self-reflective process that Naikan offers was instrumental in his ongoing recovery, as it allowed him to externalize blame and move toward a mindset of accountability and gratitude (Levine, 2020).

Integration with Other Therapies in Addiction Treatment

In Western rehabilitation settings, Naikan therapy is sometimes used in conjunction with other therapeutic modalities, such as cognitive-behavioral therapy (CBT) and 12-step programs. While CBT focuses on changing thought patterns and behaviors, Naikan adds an emotional and relational dimension, encouraging patients to focus on their past actions and relationships (Muramoto, 2020). This dual approach—changing present behaviors while reflecting on past relationships—can provide a comprehensive framework for addiction recovery.

However, the silent, introspective nature of Naikan therapy can be challenging for some Western patients who are used to more interactive and dialogue-based therapies. In response, therapists have adapted Naikan by integrating guided reflection with verbal processing, offering patients the opportunity to share their reflections with their therapist during or after the self-reflection period (Reynolds, 2017).

Efficacy in Addiction Recovery

Research suggests that Naikan therapy can be particularly effective for individuals recovering from addiction, especially when combined with other therapeutic approaches. A study by Sugimoto (2015) found that patients who participated in Naikan therapy as part of their addiction recovery program showed higher rates of emotional resilience and longer periods of sobriety than those who did not. The self-reflective focus on gratitude and responsibility appeared to foster a more positive emotional state, which was crucial in helping patients maintain their recovery.

Naikan therapy's ability to address relational issues—a common area of distress for individuals with addiction—provides a powerful tool for recovery. By acknowledging the support they have received and the harm they have caused, patients can move toward a more balanced emotional state and develop healthier relational patterns that support long-term sobriety (Levine, 2020).

Morita Therapy for Mood Disorders

Morita Therapy, grounded in Zen Buddhist philosophy, has gained recognition as an effective treatment for mood disorders, particularly depression and anxiety. It focuses on teaching patients to accept their feelings without resistance while emphasizing the importance of purposeful action.

Rather than attempting to change or suppress negative emotions, Morita Therapy guides patients in learning to coexist with these emotions and refocus on constructive behavior (Morita, 1998).

Core Principles of Morita Therapy for Mood Disorders

In contrast to many Western approaches that focus on emotional regulation or cognitive restructuring, Morita Therapy encourages patients to accept uncomfortable emotions and distressing thoughts as part of the human experience. This acceptance allows patients to focus their energy on behaviors that align with their life goals and responsibilities, rather than attempting to avoid or control their feelings (LeVine, 2017).

The therapy operates on the principle that feelings are transient, and emotional fluctuations are a natural part of life. Instead of seeking to eliminate unpleasant emotions like anxiety or sadness, patients are taught to engage in purposeful work and allow their feelings to pass naturally (Kora, 2007). This approach is particularly effective in treating patients with mood disorders such as depression, where avoidance behaviors often exacerbate feelings of helplessness and hopelessness.

Efficacy of Morita Therapy in Treating Depression

Research supports the efficacy of Morita Therapy for patients with mood disorders, particularly those who struggle with avoidance behaviors. A study by Ishiyama (1990) found that patients undergoing Morita Therapy reported a significant improvement in functionality and life satisfaction even when depressive symptoms persisted. This contrasts with traditional Western approaches that focus on symptom reduction as a primary goal.

Additionally, Morita Therapy's focus on action without reliance on emotions aligns with recent findings in behavioral activation, which is recognized as an effective treatment for depression in both Eastern and Western settings (Kanter et al., 2010). The therapy's practical approach helps patients regain control over their actions and responsibilities, providing a pathway to functional improvement even in the presence of ongoing emotional distress.

Challenges in Applying Eastern Therapies in Western Settings: Differences in Cultural Expectations, Challenges in Adaptation

When Eastern psychotherapies like Naikan and Morita therapy are introduced in Western clinical settings, significant challenges arise due to differences in cultural expectations and therapeutic norms. These therapies, rooted in Japanese culture and philosophical traditions like Buddhism, emphasize self-reflection, acceptance of emotions, and a deep sense of responsibility. In contrast, Western therapeutic models often prioritize emotional regulation, cognitive restructuring, and self-expression (LeVine, 2017). The integration of these contrasting worldviews creates a set of challenges that therapists and clients must navigate.

Cultural Expectations in Therapy

One of the most prominent challenges in applying Naikan and Morita therapies in Western contexts is the difference in cultural expectations regarding emotions and their management. In Eastern philosophies, emotions are often seen as transient and uncontrollable, and the emphasis is placed on accepting them rather than trying to change them. For instance, Morita therapy teaches that individuals should not seek to eliminate anxiety or sadness, but rather learn to act despite these emotions (Kora, 2007). In contrast, Western therapies tend to emphasize the regulation and modification of emotions, using techniques like cognitive-behavioral therapy (CBT) to challenge irrational thoughts and reduce emotional distress (Beck, 2011).

This difference in how emotions are approached can be challenging for Western patients who may expect therapies to focus on alleviating distress or providing emotional insight. Morita's approach, for example, might seem counterintuitive to Western clients who are accustomed to the idea that therapy is meant to make them feel better. In Naikan therapy, where the focus is on reflecting on the impact of one's actions on others rather than discussing one's emotions directly, Western clients may feel a lack of emotional catharsis or resolution (LeVine, 2017). The introspective and non-verbal nature of Naikan also contrasts sharply with the Western expectation of dialogue and verbal expression in therapy sessions (Sugimoto, 2015).

Adaptation of Eastern Therapies in Western Settings

While Naikan and Morita therapies have seen some success in Western clinical settings, their application requires careful adaptation to meet the expectations of Western patients. One significant challenge is the difference in therapeutic goals. In Western settings, therapy often aims at symptom reduction, particularly in disorders such as anxiety and depression. The success of treatment is typically measured by a decrease in symptoms, whereas in Morita therapy, the primary goal is not the elimination of symptoms but rather the functional engagement with life despite them (Ishiyama, 1990).

To make Eastern therapies more accessible in Western contexts, some therapists have modified Morita therapy by incorporating elements of behavioral activation or mindfulness-based approaches, both of which share similarities with Morita's emphasis on action without emotional reliance. Behavioral activation, for example, encourages individuals to engage in meaningful activities regardless of their emotional state, a concept that parallels Morita's core principles (Kanter et al., 2010). This blending of approaches can help Western clients feel more aligned with the therapy's goals while preserving the essence of Morita's teachings.

Similarly, Naikan therapy has been adapted to include more verbal processing to meet the expectations of Western clients who may feel uncomfortable with prolonged silent reflection. Therapists often guide patients in discussing their reflections, which provides a space for emotional expression while still maintaining the focus on gratitude and self-responsibility (Muramoto, 2020). This adaptation makes Naikan more approachable for Western clients without losing the therapy's introspective core.

Challenges in Therapist Training and Cultural Competency

Another significant challenge in applying Naikan and Morita therapies in Western settings is the need for adequate therapist training in these Eastern modalities. Western therapists may not be familiar with the philosophical underpinnings of these therapies, such as the Buddhist concepts of impermanence and non-attachment that guide Morita therapy. Without a deep understanding of these philosophies, therapists may struggle to effectively implement the techniques or convey the therapeutic goals to their clients (LeVine, 2017).

Moreover, the success of Naikan and Morita therapies in Western settings often depends on the therapist's ability to navigate cultural differences and tailor the treatment to the individual needs of Western clients. For instance, therapists need to be culturally sensitive to the fact that Western clients may be less familiar with the concept of collectivism, which plays a central role in both Naikan and Morita therapies. These therapies emphasize the interconnectedness of relationships and the importance of one's actions on the well-being of others, whereas Western cultures often prioritize individualism and personal well-being (Reynolds, 2017).

Therapists trained in these Eastern modalities must also be prepared to address potential resistance from clients who may find the practices of silent reflection or acceptance of distressing emotions difficult or counterproductive. Without proper training and cultural competency, therapists risk misunderstanding the core principles of Naikan and Morita therapies or failing to adapt them appropriately for their Western clients (Sugimoto, 2015).

Efficacy and Future of Eastern Therapies in Western Settings

Despite these challenges, studies suggest that with proper adaptation, Naikan and Morita therapies can be highly effective in treating mood disorders and anxiety in Western clients. Research conducted by Ishiyama (1990) showed that Morita Therapy's emphasis on purposeful action rather than emotional avoidance can lead to significant improvements in patients' functionality, even when depressive symptoms persist. Similarly, Naikan therapy has been shown to improve interpersonal relationships and reduce emotional distress by fostering a sense of gratitude and responsibility (Levine, 2020).

Moving forward, the integration of Eastern psychotherapies into Western clinical settings will likely continue to grow, particularly as mental health practitioners become more aware of the value of holistic approaches that incorporate both cognitive and emotional acceptance. The challenge remains, however, in balancing cultural differences and ensuring that the core principles of these therapies are not lost in the adaptation process.

Comparative Studies and Integrated Approaches

Several studies have examined the combination of Naikan and Morita therapies, particularly for individuals with complex psychological conditions that involve both emotional distress and behavioral avoidance. A study by Uehara et al. (2020) explored the integrated use of Naikan and Morita therapies in a clinical setting, treating patients with Mixed Anxiety and Depressive Disorder (MADD). The study found that the combination of these therapies helped patients achieve both emotional clarity (through Naikan's reflective practice) and behavioral activation (through Morita's focus on action). Patients who received this combined approach showed more significant improvements compared to those who received only one type of therapy, with many reporting increased life satisfaction and a more balanced emotional outlook (Uehara et al., 2020).

Another comparative study by Miyamoto and Hashimoto (2019) focused on the integration of Naikan and Morita therapies within Western clinical settings. The study highlighted several challenges, particularly in adapting the cultural underpinnings of these therapies to Western patients. However, it also noted that patients who were open to Eastern philosophies, such as mindfulness and acceptance, responded positively to the integrated approach. The researchers found that the dual focus on self-reflection (Naikan) and purposeful action (Morita) allowed for more comprehensive treatment, particularly for patients dealing with chronic emotional distress and behavioral stagnation (Miyamoto & Hashimoto, 2019).

Future of Eastern Therapies in Global Mental Health

The landscape of mental health care is evolving, with increasing recognition of the need for diverse therapeutic approaches that cater to the unique cultural, psychological, and social needs of individuals.

Potential for Broader Acceptance

1. ***Growing Interest in Holistic Approaches:*** There is a burgeoning interest in holistic and integrative approaches to mental health that go beyond traditional Western modalities. Practitioners and researchers are increasingly recognizing the value of therapies that emphasize self-reflection, acceptance, and mindfulness.
2. ***Cultural Adaptation and Integration:*** The successful integration of Eastern therapies into Western contexts hinges on cultural adaptation. This adaptation involves modifying therapeutic techniques to resonate with clients' values and cultural backgrounds. As therapists become more skilled in cross-cultural practice, the acceptance of these Eastern modalities is likely to increase.
3. ***Research and Evidence-Based Practice:*** As the body of research supporting Naikan and Morita therapies continues to grow, evidence-based practice will play a crucial role in their acceptance. Clinical trials, meta-analyses, and systematic reviews showcasing the effectiveness of these therapies will enhance their credibility among mental health professionals.
4. ***Global Mental Health Initiatives:*** With the increasing focus on global mental health initiatives, there is a unique opportunity to incorporate Eastern therapies into mental health strategies across different countries. The World Health Organization's efforts to promote mental health interventions that are culturally appropriate can facilitate the integration of Naikan and Morita therapies in regions where such practices resonate with traditional beliefs (WHO, 2021).
5. ***Training and Education:*** The future acceptance of Naikan and Morita therapies will also depend on the training and education of mental health professionals. Integrating these therapies into psychology and counseling programs can expose students to diverse therapeutic approaches, equipping them with the skills to apply them effectively in practice.

The Role of Introspection in Healing

1. **Self-Discovery and Understanding:** Introspection, or self-reflection, is a foundational aspect of both Naikan and Morita therapies. By encouraging individuals to engage in deep self-examination, these therapies promote self-discovery, enabling patients to gain insights into their thoughts, feelings, and behaviors. This process allows individuals to understand the roots of their suffering and cultivate a greater sense of self-awareness.

2. **Empathy and Compassion:** Naikan therapy, in particular, fosters empathy and compassion towards oneself and others through structured reflection on one's relationships. This process often involves acknowledging the contributions of others and recognizing the impact of one's actions. Such reflections can facilitate forgiveness, both of oneself and others, which is essential for emotional healing.
3. **Enhanced Coping Mechanisms:** Introspective practices empower individuals to develop better coping strategies. By identifying negative thought patterns and understanding their origins, patients can work towards replacing maladaptive behaviors with healthier alternatives.

The Importance of Acceptance in Mental Health

4. **Reducing Resistance to Emotions:** Acceptance is a core principle of both Naikan and Morita therapies. By encouraging individuals to accept their thoughts and feelings without judgment, these therapies reduce resistance to difficult emotions. This acceptance fosters a non-reactive stance towards distressing experiences, enabling individuals to process their emotions more effectively.
5. **Promoting Psychological Flexibility:** Acceptance facilitates psychological flexibility, which is the ability to adapt one's thoughts and behaviors in response to changing circumstances. Morita therapy emphasizes the importance of accepting one's feelings and engaging in meaningful activities regardless of emotional states. This perspective encourages individuals to move forward in life, even in the face of discomfort, fostering a proactive approach to mental health.
6. **Cultivating Mindfulness:** Acceptance is closely linked to mindfulness, a practice that involves being present and fully engaged in the moment. Both Naikan and Morita therapies promote mindfulness through introspective reflection and acceptance of one's current state.

Relevance in Today's Mental Health Landscape

In today's mental health landscape, where individuals often grapple with stress, anxiety, and existential concerns, the principles of introspection and acceptance offer valuable tools for healing. Naikan and Morita therapies provide frameworks that encourage individuals to look inward, understand their emotions, and accept their experiences without judgment. As mental health professionals increasingly recognize the importance of holistic approaches, the relevance of these therapies will continue to grow.

Moreover, the ongoing integration of Eastern therapeutic practices into Western contexts highlights the global shift towards embracing diverse healing modalities. This integration fosters a more inclusive understanding of mental health, allowing for personalized and culturally sensitive approaches to therapy.

Conclusion

In this chapter, we have explored the intricate and transformative nature of Naikan and Morita therapies, two significant Eastern psychotherapeutic approaches rooted in profound philosophical principles and cultural traditions.

As we have seen, Naikan therapy's emphasis on introspection, gratitude, and interpersonal relationships encourages individuals to cultivate a deeper awareness of their thoughts, emotions, and behaviors. This therapeutic modality empowers clients to recognize their connections to others, facilitating a shift towards greater emotional resilience and well-being. Similarly, Morita therapy's focus on acceptance, commitment, and engagement with life despite discomfort allows individuals to embrace their experiences fully, fostering a sense of agency and purpose.

The integration of these Eastern psychotherapies into Western mental health practices presents exciting opportunities for expanding the therapeutic landscape. By recognizing and addressing the unique needs of clients through an integrative approach, practitioners can harness the strengths of both Eastern and Western methodologies.

Looking ahead, the future of Naikan and Morita therapies lies in continued research, adaptation, and collaboration. By fostering an environment of inquiry and exploration, mental health professionals can contribute to a more nuanced understanding of these therapies, ultimately enhancing their efficacy and accessibility.

In conclusion, Naikan and Morita therapies offer valuable insights and techniques that can significantly enhance the practice of psychotherapy. By continuing to explore, integrate, and innovate within this rich tradition, we can pave the way for a more inclusive and effective mental health care system that honors the diverse pathways to healing and growth.

References

Beck, A. T. (2011). *Cognitive therapy of depression*. Guilford Press.

Beck, A. T., Rush, A. J., Shaw, B. F., & Emery, G. (1979). *Cognitive therapy of depression*. Guilford Press.

Cheng, H. (2021). The importance of holistic approaches in mental health care: A global perspective. *Journal of Integrative Medicine*, 19(3), 199-205.

Crane, R. S., Kuyken, W., Williams, J. M., Hastings, R. P., Cooper, L., & Fennell, M. J. (2014). Competence in teaching mindfulness-based courses: Concepts, development and assessment. *Mindfulness*, 3(1), 76-84.

Dimidjian, S., Barrera, M., Martell, C., Muñoz, R. F., & Lewinsohn, P. M. (2011). The origins and current status of behavioral activation treatments for depression. *Annual Review of Clinical Psychology*, 7(1), 1-38.

Hara, T., & Sato, M. (2020). The role of acceptance in psychological well-being: Implications for therapy. *Journal of Counseling Psychology*, 67(2), 159-171.

Hayes, S. C., Strosahl, K. D., & Wilson, K. G. (1999). *Acceptance and commitment therapy: An experiential approach to behavior change*. Guilford Press.

Ishii, M., Yamaguchi, S., & Okada, K. (2013). The effectiveness of Naikan therapy in reducing rumination and self-blame in depressive patients. *Journal of Asian Psychotherapy*, 14(2), 89-102.

Ishikawa, Y. (2015). The role of Naikan Therapy in contemporary family and relationship counseling. *Journal of Asian Psychotherapy*, 41(3), 45-60.

Ishiyama, F. I. (1990). Morita therapy and the process of constructive living. *Journal of Counseling & Development*, 68(4), 402-407.

Ishiyama, I. (2019). Nature as a therapeutic agent: Morita therapy and Japanese culture. *Journal of Japanese Psychological Studies*, 27(2), 85-102.

Ishiyama, I. F. (1986). Morita therapy: A psychotherapeutic system for neurosis. *Psychotherapy: Theory, Research, Practice, Training*, 23(4), 575-582.

Kabat-Zinn, J. (1990). *Full catastrophe living: Using the wisdom of your body and mind to face stress, pain, and illness*. Delta.

Kabat-Zinn, J. (2003). Mindfulness-based interventions in context: Past, present, and future. *Clinical Psychology: Science and Practice*, 10(2), 144-156. https://doi.org/10.1093/clipsy/bpg016

Kabat-Zinn, J. (2013). *Full catastrophe living: Using the wisdom of your body and mind to face stress, pain, and illness*. Bantam Books.

Kanter, J. W., Puspitasari, A. J., Santos, M. M., & Nagy, G. A. (2010). Behavioral activation: History, evidence, and promise. *The Behavior Analyst*, 33(2), 279–299.

Kanter, J. W., Puspitasari, A. J., Santos, M. M., & Nagy, G. A. (2010). Behavioral activation: History, evidence, and promise. *The Behavior Analyst*, 33(2), 279–299.

Kawai, H. (2005). *Buddhism and psychotherapy*. University of Tokyo Press.

Kawai, H. (2016). Eastern Psychotherapy: Insights from Japanese Traditions. *Journal of Cross-Cultural Psychology*, 47(8), 1-17. https://doi.org/10.1177/0022022116669057

Kawai, H. (2016). Eastern Psychotherapy: Insights from Japanese Traditions. *Journal of Cross-Cultural Psychology*, 47(8), 1-17. https://doi.org/10.1177/0022022116669057

Kawai, H. (2016). Eastern Psychotherapy: Insights from Japanese Traditions. *Journal of Cross-Cultural Psychology*, 47(8), 1-17. https://doi.org/10.1177/0022022116669057

Kawakami, M. (2018). The role of cultural values in Naikan and Morita therapies. *International Journal of Eastern Psychology*, 32(1), 45-60.

Kawasaki, K., & Kato, T. (2018). The impact of introspection on emotional regulation: A review of literature. *Psychological Reports*, 121(5), 849-865.

Kirmayer, L. J. (2007). Psychotherapy and the cultural concept of the person. *Transcultural Psychiatry*, 44(2), 232-257. https://doi.org/10.1177/1363461507077717

Kirmayer, L. J. (2007). Psychotherapy and the cultural concept of the person. *Transcultural Psychiatry*, 44(2), 232-257. https://doi.org/10.1177/1363461507077717

Kitanishi, K. (2018). Morita therapy: Accepting emotions and finding meaning through action. *Asian Journal of Psychiatry*, 36, 50-57. https://doi.org/10.1016/j.ajp.2018.08.010

Kitanishi, K., & Kondo, M. (2017). Morita Therapy in Japan and its adaptation in Western countries. *Journal of Psychotherapy Integration*, 27(3), 307-320. https://doi.org/10.1037/int0000058

Kitanishi, K., & Mori, T. (2016). The development of Naikan therapy in the context of Japanese culture. *Asian Journal of Psychiatry*, 20(4), 76-82. https://doi.org/10.1016/j.ajp.2016.01.004

Kondo, Y., & Kurosawa, H. (2018). Morita therapy: Clinical applications in modern psychological practice. *Journal of Japanese Psychotherapy*, 53(2), 22-34.

Kora, T. (2007). Understanding the principles of Morita therapy: A guide for therapists. *Asian Journal of Psychotherapy*, 19(3), 123-138

Kora, T. (2015). A historical review of Morita Therapy and its application in modern clinical settings. *Journal of Japanese Psychosomatic Medicine*, 55(3), 143-151.

Kora, T., & Tanaka, Y. (2017). A randomized controlled trial comparing Morita therapy and CBT for depression and avoidance. *Journal of Clinical Psychology*, 26(5), 279-292.

Levine, A. (2020). The principles and practices of Morita therapy. *International Journal of Psychotherapy*, 25(2), 19-30.

Levine, A. (2020). The role of Naikan in addiction recovery: A case study approach. *Journal of Eastern Psychotherapy*, 27(2), 142-155.

Levine, M. (2020). Eastern psychotherapeutic approaches and their integration into Western practices. *International Journal of Clinical Practice*, 74(4), e13479. https://doi.org/10.1111/ijcp.13479

LeVine, P. (2017). Morita therapy in the treatment of depression: Acceptance, action, and purpose. *International Journal of Eastern and Cross-Cultural Psychology*, 35(2), 199-213.

Miyamoto, S., & Hashimoto, T. (2019). The integration of Naikan and Morita therapy in Western clinical settings: Challenges and potential. *International Journal of Cross-Cultural Psychology*, 30(3), 122-135.

Miyamoto, S., & Hashimoto, T. (2019). The integration of Naikan and Morita therapy in Western clinical settings: Challenges and potential. *International Journal of Cross-Cultural Psychology*, 30(3), 122-135.

Morita, S. (1928). *Morita therapy: A Japanese psychotherapeutic method*. Shinchosha.

Morita, S. (1998). *Morita therapy and the nature of anxiety-based disorders (Shinkeishitsu)*. State University of New York Press.

Morita, S., Harada, M., & Yamamoto, R. (2018). The effectiveness of Morita therapy in treating psychosomatic disorders: A longitudinal study. *Journal of Somatic Therapy*, 10(1), 35-47.

Muramoto, Y. (2020). Silence in Japanese culture: Implications for psychotherapy. *Journal of Eastern Therapy Practices*, 16(4), 101-118.

Muramoto, Y. (2020). Silence in Japanese culture: Implications for psychotherapy. *Journal of Eastern Therapy Practices*, 16(4), 101-118.

Muramoto, Y. (2020). The integration of Naikan therapy in Western clinical practices: Challenges and successes. *International Journal of Cross-Cultural Psychology*, 43(1), 112-128.

Muramoto, Y. (2020). The integration of Naikan therapy in Western clinical practices: Challenges and successes. *International Journal of Cross-Cultural Psychology*, 43(1), 112-128.

Nakamura, T., Uehara, S., & Fujita, H. (2020). Empathy and mental health: A study on the effects of Naikan therapy. *Japanese Journal of Psychotherapy*, 29(1), 45-58.

Noda, A. (2016). Morita therapy for anxiety disorders: A meta-analysis. *Journal of Psychotherapy Research*, 22(4), 423-435.

Pope, K. S., Smith, R. L., & Holroyd, K. (2022). Cultural competence in psychotherapy training: An overview of the current state and future directions. *Journal of Counseling Psychology*, 69(1), 12-25.

Rao, K. R., & Paranjpe, A. C. (2016). *Psychology in the Indian tradition*. Springer.Reynolds, D. K. (2017). *Morita therapy: A practical guide to acceptance and purposeful living*. University of Hawaii Press.

Reynolds, D. K. (2017). *Naikan therapy and the healing power of introspection*. University of Hawaii Press.

Reynolds, W. (2017). Exploring the use of Naikan therapy in addiction rehabilitation: Gratitude and responsibility. *Journal of Addiction Therapy*, 11(4), 78-89.

Seligman, M. E. (2011). *Flourish: A new understanding of happiness and well-being—and how to achieve them*. Free Press.

Shirahase, K. (2014). Naikan therapy in addiction rehabilitation: A study of motivation for change. *Asian Journal of Psychotherapy*, 15(3), 145-159.

Sugimoto, H., & Green, P. (2019). Applications of Eastern psychotherapeutic principles in corporate wellness programs. *Mindfulness & Wellbeing Journal*, 29(1), 91-103.

Sugimoto, T. (2015). Gratitude and Responsibility: The Core of Naikan Therapy. *International Journal of Therapy and Counseling*, 9(2), 121-133.

Sugimoto, T. (2015). Long-term effects of Naikan therapy on emotional regulation in patients with borderline personality disorder. *Journal of Japanese Psychology*, 21(1), 67-79.

Sugimoto, T. (2015). Naikan therapy and its clinical applications in addiction treatment. *Asian Journal of Psychotherapy*, 19(3), 98-109.

Suzuki, T. (2000). Zen and Morita therapy: The philosophical underpinnings of acceptance and action. *Eastern Philosophy Journal*, 38(3), 101-113.

Tanaka, Y., Matsumoto, K., & Nishida, K. (2019). Coping mechanisms and their relation to self-reflection in therapy. *International Journal of Psychology*, 54(4), 553-561.

Uehara, S., Fujita, H., & Nakamura, T. (2020). Integrated approach using Naikan and Morita therapy in treating mixed anxiety and depressive disorder. *Japanese Journal of Psychotherapy*, 29(2), 202-217.

Uehara, S., Fujita, H., & Nakamura, T. (2020). Integrated approach using Naikan and Morita therapy in treating mixed anxiety and depressive disorder. *Japanese Journal of Psychotherapy*, 29(2), 202-217.

Wood, A. M., Froh, J. J., & Geraghty, A. W. (2010). Gratitude and well-being: A review and theoretical integration. *Clinical Psychology Review*, 30(7), 890-905. https://doi.org/10.1016/j.cpr.2010.03.005

World Health Organization. (2021). Global mental health: Strengthening our response. Retrieved from https://www.who.int/

Yoshida, Y., Takahashi, K., & Yamamoto, S. (2021). Psychological flexibility and its relation to mental health: A review of empirical studies. *Psychological Science*, 32(3), 301-312.

Chapter 12

Naikan Therapy

Rudranshi Bhati School of Liberal Studies (SLS), CMR University, Bangalore

Introduction

The Eastern approach towards psychology has long been generating insights that transcend conventional western understanding of mental health to focus on the holistic integration of mind, body, and spirit. Generally, this approach fosters introspection, interdependence, and the growing sense of empathy. Developed in Japan during the 1940s by Yoshimoto Ishin, Naikan was based on principles of Jōdo Shinshū Buddhism in the attempt to help people introspect over their past encounters and learn from them. In fact, the word "Naikan" literally means "inner looking," emphasising intense, structured self-examination.

The guiding questions for this therapy are: "What have I received from others?" "What have I given to others?", and "What troubles and difficulties have I caused?

Tonglen" which in Tibetan means "giving and taking," is a Tibetan Buddhism practice, notably attributed to Lojong mind training. They inhale into their suffering the suffering of others, or their own, and exhale relief, compassion, and kindness. This process concretizes the Buddhist ideals of service for the self and connection to others, making one's own suffering a spark of compassion and love. The combination of **Naikan** and **Tonglen** therapy offers a holistic approach that not only prompts the individual to reflect on his past but also inspires him to engage with the present in a compassionate, proactive manner. When the individual acknowledges his actions through Naikan and then applies the method of Tonglen's exchange of suffering for kindness, he cultivates both retrospective and forward-looking thinking.

This integrated approach develops the emotional sense and resilience by equipping one with the ability to address existing and future emotional obstacles. Integrating the Naikan with the Tonglen will thus meet both the reflection and expression components of psychological development.Naikan encourages people to actually and sometimes painfully audit their relationships or choices in life, which enables people to grow gratitude and responsibility.

Meanwhile, Tonglen takes the fruit of Naikan awareness in becoming compassionate action. For example, a man who gained from Naikan that he accepted more than he gave could practise Tonglen by contemplating relieving the suffering of those whom they may have influenced, thus further developing a cycle of compassion and self-change. The appeal of such Eastern practices has grown, as people seek holistic and sustainable ways to manage stress, emotional difficulties, and complexities in life. While there have been great strides for Western psychology in cognitive-behavioural methods and psychodynamic theories, it does sometimes forget the benefits that can be achieved by meditative and introspective practice, focusing on emotional interconnectedness. The two are Naikan and Tonglen.

Given by Whom and the Country of Origin

Originators and key players of Naikan Therapy Naikan therapy was created in Japan in the early 1940s by a man named Yoshimoto Ishin(1916–1988). Its originator was born into a poverty-stricken family and, consequently, was nurtured within the context of the Jōdo Shinshū sect of Buddhism, which centres on human interdependence and gratitude as means to enlightenment.The concept behind Naikan therapy was taken from the Mishirabe, a type of strict self-reflection practice monks would undergo for purification of the spirit.

Yoshimoto translated the Mishirabe into an understandable form to assist, other than religion followers, the common public in developing self-reflection for their growth.

Yoshimoto "wanted to enable people to realise that the giving and the payback were equally important and that the payback was something the person receiving support depended upon throughout his or her life." He then developed Naikan as a self-guided introspective exercise, framed around three big questions that would stir deep reflection and advocate for emotional balance:

1. What have I received from others?
2. What have I given to others?
3. What problems and pains have I caused others?

These questions were to be faced with the unattended graciousness of others and make the individual responsible for the wrongdoing of their deeds that bring bad effects. Naikan therapy eventually gained exposure outside of their religious and spiritual domain. It was adapted to be used within prisons and rehabilitation centres in Japan to help individuals shift their focus from being self-centred whining to becoming aware of support and community.

Yoshimoto's dedication to the expansion of Naikan is very well seen in the development of Naikan centres and retreats under which people would spend days in deep reflection. Years-on years since their creation, these retreats have been arguably surprisingly successful in aspects related to gratitude, relationships, and sentiments of resentment. Because of its affinity with the deeply held Japanese values of humility, respect for others, and the harmony of community, the message of Naikan came as something culturally relevant to improve personal and collective well-being.

Tonglengen: Origins and famous teachers were like the Naikan is about systematic introspection, Tonglen is a meditation that pushes mindfulness further to become compassionate action. The origins of Tonglen trace back to **Tibetan Buddhism** through Atisha Dipankara Shrijnana (980–1054 AD), a prominent Buddhist scholar and teacher directed his teachings towards cultivating **Bodhicitta**, the awakened mind that strives for the welfare of all sentient beings.This practice became the heartbeat in seeking this practice: tonglen has a method for practitioners to transform their suffering and empathise with compassion by exchanging self-focus for compassion.

Tonglen is the practice of imagining and visualising breathing in the suffering of others or personal pain and breathing out relief and compassion. This visualisation and breathing process counters the innate tendency to protect oneself from discomfort and pain.

Tsong Khapa's practice of tonglen, actively participating in suffering and letting compassionate feelings out, deepens empathy and builds emotional resilience. The 8th-century Buddhist master Shantideva practised in his seminal work, The Way of the Bodhisattva, that compassion and altruism are necessary for spiritual development.

Prominent Modern Teachers: One of the most well-known leaders who brought Tonglen to the international centre is an American Buddhist nun and disciple of Chögyam Trungpa Rinpoche Pema Chödrön. Her teachings and books, like *When Things Fall Apart*, and *The Places That Scare You*, presented her enlightenment in the form of practice by incorporating Tonglen into the everyday contexts. Pema Chödrön's work emphasised how Tonglen can help people respond to challenges with an open heart and strengthen their ability to face personal and collective suffering.

Integration with Modern Psychology

Naikan Therapy and Contemporary Practice

Naikan therapy has been popularised and spread from its roots in the religious and cultural practices of Japan into other contemporary therapeutic contexts around the world. Its foundational features of self-reflection, gratitude, and personal responsibility resonate well with contemporary psychological practice, allowing for mindfulness, cognitive restructuring, and emotional regulation.

Especially good practices in correction and rehabilitation areas, Naikan has revealed its strong side. Encouraging such people in the understanding that they could have influenced so many through their negative thinking and therefore should show great appreciation and gratitude toward many who showed them kindness over the course of their lives also helps cultivate empathy in this practice. Therapists have discovered that leading those inmates in recovery through a series of structured questions to Naikan improves their changes in behaviours, minimises recidivism rates among participants, and even results in renewed personal responsibility by the recipients.

Naikan Retreats: There are traditional retreats held in Japan and then modified retreats that happen in the West. For these retreats, usually several days are involved where individuals are placed under high silent introspection. These are usually overseen by a qualified therapist or Naikan practitioner. Experience-that can take someone deep into their past and relationships -has a great insight leading to a significant shift in emotions and cognition. Participants often comment on feeling greater peace, resentment reduction, and appreciation for people who helped them through life.

Integrative Psychological Practices: Naikan can be integrated in contemporary clinical psychology with the following practices: cognitive-behavioural therapy, encouraging examination of distorted thoughts and challenging to alter them; and mindfulness-based stress reduction, which focuses on present-moment awareness, like the call of Naikan to reflect mindfully on life's interactions.

Tonglen in Therapeutic and Clinical Use

Tonglen meditation, which originated from Tibetan Buddhism, has been widely used in therapeutic and counselling applications, especially in trauma therapy and emotional resilience programs.

Trauma Therapy: Tonglen's approach, in which pain is to be included rather than avoided, is highly fruitful in trauma work where avoidance and repression can be in itself very painful. During the practice of Tonglen as a therapist, the client is guided by the visualisation practice to breathe in their pain or others' suffering and exhale compassion and relief; this practice may even treat trauma with some grace, thereby lessening the impact of shame and guilt.

Mindfulness and Compassion Training: Tonglen has been incorporated into mindfulness-based interventions and compassion-focused therapy. Practitioners in these applications use Tonglen to train clients in developing a compassionate stance toward their own pain and the suffering of others. The practice enhances emotional resilience by shifting the focus from self-criticism and avoidance to acceptance and empathetic action. Drawing from practices such as Tonglen, Paul Gilbert's Compassion-Focused Therapy (CFT) based on building compassion as the fight against shame and self-criticism may serve as just an example of efforts deepened within the therapeutic outcome.

Health and Palliative Care: The outward flow of compassion, as found in Tonglen, can be applied in health care, specifically to caregivers and palliative care workers who suffer emotional burnout. Practitioners of Tonglen could cultivate empathy for themselves as well as their patients while holding onto emotional balance. The act of visualising the inflow of suffering and outflow of compassion may serve caregivers in managing their own stress and keeping purpose and fulfilment in their work.

It can also be practised in the group therapy context, such as people all breathing together in the shared suffering but breathing out the relief so that people do not find themselves in this isolation because everyone, again healing is both personal and common. It was used also in places like grief counselling to disaster recovery communities, particularly where collective response is fundamental to emotional healing.

Synergy of Naikan and Tonglen in Modern Therapeutics

Combining the structure of Naikan's self-reflection with the practice of Tonglen's active compassion brings together a powerful tool kit for emotional and psychological growth. While Naikan will allow the individual to critique and gratefully consider the relationships and past actions involved, Tonglen asks him or her to respond with a compassionate heart to these reflections. This approach helps clients not only process and accept their past but also develop proactive ways to change emotional pain into positive energy.

Case Applications: For instance, individuals who have problems in their family relationships can utilise Naikan to reflect upon what their parents or spouses had sacrificed for them. This reflection would possibly evoke feelings of guilt or sadness, which would be processed using Tonglen to transform these emotions into compassionate intentions to mend relationships. Similarly, those who are suffering from loss or grief can do Tonglen so that they can feel a connection with others who have the same pain, which otherwise would leave them feeling isolated with their suffering.

Applications of Naikan Therapy

Addiction Recovery

Naikan therapy has earned its share of other therapies aimed at eradicating additions like drug abuse using Japan-based rehabilitation centers, which incorporated substance use disorder into their programmes for the affected patients. The backbone therapeutic intervention in Naikan is self-reflection wherein a client examines ways of life and realizes ways those habits hurt other individuals through substances abused.

Literature Evidence: In Ishii et al. (2012) it demonstrated how Naikan therapy can be applied in Japanese rehabilitation settings for recovering addicts. Through Naikan therapy, authors found that there was a statistically significant decrease in the percentage of individuals who experienced a relapse because individuals learned to face the emotional impacts on family members and close relatives whom their addiction has affected. Creating a sense of empathy and responsibility made people socialised into becoming responsible individuals who remained more in recovery for the long run.

Application in Practice: For instance, a recovering alcoholic contemplating the pain he caused his loved ones may experience a sense of emotional responsibility because, once he realises the emotional toll that his addiction has taken on others, he will want to stay sober.

Challenges: Even though Naikan is effective, it can evoke some pretty agonising emotions such as guilt, regret, or shame that may be too painful for some recovering addicts. For example, a person who has alienated loved ones due to addiction might find it difficult to cope with intense self-blame.

Family and Relationship Therapy

The value of Naikan therapy has been found in the use of it for family therapy and relationship counselling with long-standing conflict, miscommunication, or emotional distance.

Literature-Based Research: In Maruyama et al. (2014), Naikan therapy was used in couple's family therapy for clients in communication breakdown and emotional estrangement. The result showed that the use of Naikan led to significantly high relationship satisfaction as both the partners were encouraged to reflect on their **mutual sacrifices** and shared emotional labour in the relationship. Such a shift in perspective enhances empathy and increases emotional intimacy while decreasing blaming.

Application in Practice: Reflective questions of Naikan assist family members to understand what the other person received due to their actions and how that affected the other. A couple in therapy may be able to use Naikan to explore the contributions each partner made to a sequence of unresolved conflicts. Understanding each's sacrifices can lead to appreciation and better communication.

Challenges: For couples with deep-seated resentment or unresolved emotional issues, Naikan may bring more tension to the surface. The practice demands a certain level of emotional maturity, and some may feel vulnerable or defensive as they work through the process.

Mental Health and Emotional Wellness

Naikan therapy is also in use as treatment of mental health disorders like depression, anxiety, and stress illnesses. Naikan therapy can help find the meanings of life because it keeps emphasis on things that make men grateful and appreciative, keeping away from negative thoughts about defeatism.

Evidence: There is evidence from Kato et al. (2006) that Naikan therapy resulted in significant symptoms reduction of depression among the participants subjected to reflective practice. As the authors point out, Naikan's approach that emphasises gratitude and self-responsibility was conducive to enhanced mood, emotional regulation, and mental well-being.

Application in Practice: With depressed patients, Naikan shifts their line of thought away from what is missing or is wrong in their life towards what they have received and to whom they have been able to give. This could be the way by which a depressed patient employs Naikan to think on how he or she receives much love and support in her family, and hence appreciate that there is something he or she is worth with.

Challenges: An individual who is depressed or suffers from anxiety may find Naikan hard to cope with since, at times, the therapy may force people to confront some uncomfortable truth regarding their relationships. A severely mentally ill person would be treated through Naikan therapy with the support of other therapy interventions, such as CBT and medication.

Cognitive and Behavioral Change

Naikan therapy enables cognitive restructuring by moving the individual from a centred self-view to a worldview of mutual interconnectedness, thus leading to behavioural change and an increase in self-awareness.

Scientific Research: The study by Sakai et al. (2015) showed that those Naikan practitioners had experienced much decreased impulsivity, improved decision-making. Reflexive action and its outcome, in this case - about others affected by said action, evokes conduct of more aware human behaviour being responsibly conscious about any actions undertaken and decisions.

Application in Practice: Where clients may receive a sense of the impact created by their impulsive acts on others through structured reflection in Naikan. For example, one with an impulsive spending habit may learn through the method about the pain and worry that his inability to handle finances aptly has caused to his family, prompting him towards more controlled actions resulting in responsible behaviours.

Problems: The major drawback of using Naikan to affect behaviour change is that reflection may take time to come out in the behavioural realm. Clients need to be supported continuously in integrating reflections into action in daily life, and a few people may not accept the emotional vulnerability that Naikan demands.

Challenges of Naikan Therapy

Cultural Adaptation

Naikan is steeped in Japanese cultural values of humility, interdependence, and gratitude. The principles of Naikan, which emphasise selflessness and the interconnectedness of all individuals, are not always compatible with more individualistic cultures, such as those found in Western countries.

Question: The Western clients, who are normally enlightened to concern themselves about their personal rights and freedoms and self expression, are likely to be surprised or even downright opposed to Naikan's approach of tackling the theme of humility and collective responsibility.

Research Insight: As commented by Maruyama et al. (2014), there should be a cultural adaptation in case of Naikan application outside of Japan because " the concept of selflessness might be too abstract in today's world ". Instead of being abstract and philosophical about values, this form of therapy should have more attention paid to the therapeutic value of introspection about a more significant relationship being constructed through better relationships.

Solution: Therapists should work from the universal benefits that derive from Naikan, namely emotional regulation, better relationship building, and resilience development. Labelling Naikan as a practice to foster personal well-being rather than as self-sacrifice can make the practice accessible to clients of different cultures.

Emotional Overload and Vulnerability

Naikan practice can also evoke strong emotional responses. For those who have experienced experiences of trauma, abuse, or disastrous relationships, recalling painful memories or even guilt/ shame might overwhelm them emotionally.

Problem: The self-reflection of Naikan therapy is so intense that individuals may get into an emotional turmoil that worsens their psychological condition. This is more so for those with deeper traumas because confrontation of past actions can be very evocative of shame, guilt, or self-blame.

Research Insight: According to Sakai et al. (2015), Naikan may be too intense for clients who have not developed adequate emotional coping strategies, especially when they have underlying trauma. The gradual integration of reflective practices combined with supportive therapy is required to ensure emotional safety.

Mitigation Strategy: To reduce this threat, therapists should create a safe environment for the processing of such intense emotions among their clients. Naikan combined with other therapies like trauma-focused therapy or mindfulness techniques will help in managing emotional stress from the process of reflection.

Time and Commitment

Naikan is intensive therapy and time and emotional involvement consuming. The process often may require long periods of introspection, sometimes lasting for days or even weeks that are impossible for busy people to accomplish.

Problem: Individuals may feel they don't have time or are unable in a chaotic, highly advanced world and therefore do not have the time needed for the lengthy process of Naikan.

Research Understanding: As noticed by authors of Kato et al. (2006) the long-term involvement of Naikan therapy may put a limitation on its accessibility and participation by individuals who often do not have sufficient space or time in their agenda for reflection.

Alternative: Naikan process may be integrated into daily lifestyles through a process of making brief reflective periods and a series of short practice sessions. This could mean journaling or meditation on a weekly basis for the experience of Naikan rather than a one-week, all-out retreat.

Can't Notice the Results Promptly

Naikan is a process-oriented therapy that stresses the long term rather than immediate returns. For this reason, frustration on the side of clients may be involved, especially if they are not given immediate relief from emotional concerns or behavioural changes.

Challenge: This slower pace can be used as a means of frustrating the impatient client who believes in cure and quick remedies for emotional and behavioural ills. In this manner, they may be dissuaded from making deeper commitments toward treatment.

Discovery: Based on the study of Ishii et al. (2012), clients feel a little uneasy or irritated before the beneficial changes can be observed. It requires a lot of time and effort to wait patiently.

Solution: The process should be initiated by giving practical expectations in the beginning. This therapeutic technique takes time and should be clarified to the clients to keep them in the process and adjust their expectations.

Case Studies

Case study 1:

Case Study 1 elucidates his treatment cycle from Naikan therapy regarding cure to addiction with stages experienced along the course and even valuable conclusions he took home during these transformation stages. His drug use had begun when he was around 22 years old as a coping mechanism for work pressures and eventually continued until he became addicted where it was becoming the focal point over everything else in his life. Hiroshi had been in and out of rehab quite a few times without much success and with each relapse, the shame and guilt continued to mount. He cut himself away from the family, his wife, Yuki, and two children, 10 and 13 years old. Mrs. Yuki was at the edge of divorce. His children vividly showed signs of emotional withdrawal. His wife issued him an ultimatum, so he agreed to undergo Naikan therapy at a special centre though he was sceptical about it.

Therapeutic Setting

The Naikan retreat centre was situated in a quiet, rural part of Japan far removed from the turmoil of city life. The place operates under very strict principles: participants have to be silent as much as possible, hold the barest contact with people, and most of their time is usually spent doing reflection in solitude. Everyone would stay in a small private room containing minimal furniture so as not to disturb them. The empty, yet tidy environment was designed to foster intense self-reflection and caring about the three driving questions of the therapy:

1. What did I receive from others?
2. What did I give to others?
3. What trouble or difficulty have I caused others?

Naikan Process of Reflection

This orientational session was guided by a therapist; she told three questions he needed to ponder over three days. Hiroshi is oriented for different time spans of his life remembering about relationships and activities engaged between him and his wife and children and parents. Throughout this time, he will provide answers to the three questions consecutively for hours.

Day 1-2: Initial Resistance and Frustration

He was quite opposed to the practice for a time. His experience of his family had been abandonment, so he resented the idea of focusing on other people. He could hardly even make a list of incidents when he had received something or given something, much less felt a sense of resonance about the process. As the hours passed him sitting in quiet stillness, his memories began to deepen. He remembered specific incidents of generosity Yuki had extended to him, including financial support and personally assuming care for the children when he was out for many periods. Though it pained him to learn this, it was somewhat surprising that he never consciously acknowledged such a pattern of behaviour during his active period of addiction.

Day 3-4: Coming to Terms with the Results of his Actions

In reflection, Hiroshi's third day proved to be more intense because he focused his thoughts on what he had given to others.

He could not pinpoint ways he had assisted his family. He was conscious of the fact that he rarely found himself available for them. This took him to the third question, "What difficulties have I caused others? "He recalls how he missed his children's birthdays, argued with his wife when drunk, and neglected the needs of his children. Every memory got him to face the repercussions of his activities and pain he had caused his loved ones.

Day 5: Feeling Remorse and Guilt

On the fifth day, Hiroshi was overwhelmed with emotions.

He confessed to the therapist feelings of guilt and remorse and deep sorrow. These were emotions that had always been simmering below but were covered up with his drinking. Now, bereft of his defences, Hiroshi was faced unblinkered with his history. He thought through hours of the times that his children pleaded for his time, which he pushed aside. The feeling of defeat as a father and husband was both painful and a landmark moment: Hiroshi felt the urge to transform himself, not to flee punishment but to regain what he had lost.

Day 6-7: From Guilt to Gratitude and Responsiveness

At this point, Hiroshi's introspection began to change and shift as he neared the end of the retreat. Through the process, he came out of self-pity and finally realised how consistently his family had supported him despite all his offences .He began to feel gratitude toward his wife for her forbearance, toward his children for their continued love, and even toward financial and emotional support his parents had shown to him. This became a new motivation: instead of focusing on his shame, he devoted himself to giving back to those who had stayed by him. He compiled a list of ways he intended to express his appreciation and make amends upon his return to his hometown. Outcome and Impact The weeklong Naikan retreat left Hiroshi with a profound emotional transformation. Instead, he perceived himself as a person who has options, able to be thankful and take good directions.When he reached home, he started by telling his wife and children from the bottom of his heart how sorry he was to them, the pain he had caused them, and all the things he vowed to do to help them move on.

Instead of grand gestures, Hiroshi continued with small, steady actions: cooking meals, helping with chores, and spending time with his family. Over time, he remarked that his relationship with his family had improved, and he found himself feeling less need to drink; he had found something new to give life purpose and meaning. The Naikan therapy that Hiroshi undertook provided him the opening to reflect from a relational vantage point on his life so he could see the behaviours that he was entwined within a bigger context: family support versus responsibility. Rather than asking himself the "why" of the addiction, where he felt completely helpless, the questions of the "what" and "how" took him down a tangible path to responsibility and gratitude.

Case Study 2: An extension of Naikan therapy in the context of family reconciliation, particularly concerning adolescent problems in behaviour.

Case Summary

Taro is a 16-year-old high school student residing in Tokyo, who has gradually become distant to his family for the past couple of years. His parents were worried because he was often absent from school, showed defiant behaviours at every turn, and did not show much respect for his parents. Keiko and Satoshi tried counselling and strict discipline with Taro, but it seemed like everything they did was having the opposite effect. Taro felt as if no one was listening; his parents felt drained and resentful. A family therapist recommended Naikan therapy, explaining that the reflective approach could offer them a way to rebuild empathy and understanding. Taking this in slowly, the family agreed to a modified Naikan program whereby both Taro and his parents participated.

Therapeutic Setting

The family participated in a one-week Naikan retreat designed specifically for the dynamics of a family. The structured, silent setting required each member of the family to reflect separately alone, but very different from their typical use of argumentative rhetoric and emotional breakdowns. The family therapist was one who had worked with families previously and kept each member focused on answering three questions:

1. What have I received from others?
2. What have I given to others?
3. What have I caused others to suffer or inconvenience?

Each member was then asked to reflect on specific memories that were related to his relationships with other members.

Naikan Reflective Process

The Naikan program divided the family for reflection hours to eliminate distractions and deepen contemplation. Week in, week out, the family gradually progressed into the three Naikan questions for each other, which unfolded layers of unacknowledged emotions and overlooked supportive acts.

Days 1-2: First Resistance, Initial Awareness

Taro initially found it hard, describing the questions as superficial and not liking the notion of self-reflection. For years, he justified his behaviour and concentrated on his complaints about his parents, mainly feeling misunderstood and dominated. But as Taro was assured to dwell exclusively on remembering times when he could recall his parents supporting him, very specific memories surfaced. Taro remembers how his mother would cook him up after long days at school, remember how his father was always present at his sports events, and recall how supportive they are of his hobbies. Keiko and Satoshi, Taro's parents, faced their set of challenges too during the early times.Having always viewed the behaviour of their son as oppositional and disrespectful, it was hard for them to accept how they could have been contributing factors to his suffering. Looking at their memory of Taro's childhood, however, they recalled how he used to be enthusiastic about participating in activities with the family and even in school events long ago. This consciousness helped them to realise how there was a gap that had developed between the boy he used to be and the teenager he has become, prompting change from anger into curiosity at what might have led to such development.

Days 3-4: Realisation of Reciprocity and Blunders

Midweek, the family investigated the question, "What have I contributed to others?

For Taro, this question was really hard to address.He realised he had given the family little support or affection; indeed, he mostly kept himself aloof, often refusing to participate in family activities. Yet, however, he remembered when he tried to express his sentiments and was dismissed by the parents. It made him think through how this defensiveness and resentment had compounded the distance between him and his family. The question proved to be open to Keiko and Satoshi. As they reflected upon their efforts to guide and discipline Taro, they began to see how well-intentioned actions could have been misinterpreted.Satoshi remembered when he lectured Taro about his school performance, many times doing so with an impatient tone. He realised that his supposed concern had probably come off as more of an attack than a declaration of support for which Taro had moved away. Keiko realised that making up for Taro's supposed bad influence from others had given off the appearance of possessiveness, especially when he needed increasing amounts of independence.

Days 5-6: Dealing with the Impact of Their Actions

During their crossing to the third question, "What troubles or difficulties have I brought to others? " the reflections deepened.Taro was stung by his conscience as he would look at things from his parents' perspective.

He recalled times when he had gone out late without informing them and had ignored them when they called him, not even to talk with his parents when they attempted to talk to him. This question enabled him to interpret his actions not simply as acts of frustration but rather as behaviours that have distressed and concerned his parents. Keiko and Satoshi also had some uncomfortable truths brought to their attention. Keiko realised she had alienated Taro through her severe boundaries and sometimes intrusive questions, while Satoshi saw how his high expectations and critiques have probably dented his son's self-esteem. Hurtful reasons: each of them believed that he was doing the best for Taro.

But in recognizing their contribution to the tension in the family, they began to see things in a new perspective concerning his behaviour. They saw that he wasn't rebelling out of sheer rebellion but the pain of having been pushed and forced to understand himself in ways he didn't. On the third day, the family sat in a moderated discussion to share their reflections. For the first time, Taro spoke out about not feeling heard; he explained how constantly focusing on academics and discipline by his parents made him feel he was not appreciated for what he was outside school.

This made Keiko and Satoshi realise that they tend to focus much more on his success rather than the psychological state of his mind.They apologised about making him feel that his feelings were not important and wished to support him not just as a student but as a human being. This dialogue marked a milestone for Taro as he finally felt his parents understood and accepted him. He confessed regret for having caused them distress and acknowledged how much they had sacrificed for him. The Naikan retreat ended with empathy and recognition among the members of the family who vowed to work on improving dialogue and showing each other more patience and compassion.

Outcome and Effect

As a fruit of Naikan therapy, once Taro returned from the retreat, his general behaviour and disposition began to change. He began attending school regularly without becoming silent with his parents but now expresses their problems. He began attending family functions. Taro's parents would gradually reduce their tendency to think in terms of punishment and increase their tendency to understand and support his needs and interests. The family said they had a more profound mutual respect and empathy that brought down the tensions that had been accumulating over the years.

This process also helped them continue practice within the family, such as check-ins in which they would report on their lives and reflect on how they could help each other more. The therapy gave the family tools for future challenges and how to work through them with greater patience and understanding; it thus became a foundation of healthier, more open communication.

Analysis

In this family setting, it is precisely in such a non-confrontational approach of Naikan therapy that makes every member reflect on his own role rather than expecting each person to focus on the faults of another member. Structured questions allow Taro and his parents to step out from reactive judgments into some space for empathy and self-awareness. This shift from accusation to introspection helped Taro overcome the feelings of resentment and helped him find out the extent to which his parent's actions had led him to his behavioural changes.

Case Study 3: Described and Explained- Naikan therapy in the healthcare of the terminally ill patient who has complex emotions and strained family relationships.

(Naikan Therapy for Terminal Illness and Family Healing)

Aiko was a 68-year-old lady from Nagoya, Japan. A few months ago, she was diagnosed with terminal pancreatic cancer. Aiko had always been withdrawn, secretive, especially when it came to her feelings. For her entire life, Aiko had put her family first and had been a dutiful wife and mother. However, she did not have a healthy relationship with her grown children; there was little to no communication, many unresolved issues, and the past was full of resentment, anger, and pain. Diagnoses coupled with isolation brought only sorrowful regrets, guilt, and sadness. Aiko had told her providers that she wanted to see peace brought back to her family and relations before she died. Her health care provider advised her Naikan therapy-a self-reflection therapy to help her deal with the complex emotions and closure with her family.

Therapeutic Setting

The therapy was personalised for Aiko, and was conducted in a quiet hospital room with minimal distractions. Due to her physical disability, her Naikan practice was dispersed over weeks, and each session lasted about two hours long. A trained facilitator guided Aiko through the three traditional questions given at the beginning of this chapter:

1. What have I received from others?
2. What have I given to others?
3. What wrongs or sufferings have I committed against others?

Since Aiko had no hope of recovery, the treatment was a reflective exercise that reached not only her familial life but also her entire lifetime considering the ways she has taken and given based on the roles of mother, sister, and friend.

Naikan Reflection Procedure

Week 1-2. Initial Reflections About the Family Relationships

Week 3-4: Confronting Regret and Unrecognised Contributions

Weeks 5-6: Evaluating any built-up emotions of guilt and regret

Weeks 7-8: Coming Towards Acceptance, Forgiveness, and Closure

Outcome and Impact

The Naikan therapy sessions made a profound impact on Aiko's final months. This process allowed her to confront long-held guilt and regret, which she was able to work through into thanksgiving and acceptance. Her reconciliation with her children brought a new closeness, especially great comfort and healing to her and her family.

Aiko's children showed readiness to spend much more time with her in her final weeks; her husband became more affectionate and recognized the depth of their shared life experiences.This case demonstrates how Naikan therapy can help terminally ill patients find emotional resolution and comfort. Naikan is a structured reflection on the journey of life, bringing out unaddressed emotions so the patients can then act meaningfully to heal the emotional wounds that exist among loved ones. For Aiko, therapy provided a way to address mortality with fulfilment and mend relationships that felt profoundly restorative for her.

Analysis

Naikan therapy is, in a way, a novel approach towards emotional healing for terminally ill patients using self-reflection and self-compassion. Aiko's case illustrates how the structured questions of Naikan guide these patients to confront left-out emotions in such a way that they might not be able to achieve closure under traditional therapies.

Techniques Used

Technique 1: The Three Central Questions in Naikan Therapy

Purpose of the Three Questions: In fact, the three questions of Naikan therapy are devised to move the focus of participants away from a self-centred perspective toward one of empathy and relational awareness. Unlike many of the therapies that start off with open-ended discussions of feelings, Naikan's questions guide participants toward examining the specifics of their interchanges with others. This structured approach helps in breaking down the complex emotional experiences and gaining insight that is based on real-life instances rather than feelings or generalised grievances.

The questions serve distinct but interconnected purposes:

1. ***"What have I received from others?***

   This question fosters gratitude. As participants consider what others have given to them in terms of support, kindness, and effort, they become aware of the web of care and assistance beneath their lives. This helps people think out of a sense of entitlement or resentment and on to what has been put into them.

2. ***"What have I given to others?***

   This question promotes accountability. It makes participants think of their own contributions to relationships in terms of either good or ill. Reflecting on this helps people see whether they are really active, reciprocal contributors to their relationships or whether they're mainly concentrated on what they get and not as much on what they give.

3. ***"What hardships or troubles have I caused others?***

   This question is the most challenging and makes the respondents face the implications that their actions bring to others. It takes participants beyond self-justification when it forces people to recognize how their behaviour might have caused pain or frustration for others. In doing so, it breeds in people a sense of responsibility and humility, thereby promoting a greater depth of empathy.

Application of the Questions in Practice

The questions can be used in a more formal setting, such as at a Naikan retreat or in therapy, but are also suitable for shorter, private reflection exercises. This is how the process usually unfolds:

1. ***Topic Selection for Reflection:***

   Participants are likely to be requested to do the reflection on a specific person, time period, or relation. For instance, they can choose one parent, sibling, spouse, or friend and reflect about it, or they can try to focus on a certain period of their life, for example, childhood or teenage years, early adulthood. This targeted view anchors the reflections into some specific memories rather than letting it become too broad, overwhelming, or hard to handle.

2. ***Reflective thinking and evoked memories:***

   Third, elicit memory of concrete events, conversations, and actions that can be illustrations of their responses to each question. Maybe they remember instances when someone out of their way helped them or when they helped someone else. Again, recalling real situations rather than abstract generalities is the point, since that concreteness makes feeling more alive and comprehension sharper.

3. ***Working Through Each Question One at a Time Systematically:***

   Participants are invited to work through each question one at a time, in a step-by-step manner. The person might spend an hour, or more, on each question, going deep on one thing before working their way through to the next. In this way, they create for themselves a pattern of systematic exploration that helps them encounter a gamut of emotions: thankfulness, accountability, even regret, and avoid defensiveness and denial.

4. ***Supportive Guidance of Facilitators :***

   In Naikan with a more formal setup, facilitators can offer questions or subtle hints to sustain participants' concentration and candour during reflection. For instance, if it's too hard for a participant to enumerate the times he or she has caused trouble, the facilitator will push him or her to think of the times when he or she became impatient, critical, or withdrawn. By this intervention, participants are nudged to confront aspects about themselves that otherwise they would shy away from.

Psychological Impact of Every Question

1. Gratitude Building (First Question):

Reflecting on what is received, then, makes this person shine with a deep appreciation and gratitude. By taking stock of events in which they have been supported, loved, helped, and more, many participants realise they might have taken such things for granted. This process may lessen resentment because one begins to look at their relationships with a better balance. For example, an over-entitled individual who tends to feel underappreciated learns to realise just how often the people around him have made themselves available to help him. That can largely help in reducing feelings of entitlement or resentment.

2. Creating Accountability (Second Question):

Encouraging self-assessment and personal responsibility, this question can easily put into one's mind thoughts of what they may have given others. It makes participants consider their contributions to the relationships they are in, whether they have been actively contributing or mainly focused on themselves. This can be a good way of improving individual awareness and prompting people to be more active in their relationships rather than passively expecting others to make the move.

3. Responsibility and Empathy Promotion- Third Question

The final question, which one has caused others trouble, encourages responsibility and empathetic power because participants always find it difficult to know how their behaviour has hurt someone negatively. It opens the door to humility and compassion while showing them the instances where they were wrong. This question deconstructs defensiveness since one learns to take responsibility without self-justification.

Example of How the Process is Applied

Hiro is reflecting on his relationship with his mother. After each question has been put aside, Hiro recalls specific instances to guide him through as follows:

"What have I received from others?"

Hiro remembers when his mother has made extra efforts for him, like staying late in work to generate enough money to fund his education or putting up with his illnesses. Now he realises he barely thanks her.

"What have I given to others?"

Reflecting on his contribution to his mother, Hiro can only recall a few times when he had assisted his mother with the household chores or spent his free time with her. He, however came to realise how those were fewer and became aware of the imbalance in their relationship by learning how rare those become as against everything he receives.

"What troubles or difficulties have I caused others?"

He remembers how many times he must have painted his mother, such as when he was inaccessible, not listening, or even worse, scolding. He can still remember those arguments where he became oblivious to her feelings and how he may have forgotten to see her whenever she invited him. That painful moment made Hiro look at things from his mother's end and made him really very sorry for all those instances wherein he took her efforts for granted.

Reflection and Outcome of the Technique

The three questions guide the participants into a meaningful understanding of themselves and their relationships, which usually ends in deep emotional and behavioural changes.

Increase in Empathy: The answer to the third question will usually bring in empathy and even compassion when the participants reflect on how their action affects others. This self-awareness could, in turn, bring about better relationships and improve the willingness to make amends.

A Sense of Fulfilment and Peace : In working through these questions, one gains a clearer sense of his or her values and role in their relationships. Many participants report that they are feeling more at peace, letting go of resentments, and gaining a more balanced view of their relationships.

Technique 2:

The second technique of Naikan therapy—Silent and Solitary Reflection—represents the core of the transformative impact of the therapy. This technique confers a definite character to the therapeutic environment by emphasising introspection and self- awareness, enabling participants to truly dive inside themselves in their thoughts and feelings, free from any extraneous stimuli that might compete for attention. Below is an elaborate discussion of the objective, technique, and the psychological impact of Silent and Solitary Reflection in Naikan therapy.

Silent and Lonely Reflection Purpose

Silent and lonely reflection in Naikan therapy helps to create an environment fully concentrated on deep reflection, away from noise and daily distraction. Unlike talk-based therapies, in which communication between therapist and patient is verbatim as much as possible, Naikan therapy takes a participant into a quiet, reflective space where he or she is left alone with memories and feelings. This kind of isolation is deliberate because it makes the participants look inside and digest emotions outside of any influence or interruption from other agents.

The purposes of silent or solitary reflection would be as follows:

1. **Increased Inner Focus:** Silent isolation eliminates all distractions outside: this environment enables a subject to focus more profoundly on personal thought and memories. The concentration is deep and important because Naikan demands that one be able to handle retro-viewing specific relationships, past actions, and experiences that make sense, are clear, and deep.
2. **Building Emotional Resilience:** Silent reflection will instill in people more willingness to face difficult emotions and less tendency to sidestep or rationalize pain, as with the example of the sit-with approach to uncomfortable feelings toward better emotional resilience.
3. **Building Self-Responsibility:**The isolation of Naikan therapy challenges the patient to own their insights and growth. With no therapist to guide the conversation, it is in this way that the

patient learns to become a little more independent and take charge of their reflection as well as emotional journey. In such independence, this freedom might allow them to really change out of their therapy.

4. **Space for Reflection:** Silence and solitude then become a safe, non-judgmental space where the participants are invited to embrace their reflections without the threat of judgment or attack from elsewhere. This allows them to deeply reflect on their experiences honestly and therefore nurture a balanced view concerning their relationships and actions.

Silent and Solitary Reflection in Practice Implementation

1. **Creating a Safe Environment:** Silent and lonely reflection normally occurs in a calm, well-controlled area such as a retreat house or private bedroom. It is in this space where things are kept simple and clean without too much sensory stimulation, thus avoiding the distraction of other things. Participants are usually asked to leave behind their electronic devices and other means of communicating through which the participants are disconnected from daily routines and responsibilities.
2. **Time Slots for Reflection:** Naikan therapy is segmented into time slots, and typically, the guardians are expected to spend hours of silent reflection without any interruption. Naikan retreat session is typical, usually when one has more than one session in a day, and the length of sessions varies between an hour and extended hours. Participants focus only on reflection of some questions (such as the three central ones as listed above) without any distraction within that time slot. The reflection period is longer than one would in traditional therapy sessions, and it encourages participants to think more deeply into what to say.
3. **Minimal Facilitator Interaction:** While a Naikan facilitator may provide general guidance at the beginning of each session or day, in silent reflection their role is quite minimal. The facilitator might occasionally ask if everyone is comfortable, but they avoid entering into a discussion about participant's reflections. This minimal contact keeps attention focused on the inner journey of the participant by embedding therapeutic thrusts into solitude.
4. **Journaling: A Tool for Self-Reflection:** During their solitary isolation, participants are advised to write a journal of their thoughts. Such journaling is private; the objective is that this would allow them to better control their reflection in a more concrete sense. In writing down their answers to the three central questions or emotional responses to memories, participants may be able to clarify and consolidate their insights better and also remember significant realisations.
5. **Lengthier Period of Isolation:** Naikan therapy usually lasts for days, and sometimes even up to a week. The time spent in isolation, in the case of such a reflective process, is important for the profundity it offers for reflection because this helps participants gradually peel away layers of emotion and memory. The length of time spent in silence during this process allows participants to move beyond surfaceful thoughts, and they can achieve deeper levels of self-realisation and acceptance.

The Psychological Effects of Silent and Solitary Reflection

Silent and private reflection in Naikan therapy has many psychologically important benefits, each amalgamated to function toward the effectiveness of the therapy:

1. **Lifting Self-Acceptance as well as Accountability:** One learns to incorporate greater acceptance of all actions, good and bad, from his or her past over extended periods of quiet contemplation. A participant does not have a chance to justify or explain away his or her behaviour to a therapist or anyone else, so they are accountable for their choices. This can contribute to increased personal responsibility and, through time, healthier choices in relationships and personal behaviour.
2. **Decrease Defensiveness and Rationalization:** Participants are less likely to go on the defensive or avoid checking their thoughts when left to themselves with their thoughts. Individuals coming in for traditional therapy often automatically diffuse or rationalize any perceived wrongdoing when getting feedback or perceived criticism from the therapist. Naikan removes these social factors that stimulate participants' sense of themselves to become defensive in reactions and truthfulness and, instead, allow individuals to confront uncomfortable truths without the impression to defend themselves. Honest and genuine insights come through with such efforts.
3. **Building emotional resilience through vulnerability:** A silent quiet time alone calls forth pain: guilt, regret, and even sorrow. From such an uninterrupted sitting period, the participants learn to tolerate and process emotions that otherwise have been suppressed or avoided. Building emotional resilience comes with such a practice of exposure to uncomfortable emotions because people learn to confront even the most painful moments of their lives.
4. **Inspirational Inner Peace and Wisdom:** The silent surroundings of Naikan therapy induce inner silence that would support acceptance of past experiences. Many have reported that being away for such long periods develops the peace of mind concerning unresolved matters since they leave behind the resurfacing of rancour or anger. The participant, by not having any outside input, provides space to come to his or her own conclusion and to give him or her his or her meaning in the experience.
5. **Accentuate a Sense of Thankfulness and Gratitude:** Participant after participant reports a renewed sense of thankfulness to what they received from others in the process, something in large part because the quiet solitude of such reflection allows the memories to dwell on what has been received without disruption to the lengthening of a sense of appreciation. Many participants report a strong sense of connection to loved ones after the therapy, as well, having been able to reflect fully on the help and kindness that they have received.

Example of the Technique in Use:

For instance, Sachiko went to a Naikan retreat. She spoke to reflect about her father whom she had never been on good terms with. The structured periods of silent reflection helped Sachiko dig deep into her memories since each period was dedicated to answering the three questions about her father. During hours that went by, she remembered from her childhood instances when her father cared and stood for her as she had never turned to those aspects earlier.

Session 1 (What have I received?):

Sachiko remembered that as a child, her father had attended to her concerning school work and taken care of the entire family despite this being a challenge for him. With time, she could think back on it uninterrupted, in memory, and appreciate these, of which she hadn't thought of for years.

Session 2 (What have I given?):

Sachiko found it hard to remember most of the things she had done good for her father. She had made it a point to criticise him almost every time and rarely said thank you. The silence has given her the chance to reflect on this and get motivated to change.

Session 3 (What difficulties have I caused?) :

Sachiko remembered a particular argument in which she had, as a matter of fact, hurt her father's feelings, mostly by ignoring his view. This silent reflection came up with the feeling of regret but brought much clarity and acceptance. She started noticing her father's problems more sympathetically. Through silence, insights and emotions that lay hidden under a mound of daily frustrations were better reached. At the end of the retreat she had regained respect and understanding for her father, which then led to reconciliation between them.

Conclusion of the Effectiveness of Silent and Solitary Reflection

With silent and solitary reflection in Naikan therapy, there is a strengthening potential that in depth gives a better therapeutic experience.Quiet, distraction-free time allows participants to come to terms with and work through their memories and emotions in a protected, reflective atmosphere. Besides leading to an in-depth self-awareness, it generates an atmosphere of appreciation, sympathy, and personal accountability. With this process, Naikan therapy frees the equations from extraneous interference, enabling one to take charge of the insights-a great foundation for life-long emotional growth and increased abilities to healthy relationships. It is not easy for some; however, silence is what catalytically forms people to find peace within themselves in a manner and under a condition that would help them gain clarity and acceptance.

Technique 3

The third is Focused Recall of Specific Interpersonal Relationships,a deep, structured recalling of specific relationships, usually with family members or very close contacts by individuals, throughout which they systematically discuss their actions, experiences, and feelings in these interactions. This method primarily points to understanding the functions we play in our relations; understanding the impact that others have on us, and the cultivation of a heightened sense of gratitude, accountability, and empathy.

Technique 3: Focused Recall of Specific Interpersonal Relationships

Purpose of Focused Recall in Naikan Therapy:

Focused recall is the technique through which the Naikan therapy helps the subjects to explore relationships in a very structured and highly defined way. Instead of focusing broadly on life, Naikan therapy asks participants to concentrate on a few very crucial persons—choose the kind of person that they can't easily categorise feelings about: parents, siblings, or spouses—and tease apart all their interactions with those people.

In this specific type of directed recall, participants gain insight into patterns of behaviour and attitude and provide healing for greater emotional insight. The two chief goals of directed recall are:

Interpersonal Contributions Awareness Enhancement:

It enables the individuals to cognitively assess whether they were a positive or negative influence in the relationships. This would be achieved through tracking of concrete activities and moments. In this manner, they can see how they have influenced other people, creating an obligation and also more balanced views of the relationships they experienced.

Gratitude and Empathy Building: Focused recall makes it easier for participants to appreciate what others have done for them and how they have benefited from others' efforts. This reflective process fosters gratitude and empathy as individuals begin to perceive their relations in a fuller, more compassionate manner.

Emotional Reconciliation:

Much of the unforgotten resentment, guilt, or anger is carried around within close relationships. Participants, when they go deeply into such relationships, can confront and work through the pain, which would lead to emotional reconciliation and often even a sense of closure.

Practice Application of Focused Recall

Choosing a Specific Relationship :

Encouragement is made to the participant to select one or more close relationship where and with whom he wishes, frequently beginning with those which are emotionally intense or challenging. These may involve a relationship with a parent, spouse, or close friend. In some cases, Naikan practitioners guide participants to reflect first on more challenging relationships because of the latter yielding the greatest transformative insight.

The Three Core Questions:

With a relationship chosen, the respondent applies the three core Naikan questions in relation to that person. If reflecting about their mother, they might ask themselves:

- What have I received from my mother?
- What have I given to my mother?
- What troubles or problems have I caused my mother?

With these questions, respondents avoid generalising and instead work to include real memories and experiences in that relationship.

Recalling Specific Events

Instead of just a laundry list of abstract feelings or vague thoughts, these respondents are led to recall specific events, conversations, and interactions that respond to each question. For instance, with the theme of "What have I received from my mother?", they can remember meals prepared for them, comfort from her, or times when she gave up her comfort to make them happy. This exercise of reviving memories makes their reflection better and gets participants a little closer to dealing with their feelings.

Recording Observations in a Journal or Reflection Log

During Naikan retreats or guided sessions, many clients write down their impressions of each memory as responses to the three questions. It acts as a written report which can be kept handy as a reminder of one's insights and may also be referred to in further follow-up therapy.

Balanced Focus on Good and Bad Aspects:

The technique does not glorify or malice anybody.Instead, invite participants to examine the constructive contributions and troubles of a relationship as a whole. For instance, when a student is asked to reflect on the support he or she has received from a sibling, that student is also reminded of the times he or she may have caused distress for his or her sibling. That balanced analysis creates a nuanced sensibility toward relationships rather than something polarised, which might impede emotional growth.

Psychological Impact of Focused Recall in Naikan Therapy

This focused recall technique brings about the amazing ability to create substantial understanding and emotional movement. The following are a number of the psychological results that have been exhibited by participants in this stage of Naikan therapy:

Heightened Sympathy and Compassion: In this regard, with focused recall, respondents are often made to understand struggles and sacrifices of loved ones in much greater detail. When thinking about specific actions, they are able to see these individuals in a more compassionate light, often realising the extent of care and effort they received without being able to appreciate it as much previously.

Transition from Entitlement to Gratitude: Focused recall frequently brings out the support and care participants have taken for granted. This shift from entitlement to gratitude is important because it enables the individual to become more connected and appreciative of those around them. For instance, a spouse might often reflect on how often they overlook the little acts of support their spouse provides.

Reducing Anger and Increasing Forgiveness: Acknowledging the good of a relationship and the efforts others have made often dissolves bitter resentment. For example, if anger is harboured against a parent, concentrated remembering may reveal moments when that parent was good to or loving toward the person. This acknowledgment can dissolve resentments, offering forgiveness.

Enabling Personal Accountability: The mere act of structured reflection of one's actions in a relationship increases self-awareness and accountability. They would be held accountable for acts which caused problems or hurt without a defensive tone, thus leading to healthier, more constructive behavior toward those relationships in the future.

Promotes Emotional Reconciliation: What really happens is that most of these targeted participants use the exercise as a form of emotional reconciliation, in which unresolved feelings of guilt, regret, or anger are therefore addressed. Closure would usually be the outcome of this reconciliation, thus enabling them to clear the baggage and move onward in life.

Example of the Technique in Action

Consider participant Mei who has chosen to reflect on her relationship with her father. Mei has always felt resentful and guilty toward him: he is emotionally distant yet guilty for not reciprocating his efforts. Using focused recall, Mei reviews some of the specific memories she must answer the three Naikan questions below:

1. **What has my father given me?**

   Mei reflects on the times her dad went to work for long hours, made sure her school project was done to perfection, drove her to various activities, and compromised his comfort. These memories help Mei perceive his action as a way of care, though he rarely showed verbal affection.

2. **What have I given to my father?**

   Mei reflects on how rarely she thanked her dad for his efforts. She basically complained about what was not good enough about him most of the time. Mei remembers instances when she overgeneralized or criticised him that created emotional distance from her dad.

3. **What am I causing my dad?**

   Mei now distinctly remembers numerous instances when her action would have hurt her dad, including when she turned a deaf ear to his advice or evaded family gatherings. She is opening to a deeper understanding of why her dad might have felt sad; it is an occasion that elicits empathy for him.

Through this focused recall, Mei underwent a massive change about her father. Structured reflection allows her to transcend from resentment and see her father as one who cared for her; though in ways she didn't recognize initially.

Conclusion on the Impact of Focused Recall in Naikan Therapy

One of the potent tools which enable Self-awareness, emotional healing, and relational understanding in Naikan therapy is the focused recall technique.Naikan therapy will assist individuals in gaining an even more balanced view of both themselves as well as of others by permitting participants to concentrate on specific relationships in an extremely structured and detailed manner. This technique brings gratitude, empathy, and forgiveness into the heart of the participants while empowering them to reconcile past emotional issues and introduce healthier, more appreciative relationships going forward. That way, focused recall serves as a steppingstone to deeper inner peace and even deeper compassionate relationships with people around them.

Conclusion

Naikan therapy, with such deep foundational principles of self-reflection and structured inquiry into interpersonal relationships, is especially a deep approach to healing of the emotions and consciousness when it comes to personal growth and self-awareness. This Japanese psychology bases its central tenets around gratitude, responsibility, and the review of one's part within an intricate network of human interdependency.

Naikan can be used for reflection on past experiences and their re-evaluation. It helps people cultivate empathy, reduce resentment, and mend old emotional wounds that never seemed to heal. Combining Tonglen therapy with Naikan practice creates an excellent doubling effect: the complementary interaction of compassionate reflection and interpersonal healing. While Naikan aims for reflection toward self within the course of interpersonal relationships, Tonglen is regarding the development of compassion for others even during bad or hurtful events. The combination of these two therapies can further strengthen emotional resilience and mental health, thereby achieving a balance between gaining insight into oneself and empathy towards others.

These two practices meet in a more holistic path toward emotional and psychological health-especially for those lingering in anger, unresolved, guilt unresolved, and the complicated relational dynamics. Applications of Naikan practice are wide-ranging. Its potential for emotional reconciliation and psychological healing has therefore been acknowledged from clinical psychology application to personal growth retreat use.

This approach can be particularly useful for people dealing with relational conflict, grief, or feelings of emotional stagnation-it's a kind of guide through complex emotions and insights that lead to emotional clarity. Yet, as is true of any therapeutic approach, Naikan encounters some challenges.

Despite these potential difficulties, Naikan has been found to be genuinely helpful in many therapy settings, such as with other therapeutic interventions and when done within a communal setting. Case studies and real-life practices show that through Naikan therapy, there would be deep, life-changing personal changes. Private learnings from these case studies reveal how Naikan is important in the resolution of feelings of resentment and guilt and misunderstanding, thereby forming healthier and more compassionate relationships.

The three techniques used in Naikan therapy—silent reflection, structured journaling, and the focused recall of interpersonal relationships—are regarded as the most powerful forms of introspection and emotional healing. These techniques guide the individual through the process of examining his contributions to the relationship and coming to an understanding of the positive and negative aspects of his presence. Hence, Naikan serves as a framework of emotional growth and personality development by allowing honest and non-judgmental reflection of the past.

It gives insights into human relationships with emotional well-being. Their application in promoting compassion and empathy, side by side with Tonglen, makes the therapeutic experiences even deeper. Despite the challenges associated with deep introspection, the therapeutic value of Naikan is substantial. Combining these two therapies provides a way into emotional healing and reconciliation as well as personal growth-longing for both the awareness of the self and the altruism of the other in a profoundly meaningful way.

References

Krech, G. (2001). Naikan: Gratitude, Grace, and the Japanese Art of Self-Reflection. Stone Bridge Press.

Reynolds, D. K. (1989). The Quiet Therapies: Japanese Pathways to Personal Growth. University of Hawaii Press.

Trungpa, C. (1991). Training the Mind and Cultivating Loving-Kindness. Shambhala Publications.

Chödrön, P. (1994). Start Where You Are: A Guide to Compassionate Living. Shambhala Publications.

Morita, S. (1998). Morita Therapy and the True Nature of Anxiety-Based Disorders (Shinkeishitsu). State University of New York Press.

Ogawa, T. (2005). "Naikan Therapy and Japanese Psychology." Journal of Japanese Clinical Psychology.

Krech, G. (2001). Naikan: Gratitude, Grace, and the Japanese Art of Self-Reflection. Stone Bridge Press.

Brown, K. W., & Ryan, R. M. (2003). "The benefits of being present: Mindfulness and its role in psychological well-being." Journal of Personality and Social Psychology, 84(4), 822–848.

Long, C. R., & Averill, J. R. (2003). "Solitude: An Exploration of the Benefits of Being Alone." Journal for the Theory of Social Behaviour*, 33(1), 21–44.

Ikemi, Y. (2004). "Naikan therapy: Discovering Japanese introspection." International Journal of Mental Health, 33(4), 32–45.

Reynolds, D. K. (1989). The Quiet Therapies: Japanese Pathways to Personal Growth*. University of Hawaii Press.

Krech, G. (2001). Naikan: Gratitude, Grace, and the Japanese Art of Self-Reflection. Stone Bridge Press.

Desbordes, G., et al. (2014). "Effects of Meditation on Emotional Processing and Well-Being: A Review of Clinical Studies on Buddhist Practices." Frontiers in Psychology.

Ikemi, Y. (2004). "Naikan therapy: Discovering Japanese introspection." *International Journal of Mental Health*, 33(4), 32–45.

Krech, G. (2001). Naikan: Gratitude, Grace, and the Japanese Art of Self-Reflection*. Stone Bridge Press.

Morita, S. (1998). Morita Therapy and the True Nature of Anxiety-Based Disorders (Shinkeishitsu)*. State University of New York Press.

Brown, K. W., & Ryan, R. M. (2003). "The benefits of being present: Mindfulness and its role in psychological well-being." Journal of Personality and Social Psychology, 84(4), 822–848.

Reynolds, D. K. (1989). The Quiet Therapies: Japanese Pathways to Personal Growth. University of Hawaii Press.

Chödrön, P. (1994). Start Where You Are: A Guide to Compassionate Living. Shambhala Publications.

Chapter 13

Psycho-Neurobics

Navisha Bajaj School of Liberal Studies (SLS), CMR University, Bangalore

Psycho-neurobics is a set of neuro-exercises which helps in utilizing spiritual energy in neuronal cells. It is a healing system that combines psychology, neurology, and energy exercises (aerobics). This technique helps in connecting our psyche to spiritual energy and aims at removing negative energy. This technique focuses on enhancing an individual's mental state and strengthening mental health through exercises which aim at 7 chakras or energy centers in the body.

The development of Psycho-Neurobics is attributed to Dr. BK Chandrashekhar, a mental health and spiritual expert from India. Dr. Chandrashekhar combined color therapy, meditation methods, and traditional yoga poses with contemporary knowledge of the mind-body relationship. He developed Psycho Neurobics, which restores positive energy flows and activates the body's own healing systems to help people deal with stress, emotional imbalance, and health difficulties.

Our body channelizes energy from the 7 centers or chakras in our bodies. To learn about those centers or chakras, it is important to learn that our body is composed of 5 elements:

1. Fire (which is regulated by Thumb)
2. Air (which is regulated by Index finger)
3. Space/ Ether (which is regulated by Middle finger)
4. Earth (which is regulated by Ring finger)
5. Water (which is regulated by Little finger).

As these elements are regulated by an assigned finger of our hand, Hasta Mudras play an active role as well to regulate these elements. Some mundras are: Gyan mudra, Vayu mudra, Akash mudra, Shoonya mudra, Prithvi mudra, Agni mudra, varun mudra, Apaan-vayu mudra, Apaan mudra, Pran mudra, Vyaan mudra and Shivlinga mudra.

It is essential to distinguish between the 7 chakras and their functions and importance in our daily lives. The 7 chakras have an assigned colour, musical notes and mudra, so psycho-neurobics functions through colour psychology, sound, and rhythmic dance as these are the basic functions of the neurobics.

The 7 chakras present in our body are: Root chakra, Hara chakra, Navel chakra, Heart chakra, Throat chakra, Third Eye chakra and crown chakra.

Root chakra: it facilitates blood circulation activation. It is also called "Muladhar Chakra" in sanskrit. Mudras play an important role in psychoneurobics and every chakra is activated by a certain mudra, for Root chakra the "Mahaveer mudra" is used for activating the chakra. All the seven chakras are located at different locations in our body . Root chakra is located at the base of the spine, which is between anus and genital. The root chakra gives the sense of "to be here" or to be present, which is why the power of this chakra is derived by Gravity. Psychoneurobics also uses sound and colour therapy, root chakra is activated through the musical note "C" and "Red" colour. The mantra that is to be chanted is "Lam/Ra". The sense that helps in activation of root chakra is smell. The relationship style of the people who are energised by activation of root chakra is Clinging. This Chakra opens by Will power, Happiness, and contentment.

Hara chakra/Sacral Plexus: it helps eliminate Many Hereditary Diseases and increases the immune system and defense mechanism of the body. It is also known as "Svadhisthana" in sanskrit. The mudra used to activate Hara chakra is "varun mudra". The Hara chakra is placed above root chakra and is found at the lower abdomen and the power for this chakra is Magnetism and attraction of Opposites. The chakra helps the individual "to feel". The musical note that activates this chakra is "D" and the colour used in therapies to activate it is "Orange". The Mantra sound to be chanted during the process of activation of this chakra is "Vam/Ma". And the sense that helps in activation of this chakra is Taste. the relationship style of people energized by activity of this chakra is an idealized fantasy. This Chakra opens by purity in life.

Navel Chakra: it helps in strengthening the digestive system. It is also known as "Manipura" in its Sanskrit translation. The mudra used for activation of Navel Chakra is "Agni mudra". It is found above Hara chakra and is located at the hollow area between the ribs and the area behind it and the power achieved through this chakra is will. The chakra helps the individual "to Act". The musical note used to activate this chakra is "E" and the colour to be used is "Yellow" colour. The Mantra sound which helps in activation of Navel Chakra is "Ram/Da". And the sense which activates it is Sight. The relationship style of people who are energized through action of this chakra is Manipulative and competitive. This Chakra opens by Joy, Happiness and contentment.

Heart chakra: It helps restore equilibrium of body temperature and increases the power of lungs and heart. It is also known as "Anahata" in sanskrit. And the mudra that activates this chakra is "Apaan-Vayu mudra". It is located above the Navel chakra at the front of the heart area. The mudra helps the individual "to Love" and the power achieved through activation of this chakra is Love. The Musical note that helps in activation of Heart chakra is "F" and the colour used in therapies for this chakra is "Green" colour. The Mantra sound that is chanted is "Yam/Sa/F". The sense that is related to this chakra is Touch. The relationship style for an individual is selfless and loving. This Chakra opens by Love, Affection, and social success in life.

Throat chakra/Visudhi: it helps clear the upper respiratory tract and clear lungs fully. It is called "Vishuddha" in Sanskrit. And the mudra that helps in activation of this chakra is "Vayu mudra" and it is located above the heart chakra in the throat area. This chakra helps the individual "to Speak" and the power achieved is Creativity. The Musical note that helps in activating this chakra is "G" and it is activated by "Sky Blue" colour. The Mantra sound to be chanted for activation of this chakra is "Ham/Se". The sense that is associated with this chakra is Hearing. The relationship style of the individual is Commitment to higher goals and communion with others. This Chakra opens by Dissolving ego, clear and effective communication.

Third Eye/ Anja chakra: It helps cure brain disorders, migraine, nerve and eye problems. It is known as Ajna Chakra in Sanskrit. The mudra that helps in activation of Anja chakra is "Pran mudra". It is located above Throat chakra and is located Between the eyebrows. This chakra helps the individual "to See" and the power achieved is imagination which further helps is visualization and meditation. The Musical note for activation of this chakra is "A" and the colour used is "Indigo". The Mantra sound to be chanted for this chakra is "Ksham/So". The sense associated with this chakra is Sixth sense. The relationship style of the individual is Complete union. This Chakra opens by Will power and intuition.

Crown chakra: It helps evoke feelings of bliss as well as dulls the perception of pain. It also helps increase memory and mind power. The Sanskriti Translation of Crown Chakra is "Sahasrara". And the mudra used for activation of this chakra is "Gyan mudra". This chakra is located above all the other chakred and is found at the Crown of the head. This chakra helps the individual "to Know" and the power achieved is Enlightenment. The Musical note used for activation of this chakra is "B" and the colour used in therapeutic healing is "Violet" colour. The Mantra sound to be chanted for this chakra is "Om/Gn". The sense associated with this chakra is oneness and unity. The relationship style for the individual is oneness and unity. This Chakra opens by eternal bliss, gratitude deep joy, compassion, and affection.

Techniques used in Psycho-neurobics

- **Raas/ rhythmic dance:** It is also called Easy psychoneurobics. It includes hand gestures also known as mudra. Hasta-mudras are effective in regulating and balancing the five elements of our body as mentioned before. Each finger corresponds to one of the elements. As our fingers are divided into three sections, touching the lower parts helps in increasing the corresponding element, middle part helps in decreasing the element and upper part helps in keeping the elements balanced. Joining fingers together is effective. For example, when we join the thumb finger (fire element) with the middle finger (space element), it increases space and sound. Whereas when we join the thumb with the index finger (Air element), it increases memory and intellect. Hence, the hasta-mudra or raas element is an important part of psycho-neurobic techniques.
- **Colour (Rang):** it is used as light psycho-neurobics. Colour plays an important role in our life. Colours add excitement in our lives. These colours can be used to activate subtle energy in our body. Light psycho-neurobics is done with colours of "VIBGYOR". Even when sunlight falls it brings positivity and confidence. Light therapy can also be associated with sunlight as it helps in curing seasonal depression. Additionally, light energy rays are attracted by the body through the chakras that are dispersed along the spine and subsequently dispersed throughout the other systems. Every chakra takes in a certain colour frequency from the white light. After that, the energy travels to the cells via the blood, organs, nervous system, and special and

regular meridians, purifying and reviving them along the way. Every vertebra, according to some colour therapists, is connected to one of the seven spectrum colours and to a certain organ or body part. Visualizing various colours with the third eye stimulates the body's subtle energy centres, which then channel energy to the appropriate bodily systems to cleanse, clear obstructions, and promote health.

- **Sound (Naad):** sound therapy uses voice, music and tone. Sound is nothing but vibration and according to some sound therapists illness occurs due to changes in energy relating to mind, body and soul, it mostly occurs due to vibration at incorrect frequencies of the three. We use more than just our ears to react to sound. The sound waves in our surroundings cause the entire human energy system to react. The body, mind, and soul are synchronized by healing sound. Certain fundamental sounds that have a strong impact on the mind, body, and soul are used in Ayurvedic treatment. During mantra-induced meditation, saying the right sound silently calms the mind and immediately slows down breathing. According to studies, these sounds can stop cancer cells from proliferating. From the simple repetition of magical phrases to the more complex rhythms and game plans of notes, sound neurobics can change our moods and behaviors, ease physical tensions, guide natural processes, and increase awareness.

Some Key Techniques used in Psycho-Neurobics

Visualization Techniques

It involves practicing visualization of images or scenarios to help create positive results by boosting optimism, energy, and awareness. Visualization techniques also help in improving mindset, bringing clarity and motivate the individual to act some of the visualization techniques are:

- ***Mental Imagery:*** Practicing visualization exercises to mentally create positive images or scenarios and healing energy. For example, visualizing oneself being surrounded by a sphere of healing light that further boosts confidence.
- ***Energy Visualization:*** Imagining specific colours or forms of energy flowing throughout the body, targeting areas that need healing or balance.

Breathing Exercises (Pranayama):

Breathing Exercises are a crucial part of psycho-neurobics. It helps in maintaining oxygen levels, stress, lungs capacity and also helps in promoting relaxation. Some of the breathing techniques used in psycho-neurobics are as follows:

- ***Deep Breathing:*** Controlled, slow inhalations and exhalations helps to increase the oxygen flow, relax the mind, and activate the parasympathetic nervous system.
- ***Rhythmic Breathing:*** Using specific rhythm as breathing patterns to calm the mind and channel energy through various parts of the body.

Colour and Sound Therapy:

Colour and Sound are two crucial elements of psycho-neurobics. Both the components are used to heal and fix the energy disturbances. Some of the techniques are as follows:

- ***Colour breathing and colour showers***: Using the visualization of specific colors, where the individual imagines breathing in a specific colour or feel the showering of colours or colours pouring, out from the divine source, on our head. The colour travels to the area of blockage or illness and helps in healing of the affected areas. The visualized colours help in nourishing the chakra and our aura, which opens the channel of energy throughout our bodies as each colour represents different types of energy, to promote healing and balance.
- ***Sound Vibrations:*** Chanting or listening to specific sounds and mantras help to align the body's energy centers (chakras) and stimulate the brain. Sound vibrations are believed to help in releasing emotional blockages. Chanting the right mantra while meditating helps still the mind and slows down the breathing, which helps the individual to relax and makes the therapy more effective.

Mudras (Hand Gestures):

Another crucial aspect of psycho-neurobics. Mudras or hasta-mudras helps in regulating the energy of our bodies. Our 5 fingers are each associated with one of the elements. And when we join the tips of the fingers or squeeze by the thumb, equalization of the element takes place. We can increase, decrease, or balance each element by touching specific points of our fingers. Specific hand positions (mudras) are used to activate certain energy circuits in the body. These mudras are practiced during meditation or breathing exercises to channel energy more effectively.

Neurobic Exercises

Neurobics are those exercises that are tailored for our brain, which further helps to stimulate our brain. These exercises involve stimulation of the brain through engaging multiple sense organs or changing routine. Neurobics helps engage the brain in active thinking and helps in strengthening neural connections. It also helps in improving memory and concentration. Neurobics are mental and physical activities that are designed to stimulate the brain by using the senses in novel ways.

Meditative Techniques

Psycho-neurobics is a meditative technique that helps in activation of energy centers or chakras in our body. Numerous meditative practices are inculcated in psycho-neurobics. It includes breathing based meditation, colour or light meditation and affirmative meditation. It also practices mindfulness meditation, which is done by practicing awareness of the present moment to reduce stress and promote mental clarity. And guided meditation which involves using specific scripts or audio recordings that guide participants through a series of visualizations aimed at relieving stress and promoting healing.

Affirmations and Positive Thinking

Psycho-neurobics uses affirmations to reprogram the subconscious mind and inculcate more positive thoughts and beliefs and improves sense of well-being. Positive thinking helps in boosting self-esteem and has an optimistic outlook in life which further helps in reducing anxiety. It also helps in improving focus and bringing clarity and also enhancing emotional well-being. Repeating positive affirmations during meditation to reinforce self-belief and create a positive mental state. The use of positive language is believed to rewire the brain for success and well-being.

Postures and Movements

These are crucial techniques as it helps in facilitating effective flow of energy throughout our bodies. Psycho-neurobics helps in combining physical movements and postures with neurobics for enhanced overall well-being. Posture is really important as it enhances flow of energy and it is also crucial to maintain spinal alignment. Spinal alignment facilitates free flow of energy and a good posture helps provide a stable base and maintain balance and makes the body relax and secure. Hence, Gentle physical movements and yoga postures are incorporated to stimulate energy flow and release tension from the body. These movements are usually synchronized with breathing exercises and mental focus to enhance our well-being.

Chakra Balancing

Its aim is to maintain balance between the energy centers of our body. It also helps in releasing energy blockages, reduces stress, and enhances well-being. Chakra balancing can be done through crystal healing where each chakra is associated with a certain crystal. Other techniques designed to align and energize the body's seven main chakras (energy centers) using a combination of visualization, sound, breathwork, and mudras. Each chakra is associated with different aspects of physical and emotional health. Chakra balancing is a transformative practice that promotes harmony between mind, body, and soul.

Benefits of Psycho-neurobics

- **Improved mental clarity and focus:** Psycho-neurobic helps inculcate meditative techniques and neurobic exercises that further helps in important focus and bring clarity.
- **Reduced stress and anxiety levels**: psycho-neurobics helps in reducing stress and anxiety by balancing chakras and through meditative exercises and visualization techniques. Alignment of chakras and flow of energy is impactful in making the body relaxed and also helps in reducing anxiety and stress.
- **Enhanced emotional well-being and resilience:** techniques used in Psycho-neurobics help in enhancing overall emotional well-being and using affirmation and positive thinking it helps in enhancing resilience.
- **Greater physical vitality and energy balance:** chakra balancing, posture and movement and various other techniques helps in improving our physical health along with emotional and mental health and helps provide greater physical vitality and helps in balancing our energy centers.
- **Better management of chronic conditions through mind-body connection:** psycho-neurobics uses techniques which help in improving not only our mental health but also our physical health. Various techniques in psycho-neurobics help improve migraines and some techniques like sound therapy even help stop proliferation of cancer cells. Hence, through mind-body connection psycho-neurobics helps in management of chronic conditions.

- **Emotional Balance:** Psycho-neurobics promote emotional healing and resilience through vario techniques like positive thinking and affirmation. Chakra alignment also helps in balancing our emotions. It helps the individual to gain emotional stability and helps in staying calm in stressful situations and it also helps in managing and regulating emotions.
- **Energy Boost:** Psycho-neurobics helps in increasing physical and mental energy levels through chakra activation and balancing. It helps in boosting energy and healing our body.
- **Spiritual Connection:** Deepens the connection to higher consciousness and universal energy. This technique helps individuals get in touch with the divine powers and energy, which have healing powers alongside meditations.

Applications of Psycho-neurobics

Psycho-neurobics helps in healing through meditation. An efficient therapeutic method for meditation is called neurobics spa. It functions by fully involving the body, mind, and spirit.

The use of colour psychology helps in mind-body health management emphasizing on chakra concentration.

- The violet hue enhances memory and helps treat issues with hormones and sleep difficulties.
- The indigo colour is used to treat neurological disorders, migraines, eye issues, and nervous system disorders.
- The colour sky blue is beneficial for issues with the thyroid, respiratory system, ears, nose, and throat.
- Green colour aids with cardiac problems, asthma, and strengthens the heart and lungs.
- The hue yellow strengthens the digestive system and treats issues with the liver, stomach, constipation, and diabetes.
- Orange strengthens the immune system and aids with issues pertaining to the blood, skin, urine, reproductive, and excretory systems.
- Red is a powerful colour that treats low blood pressure, strengthens bones and muscles, and empowers people.

Challenges of Psycho-neurobics

Complexity for Beginners:

Psycho-Neurobics combines elements like meditation, energy healing, sound, mudras, colour therapy, and neurobiology, which may be overwhelming and confusing for new practitioners to practice. Understanding and mastering these techniques may require time, effort and proper guidance.

Lack of Scientific Evidence:

Psycho-Neurobics is based on the mind-body healing concept and lacks the required scientific validation. The benefits from this technique are based on either anecdotal evidence or subjective experiences, which can be one of the barriers for those who seek empirical proof of the effectiveness and efficiency of this method.

Consistency and Discipline:

Like any other mind-body practices, Psycho-Neurobics requires consistently practicing is required for noticeable benefits. Discipline is essential to regularly engage in exercises, especially in a fast-paced or stressful lifestyle, where it can be challenging for many people to be motivated.

Subjectivity of Experience:

The effectiveness of Psycho-Neurobics can vary from individual to individual. What works for one individual may not work for another, making it difficult to predict outcomes.

Expert Guidance:

Properly practicing Psycho-Neurobics requires guidance from trained instructors or experts, as incorrect application of techniques may lead to ineffective results, failure, frustration or even negative emotional experiences.

Misunderstanding the Scope:

Some practitioners may expect quick results for physical healing from Psycho-Neurobics, but its primary focus is on mental and emotional well-being. Unnecessary expectations can lead to disappointment if the deeper healing process or time needed for results is misunderstood.

Cultural Barriers:

Psycho-neurobics has roots in yogic and spiritual traditions, which might not resonate with individuals from different cultural or religious backgrounds. This can make adoption challenging in contexts where these concepts are unfamiliar or viewed skeptically.

Integration with Medical Treatment:

While Psycho-Neurobics emphasizes mental healing, it should not be used as a substitute for conventional medical treatment for serious physical or mental health conditions. Balancing the practice with professional medical care can be a challenge for some practitioners.

Case Studies

Case study 1: Boosting Psychological well-being through Psycho-Neurobics intervention.

In Delhi NCR, Psycho-Neurobics interventions were tested on 60 participants which included both males and females, with the age between 15 to 17 years. After selection of the participants, the Ryff scale of psychological well-being was administered, which measures wellness of individuals in 6 dimensions, i.e., Self-acceptance, Positive relationships, Autonomy, Purpose in life, Environmental Mastery and Personal Growth. These 6 dimensions have 7 statements each making this 42-item scale, developed by Dr. Carol Ryff & Keyes. It scores on the basis of 6-point scale, from strongly disagree to strongly agree, ranging from 0 to 6, so the highest score anyone can score is 252 and the lowest is 0. High scores indicate high quality of psychological well-being whereas low scores show deteriorated psychological well-being.

Neurobic machines were also used to measure the state of mind and mood of the participants. It measures electro dermal activity which results from changes in bio-electrical impulses due to mood swings or agitated mind. It ranges from 0-100, the higher the score, the higher the agitation and chaos in mind whereas lower scores indicate calmness and peace of mind. After the administration of both the scale and neurobic machine. The participants were divided into three intervention groups, group 1 received psychoneurobic interventions, group 2 received mindfulness training and group 3 was a control group which received no intervention.

Group 1 and group 2 received 1 hour intervention once a week for 4 months which was administered by the field expert and they practiced intervention for half an hour daily by themselves. After 4 months, both the scale and neurobic machines were administered again on the participants.

The groups undergoing psychoneurobic intervention and mindfulness training showed improved results as compared to the control group. One way ANOVA was used to compare the scores of psychoneurobic interventions and mindfulness training and it was found that the mean score of psychoneurobic intervention group was greater than mindfulness training group. Even though both groups show improvement in psychological well-being, data analysis of the psychoneurobic intervention group shows significant improvement in each dimension of the psychological well-being scale which was not the case for mindfulness training. Hence, psychoneurobic can help in attainment of self-acceptance, positive relationships, autonomy, purpose in life, environmental mastery and personal growth.

Case study 2: Effect of Psycho-neurobics on status of anxiety in patients undergoing cataract surgery

In Raipur, people above 40 years old were taken under the study. The other inclusive criteria were that they were all going through cataract surgery and it was checked that their hypertension and diabetes or blood sugar level were under control. People having traumatic cataract or associated ocular or systemic comorbidities and mental illness were excluded.

50 patients each were allocated to two groups, one experimental group which received psycho-neurobics intervention and the other became a control group. And both the groups were sent into separate rooms for pre-intervention assessments.

Experimental group received psycho-neurobic medication along with counseling for the surgery whereas the control group only received counseling. Recordings of pre-operative physiological parameters including blood pressure, blood sugar, heart rate, and respiration rate was done. The Amsterdam Preoperative Anxiety and Information Scale (APAIS), created in 1996 by a Dutch team from the University of Amsterdam in the Netherlands, Moermann, served as the study's instrument. Anxiety levels in patients before anesthesia and surgery can be assessed with the APAIS.

APAIS has 6 statements and is rated on the basis of 5-point likert scale. It has three subscales: anesthesia related anxiety, surgery related anxiety and need for information. It overall has 2 scales: combines anxiety and need for information. For any subscale, the minimum score was 2 whereas maximum score was 10. Whereas, for combined anxiety, the minimum score was 4 and maximum score was 20. The higher the score, the greater the degree of anxiety. A total of two scales were taken to get the total value. If the patient scores more than 11, then the patient was anxious and if the score was more than 5, then the patient required more information about the surgery and anesthesia.

The experimental group underwent psycho-neurobic training where the patients along with their family members were instructed to follow certain protocols. The patients were advised to practice psycho-neurobic meditation in a dimly lit room in a hospital setting for half an hour. It was a simple technique for preserving a harmonious relationship between the body, mind, soul, and the cosmos. By employing certain meditation techniques and exercises that use particular colours, sounds, and "mudras," the soul receives holy energy from the universe or Supreme God, which then travels to the mind. This increases the subconscious mind's frequency, which strengthens the will and mental fortitude and promotes physical healing. This passive energy is replaced by a more active form of energy when done consistently throughout time. The control group did not undergo any such intervention but they along with their caretaker or family members were counseled about the surgery and the procedure in the same room.

Most individuals in both the experimental and control groups were anxious, according to the preoperative pre-interventional anxiety assessment, The experimental group had a higher initial pre-interventional mean score for the combined anxiety scale and score than the control group. The pre and post test results indicates that patients were still worried about surgery and anesthesia after intervention in both groups, but the experimental group that had received psycho-neurobics meditation experienced a greater decrease in the number of patients with anxiety and comparatively had lower anxiety score than the control group, and this difference was statistically significant.

In the experimental group, pre-interventional anxiety was found to be 90%, need for information totaled up to 98%, and mean of combined anxiety score was 15.36 and mean of need for informacion score was 6.86 which decreased after psycho-neurobics meditation to the scores of 12%, 16%, 7.74 and 3.3 respectively. But in the control group, this decline went from 84% to 74% in anxiety, 96% to 94% in need for information, 12.78 to 12.2 for mean of combined anxiety score and 6.52 to 6.32 was the mean of need for information score only. This was very low decline. This indicates that the patients in the control group continued to feel anxious about the surgery. It can be said that psycho-neurobic training is effective as it makes the body calm, quiet and relaxed and helps control our thought patterns and helps the individual to indulge in positive thinking.

It can be concluded that patients who receive psycho-neurobics prior to surgery may experience less tension and anxiety. By regulating blood pressure and anxiety levels, it lowers the preoperative cancellation rate of procedures. Additionally, it can make them more cooperative throughout surgery and more comfortable with the surgical process.

References

Chandrashekhar, B., K. Health in Your Hand. Teenage Publishers.

Agrawal, S., Kashyap, P., & Chauhan, B. (2021). Effect of Enlightening Psycho Neurobics Exercises on Migraine patient. International Journal of Research Publication and Reviews 2(11):919-927.

Khanna, D. (2023). Psychoneurobics study on the mental instability of students pursuing higher education. Journal of Management & Technology

Gupta, S., A., & Pradhan, S., K. (2018). Effect of Psychoneurobics (Meditation Technique) on the status of Anxiety in Patients undergoing cataract surgery: A randomized controlled trial. International Journal of Preventive Curative & Community Medicine 04(03):36-42

Kumeriya, R., & Chopde, Y. (2019). Therapeutics Impact of Psychoneurobics on Mind-Body Management and Its Possible Scientific Mechanisms. Journal of Scientific Research in Allied Sciences 7(3): 113-120.

Dhankhar, D., & Kumeriya, R. (2020). Analysis on Effectiveness of Psycho-neurobics on Mental Concentration and Memory Betterment. Medico Research Chronicles 7(1): 33-40.

Gupta, A. (2018). Boosting Psychological Well Being of Adolescent: Psychoneurobics Intervention Versus Mindfulness Training. Journal of Social Sciences 4(3): 682-699.

Dhankhar, D., Kumeriya, R., & Chopde, Y. (2020). Psycho Neurobics Practices For Self Healing for Individual Seafarer: Wellness at Sea. Medico Research Chronicles 7(2): 87-101.

Chapter 14

Qigong Therapy

Palak Shori School of Liberal Studies (SLS), CMR University, Bangalore

Definition

Qigong pronounced "chi gong," was developed in China thousands of years ago as part of traditional Chinese medicine. It involves using exercises to optimize energy within the body, mind, and spirit, with the goal of improving and maintaining health and well-being. Qigong therapy is a holistic practice rooted in Traditional Chinese Medicine (TCM) that focuses on cultivating and balancing *qi* (pronounced "chee"), often translated as "vital life energy." The practice combines physical postures, breathing techniques, meditation, and sometimes guided imagery to improve physical and mental well-being. Qigong therapy is used as both a preventive health measure and a complementary treatment for various ailments.

Key Components for Qigong Therapy

Physical Movements can range from gentle, slow motions to more active exercises, depending on the style. The goal is to promote the smooth flow of *qi* through energy pathways (or meridians) in the body. Movements are often circular and graceful, designed to encourage relaxation and energy flow. Breathing Techniques in Qigong are typically slow, deep, and mindful, aimed at harmonizing breath with movement. Different breathing techniques are used depending on the goals of the practice, such as reducing stress or increasing vitality.

Benefits of Qigong Therapy

Physical Health Benefits

Qigong involves slow, controlled movements that help stretch and strengthen muscles, improving flexibility and mobility. Over time, these movements can increase joint mobility and muscle tone, particularly in older adults or those with limited physical activity. The slow, deliberate movements of Qigong are especially beneficial for improving balance. This can reduce the risk of falls in older adults and enhance coordination, which is also beneficial for athletes or those recovering from injuries. Qigong has been shown to reduce chronic pain, including pain related to conditions such as arthritis, fibromyalgia, and back pain. The gentle movements, combined with deep breathing and mental focus, can help relax tense muscles, improve blood circulation, and reduce inflammation. Regular practice of Qigong can improve blood flow and oxygenation throughout the body. This helps to nourish tissues, promote detoxification, and strengthen the cardiovascular system.

Mental Health Benefits

One of the most well-known benefits of Qigong therapy is its ability to reduce stress and anxiety. The slow movements, focused breathing, and meditative aspect of Qigong activate the parasympathetic nervous system, which helps lower cortisol levels and promote relaxation. Qigong practice can improve sleep quality by calming the mind and relaxing the body. Its meditative aspects help ease anxiety and stress, which are often the underlying causes of sleep disturbances. The combination of mindfulness, physical exercise, and controlled breathing helps regulate mood and foster a sense of calm and emotional stability.

Emotional and Spiritual Benefits

Regular practice of Qigong can help balance emotional energy, promoting feelings of calm, peace, and contentment. It can assist in releasing pent-up emotions, such as anger, frustration, or sadness, helping individuals achieve emotional resilience. The meditative aspect of Qigong encourages introspection and mindfulness. By becoming more attuned to your body's energy flow and mental state, you can foster greater self-awareness and emotional intelligence. For those who practice Qigong from a spiritual perspective, it can lead to a sense of connectedness with oneself, others, and the universe.

Chronic Disease Management

Qigong has been used in conjunction with conventional treatments like chemotherapy and radiation to help cancer patients manage symptoms such as fatigue, nausea, pain, and anxiety. Some studies suggest that Qigong can enhance energy levels, improve mood, and support immune function during cancer recovery. Studies have shown that Qigong can lower high blood pressure, reduce the risk of cardiovascular disease, and improve overall heart health. It has a calming effect on the heart rate and can help reduce stress-related cardiovascular risks.

Holistic Health and Prevention

Regular Qigong practice is viewed as an effective preventive health measure. By improving energy flow and enhancing circulation, Qigong can help maintain health, prevent disease, and delay the aging process. It encourages the balance of yin and yang in the body, which is believed to help prevent the onset of illness. Qigong is often associated with longevity and anti-aging practices. The gentle, flowing movements combined with deep breathing help to nourish the body, improve circulation, and increase vitality, all of which contribute to the aging process. By promoting smooth energy flow, improving circulation, and enhancing lymphatic drainage, Qigong can aid in detoxification and the removal of waste products from the body.

Greater Resilience and Adaptability

The combination of breath control, movement, and mental focus in Qigong helps increase resilience to stress and pain. Over time, practitioners develop a greater ability to cope with physical and emotional challenges. As Qigong improves both physical fitness and mental fortitude, it can increase endurance, stamina, and the ability to handle both physical exertion and stressful situations with greater ease.

History of Qigong Therapy

Ancient Beginnings (Circa 4,000-5,000 Years Ago)

The origins of Qigong can be traced back to ancient China, where early practices focused on exercises, breath control, and meditation as means of connecting with nature and balancing bodily energy. Ancient records like the *I Ching* (Book of Changes), dating back to around 1122 BCE, include early references to concepts that became foundational to Qigong, such as the balance of yin and yang and the flow of *qi*. During this period, early forms of Qigong were known by various names, including *daoyin* ("guiding and pulling") and *tuna* ("exhalation and inhalation"), and were primarily used for health and spiritual development.

Early Medical and Daoist Influences (770-221 BCE, Warring States Period)

Daoism, one of the major philosophical schools in China, promoted the idea of harmony with the natural world and internal energy cultivation, both of which are central to Qigong practices. The *Huangdi Neijing* (Yellow Emperor's Inner Canon), written around 200 BCE, is one of the earliest foundational texts of Chinese medicine and describes the importance of *qi* and its role in health and disease. It also references exercises like Qigong. During this period, Qigong was integrated into early Chinese medicine to balance the body's *qi* and to treat various ailments.

Buddhism and Martial Arts Influence (200-500 CE)

With the introduction of Buddhism to China, Qigong incorporated meditation and physical conditioning techniques used by Buddhist monks, particularly in the Shaolin Temple. Buddhist monks, including the famous monk Bodhidharma, are credited with introducing exercises to improve physical health and support long meditation practices, blending spiritual, martial, and health-based elements of Qigong. Qigong practices within the martial arts also evolved during this time, with exercises used to enhance physical strength, flexibility, and concentration.

Systematization and Popularization (Tang and Song Dynasties, 618-1279 CE)

During the Tang and Song dynasties, Qigong was systematically developed and classified. Various schools and styles of Qigong emerged, focusing on healing, spiritual growth, and martial arts. The *Daoist Canon* (Daozang), a collection of Daoist scriptures, includes many texts on Qigong practices that emphasize meditation, energy circulation, and breath control. These practices were popularized as methods for self-cultivation, health maintenance, and extending longevity. Qigong techniques became a part of everyday life for both monks and laypeople.

Ming and Qing Dynasties (1368-1912)

This period marked a flourishing of Qigong theory and practice, with the publication of numerous books on energy cultivation and martial arts. Medical Qigong became more formalized, and specific exercises were designed to treat various diseases based on TCM theories of qi flow and meridians. The *Baduanjin* (Eight Brocades), a popular Qigong sequence still widely practiced today, was developed to enhance both martial and health benefits.

Modern Revival and Scientific Study (20th Century - Present)

In the 1950s, Qigong was popularized in mainland China as part of national health campaigns. Medical Qigong began to be practiced widely in hospitals and clinics as a preventive and therapeutic practice. The 1980s and 1990s saw a "Qigong fever" in China, with millions practicing Qigong, and various schools emerging. Qigong also gained international recognition and started to be practiced worldwide. Qigong's health benefits attracted the attention of researchers globally, leading to scientific studies on its effects on chronic diseases, pain management, and mental health. Though research is ongoing, some studies have suggested that Qigong can positively impact stress reduction, cardiovascular health, and immune function.

Contemporary Qigong Therapy

Today, Qigong therapy is integrated into both alternative and complementary medicine and is widely practiced across the world. It is used in clinics, hospitals, wellness centers, and community centers as part of integrative health practices. Many forms of Qigong are available, from simple exercises for beginners to advanced Medical Qigong used by TCM practitioners to treat specific conditions.

Theoretical Background of Qigong Therapy

The theoretical background of Qigong therapy is based on Traditional Chinese Medicine (TCM) principles, Daoist and Buddhist philosophies, and the understanding of energy dynamics within the body.

Concept of Qi (Vital Energy)

In Chinese culture, *qi* is understood as the essential life energy or vital force that flows through all living things. It is considered the basis of life and health, circulating within the body along energy pathways called *meridians*. Good health is thought to result from a smooth, balanced flow of *qi*. Conversely, illness or discomfort is often attributed to blockages, deficiencies, or imbalances in *qi*. Qigong therapy is designed to cultivate, harmonize, and regulate *qi* through movement, breathing, and meditation. These practices are believed to strengthen the body's energy, improve vitality, and promote healing.

Yin-Yang Theory

Yin and Yang represent opposing but complementary forces in the universe and within the body. Yin is associated with qualities such as coolness, calmness, and passivity, while Yang represents warmth, energy, and activity. Health is viewed as a state of dynamic balance between Yin and Yang within the body's *qi*. Imbalance in these forces leads to illness, and Qigong therapy aims to restore this balance by harmonizing Yin and Yang energy. Qigong exercises are often designed to stimulate either Yin or Yang aspects of the body, depending on the individual's needs. For example, a person with excessive Yang energy may practice more calming, Yin-based Qigong exercises, and vice versa.

The Five Elements Theory

The Five Elements (Wood, Fire, Earth, Metal, and Water) are seen as different aspects or phases of *qi* and are linked to various organs, emotions, and seasons in TCM. Each element is associated with particular organs and emotional states (e.g., Wood with the liver and anger, Fire with the heart and joy). The theory describes both generative and controlling cycles among the elements, which explain how energy flows and regulates bodily systems. An imbalance in one element can affect others, contributing to health or disease. Specific Qigong exercises, meditations, and breathing techniques are used to balance the Five Elements within the body.

Meridian Theory

According to TCM, *qi* flows through channels or meridians in the body that connect to specific organs and systems. These meridians act as pathways for energy circulation, enabling different parts of the body to communicate and balance each other. If a meridian becomes blocked or depleted, it can lead to physical and emotional symptoms. Qigong therapy incorporates movements, breathing, and acupressure to help open, clear, and stimulate the meridians, promoting a free flow of *qi*. Qigong exercises often target meridians related to specific health goals.

Role of Consciousness and Intention

In Qigong, the role of intention (known as *yi*) is crucial for guiding *qi* within the body. The belief is that the mind can direct the flow of *qi*, enabling practitioners to focus energy where healing is needed. By cultivating a mindful awareness of the body and its energy, practitioners can regulate and balance *qi* more effectively. Visualization and concentration are therefore key components of Qigong practice.

Daoist and Buddhist Influences

Daoism emphasizes harmony with the natural world, the balance of Yin and Yang, and the concept of *wu wei* (effortless action). These ideas shape Qigong's focus on relaxed, flowing movements, natural breathing, and spontaneous adaptability in energy flow. Buddhism's introduction to China influenced Qigong through meditative practices that cultivate mindfulness and compassion. Buddhist monks adapted Qigong to enhance physical and mental resilience for long meditation practices, blending spiritual development with health benefits. Advanced Qigong practices, known as *Neidan* or inner alchemy, are based on Daoist concepts.

Psychophysiological Effects and Modern Interpretations

Modern research suggests that Qigong practices influence the nervous, endocrine, and immune systems, supporting the body's stress response, reducing inflammation, and promoting relaxation. These findings are compatible with TCM's view of mind-body interdependence. Some researchers view Qigong from a bioenergetic perspective, suggesting that the practice might enhance bioelectric activity within the body. Though not fully understood scientifically, this aligns with TCM's understanding of *qi* as a form of bioenergy.

Self-Regulation and Preventive Medicine

In TCM, health maintenance and disease prevention are central concepts. Qigong therapy is seen as a form of self-cultivation, in which regular practice strengthens the body, mind, and immune system. By balancing *qi*, Qigong aims to prevent disease before it manifests physically. Practitioners believe that harmonizing internal energy can correct small imbalances before they lead to significant health issues, making Qigong a preventive therapy.

Applications of Qigong Therapy

Chronic Disease Management

Qigong therapy can help lower blood pressure, reduce heart rate, and improve circulation, making it beneficial for managing hypertension, coronary artery disease, and other cardiovascular issues. Certain Qigong practices can help stabilize blood sugar levels, improve insulin sensitivity, and aid in weight management. The practice of Qigong can also reduce stress, which is beneficial for controlling blood sugar levels in diabetics. Qigong therapy is often used as a complementary approach to manage symptoms of cancer and side effects of treatments like chemotherapy and radiation. It can help with fatigue, nausea, pain, and mental health issues, such as anxiety and depression, common among cancer patients.

Pain Management

Qigong has been shown to reduce symptoms in people with chronic pain conditions such as arthritis, fibromyalgia, and back pain. The gentle movements and meditative aspects of Qigong can alleviate muscle tension, improve circulation, and release endorphins to reduce pain. Regular Qigong practice can help reduce the frequency and severity of migraines and tension headaches by balancing energy flow, reducing stress, and promoting relaxation. For individuals recovering from injuries or surgeries, Qigong offers gentle, low-impact exercises that aid in the healing process, increase joint mobility, and improve muscle tone, all while minimizing the risk of re-injury.

Mental Health and Emotional Well-being

One of the primary applications of Qigong is reducing stress. Through deep breathing and relaxation techniques, Qigong activates the parasympathetic nervous system, lowering cortisol levels and promoting a state of calm. Qigong's focus on mindfulness, intentional movement, and breathing can help alleviate symptoms of depression. Studies show that the practice can improve mood and provide a sense of accomplishment, which can be uplifting for those experiencing depressive symptoms. By fostering awareness of bodily sensations and emotions, Qigong helps individuals better regulate their emotional responses. This makes it beneficial for people dealing with high-stress situations, PTSD, and emotional burnout.

Respiratory Health

Qigong breathing exercises can improve lung function, increase lung capacity, and reduce shortness of breath in individuals with respiratory conditions like Asthma and Chronic Obstructive Pulmonary Disease (COPD). The gentle exercises promote oxygenation and can help reduce symptoms such as wheezing and coughing. Regular practice of Qigong breathing techniques helps keep the respiratory system in optimal condition, which can be beneficial for improving endurance, managing seasonal allergies, and promoting recovery from respiratory infections.

Immune System Support

Studies have shown that Qigong can strengthen immune function, potentially reducing the risk of infections and illnesses. It is used as a preventive approach to maintain immune resilience, especially in older adults. By reducing stress and promoting balance in the body, Qigong may benefit people with autoimmune disorders, such as rheumatoid arthritis or lupus, by reducing flare-ups and alleviating symptoms.

Musculoskeletal Health and Physical Fitness

Qigong's gentle movements enhance flexibility and joint mobility, making it suitable for individuals with joint stiffness, osteoarthritis, or limited mobility. Qigong's emphasis on controlled, mindful movements makes it effective for improving balance and coordination, which can be particularly beneficial for older adults and those with a high risk of falls. Weight-bearing Qigong exercises are beneficial for bone density, making them suitable for preventing osteoporosis and improving skeletal health.

Sleep and Insomnia

Qigong helps activate the parasympathetic nervous system, which can lower cortisol levels and calm the mind, promoting deeper and more restful sleep. For people with insomnia, regular practice can help establish a better sleep cycle. Qigong's relaxation and breathing techniques can help manage nighttime anxiety and racing thoughts, making it easier to fall asleep and stay asleep.

Digestive Health

Qigong can help relieve stress and anxiety, which are common triggers for IBS (Irritable Bowel Syndrome). The abdominal movements and breathing techniques in Qigong may also improve digestion and reduce bloating. The gentle massaging effect of Qigong exercises on the abdomen can help promote efficient digestion, increase peristalsis, and alleviate symptoms like constipation and indigestion.

Longevity and Anti-Aging

Qigong is often practiced improving longevity by enhancing vitality, improving circulation, and supporting hormonal balance. It helps preserve muscle strength, joint flexibility, and cognitive function, contributing to a healthy aging process. Qigong's mindfulness practice can help improve memory, attention, and cognitive function, which is beneficial for older adults aiming to maintain mental clarity.

Workplace Wellness and Burnout Prevention

Qigong is increasingly being integrated into workplace wellness programs as a tool for reducing stress, boosting mental clarity, and enhancing focus. Short Qigong sessions can provide employees with a mental break and help prevent burnout. By reducing mental clutter and enhancing relaxation, Qigong can improve concentration, decision-making, and creativity, making it beneficial for people in high-stress or high-demand professions.

Rehabilitation and Recovery

Qigong therapy can support healing after surgery by enhancing circulation, reducing pain, and promoting relaxation. It is also a gentle way for patients to regain physical function gradually. Qigong is sometimes used as part of addiction recovery programs. Its ability to reduce cravings, alleviate stress, and promote mindfulness can support individuals in managing withdrawal symptoms and maintaining sobriety.

Spiritual Development and Self-Cultivation

Qigong therapy is also practiced for spiritual growth and self-awareness. It encourages introspection and a sense of unity with the natural world, which can foster peace, compassion, and a deeper connection with oneself. For people interested in meditation, Qigong offers an active form of mindfulness that integrates body movement with mental focus, creating a state of meditative awareness that can be easier for some than seated meditation.

Post-Traumatic Stress Disorder (PTSD) and Trauma Recovery

Qigong's combination of slow, rhythmic movements and mindfulness can help individuals manage PTSD symptoms by promoting relaxation and reducing hyperarousal. By helping trauma survivors reconnect with their bodies in a safe, gradual manner, Qigong provides a therapeutic approach that can help reduce flashbacks, nightmares, and anxiety linked to traumatic experiences.

Steps/ Process of Qigong Therapy

Preparation and Grounding

Before starting, practitioners take a few moments to settle their mind, relax the body, and enter a calm, focused state. This is often done through slow, deep breathing to transition from daily activities to a meditative mindset. Many Qigong practices begin with setting an intention, such as healing, relaxation, or energy cultivation. This intention helps direct *qi* and enhances focus throughout the session. A balanced, relaxed posture is essential in Qigong. Practitioners stand with feet shoulder-width apart, knees slightly bent, and shoulders relaxed. The head is positioned as if suspended from above, creating a natural alignment of the spine.

Breathing Techniques

In Qigong, breathing deeply and rhythmically into the abdomen is essential. This breathing technique enhances oxygen intake, helps calm the nervous system, and promotes relaxation. Practitioners learn to synchronize their movements with their breath, which promotes a smooth flow of *qi*. Typically, inhalation is paired with upward or outward movements, while exhalation corresponds with downward or inward motions. Slowing down the breath allows practitioners to become more aware of their energy flow, fostering a meditative state. This type of breathing helps deepen focus and supports energy cultivation.

Basic Movements and Postures

Qigong movements are generally slow, gentle, and repetitive, focusing on specific body parts or energy channels. These movements stimulate energy flow in the meridians, increase circulation, and relax muscles. The continuous, flowing nature of Qigong movements is designed to create a seamless connection between the body and breath, which encourages a smooth flow of *qi*. Some Qigong practices include standing or seated postures that promote energy accumulation in specific areas. Practitioners hold these positions for a few minutes to enhance concentration, build strength, and cultivate *qi* in the lower abdomen or other key areas.

Energy Awareness and Visualization

Practitioners are encouraged to develop awareness of *qi* sensations in the body, such as warmth, tingling, or a subtle flow of energy. This process is called "feeling the *qi*," and it enhances one's sensitivity to internal energy. Through focused intention (or *yi*), practitioners learn to direct *qi* to specific body areas or along meridians. For example, if a person is working on healing their shoulder, they might visualize *qi* flowing to that area, aiding recovery. Visualization often includes imagining energy circulating within the body, connecting with the earth, or aligning with the universe's energy. These visualizations help deepen the mind-body connection and enhance the effectiveness of Qigong therapy.

Meditation and Mindfulness

In many forms of Qigong, standing meditation is practiced cultivating a state of inner stillness and awareness. This posture, known as *Zhan Zhuang* (standing like a tree), strengthens the body, improves energy flow, and promotes mental clarity. Some Qigong practices incorporate seated meditation, where practitioners focus on breathing, energy sensations, and stillness. This meditation develops concentration and fosters mental peace. Practicing mindfulness while observing one's breathing, posture, and movements helps calm the mind and regulate emotions, which is essential for energy balance and healing.

Closing the Practice and Grounding

After a Qigong session, practitioners often perform a closing ritual, such as rubbing the hands together or gently patting specific body areas to "seal" the *qi* gathered during the practice. This helps retain the energy in the body and completes the session. In some practices, practitioners massage specific points, such as the lower abdomen (known as *Dantian*) or other energy centers, to settle the *qi* and improve circulation. Practitioners take a moment to relax, slowly transition their mind and body back to their everyday state, and express gratitude. This helps them maintain the benefits of Qigong and allows a smooth return to daily activities.

Regular Practice and Integration

For best results, Qigong should be practiced regularly. Many practitioners create a daily routine, even if it's only a few minutes each day, to maintain energy flow, reduce stress, and continue improving. Advanced practitioners often integrate Qigong principles into their daily activities, such as mindful breathing, posture awareness, and relaxation techniques. This makes it easier to apply the benefits of Qigong therapy in daily life. Practitioners regularly assess their energy levels, emotional state, and physical health to determine which Qigong practices suit their needs best. This allows them to adapt their practice according to their changing needs and goals.

Case Studies

Case Study 1: The Impact of Qigong Therapy on Chronic Pain and Anxiety in Adults with Fibromyalgia

Background

Fibromyalgia is a chronic condition characterized by widespread musculoskeletal pain, fatigue, and tenderness in localized areas. Patients often experience accompanying mental health symptoms, such as anxiety and depression, due to the condition's debilitating nature. Standard treatment includes pain relievers, antidepressants, physical therapy, and lifestyle modifications. However, these interventions often provide limited relief, prompting patients to explore alternative therapies like qigong.

Purpose of the Study

The purpose of this study is to evaluate the impact of regular qigong practice on pain levels, quality of life, and anxiety symptoms in adults with fibromyalgia. The study focuses on understanding the physiological and psychological effects of qigong therapy and its viability as a complementary intervention.

Methodology

The sample size was 50 participants diagnosed with fibromyalgia. The age range was from 30 to 60 years. The selection criteria were participants who had persistent symptoms for over one year and expressed interest in alternative therapy.

Intervention

A standardized qigong program consisting of gentle movements, breathing exercises, and meditation, held twice a week over 12 weeks. Participants were encouraged to practice qigong at home for an additional 15 minutes each day. The duration for each session lasted 60 minutes. Certified qigong therapist with experience in working with chronic pain patients working as instructor.

Measurements

Pain levels were assessed using the Visual Analog Scale (VAS) before and after the 12-week intervention. Anxiety levels were measured through the Generalized Anxiety Disorder 7-item (GAD-7) scale. Quality of Life was evaluated by using the Fibromyalgia Impact Questionnaire (FIQ).

Results

Participants experienced an average reduction in pain levels by 30% over the 12-week period. 35 out of 50 participants reported a moderate reduction in their pain intensity, and 10 participants reported significant pain relief. The average anxiety score decreased by 25%. Notably, participants who practiced qigong more frequently reported greater improvements in managing anxiety symptoms. Quality of life improved, with 40% of participants reporting greater physical ease in performing daily tasks. Participants cited enhanced sleep quality, increased energy, and a greater sense of overall well-being.

Discussion

Qigong is believed to stimulate the release of endorphins and decrease the release of stress hormones like cortisol. This effect could help reduce perceived pain and improve mood. Qigong's slow, flowing movements may enhance blood and lymphatic flow, potentially aiding in pain reduction. The meditative aspects of qigong can activate the parasympathetic nervous system, promoting relaxation and reducing anxiety. The gentle stretching and movements associated with qigong help to relieve muscle stiffness and increase flexibility, which are beneficial for fibromyalgia patients who often have muscle tension.

Limitations

Pain and anxiety levels are subjective, and reliance on self-reported data introduces a risk of bias. A larger study could better determine the generalizability of these findings. Participants who practiced qigong more frequently at home tended to have better outcomes, suggesting variability in adherence to the program may influence results.

Conclusion

This case study suggests that qigong therapy could be an effective complementary approach for managing pain, reducing anxiety, and improving the quality of life in individuals with fibromyalgia. Regular practice, even at low intensity, seems to offer physical and psychological benefits. Although further research with larger samples and control groups is necessary, qigong presents a low-risk, accessible option for those seeking alternative methods to complement traditional fibromyalgia treatment.

Case Study 2: Effects of Qigong Therapy on Quality of Life and Immune Function in Cancer Patients

Background

Cancer patients often experience a range of symptoms, including fatigue, pain, anxiety, and reduced immune function, especially those undergoing chemotherapy or radiation therapy. These treatments can weaken the immune system, making patients more vulnerable to infections and affecting overall quality of life. There has been increasing interest in qigong therapy as a complementary treatment to improve physical and mental health outcomes in cancer patients.

Purpose of the Study

This study aims to evaluate the impact of qigong therapy on immune function, quality of life, and psychological well-being in cancer patients undergoing treatment. It explores whether qigong therapy can help mitigate the side effects of conventional treatments and support overall recovery.

Methodology

Sample Size was 60 cancer patients (various types and stages). Selection criteria were of patients currently receiving chemotherapy or radiation therapy, and experiencing symptoms such as fatigue, anxiety, or low immunity.

Intervention

A structured qigong program involving gentle exercises, breathing techniques, and meditation. The sessions were held three times a week, each lasting 45 minutes, over a period of 8 weeks. Patients were encouraged to practice for 10–15 minutes daily at home. Certified qigong therapist with expertise in working with cancer patients.

Measurements

Blood tests measuring immune markers, including white blood cell count and natural killer (NK) cell activity, were conducted at the beginning and end of the study. Quality of Life was assessed using the

Functional Assessment of Cancer Therapy-General (FACT-G) questionnaire. Anxiety and depression were measured using the Hospital Anxiety and Depression Scale (HADS).

Results

45 out of 60 patients showed a mild to moderate increase in white blood cell count, indicating improved immune resilience. NK cell activity improved in 38 participants, suggesting a potential benefit for the body's ability to target and destroy cancer cells. Quality of life improved in 78% of participants, with significant increases in emotional well-being, physical health, and social interactions. Many patients reported feeling more energetic and less fatigued. The HADS scores showed a 30% average reduction in both anxiety and depression symptoms across the group. Patients commonly reported feeling more relaxed, less anxious about their treatment, and more positive overall.

Discussion

Qigong's combination of gentle movement and deep breathing may help reduce stress, which in turn can boost immune function by reducing cortisol levels and other stress hormones that weaken immunity. The focus on balancing "Qi" (energy flow) is thought to aid the body's natural healing processes and reduce blockages that may contribute to fatigue and other symptoms. Qigong's meditative component fosters mindfulness, which may improve mental resilience and emotional control, particularly helpful for those facing serious health challenges.

Limitations

While promising, the sample size is small, and further studies with larger, more diverse groups would help confirm findings. Some observed benefits might stem from increased physical activity, social support from group sessions, or the placebo effect. Not all patients practiced qigong consistently at home, which may affect the results.

Conclusion

This case study suggests that qigong therapy has potential benefits for improving immune function, quality of life, and mental health in cancer patients undergoing treatment. Although more research is needed, qigong therapy appears to be a low-risk, accessible intervention that could complement conventional cancer treatments, helping to manage symptoms and support overall well-being.

References

Chan, C. L. W., Wang, C. W., Ho, R. T. H., Ng, S. M., & Chan, J. S. M. (2012). Qigong exercise on quality of life, anxiety, and depressive symptoms in cancer patients: A systematic review and meta-analysis. *Evidence-Based Complementary and Alternative Medicine*, 2012.

Chen, K. W., Liu, T., Zhang, H., Lin, Z., Lee, Y., & Thompson, E. A. (2020). Qigong exercise for the treatment of fibromyalgia: A systematic review of randomized controlled trials. *Journal of Pain Research*, 13, 343-352.

Cohen, M. H., & McCarthy, E. P. (2015). Complementary therapies in cancer care: Evidence for qigong and tai chi. *Current Oncology Reports*, 17(3), 25.

Jahnke, R., Larkey, L., Rogers, C., Etnier, J., & Lin, F. (2010). A comprehensive review of health benefits of qigong and tai chi. *American Journal of Health Promotion*, 24(6), e1-e25.

Lam, L. C., & Kwan-Ho, Y. L. (2018). The impact of qigong on dementia: A systematic review and meta-analysis. *Journal of Alzheimer's Disease*, 64(1), 245-253.

Larkey, L., Jahnke, R., Etnier, J., & Gonzalez, J. (2009). Meditative movement as a category of exercise: Implications for research. *Journal of Physical Activity and Health*, 6(2), 230-238.

Lee, M. S., & Ernst, E. (2012). Systematic reviews of tai chi: An overview. *British Journal of Sports Medicine*, 46(10), 713-718.

Liu, X., Clark, J., & Siskind, D. (2015). The efficacy of qigong on mental health outcomes: A systematic review and meta-analysis. *Medicine*, 94(39), e1500.

Oh, B., Butow, P., Mullan, B., Clarke, S., Beale, P., & Pavlakis, N. (2012). Impact of medical qigong on quality of life, fatigue, mood, and inflammation in cancer patients: A randomized controlled trial. *Annals of Oncology*, 23(2), 508-513.

Rogers, C. E., Larkey, L. K., & Keller, C. (2009). A review of clinical trials of tai chi and qigong in older adults. *Western Journal of Nursing Research*, 31(2), 245-279.

Tsang, H. W., Fung, K. M., Chan, A. S., Lee, G., & Chan, F. (2006). Effect of qigong on depressive and anxiety symptoms: A randomized controlled trial. *Journal of Affective Disorders*, 90(1), 13-16.

Wang, F., Lee, E. K., Wu, T., Benson, H., Fricchione, G., Wang, W., & Yeung, A. (2014). The effects of tai chi on depression, anxiety, and psychological well-being: A systematic review and meta-analysis. *International Journal of Behavioral Medicine*, 21(4), 605-617.

Zeng, Y., Luo, T., Xie, H., & Huang, M. (2014). Health benefits of qigong or tai chi for cancer patients: A systematic review and meta-analyses. *Complementary Therapies in Medicine*, 22(5), 809-817.

Chapter 15

Reiki Healing

Preetha D.V School of Liberal Studies (SLS), CMR University, Bangalore

Introduction to Reiki Healing: An Eastern Perspective on Healing and Therapy

Reiki, a form of energy healing that originated in Japan, is based on the belief in an unseen life force energy that flows through us and is responsible for our vitality. This healing system aligns with many traditional Eastern practices, where the mind, body, and spirit are seen as interconnected aspects of health. The word "Reiki" comes from two Japanese words: "Rei," meaning universal, and "Ki," meaning life force energy. Reiki has gained global recognition as a complementary therapy, appealing to those seeking holistic, non-invasive treatments that focus on spiritual well-being.

The Origin of Reiki

Reiki, a healing practice that focuses on channeling universal life energy, has gained global recognition as an alternative therapy. Rooted in ancient Eastern philosophies, Reiki was rediscovered and formalized in Japan in the early 20th century by Dr. Mikao Usui.

The Life of Dr. Mikao Usui: The Founder of Reiki

Dr. Mikao Usui (1865-1926), the founder of the Reiki system, was born in the village of Taniai, Japan, during a time of cultural and spiritual transition in Japan. Usui grew up in a family that valued education and spirituality, which set the foundation for his later pursuits. He was a seeker of spiritual knowledge, and his studies covered a wide range of subjects, including medicine, psychology, theology, and various spiritual disciplines.

The Spiritual Awakening on Mount Kurama

The turning point in Dr. Usui's life occurred in 1922 when he embarked on a spiritual retreat to Mount Kurama, a sacred site near Kyoto, Japan. Mount Kurama has long been associated with spiritual enlightenment and is believed to be home to powerful spiritual energies. During his 21-day retreat, Usui fasted, meditated, and engaged in deep reflection, seeking answers to questions about life, health, and spirituality.

According to Reiki tradition, on the 21st day of his retreat, Usui experienced a profound spiritual awakening. As the story goes, he felt a powerful flow of energy enter his body through his crown chakra, granting him insight into the nature of universal life energy and how to channel it for healing purposes. This experience marked the birth of Reiki, which translates to "universal life energy" (with "Rei" meaning universal and "Ki" meaning life force energy) (Rand, 2011).

Establishing the Usui System of Natural Healing

Upon returning from Mount Kurama, Dr. Usui dedicated himself to developing a system of healing that anyone could practice. He called it Usui Reiki Ryoho or the Usui System of Natural Healing. His method involved the use of specific hand placements to channel Reiki energy into the body, helping to remove energy blockages and promote healing (Rosenthal, 2016). Reiki, according to Usui, not only addressed physical ailments but also supported emotional and spiritual healing.

To ensure that his system was accessible to everyone, Usui formalized Reiki training into a series of attunements and techniques. Attunements are energetic transmissions from a Reiki master to a student, enabling the student to connect to the universal life force and channel it for healing. These attunements became an essential part of Reiki's transmission from teacher to student.

The Role of Chujiro Hayashi and Hawayo Takata in Spreading Reiki

Dr. Usui began to teach Reiki to others and, over time, attracted a dedicated group of students. One of his most prominent students was Chujiro Hayashi, a former naval officer. Hayashi played a significant role in systematizing Reiki by refining Usui's teachings into a structured practice, including detailed hand positions and protocols for treating specific ailments. In 1925, Usui initiated Hayashi as a Reiki master, ensuring the continuation of Reiki after his death.

Hayashi went on to open a Reiki clinic in Tokyo, where he treated patients and trained students. He further systematized the practice of Reiki, making it more accessible to people seeking alternative forms of healing. His efforts in structuring the practice contributed to Reiki's growth in Japan (Miles & True, 2003).

The global spread of Reiki can largely be attributed to Hawayo Takata, a Japanese American woman who learned Reiki from Hayashi in the 1930s. Takata had traveled to Japan for surgery but, after receiving Reiki treatments, decided to study the practice under Hayashi. Takata was instrumental in bringing Reiki to the West, where it became widely recognized as a form of complementary therapy.

Takata's teachings helped bridge the gap between Eastern and Western medicine, and she adapted some of the practices to make Reiki more accessible to Western audiences. She simplified the explanations of Reiki's spiritual components, focusing on its practical benefits for healing and stress relief (Rosenthal, 2016). By the time of her death in 1980, Takata had trained 22 Reiki masters, ensuring the continuation of Reiki's global spread.

Reiki's Connection to Ancient Eastern Healing Traditions

While Dr. Usui formalized the practice of Reiki in the early 20th century, its philosophical roots can be traced back to ancient Eastern healing systems. The concept of Ki (life force energy) is central to many Eastern healing traditions, such as Traditional Chinese Medicine (TCM) and Ayurveda. In TCM, the life force energy is called Qi, and it flows through energy pathways known as meridians. Similarly, in Ayurveda, the life force is known as Prana, which flows through the body's energy centers, or chakras (Baldwin, Wagers, & Schwartz, 2008).

In these traditions, health is understood as a state of balance, where energy flows freely without blockages. Illness arises when the flow of energy is disrupted, and healing occurs when balance is restored. Reiki shares this fundamental belief: when Ki flows harmoniously through the body, health is maintained; when it is blocked or imbalanced, disease and emotional distress can result (Rand, 2011). Reiki practitioners aim to restore this balance by channeling universal life energy into the body, promoting healing at the physical, emotional, and spiritual levels.

Reiki's origins lie in Dr. Mikao Usui's spiritual quest for a healing method that could transcend conventional medicine and address the whole person—body, mind, and spirit. His discovery of Reiki on Mount Kurama in 1922 marked the beginning of a healing tradition that would spread from Japan to the rest of the world. Through the efforts of Dr. Usui, Chujiro Hayashi, and Hawayo Takata, Reiki became a global phenomenon, practiced by millions seeking holistic health and emotional well-being.

The Philosophy of Reiki Healing

Reiki, a healing practice rooted in the concept of universal life energy, embodies a unique philosophical foundation that integrates spiritual, emotional, and physical healing. At its core, Reiki is not merely a method of healing but a holistic way of understanding the self and the universe. It teaches that the flow of life energy, or Ki, is essential for maintaining harmony within the body and between individuals and their environment.

The Central Concept of Ki (Life Force Energy)

The fundamental concept behind Reiki is Ki, the vital life force energy that flows through all living beings. This idea is not unique to Reiki but is shared across many Eastern healing traditions. In Traditional Chinese Medicine (TCM), it is known as Qi, and in the Indian system of Ayurveda, it is referred to as Prana (Baldwin, Wagers, & Schwartz, 2008). Reiki views Ki as the essential energy that sustains life and supports overall well-being. When Ki flows freely, it nourishes the body, mind, and spirit. However, when this energy is blocked or stagnant, it leads to illness, stress, and emotional imbalance.

Reiki practitioners believe that through the gentle laying on of hands, they can channel universal energy into the recipient, helping to restore the natural flow of Ki. This is not a religious belief but a spiritual understanding of the interconnectedness between energy, health, and consciousness. Ki is seen as the bridge between the physical and spiritual worlds, flowing through all living things and connecting them to the universal source of energy, often referred to as Rei (Rand, 2011).

Reiki's Holistic Worldview: Body, Mind, and Spirit

Reiki philosophy is fundamentally holistic, meaning that it views the individual as a whole—body, mind, and spirit—rather than focusing solely on physical symptoms. In this perspective, illness is not just a physical condition but often reflects deeper emotional or spiritual imbalances. Healing, therefore, must occur at multiple levels: physical, emotional, and spiritual.

According to Reiki's philosophy, emotional and mental stress can manifest in the body as illness or discomfort. For example, chronic stress might lead to physical ailments like headaches or digestive problems. Reiki aims to address these deeper sources of disharmony by calming the mind, clearing emotional blockages, and promoting spiritual growth (Rosenthal, 2016). This holistic approach is also seen in many other alternative therapies, such as Ayurveda and traditional Japanese medicine, which emphasize the importance of treating the root cause of an issue rather than just the symptoms.

The Five Reiki Principles

The Five Reiki Principles are a central part of Reiki philosophy. These principles, established by Dr. Mikao Usui, serve as a guide for living a balanced and harmonious life.

1. **Just for today, do not anger**

   Anger, according to Reiki, is one of the most destructive emotions. It not only disrupts emotional balance but can also block the flow of Ki in the body. By practicing non-anger, Reiki encourages individuals to let go of resentment and frustration, creating space for healing and compassion.

2. **Just for today, do not worry**

   Worrying is seen as a misuse of mental energy, focusing on potential future problems rather than the present moment. Reiki teaches that excessive worrying can deplete one's energy reserves, leading to physical and emotional exhaustion. Practicing mindfulness and focusing on the present can alleviate the burden of worry.

3. **Be grateful**

   Gratitude is a powerful emotion that shifts focus away from what is lacking and towards the abundance already present in life. Reiki practitioners are encouraged to cultivate an attitude of gratitude, which helps raise their energetic frequency and strengthens their connection to the universal energy.

4. **Work with integrity**

   Integrity, in Reiki philosophy, refers to being honest with oneself and others. It encourages practitioners to live authentically and to honor their responsibilities. Working with integrity also means respecting the energy of others and not using Reiki for selfish purposes.

5. **Be kind to others**

   Kindness and compassion are central to the practice of Reiki. By extending kindness to others, Reiki practitioners help foster a sense of unity and interconnectedness. The energy of kindness promotes healing and strengthens the flow of Ki within both the practitioner and the recipient.

The Role of the Practitioner in Reiki Healing and the Techniques Used

Reiki is a gentle, non-invasive energy healing practice that relies on the practitioner as a conduit for universal life energy. The role of the Reiki practitioner is not to manipulate or force healing, but to facilitate the natural flow of energy in a way that supports the body's innate ability to heal itself. In this article, we will delve into the key responsibilities of the Reiki practitioner, the qualities they must cultivate, and the specific techniques they employ during healing sessions.

The Role of the Reiki Practitioner

Reiki practitioners are essentially channels for healing energy. Their main responsibility is to access and direct universal life energy (often referred to as "Ki") to the recipient, allowing this energy to flow through the body and restore balance. The practitioner does not control or manipulate the energy but instead allows it to be drawn to where the recipient needs it most.

This dynamic underscore one of the most important aspects of the Reiki practitioner's role: they are facilitators rather than healers in the traditional sense. Reiki philosophy teaches that healing is a natural process driven by the body's own energy system, and the practitioner's role is to clear blockages and support the recipient's ability to heal.

Establishing a Healing Space

Before starting a Reiki session, practitioners are responsible for creating a calm, safe, and sacred space where the recipient can relax. The environment plays an important role in facilitating healing, as Reiki encourages the recipient to release stress and tension. Practitioners often prepare the space by:

- Dimming the lights to create a serene atmosphere
- Playing soft, meditative music
- Using calming scents, such as essential oils or incense
- Ensuring the room is free from distractions and interruptions

Attunement and Connection to Universal Energy

The ability to channel Reiki energy is developed through a process called attunement. Attunements are performed by Reiki masters and involve a spiritual initiation that opens the practitioner's energy channels, allowing them to connect to the universal life force. This connection is crucial, as the practitioner does not use their own energy to heal but acts as a conduit for the energy that flows from the universal source (Rosenthal, 2016).

Practitioners must maintain a high degree of spiritual alignment and mindfulness to channel Reiki effectively. This means practicing regular meditation, self-care, and adherence to the Five Reiki Precepts (do not anger, do not worry, be grateful, work with integrity, be kind to others), which ensure that the practitioner approaches healing with a balanced mind and heart (Rand, 2011).

The Importance of Compassion and Intention

A key role of the Reiki practitioner is to hold space for the recipient with compassion and non-judgment. Unlike conventional medical practitioners, who may diagnose or prescribe, Reiki practitioners remain open and accepting, trusting that the recipient's body knows how to heal itself when provided with the right energetic support.

Compassion is central to the practice of Reiki because the practitioner's intention significantly impacts the flow of energy. Reiki philosophy teaches that energy is most effectively channeled when the practitioner's intention is rooted in pure love and concern for the recipient's well-being. In this way, Reiki is not just a technical skill but also a deeply empathic practice that nurtures emotional and spiritual healing as much as physical recovery (Rand, 2011).

The Techniques Used in Reiki Healing

Reiki practitioners use a variety of techniques to channel healing energy into the recipient's body. The techniques are gentle and non-invasive, involving the laying on of hands or hands hovering just above the body. Below, we explore the main techniques employed in Reiki healing sessions.

The Laying on of Hands

One of the most common techniques in Reiki is the laying on of hands. During a Reiki session, the practitioner places their hands on or near specific areas of the recipient's body, typically focusing on the energy centers known as chakras. The goal is to channel energy to these areas, helping to release blockages and restore a balanced flow of Ki (Baldwin, Wagers, & Schwartz, 2008).

There are twelve standard hand positions used in Reiki, covering the head, torso, and back. The practitioner typically holds each hand position for three to five minutes, depending on the recipient's needs. Practitioners are trained to allow the body's energy field to "pull" the energy from their hands rather than actively pushing energy into the recipient.

Scanning the Energy Field (Byosen Scanning)

Another important technique in Reiki healing is Byosen Scanning, a process where the practitioner scans the recipient's energy field with their hands to detect areas of imbalance. Byosen is a Japanese word meaning "disease line" or "sick line," and it refers to the subtle sensations a practitioner feels when they come across areas where the energy is stagnant or imbalanced.

During this process, the practitioner hovers their hands several inches above the body and moves them slowly, paying attention to any sensations such as tingling, heat, or coolness. These sensations provide clues about where healing energy may be needed. Once identified, the practitioner may focus on these areas during the session, directing extra energy to restore balance.

The Chakras and Energy Centers

Reiki healing is closely tied to the concept of chakras, which are energy centers located throughout the body. According to Reiki philosophy, there are seven major chakras that align along the spine, each corresponding to different physical, emotional, and spiritual aspects of a person.

Practitioners often focus on balancing the chakras during Reiki sessions. Blocked or imbalanced chakras are believed to contribute to physical or emotional issues, so the practitioner works to clear these blockages and restore a healthy flow of energy. This can be done through specific hand placements over the chakra points, combined with focused intention and energy transmission (Rosenthal, 2016).

Distance Healing (Enkaku Chiryo)

Reiki is unique in that it offers a method for distance healing, known as Enkaku Chiryo. This technique allows the practitioner to send healing energy to a recipient who is not physically present. Distance healing operates on the premise that energy is not confined by space or time and can be sent across distances just as effectively as when performed in person.

The practitioner typically uses symbols (known as the Reiki symbols) that were taught during their attunement to connect with the recipient's energy field. They visualize the person and direct healing energy to them, often using a photograph or an object that represents the recipient. Many Reiki practitioners find that distance healing is just as powerful as in-person sessions and can be a valuable tool for those who are unable to attend in person due to physical limitations or geographical distance (Rand, 2011).

Intuitive Reiki Techniques

While traditional Reiki techniques follow specific hand positions and protocols, advanced practitioners often incorporate intuitive techniques into their practice. After years of working with energy, some practitioners develop a heightened sensitivity to the recipient's needs and may choose to adjust their hand positions or use different methods based on the energy they feel during the session.

This intuitive approach reflects Reiki's emphasis on attunement and connection with the universal life force. Reiki encourages practitioners to trust their intuition, allowing the energy to guide them to where it is needed most. This is a hallmark of Reiki's flexible and adaptive nature, which distinguishes it from more rigid healing modalities.

Self-Reiki: Empowering the Practitioner's Own Healing

In addition to offering Reiki to others, practitioners are encouraged to practice self-Reiki as part of their own spiritual and healing journey. Self-Reiki involves applying the same hand positions and techniques to oneself, focusing on promoting personal balance, relaxation, and well-being. Practitioners are taught that before they can heal others, they must take care of their own energy, ensuring they remain clear channels for healing (Rosenthal, 2016).

The role of the Reiki practitioner is both humble and profound. As a conduit for universal life energy, the practitioner facilitates the natural healing process, helping to restore balance and harmony within the recipient. Through compassionate intention, mindfulness, and the application of specific techniques such as the laying on of hands, Byosen Scanning, and chakra balancing, the practitioner supports the recipient in releasing blockages and promoting overall well-being.

Reiki practitioners must cultivate compassion, intuition, and spiritual alignment, recognizing that they are not the source of the healing but simply a channel for it.

Reiki and Its Connection to Other Eastern Healing Systems:

Reiki, a form of energy healing developed in Japan by Dr. Mikao Usui in the early 20th century, is deeply rooted in the spiritual and healing traditions of the East. Although Reiki is unique in its practice and philosophy, it shares several fundamental principles with other ancient Eastern healing systems such as Traditional Chinese Medicine (TCM), Ayurveda, and Tibetan healing traditions. These systems emphasize the flow of energy through the body, the interconnectedness of body, mind, and spirit, and the belief that health is achieved by maintaining balance within the body's energy systems.

The Concept of Universal Life Energy

One of the most significant connections between Reiki and other Eastern healing systems is the concept of universal life energy. Reiki is based on the belief that there is a vital life force energy, known as Ki in Japanese, that flows through all living beings. This energy is what sustains life, and when its flow is disrupted, illness or emotional imbalance can result. The practitioner channels Ki into the recipient's body to restore balance and promote healing.

The concept of life force energy is not unique to Reiki. In Traditional Chinese Medicine (TCM), this same energy is referred to as Qi (also spelled "Chi"), which is believed to flow through meridians or energy pathways in the body. In Ayurveda, the ancient healing system from India, this energy is known as Prana, which moves through the body's nadis (energy channels). Tibetan Medicine also speaks of a subtle life force energy that connects all things and flows through the body's channels.

Although these systems use different names for life energy, the underlying principle is the same: the free flow of energy is essential for health, while blockages or imbalances in this flow lead to illness. Reiki, TCM, and Ayurveda all focus on removing these blockages and restoring balance to promote physical, emotional, and spiritual well-being (Rand, 2011).

Chakras and Meridians: Pathways of Energy

Reiki shares a close connection with the concept of chakras—energy centers in the body that originate in Hindu and Buddhist traditions. According to these traditions, there are seven major chakras that run along the spine, from the base to the crown of the head. Each chakra corresponds to different aspects of physical, emotional, and spiritual health, and when these chakras are blocked or imbalanced, it can lead to illness.

In Ayurveda and Yoga, practitioners focus on balancing the chakras to maintain the free flow of Prana (life energy) throughout the body. Similarly, in Reiki, practitioners often direct energy to the chakras to clear blockages and restore balance. While Reiki does not focus exclusively on the chakras, many practitioners incorporate chakra healing into their sessions, recognizing that these energy centers are crucial for overall health and well-being.

In Traditional Chinese Medicine (TCM), the concept of energy flow is represented by meridians—invisible channels through which Qi flows. Acupuncture, a core practice in TCM, aims to balance Qi by inserting fine needles into specific points along the meridians to release blockages and stimulate the flow of energy. Reiki practitioners, though they do not use needles, also aim to restore the free flow of Ki by working with the body's energy field, often focusing on areas where they sense blockages or imbalances (Baldwin, Wagers, & Schwartz, 2008).

Holistic View of Health: Body, Mind, and Spirit

Another commonality between Reiki and other Eastern healing systems is the holistic approach to health. In the West, medicine often focuses on treating physical symptoms, whereas Eastern traditions, including Reiki, recognize that health is a product of the balance between body, mind, and spirit.

In Ayurveda, health is achieved through the balance of the three doshas: Vata (air), Pitta (fire), and Kapha (earth). Each person has a unique constitution, and imbalance in the doshas can lead to illness. Ayurvedic treatments aim to restore harmony by balancing these forces through diet, lifestyle changes, herbal remedies, and energy work.

Similarly, Traditional Chinese Medicine views health as the balance of Yin and Yang, the complementary forces that make up all aspects of life. Imbalance between these forces leads to illness, and treatments such as acupuncture, herbal medicine, and Tai Chi aim to restore this balance.

Reiki also adopts a holistic philosophy, viewing illness not just as a physical issue but as the result of imbalances in the emotional, mental, or spiritual realms. Reiki practitioners work to address the root cause of these imbalances, promoting healing on all levels. For example, a Reiki practitioner might sense an emotional blockage in a person's heart chakra that corresponds to grief or heartache, and by channeling healing energy, they help the individual release this emotional burden, which in turn may improve their physical health (Rosenthal, 2016).

Healing Through Intention and Compassion

A distinguishing feature of Reiki, which aligns with many Eastern traditions, is the emphasis on intention and compassion in healing. Reiki practitioners believe that healing energy is guided by the highest intention of the practitioner and recipient. The practitioner serves as a channel for universal life energy, and the energy flows where it is most needed, based on the intention of healing.

In Ayurveda and Tibetan Medicine, healing is also a spiritual process that involves cultivating compassion and mindfulness. Tibetan healers, for example, often incorporate meditation and mantras into their practice, believing that healing cannot occur without spiritual awareness and a compassionate heart.

Similarly, in Traditional Chinese Medicine, treatments such as Qi Gong—a practice that combines movement, meditation, and breath control—focus on cultivating inner peace and balance. The intention behind Qi Gong is not just to treat the physical body but to harmonize the mind and spirit as well.

Distance Healing and Universal Connectivity

One of the unique aspects of Reiki is its use of distance healing, a practice that allows practitioners to send healing energy to someone who is not physically present. This concept is based on the belief that universal life energy transcends physical boundaries and can be directed across time and space.

The idea of energy operating beyond physical proximity is also present in Eastern spiritual traditions. In Buddhism, for example, the concept of interconnectedness suggests that all beings are connected through the fabric of the universe. Similarly, in Ayurveda, it is believed that the energy of the universe is omnipresent and can be accessed by those who are attuned to it. Practices like meditation and prayer in many Eastern traditions also embody this idea of sending healing intentions across distances.

Reiki's distance healing aligns with these beliefs, as it is rooted in the idea that energy is not limited by physical constraints. Reiki practitioners often use symbols and visualization techniques to send healing energy to a recipient, trusting that the energy will reach them wherever they are. This reflects the broader Eastern worldview that energy and consciousness are interconnected, transcending the physical limitations of time and space (Miles & True, 2003).

The Healing Power of Meditation

Meditation plays a key role in many Eastern healing systems, including Reiki. In Reiki, meditation is used to attune practitioners to the universal life energy, clear their own energy field, and enhance their intuitive abilities. Practitioners often meditate before and during healing sessions to ensure that they are centered and open to receiving and transmitting healing energy.

Meditation is equally important in Buddhist and Hindu traditions, where it is viewed as a path to spiritual enlightenment and healing. In Ayurveda, meditation is used to calm the mind and balance the doshas, while in Tibetan Medicine, meditation is seen as a tool for connecting with the deeper layers of consciousness and facilitating emotional and spiritual healing.

Reiki's connection to meditation highlights its emphasis on mindfulness and presence during the healing process. Just as in these other traditions, Reiki practitioners believe that healing can only occur when the mind is still, the heart is open, and the practitioner is fully present in the moment (Rosenthal, 2016).

Reiki is more than just a standalone healing system; it is deeply connected to the broader traditions of Eastern philosophy and medicine. Whether through the shared belief in the flow of life energy (Ki, Qi, or Prana), the importance of balance within the body's energy systems, or the role of intention and compassion in healing, Reiki reflects many of the core principles found in other Eastern healing systems such as Traditional Chinese Medicine, Ayurveda, and Tibetan healing practices.

Although Reiki has its own unique methods, such as the laying on of hands and distance healing, it resonates with the holistic, spiritual approach to health that characterizes Eastern medicine.

Reiki in the Modern Context

The journey of Reiki from a spiritual practice in Japan to a global healing modality reflects its ability to adapt and evolve. Originally rooted in Eastern philosophy, Reiki was primarily a spiritual practice focused on balancing the body's energy and facilitating healing on multiple levels—physical, emotional, and spiritual. Reiki was not intended to replace conventional medicine but to complement it by supporting the body's natural ability to heal itself.

In the mid-20th century, Reiki was introduced to the West by Hawayo Takata, a Japanese American woman who learned Reiki in Japan and brought it to the United States. Through Takata's efforts, Reiki spread across North America and Europe, eventually becoming a popular alternative therapy. Since then, Reiki has continued to evolve, with various styles and approaches emerging, such as Usui Reiki, Karuna Reiki, and Tibetan Reiki. Each adaptation maintains the core principles of Reiki while incorporating new insights and techniques to address the needs of modern practitioners and recipients (Rand, 2011).

Reiki in Healthcare: A Growing Integration

One of the most significant developments in Reiki's modern context is its increasing integration into the healthcare system. Reiki is now used in hospitals, hospices, and wellness centers as a complementary therapy for patients dealing with a variety of conditions, including chronic pain, cancer, stress, and anxiety. This integration is part of a broader trend toward holistic health in modern medicine, where practitioners recognize that healing involves more than just treating physical symptoms. It requires addressing the emotional, mental, and spiritual aspects of health as well.

In hospitals, Reiki is often used to help patients manage pain and reduce anxiety before and after surgery. It is also employed in palliative care to provide comfort and emotional support to patients with terminal illnesses. Many hospitals now offer Reiki as part of their integrative medicine programs, recognizing its potential to improve patients' quality of life (VanderVaart, et al., 2009). The incorporation of Reiki into medical settings represents a shift toward patient-centered care, where the well-being of the whole person—body, mind, and spirit—is considered.

Reiki and Scientific Research: Growing Evidence for Its Benefits

While Reiki is often classified as a complementary or alternative therapy, a growing body of research has begun to explore its efficacy in improving health outcomes. Although Reiki's mechanisms remain largely unexplained from a scientific perspective, studies suggest that Reiki may offer several benefits, particularly in stress reduction, pain management, and emotional well-being.

One of the most well-documented effects of Reiki is its ability to induce a state of deep relaxation, which can help alleviate stress and anxiety. Stress is widely recognized as a contributing factor to a range of health problems, including cardiovascular disease, depression, and weakened immune function. By promoting relaxation, Reiki may help reduce the physiological and emotional effects of stress. A study published in the Journal of Alternative and Complementary Medicine found that Reiki significantly lowered stress levels and improved the mood of participants (Baldwin, Wagers, & Schwartz, 2008).

Reiki has also been studied for its potential role in pain management. A randomized controlled trial conducted at Hartford Hospital in Connecticut found that patients who received Reiki treatments experienced a reduction in pain, anxiety, and fatigue. The study concluded that Reiki could be a useful adjunct to conventional medical treatments for pain management, particularly for patients undergoing surgery or chemotherapy (Thrane & Cohen, 2014).

Additionally, Reiki's impact on emotional healing is of particular interest in modern psychological care. Many Reiki practitioners report that their clients experience emotional release and healing, especially in cases of trauma, grief, or depression. Although the exact mechanisms are still not fully understood, it is believed that Reiki helps to rebalance the body's energy, allowing emotional blockages to be released and promoting a sense of calm and well-being (Miles & True, 2003).

Reiki in Mental Health and Emotional Well-being

In the modern context, where mental health has become a critical concern, Reiki offers a non-invasive and compassionate approach to emotional healing. In today's fast-paced world, stress, anxiety, and depression are prevalent. Many people are searching for holistic methods to manage their mental health, and Reiki's focus on energy balance provides an alternative to pharmaceutical treatments.

Reiki helps address mental health challenges by promoting emotional balance and inner peace. Recipients often report feeling a sense of calm and clarity after a session, which can be particularly helpful for individuals dealing with chronic stress or anxiety. Some therapists and counselors integrate Reiki into their mental health practices, using it to support clients in managing emotional overwhelm and finding a sense of grounding (Rosenthal, 2016).

Furthermore, Reiki's gentle and nurturing nature makes it especially appealing to those who may feel uncomfortable with more intrusive forms of therapy. It offers a safe space for individuals to relax, connect with their inner selves, and begin the process of emotional healing without feeling judged or pressured.

Reiki in Corporate and Workplace Settings

In recent years, Reiki has also found its way into the corporate world, as more companies recognize the importance of supporting their employees' mental and emotional well-being. Reiki is increasingly being offered in workplace wellness programs to help employees manage stress, improve focus, and enhance productivity.

The modern workplace is often characterized by high levels of stress, long hours, and fast-paced environments, all of which can take a toll on employees' mental and physical health. Reiki provides a means of stress reduction that helps employees feel more relaxed and energized, which in turn can lead to improved job satisfaction and performance.

Some organizations have introduced Reiki workshops or in-office sessions as part of their wellness initiatives, allowing employees to receive Reiki treatments during the workday.

Reiki and the Global Wellness Movement

Reiki's rise in popularity in modern times can also be attributed to the broader global wellness movement, which emphasizes the importance of holistic approaches to health. As people become more interested in wellness practices that address the whole person—body, mind, and spirit—Reiki fits naturally into this paradigm.

The wellness movement is driven by a growing awareness of the limitations of conventional medicine in addressing chronic conditions such as stress, anxiety, and burnout. Reiki, with its emphasis on balance, relaxation, and spiritual well-being, resonates with individuals seeking alternative methods of healing that align with the principles of self-care and mindfulness.

The Future of Reiki in the Modern World

As Reiki continues to evolve in the modern context, its role in healthcare, mental health, corporate wellness, and the global wellness movement will likely continue to grow. With increasing research supporting its benefits and more people seeking holistic approaches to health, Reiki is poised to play a significant role in integrative medicine in the years to come.

The future of Reiki may also involve greater standardization and regulation as it becomes more widely accepted in healthcare settings. While Reiki remains largely unregulated, some countries and states have begun to introduce certification processes to ensure that practitioners meet certain standards of training and professionalism. This development may help Reiki gain further credibility and acceptance within the medical community (Thrane & Cohen, 2014).

As scientific research continues to explore its benefits and as more people experience the profound effects of energy healing, Reiki's place in the modern world is becoming more firmly established. By addressing the interconnectedness of body, mind, and spirit, Reiki offers a pathway to well-being that complements conventional medicine and aligns with the modern understanding of health as a dynamic, holistic process.

Reiki Healing and Psychological Disorders:

Reiki, a Japanese form of energy healing, is becoming increasingly recognized as a complementary therapy for addressing psychological disorders such as anxiety, depression, and trauma. While Reiki is often viewed as a method for promoting relaxation and enhancing physical well-being, its impact on mental and emotional health is gaining attention in both alternative and conventional healthcare settings. By working with the body's energy field and promoting balance, Reiki provides a non-invasive and holistic approach to healing that resonates with individuals suffering from psychological distress.

Understanding Psychological Disorders and Energy Imbalance

Psychological disorders such as anxiety, depression, post-traumatic stress disorder (PTSD), and stress-related conditions are often viewed through a purely medical or psychological lens in Western healthcare. Treatment usually involves psychotherapy, medication, or a combination of both. While these treatments can be effective, they sometimes focus solely on symptoms rather than addressing the root cause of the issue or the individual's overall well-being.

Reiki, however, approaches psychological disorders from a holistic perspective. It operates on the belief that emotional and mental imbalances are linked to disruptions in the body's energy flow. Reiki practitioners aim to clear these blockages and restore balance to the energy system, which can have a positive effect on mental and emotional health.

Reiki for Anxiety and Stress Reduction

One of the most well-documented benefits of Reiki is its ability to induce a state of deep relaxation, which can help alleviate symptoms of anxiety and stress. Anxiety disorders are characterized by excessive worry, fear, and tension, and are often accompanied by physical symptoms such as a racing heart, rapid breathing, and muscle tension. Reiki helps to calm the body's nervous system, promoting a sense of inner peace and grounding.

The relaxation response triggered by Reiki sessions is similar to the effects of meditation and mindfulness practices. Reiki encourages the recipient to enter a state of rest, allowing the parasympathetic nervous system to engage, which slows the heart rate, lowers blood pressure, and calms the mind. A study conducted by Baldwin et al. (2008) found that Reiki was effective in reducing anxiety in patients, supporting its use as a complementary therapy for stress-related psychological disorders.

Many individuals who receive Reiki for anxiety report feeling more centered and present after a session, which helps them manage their symptoms more effectively. For people with generalized anxiety disorder (GAD), where worry and fear become chronic and pervasive, Reiki can offer a safe space to release pent-up energy and emotions, providing relief from the constant tension they experience (Shore, 2004).

Reiki for Depression: Emotional Release and Energy Balance

Depression is a psychological disorder marked by feelings of sadness, hopelessness, and disinterest in life. It often involves deep emotional pain and disconnection from one's sense of purpose. From an energetic standpoint, depression can be seen as a condition where the life force energy (Ki) is depleted or blocked, particularly in the heart and crown chakras. These energy centers are associated with love, emotional healing, and spiritual connection.

Reiki works by channeling healing energy into these areas, helping to lift the emotional weight that often accompanies depression. Through gentle, non-invasive touch, Reiki practitioners facilitate the release of emotional blockages that may be contributing to the condition. This can create a shift in the recipient's emotional state, allowing them to experience a renewed sense of vitality and hope.

A pilot study conducted at the Hartford Hospital in Connecticut explored the impact of Reiki on patients suffering from depression. The study showed that participants who received Reiki experienced a significant reduction in their depressive symptoms, as well as improvements in their overall mood and energy levels (Thrane & Cohen, 2014). These results suggest that Reiki can be a valuable complementary therapy for individuals struggling with depression, particularly when combined with conventional treatments like psychotherapy or medication.

Reiki's emphasis on emotional healing is particularly helpful for individuals who feel disconnected from their emotions or who struggle with expressing feelings such as grief, anger, or shame. By restoring balance to the energy body, Reiki allows emotions to flow more freely, which can lead to greater emotional clarity and healing (Miles & True, 2003).

Reiki for Trauma and PTSD

Trauma and post-traumatic stress disorder (PTSD) are complex psychological conditions that involve the body's inability to process and release the emotional impact of traumatic events. Individuals with PTSD often experience flashbacks, nightmares, and heightened anxiety, and they may feel trapped in a constant state of hyperarousal. This condition is not just emotional but deeply physiological, as trauma affects both the body and the mind.

Reiki offers a gentle approach to healing trauma by working with the body's energy field to release stored emotional and physical tension. Trauma can create energetic blockages, particularly in areas associated with safety and emotional security, such as the root chakra. Reiki helps to restore a sense of grounding and safety in the body, allowing individuals to release the trauma in a way that feels manageable and supportive.

Unlike talk therapy, which can sometimes feel overwhelming for trauma survivors, Reiki allows healing to occur without the need for verbal processing. This can be particularly beneficial for individuals who are not yet ready or able to discuss their traumatic experiences. Reiki practitioners create a safe, non-judgmental space for recipients to begin the healing process at their own pace, using energy rather than words (Van der Kolk, 2014).

A study by Schiff & Moore (2006) explored the use of Reiki in treating PTSD and found that participants reported feeling more relaxed, less anxious, and more in control of their emotions after receiving Reiki treatments. These findings support the use of Reiki as a complementary therapy for trauma survivors, helping them to reconnect with their bodies and begin the process of emotional healing.

Reiki and Emotional Regulation

One of the key benefits of Reiki for individuals with psychological disorders is its ability to promote emotional regulation. Emotional dysregulation, where individuals have difficulty managing or controlling their emotions, is a hallmark of many psychological disorders, including borderline personality disorder (BPD) and bipolar disorder. Individuals with these conditions may experience intense emotional swings, from anger and sadness to euphoria and anxiety.

Reiki helps to calm the emotional body, bringing balance and stability to the individual's energy field. By addressing the underlying energetic imbalances, Reiki can help individuals gain greater control over their emotional responses. Over time, this increased emotional regulation can lead to improved relationships, a better sense of self-worth, and a more balanced mood.

In addition to its impact on emotional regulation, Reiki is also used to help individuals with attachment issues or a history of relational trauma. By working with the heart chakra, Reiki can foster a deeper sense of self-love and compassion, which is essential for healing relational wounds and developing healthier relationships with others.

Reiki in Modern Mental Health Care

As the understanding of mental health evolves, more therapists and healthcare providers are recognizing the value of integrating energy healing modalities like Reiki into their practice. While Reiki is not meant to replace traditional psychotherapy or medication, it can serve as a powerful complement to these treatments by addressing the energetic and spiritual dimensions of psychological disorders.

Several mental health professionals have begun incorporating Reiki into their therapeutic work, offering it alongside talk therapy to support emotional healing. Reiki can help individuals process difficult emotions, cope with trauma, and find inner peace, making it a valuable tool in modern mental health care.

Additionally, Reiki's emphasis on self-healing empowers individuals to take an active role in their recovery. By learning Reiki techniques for self-care, individuals with psychological disorders can continue their healing journey outside of therapy sessions. This sense of empowerment and control can be particularly beneficial for individuals who feel helpless or overwhelmed by their mental health challenges.

Case Studies

Case Study 1: Reiki for Generalized Anxiety Disorder (GAD)

Background

Patient: Sarah, 32-year-old woman

Diagnosis: Generalized Anxiety Disorder (GAD)

Symptoms: Chronic worry, restlessness, muscle tension, difficulty concentrating, and sleep disturbances.

Sarah had been struggling with GAD for several years. She was constantly on edge, worried about various aspects of her life, including work, relationships, and health. She often experienced physical symptoms such as a racing heart, shallow breathing, and muscle tension. Although Sarah was undergoing cognitive-behavioral therapy (CBT) and taking anti-anxiety medication, she felt that something was missing from her treatment. A friend recommended Reiki as a complementary therapy, so Sarah decided to give it a try.

Reiki Treatment

Sarah attended weekly Reiki sessions with a certified practitioner. During each session, she lay fully clothed on a massage table while the practitioner placed their hands over various points on her body, focusing on areas where energy blockages were detected, especially around the solar plexus chakra (associated with personal power and anxiety) and the heart chakra (related to emotional well-being).

The sessions lasted about 60 minutes, during which Sarah reported feeling warm sensations and a sense of deep relaxation. Over time, she noticed that her physical symptoms began to subside, and her mind became quieter and more focused. After eight sessions, Sarah felt a noticeable reduction in her overall anxiety levels.

Case Analysis

In Sarah's case, Reiki seemed to address the physical manifestations of anxiety by calming her nervous system and releasing energy blockages in the areas most affected by stress. According to Baldwin et al. (2008), Reiki is particularly effective in promoting the body's relaxation response, which is essential for individuals with anxiety disorders. Sarah's experience supports this, as she felt a significant reduction in muscle tension, improved sleep, and a sense of inner calm after her sessions.

While Sarah continued her CBT and medication regimen, Reiki provided a complementary benefit by helping her manage the physiological and emotional aspects of her anxiety. This case highlights how Reiki can be integrated into a broader treatment plan for anxiety disorders, addressing both emotional and energetic imbalances.

Case Study 2: Reiki for Depression

Background

Patient: James, 45-year-old man

Diagnosis: Major Depressive Disorder

Symptoms: Low mood, fatigue, loss of interest in activities, feelings of hopelessness, and difficulty concentrating.

James had been battling depression for several years. He felt weighed down by his emotions and had lost interest in his usual activities. Despite taking antidepressant medication and attending regular psychotherapy, James continued to struggle with low energy and persistent feelings of sadness. He sought out Reiki as an alternative form of healing, hoping it might help him feel more connected to himself and others.

Reiki Treatment

James began Reiki treatments with a focus on rebalancing his heart chakra and solar plexus chakra, both of which are closely tied to emotional well-being and personal empowerment. The practitioner also paid special attention to his crown chakra, which is associated with spiritual connection and a sense of purpose, as depression often involves a deep sense of disconnection from these aspects of life.

Over the course of 10 weekly sessions, James began to notice subtle shifts in his mood and energy levels. He reported feeling lighter after each session and found that he was more open to discussing his feelings in therapy. His depressive symptoms began to lift, and he felt a renewed sense of purpose in his life.

Case Analysis

In James's case, Reiki appears to have helped lift the energetic blockages that were contributing to his depression. Depression is often associated with a depletion of life force energy, particularly in the heart and solar plexus chakras. Through Reiki, James was able to reconnect with these energy centers, facilitating emotional release and healing.

The deep relaxation and emotional release provided by Reiki likely helped James access his emotions more readily in psychotherapy, which may have contributed to the improvement in his symptoms. Research by Thrane & Cohen (2014) suggests that Reiki can be an effective adjunct therapy for individuals with depression, particularly when combined with conventional treatments like medication and therapy. James's case demonstrates how Reiki can provide a gentle yet powerful form of emotional support for individuals suffering from depression, complementing other treatment modalities.

Challenges and Limitations of Reiki Healing

Lack of Scientific Validation and Empirical Evidence

One of the most significant challenges Reiki faces is the lack of robust scientific validation. Reiki operates on the principle that the practitioner channels "universal life force energy" (Ki) to the recipient, restoring balance and promoting healing. However, this concept of energy is not measurable by scientific instruments, which makes it difficult to validate Reiki using traditional research methods (Miles & True, 2003).

The absence of a well-defined mechanism of action for Reiki also poses a challenge. Unlike conventional medical treatments, where the biological processes involved are understood and observable, Reiki's effects are attributed to metaphysical concepts that are difficult to study through empirical research. This has led to skepticism among medical professionals and scientists, with some dismissing Reiki as a form of pseudoscience.

Standardization of Training and Practice

Reiki training and practice lack standardization, leading to variations in how practitioners are trained and how treatments are administered. Unlike regulated healthcare professions, where there are clear educational pathways and licensure requirements, Reiki training often varies widely between different schools and lineages. Some practitioners may undergo years of training, while others may become certified in a weekend workshop (Wittine, 2020). This inconsistency in training creates challenges for establishing Reiki as a credible therapeutic modality.

Furthermore, there is no governing body or regulatory framework that oversees Reiki practice, making it difficult to ensure that practitioners adhere to ethical standards or maintain their professional development.

Integration into Conventional Healthcare

Another significant limitation of Reiki is its slow integration into conventional healthcare systems. Despite growing interest in integrative and complementary medicine, Reiki is still considered an "alternative" practice rather than a mainstream therapeutic option. Hospitals, clinics, and healthcare providers are often hesitant to incorporate Reiki into their treatment plans due to the lack of scientific evidence and the concerns over practitioner training and regulation.

Some hospitals and hospices have begun offering Reiki to patients as part of palliative care or stress-reduction programs, but it remains largely viewed as a supplementary therapy rather than a core treatment.

Placebo Effect and Subjectivity of Results

Reiki's effectiveness is often attributed to subjective experiences and may be influenced by the placebo effect. Recipients frequently report feeling relaxed, peaceful, and more balanced after a Reiki session, which are valuable outcomes but difficult to quantify in clinical studies. The placebo effect can play a significant role in how patients perceive the benefits of Reiki, particularly because Reiki treatments involve non-invasive touch and the calming presence of the practitioner.

While the placebo effect can lead to real improvements in symptoms such as pain, anxiety, and stress, critics argue that Reiki's reliance on subjective reports makes it challenging to establish its efficacy in treating more complex psychological or physical disorders.

Ethical Concerns and Cultural Sensitivity

Reiki's roots in Japanese spirituality and its association with energy healing raise ethical concerns, particularly when it is practiced in cultures where these concepts may be unfamiliar or misunderstood. Some critics argue that Reiki has been Westernized and stripped of its cultural and spiritual context, leading to concerns about cultural appropriation. In Western Reiki practices, the spiritual teachings of Mikao Usui, Reiki's founder, are sometimes downplayed in favor of a more secular or clinical approach, which can lead to a loss of authenticity and misinterpretation of the practice's true intent (Beeler, 2015).

Over-Reliance on Reiki and Avoidance of Conventional Medical Care

Another limitation of Reiki is the potential for individuals to become overly reliant on it and avoid seeking conventional medical care. While Reiki can offer valuable support for stress management, emotional healing, and physical well-being, it is not a substitute for evidence-based medical treatments. Some individuals, particularly those with chronic illnesses or mental health disorders, may turn to Reiki in the hope of a "miracle cure," which could delay or prevent them from receiving appropriate medical intervention.

Conclusion

Reiki, rooted in Eastern traditions, represents a unique blend of spirituality and healing that offers a non-invasive, holistic approach to well-being. Over the past century, Reiki has evolved from a Japanese spiritual practice into a widely used form of complementary therapy, with increasing interest in its ability to promote relaxation, reduce stress, and support emotional and physical healing.

Despite its origins in Japan under the teachings of Mikao Usui, Reiki has become a global phenomenon, particularly embraced in Western countries where it is often practiced alongside or as an adjunct to conventional medical treatments. However, its acceptance in mainstream healthcare is still limited due to several factors, including the lack of scientific validation, difficulties in standardization of training, and concerns about the placebo effect.

From my perspective, the beauty of Reiki lies in its emphasis on balance—not just physical balance, but a balance between the mind, body, and spirit. This holistic focus is a cornerstone of many Eastern healing traditions, which view health as a state of energetic harmony within the body. Unlike Western medicine, which often compartmentalizes illnesses and focuses on treating symptoms, Reiki aims to address the underlying energetic imbalances that may contribute to dis-ease.

That said, Reiki is not without its challenges. Its esoteric nature and the inability to measure the energy it works with make it difficult to prove through the lens of modern science. This creates a disconnect between the profound experiences of individuals who benefit from Reiki and the skepticism of those who rely on empirical evidence. Moreover, the lack of regulation and standardization raises questions about the consistency and quality of care provided by practitioners.

At the same time, Reiki's gentle and non-invasive approach to healing makes it a safe complement to more conventional treatments. As the world increasingly embraces integrative medicine, which combines the best of Eastern and Western healing traditions, Reiki's role could continue to expand. It can serve as a valuable tool for patients looking to manage chronic stress, process emotional trauma, or simply reconnect with their sense of well-being in a deeply spiritual way.

To sum up, Reiki is a gentle yet powerful healing modality, rooted in Eastern philosophy but increasingly adopted worldwide. While it faces challenges in gaining full acceptance within the scientific and medical communities, its focus on holistic well-being offers a refreshing contrast to the symptom-focused nature of Western medicine. For those open to its principles, Reiki provides a unique path to healing—one that acknowledges not just the physical body, but also the energetic and emotional dimensions of health.

References

Baldwin, A. L., Wagers, C., & Schwartz, G. E. (2008). Reiki improves heart rate homeostasis in laboratory rats. Journal of Alternative and Complementary Medicine, 14(4), 417–422. https://doi.org/10.1089/acm.2007.0736

Beeler, D. (2015). Reiki: An introduction to energy medicine. Llewellyn Publications.

Bowden, D., Goddard, L., & Gruzelier, J. (2011). A randomized controlled single-blind trial of the effects of Reiki and positive imagery on well-being and salivary cortisol. Brain Research Bulletin, 85(3-4), 153–156. https://doi.org/10.1016/j.brainresbull.2010.12.010

Cuneo, C. L., Curtis Cooper, M. R., Drew, C. S., Naoum-Heffernan, C., Sherman, T., & Walz, K. P. (2011). The effect of Reiki on work-related stress of the registered nurse. Journal of Holistic Nursing, 29(1), 33–43. https://doi.org/10.1177/0898010110376944

Lee, M. S., Pittler, M. H., & Ernst, E. (2008). Effects of Reiki in clinical practice: A systematic review of randomized clinical trials. International Journal of Clinical Practice, 62(6), 947–954. https://doi.org/10.1111/j.1742-1241.2008.01729.x

Miles, P., & True, G. (2003). Reiki—Review of a biofield therapy history, theory, practice, and research. Alternative Therapies in Health and Medicine, 9(2), 62–72.

Rand, W. L. (2011). The Reiki touch: Complete home learning system. Sounds True.

Rosenthal, J. (2016). Reiki: The ultimate guide to mastering Reiki for beginners in 30 minutes or less!. CreateSpace Independent Publishing Platform.

Schiff, E., & Moore, T. (2006). The effects of Reiki: A practice-based study. Journal of Holistic Nursing, 24(3), 201–206. https://doi.org/10.1177/0898010106289835

Shore, A. G. (2004). Long-term effects of energetic healing on symptoms of psychological depression and self-perceived stress. Alternative Therapies in Health and Medicine, 10(3), 42–48.

Thrane, S., & Cohen, S. M. (2014). Effect of Reiki therapy on pain and anxiety in adults: An in-depth literature review of randomized trials with effect size calculations. Pain Management Nursing, 15(4), 897–908. https://doi.org/10.1016/j.pmn.2013.07.008

Van der Kolk, B. A. (2014). The body keeps the score: Brain, mind, and body in the healing of trauma. Penguin Books.

VanderVaart, S., Gijsen, V. M., de Wildt, S. N., & Koren, G. (2009). A systematic review of the therapeutic effects of Reiki. Journal of Alternative and Complementary Medicine, 15(11), 1157–1169. https://doi.org/10.1089/acm.2009.0036

Vitale, A. (2007). An integrative review of Reiki touch therapy research. Holistic Nursing Practice, 21(4), 167–179. https://doi.org/10.1097/01.hnp.0000280924.70899.4c

Warber, S. L., Cornelio, D., & Straughn, J. (2004). Biofield energy healing from multiple perspectives: An integrative review of Reiki touch therapy research. Annals of Behavioral Medicine, 28(2), 117–127. https://doi.org/10.1207/s15324796abm2802_7

Chapter 16

Tai Chi Chuan - An Integrative Mind-Body Practice

Priyanka Barman School of Liberal Studies (SLS), CMR University, Bangalore

Introduction

Tai Chi can also be referred to as Tai Chi Chuan/Quan or Taiji. Several various definitions of Tai Chi exist: "a Chinese system of physical exercises designed especially for self-defense and meditation," "a Chinese system of slow meditative physical exercise designed for relaxation and balance and health," or as "an internal Chinese martial art practiced for both defensive training and its health benefits." Tai Chi is actually abbreviation for Tai Chi Chuan, which can be stated like this in Chinese: 太極拳

Tai means supreme, grand, or great. *Chi* means ultimate, extreme, or what is on top. *Chuan* means fist, palm, or boxing.

More specifically, the words "tai" and "chi" imply "Supreme Ultimate," which depicts the "Cosmos" and its operational principles of yin and yang. Chuan is an abbreviated form of "Chuan Fa," which literally translates to "fist techniques." By simplifying Tai Chi Chuan to Tai Chi, we eliminate the martial part of the practice and accentuate its health and harmony virtues.

Tai Chi practices, which was born in China, involve purposeful and graceful bodily movements that aim to relax both the body and the mind. It consists of an assortment of postures combined in slow, seamless, effortless motions and is regarded as a low intensity workout that is intended to encourage balance and coordination, as well as help preserve strength and psychological wellness (Koh, 1981; Brown et al., 1989; Wolf et al., 1997; Li, J. X. et al., 2001; Wolf et al., 2001; Wu, 2002).

Tai Chi's slow, fluid, and beautiful movements have their roots in Taoism. Taoism is an ancient Chinese philosophy that was introduced by Lao Tze in the 5th 4th centuries BCE. The Taoist doctrine highlights mental tranquilly and aspires to achieve longevity through meditation and lifestyle changes.

Tai Chi, a form of internal martial arts practice, has remained prominent in China for generations of years.

History and Origin

Taijiquan's origins, like those of many other conventional forms of therapy around the world, have their foundations in myth and folklore. Tai Chi is believed to have emerged with Daoist monk Zhang Sanfeng (张三丰). Zhang was believed to have lived during the Song (9601 to 279) or Yuan Dynasties (1271 to 1368), but evidence from history of his existence is undetermined. The folklore tells how Zhang Sanfeng observed a battle between a crane and a snake. He was influenced by the snake's smooth and delicate movements, which signified yielding and tenderness triumphing over sheer force. This understanding formed the philosophical underpinning for Tai Chi's emphasis on softness overcoming hardness.

According to Tang Hao, during the 1930s, Tai Ji Quan, which fits within the general umbrella of Chinese Wushu (martial arts), was widely believed to have originally developed in the village of Chenjiagou in Wenxian county, Henan province, around the late Ming and early Qing dynasties.

He integrated traditional martial arts together with Chinese medical practices, which included Dao Yin Shu (the art that strengthened internal circulation) integrated various physical movements including bending, expanding, contracting, and extending with breathing techniques promoting the Qi circulation, and the "Tuna" (breathing exercises), alongside principles of Yin Yang and the Five Elements. Hua Tuo(华佗 141208 A.D.), created the form of Wu Qin Xi(五禽戏 Five Animal Play) by devising movements that were similar to the movements of five different animals (tiger – 虎, deer –鹿, bear – 熊, ape –猿 and bird – 鹤) and integrating them with breathing techniques.

All through Chinese history, the practice of Five Animal Play has long been one of the oldest and most common disease prevention and life prolonging practices due to the effectiveness it has in regulating Qi and blood movements, nourishing the viscera, and building muscle and bones.

Different Styles of Tai Chi Chuan

Chen Style (陳氏) by Chen Wangting (1580 to 1660):

Originating in the 16th century, Chen style is considered the oldest Tai Chi style. The Chen style, more close to the martial art concept, has low positions, changing rhythms with smooth and explosive movements, jumps, and more use of joint rotation (Wang et al., 2004, Wang et al., 2010, Chen et al., 2006, Yeh et al., 2009, Chang et al., 2010).

Yang Style (楊氏) by Yang Lu Chan (1800 to 1873) , Yang Chen Fu (1883 to 1936):

Developed in the 19th century, Yang Lu Chan popularized the name "tai chi chuan" (supreme ultimate fist). Yang style is the most widely practiced Tai Chi style. It focuses on large, open movements that are smooth and steady, emphasizing relaxation and continuity of motion. It lacks the explosive movements found in Chen style, making it more accessible.

Wu/Hao Style (武氏/郝氏) by Wu Yu Xian – also spelled Xiang or Hsiang – (1813 to 1880), Hao Wei Chen – or Zheng or Zhen – (1849 to 1920):

Wu/Hao style, developed in the mid19th century, emphasizes small, precise movements and a higher posture compared to other styles. The style is characterized by its emphasis on internal cultivation and subtle weight shifts.

Wu Style (吳氏) by Wu Jian Quan – or Wu Chien Chuan – (1870 to 1942):

Originating in the late 19th century, Wu style is the second most popular Tai Chi style after Yang. It features small, compact movements with a forward leaning posture. It emphasizes close range combat applications and is known for its focus on "sticky" energy.

Sun Style (孫氏) by Sun Lu Tan (1861 to 1933):

Created in the early 20th century, Sun style combines elements of Tai Chi with movements from Xing Yi Quan and Ba Gua Zhang. It features smooth, flowing steps with agile footwork, and emphasizes continuous movement without pauses. The style is suitable for older practitioners and those seeking gentle exercise.

24 Postures of Taijiquan

The simplified form Taijiquan (Tai Chi Chuan) was created by the Chinese Sports Commission in 1956 with the purpose of standardising and popularising taijiquan. It includes twenty various postures from the Yang Style Long Sequence. Three of the postures are performed on both the left and right sides, and one has been repeated, for a total of twenty-four postures. This is why it is generally referred to as 24Posture Taijiquan.

24 Postures of Taijiquan (Simplified Taijiquan) posture names:

1. Commencing (Qi Shi)
2. The Wild Horse Parts Its Mane (Ye Ma Fen Zong)
3. White Crane Spreads Its Wings (Bai He Liang Chi)
4. Brush Knee and Step Forward (Lou Xi Ao Bu)
5. Playing the Lute (Shou Hui Pipa)
6. Reverse Reeling Forearm (Dao Juan Gong)
7. Left Grasp Sparrow's Tail (Zuo Lan Que Wei)
8. Right Grasp Sparrow's Tail (You Lan Que Wei)
9. Single Whip (Dan Bian)
10. Wave Hands Like Clouds (Yun Shou)
11. Single Whip (Dan Bian)
12. High Pat on Horse (Gao Tan Ma)
13. Right Heel Kick (You Deng Jiao)
14. Strike to Ears with Both Fists (Shuang Feng Guan Er)
15. Turn Body and Left Heel Kick (Zhuan Shen Zuo Deng Jiao)
16. Left Lower Body and Stand on One Leg (Zuo Xia Shi Du Li)
17. Right Lower Body and Stand on One Leg (You Xia Shi Du Li)
18. Shuttle Back and Forth (Chuan Suo)
19. Needle at Sea Bottom (Haidi Zhen)
20. Fan through Back (Shan Tong Bei)
21. Turn Body, Deflect, Parry, and Punch (Zhuan Shen Ban Lan Chui)
22. Appears Closed (Ru Feng Si Bi)
23. Cross Hands (Shi Zi Shou)
24. Closing (Shou Shi)

Tai Chi Chuan for Different Ages

Tai Chi has grown in popularity throughout the years (Clarke et al. 2015), especially among middle aged and senior citizens (Wang et al. 2004). Today, millions of people throughout the world practice Tai Chi. Some people begin practicing when they are five years old, nonetheless many people are 85 years or older and continue their practise. Tai Chi is practiced by multiple generations of people in many Asian and other families.

Younger generation:

Tai Chi offers remarkable benefits for young people. Classes designed for younger practitioners often emphasize physical challenges and athletic growth. Many young participants are encouraged to learn Chen Style Tai Chi, which is known for its dynamic and physically demanding nature, featuring low stances, powerful bursts, and broad, vigorous movements. This style promotes strengthening and stretching of the lower body and core (dantian), making it particularly suited for active, growing bodies, while keeping younger practitioners engaged. Tai Chi also provides valuable support for children with ADHD through its graded movements, focus on deep breathing, and meditation elements that help calm the mind. Children with motor planning challenges benefit from practicing slow, controlled movements, while anxious children gain from the stress relief effects of Tai Chi. This practice is beneficial for all children, as it enhances mental alertness, improves concentration, reduces anxiety, and supports physical health by boosting circulation, reducing muscle tension, and lowering blood pressure and heart rate. Additionally, Tai Chi promotes better balance and reinforces proper posture, a foundational habit that is essential for young people to develop early on.

Young Adult generation:

Tai Chi also supports young adults in managing stress related to academics or career pursuits. The practice of deep breathing and slow, deliberate movements promotes relaxation and has been shown to lower cortisol levels. Additionally, Tai Chi has been associated with enhanced cognitive performance, including memory and attention—benefits that are particularly valuable in academic and professional settings.

At a more advanced stage, the Tai Chi journey focuses on developing internal intention, a critical component of personal growth within the practice. While children may initially mimic Tai Chi movements with impressive physical outcomes, mature practitioners learn the importance of cultivating intention from within. This internal focus shapes external movement, teaching practitioners to channel their energy toward purposeful actions and to remain undistracted by external or trivial matters. Through this disciplined practice, Tai Chi offers a profound approach to selfawareness, mindfulness, and the intentional alignment of inner and outer life.

Middle age generation:

Approximately 40% of adults in the United States engage in complementary and alternative medicine practices (Harris et al., 2012), with around 25% of these individuals participating in mind–body activities (Chacko et al., 2014). The desire to maintain physical capability and avoid premature aging becomes increasingly important. For middle aged adults who may encounter stressors related to work, family, or health, Tai Chi supports cognitive function and may help delay the onset of age-related cognitive decline, making it a beneficial practice for maintaining mental acuity during middle age. By fostering mindfulness and self-compassion, Tai Chi can aid individuals in managing midlife challenges and stressful life transitions.

In addition to improving fitness, Tai Chi helps individuals maintain core strength without the high impact stress on joints—such as the back, knees, and hips—that can accelerate deterioration with age. Unlike in their 20s, adults in middle age often find that their bodies take longer to recover, making gentle, slower paced exercise a better fit. Despite its slower pace, Tai Chi raises the heart rate, offering an effective cardiovascular workout. Although it may seem counterintuitive, the practice's gentle movements enhance circulation, and many participants experience a noticeable rise in core temperature after a one-hour session.

Older generation:

For older adults, learning and engaging in Tai Chi provides numerous advantages. Seniors who experience a fall often suffer from a range of physical ailments that are slow to heal, and many find that their overall health declines significantly after such an incident. However, by maintaining good health, core strength, upright posture, and the ability to regain balance swiftly, older adults can reduce their risk of falling. This preventive approach greatly enhances their quality of life in later years.

Tai Chi offers not only physical benefits but also mental stimulation and social engagement, helping to mitigate some of the primary mental health concerns that older adults face, such as depression and dementia. Research suggests that individuals who regularly practice Tai Chi are less likely to experience these conditions or can alleviate their symptoms. A contributing factor is the social environment of Tai Chi, which is often practiced in groups, fostering connections with friends, family members, and individuals of diverse age groups.

Tai Chi Practice in Psychotherapy

Tai chi is increasingly being incorporated into psychotherapy as a complementary method to enhance mental health.

- **Stress Relief:** Tai chi aids in alleviating stress and anxiety by fostering relaxation and a meditative state. The practice of deep, rhythmic breathing and mindful movements activates the parasympathetic nervous system, leading to a calming effect.
- **Emotional Self-Regulation:** Practicing tai chi increases awareness of one's physical and emotional state, enhancing emotional regulation. This self-awareness helps clients manage their emotions more effectively in stressful situations.
- **Trauma Sensitive Approach:** Tai chi is used in trauma therapy to help clients reconnect with their bodies in a gentle and safe way. The slow, continuous movements provide a sense of security and stability, supporting trauma survivors in rebuilding trust with their physical selves.

- **Easing Depression and Anxiety Symptoms:** Studies indicate that consistent tai chi practice can reduce symptoms of depression and anxiety by increasing endorphin levels and promoting relaxation. It offers a structured activity that can uplift mood and build resilience.
- **Mindfulness and Present Moment Awareness:** Tai chi emphasizes being in the moment and maintaining focus, aligning well with mindfulness strategies used in therapy. This helps clients enhance their attention skills and minimize rumination.
- **Grounding Practices:** Tai chi's focus on movement and body awareness can act as an effective grounding method for individuals experiencing dissociation or intense emotions, helping them reconnect with the present moment and their physical self.
- **Boosting Self Esteem:** Mastering tai chi routines can enhance self-confidence and a sense of accomplishment. This progress can build a more positive self-image and reinforce self-efficacy.
- **Improving Sleep:** Regular tai chi practice has been shown to improve sleep by fostering relaxation and reducing stress. Enhanced sleep quality supports emotional regulation and better mental health outcomes, aiding clients with sleep disorders.
- **Body-Mind Integration:** For clients dealing with body image issues or feeling disconnected from their physical selves, tai chi helps cultivate a healthier connection to their body. It emphasizes the unity of body and mind, encouraging acceptance and integration.
- **Supporting Brain Plasticity:** Mindful movement practices like tai chi may enhance neuroplasticity, helping the brain form new neural pathways. This can assist clients in developing healthier emotional and cognitive patterns.
- **Fostering Patience and Tolerance:** Tai chi's slow and repetitive nature requires patience and perseverance, teaching clients to be more patient with themselves and others while reducing impulsivity.
- **Enhancing Cognitive Skills:** Tai chi can help improve cognitive functions, such as memory, attention, and executive functioning, which is particularly beneficial for older adults or those experiencing cognitive decline.

Applications

Hypertension:

Hypertension is a significant risk factor for various cardiovascular conditions, including coronary artery disease, heart failure, stroke, and peripheral vascular disease. Approximately 54% of strokes and 47% of cases of ischemic heart disease globally can be attributed to hypertension. Reducing blood pressure (BP) in individuals with hypertension is associated with a substantial decrease in cardiovascular morbidity and mortality. Most studies investigating the effects of Tai Chi have implemented training programs lasting between 6 to 12 weeks, demonstrating a reduction in both systolic and diastolic BP, whether at rest or post exercise. Notably, hypertensive patients exhibit the most significant improvements in blood pressure control. Research conducted by Yeh and colleagues has reported favourable outcomes associated with Tai Chi in managing BP.

Stress:

Research indicates that prolonged stress may trigger cognitive, emotional, and biological processes that heighten the risk of developing depression, with inflammation potentially playing a role in this mechanism. Specifically, neuroinflammatory sensitization induced by stress can result in substantial behavioural changes and the emergence of common depressive symptoms. Recent studies suggest that mind–body interventions, such as Tai Chi, may alleviate stress and influence the inflammatory response.

Major depressive disorder (MDD):

Major depressive disorder is a prevalent mental illness in the United States, and it is particularly common among older adults. Brown et al. conducted a study comparing the psychological effects of 16 weeks of moderate intensity walking (MW), low intensity walking (LW), low intensity walking combined with relaxation response (LWR), and Tai Chi among healthy, sedentary adults. Their findings indicated that women participating in the Tai Chi group experienced a significant reduction in mood disturbances, including tension, depression, anger, confusion, and overall mood disturbance, as well as an improvement in general mood. Additionally, women in the MW group reported enhanced satisfaction with their physical attributes (body cathexis), while men in the same group experienced increased positive affect.

Anxiety disorders:

Depression and anxiety disorders rank among the most prevalent and burdensome psychiatric conditions globally, impacting approximately 1 in 10 individuals. Notably, anxiety disorders currently represent the sixth leading cause of nonfatal health loss. In response to these challenges, mind–body interventions have garnered increasing attention as potential alternative treatments for a range of psychiatric disorders, particularly depression and anxiety. These interventions adopt a holistic framework that integrates the brain, mind, body, and human behaviour. Among these, Tai Chi and qigong stand out as practices that emphasize self-awareness, intrapersonal mind–body alignment, mental concentration, fluid body movements, breathing techniques, and attentional training.

Immune function and inflammation:

Tai Chi practices enhance the efficiency of the immune system, primarily by increasing the levels of immune cells, decreasing inflammation markers, and positively influencing virus specific immune responses during vaccinations.

Stroke:

It is estimated that approximately 15 million individuals worldwide experience a stroke annually. In the United States alone, around 795,000 people suffer either a new or recurrent stroke, which can be classified as either ischemic or hemorrhagic. Stroke significantly diminishes quality of life, a decline that is influenced not only by neurological deficits but also by cognitive impairments.

Parkinson's disease:

A study conducted in 2012 indicated that Tai Chi training effectively reduces balance impairments in patients with mild to moderate Parkinson's disease (PD). Furthermore, it offers additional benefits such as enhanced functional capacity and a decreased incidence of falls. Impaired mobility is frequently observed in individuals with PD, necessitating normal sensorimotor agility and dynamic control to maintain balance during both motor and cognitive tasks. Common gait alterations in these patients include difficulties with initiating steps, shuffling, and experiencing freezing of gait. Balance challenges are particularly evident during turning and backward walking, contributing to a heightened risk of falls among individuals with PD. Tai Chi has the potential to improve balance, kinesthetic awareness, and muscular strength, and therefore may be recommended as a sensorimotor agility program for patients diagnosed with Parkinson's disease.

Traumatic Brain Injury:

Exercise therapy has shown promise in enhancing motor function and promoting independence in individuals with TBI. Shapira and colleagues conducted a study on the long-term effects of Tai Chi training in three patients with severe TBI. Following a training period of 2 to 4 years, all patients demonstrated the ability to walk unassisted, experienced a reduction in falls, and reported increased confidence while walking. Notably, one patient regained the ability to perform daily activities independently and was able to resume driving.

Multiple Sclerosis:

Husted and colleagues conducted a study involving 19 patients with multiple sclerosis who participated in an 8-week Tai Chi program. Following the training, the participants demonstrated a 21% increase in walking speed and a 28% improvement in hamstring flexibility. These outcomes may be attributed to the effects of neuromuscular facilitation experienced during Tai Chi practice, which promotes enhanced motor control and coordination. The slow, deliberate movement characteristic of Tai Chi may stimulate the nervous system, thereby improving neuromuscular responses and overall physical function.

Osteoarthritis:

Patients with osteoarthritis (OA) have demonstrated improvements following 6 to 20 weeks of Tai Chi training. The initial randomized trial examining the effects of Tai Chi on osteoarthritis was conducted by Hartman and colleagues. In this study, 33 older adults diagnosed with lower extremity OA were randomly assigned to either a Tai Chi group or a control group. The Tai Chi intervention consisted of two one-hour classes per week over a duration of 12 weeks. Post training assessments revealed that participants in the Tai Chi group experienced significant enhancements in self efficacy regarding arthritis symptoms, overall arthritis selfefficacy, levels of tension, and satisfaction with their general health status.

Musculoskeletal Disorder:

Musculoskeletal disorders are a primary contributor to work related disability and productivity losses in industrialized countries. Tai Chi presents a straightforward and convenient intervention that can be implemented in the workplace to enhance musculoskeletal health, requiring no special equipment. A recent study focused on female computer users, involving 52 participants who attended a 50minute

Tai Chi class once a week for a duration of 12 weeks. The findings indicated significant improvements in heart rate, waist circumference, and handgrip strength, suggesting that Tai Chi is effective in enhancing musculoskeletal fitness.

Diabetes mellitus:

Diabetes mellitus is an increasingly significant risk factor for cardiovascular disease, with an estimated 19.7 million American adults diagnosed with diabetes. Furthermore, the prevalence of pre-diabetes among the U.S. adult population stands at 38%. Previous research has demonstrated that physical exercise provides substantial benefits for individuals with diabetes or impaired glucose tolerance.

Moreover, several studies have highlighted the advantages of Tai Chi for patients with diabetes. In a pilot study involving 12 diabetic patients, Wang reported that an 8week Tai Chi program resulted in decreased blood glucose levels.

Cancer:

Cancer remains one of the leading causes of mortality globally. Exercise therapy has emerged as a safe adjunctive treatment that can alleviate common side effects associated with cancer therapies. Furthermore, engagement in exercise has been shown to positively impact various aspects of health-related quality of life (QOL), including physical functioning, role functioning, social functioning, and levels of fatigue.

Benefits

Improved Balance and Coordination:

Research has established that Tai Chi notably decreases the risk of falls in older adults by improving balance and coordination. A comprehensive study in the Journal of the American Geriatrics Society found that "Tai Chi practice reduced the incidence of falls in this group by approximately 47%." (Li, Harmer, & Fitzgerald, 2010).

Stress Reduction:

The practice of Tai Chi has been associated with lower cortisol levels and higher serotonin levels, contributing to enhanced wellbeing. Research published in the American Journal of Health Promotion reported "significant reductions in symptoms of anxiety and depression among individuals who practice Tai Chi regularly". According to Dr. Paul Lam, "Tai Chi resembles meditation in motion, as it facilitates stress relief and brings a calming effect to the mind."

Enhanced Flexibility:

The fluid movement characteristic of Tai Chi promotes muscle elongation and joint flexibility. A study published in the Journal of Physical Activity and Health reported that individuals who practiced Tai Chi regularly experienced a 20% improvement in flexibility compared to those who did not. Increased flexibility contributes to a greater range of motion and reduced joint stiffness.

Increased Strength:

Tai Chi enhances muscular strength through bodyweight resistance training, focusing particularly on strengthening the lower body—a critical factor in preserving mobility among older adults. Research published in The Journals of Gerontology reports that "older adults who engaged in Tai Chi practice saw a 28% increase in muscle strength". This practice is especially beneficial in rehabilitation settings, providing a safe and controlled method for individuals to regain strength and mobility following surgery or injury.

Improved Cardiovascular Health:

Tai Chi is recognized as a moderate intensity exercise that offers cardiovascular benefits like those of walking. The American Heart Association states, "Tai Chi is a valuable form of exercise that improves cardiovascular health, reduces blood pressure, and enhances overall wellbeing." Integrating Tai Chi sessions into a weekly exercise routine can complement other aerobic activities, thereby improving overall cardiovascular fitness.

Pain Management:

Tai Chi has demonstrated effectiveness in the management of chronic pain conditions, including arthritis. A review published in Pain Medicine reported a 40% reduction in pain symptoms among individuals who engage in Tai Chi practice. The gentle, controlled movements associated with Tai Chi contribute to alleviating stiffness and promoting relaxation, positioning it as a viable option for pain relief.

Mental Focus and Clarity:

Engaging in Tai Chi has been shown to enhance mindfulness, a quality that is linked to improved cognitive function and emotional regulation. According to Xu and Wang (2018), "Tai Chi practice can enhance cognitive function and mental clarity, making it beneficial for older adults." Consequently, practicing Tai Chi can serve as an effective method for cultivating mindfulness, which may lead to increased focus in daily activities and tasks.

Enhanced Immune Function:

Tai Chi practice has been demonstrated to possess immunomodulatory effects. A study published in The Journal of Immunology revealed that individuals who regularly engage in Tai Chi exhibited improved immune responses compared to those who do not practice. Dr. Helen Lavretsky, a geriatric psychiatrist, affirms, "Tai Chi enhances the body's immune response, highlighting its significant influence on overall health and wellbeing."

Emotional Well-Being:

"Tai Chi practice is associated with notable enhancements in emotional wellbeing and a decrease in depressive symptoms" (O'Brien, S., & Janus, M., 2019). The meditative nature of Tai Chi promotes a positive mental state, and research has established a correlation between its practice and improvements in mood, as well as a reduction in depressive symptoms. Individuals may utilize Tai Chi as an effective coping strategy during periods of stress, thereby cultivating emotional resilience through its soothing effects.

Challenges

Accessibility and Learning Curve:

For newcomers, the process of learning Tai Chi can be challenging. The slow and deliberate movements demand considerable time and practice to master, which may discourage some individuals from persisting in their practice. A survey conducted among Tai Chi participants indicated that 35% experienced difficulties in initially learning the forms, resulting in frustration and a potential risk of dropout.

Physical Limitations:

Certain individuals may experience physical limitations or health conditions that complicate their ability to practice Tai Chi. Conditions such as severe arthritis, joint pain, or mobility impairments can significantly impede participation. Research has shown that approximately 30% of older adults with chronic health issues encounter difficulties in engaging with Tai Chi due to these physical constraints.

Motivation and Consistency:

Maintaining motivation and consistency in Tai Chi practice can be a significant challenge, particularly for individuals who do not observe immediate results. The full benefits of Tai Chi may not be attained without regular practice. Additionally, the demands of daily life can disrupt participation in classes or self-practice. Many practitioners have reported difficulties in sustaining a consistent Tai Chi routine following their initial lessons.

Space and Environment:

Practicing Tai Chi necessitates adequate space to execute movements safely and effectively. Individuals residing in crowded or confined environments may encounter difficulties in maintaining a consistent practice. A survey revealed that 28% of practitioners identified limited space as a significant barrier to regular engagement, hindering their ability to move freely. Tai Chi instructor Martin Lee observes, "The beauty of Tai Chi lies in its fluidity; however, a lack of sufficient space can create a sense of restriction and frustration."

Instructors' Expertise:

The effectiveness of Tai Chi practice is frequently influenced by the instructor's level of experience and teaching methodology. Instructors who lack adequate training or experience may struggle to communicate the fundamental principles effectively, resulting in misunderstandings and mislearning among students. Additionally, in certain regions, the availability of qualified Tai Chi instructors may be restricted, which can adversely impact the quality of training and guidance that practitioners receive. This limitation may lead to incorrect execution of forms or techniques.

Perceived as Low Intensity:

Some individuals may regard Tai Chi as a low intensity form of exercise and may not consider it as seriously as more vigorous activities. This misconception can result in a diminished commitment to the practice, leading individuals to overlook the profound benefits that Tai Chi can offer. While the movements may appear gentle and fluid, Tai Chi requires a significant degree of mental focus, physical control, and body awareness.

Case Studies

Case Study1: Parkinson's Disease Symptoms with Tai Chi Exercise Program

Client A, 67years old retired teacher Diagnosed with Parkinson's Disease (PD) for six years, with recent decline in gait, mobility, and increased hand tremors.

Present Complaints:

Difficulty with walking, mobility, and fine motor tasks (e.g., cooking, shopping, dressing). Increased tremors and challenges with overhead movements.

Assessment Results:

MDSUPDRS indicated mild impairments in motor aspects, daily living, and motor complications. PDQ39 scores showed challenges in mobility, daily activities, emotional wellbeing, and stigma. FOGQ score was 11/24, indicating freezing of gait.

Intervention Plan:

1. **Goals**: Improve ambulation, maintain upper extremity range of motion, reduce fall risk.
2. **Treatment**: Tai Chi sessions (5 sessions per week for 24 weeks).

Outcome:

Significant improvements in balance, mobility, and motor functions. TUG score improved from 13 to 9 seconds, FOGQ score improved to 9/24. Enhanced confidence, emotional wellbeing, and quality of life. Continued fine motor difficulties but improved gait speed, stride, trunk rotation, and arm swing.

Case study 2: Progressive Supranuclear Palsy (PSP)

Client K, Age 61, Married, Retired farmer. Diagnosed with Parkinson's disease (PD) 6 years ago, experiencing a recent decline in gait, mobility, and hand tremors.

History of Present Illness:

J experienced a gradual decline in balance, leading to frequent falls, reduced walking speed, mild hand tremors, blurred vision, and neck stiffness over the past two years.

Present Complaints:

Increased falls, slower gait, tremors when gripping objects, spastic speech, and irritability affecting relationships.

Medical Evaluation:

Initially suspected Parkinson's disease but diagnosed with PSP based on MRI findings and lack of response to Levodopa. Physiotherapy recommended for balance improvement.

Physical & Neurological Assessments:

Symptoms include spastic speech, stooped posture, kyphosis, positive Babinski sign, bradykinesia, and moderate fall risk (BERG Balance Score: 36/56). Gait analysis showed instability and stiffness.

Intervention Strategy:

1. Long-term: Improve balance and mobility, range of motion, and reduce fall risk within specified timeframes.
2. Short-term: Weekly Tai Chi and Qi Gong sessions with spouse, physiotherapy involving warmups, parallel bar training, TUG practice, and treadmill use.

Outcomes after 16 Weeks:

Pain reduced to 0/10 at rest, TUG time improved to 25 seconds, Berg Balance Score increased to 41/56, and PSP Rating decreased to 26/100. Gait confidence improved with reduced fear of falls, but gait remained broad.

Case Study 3: A Customized Tai Chi for Multiple Sclerosis (MS) Program

Client L, 43years old female, married, fulltime professional. Diagnosed with Multiple Sclerosis (MS) 5 years ago, experiencing balance issues, fatigue, muscle weakness, sensory symptoms, and cognitive difficulties impacting her work.

Present Complaints:

Persistent fatigue, balance instability, cognitive difficulties, and mood fluctuations. Struggles with job performance and work-life balance due to MS.

Evaluation:

Difficulty with Tai Chi movements due to poor balance, Observed gait instability and muscle weakness.

Initial Exercise Program (3 months):

1. Objectives: Improve stamina, leg and hip strength, balance, and body awareness.
2. Frequency: Twice a week, with home practice.
3. Duration: 515 minutes per activity, 60 minutes per session.

Intervention:

Focus on simplified and modified Tai Chi for balance and coordination, along with hip strengthening exercises.

Outcomes:

Progress measured by sustained activity and total exercise time per session, showing improvements in stamina and overall exercise tolerance.

Conclusion

Taijiquan (Tai Chi Chuan), combined martial techniques with meditative movements to cultivate physical strength, mental clarity, and spiritual harmony. Influenced by Chinese medicine and Taoist principles, Tai Chi underscores the importance of balance, energy flow, and the interconnection between mind and body.

Practitioners emphasize slow, deliberate movements, breath control, and inner mindfulness. This transformation has made Tai Chi accessible to a broader audience. Today, Tai Chi Quan is practiced worldwide and is valued as a holistic exercise that harmonizes body, mind, and spirit. Its deep roots in Chinese philosophy, coupled with evidence-based health benefits, confer a timeless appeal, offering a serene yet powerful practice for individuals seeking resilience, mental tranquility, and a sense of inner balance amidst the demands of modern life. The fluid movements inherent in Tai Chi reflect the natural rhythms of life, teaching practitioners to navigate challenges with grace and resilience. Just as the body transitions smoothly through each posture, individuals are encouraged to adapt to life's changes, embracing uncertainty rather than resisting it. This philosophy of acceptance and adaptability nurtures a mind-set applicable beyond the practice itself, promoting a calm and flexible approach to daily life.

Ultimately, Tai Chi represents a synthesis of ancient wisdom and modern perspectives on health and wellness. It conveys that health is not merely the absence of illness but a dynamic state of balance and harmony. As individuals continue to seek natural and sustainable methods to enhance their wellbeing, Tai Chi will undoubtedly remain a cherished and enduring practice, providing a pathway to strength, serenity, and self-awareness. By embracing Tai Chi, practitioners open themselves to a deeper understanding of both them and the world around them, enabling them to navigate life's challenges with grace and resilience.

References

Bongi, S., et al. (2016). Efficacy of Rehabilitation With Tai Ji Quan In An Italian Cohort Of Patients With Fibromyalgia Syndrome. *Complementary Therapies in Clinical Practice*, 23, 109115. https://doi.org/10.1016/j.ctcp.2016.05.010

Dechamps, A., Lafont, L., & BourdelMarchasson, I. (2007). Effects of Tai Chi Exercises On Self Efficacy and Psychological Health. *European Review of Aging Physical Activity,* 4, pp: 2532. https://doi.org/10.1007/s1155600700150

Guyon, A. (2024). Benefits of Tai Chi for Physical and Mental Health. *Future Integrative Medicine,* 3(1), pp: 6973. https://doi.org/10.14218/FIM.2023.00088

Jahnke, R., Larkey, L., Rogers, C., Etnier, J., & Lin, F. (2010). A Comprehensive Review of Health Benefits of Qigong and Tai Chi. *American Journal of Health Promotion,* 24(6), e1e25. https://doi.org/10.4278/ajhp.081013LIT248

Kong, J., Wilson, G., Park, J., Pereira, K., Walpole, C., & Yeung, A. (2019). Treating Depression With Tai Chi: State of The Art and Future Perspectives. *Frontiers in Psychiatry,* 10, 237. https://doi.org/10.3389/fpsyt.2019.00237

Kuramoto, A. (2006). Therapeutic Benefits of Tai Chi Exercise: Research Review. *Wisconsin Medical Journal,* 105(7), 4246.

Lan, C., Chen, Y., Lai, J., & Wong, K. (2013). Tai Chi Chuan In Medicine And Health Promotion. *EvidenceBased Complementary and Alternative Medicine,* Article 502131. https://doi.org/10.1155/2013/502131

Li, Y., Su, Q., Guo, H., Du, H., Yang, G., Meng, G., Li, C., Nagatomi, R., & Niu, K. (2014). LongTerm Tai Chi Training Is Related To Depressive Symptoms Among Tai Chi Practitioners. *Journal of Affective Disorders,* 169, 3639. https://doi.org/10.1016/j.jad.2014.07.029

Lihua, Z. (2024). The Enlightenment of Tai Chi Philosophical World View on Human Peace. *International Relations and Diplomacy,* 12(3), 9197. https://doi.org/10.17265/23282134/2024.03.001

Mahalakshmi, A. L., & Shaji, J. C. (2024). Tai Chi and Its Impact on Health. *Journal of Datta Meghe Institute of Medical Sciences University,* 19(3), 402405. https://doi.org/10.4103/jdmimsu.jdmimsu_109_24

McGee, R. (2021). Tai Chi, Qigong and The Treatment of Disease. *Biomedical Journal of Science & Technical Research,* 34(2), BJSTR.MS.ID.005531. https://doi.org/10.26717/BJSTR.2021.34.005531

Malgorzata, S., Romuald, W., Teresa, P., Katarzyna, W., Katarzyna, P., Wojciech, R., & Wojcieh, C. (2021). Ido Movement for Culture. *Journal of Martial Arts Anthropology,* 21(3), 6778. https://doi.org/10.14589/ido.21.3.9

Niu, Y., Buranarugsa, R., & Kuhirunyartn, P. (2024). Tai Chi: Definition, History, Style, Principles, And Health Benefits. *AsiaPacific Journal of Science and Technology,* 29(3), Article APST290301.

Riskowski, J. L., & Almeheyawi, R. (2019). Effects of Tai Chi and Qigong In Children And Adolescents: A Systematic Review of Trials. *Adolescent Research Review,* 4, 7391. https://doi.org/10.1007/s408940170067y

Xianjian, C., & Datao, X. (2021). Effects of Tai Chi Chuan On The Physical And Mental Health of The Elderly: A Systematic Review. *Physical Activity and Health,* 5(1), 2127. https://doi.org/10.5334/paah.70.

Chapter 17

The Bhagavad Gita - Integrating Ancient Wisdom into Psychotherapy

Suhasini DR School of Liberal Studies, CMR University, Bangalore

Introduction

The Bhagavad Gita, regularly cited virtually because the Gita, is a 700-verse Hindu scripture this is a part of the Indian epic, the Mahabharata. It is a verbal exchange among Prince Arjuna and the god Krishna, who serves as his charioteer. The Gita addresses the ethical and philosophical dilemmas confronted through Arjuna at the battlefield of Kurukshetra, in which he's torn among his obligation as a warrior and his preference to keep away from the destruction of his cherished ones in war. Through this dialogue, Krishna imparts religious wisdom, guidance, and the standards of righteous action, devotion, and selfless service.

The Gita explores numerous center themes, along with the character of the self (atman), the significance of obligation (dharma), the route to liberation (moksha), and the special styles of yoga (religious practice), along with karma yoga (the yoga of selfless action), bhakti yoga (the yoga of devotion), and jnana yoga (the yoga of knowledge).

The Bhagavad Gita`s teachings preserve to offer undying Insights into human nature and the demanding situations of dwelling a significant and moral lifestyles withinside the face of adversity. Beyond its religious dimensions, the Gita addresses essential components of human psychology, along with self-doubt, fear, emotional regulation, and moral decision-making. These teachings resonate a long way past spiritual or historic contexts, referring to regular standards that stay applicable for addressing present day lifestyle's complexities. Through its exploration of obligation (dharma), detachment, and self-knowledge, the Gita affords a dependent method to handling internal conflicts and reaching intellectual clarity, aligning intently with mental practices targeted on non-public increase and resilience (Sarma, 2019).

Relevance of Ancient Wisdom in Modern Therapy

Ancient wisdom, particularly from spiritual and cultural texts, has found increasing relevance in contemporary therapeutic practices. These age-old teachings provide valuable insights into addressing psychological needs that often encompass spiritual, emotional, and existential dimensions. Research in cultural psychology suggests that therapies aligning with clients' cultural and spiritual frameworks foster stronger engagement and lead to better therapeutic outcomes. Clients facing existential or spiritual challenges especially benefit from approaches that incorporate their cultural or spiritual traditions (Wong, 2015).

Non-Attachment and Emotional Regulation

A fundamental principle of the Bhagavad Gita is non-attachment, which emphasizes engaging wholeheartedly in meaningful actions without being overly fixated on outcomes. This aligns closely with ACT, which teaches individuals to accept challenging thoughts and emotions without letting them dictate their actions. In ACT, techniques like cognitive defusion help clients observe their thoughts without becoming overly entangled in them—mirroring the Gita's call for detachment from desires and transient emotions (Hayes et al., 2011).

Self-Awareness and Cognitive Flexibility

Self-awareness, another core teaching of the Bhagavad Gita, is essential in therapeutic work. The Gita emphasizes self-reflection and understanding one's inner nature, which parallels the goals of CBT and ACT. CBT, for instance, helps individuals recognize and modify unhelpful thought patterns through introspection and insight (Beck, 2011). Similarly, ACT encourages mindfulness and acceptance, fostering cognitive flexibility.

Purposefulness and Values-Driven Action

The Bhagavad Gita underscores the importance of dharma, or fulfilling one's purpose and responsibilities, without attachment to the results. This concept resonates with ACT's emphasis on identifying core values and committing to value-driven actions, even in the face of discomfort or challenges (Hayes et al., 2006).

Culturally Relevant Approaches and Therapeutic Engagement

Therapeutic approaches that respect and incorporate clients' cultural and spiritual values tend to foster better engagement and outcomes (Sue et al., 2009). For individuals from Eastern or Hindu backgrounds, incorporating concepts from the Gita into therapy can create a sense of familiarity and trust. This alignment can strengthen the therapeutic alliance and enhance participation in the therapeutic process.

Core Teachings of the Bhagavad Gita and Empirical Evidence

The Bhagavad Gita, a cornerstone of Hindu philosophy, offers timeless wisdom on life, duty, and human psychology. Its teachings, deeply rooted in spirituality and ethics, resonate with modern therapeutic practices. Below is a discussion on some key principles of the Gita, their psychological relevance, and the empirical evidence supporting their role in mental health.

Non-Attachment (Detachment from Outcomes)

The Bhagavad Gita emphasizes the principle of non-attachment, urging individuals to perform their duties selflessly without being fixated on the results. Krishna's advice to Arjuna to focus on action without being swayed by success or failure encapsulates this teaching (Chapter 2, Verse 47).

Psychological Relevance: Non-attachment aligns with the core principles of acceptance and mindfulness in therapy. Acceptance and Commitment Therapy (ACT), for example, encourages clients to acknowledge their thoughts and emotions without clinging to them, thereby fostering psychological flexibility (Hayes et al., 2006). Similarly, the Gita's emphasis on performing actions with integrity, free from outcome-based anxiety, mirrors these therapeutic goals.

Empirical Evidence: Research demonstrates that adopting a stance of non-attachment can significantly improve mental health. Studies on ACT reveal that distancing oneself from intrusive thoughts and outcome-driven anxiety reduces emotional reactivity and enhances resilience (Forman et al., 2007). Cognitive diffusion techniques within ACT further empower individuals to observe their thoughts without becoming overly influenced by them, a practice that resonates with the Gita's teachings (Hayes, 2004).

Self-Awareness and Introspection

The Gita underscores the importance of self-awareness and self-reflection. Krishna encourages individuals to elevate themselves through their own minds, emphasizing the need for introspection and mastery over one's thoughts and emotions (Chapter 6, Verse 5).

Psychological Relevance: This principle parallels therapeutic practices like Cognitive Behavioral Therapy (CBT), which helps clients recognize and reframe unhelpful automatic thoughts. CBT emphasizes self-understanding as a critical step toward emotional regulation and behavior change (Beck, 2011).

Empirical Evidence: Studies confirm that self-awareness is a key factor in improving mental health. Mindfulness-based interventions, which promote introspection and present-moment awareness, are effective in treating mood disorders (Zeidan et al., 2010). Additionally, heightened self-awareness has been linked to better emotional regulation and fewer cognitive distortions, which are central in addressing anxiety and depression (Gross, 2002).

Purposefulness and Duty (Dharma)

The concept of dharma—one's duty and life purpose—is a central theme in the Gita. Krishna advises Arjuna to act according to his dharma with dedication, irrespective of external difficulties, as this brings inner peace and fulfillment (Chapter 2, Verse 31).

Psychological Relevance: The Gita's emphasis on duty and purpose aligns with modern approaches like Logotherapy and ACT. Logotherapy focuses on finding meaning and purpose as a pathway to psychological well-being, while ACT encourages individuals to identify their values and take committed action in alignment with those values (Hayes et al., 2006).

Empirical Evidence: A strong sense of purpose has been consistently associated with better mental health. Research shows that individuals with meaningful life goals experience reduced psychological distress and lower levels of depression and anxiety (Steger et al., 2006). Values-based interventions, as seen in ACT, further enhance psychological flexibility and life satisfaction (Hayes et al., 2011).

Mind Control and Emotional Regulation (Meditation and Mindfulness)

Krishna highlights the importance of mastering the mind for personal growth and inner peace. He advises Arjuna to bring a wandering mind back to focus through meditation and intellect (Chapter 6, Verse 26).

Psychological Relevance: This teaching resonates with modern practices like mindfulness and meditation, which are widely used in therapeutic settings. Mindfulness-Based Stress Reduction (MBSR) programs encourage individuals to observe their thoughts nonjudgmentally, promoting better emotional regulation and mental clarity.

Empirical Evidence: Research validates the effectiveness of mindfulness and meditation in managing anxiety, depression, and emotional dysregulation. Studies show that regular mindfulness practice enhances cognitive control, reduces impulsive reactions, and improves emotional resilience (Zeidan et al., 2010; Jha et al., 2010). The Gita's emphasis on disciplined mental focus complements these therapeutic methods.

Equanimity (Emotional Balance)

The Gita advocates for equanimity, a balanced state of mind that remains steady amid life's dualities—pleasure and pain, success, and failure (Chapter 2, Verse 14).

Psychological Relevance: Equanimity is central to approaches like Dialectical Behavior Therapy (DBT), which teaches emotional regulation and the acceptance of intense emotions without becoming overwhelmed. DBT emphasizes finding balance in emotional experiences, much like the Gita's philosophy of steadiness in life's ups and downs.

Empirical Evidence: Emotional regulation is critical for maintaining mental health. Research indicates that individuals who regulate their emotions effectively are less prone to mood disorders and experience greater resilience (Gross & John, 2003). Mindfulness practices, which promote acceptance of all emotional states, have also been shown to enhance overall well-being (Keng et al., 2011). The Gita's insights on emotional steadiness provide a valuable framework for cultivating emotional balance in therapy.

Clinical Applications of the Bhagavad Gita in Therapy

The Bhagavad Gita offers profound philosophical teachings that can be used in psychotherapy to enhance emotional resilience, promote personal growth, and foster better mental health. Its emphasis on concepts such as dharma (life purpose), non-attachment, meditation, and self-awareness resonates with many modern therapeutic practices.

Applying Dharma and Non-Attachment to Clinical Practice

In the Bhagavad Gita, dharma is described as one's life purpose or duty, and practicing non-attachment involves engaging with life's challenges without being overly attached to the outcomes. These teachings can be directly applied in therapy to help clients reduce stress, find meaning in difficult situations, and improve emotional well-being.

Case Example: Career-Related Stress – A case study by Rangan and George (2018) showed that incorporating the Gita's concept of dharma into therapy helped clients struggling with career-related anxiety. The clients were encouraged to reframe their careers not as sources of self-worth but as opportunities for personal growth and service. This shift in perspective allowed them to engage with their work more meaningfully and with less anxiety, reducing overall stress and improving life satisfaction.

Meditation and Mindfulness Practices from the Gita

The Bhagavad Gita encourages meditation as a tool for mental clarity, emotional balance, and spiritual growth. Krishna instructs Arjuna to cultivate a focused, tranquil mind to better understand the nature of the self and the world. Modern therapies like Mindfulness-Based Stress Reduction (MBSR) and Mindfulness-Based Cognitive Therapy (MBCT) align with these teachings, showing substantial benefits for mental health, including reductions in anxiety, depression, and stress.

Meditation Practices in the Gita and Clinical Applications

The meditation practices described in the Gita emphasize cultivating inner awareness and focusing on the present moment, which is also central to mindfulness techniques used in contemporary therapy. In clinical settings, clients can be taught to focus on their breath or engage in meditative practices that help them observe their thoughts without judgment.

Fostering Self-Awareness and Self-Acceptance through the Gita

A core teaching of the Bhagavad Gita is the importance of self-awareness and self-acceptance. Krishna advises Arjuna to observe his emotions and thoughts without judgment, to accept his situation as it is, and to remain true to his inner nature. These principles align with modern therapeutic approaches that encourage clients to practice self-compassion and develop a non-judgmental awareness of themselves.

Self-Acceptance and Positive Psychology Interventions

Research in positive psychology emphasizes the importance of self-compassion and self-acceptance for emotional well-being. The Gita's focus on non-judgmental self-awareness supports the development of a healthier self-concept, helping individuals overcome self-criticism and enhance resilience.

Implementing the Bhagavad Gita's Teachings in Therapeutic Practice

The Bhagavad Gita, a timeless philosophical text, offers profound insights into human psychology and behavior. Its teachings align remarkably well with modern therapeutic approaches.

Personal Study and Understanding:

- ***Deepen Your Knowledge:*** Therapists should engage in a comprehensive study of the Gita to ensure accurate and ethical application.
- ***Cultural Sensitivity:*** Understand the cultural and philosophical context of the Gita to apply its principles respectfully and effectively.
- ***Ethical Application:*** Use the Gita's teachings responsibly, avoiding oversimplification or misinterpretation.

Assessing Client Openness:

- ***Client's Perspective:*** Engage in open dialogue with clients about their spiritual beliefs and comfort level with philosophical concepts.
- ***Tailored Approach:*** Adapt the application of the Gita's teachings to the client's specific needs and preferences.
- ***Respectful Integration:*** If the client is open to spiritual concepts, integrate them thoughtfully; if not, focus on secular mindfulness techniques and psychological interventions.

Tailoring the Gita's Teachings to Individual Needs:

- ***Personalized Approach:*** Consider the client's specific challenges and tailor the application of the Gita's principles accordingly.
- ***Alignment with Modern Therapies:*** Integrate the Gita's teachings with contemporary therapeutic approaches like ACT and CBT.
- ***Evidence-Based Support:*** Utilize research findings to support the effectiveness of mindfulness and non-attachment practices.

Ethical Considerations:

- ***Informed Consent:*** Obtain informed consent from clients about the potential use of spiritual or philosophical concepts in therapy.
- ***Therapist Qualifications:*** Ensure that therapists have the necessary training and expertise to apply the Gita's teachings ethically and effectively.
- ***Boundary Setting:*** Maintain clear professional boundaries and avoid imposing personal beliefs or values on clients.

Specific Applications in Therapy

- ***Mindfulness and Meditation:*** The Gita emphasizes mindfulness and meditation for mental clarity and emotional well-being. These practices can be incorporated into therapy sessions to reduce stress, anxiety, and depression.
- ***Cognitive-Behavioral Therapy (CBT):*** The Gita's teachings on karma yoga can be used to help clients challenge negative thought patterns and develop more adaptive behaviors.
- ***Acceptance and Commitment Therapy (ACT):*** The Gita's emphasis on non-attachment aligns with ACT's core principles of acceptance and commitment.
- ***Existential Therapy:*** The Gita's exploration of the nature of reality and the human condition can be used to help clients address existential concerns and find meaning in life.

Benefits of Integrating the Gita in Therapy

Building Resilience

Resilience is the ability to adapt to challenges, bounce back from adversity, and maintain emotional well-being during difficult times. The Bhagavad Gita offers powerful teachings on resilience through its emphasis on detachment, acceptance of impermanence, and embracing duty (dharma) without attachment to outcomes. By adopting a mindset of equanimity—accepting life's ups and downs without being overwhelmed—clients can develop stronger emotional resilience.

Enhanced Emotional Regulation

Emotional regulation is the ability to manage one's emotional responses to stimuli in a healthy way, a critical factor in mental health. The Bhagavad Gita teaches emotional regulation through practices such as mindfulness, equanimity, and non-reactivity, all of which help individuals maintain balance and clarity in the face of strong emotions. These practices are increasingly integrated into modern psychological approaches, particularly in Mindfulness-Based Cognitive Therapy (MBCT) and Dialectical Behavior Therapy (DBT), which have shown promise in treating anxiety, depression, and other mood disorders.

Research Gap and Justification

While there is a growing body of literature on the intersection of spiritual philosophies and modern psychotherapeutic practices, empirical studies directly examining the integration of the Bhagavad Gita's teachings into psychotherapy remain scarce. Much of the existing research on culturally or spiritually adapted therapies has focused primarily on mindfulness practices rooted in Buddhist traditions (Grossman et al., 2004; Hofmann et al., 2010) and, to a lesser extent, on Islamic and Christian frameworks (Wong, 2015). However, despite its rich insights into human psychology and coping strategies, the Gita has been relatively underexplored in terms of structured, evidence-based therapeutic interventions.

The lack of empirical studies on Gita-based therapeutic applications leaves an unexplored avenue in psychology for culturally relevant, client-centered care—particularly in regions where Hinduism is prevalent or among individuals who identify with or have an openness to Eastern philosophies. Culturally congruent therapies have shown to enhance engagement, satisfaction, and outcomes for clients, particularly those from non-Western backgrounds (Sue et al., 2009). However, without systematic research, therapists have limited guidance on how to incorporate the Gita's teachings ethically and effectively into therapeutic frameworks, leaving a notable gap in culturally inclusive care models.

Potential Areas for Future Research

Developing and Testing Gita-Based Interventions: Pilot studies and randomized controlled trials could evaluate specific therapeutic interventions derived from the Gita's teachings on non-attachment, purpose, and self-realization. Such studies could assess the effectiveness of Gita-based practices in reducing symptoms of anxiety, depression, and stress.

Comparative Studies with Established Therapies: Research comparing the outcomes of Gita-based approaches to those of well-established models like CBT, ACT, and mindfulness could offer valuable insights into the efficacy and unique contributions of Gita teachings in therapeutic contexts.

Longitudinal Impact on Spiritual and Existential Well-Being: Longitudinal research on individuals undergoing Gita-informed therapies could provide evidence on how these approaches impact long-term well-being, especially for clients seeking support for existential or spiritual concerns.

Case Studies

Case Study 1: Application of Karma Yoga in Therapy

Client Background :

Client Profile: Ravi, a 32-year-old professional, came to therapy struggling with existential anxiety, primarily around the purpose of his work and the pressure to meet personal and societal expectations. Despite being a high achiever in his career, he felt a constant sense of unease, questioning the value of his work and fearing failure in the eyes of others. Ravi also reported high levels of performance-related anxiety, often feeling trapped by the desire for external validation and success.

Therapeutic Approach :

Given Ravi's cultural background and openness to spiritual ideas, the therapist decided to integrate the Bhagavad Gita's teachings on Karma Yoga (selfless action) into the therapeutic process. Karma Yoga, as described in the Gita, teaches that one should focus on actions without attachment to their outcomes, doing one's duty without expecting personal rewards. This concept was chosen because it directly addressed Ravi's fixation on outcomes, which was contributing to his anxiety.

Intervention Strategy

- **Introduction to Karma Yoga:** The therapist introduced Ravi to the core concept of Karma Yoga: performing actions as a duty without attachment to success or failure. Ravi was taught to focus on the process of his work, not the results, helping him find intrinsic value in the act of working rather than attaching his sense of self-worth to external achievements.
- **Cognitive Reframing:** The therapist helped Ravi reframe his thoughts surrounding success and failure. Instead of viewing his work to an end, Ravi was encouraged to engage with it as an expression of personal growth and selfless service, thereby shifting focus from external validation to personal fulfillment and purpose (Hayes et al., 2006).
- **Mindfulness and Acceptance:** As part of the intervention, Ravi was trained in mindfulness techniques. He learned to be present in the moment, focusing on the task at hand, and acknowledging any anxious thoughts that arose without judgment. This helped him practice non-attachment to the outcomes of his actions, aligning with the Gita's teachings on detachment and mindfulness (Zeidan et al., 2010).
- **Emotional Regulation:** The therapist guided Ravi in building emotional resilience through acceptance-based strategies. Ravi was encouraged to accept that uncertainty and imperfection were natural parts of life, which helped him reduce his anxiety over performance and success (Forman et al., 2007).

Follow-Up Assessments and Outcomes

After eight sessions, follow-up assessments revealed significant changes in Ravi's psychological state and coping mechanisms:

- **Reduced Anxiety:** Ravi's scores on standardized anxiety assessments showed a significant decrease in anxiety levels. His existential worries about the meaning of his work diminished, and he reported feeling less overwhelmed by the pressure to succeed.
- **Improved Coping Skills:** Ravi demonstrated improved coping strategies for handling workplace stress. Instead of feeling paralyzed by performance pressure, he became more focused on the process and his personal growth. His ability to manage stress in high-pressure situations improved, and he described feeling more balanced and in control.
- **Increased Life Satisfaction:** Ravi reported a newfound sense of inner peace. He no longer tied his self-worth solely to his career achievements, and he felt more fulfilled by the work itself. This shift toward intrinsic motivation mirrored the self-acceptance promoted by the Gita and was reflected in Ravi's increased satisfaction with both his professional and personal life (Gu et al., 2015).
- **Enhanced Sense of Purpose:** Through the practice of Karma Yoga, Ravi began to view his professional tasks as opportunities for growth, rather than burdens. This led to an increased sense of meaning and purpose in his work, contributing to his overall psychological well-being.

Reflection and Conclusion

This case study illustrates how Karma Yoga can be an effective therapeutic intervention for clients experiencing existential anxiety or performance-related stress. By focusing on selfless action and detaching from the results of one's efforts, Ravi was able to reduce his anxiety and improve his coping skills.

This outcome is consistent with research in acceptance-based therapies, which emphasize non-attachment to outcomes and mindfulness to alleviate stress and improve emotional regulation (Hayes et al., 2006). The case also underscores the importance of integrating spiritual and philosophical teachings into psychotherapy, particularly for clients who resonate with such practices.

The integration of Karma Yoga in therapeutic practice offers a unique way to address existential concerns and performance anxiety, providing clients with a deeper sense of purpose, acceptance, and emotional resilience. This approach aligns well with modern therapeutic interventions such as Acceptance and Commitment Therapy (ACT), which focuses on values-driven actions and psychological flexibility (Forman et al., 2007).

Case Study 2: Bhakti Yoga and Depression

Context:

A 28-year-old woman was struggling with depression and feelings of emptiness following a series of personal setbacks, including a breakup and job loss. She experienced pervasive sadness, lack of motivation, and a sense of being disconnected from the world around her. Bhakti yoga, with its focus on devotion and connecting to a higher power, was introduced as a potential therapeutic tool.

Application:

The therapist guided the client to cultivate a sense of devotion and love towards a higher power or universal consciousness, in line with the teachings of the Bhagavad Gita. This process involved prayer, meditative rituals, and focusing on surrendering personal control to a higher purpose. Bhakti yoga's practice of cultivating love and devotion helped the client reconnect with a sense of meaning beyond personal struggles.

Outcome:

After eight weeks of incorporating bhakti yoga practices, the client reported a marked improvement in mood, with a significant decrease in depressive symptoms. They reported feeling a deeper sense of peace and acceptance, and began engaging in daily devotional practices that helped them cope with challenges. The client also expressed a renewed sense of connection with others, and described a shift from self-centered thinking to a more expansive, spiritually inclusive perspective. This is consistent with research demonstrating that spiritual practices can provide individuals with resilience and emotional regulation, as seen in studies on religious coping mechanisms (Pargament et al., 2004).

Reflection:

This case highlights how Bhakti yoga can be a powerful tool for individuals experiencing depression, particularly when they feel disconnected or disillusioned by life's challenges. By fostering a sense of devotion and connection to a higher power, clients can gain perspective, find meaning, and restore their emotional balance. The therapeutic application of bhakti yoga provides a bridge between ancient spiritual wisdom and modern therapeutic practices, demonstrating the efficacy of spiritual practices in enhancing psychological well-being (Koenig et al., 2012).

Conclusion

This study explored the potential of the Bhagavad Gita's ancient wisdom to enrich modern therapeutic practices. With its teachings on non-attachment, self-awareness, emotional regulation, and the pursuit of purpose, the Gita offers principles that resonate with established therapeutic approaches like Cognitive Behavioral Therapy (CBT), Acceptance and Commitment Therapy (ACT), and Logotherapy. Each of these modern practices shares the Gita's focus on mindfulness, values, resilience, and acceptance—concepts that support clients in developing coping mechanisms, reducing stress, and fostering mental well-being.

The Gita's approach to non-attachment, which encourages individuals to act with intention rather than fixation on outcomes, has proven effective in reducing anxiety and enhancing resilience. Similarly, the Gita's theory of the three gunas offers a meaningful lens for understanding personality and behavior, enabling therapists to create culturally relevant and personalized interventions. Case studies and empirical evidence indicate that incorporating these principles can support clients facing existential concerns, emotional dysregulation, and performance-related pressures.

However, integrating spiritual texts like the Gita into therapy requires a thoughtful approach. Therapists must ensure cultural sensitivity, accurately interpret the teachings, and evaluate each client's openness to spiritual or philosophical interventions. Research suggests that when spiritual principles are appropriately integrated, they can lead to improved outcomes by fostering respect, engagement, and a sense of meaning for clients.

In conclusion, the Bhagavad Gita provides timeless insights that can enhance the therapeutic process by addressing both the psychological and spiritual needs of clients. By blending the Gita's wisdom with evidence-based practices, therapists can offer a holistic approach that fosters resilience, emotional balance, and a purposeful life. This integration creates a unique therapeutic path that honors the client's cultural background while promoting personal growth and mental well-being.

References

Bhattacharyya, N. (2001). The Bhagavad Gita: A Study in the Philosophy of Life. Calcutta: Sanskrit Pustak Bhandar.

Radhakrishnan, S. (1993). The Bhagavad Gita: With an Introduction and Commentary. Harper Collins.

Forman, E. M., Herbert, J. D., & Gaudiano, B. A. (2007). The acceptance and commitment therapy (ACT) approach to treating anxiety and depression. Journal of Cognitive Psychotherapy, 21(2), 106–121.

Hayes, S. C., Strosahl, K. D., & Wilson, K. G. (2006). Acceptance and Commitment Therapy: An Experiential Approach to Behavior Change. The Guilford Press.

Gu, J., Strauss, C., Bond, R., & Cavanagh, K. (2015). Mindfulness-based interventions for mental health problems in children and adolescents: A systematic review. Journal of Child Psychology and Psychiatry, 56(8), 708-722.

Zeidan, F., Johnson, S. K., Diamond, B. J., & David, Z. (2010). Mindfulness meditation improves emotion regulation and reduces stress in non-clinical populations. Journal of Consulting and Clinical Psychology, 78(3), 434-444.

Forman, E. M., Herbert, J. D., & Gaudiano, B. A. (2007). The acceptance and commitment therapy (ACT) approach to treating anxiety and depression. Journal of Cognitive Psychotherapy, 21(2), 106–121.

Arch, J. J., & Craske, M. G. (2008). Acceptance and commitment therapy and cognitive behavioral therapy for anxiety disorders: Different treatments, similar mechanisms? Clinical Psychology: Science and Practice, 15(4), 263-279.

Damon, W., Menon, J., & Bronk, K. C. (2003). The development of purpose during adolescence. Applied Developmental Science, 7(3), 119-128.

Deci, E. L., & Ryan, R. M. (2008). Self-determination theory: A macrotheory of human motivation, development, and health. Canadian Psychology/Psychologie Canadienne, 49(3), 182-185.

Grossman, P., Niemann, L., Schmidt, S., & Walach, H. (2004). Mindfulness-based stress reduction and health benefits: A meta-analysis. Journal of Psychosomatic Research, 57(1), 35-43.

Grover, S., & Ghosh, A. (2021). Cultural aspects of psychiatric disorders. In Sadock, B. J., Sadock, V. A., & Ruiz, P. (Eds.), Kaplan & Sadock's Comprehensive Textbook of Psychiatry (11th ed.). Wolters Kluwer.

Gu, J., Strauss, C., Bond, R., & Cavanagh, K. (2015). How do mindfulness-based cognitive therapy and mindfulness-based stress reduction improve mental health and wellbeing? A systematic review and meta-analysis of mediation studies. Clinical Psychology Review, 37, 1-12.

Hill, P. L., & Turiano, N. A. (2014). Purpose in life as a predictor of mortality across adulthood. Psychological Science, 25(7), 1482-1486.

Hofmann, S. G., Sawyer, A. T., Witt, A. A., & Oh, D. (2010). The effect of mindfulness-based therapy on anxiety and depression: A meta-analytic review. Journal of Consulting and Clinical Psychology, 78(2), 169-183.

Kabat-Zinn, J. (2003). Mindfulness-based interventions in context: Past, present, and future. Clinical Psychology: Science and Practice, 10(2), 144-156.

Kumar, A., & Gopalan, T. (2020). Guna personality in the Bhagavad Gita: Implications for clinical psychology. Indian Journal of Psychiatry, 62(2), 151-160.

Neff, K. D. (2003). The development and validation of a scale to measure self-compassion. Self and Identity, 2(3), 223-250.

Pargament, K. I., Murray-Swank, N. A., & Tarakeshwar, N. (2004). An empirically-based rationale for a spiritually-integrated psychotherapy. Mental Health, Religion & Culture, 7(3), 225-239.

Patel, V., & Sharma, M. (2022). Bridging spirituality and psychotherapy: Ethical considerations and potential benefits. Journal of Spirituality in Mental Health, 24(3), 186-202.

Rangan, V., & George, S. (2018). Addressing career stress through the concept of dharma: A case study approach. Journal of Career Development, 45(2), 147-158.

Shapiro, S. L., Carlson, L. E., Astin, J. A., & Freedman, B. (2006). Mechanisms of mindfulness. Journal of Clinical Psychology, 62(3), 373-386.

Sue, S., Zane, N., & Young, K. (2009). Research on psychotherapy with culturally diverse populations. In Norcross, J. C., VandenBos, G. R., & Freedheim, D. K. (Eds.), History of Psychotherapy: Continuity and Change (pp. 521-547). American Psychological Association.

Seligman, M. E. P. (2002). Positive psychology, positive prevention, and positive therapy. In Snyder, C. R., & Lopez, S. J. (Eds.), Handbook of Positive Psychology (pp. 3-9). Oxford University Press.

Tusaie, K., & Dyer, J. (2004). Resilience: A historical review of the construct. Holistic Nursing Practice, 18(1), 3-10.

Wong, Y. J. (2015). The role of culture in psychotherapy: A review of the cultural adaptations of psychotherapy. Clinical Psychology Review, 35, 15-25.

Zeidan, F., Johnson, S. K., Diamond, B. J., David, Z., & Goolkasian, P. (2010). Mindfulness meditation improves cognition: Evidence of brief mental training. Consciousness and Cognition, 19(2), 597-605.

Chapter 18

The Noble Eightfold Pathway

Noyanika Karmakar School of Liberal Studies (SLS), CMR University, Bangalore

Introduction

Buddhism, one of the world's oldest spiritual traditions, was founded in the 6th century BCE by Siddhartha Gautama, known as the Buddha, in what is now modern-day Nepal and India. Born a prince, Siddhartha renounced his privileged life to seek the truth behind human suffering. After years of ascetic practices and meditation, he attained enlightenment and dedicated his life to teaching others a path to liberation from suffering. At the heart of his teachings are the Four Noble Truths, which diagnose the existence and nature of suffering and prescribe a way to overcome it. The Fourth Noble Truth outlines the Noble Eightfold Path (NEP)—a guide to ethical and mental discipline that leads to insight, peace, and ultimately, enlightenment.

The Noble Eightfold Path is an early summary of the path of Buddhist practices leading to liberation from samsara, the painful cycle of rebirth which teaches that by restraining oneself, cultivating discipline, and practicing mindfulness and meditation, house-leavers (monks and nuns) attain nirvana and stop their craving, clinging and karmic accumulations, thereby ending their rebirth and suffering. This is a central teaching in Buddhism, offering a guide to ethical and mental development with the goal of freeing individuals from suffering (dukkha). While not commonly referred to as a "healing method" in modern therapeutic practices, it can be interpreted as a method for healing the mind, spirit, and even interpersonal relationships.

In Buddhist symbolism, the NEP is often represented by means of the dharma wheel (dharmachakra), whose eight spokes represent the eight elements of the path.

Origin of The Noble Eightfold Path

According to Vetter, the description of the Buddhist path may initially have been as simple as the term "the middle way". In time, this short description was elaborated, resulting in the description of the eightfold path. Vetter and Bucknell both note that longer descriptions of "the path" can be found, which can be condensed into the eightfold path.

The origin of the NEP lies in the foundational teachings of the Buddha, Siddhartha Gautama, who lived in the 6th century BCE. Born into a royal family in what is now Nepal, Siddhartha was shielded from the hardships of life. However, upon encountering the realities of aging, illness, and death, he felt compelled to understand the nature of suffering and the means to transcend it. Renouncing his life as a prince, he embarked on a spiritual quest that led him through years of extreme ascetic practices. Despite his intense efforts, he found that self-denial did not bring him the insight he sought.

This realization led him to discover the "Middle Way," a balanced approach between indulgence and extreme asceticism. He adopted this Middle Way and sat in meditation under the Bodhi tree in Bodh Gaya, India, where he ultimately attained enlightenment. In his enlightenment experience, the Buddha realized the Four Noble Truths, which outline the nature of suffering (dukkha), its origin in desire and attachment, its cessation, and the path to end suffering. The Noble Eightfold Path is the fourth of these truths and serves as a practical guide for ethical and spiritual development that leads to liberation. The Buddha first introduced the *Dhammacakkappavattana Sutta* (The Setting in Motion of the Wheel of Dharma), delivered to five of his former companions in Sarnath, near Varanasi. This sermon marks the beginning of his teaching career and the birth of the Buddhist community.

The Eight Divisions

Right View (Samma Ditthi) - Our actions have consequences; death is not the end, and our actions and beliefs have also consequences after death; the Buddha followed and taught a successful path out of this world and the other world (heaven and underworld/hell) Later on, right view came to explicitly include karma and rebirth, and the importance of the Four Noble Truths, when "insight" became central to Buddhist soteriology.

Right Resolve (Samma Sankappa) - The giving up home and adopting the life of a religious mendicant in order to follow the path; this concept, states Harvey, aims at peaceful renunciation, into an environment of non-sensuality, non-ill-will (to loving kindness), away from cruelty (to compassion). Such an environment aids contemplation of impermanence, suffering, and non-Self.

Right Speech (Samma Vaca) - No lying, no rude speech, no telling one person what another says about him, speaking that which leads to salvation.

Right Conduct (Samma Kammanta) - no killing or injuring, no taking what is not given, no sexual acts.

Right Livelihood (Samma Ajiva) - beg to feed, only possessing what is essential to sustain life.

Right Effort (Samma Vayama) - guard against sensual thoughts; this concept, states Harvey, aims at preventing unwholesome states that disrupt meditation.

Right Mindfulness (Samma Sati) - never be absent minded, being conscious of what one is doing; this, states Harvey, encourages the mindfulness about impermanence of body, feeling and mind, as well as to experience the five aggregates (skandhas), the five hindrances, the four True Realities and seven factors of awakening.

Right concentration (Samma Samadhi) - practicing four stages of meditation (dhyāna) culminating into unification of the mind.

Components of Path as Developmental Stages

In Buddhism, the teachings of the NEP are often organized into a "Threefold Division," which categorizes the eight aspects of the path into three key areas of practice.

Wisdom (Paññā)

Right View- This is the understanding of the nature of reality and the Four Noble Truths. Right View involves seeing things as they truly are, recognizing the existence of suffering, its causes, and the path to its cessation. It is foundational, as wisdom guides ethical and mental discipline.

Right Intention- This focuses on cultivating thoughts and intentions that are free from desire, ill-will, and harmful inclinations. Right Intention promotes kindness, compassion, and non-attachment, supporting a mental state conducive to spiritual growth.

The wisdom components guide practitioners to a deep understanding of the causes of suffering and the nature of existence, laying the groundwork for ethical behavior and mental focus.

Ethical Conduct (Sīla)

Right Speech- This encourages truthful, kind, and constructive communication, avoiding falsehoods, gossip, or harmful speech.

Right Action- Right Action involves behaving in a morally upright way by avoiding harm to others, stealing, and engaging in misconduct. It emphasizes compassion and respect for all life.

Right Livelihood- Right Livelihood means choosing a profession or means of living that does not harm others and is in line with ethical principles. This includes avoiding occupations that exploit, harm, or deceive.

Ethical conduct is essential for creating harmonious relationships and a peaceful society. It helps prevent harm and cultivates positive interactions, setting a foundation for mental stability and inner peace.

Mental Discipline (Samādhi)

Right Effort- It involves the intentional cultivation of positive states of mind and the prevention of unwholesome or harmful thoughts. It is the effort to foster good mental qualities like patience and compassion, while also working to diminish negative traits like anger or jealousy.

Right Mindfulness- This encourages full awareness and attention to the present moment, without attachment or judgment. Mindfulness is practiced through observing the body, feelings, mind, and phenomena, allowing one to cultivate clarity and reduce suffering.

Right Concentration- Right Concentration refers to developing a focused and stable mind, usually through meditation practices. This practice helps calm and center the mind, preparing it for deeper insight and wisdom.

Mental discipline helps refine the mind, fostering inner stillness and focus. It allows practitioners to see reality more clearly and develop insight, supporting the goal of liberation.

Application of Path as an Emerging Therapeutic Intervention

Right View

It helps in developing insight and self-awareness and clients gain a clear understanding of how their beliefs, perceptions, and cognitive biases contribute to their suffering. The aim is to foster self-awareness and insight into the nature of their challenges. Therapists work with clients to identify and challenge distorted thinking patterns, like the cognitive restructuring techniques used in Cognitive Behavioral Therapy (CBT) and educating clients about how thought patterns affect emotions and behaviors, encouraging a realistic and compassionate view of themselves and their experiences. Clients develop healthier cognitive patterns, gain a deeper understanding of their emotional responses, and start seeing issues from a balanced perspective.

Right Intention

It helps in cultivating positive motivation and intentions in clients. It encourages clients to set intentions that align with kindness, compassion, and non-harm, focusing on values that promote mental health and positive relationships. Therapists help clients explore their values and motivations, clarifying what they truly want in their lives and relationships and set short-term and long-term goals based on compassionate and constructive intentions. Clients are encouraged to pursue goals that promote inner peace and resilience. Thus, clients feel more motivated and intentional, better able to act in alignment with their values, and more resilient when facing life's challenges.

Right Speech

It helps in improving communication and self-talk and promotes clear, compassionate, and constructive communication, both in relationships and within oneself (self-talk). Therapists teach clients techniques for assertive, honest, and kind communication to improve relationships and resolve conflicts and help clients identify negative internal dialogues and replace them with supportive, affirming statements. Thus, clients improve their interpersonal communication skills, experience enhanced relationships, and develop a kinder inner dialogue that supports self-esteem and resilience.

Right Action

It encourages ethical and self-respectful behavior to guide clients to adopt behaviors that are ethical, self-respectful, and promote personal integrity. Clients engage in activities that align with their values, enhancing motivation and reducing avoidance behaviors. This is particularly effective in addressing depression and promoting responsible decision-making and helping clients set healthy boundaries to protect their well-being and act in ways that reflect self-respect and self-care. Thus, clients feel more in control of their lives, make choices that align with their values, and build self-respect through integrity and ethical action.

Right Livelihood

It fosters purpose and balance in life and encourages clients to find or create a sense of purpose in their work and ensure that it contributes positively to their lives and well-being. Therapists further support clients in exploring their career satisfaction, purpose, and the impact of their work on their mental health. Clients find greater purpose and satisfaction in their daily lives, reducing feelings of meaninglessness and burnout, and increasing overall life satisfaction.

Right Effort

It helps in developing healthy mental habits and guide clients to cultivate positive mental habits while reducing negative, unhelpful ones. It further encourages clients to engage in practices such as gratitude journaling, cultivating optimism, focusing on strengths and teaching clients techniques for managing negative emotions, such as stress and anger, and reinforcing positive emotions. Clients develop greater resilience and emotional stability, able to replace negative habits with constructive ones that enhance their mental well-being.

Right Mindfulness

It helps in building present-moment awareness and clients become aware of their thoughts, emotions, and physical sensations in a non-judgmental way, allowing them to respond rather than react impulsively. Clients also practice mindfulness meditation to build awareness of the present moment, observing thoughts and emotions without attachment further incorporating methods from Mindfulness-Based Stress Reduction (MBSR) and Mindfulness-Based Cognitive Therapy (MBCT) to help clients manage stress, anxiety, and depression that helps them gain control over automatic reactions, reduce symptoms of anxiety and depression, and experience increased clarity, focus, and emotional regulation.

Right Concentration

It enhances focus and inner calm and develop clients' capacity for sustained attention and mental calmness, promoting a more focused, serene mind by practicing single-pointed focus meditation techniques and relaxation techniques, such as focusing on the breath, which can improve attention and calmness which helps them manage stress, reduce symptoms of ADHD, and make more mindful decisions.

Sacred Sites for Path

The NEP, as part of the core teachings of Buddhism, has historically been practiced and taught in regions where Buddhism has spread and taken root. From ancient India, where the Buddha first introduced this path, to its presence across various countries and cultural settings, the Eightfold Path has been central to Buddhist practice, monastic life, and lay community traditions. Here are some notable regions and historical places where the Eightfold Path has been practiced-

India (Ancient and Modern) - Bodh Gaya is the place of the Buddha's enlightenment under the Bodhi tree. Sarnath, near Varanasi is one of the key pilgrimage sites in Buddhism. Nalanda was once a renowned center of learning in ancient India.

Sri Lanka - It is one of the oldest continuous centers of Theravāda Buddhism. The Eightfold Path has been a core element of Theravāda teachings in the Pali Canon.

Myanmar - Formerly Burma has a rich tradition of Theravāda Buddhism. Notable centers include Shwedagon Pagoda in Yangon and meditation centers like Mahasi Monastery and Panditarama Monastery.

Thailand - It is predominantly a Theravāda Buddhist country. Notable places include Wat Phra Dhammakaya and Wat Suan Mokkh and Thai Forest Tradition monasteries, like Wat Pah Nanachat.

Tibet - Tibetan Buddhism incorporates the Eightfold Path as part of the broader Mahāyāna tradition, though it is often taught in conjunction with other Mahāyāna and Vajrayāna paths to enlightenment. Lhasa and Samye Monastery, the first Buddhist monastery in Tibet.

China - Buddhism entered China around the 1st century CE, and the Eightfold Path became part of the core teachings alongside the Mahāyāna sutras. Notable centers of practice include Shaolin Monastery and Mount Wutai, where monastics practiced meditation, ethics, and wisdom following the principles of the Path.

Present Day Retreats for Path

Theravāda Buddhist Countries

Sri Lanka- The Eightfold Path is a core aspect of Buddhist practice in Sri Lanka, with temples, monasteries, and meditation centers across the country promoting its principles. Notable centers include the Nilambe Meditation Centre and Kandy's Buddhist Publication Society, which offers resources on the Path.

Myanmar- Monasteries and meditation centers in Myanmar, such as Mahasi Monastery in Yangon and Panditarama Meditation Center, focus on Vipassana (insight meditation) and follow the Eightfold Path closely.

Thailand- Thailand's Wat Suan Mokkh and Wat Pah Nanachat are known for their emphasis on mindfulness and ethical conduct as part of the Path. The Thai Forest Tradition, led by respected monks like Ajahn Chah and Ajahn Sumedho, practices the Path in forest monasteries throughout Thailand.

Laos and Cambodia- The Eightfold Path is also fundamental in Laos and Cambodia, where it is practiced in local monasteries and lay communities as part of daily life, integrating ethical living, mindfulness, and meditation.

Mahayana and Vajrayana Buddhist Countries

Tibet- Tibetan Buddhist monasteries, such as Drepung Monastery and Ganden Monastery, incorporate the Eightfold Path within a broader framework of Mahāyāna and Vajrayāna teachings. Tibetan Buddhism emphasizes the Path along with bodhisattva practices and compassion-based meditations.

China- In China, the Eightfold Path is practiced in both Chan (Zen) and Pure Land traditions. Temples like Shaolin Monastery and Mount Wutai continue to incorporate the Path into their spiritual practices, especially through mindfulness, meditation, and ethical conduct.

Japan- Japanese Zen Buddhism, including centers like Eiheiji and Myoshin-ji, integrates the Path into zazen (seated meditation) and mindful, ethical living. Pure Land and Nichiren traditions also respect the Path as part of broader Buddhist teachings.

Modern Mindfulness Programs and Therapeutic Settings

Mindfulness-Based Programs- The Eightfold Path, especially its components of Right Mindfulness and Right Concentration, serves as a foundation for mindfulness-based interventions like MBSR and MBCT. These programs are widely used in hospitals, therapy centers, and schools globally to reduce stress and promote mental health.

Digital and Online Platforms

With the rise of digital platforms, people around the world now practice the Eightfold Path through online meditation communities, apps, and resources. Platforms like Insight Timer, Dharma Seed, and Mindful Schools offer guided teachings and meditations based on the Path, making it accessible to practitioners globally.

Case Studies

Case Study 1: Application of the Eightfold Path in Overcoming Chronic Anxiety

Presenting Problem:

A client in their late twenties experienced chronic anxiety, which impacted their personal relationships, professional life, and overall well-being. The anxiety manifested in overthinking, excessive worry about future scenarios, and avoidance of social situations.

Background:

The client had a history of anxiety and had tried several forms of therapy but found limited success. They sought help specifically to manage anxiety without reliance on medication.

Methodology:

The therapist introduced the Eightfold Path with a focus on:

- Right View to help the client understand how their thoughts fueled anxiety.
- Right Intention to cultivate a mindset of letting go and acceptance.
- Right Mindfulness to observe anxious thoughts without judgment or reaction.
- Right Effort to gently challenge avoidance behaviors and build new habits.

The therapist used cognitive restructuring exercises combined with mindfulness practices, such as breath awareness and body scans. Journaling was encouraged to track the client's progress, particularly their insights on how perceptions and intentions influenced their anxiety.

Outcome:

The client reported a noticeable reduction in anxiety. They learned to observe anxious thoughts with less reactivity, finding it easier to let go of catastrophic thinking. Over time, they became more comfortable in social situations and expressed gratitude for the deeper sense of peace and clarity cultivated through the Eightfold Path.

Case Study 2 : Family Therapy Utilizing the Eightfold Path for Conflict Resolution

Presenting Problem:

A family of four, including two parents and two teenage children, struggled with constant arguments, misunderstandings, and strained relationships. The parents felt disrespected by the teens, while the teens felt unheard and overly criticized.

Background:

The family had tried traditional family therapy before but found it didn't lead to lasting changes. They sought a new approach to create deeper respect and understanding among family members.

Methodology:

The therapist integrated the Eightfold Path into family therapy sessions, emphasizing:

- Right Speech to teach family members honest but respectful communication.
- Right View to foster empathy and understanding for each other's perspectives.
- Right Effort to encourage each family member to consciously maintain positive interactions and avoid conflict.

Outcome:

The family experienced a significant decrease in arguments. They reported that Right Speech improved their ability to listen and express themselves without judgment or resentment. Parents felt more respected, and the teens felt more valued, leading to a harmonious environment. The family developed tools to manage future disagreements constructively.

Conclusion

The Eightfold Path, when applied therapeutically, encourages clients to lead a more mindful, ethical, and balanced life. Each component of the Path contributes to emotional healing and mental health by cultivating awareness and insight, clarifying intentions and values, improving relationships and communication, fostering ethical behavior and integrity, promoting work-life balance and purpose, building positive mental habits, enhancing focus and inner peace.The Eightfold Path as a therapeutic framework provides a flexible and holistic approach that can meet clients where they are, helping them to reduce suffering and build a life of resilience, peace, and purpose.

References

Barrett, R. (1996). *The Buddha's teachings on the Four Noble Truths and the Eightfold Path.* Wisdom Publications.

Batchelor, S. (1994). *The awakening of the West: The encounter of Buddhism and Western culture.* Continuum.

Bodhi, B. (2000). *The connected discourses of the Buddha: A new translation of the Samyutta Nikaya.* Wisdom Publications.

Goldstein, J. (2002). *The experience of insight: A simple and direct guide to Buddhist meditation.* Shambhala Publications.

Hayes, R. (2007). The Eightfold Path as a psychotherapeutic model. *Journal of Buddhist Psychology, 3*(2), 240-259. https://doi.org/10.1002/jbps.242

Gelek Rimpoche, G. (2016). *The Eightfold Path: The key to enlightenment.* Clear Light Publishers.

Gethin, R. (1998). *The foundations of Buddhism.* Oxford University Press.

Ingram, D. (2009). The path of purification: The Four Noble Truths and the Eightfold Path. *Journal of Contemplative Practice, 5*(4), 8-22. https://doi.org/10.1002/jcps.510

Kiernan, T. (2007). *The Eightfold Path as an Ethical Compass in the Therapeutic Environment*. Sacred Stream.

Kornfield, J. (2008). *The wise heart: A guide to the universal teachings of Buddhist psychology*. Bantam.

Segal, Z. V., Williams, J. M. G., & Teasdale, J. D. (2002). *Mindfulness-based cognitive therapy for depression: A new approach to preventing relapse*. The Guilford Press.

Seligman, M. E. P. (2011). *Flourish: A visionary new understanding of happiness and well-being*. Free Press

Chapter 19

Tibetan Singing Bowl Sound Therapy

Prarthana Mazumdar School of Liberal Studies (SLS), CMR University, Bangalore

Tibetan Singing Bowl Sound Therapy

Tibetan singing bowl sound therapy, also known as "vibrational sound healing," is a holistic therapeutic approach where metal bowls, typically made from a combination of metals, are used to produce sounds and vibrations that impact both the mind and body. Practitioners strike or circle the bowls with a mallet, creating a resonant tone that emits harmonics believed to interact with the body's natural energy fields. This phenomenon is backed by the belief that different sound frequencies impact the body's physiological and psychological states, potentially reducing stress, anxiety, and physical pain by promoting homeostasis within the body's systems (Goodin et al., 2012; Canete et al., 2023). The vibrations produced by these bowls are believed to affect both the physical body and the "subtle" body, which in Eastern philosophies includes layers of energy beyond the physical form.

From an Eastern perspective, Tibetan singing bowls hold spiritual significance and are rooted in centuries-old traditions of Buddhist and Himalayan culture. Traditionally, these bowls were crafted with precise metal combinations and used by monks and spiritual practitioners in rituals and meditation, symbolizing purity, wisdom, and the transmutation of consciousness. Within the Buddhist philosophy, sound is believed to be an expression of emptiness (śūnyatā), a concept that underpins the idea of interconnectedness and the transient nature of existence.

Benefits

Tibetan singing bowl sound therapy offers a range of physical, mental, and emotional benefits supported by both anecdotal and clinical evidence. This therapy is particularly known for its effectiveness in promoting relaxation and reducing stress. Studies show that the tones and vibrations of the singing bowls can influence brainwave activity, leading to shifts into more relaxed alpha and theta states. These brainwave states are often associated with meditative, relaxed mindsets and help reduce the production of stress hormones like cortisol.

Another significant benefit of Tibetan singing bowl therapy is pain relief. The sound waves produced by the bowls are believed to penetrate the body, creating micro-vibrations that can reduce physical discomfort and improve circulation.

Tibetan singing bowl therapy is also known to enhance emotional well-being. The sound and vibration from the bowls can promote a state of mental clarity and emotional balance by harmonizing the mind and body. Research suggests that this therapy helps individuals access deeply buried emotions and gain clarity on unresolved feelings, facilitating emotional release and healing.

On a spiritual level, Tibetan singing bowl therapy supports deeper meditation and mindfulness practices. The resonant sounds are thought to help practitioners enter meditative states more easily, which can lead to greater introspection and a heightened sense of connection with the self and surroundings.

History

The origins of Tibetan singing bowl therapy trace back several millennia and are deeply rooted in the spiritual traditions of the Himalayan region, including Tibetan Buddhism and Bon, the indigenous religion of Tibet. Tibetan singing bowls were initially crafted as tools for ritual and spiritual practices, often used by Buddhist monks and other spiritual leaders in meditation and healing rituals. These bowls are thought to have evolved from various metalworking traditions in Asia and were historically constructed from a unique seven-metal alloy. Each metal in this alloy was symbolically linked to celestial bodies: gold for the Sun, silver for the Moon, mercury for Mercury, copper for Venus, iron for Mars, tin for Jupiter, and lead for Saturn. This blend of metals was believed to enhance the spiritual potency of the bowls, lending them an almost alchemical significance (Canete et al., 2023)

Initially, the precise role of singing bowls within Tibetan culture was somewhat shrouded in mystery due to the secretive nature of Tibetan Buddhism's monastic practices, which were often reserved for monks and spiritual leaders. It wasn't until the 1970s, following a greater Western interest in Eastern spiritual traditions, that Tibetan singing bowls gained widespread recognition. Western travelers and scholars studying Buddhist and Himalayan spiritual practices brought these instruments to the attention of holistic healers, meditators, and musicians worldwide. At the same time, New Age movements began adopting Tibetan singing bowls as a means of promoting inner peace, meditation, and vibrational healing. This exposure led to further exploration and research into their healing properties, as Western practitioners experimented with the bowls' applications in alternative therapies, integrating them into modern wellness practices (Goodin et al., 2012; Beri, 2018)

Within Tibetan Buddhism and other Eastern philosophies, singing bowls were traditionally believed to assist practitioners in achieving higher states of consciousness. Their sounds, symbolizing the universal energy of "emptiness" (śūnyatā), were used to aid in meditation and prayer, allowing monks to deepen their spiritual focus and transcend the material world. In the Bon tradition, the vibrations from the bowls were used in healing rituals and as protective charms to ward off negative energies, aligning with the belief that sound could purify and protect the soul. With this perspective, sound was not only a tool for relaxation but a means of spiritual evolution and protection, connecting the user to cosmic energies and supporting the soul's journey toward enlightenment (Miles & True, 2003)

Today, Tibetan singing bowls are recognized worldwide for their therapeutic applications, from meditation and mindfulness practices to clinical sound therapy. In modern sound healing, their traditional uses have expanded to include vibrational sound therapy techniques for managing stress, anxiety, and physical ailments. This evolution from a sacred spiritual tool to a widely recognized healing modality highlights both the adaptability of Tibetan singing bowls and the deep cultural respect surrounding their continued use. The historical significance of Tibetan singing bowls thus continues, bridging ancient spiritual practices with contemporary therapeutic applications in integrative health and wellness.

Theoretical Background

The theoretical foundation of Tibetan singing bowl therapy lies primarily in principles of vibrational healing, sound wave entrainment, and concepts from Eastern spirituality, including chakras and the human biofield. The therapy operates on the understanding that sound vibrations have a direct impact on the body, mind, and energy fields, which can influence a person's overall well-being. According to vibrational healing theory, each organ and cell in the body resonates at a particular frequency, and when this frequency is disrupted by stress, illness, or negative emotions, imbalances and disease may manifest. Sound therapy, particularly through Tibetan singing bowls, aims to restore these frequencies, promoting harmony and balance within the body (Gal & Elefant, 2024; Beri, 2018)

One of the most critical theoretical elements of Tibetan singing bowl therapy is sound wave entrainment. This principle posits that the brain can synchronize with external frequencies. The resonant sounds of singing bowls produce harmonic frequencies that induce states of relaxation and meditation by bringing the brain into alpha and theta wave states, which are associated with calmness, relaxation, and focused mindfulness. These sound frequencies encourage a deep meditative state, like what is achieved in mindfulness practices. The steady, rhythmic vibrations created by the bowls are thought to allow the mind and body to "entrain" to a calmer frequency, reducing stress and promoting emotional regulation (Canete et al., 2023; Goodin et al., 2012)

From an Eastern perspective, Tibetan singing bowl therapy is linked to the concept of chakras, or energy centers, originating from yogic traditions and integrated into Tibetan Buddhism. Chakras are believed to be points of energy along the spine, each resonating at a particular frequency and associated with specific physical, emotional, and mental functions. Practitioners believe that Tibetan singing bowls can help balance these chakras by emitting frequencies that resonate with each center, leading to improved health and well-being. This concept aligns with the idea that illness or discomfort in the body can result from blockages or imbalances in the body's energy system. By placing the bowls near or on the body, sound therapists aim to "tune" these chakras, allowing energy to flow freely and aiding in the release of emotional or energetic blockages (Miles & True, 2003; Goodin et al., 2012)

Another crucial component of the theoretical background is the human biofield, an energy field to surround the body and connect all living beings, according to Eastern healing philosophies. Tibetan singing bowls are thought to interact with this biofield, which encompasses both the physical and subtle bodies, including mental and spiritual aspects. Vibrational frequencies from the bowls are believed to positively impact the biofield, restoring balance and harmony. This perspective has gained support in integrative medicine, where biofield therapies like sound therapy, Reiki, and acupuncture are recognized as potentially effective complementary treatments for mental health and stress-related conditions. Tibetan singing bowl therapy, therefore, bridges ancient Eastern philosophies and contemporary biofield science, reflecting its relevance in both traditional and modern wellness practices (Beri, 2018; Gal & Elefant, 2024)

In summary, the theoretical basis of Tibetan singing bowl therapy incorporates vibrational healing, entrainment, chakras, and the biofield. Together, these principles form a holistic view that considers physical, emotional, and spiritual aspects, emphasizing the interconnectedness of body and mind. The therapy's theoretical grounding in both Eastern spirituality and modern sound science supports its wide application, providing a comprehensive approach to healing that integrates the physical and subtle energies of the human experience.

Applications

Mental Health and Emotional Well-being

Tibetan singing bowl therapy is widely used to reduce stress, anxiety, and symptoms of depression. The therapy's calming effects, achieved through brainwave entrainment, can help shift the mind into a more relaxed, meditative state, which has been shown to reduce the production of stress hormones. This application is particularly valuable for individuals experiencing high stress levels, generalized anxiety disorder, and post-traumatic stress disorder (PTSD). Studies suggest that sessions involving Tibetan singing bowls can improve mood, decrease tension, and promote emotional release, making it a useful complementary therapy for mental health management (Goodin et al., 2012; Gal & Elefant, 2024)

Pain Relief and Physical Rehabilitation

Tibetan singing bowl therapy is also used to address physical pain, particularly chronic pain conditions such as fibromyalgia, arthritis, and migraines. The sound and vibration from the bowls are believed to help reduce muscle tension, improve circulation, and stimulate the nervous system, which can alleviate physical discomfort. Sound therapy involving singing bowls has been shown to help release endorphins, the body's natural pain-relief hormones, making it effective for managing acute and chronic pain. In physical rehabilitation, sound therapy can be an adjunct to physiotherapy, enhancing relaxation and supporting recovery in patients with musculoskeletal injuries (Canete et al., 2023; Beri, 2018)

Meditation and Mindfulness Practices

Tibetan singing bowl therapy is commonly incorporated into meditation practices to enhance focus, mindfulness, and deep relaxation. The resonant sounds of the bowls aid in reaching deeper states of meditation, often required for practices such as mindfulness-based stress reduction (MBSR) and transcendental meditation. In these contexts, the sound acts as an anchor, guiding the meditator back to awareness when distractions arise. Practitioners use the sound's consistency to maintain focus and achieve a state of mindfulness, which can help reduce stress and cultivate present-moment awareness. This application aligns with both therapeutic and spiritual goals, as it fosters inner peace and heightened self-awareness (Miles & True, 2003; Goodin et al., 2012)

Energy Healing and Chakra Balancing

Tibetan singing bowls are also widely used in energy healing and chakra alignment. According to Eastern healing philosophies, chakras are energy centers along the spine that influence physical, emotional, and mental well-being. Practitioners of chakra healing believe that each chakra resonates at a specific frequency, and Tibetan singing bowls can emit sounds that help balance these frequencies. By placing bowls near or on the body in alignment with chakras, therapists aim to clear blockages and balance energy, which is thought to improve health, emotional balance, and spiritual connection. Chakra-focused sound therapy is often used in Reiki, yoga, and holistic healing practices, reflecting its compatibility with various energy healing methods (Beri, 2018; Canete et al., 2023)

Sleep Improvement and Insomnia Relief

Tibetan singing bowl therapy has shown promise in improving sleep quality and addressing issues like insomnia. The therapy's impact on brainwave patterns, particularly its ability to encourage alpha and theta brain states, can help the mind transition into deeper stages of sleep. Regular use of singing bowls as part of a relaxation routine before bed can help calm the nervous system, reduce racing thoughts, and promote more restful sleep. This application is beneficial for individuals with sleep disorders or those struggling with insomnia due to stress or anxiety (Gal & Elefant, 2024; Miles & True, 2003)

Integrative Medicine and Complementary Therapy

In clinical settings, Tibetan singing bowl therapy is increasingly recognized as a complementary approach alongside traditional medical treatments. Hospitals and wellness centers have incorporated sound therapy sessions to help patients manage symptoms, improve mood, and enhance overall quality of life. For patients undergoing chemotherapy or recovering from surgery, sound therapy can provide relaxation, alleviate anxiety, and improve their tolerance to treatments. Studies suggest that sound-based therapies, including Tibetan singing bowls, can reduce discomfort and provide a holistic complement to conventional treatment, enhancing the patient's experience (Goodin et al., 2012; Beri, 2018)

Enhancing Creativity and Focus

Some practitioners use Tibetan singing bowls to stimulate creativity and improve focus. By inducing a relaxed yet alert brain state, the sounds from singing bowls are thought to help individuals access a flow state, where they can think more freely, brainstorm effectively, and develop innovative ideas. This application is particularly useful for artists, writers, and professionals seeking to overcome creative blocks or improve mental clarity. Singing bowls are also employed in educational settings as tools for focus enhancement, promoting a calm learning environment that encourages concentration (Canete et al., 2023; Gal & Elefant, 2024)

Steps

Preparation of the Space and Instruments

The first step involves preparing a calm, safe environment conducive to relaxation and healing. The room should be quiet and free from distractions, with dim lighting to foster a peaceful atmosphere. Practitioners may also choose to use aromatherapy, such as essential oils or incense, to enhance relaxation. The Tibetan singing bowls are usually placed around the client or on their body in specific positions. These bowls are often set according to specific chakras or energy centers, depending on the therapeutic goal (Goodin et al., 2012; Miles & True, 2003)

Setting an Intention

Many sessions begin by setting an intention, a process that allows the client to focus on a particular area of healing or personal growth. The practitioner may guide the client in identifying their goals for the session, such as stress reduction, pain relief, emotional release, or spiritual clarity. This intention helps to direct the energy and focus of the session, aligning the client's mindset with the healing process (Canete et al., 2023)

Beginning the Sound Therapy with Gentle Tones

The session typically begins with gentle strikes or circles on the rim of the singing bowls to produce initial tones. These introductory sounds are often soft and low-pitched to ease the client into a state of relaxation. The practitioner may use a mallet to either tap or circle the bowls, creating a range of vibrations that resonate through the room. These initial sounds are meant to ground the client and help them release tension as they focus on the vibrations and tones produced by the bowls (Beri, 2018; Goodin et al., 2012)

Deepening the Sound with Varying Frequencies and Patterns

As the session progresses, the practitioner typically introduces more varied tones by changing the rhythm, volume, and intensity of the sounds. This often involves alternating between bowls of different sizes and frequencies, each associated with different chakras or energy points. This step encourages a deepening of relaxation and allows the client's brainwaves to entrain to the soothing frequencies, gradually shifting to alpha or theta states associated with meditation and mental clarity. Practitioners may place bowls on different parts of the client's body to stimulate specific areas with vibrations, which is believed to aid in releasing blocked energy and harmonizing the body's energy flow (Gal & Elefant, 2024)

Creating a Rhythmic Flow for Healing and Energy Balance

The therapist then follows a rhythmic pattern, focusing on achieving a harmonious flow that aligns with the client's energy. This process often includes a specific sequence of strikes that can be tailored to target physical or emotional issues, promoting a balanced distribution of sound energy across the body. The practitioner's focus on rhythm and timing helps to establish a resonance that resonates within the client's biofield, encouraging energy balance and relaxation (Miles & True, 2003; Canete et al., 2023)

Encouraging Meditative and Mindful Focus

Throughout the session, the therapist may encourage the client to focus on their breath, maintain awareness of the sounds, and observe any sensations or emotions that arise. This mindfulness aspect helps the client stay present and promotes emotional release and healing. Clients are often guided to observe without judgment, fostering a sense of inner peace and introspection that aligns with the therapeutic goals of sound therapy (Goodin et al., 2012)

Gradual Conclusion and Integration

As the session draws to a close, the therapist gradually decreases the intensity and volume of the sounds, easing the client out of the deep relaxation state. The tones become softer and less frequent, helping the client transition back to a normal waking state. The practitioner may encourage the client to take a few deep breaths and slowly become aware of their surroundings, allowing time for the experience to integrate into their body and mind.

Reflection and Feedback

Finally, the session often ends with a brief period of reflection where the client can share any sensations, thoughts, or emotions that arose during the therapy. This reflection is a valuable part of the healing process, as it helps clients process their experiences and gain insights into their own emotional and physical state. Some practitioners offer advice on integrating the therapy's effects into daily life, suggesting practices like journaling, continued meditation, or future sound therapy sessions to maintain the benefits achieved.

Case studies

Case Study 1: Tibetan Singing Bowl Therapy for Chronic Pain Management in Fibromyalgia

Profile:

- Patient: Female, 52 years old
- Diagnosis: Fibromyalgia (Chronic Pain Syndrome)
- Duration of Treatment: 6 weeks
- Frequency: 2 sessions per week

Executive Summary:

This case study explores the use of Tibetan singing bowl therapy as a complementary treatment for a 52-year-old woman with fibromyalgia, a condition characterized by chronic widespread pain, fatigue, and sleep disturbances. The study aimed to assess the effectiveness of sound therapy in reducing pain and improving sleep quality.

Background Information about the Client:

The patient had been living with fibromyalgia for over 10 years. Despite trying various conventional treatments, including medications and physical therapy, she found little relief from her symptoms. Her pain was primarily concentrated in the neck, shoulders, and lower back, areas commonly affected by fibromyalgia. Additionally, she struggled with insomnia and fatigue, which compounded the physical discomfort.

Problem Statement:

The client's chronic pain and poor sleep were significantly impacting her daily life. Conventional treatments had not provided long-term relief, and she sought alternative therapies that could address both the physical and emotional components of her condition.

Analysis:

Fibromyalgia is a complex condition that often resists traditional pain management treatments. The disorder is associated with central nervous system abnormalities that amplify pain signals, making it a challenging condition to manage. Tibetan singing bowl therapy offers a holistic approach, using sound vibrations and frequencies to stimulate relaxation, reduce stress, and help balance the body's energy fields.

Interventions:

The patient participated in Tibetan singing bowl therapy for six weeks, attending two sessions each week. During the sessions, the therapist placed the singing bowls on and around the patient's body, focusing on the areas of pain. The vibrations from the bowls were intended to promote relaxation, stimulate circulation, and release muscle tension. The therapy also aimed to improve sleep by calming the nervous system and reducing anxiety.

Outcomes:

By the end of the treatment period, the patient reported significant improvements in her condition:

- **Pain Reduction:** The patient experienced a noticeable decrease in the intensity of her chronic pain, especially in the areas where the bowls were placed (neck and lower back).
- **Improved Sleep:** The patient reported fewer disruptions during the night and felt more rested upon waking.
- **Increased Energy:** She also noticed a gradual increase in energy levels and reported feeling less fatigued during the day.
- **Emotional Well-being:** The patient described feeling more emotionally balanced and less stressed, as the therapy helped her enter a deeply relaxed state.

Discussion:

Tibetan singing bowl therapy can be a useful complementary treatment for chronic pain conditions like fibromyalgia. The sound frequencies from the bowls may help regulate the autonomic nervous system, leading to a reduction in pain and stress. Additionally, the vibrations promote better circulation and can encourage the body's natural healing processes. The success of the therapy in this case underscores its potential as a non-invasive, holistic treatment for managing chronic pain and associated symptoms.

Conclusion:

Tibetan singing bowl therapy proved to be an effective complementary treatment for managing chronic pain and sleep disturbances in a fibromyalgia patient. Regular sessions led to significant pain relief, improved sleep quality, and greater emotional well-being. This case suggests that Tibetan singing bowl therapy could be a valuable addition to traditional fibromyalgia treatments, offering a holistic approach to symptom management.

Case Study 2: Tibetan Singing Bowl Therapy for Anxiety and Stress Management

Profile:

- Patient: Male, 34 years old
- Diagnosis: Generalized Anxiety Disorder (GAD) and mild depression
- Duration of Treatment: 8 weeks
- Frequency: 2 sessions per week

Executive Summary:

This case study examines the effectiveness of Tibetan singing bowl therapy in treating anxiety and mild depression in a 34-year-old man. The therapy aimed to reduce his anxiety levels, improve emotional regulation, and enhance overall mental well-being.

Background Information about the Client:

The patient had a history of generalized anxiety disorder, which manifested as constant worry, restlessness, and an inability to relax. He also experienced episodes of mild depression, which contributed to feelings of hopelessness and low energy. Traditional therapy, including medication, helped to some extent but did not fully alleviate his symptoms. The patient sought alternative treatments to manage his anxiety and improve his overall mental health.

Problem Statement:

The patient's anxiety and depression symptoms were significantly impacting his daily life, leading to difficulties at work and strained personal relationships. He felt that traditional treatment options were insufficient, and he sought a natural therapy to complement his current treatment plan.

Analysis:

Anxiety and depression are often interconnected, and individuals with anxiety disorders may experience chronic stress and emotional instability. Tibetan singing bowls, through their vibrational properties, are thought to influence brainwave patterns, inducing relaxation and calming the mind. This form of sound therapy can help the body and mind return to a balanced state, potentially alleviating symptoms of anxiety and depression.

Interventions:

The patient participated in twice-weekly Tibetan singing bowl sessions for eight weeks. During the sessions, the therapist used different-sized singing bowls placed around the client's body, focusing on his chest, head, and abdominal areas. The sound vibrations were aimed at inducing a meditative state, calming the nervous system, and promoting relaxation. The patient was also guided in deep breathing techniques to enhance the effects of the therapy.

Outcomes:

At the end of the therapy, the patient reported the following improvements:

- **Reduced Anxiety:** The patient noted a significant decrease in feelings of restlessness and worry. He felt more in control of his anxiety and was able to handle stress more effectively.
- **Improved Mood:** Symptoms of mild depression improved, with the patient feeling more hopeful and less emotionally fatigued.
- **Better Sleep:** Sleep quality improved as anxiety levels decreased, allowing for deeper and more restful sleep.
- **Enhanced Emotional Regulation:** The patient found it easier to manage his emotions and was better equipped to handle stressful situations.

Discussion:

The results of this case suggest that Tibetan singing bowl therapy can be highly effective in treating anxiety and stress. The sound therapy works by facilitating a relaxation response in the body, which helps lower the production of stress hormones. Additionally, the entrainment of brainwave patterns to a calmer state is likely to reduce anxiety and depression symptoms over time. The use of sound vibrations to promote emotional and physical well-being offers a promising alternative to traditional methods of managing anxiety.

Conclusion:

Tibetan singing bowl therapy was effective in reducing anxiety and improving emotional regulation in a patient with generalized anxiety disorder and mild depression. The therapy provided significant benefits, including improved sleep, decreased anxiety levels, and enhanced mood. Tibetan singing bowls offer a valuable complementary treatment for anxiety and depression, promoting overall mental and emotional well-being.

References

Cañete, T., Sotomayor, J., & Fernández-Teruel, A. (2023). Acute relaxation response induced by Tibetan singing bowl sounds: A randomized controlled trial. *European Journal of Investigative Health Psychology and Education, 13*(2), 317–330. https://doi.org/10.3390/ejihpe13020024

Gal, H., & Elefant, C. (2024). A qualitative pilot study examining Tibetan bowls and monochord sound meditation with adults with mental health conditions and intellectual disabilities. *Approaches: An Interdisciplinary Journal of Music Therapy.* https://doi.org/10.56883/aijmt.2024.320

Goodin, P., Lavallee, C., Wahbeh, H., & Norhazman, F. (2012). Sound healing: Mood, emotional, and spiritual well-being interrelationships. *Psychology Today.* Retrieved from https://www.psychologytoday.com

Chapter 20

Tui Na

Pratheeksha P School of Liberal Studies (SLS), CMR University, Bangalore

Tui Na

Tui Na is a traditional Chinese manipulative therapy designed to stimulate the body's defensive energy, or Wei Qi, and enhance the flow of energy (Qi) through the body's meridians and muscles. The name "Tui Na" is derived from two fundamental actions: "Tui" meaning "to push" and "Na" meaning "to lift and squeeze." Practitioners use a wide array of techniques, including pressing, rolling, kneading, rubbing, brushing, shaking, and tapotement (percussive tapping) to treat both acute and chronic musculoskeletal issues.

Tui Na is frequently combined with other Traditional Chinese Medicine (TCM) modalities, such as acupuncture, t'ai chi, qigong, herbal treatments, and cupping, as well as Western methods like traction and range-of-motion exercises. It is a versatile therapy, commonly used for ailments like headaches, digestive issues (e.g., constipation, irritable bowel syndrome), sleep disorders, psychological conditions, vascular health problems, and premenstrual syndrome.

There is some evidence to suggest that Tui Na may be more effective than Western-style massage for conditions like back pain, but questions remain about its long-term efficacy. As research continues, Tui Na remains a popular, holistic therapy for addressing a variety of physical and energetic imbalances.

History

Archaeological evidence dates Tui Na therapy back to approximately 2700 BC, making it one of the oldest known forms of bodywork and a precursor to many modern therapies like shiatsu and osteopathy. One of the foundational texts of Traditional Chinese Medicine (TCM), the *Huang Di Nei Jing* (The Yellow Emperor's Classic of Internal Medicine), written between the 1st century BC and the 1st century AD, documented the use of massage for treating various diseases, underscoring its long-standing role in Chinese healthcare.

During the Sui (581–618) and Tang (618–906) dynasties, a department dedicated to massage therapy was established within the Office of Imperial Physicians, signalling the formalisation of Tui Na as a respected medical practice. A prominent figure during this time, Dr. Sun Si Miao, further developed Tui Na by introducing new techniques and systematising its use in paediatric care, expanding its therapeutic applications.

In the Song (960–1279) and Yuan (1280–1368) dynasties, Tui Na underwent significant refinement, particularly in the areas of bone-setting and paediatrics, becoming a central treatment within the

Imperial Physicians' Institute. These periods saw in-depth analyses and improvements to the techniques, solidifying Tui Na's importance in Chinese medicine.

The Ming dynasty (1368–1644) was a pivotal time for Tui Na, as the therapy gained its formal name and saw an expansion of literature, particularly on paediatric applications, which became increasingly popular. However, the rise of Western medicine in the early 20th century posed a significant challenge to Traditional Chinese Medicine (TCM), including Tui Na. A push to ban TCM, including Tui Na, emerged between 1912 and 1948 but was successfully opposed in 1929, preserving TCM's role in Chinese healthcare. This victory is commemorated annually as Chinese Doctors' Day.

Mao Zedong's view of TCM changed dramatically during the Long March (1934–35), when TCM practitioners, including those skilled in Tui Na, provided essential care for wounded soldiers in the absence of modern medical supplies. Their success in treating large numbers of injured and ill soldiers led to a resurgence of TCM under Mao's leadership.

Following the establishment of the People's Republic of China in 1949, TCM received renewed support, and in 1956, the first official training course in Tui Na was launched in Shanghai. By 1974, Tui Na departments had been integrated into hospitals across China, solidifying its place within modern Chinese healthcare as an essential therapeutic practice that bridges ancient wisdom and contemporary medicine.

Different Styles of Tui Na

Over the centuries, as Tui Na evolved, various styles or schools emerged. Practitioners are trained in a range of techniques to stimulate meridians, relax muscles, relieve pain, and stretch joints.

Yin Style

Yin style Tui Na, sometimes referred to as Qi Gong Tui Na, emphasises a calm, focused, and meditative approach. The practitioner works from a deeply relaxed and centred state, with very little external physical movement. Instead of vigorous techniques, a smaller and more subtle set of motions is used, applying gentle and slow pressure to specific areas, acupuncture points, channels, or organs for a prolonged period.

In this method, the practitioner channels their own Qi (vital energy) into the patient's body, directing it toward the affected points or meridians. This careful and focused energy work is designed to soothe, calm, cool, sedate, nourish, and contain the patient's internal energy.

Yang Style

Yang style Tui Na is characterised by its dynamic, physically demanding approach and is frequently practised in Tui Na departments of Traditional Chinese Medicine (TCM) hospitals across China. This style involves a wide range of powerful massage techniques, which are applied with significant force to stimulate acupuncture points and meridians. These vigorous manipulations aim to enhance energy flow, break up tension, and address musculoskeletal issues.

Techniques

Tuina practitioners use a diverse combination of hand and arm techniques to manipulate and realign the recipient's muscles, bones, ligaments, and tendons. These techniques often include kneading, pressing, rolling, shaking, and stretching, each targeting different aspects of musculoskeletal health.

Much like acupuncture, Tuina aims to stimulate specific pressure points on the body, seeking to regulate the flow of Qi (vital energy) through the meridians, which are the energy pathways in the body. By influencing the Qi, practitioners work to restore balance and promote healing.

In addition to manual techniques, Tuina may incorporate the use of herbal poultices, compresses, and salves. These herbal remedies are applied externally to enhance the massage's therapeutic effects, providing additional benefits such as pain relief, muscle relaxation, and enhanced circulation.

Practitioners often tailor their techniques to focus on aspects of the therapy, depending on the patient's condition. For example:

- **The Rolling Method:** This technique is primarily used to address soft tissue injuries, such as muscle sprains or joint problems. It involves rhythmic rolling motions over muscles and joints to alleviate pain, reduce swelling, and promote recovery.
- **The One-Finger Pushing Method:** This acupressure technique focuses on treating internal diseases by applying concentrated pressure with a single finger. The goal is to stimulate specific acupuncture points related to internal organ function and overall health.
- **The Nei Gung Method:** Nei Gung, or "internal energy work," involves exercises designed to cultivate and move Qi from within the body outward. This method, combined with targeted massage, aims to replenish depleted energy systems and revitalise the patient, helping to address conditions of fatigue or energy imbalances.
- **Bone-Setting Methods:** These techniques are used to realign the musculoskeletal system, particularly in cases of joint injuries, nerve pain, or dislocated bones. By manipulating the bones and joints, practitioners aim to restore structural integrity and reduce pain caused by misalignment or nerve compression.

Applications

Advocates of Tuina massage assert that it is effective in treating a wide range of pains and ailments, particularly those related to the musculoskeletal and nervous systems. This ancient Chinese therapy is often used to address physical discomfort, promote healing, and enhance overall well-being.

Tuina is commonly applied to conditions such as neck and back pain, where the massage techniques help relieve tension and improve mobility. It is also used to treat various musculoskeletal disorders, providing relief from joint stiffness, muscle strain, and other soft tissue injuries. Beyond physical ailments, Tuina is believed to support the management of premenstrual syndrome (PMS) by balancing energy flow and alleviating discomfort.

For those experiencing chronic fatigue and insomnia, Tuina is said to promote relaxation, improve energy levels, and restore healthy sleep patterns. It may also be beneficial for conditions like carpal tunnel syndrome by improving circulation and reducing inflammation in affected areas.

Other conditions that Tuina practitioners claim it can help with include headaches, arthritis, and even osteoporosis, where gentle manipulation may assist in alleviating pain and improving flexibility. Tuina is also used to address stress and anxiety, helping to calm the nervous system and promote mental well-being.

In addition to these benefits, Tuina is thought to aid in the treatment of digestive issues, such as indigestion and bloating, as well as certain respiratory conditions, like asthma and bronchitis. By stimulating specific meridians and energy points, Tuina is believed to restore balance in the body's systems and promote overall health.

However, since Tuina is considered an alternative therapy, it's important to consult with a healthcare professional before using it to manage any medical condition. This ensures that it complements conventional treatments and doesn't interfere with ongoing medical care.

Psychological Impact

Tui Na therapy and psychotherapy, though distinct, do complement each other particularly in holistic treatments that address both the mind and body.

Mind-Body Connection:

Tui Na, although a physical therapy, inherently acknowledges the interconnectedness of the body, mind, and emotions. According to Traditional Chinese Medicine (TCM), physical ailments are often a manifestation of blocked or imbalanced energy, which tend to be influenced by emotional stress or psychological issues. By physically unblocking Qi and relieving tension in the body, Tui Na may help alleviate some emotional burdens or stress, thus indirectly supporting mental health. The physiology and psychology go hand in hand, helping alleviate each other. Psychotherapy works on mental and emotional well-being directly, but it does not fail to acknowledge the physiological symptoms of psychological distress,which include muscle tension, headaches, or digestive issues. Tui Na while focusing on the body by relieving the physical distress helps relieve the psychological distress.

Stress and Anxiety Relief:

Tui Na is widely used for reducing stress and anxiety by calming the nervous system and relaxing the body. Psychotherapy often treats anxiety by addressing cognitive patterns and emotional responses. Together, Tui Na can help relax the body, which in turn relaxes the individual. Amy distress caused by the stress and anxiety of the physical ailment is significantly reduced, which helps assuage the psychological unease.

Treating Psychosomatic Symptoms:

Many physical symptoms, such as chronic pain, headaches, or digestive issues, are closely linked to emotional or psychological stress. Tui Na can relieve these physical symptoms, which frees the individual of their emotional agony.

Trauma-Informed Approaches:

In cases of trauma, emotions are often stored in the body, leading to chronic pain or tension. Tui Na can help release physical tension,this combined with psychotherapy can succor in processing the emotional impact of trauma. Various psychotherapeutic approaches, such as body-centred or somatic therapies, also emphasise the importance of treating the body alongside the mind, akin to Tui Na's holistic principles.

Emotional Regulation:

Tui Na can help regulate the flow of Qi, which in TCM is thought to affect emotional stability. When Qi is balanced, emotional regulation improves. Psychotherapy complements this by teaching coping skills, improving emotional awareness, and helping patients manage difficult emotions.

Case Studies

Case Study 1: Evaluating Tuina Therapy's Effectiveness on Insomnia

Background

Insomnia is a prevalent condition affecting millions globally, often associated with various emotional and psychological complications like anxiety and depression. While pharmacological treatments for insomnia, including benzodiazepines and nonbenzodiazepines, are commonly prescribed, they may lead to adverse effects such as headache, vertigo, and dependency. Therefore, alternative therapies like tuina—a traditional Chinese manual therapy involving specific manipulations of the body—have gained interest for their reported benefits in improving sleep quality and psychological well-being.

Studies suggest that tuina can regulate neurotransmitter levels, especially 5-hydroxytryptamine (5-HT), a monoamine neurotransmitter closely linked with sleep regulation. This case study investigates the efficacy and safety of tuina for insomnia by summarising the findings of a recent meta-analysis.

Objectives

To systematically evaluate the effects of tuina therapy on sleep quality, psychological states (anxiety and depression), and neurotransmitter levels in individuals diagnosed with insomnia.

Methods

A meta-analysis was conducted, including a comprehensive search across eight databases for randomised controlled trials (RCTs) published up to July 2023. The primary outcomes were improvements in sleep quality measured by the Pittsburgh Sleep Quality Index (PSQI) and Athens Insomnia Scale (AIS), as well as changes in psychological states and 5-HT levels. A total of 23 studies with 1,780 participants met the inclusion criteria, with 892 in the experimental group (tuina therapy) and 888 in control groups (pharmacotherapy or acupuncture).

Data were analysed using statistical software, and risk of bias was assessed. Sensitivity analyses and subgroup analyses were also conducted to ensure the robustness of results, and publication bias was checked.

Results

- **Efficacy in Sleep Quality:** Tuina was found to significantly improve sleep quality. Participants receiving tuina had notably lower PSQI and AIS scores compared to those in control groups.

- **Psychological State Improvements:** Anxiety and depression levels, measured by self-rating scales, were significantly reduced in the tuina group.
- **Neurotransmitter Levels:** 5-HT levels increased in patients treated with tuina, supporting its potential role in the regulation of sleep and mood.
- **Comparison with Other Therapies:** Subgroup analysis indicated that tuina alone or in combination with other therapies was superior to pharmacological treatment or acupuncture alone.
- **Safety Profile:** Only two studies reported minor adverse events related to tuina, suggesting a high safety profile.

Conclusion

The meta-analysis provides robust evidence supporting the therapeutic advantages of tuina for insomnia, including its effects on sleep quality, psychological well-being, and 5-HT regulation. However, limitations in study quality necessitate further high-quality clinical trials for confirmation.

Practical Implications

1. **For Patients:** Tuina may serve as a safer alternative to pharmacological options for insomnia, with additional benefits for mood regulation.
2. **For Practitioners:** Incorporating tuina into treatment plans for insomnia could enhance patient outcomes, especially for those unable to tolerate conventional medications.
3. **For Future Research:** Further trials should focus on optimising tuina techniques, dosage, and treatment duration to establish standardised protocols for insomnia management.

This case highlights the growing importance of integrating traditional therapies with modern clinical practices, especially where conventional treatments pose safety risks or limitations in efficacy.

Case Study 2: Application of Tuina Therapy for Insomnia in a 45-Year-Old Woman with Chronic Anxiety and Depression

Background

Ms. Zhang, a 45-year-old woman, has struggled with chronic insomnia for over five years. Her condition involves difficulty falling asleep, frequent night awakenings, and early morning waking, which has significantly impacted her daily life. Ms. Zhang also experiences high levels of anxiety and mild depression, which have worsened over time due to sleep deprivation.

Despite trying various treatments, including benzodiazepines and cognitive-behavioural therapy (CBT), she continued to experience side effects from medication (such as dizziness and grogginess) and only moderate relief from CBT. At this point, Ms. Zhang sought alternative treatments and was referred to a traditional Chinese medicine clinic for tuina therapy as a natural, non-pharmacological intervention for her insomnia and related psychological symptoms.

Objectives

The goal was to evaluate the effectiveness of tuina therapy in improving Ms. Zhang's sleep quality and reducing her anxiety and depression symptoms without the adverse effects she experienced from medication.

Treatment Plan

1. **Duration and Frequency:** Ms. Zhang received tuina therapy sessions three times a week for six weeks.
2. **Intervention:** Each session lasted approximately 45 minutes and included targeted techniques to stimulate specific acupoints associated with sleep regulation and emotional balance. Techniques included pressing, rubbing, and kneading along the meridians linked to calming the mind and promoting relaxation.
3. **Follow-Up Assessments:** Ms. Zhang's sleep quality was assessed before, during, and after treatment using the Pittsburgh Sleep Quality Index (PSQI) and Athens Insomnia Scale (AIS). Anxiety and depression were monitored using the Self-Rating Anxiety Scale (SAS) and Self-Rating Depression Scale (SDS).

Results

After six weeks of tuina therapy, Ms. Zhang reported notable improvements in her sleep patterns and mental state:

- **Sleep Quality:** Her PSQI score dropped from 14 to 7, indicating a reduction in sleep disturbances and improvement in overall sleep quality. She reported that it took less time to fall asleep, and she experienced fewer night awakenings.
- **Anxiety and Depression:** Ms. Zhang's SAS and SDS scores both decreased significantly. Her anxiety reduced from a score of 55 to 38, and her depression score improved from 48 to 32, indicating her symptoms had moved from moderate to mild levels.
- **Neurotransmitter Balance (5-HT):** Although direct measurement of neurotransmitter levels was not available in this clinical setting, Ms. Zhang described feeling calmer and more emotionally stable, which aligns with the effects associated with improved 5-HT regulation.

Follow-Up and Long-Term Outcomes

At her two-month follow-up, Ms. Zhang reported that she was able to maintain her improved sleep quality and mental health with reduced frequency of tuina sessions (once weekly). She also incorporated some self-care practices taught during her therapy, such as acupressure and breathing exercises, which helped her manage stress and maintain emotional balance.

Conclusion

Tuina therapy significantly improved Ms. Zhang's insomnia, anxiety, and depression with no adverse effects. The therapy provided a safe and effective alternative to medications, which had previously caused her unwanted side effects. The case illustrates how tuina can be a valuable, natural intervention for individuals with insomnia, especially those with concurrent psychological conditions.

Clinical Implications

For patients like Ms. Zhang, tuina offers a dual benefit by addressing both insomnia and psychological distress, presenting a holistic approach to treatment that combines physical manipulation with mental relaxation techniques. This case supports integrating tuina therapy in broader insomnia treatment plans, particularly for those seeking non-drug interventions.

Benefits Of Tui Na

Tuina therapy, a traditional Chinese manual therapy, has long been valued for its holistic approach to health. Unlike many Western medical treatments that focus solely on specific symptoms, Tuina seeks to address the body's balance, offering several unique advantages in pain relief, stress reduction, and preventative care.

One of the primary benefits of Tuina therapy is its effectiveness in managing musculoskeletal pain. Techniques such as kneading, pressing, and stretching help alleviate discomfort in areas like the back, neck, and joints. By enhancing blood flow and targeting tight muscles, Tuina can relieve pain associated with chronic conditions such as arthritis, making it an appealing alternative to medications or invasive procedures.

Stress reduction is another key advantage. Tuina works to stimulate points that promote relaxation, activating the body's parasympathetic response. This release of tension contributes to lower stress levels and improvements in conditions like insomnia and anxiety. Patients often report feeling balanced and recharged after a session, which enhances both mental and physical wellbeing.

Tuina's holistic and preventative approach also sets it apart. Practitioners focus on the interconnectedness of the body, working to restore balance and prevent illnesses by addressing minor imbalances before they develop into larger issues. Regular Tuina sessions are believed to improve circulation, support immune function, and boost overall energy, fostering long-term health.

In addition, Tuina is highly compatible with other therapies, including acupuncture, herbal medicine, and Western physical therapies. This adaptability allows it to complement other treatments, providing more comprehensive care and encouraging faster recovery.

Critique of Tui Na

Tuina therapy, an ancient Chinese therapeutic practice, has grown in popularity worldwide, yet it faces significant criticism, particularly within Western medical communities. While some view Tuina as a valuable alternative or complementary therapy, sceptics raise concerns regarding its scientific validity, training standards, and safety.

One major criticism of Tuina is the lack of rigorous scientific evidence supporting its effectiveness. Most studies on Tuina are small-scale or lack the robust controls found in Western clinical trials, making it challenging to determine its efficacy. While some patients report relief from musculoskeletal pain and stress, sceptics argue that the improvements may stem more from the placebo effect than from any specific therapeutic benefits.

Inconsistent training and regulatory standards also pose problems for Tuina. Unlike other manual therapies that require licensing, Tuina training varies widely by location and institution, leading to discrepancies in practitioners' skills and qualifications. This lack of standardisation can result in inconsistent quality of care, which is concerning for those seeking safe and effective treatment.

Additionally, there are risks associated with Tuina therapy. Because it involves deep manipulation of muscles and tissues, improper technique or excessive pressure can lead to soreness, bruising, or even injury. These risks are especially relevant for vulnerable populations, such as the elderly or individuals with preexisting health conditions.

Conclusion

In conclusion, Tuina therapy stands out as a holistic and integrative approach to health that emphasises balance, pain relief, and stress reduction. Its centuries-old methods offer a unique alternative to Western medicine, particularly for individuals seeking non-invasive, natural treatment options. Despite these strengths, Tuina faces legitimate criticisms that highlight challenges in its broader acceptance within modern healthcare systems. The limited scientific evidence supporting its efficacy, inconsistent practitioner training standards, and the potential for injury have led some to question its reliability and safety. Additionally, cultural, and conceptual differences—such as the emphasis on Qi and meridian channels, which lack a foundation in Western medical science—create obstacles to Tuina's integration into evidence-based practices.

Addressing these issues through rigorous research, standardised training programs, and improved safety protocols could help bridge the gap between traditional and modern medicine. If Tuina can evolve to meet contemporary healthcare standards while maintaining its holistic approach, it holds the potential to serve as a respected complement to conventional treatments, providing patients with a balanced and accessible path to wellness.

References

Mohammed Al-Bedah, Abdullah, Gazzaffi Ibrahim Ali, Tamer Shaban Abushanab, and Naseem Akhtar Qureshi. 2017. "Tui Na (or Tuina) Massage: A Minireview of Pertinent Literature, 1970-2017". *Journal of Complementary and Alternative Medical Research* 3 (1):1-14.

Tao, W.-W., Jiang, H., Tao, X.-M., Jiang, P., Sha, L.-Y., & Sun, Wang Z, Xu H, Zhou H, Lei Y, Yang L, Guo J, Wang Y and Zhou Y (2023) A systematic review with meta-analysis: Traditional Chinese tuina therapy for insomnia. *Front. Neurosci.* 16:1096003.

X.-C. (2016). Effects of acupuncture, tuina, tai chi, qigong, and traditional Chinese medicine five-element music therapy on symptom management and quality of life for cancer patients: A meta-analysis. *Journal of Pain and Symptom Management, 51*(4), 728–747.

Lee, M.S., Pittler, M.H. & Ernst, E. Is tai chi an effective adjunct in cancer care? A systematic review of controlled clinical trials. *Support Care Cancer* 15, 597–601 (2007).

Huang, F., Zhao, S., Dai, L., Feng, Z., Wu, Z., Chen, J., Guo, R., Tian, Q., Fan, Z., & Wu, S. (2020). Tuina for cervical vertigo: A systematic review and meta-analysis of randomised controlled trials. *Complementary Therapies in Clinical Practice, 39*, 101115.

Atchison, J. W., & Eubanks, J. E. (2021). Manipulation, traction, and massage. In *Braddom's Physical Medicine and Rehabilitation* (6th ed.). Elsevier.

Irnich, D. (2013). Complementary and alternative therapies and naturopathic treatments. In *Myofascial Trigger Points*. Elsevier. de Ferrieres, M. (n.d.). Tui Na: The ancient art of Chinese massage - History, method, and healing benefits. *Wellnex*.

Medical News Today. (n.d.). Tuina massage: Uses, benefits, and risks. *Medical News Today.*

Healthline. (n.d.). Tuina: What it is, how it works, and what it treats. *Healthline.*

Cheng, Z.-J., Zhang, S.-P., Gu, Y.-J., Chen, Z.-Y., Xie, F.-F., Guan, C., Fang, M., & Yao, F. (2022). Effectiveness of Tuina therapy combined with Yijinjing exercise in the treatment of nonspecific chronic neck pain: A randomised clinical trial. *JAMA Network Open, 5*(12), e2246538.

Wang Z, Xu H, Wang Z, Zhou H, Zhang L, Wang Y, Li M and Zhou Y (2024) Effect of tuina on sleep quality, psychological state and neurotransmitter level in patients with insomnia: a systematic review and meta-analysis. *Front. Neurol.* 15:1273194.

Lee, N.-W., Kim, G.-H., Heo, I., Kim, K.-W., Ha, I.-H., Lee, J.-H., Hwang, E.-H., & Shin, B.-C. (2017). Chuna (or Tuina) manual therapy for musculoskeletal disorders: A systematic review and meta-analysis of randomised controlled trials. *Evidence-Based Complementary and Alternative Medicine.*

Fan, Z., Di, A., Huang, F., Zhao, S., Qiu, M., Wu, C., Huang, C., Guo, R., Tian, Q., & Wu, S. (2020). The effectiveness and safety of Tuina for tension-type headache: A systematic review and meta-analysis. *Complementary Therapies in Clinical Practice, 40*, 101293.

Tong C, He Q, Ho M, Zhong Z, Wu Q and Chen M (2022) Tuina for Enuresis in Children: A Systematic Review and Meta-Analysis of Randomised Controlled Trials. *Front. Public Health* 10:821781.

Yin, Z., Shuaipan, Z., He, P., Zhang, Q., Fang, M., & Lu, P. (2023). Efficacy of Tuina in chronic low back pain with anxiety: Study protocol for a randomised controlled trial. *BMJ Open, 13*(10), e073671.

Chapter 21

Yoga Therapy

Reema Sabrin M R School of Liberal Studies (SLS), CMR University, Bangalore

Brief Historical Background

Yoga is derived from the Sanskrit word Yuj', meaning 'to join' to unite' or 'to yoke' which is interpreted as the union of individual self to supreme self. It is regarded as the foundation of the ancient Indian civilization and has developed for at least five millennia. It also refers to enormous wealth of psychological, spiritual, and philosophical knowledge. The history of Yoga also traces back to the period of Bhagavad Gita. It is believed that every title of the chapters in Bhagavad Gita is a sort of yoga such as knowledge-yoga, action-yoga, devotional yoga, royal science yoga etc. Ancient texts such as the Ramayana, the Mahabharatha, the puranas and the Brahmanas, the Yoga-sutra by patanjali and the Bhagavad Gita have contributed to the yogic tradition. The concept of "Yoga-Sutra" compiled by Patanjali led to the long development of yogic tradition in india. He was the first one to codify classical yoga. Patanjali is considered as the father of yoga and his Yoga-Sutras still strongly influence most of modern yoga. Patanjali yoga consists of 8 limbs such as Yama, Niyama, Asana, Praṇayama, Pratyahara, Dharṇa, Dhyana, and Samaḍhi.

In the earlier period, yoga was a practical discipline with a goal to enhance the development of mental and physical health, well-being, and inner harmony. Yoga practices are believed to have started in early civilization on the Indian subcontinent and they have been practiced historically throughout East Asia and India and they have said to evolve separately from Oriental religions. In the late 1800s and 1900s, yoga practitioners traveled around the west attracting and gaining attention.

Limbs of Yoga

Pathajali outlined eight limbs of yoga that direct individuals to live a meaningful and purposeful life. It also shifts our attention to our health and guides us to acknowledge the spiritual view of our nature and assist us in living a life of connectedness and balance. The eight limbs of yoga include the yamas, the niyamas, asana, pranayama, pratyahara, dharana, dhyana, and samadhi.

The yamas and niyamas are the concept for living that incorporates ethics or morality, concentration or meditation and wisdom. The practice of asana is a way to align, strengthen and balance the body. And the focus is to keep the body healthy and train the body to be able to sit still for deep meditation. Pranayama involves channeling and releasing prana which the body's life force to nurture mental clarity and optimal physical health and that help us to have self-knowledge and an authentic life. The practice of pratyahara involves making a conscious effort to shift our awareness away from external stimuli or away from the world and to draw our senses inward. It helps us to look within ourselves, our habits, our cravings that may be detrimental to our health and that might influence our inner growth. Dharana and dhyana are related. Most meditation requires concentration exercise in an untrained mind. Samadhi is the transcendence of self when the individual recognizes a profound connection to the divine and to all living beings.

Branches of Yoga

The branches of yoga include hatha yoga, karma yoga, mantra yoga, bhakthi yoga, raja yoga and guyana yoga. Hatha yoga incorporates purification of the mind and the body. Karma yoga involves dynamic meditation which refers to the yoga of action that is performed with meditative awareness. Mantra yoga includes chanting mantra, combination of songs or subtle suns that are used for the liberation of consciousness from the limitation of mundane awareness. Bhakthi yoga consists of intense, pure, inner devotion or love and channeling of the emotions, intellect and the self towards a higher purpose which is the yogic path of devotion. Raj yoga aims to gain access into the realm of psychic consciousness to uncover the dormant areas of min and the consciousness. Guyana yoga involves the process of meditative awareness that guides one closer to one's higher self.

Types of Yoga

Hatha Yoga

The term Hatha which means the 'the practice of physical postures' is made up of two components "HA" which means "Sun", the positivity energy in the body and "THA" which means moon, the negative energy in the body. It symbolizes the equilibrium or balance between these two energies. The regular practice of this yoga enhances flexibility, strength and balance. Other benefits may be obtained from incorporating breath work (pranayam) and meditation in addition to hatha yoga. The beneficial effects of hatha yoga has been seen in numerous health conditions including cancer, asthma, insomnia, heart disease, infertility, pregnancy, chronic back pain, arthritis, carpal tunnel syndrome and fibromyalgia.

Kundalini Yoga

Kundalini yoga, the so-called "Kundalini awakening" focuses on psychosocial growth and the body's potential for maturation. Kundalini yoga as a psychic nerve energy helps us to raise our consciousness through the chakras that helps us to transform our heightened spiritual awareness into constructive actions. It gives special consideration to the role of the endocrine system and spine in understanding yoga awakening. The practices of kundalini yoga consist of number of bodily postures, expressive movements, breathing patterns, cultivation of character and degrees of concentration. The benefit of Kundalini yoga includes relief from stress and anxiety, improves cognitive functioning, boosts self-perception and enhances spiritual enlightenment etc.

Yin Yoga

Yin Yoga is associated with the concept of Taoist, the "yin and yang". They are described as two variables. Yin can be characterized as stable, feminine, immobile, cold, and downward moving whereas yang can be characterized by changing, masculine, active hot and upward moving. Too much of yin or too much of yang creates imbalances. They need to co-exist side by side for us to live our lives in balance and harmony. The yin styles of yoga are the modest form of yoga where the focus is to relax muscles to increase circulation in the connective joints, tissues and organs and to develop the ability to yield, observer and accept what is in the present moment. The Yin Yoga practices are highly beneficial for the nervous system and brain where it reduces stress, tension and balances the mind to reach our higher self. It is a more mindful practice that creates understanding of our present condition and of the reluctance of being in what we perceive as an unpleasant experience.

Yoga- Nidra

Yoga-Nidra, often referred to as yogic sleep, restless sleep, conscious sleep, psychic sleep, dynamic sleep, or profound relaxation, is a remarkable mental condition that exists between sleep and wakefulness. The state of inner quiet and stillness in yoga nidra helps us to relax, maintain high level awareness and manage stress. It promotes mental clarity, [physical relaxation and inner peace. It is said to be used for the treatment of mental illness including depression, stress and post traumatic disorder and other psychophysiological disorders. It also has a major influence on the development of cognitive abilities such as concentration, attention, and memory. It also helps us to mitigate the effects of anxiety, stress, anger, fear, depression, and sleep disorders. Yoga nidra helps individuals to attain a state of equilibrium and overall welfare. Research suggests that yoga nidra has a positive influence on mental health problems.

Ashtanga Yoga

Jois (2010) developed Ashtanga yoga at the beginning of the twentieth century. It shares some characteristics with other current yoga practices such as Iyengar, but also encompass unique characteristics that may make it particularly potent to improve anxiety, depression, self-esteem, and interpersonal functioning. It is beneficial for improving self-esteem and self-efficacy. This practice allows for more mindful interaction that's has been shown beneficial to interpersonal relationships. Particularly, high dispositional mindfulness is linked with higher empathy, self-expression and reduce social anxiety.

Psychological Benefits of Yoga

The psychological benefits of yoga include:

- Increase in mood
- Increase in subjective well being
- Increase social adjustment
- Increase self acceptance
- Increase in Somatic and kinesthetic awareness
- Improves psychomotor functioning,
- Improves eye hand coordination,
- Improves steadiness,
- Improves grip strength,
- Improves Balance
- Improves depth perception

- Improves cognitive functioninG
- Enhance Attention
- Enhance Concentration
- Enhance Learning efficiency
- Reduce hostility
- Reduce anxiety and depression
- Improves integrated functioning of body parts

Yoga Psychology

According to yoga, most psychological issues are caused by the involvement of ego and overidentification with pain, pleasure, failure, and success. Psychological problems because of nonacceptance of the present, false ideas about the self, others or situation and reaction in the form of anger, jealousy, hatred, indifference, anxiety, fear, and repulsion. Yoga psychotherapy is a more ancient form of psychotherapy. It is based on the principle that self-realization is a process of purification and the removal of impurities to be free of all distress and suffering. Yoga psychology considers consciousness to be the essence of a person and everything else to be the environment in which consciousness is embedded. The aim of yoga is liberation through self-realization.

Certain elements of yogic concept of karma can be seen in Jung and Freud's concept of memory. Both Freud and yoga agree that motivation and memory are parts of a single psychic process that also embodies selection. However, there is a drift in opinion in the concept of yoga and Freud to which this choice process is free or determined.

According to Swami Ajaya (1983), the most part of psychotherapy is oriented towards the development and strengthening of the ego. He also explains that yoga therapy also helps those who are functioning at those levels to build their yoga capacities but however the present models of psychotherapy generally neglect to help people reach beyond identification with ego. Yoga also helps the ego to surrender its authority and embrace a universal nurturing of wisdom and love. According to Swami Niranjanananda Saraswati (1993), by using yogic techniques, we can develop the ability to relax under any circumstances and under any condition and we can also develop the capacity to concentrate and to collect all our disputed energies to focus them at one point and by doing that, the combination of mental force and vital force becomes very powerful tool in discovering the different dimensions of human personality.

The scientific study of yoga has been constructed across the globe and the studies based on the effects of āsana, dhārana, prānāyāma, and dhyāna are reported under the heading of meditation.

Cognitive, Behavioral, Psychodynamic, transpersonal, and humanistic-existential perspectives were used in understanding the process and nature of meditative process (Salagame, 2002).

One of the main limitations in evaluating the therapeutic efficacy of yoga is the lack of commonality in the procedure. "Induced Yogic Relaxation Training", "Yogic lifestyle", "Yoga practice", "Yoga training", "Yoga Based Isometric Relaxation", "Yoga Nidra" and "Sudarshana Kriya" are some of the terms used by different researchers that involves one or more techniques. Almost all studies report improvement in the well-being and health of the participants. It is complex to examine precisely about the core components or competencies of yoga that brings about such results. Most researchers demonstrated the therapeutic efficacy of yoga without attempting to understand the mechanism underpinning the relation between the procedure and the psychological, neurochemical, and neurophysiological processes. Hence, it is difficult to explain which techniques work with whom and when. In this context, yoga instructors seem to have clear understanding from their practical experience with practitioners rather than researchers highlighting the need to develop theory driven research design to study the efficacy of yoga techniques.

Yoga Therapy

According to Brownstein, an American Physician with a diploma in yogic education from the government of India explained that Yoga therapy is preventive in nature and as yoga and is restorative in many instances. The practices of yoga therapy help people find balance. It also acknowledges the multidimensional nature including physiological, anatomical, emotional, spiritual, and intellectual dimensions of an individual. It includes techniques such as grounding exercises, asanas, mantras, guided meditation and visualization and yoga nidra etc.

The recent emergence of "yoga therapy" has posed great challenges in the study determining the useful effects of the practice. There is increasing evidence for the use of yoga intervention in enhancing mental and physical health. The literature into the yoga interventions for psychological well-being is limited by the lack of randomized trials that compares yoga intervention with medical or psychological treatments. And the research that is available often involves small samples and assess yoga as an adjunctive treatment as opposed to a stand-alone intervention.

Yoga Therapy and Psychological Disorders

Yoga and Stress

The psychological mechanisms that have been proposed as means through which yoga reduces stress include the positive attitude towards stress, coping, self-awareness, spirituality, calmness, compassion, and mindfulness. Many researchers have suggested that mindfulness is a powerful link between yoga practice and stress reduction.

The biological mechanisms underpinning yoga that may reduce stress include the autonomic nervous system, HPA axis, inflammatory and endocrine responses, endothelial function and release of nitric oxide, limbic system activity, the peripheral nervous system including GABA and gene expression. In the Autonomic nervous system, both parasympathetic and sympathetic nervous systems are often posited as the mechanism through which yoga reduces stress. Yoga training has been shown to decrease sympathetic responses after experimental stressors. In HPA Axis, the practice of yoga regulates HPA axis and sympathetic nervous system that prevent the release of catecholamines and cortisol which is also known as stress hormone.

Yoga and Anxiety

Yoga may minimize pathophysiological symptoms that contribute to anxiety through both top-down and bottom-up mechanisms by balancing stress response systems that increase parasympathetic activity and reduce sympathetic overactivity. Research studies show that yoga techniques, particularly breathing techniques can have normalizing effects on ANS. Repeated practice of yoga can alter threshold needed to initiate the stress response which may be a biological mechanism underpinning the benefits of yoga. It also minimizes limbic system overactivity and emotion regulatory circuits dysfunction. It improves cognitive function and corrects the misappraisal of threats. It also increases the capacity of the higher brain center such as (eg., prefrontal) to modulate lower brain systems (eg., amygdala). It also reduces ruminative anxious thoughts and worries. Vagal nerve - stimulation studies and preliminary clinical evidence suggests that yoga programs especially slow breathing practices may increase the release of oxytocin which is a prosocial bonding hormone which helps with anxiety to form a close loving relationship and enhance the ability to trust.

Yoga and Depression

Research suggests that yoga increases GABA levels in the thalamus and that these increases are correlated with improved mood. It also influences the neurotransmitter system involved in the regulation of mood, reward or pleasure and motivation which are impaired in individuals with depression. Studies also show that yoga practices are as effective as antidepressant medication and are linked with reducing the severity of depressive symptoms and increased treatment remission. Yoga based Intervention (YBI) has an influence on the HPA axis by reducing the peripheral inflammation and heightened neurotrophic factor production that may be linked to their benefits in patients with depression. People who were diagnosed with Major Depressive Disorder said to experience less rumination, increased feeling of connectedness especially women. Yogic diaphragmatic breathing increases ego strength, confidence, stability, alertness, and perceived control over one's environment as well as reducing depression, anxiety, psychosomatic problems and phobic behavior.

Yoga and Attention Deficit Hyperactivity Disorder

Yoga practice has been shown to reduce hyperactivity and impulsivity, stabilize emotions, increase attention span, feelings of calmness and confidence, and improve social skills. It also has said to improve sleep patterns, the quality of the parent-child relationship, and positively change the child's approach to school (Abadi, Madgaonkar, & Venkatesan, 2008)

Yoga and Eating Disorder

In eating disorders such as anorexia nervosa, bulimia nervosa, and eating disorders not otherwise specified, yoga has shown to decrease eating disorder symptoms, improve mood, increase physical and emotional awareness. It is also said to decrease the levels of food preoccupation, body concerns, and dissatisfaction, binge eating frequency, drive for thinness, self-criticism, and emotion regulation difficulties. Yoga is thought to facilitate positive changes by guiding individuals to directly experience the body which in turn promotes mindfulness, body connectedness, self-compassion, positive affect, and functionality appreciation.

Case Studies

Case study on the effects on yoga on Anxiety

Introduction

This interventional study was undertaken in the Department of Physiology, R.V.M. Institute of Medical Sciences and Research Center, Siddipet, to evaluate the influence of yoga and yoga nidra on levels of anxiety and cardiorespiratory parameters among college-going students. Total 125 volunteer students of age range between 18 to 25 years were enrolled after the application of some special criteria for inclusion and exclusion. The objectives were to evaluate the changes in anxiety on the Generalized Anxiety Disorder-7 (GAD-7) scale and Beck's Anxiety Inventory (BAI) at baseline and at the end of a 12-week yoga and yoganidra intervention.

Study Design

Participants: 125 students aged 18-25 years (both genders).

Inclusion Criteria

Students who had not practiced yoga or yoga nidra for the last six months and Students aged between 18-25 years.

Exclusion Criteria

History of organic diseases, hypertension, diabetes mellitu, Psychiatric disorders, smoking or alcohol addiction, Practice of yoga nidra within the last 3 months.

Protocol

All volunteers were informed and oriented towards the objective of the research study. Parameters like Pulse Rate, Respiratory rate and Blood Pressure were considered. The Anxiety levels had to be rated with both the GAD-7 and Beck's Anxiety Inventory (BAI) scoring tools. The volunteers for 3 to 5 days had to be introduced and made to feel free to understand and be more relaxed and receptive to all sessions of yoga and Yoga Nidra.

Treatment Interventions

Yoga Practice: Was done for an hour, 5 times a week for 12 weeks in the afternoon at between 4-5 pm. The following were undertaken during the session:

- Relaxation Prayer and mantras
- Two rounds of 12-step Surya Namaskar
- The meditation postures that would be done are Vajrasana, Padmasana, Simhasana, and Swastikasana

Yoga Nidra Training: Procedure takes 30 minutes right after the yoga practice has taken place with seven steps of it

Internalization: Conscious awareness of calm, relaxation, and outer disturbances

Sankalpa (Resolution): Formulated intention as if it says "I will be vigilant.

Rotation of Consciousness: Consciousness travelled through different parts of the body.

Breath Awareness: Awareness of natural Inhalation and Exhalation

Emotional Sensation: Practice of awareness regarding opposing emotions

Visualization: The creation of images in mind's inner space relating to objects or stories.

Externalization: Gradually getting back to the wakeful consciousness of surroundings

All participants fell asleep initially during the yoganidra session for the first 3-4 days after which they adapted and began staying conscious during the whole session.

After 12 weeks of practice of yoga and yoganidra the same cardio-respiratory variables were measured and re-assessed the anxiety scale using GAD-7 and BAI.

It carried out data analysis through paired t-tests using SPSS version 20. In that, a p-value < 0.0001 suggests that the improvement is statistically highly significant at an extremely low level.

The results of the study showed a significant improvement in both the physical (cardio-respiratory) and psychological (anxiety) measures of the subjects after the yoga and yoga nidra intervention. Students reported a high degree of relaxation, centeredness, and improved anxiety management skills. It seems that prolonged practice of yoga nidra has an even stronger effect on moderate to severe levels of anxiety as there is a marked improvement in scores of GAD-7 and BAI.

Conclusion

The anxiety level among college students was reported to be statistically significantly reduced at the end of the 12-week yoga and yoga nidra intervention. Therefore, these mind-body practices could represent effective, non-pharmacological interventions in young adults for the treatment of anxiety.

Case study on the effects of yoga on ADHD

Background

ADHD is one of the common disorders, with an estimated prevalence of approximately 5% of children worldwide. It is associated with severe impairments in attention, impulsivity, and hyperactivity. Poor academic performance and other disruptive classroom behaviors are often the result. A wide range of school-based interventions has been developed to address the challenges; however, most are expensive, time-consuming, or associated with less desirable side effects, such as issues with medication.

Objective

This case study explores how effective yoga is as an adjunctive intervention in augmenting attention and on-task behaviors in children with attention deficit hyperactivity disorder. It targets the video "Yoga Fitness for Kids" as an adjunctive intervention for students who have been diagnosed with attention deficit hyperactivity disorder.

Participants

The study comprised four second-grade boys aged 7-8 years, all with ADHD diagnoses. The children were on regular medication for ADHD but still could not concentrate and maintain on-task behaviors in the classroom.

Participant A: Moderate symptoms of ADHD with frequent inattentiveness and restlessness.

Participant B: Severe symptoms of ADHD with impulsivity and poor self-regulation.

Participant C: Mild symptoms of ADHD but constantly distracted and off-task.

Participant D: Somewhat hyperactive for ADHD, who is restlessly fidgety and can't sit for a long time.

Intervention

The intervention video "Yoga Fitness for Kids" was taken as school-based intervention on all participants. Every session of the intervention lasted for 30 minutes and was attended twice in a week over six weeks. Various yoga techniques used included rest, breath, and some postures that would allow for good concentration and concentration. They would supplement these sessions with their other classroom work. The intervention was therefore supposed to complement their previously taken ADHD medication regimens and provide a non-pharmacological means of boosting their attention.

Methods

To measure on-task behaviors during class, researchers used direct observation methods, monitoring the percentage of intervals in which each student was focused and attentive to the task. Data were collected over two phases: baseline (before the yoga intervention) and intervention (during and after yoga sessions).

Results

Scores showed improvement in three participants. There was a significant rise in on-task behavior during the intervention from the very beginning.

Participant A. Important change from baseline to intervention: Percentage of intervals increases from 50% to 80%.

Participant B. Moderate change from baseline to intervention: Changes from 40% to 70%.

Participant C. Sharp rise with the increase in intervals from baseline of 55% to 90% during intervention.

Participant D. Little increase with intervals increasing from 60% to 65%. It reflects that the treatment was not that effective on this student.

The effect size of the intervention, as applied on each individual, was computed by taking Tau-U statistics.

Participant A: 0.85

Participant B: 0.75

Participant C: 1.00

Participant D: 0.60

The weighted average Tau-U score across the participants was 0.79, indicating a very large overall effect of intervention.

Discussion

This seems to indicate that yoga would be a good school-based intervention that may help these ADHD-afflicted students, thereby improving their attentional abilities and concentration. With regard to three of four participants, the on-task behavior improved considerably when an intervention was implemented. In fact, such findings match those of prior research concerning the effectiveness of yoga in terms of a therapeutic technique to manage ADHD symptoms.

However, variability in effectiveness among participants is a pointer towards individualization. For instance, while Participant D's response was minimal, there may be a need for some other strategies or modifications to other students.

Conclusion

Yoga is a promising and low-cost alternative to more traditional ADHD interventions in the school setting. It's not a replacement for drugs, but it can play a very useful role especially in enhancing the attention level and concentration of students suffering from ADHD. Further studies are recommended to be able to know the long-run effects of yoga on symptoms of ADHD and which pupils would benefit most from the intervention.

References

Bennetts, A. (2021). How does yoga practice and therapy yield psychological benefits? A review and model of transdiagnostic processes. *Complementary Therapies in Clinical Practice*, *46*, 101514. https://doi.org/10.1016/j.ctcp.2021.101514

Dekeyser, M., Raes, F., Leijssen, M., Leysen, S., & Dewulf, D. (2008). Mindfulness skills and interpersonal behaviour. *Personality and Individual Differences*, *44*(5), 1235–1245. https://doi.org/10.1016/j.paid.2007.11.018

Goretzki, M., Thalbourne, M. A., & Storm, L. (2013). Development of a spiritual emergency scale. In *THE JOURNAL OF TRANSPERSONAL PSYCHOLOGY* (Vol. 45, Issue 2). https://www.atpweb.org/jtparchive/trps-45-13-02-000.pdf#page=38

Hagen, I., & Hagen, Ø. (2024). The impact of yoga on occupational stress and wellbeing: exploring practitioners' experiences. *Frontiers in Public Health*, *12*. https://doi.org/10.3389/fpubh.2024.1352197

Hermann, K. S., & Betz, N. E. (2006). Path models of the relationships of instrumentality and expressiveness, social Self–Efficacy, and Self–Esteem to depressive symptoms in college students. *Journal of Social and Clinical Psychology*, *25*(10), 1086–1106. https://doi.org/10.1521/jscp.2006.25.10.1086

Hofmann, L. (2013). The impact of Kundalini yoga on concepts and diagnostic practice in psychology and psychotherapy. In *Transcultural research - Heidelberg studies on Asia and Europe in a global context* (pp. 81–106). https://doi.org/10.1007/978-3-319-00315-3_4

Jarry, J.L., Chang, F.M. & La Civita, L. Ashtanga Yoga for Psychological Well-being: Initial Effectiveness Study. Mindfulness 8, 1269–1279 (2017). https://doi.org/10.1007/s12671-017-0703-4

Kamble, P., Daulatabad, V. S., Tandra, H., Singhal, A., U, M., & John, N. A. (2023). Yoganidra to Alleviate anxiety: an interventional study. *Cureus*. https://doi.org/10.7759/cureus.45083

Khalsa, S. B., Cohen, L., McCall, T., Telles, S., & Cramer, H. (2024). The principles and practice of yoga in health care. Jessica Kingsley Publishers. https://www.google.co.in/books/edition/The_Principles_and_Practice_of_Yoga_in_H/P9XXEAAAQBAJ?hl=en&gbpv=0

Kinsley, S. (2013). Yoga therapy. Diversity, Culture and Counselling: A Canadian Perspective, 310.https://www.google.co.in/books/edition/Diversity_Culture_and_Counselling_3rd_Ed/WH86EAAAQBAJ?hl=en&gbpv=0

Lamb, T. (2001). Health benefits of yoga. Yoga world, 16, 6. https://d1wqtxts1xzle7.cloudfront.net/58388419/kellypinzak-pdf_9748169-libre.pdf?1550004580=&response-content-disposition=inline%3B+filename%3Dkellypinzak_pdf_9748169_pdf.pdf&Expires=1730649512&Signature=bovRFX-ctM6RLbQjDrGzZPZyfeeogOnAiJFAGwFNOeA9dEIkeqlFyFIyH1jLEshD-S5ef7AfEvZ4shVYDA5vYuS8aqcS49ahPPU30Xavv9Tl2Q-eHaUUsRKq3wfNQpYStbww1GI1f9i8BbUtH-gHaeV7LgePAIAUy5lcQaHArg18J4uUC1LikMV78XuoHYeOVN9-ioMlyzvr-WGu17gsCsWzLBetEpskdxQESyGu8D817S4sR1qFQckWc8KNqx4JI1Pg5GlQQhX~K1JmHKaKJPJ63ps6K0YEJyPDpwUnHTqqDRcN0mNohbesgtXfkvWekP7EMd-ws0-giJ-Mm9D9hw__&Key-Pair-Id=APKAJLOHF5GGSLRBV4ZA

Lehrer, P. M. (2007). Principles and Practice of Stress Management, Third Edition. United States: Guilford Publications.

Markil, N., Geithner, C. A., & Penhollow, T. M. (2010). HATHA YOGA. *ACSM's Health & Fitness Journal*, *14*(5), 19–24. https://doi.org/10.1249/fit.0b013e3181ed5af2

MILLER, R. C. (1994). The breath of life: Through the practice of pranayama, the regulation of the breath, we can learn to bring forth and direct the spiritual energy that underlies all life. Yoga Journal, 116, 82. Retrieved from EBSCOhost: Alt HealthWatch database (Accession No. 6175923)

Moodley, R., & West, W. (Eds.). (2005). Integrating traditional healing practices into counseling and psychotherapy (Vol. 22). Sage.

Norberg, U. (2014). Yin Yoga: an individualized approach to balance, health, and whole self well-being. Simon and Schuster.https://www.google.co.in/books/edition/Yin_Yoga /HlyCDwAAQBAJ?hl=en&gbpv=1&dq=yin+yoga+&pg=PT8&printsec=frontcover

Nunez, K. (2020, July 16). *What is Kundalini yoga and what are the benefits?* Healthline. https://www.healthline.com/health/kundalini-yoga

O'Keeffe, D., & Khalsa, G. D. S. (2010). The kundalini yoga experience: Bringing body, mind, and spirit together. Simon and Schuster. https://www.google.co.in/books/edition/The_Kundalini_Yoga_Experience/cnV_XGs9lHgC?hln&gbpv=1&dq=Kundalini+yoga+benefits+&pg=PA3&printsec=frontcover

Petsche, A. (2016). The effect of yoga on attention in students diagnosed with ADHD. *Digital Commons @ UConn.* https://digitalcommons.lib.uconn.edu/dissertations/1141/ .

Rani, S. (2022). Yoga: its origin, history and development. In *RICERCA INTERNATIONAL JOURNAL OF MULTIDISCIPLINARY RESEARCH AND INNOVATION* [Journal-article]. https://rijmri.com/wp-content/uploads/2023/01/Yoga.pdf

Rhoads, M. C., Grevstad, N., Kirkland, R. A., Barber, M. E., Myers, S., & Lundstrom, T. (2023). The benefits of yoga as an intervention for depression: a meta–analysis. Int J Complement Alt Med, 16(1), 19-30.

Riley, Kristen E.; Park, Crystal L. . (2015). How does yoga reduce stress? A systematic review of mechanisms of change and guide to future inquiry. Health Psychology Review, (), 1–18. doi:10.1080/17437199.2014.981778

R, P., Kumar, A. P., S, N. D. K., Venugopal, V., Silambanan, S., K, M., & Shah, P. (2023). Role of yoga in stress management and implications in major depression disorder. *Journal of Ayurveda and Integrative Medicine*, *14*(5), 100767. https://doi.org/10.1016/j.jaim.2023.100767

Salagame, K. K. K. (2010). Psychology of yoga and yoga psychology. Yoga—The light of microuniverse.

Streeter, C. C., Gerbarg, P. L., Saper, R. B., Ciraulo, D. A., & Brown, R. P. (2012). Effects of yoga on the autonomic nervous system, gamma-aminobutyric-acid, and allostasis in epilepsy, depression, and post-traumatic stress disorder. Medical hypotheses, 78(5), 571-579.

Suresh, A., Ramachandran, K., & Jayachander, M. (2013). Effect of kundalini yoga on psychological health in young adults. Indian Journal of Positive Psychology, 4(1), 7.chrome-extension://kdpelmjpfafjppnhbloffcjpeomlnpah/ https://www.researchgate.net/profile/Suresh-Arumugam-2/publication/265111583_EFFECT_OF_KUNDALINI_YOGA_ON_PSYCHOLOGICAL_HEALTH_IN_YOUNG_ADULTS/links/53ff11f70cf21edafd15b822/EFFECT-OF-KUNDALINI-YOGA-ON-PSYCHOLOGICAL-HEALTH-IN-YOUNG-ADULTS.pdf

Trethewey, E., Evans, S., McIver, S., O'Brien, J., Lowndes, J., Pepin, G., & O'Shea, M. (2023). One size may not fit all: A mapping review of yoga-based interventions for the treatment of eating disorders. *Complementary Therapies in Clinical Practice*, *53*, 101779. https://doi.org/10.1016/j.ctcp.2023.101779

Yang, Y., Cao, D., Lyu, T., & Gao, W. (2023). Meta-analysis of a mindfulness yoga exercise intervention on depression – based on intervention studies in China. *Frontiers in Psychology*, *14*. https://doi.org/10.3389/fpsyg.2023.1283172

Chapter 22

Zen Therapy

Saheen Nasreen School of Liberal Studies (SLS), CMR University, Bangalore

Introduction

Zen therapy is a modern therapeutic approach that integrates principles from Zen Buddhism with contemporary psychological practices. Zen's emphasis on mindfulness, presence, and direct experience, Zen Therapy seeks to help individuals find peace, clarity, and a deeper understanding of themselves through a blend of meditation, mindfulness, and psychotherapeutic techniques.

The core premise of Zen Therapy is that much of human suffering arises from attachment to thoughts, emotions, and the ego. By practicing mindfulness and meditation, individuals can learn to observe their mental states without identifying with them or becoming overwhelmed by them. Unlike traditional therapy, which often focuses on analyzing past events and cognitive patterns, Zen Therapy emphasizes the importance of the present moment.

History

Zen Buddhism: Origins and Development

Zen Buddhism originated in China during the Tang Dynasty (7th-9th centuries) as a school known as Chan Buddhism. It emerged as a synthesis of Indian Mahayana Buddhism, particularly influenced by the teachings of the Mahayana sutras, and elements of Taoism, which emphasized naturalness, spontaneity, and the rejection of rigid dogma. The word "Chan" itself is derived from the Sanskrit word "Dhyana", meaning meditation, which was central to the Chan practice.

Chan Buddhism spread to Japan during the 12th century, where it evolved into Zen Buddhism. In Japan, Zen was shaped by the country's existing cultural practices, including the aesthetic values of wabi-sabi (the appreciation of imperfection and transience) and the samurai ethos, which valued discipline and directness. Over time, Zen Buddhism developed two main schools in Japan: the Rinzai school, which emphasizes koan practice and sudden insight, and the Soto school, which focuses on shikantaza (just sitting) and gradual, sustained mindfulness.

Zen's spread to the west

Zen Buddhism made its first significant inroads into the West in the 20th century, particularly after figures like D.T. Suzuki, a Japanese scholar and Zen teacher, began to lecture in the United States and Europe. Suzuki's writings, especially *An Introduction to Zen Buddhism* (1934), played a crucial role in introducing Zen philosophy to a Western audience. Zen's emphasis on direct experience, meditation, and the non-conceptual nature of reality resonated with the modernist intellectual climate of the time.

Zen's Influence on Psychology

Zen Buddhism's emphasis on mindfulness, meditation, and the cultivation of a direct, experiential awareness of reality has had a significant impact on Western psychology, particularly in the areas of mindfulness-based therapy and cognitive behavioral therapy (CBT).

The key concept that Zen Buddhism has contributed to psychology is mindfulness. The Zen practice of mindfulness (sati in Pali, or *sati* in Zen) involves paying attention to the present moment, often through techniques like breath awareness and body scanning, without attachment to thoughts or judgments. In the late 20th century, psychologists began to integrate mindfulness into therapeutic practices, especially with the development of Mindfulness-Based Stress Reduction (MBSR), created by Jon Kabat-Zinn in the late 1970s. MBSR, which was initially designed to help patients manage chronic pain, became a widely used therapeutic tool for reducing stress, anxiety, and depression.

Mindfulness practices, inspired in part by Zen meditation, have since been incorporated into various psychological therapies, such as Mindfulness-Based Cognitive Therapy (MBCT), developed by Zindel Segal, John Teasdale, and Mark Williams.

Although Zen and CBT are often seen as stemming from different traditions, there are notable overlaps in their approaches. Both emphasize the importance of present-moment awareness and non-attachment. Additionally, Zen's concept of emptiness which teaches that our sense of self and the world is fluid, interdependent, and impermanent, finds parallels in CBT's cognitive restructuring.

Zen's influence can also be seen in humanistic psychology, which emphasizes selfawareness, authenticity, and personal growth. Psychologists like Carl Rogers and Abraham Maslow, who were central figures in humanistic psychology, shared Zen's emphasis on personal transformation and self-actualization. Humanistic psychology, with its focus on the here-and-now and the self's experiential truth, bears similarities to Zen's non-conceptual approach to reality and its belief in the potential for deep transformation through direct experience.

Psychodynamic therapy has also seen intersections with Zen in its exploration of the unconscious mind and the integration of the conscious and unconscious aspects of the self.

Zen and the Emerging Field of Ecopsychology

Another area where Zen has influenced psychological thought is in ecopsychology, the study of the relationship between human beings and the natural environment. Zen practice encourages an intimate connection with the present moment and the world around us, fostering a sense of belonging and interconnectedness with nature. In turn, this can help address ecological crises by cultivating a deeper respect for the natural world and a more sustainable, mindful way of living.

Core Concepts in Zen Therapy

Sati (Mindfulness)

Mindfulness, or sati in Pali, plays a central role in Zen practice. In Zen, mindfulness refers to the practice of being fully present in the current moment, without attachment to memories or future expectations. This form of awareness is not limited to formal meditation sessions but is extended to every aspect of daily life. Practitioners strive to engage in each action—whether walking, eating, or working—with full attention, observing without distraction or judgment. This cultivation of mindful awareness leads to greater insight into the nature of one's mind and the world. The Zen saying, "When walking, walk. When sitting, sit.", captures the essence of mindfulness in Zen: complete immersion in the present moment.

Meditation (Zazen)

At the heart of Zen practice is zazen, or seated meditation. Zazen is a practice in which one sits in stillness, often with a focus on the breath or simply on the act of sitting itself. The objective of zazen is not to achieve a specific mental state or experience but to let go of distracting thoughts and the continuous chatter of the mind. In Zen, the process of sitting becomes a way to observe the mind's natural activity, allowing thoughts to arise and pass without attachment. Through regular practice, zazen leads to insight into the impermanence of all things and the illusory nature of the self. The Zen teaching "The truth is beyond words and concepts" emphasizes that direct experience, rather than intellectual understanding, is the path to enlightenment.

Emptiness (Śūnyatā)

The concept of emptiness (Sanskrit: śūnyatā) is central to Zen and Mahayana Buddhism. Emptiness refers to the lack of inherent, independent existence in all phenomena. According to this view, things do not exist in isolation but are interdependent and contingent upon a web of causes and conditions. In Zen, this concept is often interpreted as the absence of a permanent, unchanging self or essence in all things. In this view, both the self and the external world are seen as fluid, impermanent, and interrelated. Realizing emptiness is not merely an intellectual exercise but an experiential realization that leads to freedom from attachment and dualistic thinking. Zen teachings on emptiness challenge the practitioner to let go of rigid concepts and experience the world as it is—unfiltered and dynamic.

Koans

A koan is a paradoxical statement or question used in Zen practice to challenge the conceptual mind and provoke direct insight. Famous examples include, "What is the sound of one hand clapping?" or "If a tree falls in a forest and no one is there to hear it, does it make a sound?" Koans are not meant to be solved by logical reasoning but to break through the limitations of intellectual thinking and bring about a deeper, non-conceptual awareness of reality.

In the Zen tradition, a Zen master may assign a koan to a student as part of their training. The student reflects on the koan during meditation, and through this practice, they can experience a moment of sudden realization or kensho.

Non-Duality

In Zen, non-duality refers to the understanding that distinctions between self and other, subject and object, or mind and body are ultimately illusory. Zen teachings emphasize the interconnectedness of all things and the transcendence of dualistic thinking. In everyday life, this means letting go of the distinctions we typically make between good and bad, success and failure, or even life and death.

This concept is closely related to the idea of emptiness, as recognizing the non-duality of existence leads to the realization that all things are interdependent and do not have separate, fixed identities. Through non-duality, one experiences a deep sense of unity with the world.

The Zen Way of Action (Wu-Wei)

In Zen, the practice is not confined to the meditation cushion. Every action—whether it's working, eating, or interacting with others—can be a form of meditation when done with full presence and mindfulness. The concept of Wu-Wei (from Taoism but deeply integrated into Zen) refers to the idea of "non-action" or "effortless action." It does not mean doing nothing, but acting in harmony with the flow of life, without striving or forcing things.

In Zen, there is a focus on being fully engaged in whatever one is doing in the present moment, without attachment to outcomes or expectations. This is often referred to as "doing without doing"—the idea that when we act without ego or attachment, our actions become harmonious and effective, almost as though they are being done through us rather than by us.

The Absence of Self (Anatta)

Zen practice often leads to the realization of Anatta (the doctrine of no-self). This teaching asserts that the "self" is an illusion, a collection of ever-changing mental and physical processes, rather than a permanent, unchanging entity. By directly experiencing the absence of a fixed self, a Zen practitioner can transcend ego-driven desires and attachments, leading to liberation from suffering.

This concept is intimately connected with the realization of emptiness. When one perceives the interdependence of all things and the lack of inherent selfhood, one experiences a profound sense of freedom and peace.

Zen Practices for Mental Health

Zazen (Seated Meditation)

Zazen, meaning "seated meditation" in Japanese, is the cornerstone of Zen practice. It involves sitting in a specific posture and focusing the mind, often on the breath or a koan (a Zen riddle), although in its simplest form, Zazen can involve just being present with whatever arises in the mind and body. Zazen is typically practiced in a quiet space, sitting on a cushion (zafu) in a cross-legged position, though the posture may vary depending on physical comfort.

Mental Health Benefits of Zazen

Zazen encourages the cultivation of mindfulness, which helps break the cycle of anxious or worrying thoughts. By staying present with the breath and accepting thoughts without judgment, you can reduce the impact of stressors. Through the non-reactive observation of thoughts and emotions, Zazen fosters emotional resilience. Practitioners learn to sit with discomfort, whether it's physical pain, emotional distress, or mental chatter, without becoming overwhelmed. Zazen develops greater self-awareness, helping individuals become more attuned to their mental and emotional states. This awareness is the first step toward identifying and addressing unhealthy patterns of thought and behavior. By engaging in focused, meditative practice, Zazen helps quiet the habitual fluctuations of the mind. This can result in a more calm, peaceful state that lasts even outside of formal practice. Regular Zazen practice enhances the ability to focus. This improved attention can carry over into daily life, helping with tasks, decision-making, and interpersonal interactions.

Kinhin (Walking Meditation)

Kinhin is the practice of walking meditation in Zen. It is typically done in between periods of sitting meditation (Zazen), although it can also be practiced independently. Kinhin is a slower, deliberate walking practice that emphasizes mindfulness in movement.

Mental Health Benefits of Kinhin

Kinhin offers a break from the stillness of Zazen, allowing the body to gently stretch and release tension. This movement promotes relaxation and can help ease physical discomfort from prolonged sitting. Walking meditation helps cultivate a sense of grounding. By paying attention to the sensation of the feet touching the ground, practitioners are reminded of their connection to the earth and the present moment. This grounding can be especially helpful in alleviating feelings of anxiety or mental disorientation. Kinhin strengthens the mind-body connection by bringing awareness to the body's movement. This increased awareness can help address issues like dissociation, body tension, or lack of body awareness that can sometimes accompany stress or trauma. The gentle motion of walking meditation can be a way to clear the mind, especially after periods of intense mental or emotional activity. The focus on breath and step-by-step movement can create a sense of calm and centeredness. Like other forms of mindfulness, Kinhin can help regulate the autonomic nervous system, shifting the body from the "fight or flight" state (sympathetic nervous system) to the "rest and digest" state (parasympathetic nervous system), helping to reduce stress and anxiety levels.

Koan Practice

Koans are paradoxical questions or statements used in Zen Buddhism to facilitate selfinquiry and spiritual growth. Unlike intellectual puzzles, koans are designed to transcend logical thinking and provoke direct, non-conceptual insight. They challenge the mind's habitual patterns, helping practitioners break through dualistic thinking and ego-based limitations.

Koans challenge ordinary, dualistic thinking, forcing the practitioner to go beyond rational analysis and engage in direct experience. By confronting paradoxes, koans prompt deep questioning of the self and the nature of reality, encouraging practitioners to look inward for wisdom beyond intellectual understanding. Koans help dissolve the sense of a fixed, separate self (ego) by leading the practitioner into moments of non-dual awareness. Working with koans can lead to profound realizations or "satori" (awakening), moments where the practitioner directly perceives the nature of existence beyond conceptual thought.

Zen Therapy in Clinical Settings

Case Study 1

Name: S.S

Age: 32

Diagnosis: Generalized Anxiety Disorder (GAD)

Symptoms:

Persistent worry, restlessness, irritability, sleep disturbances, muscle tension, difficulty concentrating.

Background:

Sarah, a successful marketing manager, had been struggling with anxiety for several years. She often felt overwhelmed by the demands of her work, her relationships, and her personal life. Her thoughts were constantly preoccupied with worst-case scenarios, and she had difficulty relaxing or being fully present in the moment. She also experienced physical symptoms of anxiety, including a racing heart, shallow breathing, and muscle tightness. While she had attended traditional therapy (CBT) and used medication for a time, she felt that her anxiety was always simmering just below the surface, and she struggled to maintain peace of mind.

Initial Assessment and Approach

During the initial intake, Sarah described her anxiety as "a constant buzz in my mind" that never seemed to go away. She felt like she was always "on edge," anticipating potential problems and worrying about what might happen next. She often tried to control her anxiety by engaging in avoidance behaviors, such as procrastinating on tasks that caused her stress, or engaging in overplanning to "prevent" things from going wrong. However, these strategies only provided temporary relief, and the anxiety would return.

Treatment Goal:

- To help Sarah develop a healthier relationship with her anxiety by fostering mindfulness, self-compassion, and non-reactivity.
- To teach Sarah how to stay present in the moment and manage the physical and emotional symptoms of anxiety more effectively.
- To reduce the intensity of her anxiety through regular meditation and mindful awareness of thoughts, emotions, and bodily sensations.

Zen Therapy Approach

Introduction to Zen Meditation (Zazen)

The first step in Sarah's treatment was introducing her to Zazen, the foundational Zen meditation practice. In Zazen, the practitioner sits in a formal posture, typically on a cushion or chair, and focuses on the breath or simply observes whatever arises in the mind without judgment. The goal is to cultivate mindfulness and awareness of the present moment. Sarah was taught to sit in an upright position with a relaxed but alert body, helping to cultivate both physical and mental stability. Initially, she struggled with discomfort in her legs, but she was encouraged to find a comfortable seated position, either on a cushion or a chair. Sarah was guided to focus on the natural rhythm of her breath. The idea was not to control the breath but to observe it with full awareness. If her mind wandered to anxious thoughts, she was instructed to gently bring her attention back to the breath without judgment. Over time, Sarah began to realize that her constant tendency to ruminate on future fears and "what-ifs" was the source of her anxiety. Through regular practice of Zazen, she started to experience brief moments of quietness, where her racing thoughts slowed down. These moments, though fleeting, were a revelation to Sarah. She had never known that it was possible to simply be present without worrying about the future.

Mindful Awareness and Non-Reactivity

In Zen therapy, a central tenet is non-reactivity—the idea that we don't have to be controlled by our thoughts and emotions. Sarah was taught that her anxious thoughts were just mental events, not reflections of reality. By observing these thoughts without judgment or attachment, she could begin to loosen their grip on her. Sarah's therapist used mindfulness practices to help her notice her anxiety without reacting to it. Each time she felt an anxious thought or physical symptom (e.g., shallow breathing or tight muscles), Sarah was encouraged to observe it with a sense of curiosity rather than fear or resistance. For example, if she noticed her heart racing, she was instructed to notice the sensation without labeling it as "bad" or "dangerous." The goal was to disidentify from the anxiety itself. Over time, Sarah became more able to simply notice anxiety without being overwhelmed by it. By cultivating non-attachment, she realized that anxiety was not something that defined her, but a passing experience she could learn to manage.

Embracing Impermanence

A crucial Zen concept in Sarah's therapy was impermanence (anicca), the understanding that all thoughts, emotions, and experiences are temporary and ever-changing. Zen teachings emphasize that nothing, including anxiety, lasts forever. This understanding was powerful for Sarah, as it helped her move from a mindset of "I can't stand this" to one of acceptance: "This too shall pass."

Sarah's therapist used this teaching to help her reframe her experiences of anxiety. When anxiety arose, instead of fearing it or trying to get rid of it, Sarah began to acknowledge it as a natural, fleeting experience. She was reminded that, just like emotions, anxiety has a beginning, a middle, and an end, and it would eventually pass without needing to control or avoid it.

Outcome: Progress and Results

After several months of Zen therapy, Sarah reported a noticeable reduction in her anxiety symptoms. Her thoughts were less intrusive, and the intensity of her physical anxiety (such as racing heartbeat and shallow breathing) decreased. She was able to stay more present during stressful moments at work and in her personal life. Sarah also developed the ability to observe anxious thoughts without being carried away by them. Through mindfulness, she cultivated a sense of emotional distance from her anxiety, which allowed her to stay calm in challenging situations. Through the practice of mindfulness and non-judgmental awareness, Sarah became more compassionate toward herself. She stopped blaming herself for feeling anxious and learned to be kind and patient with herself during moments of discomfort.

Case Study 2

A 45-year-old male taxi driver developed chronic low back pain following a car accident in 2015. Despite various treatments (e.g., orthopedic surgery, massage), he continued to experience cramp-like pain centered around the L4-5 region. His medical imaging (X-ray and MRI) showed no structural abnormalities, and the pain was diagnosed as nonspecific chronic low back pain.

Treatment Approach: Zen Therapy Integration

In January 2020, the patient was enrolled in a 3-month Zen meditation-integrated CBT program alongside conventional treatments like pharmacotherapy (Duloxetine) and physiotherapy. The Zen-based approach focused on mindfulness and non-reactivity to pain. The patient practiced Zen breath counting meditation daily for 15 minutes, twice a day. This practice encouraged him to focus on his breath while acknowledging pain without judgment or avoidance. The mantra used was: "Leave pain alone. Do not fight against or escape from pain. Enjoy a bright and cheerful life." This helped the patient develop a non-reactive attitude toward his pain, reducing emotional and psychological distress. The patient was taught to observe pain without becoming attached to it or trying to control it. This helped reduce the intensity of pain experiences by promoting acceptance rather than resistance. A primary goal of the Zen meditation was to normalize brain function, particularly in areas involved in pain perception. Brain SPECT scans showed improvement in blood flow to the temporoparietal junction (TPJ), suggesting that Zen practice helped regulate pain-related brain activity.

Outcomes

The patient reported a significant decrease in both the frequency and intensity of pain, as measured by the Numerical Rating Scale (NRS). Psychological assessments showed improvements in mood, self-efficacy (ability to cope with pain), and reduced pain catastrophizing. Post-treatment SPECT scans revealed improved brain blood flow, suggesting that the Zen practice had a positive impact on pain processing regions of the brain.

Conclusion

The future of Zen therapy in mental health holds great potential as a holistic approach that integrates mindfulness, meditation, and the principle of non-attachment. By combining mind, body, and spirit, it offers a comprehensive framework for healing that can complement traditional therapies like cognitive-behavioral therapy (CBT). Zen practices are particularly effective for managing stress, anxiety, and depression by encouraging present-moment awareness and reducing rumination. Moreover, Zen therapy emphasizes the importance of the therapeutic relationship, fostering authenticity, presence, and compassion between therapist and client. It also provides tools for transcending rigid self-identities, promoting healing through acceptance and impermanence, and facilitating a deeper understanding of one's place in the world. Zen's focus on interconnectedness—both within the self and with the community—can broaden the scope of mental health care, supporting not only individual well-being but also relational and systemic health. As a complementary approach to conventional treatment, Zen therapy offers a path to greater self-awareness, inner peace, and freedom from suffering, making it a promising addition to the future of mental health practices.

Future of Zen Therapy

Zen therapy, blending traditional Zen Buddhist practices with modern psychological techniques, has the potential to significantly shape the future of mental health care. As mental health awareness grows, Zen therapy's emphasis on mindfulness, present-moment awareness, and selfcompassion could offer an effective, holistic approach to treating conditions like anxiety, depression, and stress-related disorders.

In the future, Zen therapy may expand beyond individual therapy to become a mainstream practice in clinical settings, integrated with cognitive-behavioral therapy (CBT) and other therapeutic modalities. Its focus on reducing the mental noise and emotional reactivity through meditation and mindful awareness could complement pharmaceutical treatments, offering patients tools for emotional regulation and resilience.

Advancements in digital mental health tools, such as apps and virtual therapy, could make Zeninspired practices more accessible to a wider audience, fostering a global movement toward integrating mindfulness and Zen principles into everyday life. By combining Eastern wisdom with Western therapeutic methods, Zen therapy may help create a more balanced and sustainable approach to mental well-being in the future.

References

Epstein, M. (2021). The Zen of therapy: Uncovering a hidden kindness in life. Flatiron Books.

Ricard, M. (2001). The art of meditation. Shambhala Publications.

Brazier, D. (2003). Zen and the art of psychotherapy. The Buddhist Society.

Hanson, R., & Mendius, R. (2009). Buddha's brain: The practical neuroscience of happiness, love, and wisdom. New Harbinger Publications.

Suzuki, S. (1970). Zen mind, beginner's mind. Weatherhill.

Kapleau, P. (1965). The three pillars of Zen. Doubleday.

Tsering, G. T. (2008). Buddhist psychology: The foundation of Buddhist thought. Wisdom Publications.

Epstein, M. (1995). Psychotherapy and Buddhism: Towards an integration. Yale University Press.

Scogin, B. T. (1992). Awakening the unconscious: A Zen approach to psychotherapy. Shambhala Publications.

Epstein, M. (1995). Psychotherapy and Buddhism: Towards an integration. Yale University

Kovacs, F. M., Llobera, J., Gil del Real, M. T., & Ballesteros, J. (2004). Prevalence of low back pain in the general population in Spain: A study of 12,000 people. Spine,29(6),609-614.

Hofmann, S. G., Sawyer, A. T., Fang, A., & Asnaani, A. (2012). The Efficacy of Cognitive Behavioral Therapy: A Review of Meta-analyses. Cognitive Therapy and Research, 36(5), 427–440.

Western Perspectives

Chapter 23

Dance Movement Therapy

Vamshitha G School of Liberal Studies (SLS), CMR University, Bangalore

Introduction

Dance Movement treatment (DMT) is an approach of therapy that integrates social, cognitive, and emotional aspects via dance and movement. It is predicated on the notion that the mind and body are intertwined, and that people may communicate emotions and experiences via movement that may be challenging to convey orally (Dosamantes-Beaudry, 1999).

Dance Movement Therapy in the West dates to the 1940s and 1950s in the United States, when pioneers such as Marian Chace, Trudi Schoop, and Mary Whitehouse combined dance with psychotherapy notions.

Key Concepts in the Western Perspective

Mind-Body Connection:

Important Ideas from a Western Perspective: The Mind-Body Connection, the connection between mental processes and bodily movement is emphasized in the Western interpretation of DMT. Practitioners feel that emotional transformation may result from changes in movement and that the body reflects interior psychological processes. The body becomes an expressive tool, and movement becomes a means of exploring unconscious emotions, traumas, and conflicts.

Psychodynamic Approach:

Psychodynamic ideas, including those of Freud and Jung, are included into the practice of many DMT practitioners in the West. This method focusses on examining unconscious content and utilising movement to reveal suppressed feelings or unsolved psychological problems. Therapists assist clients understand their mental and emotional lives by using symbolic gestures and motions.

Nonverbal Communication:

Western DMT emphasizes movement as a means of communication, especially when verbal expression is inadequate or challenging. People with autism spectrum disorders, trauma, or those who have trouble expressing themselves verbally because of psychological, developmental, or cultural difficulties may benefit from this.

Client-Centered and Creative Expression:

DMT supports self-discovery, artistic expression, and emotional release via movement, all of which are in line with humanistic psychological theories. It is regarded as a client-centered type of therapy that enables people to express themselves honestly and establish a therapeutic partnership founded on empathy, trust, and nonjudgment.

Evidence-Based Practice:

Western DMT has tried to position itself as an evidence-based therapy approach in recent years. Studies have shown how beneficial it is for enhancing social functioning, body image, and emotional control, especially in populations coping with chronic disease, PTSD, depression, and anxiety.

Case Studies

Case Study 1: Divergent Cultural Self Construals - Implications for the Practice of Dance/ Movement Therapy

This case study compares the expressive behaviours of participants from Taiwan and Western Europe in two Dance/Movement Therapy (DMT) workshops taught by Irma Dosamantes-Beaudry. Through an exploration of how cultural variations affected emotional expression during the sessions, the seminars sought to familiarise participants with American DMT practices.

Details of the Workshop:

Participants: Twenty to twenty-five self-selected experts with backgrounds in dance and mental health attended each course.

Demographics: Participants in the Taipei workshop included Taiwanese, but the Zurich workshop was primarily composed of Western Europeans.

Duration: The Taipei course was a one-day introduction session, whereas the Zurich program lasted five days.

Cultural Perspective: The workshops revealed disparities in how participants viewed themselves, with Taipei participants displaying collectivist inclinations and Zurich participants displaying individualistic features.

Observations of Expressive Behaviour:

Zurich Workshop:

Participants showed minimal reluctance to publicly voice their feelings. There was a broad spectrum of emotional expressiveness seen. Open communication and excitement were displayed by participants when they orally shared their movement experiences.

In keeping with Western standards of emotional transparency, the atmosphere promoted personal expression.

Taipei Workshop:

Even among acquaintances, participants showed a great deal of hesitancy while expressing their emotions. Instead of expressing themselves separately, the group preferred to observe and mimic one another's gestures.

Most of the emotions expressed were pleasant, and humor was frequently used as a stress reliever. The early absence of vocal input reflected a culture that values emotional control and seclusion.

Reflection from above Case Study:

The case study clearly depicts how cultural variations influence expressive behaviour in therapeutic settings. It presents beneficial perspectives for Dance/Movement Therapy practitioners and highlights the need of culturally sensitive techniques to facilitating emotional expression and participation across varied populations.

Case Study 2: Using a Dance/Movement Therapy-Based Wellness Curriculum: An Adolescent Case Study

This case study is on an eight-year-old girl called Alex who took part in a holistic wellness program based on dance/movement therapy (DMT). The story is told over the course of many sessions intended to examine several wellness-related topics, such as friendships, body image, movement, mindfulness, and nutrition.

During the first appointment, Alex seemed worn out and unsure of why she was meeting with the researcher. Playful activities like creating a personalised folder and tote bag while listening to Michael Jackson songs helped to lighten the mood. Alex and the researcher were able to build rapport through this light-hearted interaction.

The researcher used concrete examples to help them comprehend the difference between packaged and whole foods while they decorated. Alex showed a thorough understanding of the distinctions between various dietary categories and how they affect the body.

To learn more about Alex's sentiments and ideas regarding the curriculum themes, the researcher conducted qualitative interviews as the sessions went on. Alex gave her rudimentary grasp of nutrition, comparing it to "eating healthy," and she also discussed her opinions about exercise to express herself.

However, Alex became very upset when the topic of body image came up, exposing her issues with how she sees herself and how she compares to her classmates. She frequently discussed how her weight impacted her sense of acceptance in her social circle.

Alex's answers during the 30-minute interview revealed a lack of clarity and confidence in her own wellness path. She often said, "I don't know," implying that she was unsure of the curriculum and why her parents had enrolled her. Since she was uncomfortable, the researcher changed the strategy for subsequent sessions, using more engaging and immersive techniques instead of the more conventional qualitative inquiry.

Reflection from above Case Study:

With an emphasis on holistic health, the case study illustrates how dance/movement therapy (DMT) affects the wellness of teenage girls. To foster self-discovery and empowerment, the curriculum places a strong emphasis on friendships, body image, movement, mindfulness, and nutrition. Adolescent girls' emotional challenges, such body image and peer comparisons, are also highlighted in the research.

The study highlights the significance of different populations and group settings, therapeutic connections, and parental participation. Despite the study's limitations, it indicates that DMT may improve adolescent girls' self-perception, mental health, and social relationships, all of which may contribute to better health outcomes.

Techniques used in Dance Movement Therapy

Mirroring:

Mirroring is a basic method in DMT. The therapist intently observes the client's actions and then mirrors or matches them. This strategy promotes rapport, validates the client's emotional condition, and increases empathy.

Purpose: To foster trust and develop a nonverbal dialogue that allows clients to feel seen and understood without the need for spoken communication.

Therapeutic Effect: Mirroring helps clients become more aware of their own actions and feelings. It helps them feel welcomed and see their emotional habits.

Movement Exploration

Movement Exploration allows clients to experiment with a variety of movements, which are typically triggered by verbal signals or music. This approach enables clients to explore new ways of moving that might reflect or reveal emotional states (Payne, 2017).

Goal: To promote self-expression and emotional flexibility. It allows individuals to examine their sentiments via physical movement rather than verbal expression.

Therapeutic Effect: Movement exploration aids in the identification of emotional blocks, the promotion of creativity, and the development of a more profound knowledge of the mind-body relationship.

Authentic Movement

Authentic Movement is a method in which clients close their eyes and move freely while following their own impulses. There is no fixed shape or pattern to follow, and the movement develops spontaneously from inside.

Purpose: To encourage profound, unconscious emotional inquiry. The therapist serves as a witness, watching without passing judgement, making the client feel supported and comfortable in exploring their feelings.

Therapeutic Effect: Authentic movement enables clients to access and process latent emotions, frequently resulting in emotional release and insight into unconscious material.

Laban Movement Analysis (LMA)

Rudolf Laban created Laban Movement Analysis (LMA), a system for watching and understanding human movement. It offers a framework for analysing motions using four components: body, effort, space, and shape. DMT therapists utilise LMA to better understand their clients' emotional, cognitive, and psychological responses to movement.

Purpose: To analyse and comprehend the symbolic significance of motions and how they represent emotional or psychological states.

Therapeutic Effect: LMA assists therapists in determining how certain movement patterns connect to underlying emotional states. Therapists can help clients improve their emotional or mental habits by supporting changes in movement quality.

Rhythmic Synchronization

Rhythmic synchronization is the process of employing rhythm to manage emotions and body sensations. In this therapy, the therapist and client may move in sync, typically employing music or body percussion to keep a constant pace.

Purpose: To assist clients in regulating internal rhythms such as respiration and heartbeat, as well as achieving emotional and physical balance.

Therapeutic Effect: Rhythmic synchronization can be especially good for people who have experienced trauma, anxiety, or stress since it calms the nervous system and promotes a sense of safety and connection.

Group Movement and Interaction

In group DMT sessions, methods like as Group Interaction or Circle Movement are employed, in which participants perform synchronized or complimentary movements in a group context. The group dynamic provides opportunities for social connection, empathy development, and community support.

Purpose: To promote social interaction and lessen feelings of loneliness. Individuals might become more conscious of their relationships with others through group movement.

Therapeutic Effect: Group activities can help to enhance interpersonal connections, encourage collaboration, and alleviate social anxiety.

Grounding

Grounding is a method in which clients focus their movements on the ground, using their feet and lower body to create a sensation of stability and support. Grounding exercises can assist clients in managing anxiety, trauma, or dissociation by focussing on body sensations in the present now.

Purpose: To assist people feel more connected to their bodies and the world, especially when they are emotionally distant or overwhelmed.

Therapeutic Effect: Grounding techniques assist clients relax, reduce tension, and establish emotional stability.

Chace Technique

The Chace Method is a group-based, participatory method named for one of DMT's pioneers, Marian Chace. It entails verbal processing, group interaction, and rhythmic movement. Through rhythmic movement, the therapist engages participants and helps them connect with themselves, the group, and their emotions.

Application: Because it encourages social connection, group cohesiveness, and emotional expression, this method works particularly well in group therapy settings, such as with mental patients or individuals who are struggling with social isolation.

Application of Dance Movement Therapy in Psychotherapy

Trauma and PTSD:

DMT is commonly utilised for trauma sufferers. Because trauma frequently affects both the body (somatic symptoms) and the mind, DMT aids individuals in processing and releasing trauma held in the body. DMT has been shown in studies to relieve symptoms of post-traumatic stress disorder (PTSD) by improving body-mind integration (Levine 1997).

Depression and Anxiety:

Research shows that DMT can enhance mood, ease symptoms of depression, and reduce anxiety. It enables people to express themselves via their bodies, breaking free from fixed mental states. Koch et al. (2014) discovered that dance therapy dramatically improved symptoms of sadness and anxiety in various investigations.

Eating Disorders:

DMT helps individuals with eating disorders reinstate a positive and impartial attachment to their bodies. This therapeutic technique promotes body acceptance and conscious awareness.

Autism Spectrum Disorders:

Children with autism frequently struggle with verbal communication and social interactions. DMT may assist enhance social skills by facilitating nonverbal communication through organised and free-form movement.

Benefits of Dance Movement Therapy (DMT)

Emotional Expression and Processing:

DMT enables people to access nonverbal communication channels, allowing them to release and express feelings that may be suppressed or difficult to convey verbally (Chaiklin and Wengrower, 2009). This nonverbal communication facilitates therapeutic understanding and emotional processing.

Reduction of Anxiety and Stress:

DMT successfully reduces tension and anxiety, especially in people with mental health issues, according to research by Koch et al. (2014). Movement-based treatment significantly improved mood regulation and reduced stress, according to the study's meta-analysis.

Improvement in Self-Esteem and Body Image:

According to Meekums (2010), DMT is especially helpful for people who are having problems with their body image. The focus on self-expression and body awareness helps people rediscover their bodies, which boosts self-esteem and fosters a positive self-concept.

Support for Trauma Healing:

Payne (2017) claims that DMT has been effectively used in trauma treatment to assist patients in resolving the physical reactions connected to traumatic events. Clients can process trauma through nonverbal and symbolic movement, which circumvents the constraints of spoken therapy alone.

Enhancing Social Skills and Communication:

According to Levy (1988), DMT's group-based approach improves social skills by fostering community and cooperation, particularly in groups with autism spectrum disorders, developmental impairments, and social isolation.

Physical Health Benefits:

According to Levy (1988), DMT's group-based approach improves social skills by fostering community and cooperation, particularly in groups with autism spectrum disorders, developmental impairments, and social isolation.

Challenges in Dance Movement Therapy

Standardization:

DMT is a highly individualised kind of treatment, and there is disagreement on how to standardise it for research purposes. The subjective aspect of movement interpretation might differ greatly among therapists.

The absence of standardised training, certification, and regulation is a major obstacle for DMT in the West. The standards for DMT practice and training might differ greatly between nations and states, despite the existence of regulatory organisations such as the American Dance Therapy Association (ADTA).

Limited Access:

DMT is still less generally available than other types of psychotherapy, owing to the specialised training necessary for dance therapists and a lack of integration into standard mental health care.

Funding constraints frequently affect mental health services in many Western nations, especially in public healthcare systems. Compared to more traditional therapies like medicine, talk therapy, or cognitive-behavioral interventions, DMT may be viewed as less necessary or economical because it is a more specialised type of therapy.

Cultural Relevance:

DMT is mostly based on Western ideas of the body and movement, which may not be universally applicable across cultures. Critics call for more culturally sensitive modifications to DMT. In conclusion, dance movement therapy is a flexible therapeutic technique that incorporates movement for cognitive and emotional recovery. It is greatly impacted by the requirements of each individual participant as well as cultural settings.

Multidisciplinary Opposition

There is also opposition from other disciplines against DMT's incorporation into the larger area of mental health. The therapeutic potential of DMT may not be completely appreciated or understood by clinicians educated in more conventional, verbal-based psychotherapies, which might prevent multidisciplinary collaboration. Psychiatrists, psychologists, and social workers can neglect DMT as a supplemental or alternative remedy in favour of evidence-based practices that are more in line with biological or cognitive paradigms.

The Stigma Associated with Movement and Dance

Sometimes the stigma associated with the word "dance" itself causes prospective consumers to misinterpret or reject DMT. Some people might not see dancing as a means of psychological therapy, but rather as an activity only appropriate for artistic or performance settings.

People may be discouraged from obtaining DMT therapies because of this stigma, especially if they are uncomfortable dancing or expressing themselves physically. Additionally, while though DMT is suitable for all bodies and abilities, those who believe they are physically limited or lack rhythm may feel frightened or alienated by the prospect of participating in therapeutic movement.

References

Arrey, S. (2017). The art and science of dance/movement therapy: life is dance. *Body Movement and Dance in Psychotherapy*, *12*(4), 290–292. https://doi.org/10.1080/17432979.2017.1345791

Bartenieff, I., & Lewis, D. (1980). *Body Movement: Coping with the Environment*. Psychology Press.

Bernstein, P. (1979). Eight theoretical approaches in dance-movement therapy. In *Kendall/Hunt Pub. Co. eBooks*. http://ci.nii.ac.jp/ncid/BA84735750

Berrol, C. F. (2006). Neuroscience meets dance/movement therapy: Mirror neurons, the therapeutic process and empathy. *The Arts in Psychotherapy*, *33*(4), 302–315. https://doi.org/10.1016/j.aip.2006.04.001

Chaiklin, S., & Wengrower, H. (2015). *The Art and Science of Dance/Movement Therapy: Life Is Dance*. Routledge.

Dosamantes-Beaudry, I. (1999b). Divergent cultural self construals: implications for the practice of dance/movement therapy. *The Arts in Psychotherapy*, *26*(4), 225–231. https://doi.org/10.1016/s0197-4556(99)00011-8

Edwards, J. (2014). Exploring sensory sensitivities and relationships during group dance movement psychotherapy for adults with autism. *Body Movement and Dance in Psychotherapy*, *10*(1), 5–20. https://doi.org/10.1080/17432979.2014.978894

Hagensen, K. P. (2015). Using a Dance/Movement Therapy-Based Wellness Curriculum: An Adolescent Case Study. *American Journal of Dance Therapy*, *37*(2), 150–175. https://doi.org/10.1007/s10465-015-9199-4

Homann, K. B. (2010). Embodied Concepts of Neurobiology in Dance/Movement Therapy Practice. *American Journal of Dance Therapy*, *32*(2), 80–99. https://doi.org/10.1007/s10465-010-9099-6

Jeong, Y., Hong, S., Lee, M. S., Park, M., Kim, Y., & Suh, C. (2005). DANCE MOVEMENT THERAPY IMPROVES EMOTIONAL RESPONSES AND MODULATES NEUROHORMONES IN ADOLESCENTS

WITH MILD DEPRESSION. *International Journal of Neuroscience, 115*(12), 1711–1720. https://doi.org/10.1080/00207450590958574

Koch, S. C., & Fischman, D. (2011). Embodied Enactive Dance/Movement Therapy. *American Journal of Dance Therapy, 33*(1), 57–72. https://doi.org/10.1007/s10465-011-9108-4

Koch, S., Kunz, T., Lykou, S., & Cruz, R. (2013). Effects of dance movement therapy and dance on health-related psychological outcomes: A meta-analysis. *The Arts in Psychotherapy, 41*(1), 46–64. https://doi.org/10.1016/j.aip.2013.10.004

Koch, S., Kunz, T., Lykou, S., & Cruz, R. (2013b). Effects of dance movement therapy and dance on health-related psychological outcomes: A meta-analysis. *The Arts in Psychotherapy, 41*(1), 46–64. https://doi.org/10.1016/j.aip.2013.10.004

Levine, P. A. (1997). Waking the tiger - healing trauma - the innate capacity to transform overwhelming experiences. In *North Atlantic Books.* http://ci.nii.ac.jp/ncid/BA69201502

Levy, F. J. (1988). *Dance/movement therapy: A healing art.* http://files.eric.ed.gov/fulltext/ED291746.pdf

Lykou, S. (2017). Relational dance movement psychotherapy. In *Routledge eBooks* (pp. 21–36). https://doi.org/10.4324/9781315452852-2

Meekums, B. (2002). *Dance Movement Therapy: A Creative Psychotherapeutic Approach.* SAGE.

Payne, H. (2009). Pilot study to evaluate Dance Movement Psychotherapy (the BodyMind Approach) in patients with medically unexplained symptoms: Participant and facilitator perceptions and a summary discussion. *Body Movement and Dance in Psychotherapy, 4*(2), 77–94. https://doi.org/10.1080/17432970902918008

Payne, H. (2017). Essentials of Dance Movement Psychotherapy. In *Routledge eBooks.* https://doi.org/10.4324/9781315452852

Payne, H., Warnecke, T., Karkou, V., & Westland, G. (2016). A comparative analysis of body psychotherapy and dance movement psychotherapy from a European perspective. *Body Movement and Dance in Psychotherapy, 11*(2–3), 144–166. https://doi.org/10.1080/17432979.2016.1165291

Porges, S. W. (2011). *The Polyvagal Theory: Neurophysiological Foundations of Emotions, Attachment, Communication, and Self-regulation.* http://ci.nii.ac.jp/ncid/BB05274933

Porges, S. W. (2011b). *The Polyvagal Theory: Neurophysiological Foundations of Emotions, Attachment, Communication, and Self-regulation (Norton Series on Interpersonal Neurobiology).* W. W. Norton & Company.

Ritter, M., & Low, K. G. (1996b). Effects of dance/movement therapy: A meta-analysis. *The Arts in Psychotherapy, 23*(3), 249–260. https://doi.org/10.1016/0197-4556(96)00027-5

Valdivia, M. E. (2010). A psychoanalytic perspective of endings in therapy: A dance movement psychotherapy case study. *Body Movement and Dance in Psychotherapy, 5*(1), 75–87. https://doi.org/10.1080/17432971003593971

Whitehouse, M. S. (1999). The Tao of the body. *Authentic Movement: Essays by Mary Starks Whitehouse, Janet Adler and Joan Chodorow.* Jessica Kingsley Publishers.

Woolf, S., & Fisher, P. (2015). The role of dance movement psychotherapy for expression and integration of the self in palliative care. *International Journal of Palliative Nursing, 21*(7), 340–348. https://doi.org/10.12968/ijpn.2015.21.7.340

Chapter 24

Family Therapy

Sanjyukta Gupta School of Liberal Studies (SLS), CMR University, Bangalore

Introduction

Family therapy, also known as family counseling or systemic therapy, is a branch of psychotherapy that works with families and couples to nurture change and development. It emphasizes family relationships as an important factor in psychological health. Rather than focusing on an individual, family therapy works with multiple family members to resolve conflicts, improve communication, and address the dynamics that contribute to issues such as mental health problems, addiction, or relational difficulties.

Historical Background and Origin of Family Therapy

United States - Nathan Ackerman

In the US, Nathan Ackerman is frequently credited with establishing family therapy as a recognized field. Many people consider Ackerman, a psychiatrist and psychoanalyst, to be one of the pioneers of family therapy. He started advocating that family dynamics are crucial to comprehending psychological difficulties in the 1930s and 1940s. Ackerman played a key role in the development of family systems theory in the 1950s, which moved the emphasis from treating individuals to comprehending the family. Later, in 1960, he established the Ackerman Institute for the Family in New York City, which went on to become one of the key hubs for the advancement of family therapy.

United Kingdom - John Bowlby and Michael Rutter

The work of John Bowlby, a British psychiatrist and psychoanalyst most recognized for his work on attachment theory in the 1950s, had an impact on family therapy in the United Kingdom. Despite concentrating on kids and their parents, Bowlby made a substantial contribution to our knowledge of family relations. In the 1960s and 1970s, systems theory and psychoanalysis had an impact on the wider development of family therapy in the United Kingdom. Another important scholar, Michael Rutter, expanded on this work with his research on mental health, family stress, and child development.

Italy - Mara Selvini Palazzoli

Mara Selvini Palazzoli was a key figure in the development of family therapy in Italy, especially as it relates to eating disorders. She established the Milan Systemic Family

Therapy technique in the 1960s and 1970s, which gained notoriety for its creative approaches to family issues, particularly those with anorexic teens.

Germany – Helm Stierlin

In the 1970s, the German psychiatrist and psychoanalyst Helm Stierlin had a significant role in the development of family therapy. To better comprehend the communication and interactional patterns within families, particularly those with psychotic diseases, he developed systemic family treatment techniques.

Applications of Family Therapy

Mental Health Issues

Depression, Anxiety, and PTSD: Family therapy is often used to support individuals suffering from mental health issues like depression, anxiety, and post-traumatic stress disorder (PTSD). The family's role in recovery is crucial, and therapy aims to improve the family's support system, communication, and coping mechanisms.

Schizophrenia and Bipolar Disorder: Family therapy has been shown to reduce relapse rates in individuals with schizophrenia or bipolar disorder by helping family members better understand the disorder, manage symptoms, and offer appropriate support.

Substance Abuse and Addiction

Family therapy is widely applied in the treatment of substance use disorders, recognizing that addiction often affects family dynamics. By involving the family in the therapeutic process, the therapy addresses enabling behaviors, codependency, and patterns of dysfunction that contribute to the addiction cycle. Therapists work with family members to develop healthier ways of supporting recovery and coping with the stress of addiction within the family unit.

Relationship Counseling and Marital Issues

Family therapy is commonly used to help couples address marital problems, including communication breakdowns, infidelity, and intimacy issues. Therapy provides a space for partners to express their feelings, understand each other's perspectives, and learn healthier ways to resolve conflicts. In cases of divorce or separation, family therapy can help mitigate the emotional impact on children and ease the transition to new family dynamics.

Child and Adolescent Behavioral Problems

Family therapy is frequently applied when dealing with children or adolescents who exhibit behavioral problems, such as defiance, aggression, or delinquency. In such cases, the therapist works with both the child and the family to identify patterns of communication and interaction that may be contributing to the behavior. It is particularly effective in cases where parents struggle with discipline, boundaries, or supporting the child's emotional needs.

Trauma and Grief Counselling

Family therapy is valuable in helping families process trauma, such as the loss of a loved one, domestic violence, or experiences of abuse. It helps family members support each other, address unresolved feelings, and develop strategies for coping with grief or trauma.

Blended Families and Step-Parenting

As family structures evolve, with more blended families and step-parenting dynamics, family therapy is often utilized to address the challenges that arise. It helps create clearer roles, boundaries, and communication strategies for new family units, addressing issues of resentment, rivalry, or adjustment difficulties.

Cultural and Intergenerational Conflicts

In families with diverse cultural or generational differences, family therapy can be used to bridge gaps in understanding, values, and expectations. For example, conflicts between immigrant parents and their children who are assimilating into a new culture can be addressed through family therapy.

Challenges of Family Therapy

Resistance from Family Members

One of the major challenges in family therapy is that not all family members may be willing or open to the process. Family members may resist participation, either due to denial about the issues or fear of facing conflicts. This resistance can limit the effectiveness of therapy. Additionally, family members may blame one person for the problems, which can create tension during therapy sessions.

Complex Family Dynamics

Families are complex systems, and deeply ingrained patterns of behavior, communication, and dysfunction can be difficult to change. Even when one member of the family begins to change, other members may unconsciously resist these changes, making progress slow. Power imbalances within the family, such as those between parents and children, or abusive relationships, can also hinder the therapeutic process and require sensitive handling by the therapist.

Cultural and Societal Factors

Cultural beliefs and expectations about family roles, gender dynamics, and privacy can influence the effectiveness of therapy. In some cultures, discussing personal or family problems with an outsider (like a therapist) is taboo, making it difficult to engage in the process fully. Similarly, therapists must be culturally sensitive and aware of how cultural norms and values affect family interactions. Lack of cultural competence can lead to misunderstandings or a failure to address the family's needs.

Confidentiality and Privacy Issues

Since family therapy involves multiple people, confidentiality and privacy issues can arise. Family members may reveal private information about each other during sessions, leading to trust issues or conflict. Therapists must navigate these concerns carefully, balancing individual and family privacy needs.

Coordination with Other Therapies

Family therapy is often used in conjunction with individual therapy, medication management, or other forms of treatment. Coordinating these different therapeutic approaches can be challenging, especially when there are conflicting views on treatment goals or methods between the therapist and other professionals involved in the care of family members.

Financial and Time Constraints

Family therapy can be time-consuming and may require ongoing sessions to produce lasting change. Some families may struggle with the time commitment or financial cost associated with therapy. This challenge is particularly relevant in lower-income families or communities with limited access to mental health services.

Diverse Family Structures

Modern family structures are becoming increasingly diverse, including same-sex parents, single-parent households, and families with non-biological members. Traditional models of family therapy may not always align with the needs and experiences of these families, requiring therapists to adapt their approaches.

Case Studies

Case Study 1: Addressing Communication Issues in a Blended Family:

Sarah (42) and Mike (45) recently married, each bringing two teenage children from previous marriages into the new household. Both sets of children had difficulty adjusting to the new family structure and often clashed with one another. Sarah and Mike noticed tension not only between their children but also between themselves when attempting to handle discipline and household rules.

Therapy Goals:

1. Improve family communication and understanding among all family members.
2. Establish clear roles and expectations for each family member.
3. Develop strategies for co-parenting effectively as a blended family.

Intervention:

The therapist used Structural Family Therapy (SFT) to help establish a healthy hierarchy within the family, ensuring that the couple operated as a unified parental unit. The therapist also encouraged the family to hold weekly "family meetings" where each member could voice concerns and express feelings constructively.

Outcome:

Over several months, Sarah and Mike reported that the household felt more cohesive, with the children interacting more amicably and fewer conflicts arising. Sarah and Mike developed greater confidence in their roles as co-parents and learned techniques for managing disagreements.

Case Study 2: Treating Adolescent Behavioral Issues:

David (17) had been exhibiting rebellious behavior, including skipping school, substance use, and arguing with his parents. His parents, Mark and Jennifer, tried various approaches to discipline him, but nothing seemed to work. The ongoing conflict was straining their marriage, and both parents felt helpless.

Therapy Goals:

1. Address and understand the underlying causes of David's behavior.
2. Improve family communication and foster empathy.
3. Develop a supportive structure to help David make healthier choices.

Intervention:

The therapist used Cognitive Behavioral Family Therapy (CBFT) to identify the negative patterns between David and his parents and to understand David's behavior triggers. The therapist worked with David on setting realistic goals for school and discussed alternative ways to cope with stress and frustration. His parents learned how to establish boundaries and communicate support without being overly critical or punitive.

Outcome:

David's behavior gradually improved, and he re-engaged with school and extracurricular activities. The family continued to work on open communication, and both parents expressed relief at the improved relationship with their son.

Case Study 3: Managing Chronic Illness in the Family

Emily (8) was diagnosed with Type 1 diabetes, a life-changing event for her parents and siblings. Her parents, Tom and Lisa, struggled to manage her care alongside work and household responsibilities. Emily's siblings also felt neglected, leading to feelings of resentment and frustration within the family.

Therapy Goals:

1. Help the family adjust to Emily's condition and develop coping mechanisms.
2. Address feelings of neglect and ensure that each family member feels valued.
3. Teach the family how to work together in supporting Emily's health needs.

Intervention:

The therapist applied Family Systems Therapy to explore how Emily's diagnosis affected each family member. The therapist encouraged family sessions to allow everyone to express their feelings and concerns openly. The family also received practical advice on how to divide responsibilities for Emily's care to avoid burnout and to provide time for other children.

Outcome:

The family's communication and empathy improved significantly. Siblings felt less neglected, and Emily's parents felt more equipped to balance her medical needs with other family obligations. The family expressed gratitude for the tools they learned to support each other effectively.

Family Therapy Techniques for Mental Health

Structural Family Therapy (SFT)

Salvador Minuchin is credited with developing structural family therapy, or SFT. It focuses on Reorganizing family relationships to create a sound hierarchy and enhance communication. By seeing how families interact, the therapist might identify problematic patterns (such as entanglement or detachment) that could be causing problems like anxiety or sadness. To encourage better communication and support networks, the therapist could suggest reorganizing the roles and limits within the family.

Bowenian Family Therapy

The creator is Murray Bowen. It focuses on fostering self-differentiation and balancing emotional distances. Methods are Genograms which make a graphic depiction of the family structure across generations to spot trends and emotional ties. Differentiation of self is for supporting family members in forging a solid sense of identity while maintaining ties to the family. Bowenian treatment works especially well for treating problems like depression or anxiety that are inherited from relationships or trauma that has occurred throughout generations.

Cognitive Behavioral Family Therapy (CBFT)

Aaron Beck created it, and family systems later adopted it. It focuses on Recognizing and changing unhelpful thought patterns that lead to mental health issues. Methods assisting family members in reframing unfavorable or illogical views is known as cognitive restructuring. Behavioral Interventions promote constructive actions that are consistent with optimistic thinking.

Narrative Therapy

Developed by: Michael White and David Epston. It Focuses on Helping individuals separate themselves from their problems by viewing them as external narratives. Techniques are Re-authoring Conversations: Family members work to redefine the story around a particular problem, often shifting blame away from the individual. Externalization treats issues (like depression or addiction) as separate from the person affected, reducing stigmatization within the family. The application of this technique is effective for families dealing with issues such as addiction or trauma, where one member's struggles might be overwhelming the family.

Emotionally Focused Family Therapy (EFFT)

Sue Johnson created it. It focuses on improving attachment and fortifying emotional ties within the family. Methods emotion coaching teaches families how to recognize and appropriately communicate their feelings. Attachment Work on Strengthening family members' sense of safety and trust. The Application is for Families suffering from trauma or attachment-related problems, including foster or adoptive families, who benefit from EFFT. It lessens problems like anxiety and depression by assisting family members in developing stable bonds, which enables people to feel more emotionally supported within the family system.

Reflection

Family therapy is a potent therapeutic method that is based on the idea that people's problems are best understood and addressed within the framework of their family systems. According to family therapy, the family is an interdependent network in which every member has a function to perform, and each person's wellbeing affects the wellbeing of the others. Understanding family relationships can reveal deeper, often hidden implications on personal issues, making this connection especially useful when addressing mental health. Another transforming aspect of family therapy is its emphasis on empathy and communication. Many families enter treatment with years' worth of unresolved issues or repressed feelings, which can lead to avoidance or conflict cycles. Family members can create new, constructive patterns by learning how to listen intently, talk honestly, and respect one another's opinions. Beyond therapy sessions, these communication skills frequently help families deal with problems on their own in the future and provide them the tools they need to withstand new stressors. Family therapy is a preventative step for future problems as well as a means of healing existing ones.

References

Minuchin, S. (1974). *Families and Family Therapy.* Cambridge, MA: Harvard University Press.

Bowen, M. (1978). *Family Therapy in Clinical Practice.* New York: Jason Aronson.

Nichols, M. P., & Davis, S. D. (2020). *Family Therapy: Concepts and Methods* (12th ed.). Pearson.

Goldenberg, H., & Goldenberg, I. (2012). *Family Therapy: An Overview* (8th ed.). Belmont, CA: Brooks/Cole.

White, M., & Epston, D. (1990). *Narrative Means to Therapeutic Ends.* New York: Norton.

Johnson, S. M. (2004). *The Practice of Emotionally Focused Couple Therapy: Creating Connection.* New York: Brunner-Routledge.

Gurman, A. S., Lebow, J. L., & Snyder, D. K. (Eds.). (2015). *Clinical Handbook of Couple Therapy* (5th ed.). New York: Guilford Press.

Satir, V. (1988). *The New Peoplemaking.* Palo Alto, CA: Science and Behavior Books.

Chapter 25

Grief Therapy

Pavita V School of Liberal Studies (SLS), CMR University, Bangalore

Introduction

Grief therapy is defined as a specialized branch of psychotherapy which has been designed for individuals who have experienced the major loss, usually loss due to death of someone whom an individual loves and this branch is used by therapy in making them overcome the emotional pain, psychological, and at times physical pain. Therapy for grieving is about helping a grieving person navigate the process of bereavement in a healthful manner and cope with life post-loss, averting secondary complications like the prolonged grief disorder, depression, or anxiety.

The key components are-

Emotional Expression and Validation

An Absolution-Free Environment to Share Emotions: Therapy offers an outlet for the person to attend and discuss his emotions of loss—grief, hurt, guilt, frustration, and confusion—with someone who is not going to judge them. This is crucially needed for those who must go ahead in life with the veiled pain.

Validation of Emotions: The counselor validated the range of emotions which happen as a direct outcome of loss. That normalizes what they experience and thus lessens feelings of isolation or abnormality.

Coping with Loss

Understanding the Nature of Grief: Therapy can understand the nature of grief, which includes emotional stages like denial, anger, bargaining, depression, and acceptance, though in varying degrees for everyone.

Finding Meaning in the Loss: The assistance of therapy, such as Narrative Therapy or Existential Therapy, can help an individual look at the meaning of the loss and how it could fit into their life story, allowing for emotional integration and acceptance.

Coping Strategies

Development of Healthy Coping Skills: Therapy teaches a person coping skills on how to cope with stress and intense feelings associated with a loss. For instance, reframing their thoughts regarding the loss or problem-solving techniques to overcome the immediate issues that have arisen while grieving.

Control of Emotions: Counseling, specifically Cognitive Behavioral Counseling (CBT), can teach individuals control over surging emotions, such as despair or anger, by enabling them to understand how thoughts influence feelings and behaviors, ultimately fostering healthier emotional responses.

Streamlining Complex Bereavement

Reducing the Risk of Continuing Grief: Some people may suffer from complicated grief-a form of intense emotional anguish that lasts for such an extended period that interferes with everyday life. Some forms of therapy can also intervene by teaching them techniques for processing their emotions and desist from avoidance behaviors that serve to disengage them further and re-engage into the mainstream of life.

Grief Triggers: The therapist will help people identify potential triggers of their grief and prepare them for times like anniversaries or holidays and other reminders and find ways to cope through these painful moments without drowning in their pain.

Maintaining Mental Well-being

Depression and Anxiety: Grief can often trigger or trigger depression and anxiety. Therapy helps resolve these secondary mental health problems by helping individuals develop coping techniques and eliminating the negative way of thinking.

Mindfulness and Stress Reduction: Techniques like MBSR help individuals stay mindful, manage anxiety related to grief, and reduce overall stress. This can promote better well-being by calming down and reducing rumination.

Building social ties

Building Social Support Building social support is a way therapy often helps individuals regain contact with their social networks and build supportive relationships-which can be very useful in the grieving process. Groups of Therapy or grief groups allow individuals to share with others who understand their pain, providing mutual support and validation.

Improve Communication: Grief counseling therapists can help individuals by enabling them to discuss conversations involving their own grief with friends and relatives, thus improving their communication, and understanding between the support system.

Rebuilding a Purpose

Restoring Meaning to Life: Loss can cause disorientation. Existential therapy allows persons to question life and death, allowing individuals to reassess meaning in one's existence and rebuild identity at the cost of loss.

Posttraumatic Growth: Therapy has been associated with post-traumatic growth-a process during which the following occurs; new strengths may emerge through coping, personal growth, and meaning following severe loss.

Supporting Transition to Life Changes

Working with Life Changes: Counseling supports the client to adjust to the practical and emotional changes that accompany loss, for example, the death of a loved one, divorce, or any significant life change. The counselor assists the client with the emotional and practical challenges of living without the deceased or adjusting to significant life changes.

Develop New Habits: Therapy helps them develop new habits to cope with life after the loss, showing them ways to get involved with the world again and guiding them in small steps in building up a meaningful life.

Resilience Building

Improving Emotional Resilience: Therapy improves a person's emotional resilience by teaching someone to deal with difficult emotions, increase problem-solving skills, and enhance recovery from disappointments.

By slowly building long-term coping abilities over a long time, therapy will help people develop a toolkit of long-term coping strategies they can use over time to address not only grief but other life challenges, thereby boosting overall mental health and adaptability.

Tailored Approach for Individual Needs

Client-centered support: Therapy will be tailored to the specific needs of the grieving person, whether more cognition-targeted technique as in CBT, more emotion-focused approach as seen in Emotion-Focused Therapy, or an expressive therapeutic intervention, such as Art Therapy or Music Therapy. Thus, the therapy shall correspond to the individual experience with grief.

The culture and spiritual dependence of grief is addressed by therapy, so that in culture-or religious-belief-dependent griefs, individuals can grieve within their context and traditions.

Elements of Bereavement Counseling

Conceptualization of Grief

Counseling often begins with the person understanding what grief is. This could be teaching him the typical steps that one follows or passes through in the process of grieving, which would be denial, anger, bargaining, depression, and acceptance, all at the same time as he recognizes that his unique journey of grief is acceptable. Grief counseling provides a safe and secure environment for the individual to express huge feelings of sadness, anger, remorse, or confusion. They facilitate the process of inducing processing that will eventually propel the client toward healing.

Working with Unresolved Issues:

It also depends upon the unsolved issues with the person who has left the world. In this case, one of the most common emotions that arises is that of guilt and remorse. Letter to the deceased can be a modality in the therapy so that people may find closure.

Establishing New Habits and Identities:

This would, therefore, mean counseling clients in the rebuilding of their lives and identities, especially since, in these cases, the person who died played a very important part in their everyday life. This can involve learning new coping strategies, finding new sources of support, and establishing new routines.

Ritual and Memorialization:

Therapy could discuss staying in touch with the deceased through rituals, memorials, or meaningful activities that would enable them to continue having some kind of connection with the deceased.

Cognitive Behavioral Techniques:

CBT techniques in the treatment for grief will be followed to reduce dysfunctional thoughts that are found to be self-blame or even catastrophizing and develop adaptive functions of coping.

Types of Grief Therapy

Complicated Grief Therapy (CGT):

Primarily designed especially for use with those diagnosed as enduring or complicated. It primarily resolves chronic symptoms of grief and gets the client re-engaged in life.

Cognitive Behavioral Therapy (CBT)

The techniques of CBT are utilized to enable them to alter the cognitive process about negative thinking, devalue the irrational beliefs around the loss, and acquire new ways of coping up with the incident.

Narrative Therapy:

This makes its application in the use by the client to rebuild and retell their personal stories within the context of loss allow them to do something outside themselves while reframing their situation in a way that heals them from the experience.

Group Grief Therapy:

Apart from that, the knowledge of how many people were at his stage could comfort a man in sorrow, and group therapy offers an opportunity for exchange of experiences and feelings with other people who might understand the same kind of loss. In this way, they have a kind of community, support, and acceptance.

Art or Expressive Therapy:

For those who cannot speak about their grief, art therapy or other expressive therapies-music or writing-can help people externalize and process their grief in another way.

Individuals who are experiencing normal grief reactions, but feel that they cannot handle the process, or even those experiencing complicated or prolonged grief. Traumatic losses, that is, sudden death of a loved one, violent loss, or loss of a child. Ambiguous loss: when a loved one is missing or incapacitated.

Grief Therapy Benefits

Grief therapy may normalize the process of grieving and will help in dispelling some myths of how a person "should" grieve. It can also offer emotional support aside from ridding those feelings of isolation.

Cognitive and Emotional Processing in Grief:

This therefore means that the PFC plays a crucial role in cognitive control and emotional regulation. In those grieving, this area helps shape their emotional responses as well as to make sense of loss. Poor functionality of the PFC could therefore result in an inability to regulate emotions related to grief. The limbic system, particularly the amygdala, is involved in the processing of emotional responses. In the grieving process, heightened activity of the amygdala is correlated with manifestations of sadness, fear, and anxiety, and the hippocampus is vital for the recall of the memory of the deceased.

Neuropsychological Impact of Grief:

Cognitive impairments: The complicated grief like normal grief causes impaired cognition which includes failure in memorizing, concentrating difficulty, and slowing the rate of information processing. These are associated with the stress response to loss.

Emotion dysregulation: Grief is associated with poor regulation of emotion because the ACC which mediates emotional regulation and social pain is disturbed.Cognitive reappraisal. Neuropsychological interventions such as cognitive reappraisal often involve the reappraisal of negative thoughts that the loss has caused. For instance, reappraising the thoughts might change some brain function in regions known to be associated with processing emotions, like the prefrontal cortex, therefore reducing distress.

Impact on Bereavement and Executive Functioning

Attention and Concentration: MTD can have a profound impact on the ability of a person to concentrate and focus on daily responsibilities and tasks, which impacts what may be considered aspects of executive function related to the changes occurring in PFC during bereavement.

Decision-Making: Emotional pain during grief reduces the ability of a person to use decision-making, whereby the emotions of grief (processed within the amygdala) may interfere with the logical thinking of the prefrontal cortex.

Complex Grief and Cognitive Overload: In complicated grief, the patient may have cognitive overload when they are repeatedly ruminating on their loss. Such ruminating could cause hyperactivity in the default mode network-a brain network associated with self-referential thought and rumination.

Working memory and cognitive flexibility: Bereaved subjects are impaired in both working memory and cognitive flexibility; both are important for the change in process as well as for the possibility of moving on. It is mediated by the DLPFC, which bears the brunt of the emotional toll experienced by the grieving individual.

Impact of Grief on Cognition and Behavior:

Rumination: One of the psychological manifestations of grief is rumination, which is the continuous contemplation of the loss. Neuropsychologically, this translates to heightened activity in the medial prefrontal cortex, which is linked to self-focused thought and emotional suffering.

Intrusive Thoughts: Grief also makes individuals have intrusive thoughts of the deceased. These are intrusive memories that are handled by the hippocampus and amygdala, areas that are responsible for memory and emotional reactivity.

Neuropsychological Interventions for Grief

Cognitive Behavioral Therapy (CBT): CBT can assist in the modification of negative thought patterns associated with bereavement. Neuropsychologically, CBT balances brain networks responsible for emotion regulation and executive function like the PFC and ACC.

Mindfulness-Based Cognitive Therapy (MBCT): Mindfulness helps people work through emotions related to grief without getting off track. Neuropsychologically, it improves the function of the PFC and decreases the activity of brain regions involved in distress such as the amygdala.

Neuropsychological Resilience during Grief:

The neuropsychology of resilience in grief will be characterized by higher activation in the PFC; their ability to control their thoughts could be better. Cognitive adaptability and shifting focus on loss to positive coping behaviors is likely to go hand-in hand with stronger pathways for supportive behaviors.

Grief Recovery and Neuroplasticity

Grief has effects on the brain but is an adaptive one because the brain can perform neuroplasticity; this means, it can produce new connections among neurons. With some years and intervention, the individual rebuilds his or her capabilities for regulating cognition as well as emotions, thus alleviating the severity of the effects of grief on the psychological aspect.

Grief counseling varies in stages according to age, primarily because cognitive development, expressions, and ways of coping are not identical in all individuals. Here's how grief counseling is usually adapted depending on age:

1. ***Children (Ages 3-12)***

   Understanding Death: Children around the age of 3 to 5 years really have no understanding of how final death is; the child may think that persons who die return to live. Children from ages 6 to 9, however, know that dying is a fact but fail to cope with the psychological stage about death.

   Between age 10 and 12, they are likely to have some concrete understanding regarding the matter of death; a child may feel mixed sentiments or feelings of sorrow, being angry, and confusion too.

Therapy Aids:

Play Therapy: In younger children, play therapy is used because they may use a toy, drawing, or story to tell their bereavement. Playing will give them an outlet to voice emotions without needing highly developed verbal skills.

Art and Music Therapy: A child can be involved in various creative activities such as drawing or music to help in expressing their grief

Storytelling and Books: Age-appropriate books or stories about loss will help the child express and understand death in more concrete terms.

Parent Involvement: Parents and other caregivers are included as it is a process, often requiring comfort and reassurance from the adults they are accustomed to.

2. ***Adolescents (13-18)***

Understanding of Bereavement: Teenagers possess a more mature understanding of death and the fact that it is irreversible. They go through various emotions like anger, guilt, and anxiety. The teenagers also feel out of sync with their peers because of the lack of shared experience regarding bereavement.

Therapeutic Methods:

CBT: It makes the teenager face the unhealthy thoughts and brings in the healthier ways of dealing with the grief-evoking feelings.

Group Counseling: The teens find it reassuring that they are not alone in their grief process. They can share their experiences with each other in group counseling where the emotions become normalized by others.

Journaling/Writing Therapy: Ask the teen to write about how they are grieving (Letter writing, journaling etc). This will help him/her to understand and even order his emotion.

Mindfulness and Relaxation Approaches: These mindfulness-intensive therapies enable the teens to focus more on the present; they remove emotional overkill and become conscious of their grieving process.

3. ***Adolescents (19-30 Years)***

Death Literacy: At this transition period, young adults may also question the very existence of life as it pertains to death, especially when they experience the loss of a close friend or family member. This transitional stage often includes education, career, and personal identity. These issues can worsen the impact of loss.

Therapeutic Interventions:

Narrative Therapy: Young adults can use the narrative method to express their grief in the form of a story or letter. This can help them process their loss and include it in the larger life story.

Support Groups: Young adults will require peer support. Grouping with other people facing similar situations will help the young adult find emotional comfort and avoid loneliness.

Emotion-Focused Therapy: This technique is done with young adults teaching them to understand and process their emotions, such as letting themselves feel sad, angry, or guilty.

Psychoeducation: Educating young adults about the grieving process, reminding them that the emotional responses are natural for healing.

4. ***4. Middle-Aged Adults (30-60)***

   Knowledge about Grief: For most middle-aged individuals, loss would be the death of many of their near and dear ones, such as their parents, spouse, or even close relatives. For most of them, it is usually the time of multiple stressors, and they would usually cope up with these losses along with other responsibilities, such as working, raising children, and taking care of the family. Inability to cope up with those several stressors would most probably lead to complicated grief.

   Treatment Approaches:

   Cognitive Behavioral Therapy: The middle-aged adult can learn to reframe negative thoughts about grief, manage distress, and regain a normal sense of life through CBT.

   Family Therapy: If the whole family is affected by grief, middle-aged adults can navigate their emotions while maintaining supportive roles for other family members, especially children or elderly relatives, through family therapy.

   Mindfulness-Based Stress Reduction (MBSR): MBSR may help middle-aged adults to handle their stress as well as emotional responses from grief since it is useful in keeping the individual in control of unmanageable emotions.

   Existential Therapy: It could be useful to middle-aged adults who are finding themselves questioning life, death, and what happened to them after losing a loved one.

5. ***Older Adults (Ages 60+)***

   Awareness of Loss: Older adults commonly experience the loss of a spouse, friends, and even children. They are most likely to be concerned with their own mortality, bringing fear, regret, or loneliness.The cognitive aspects of aging, such as forgetting or dementia, may present a challenge to their process of grieving.

   Therapeutic Interventions:

   Reminiscence Therapy: This is assisting older adults to work through positive recollections of the deceased. It enables them to include that loss in their life story while remaining close to loved ones.

   Elderly Support Groups: The peer support groups are for older adults to help share grief with those who understand the uniqueness of conditions in aging and loss.

Case Studies

Case Study 1

- Name: J M
- Age: 15 years
- Gender: Male
- Presenting Problem: James presented with depression, school refusal, and social withdrawal following the death of his mother due to cancer six months earlier. He struggled with feelings of abandonment and guilt for not being able to "save" her.

Clinical Assessment:

- **Symptoms:**
    - Persistent feelings of sadness and guilt
    - Decline in academic performance
    - Social isolation from peers
    - Irritability and outbursts at home
    - Sleep difficulties (both insomnia and hypersomnia)

Diagnostic Criteria:

- **DSM-5 Diagnosis:**
    - Major Depressive Disorder (MDD): J exhibited a depressed mood, feelings of guilt, social withdrawal, and academic decline lasting for more than two weeks.
    - Comorbid Condition: Prolonged Grief Disorder (PGD) was also considered, given the prolonged grieving period and functional impairment.

Therapeutic Approach:

- **Therapy Type:** Cognitive Behavioral Therapy (CBT)
    - Goal: To challenge James' maladaptive beliefs about his mother's death and improve coping skills.
    - Techniques:

      Cognitive Restructuring: The therapist helped J identify and challenge his irrational thoughts, such as "If I had been a better son, my mother would have survived." He learned to replace these thoughts with more realistic ones, recognizing that his mother's illness was beyond his control.

      Behavioral Activation: J was encouraged to re-engage in social and academic activities, starting with small, manageable tasks to build a sense of accomplishment and reduce withdrawal.

Outcome:

- Short-term Results: After 12 weeks of CBT, J showed significant improvement in mood and academic performance. His sense of guilt decreased, and he became more involved with his peers and schoolwork.

- Long-term Outcome: By the end of therapy, J reported a renewed sense of normalcy, decreased feelings of abandonment, and better emotional regulation.

Case Study 2

Anna, a 28-year-old woman, lost her best friend in a car accident. She struggled with feelings of isolation, guilt, and the thought that she would never find a friendship as deep again. Anna believed that she should have been present on the day of the accident and blamed herself for not preventing it.

- **Narrative Approach:**
  - ***Externalization:*** Anna's therapist helped her to externalize her grief and guilt, discussing these as external forces rather than intrinsic flaws. Anna began to say, *"Grief is making me feel disconnected, but it's not who I am."*
  - ***Letter Writing:*** Anna wrote a series of letters to her friend, expressing her pain and guilt. In later letters, she began to share positive memories and express gratitude for the friendship. This allowed Anna to move from focusing solely on the loss to remembering the meaningful moments they had shared.
  - ***Re-storying:*** Through the therapeutic process, Anna reconstructed her narrative from *"I failed her"* to *"I was a good friend to her, and her friendship shaped who I am today."* She was able to reframe the relationship in a way that honored both the loss and the lasting impact her friend had on her life.
- **Outcome:** Anna reported feeling lighter, less burdened by guilt, and more connected to her friend in a way that focused on positive memories rather than solely on her absence.

References

Bonanno, G. A. (2004). Loss, trauma, and human resilience: Have we underestimated the human capacity to thrive after extremely aversive events? *American Psychologist, 59*(1), 20–28. https://doi.org/10.1037/0003-066X.59.1.20

Bonanno, G. A., & Kaltman, S. (1999). Toward an integrative perspective on bereavement. *Psychological Bulletin, 125*(6), 760–776. https://doi.org/10.1037/0033-2909.125.6.760

Boelen, P. A., van den Hout, M. A., & van den Bout, J. (2006). A cognitive-behavioral conceptualization of complicated grief. *Clinical Psychology: Science and Practice, 13*(2), 109–128. https://doi.org/10.1111/j.1468-2850.2006.00013.x

Currier, J. M., Holland, J. M., & Neimeyer, R. A. (2007). The effectiveness of bereavement interventions with children: A meta-analytic review of controlled outcome research. *Journal of Clinical Child and Adolescent Psychology, 36*(2), 253–259. https://doi.org/10.1080/15374410701279669

Currier, J. M., Neimeyer, R. A., & Berman, J. S. (2008). The effectiveness of psychotherapeutic interventions for bereaved persons: A comprehensive quantitative review. *Psychological Bulletin, 134*(5), 648–661. https://doi.org/10.1037/0033-2909.134.5.648

Field, N. P., Gal-Oz, E., & Bonanno, G. A. (2003). Continuing bonds and adjustment at 5 years after the death of a spouse. *Journal of Consulting and Clinical Psychology, 71*(1), 110–117. https://doi.org/10.1037/0022-006X.71.1.110

Folkman, S. (2001). Revised coping theory and the process of bereavement. *Death Studies, 25*(4), 277–289. https://doi.org/10.1080/07481180126191

Klass, D., Silverman, P. R., & Nickman, S. L. (Eds.). (1996). *Continuing bonds: New understandings of grief.* Taylor & Francis.

Lazarus, R. S., & Folkman, S. (1984). *Stress, appraisal, and coping.* Springer.

Neimeyer, R. A. (2001). *Meaning reconstruction & the experience of loss.* American Psychological Association. https://doi.org/10.1037/10397-000

Prigerson, H. G., & Maciejewski, P. K. (2008). Grief and acceptance as opposite sides of the same coin: Setting a research agenda. *Psychiatry Research, 168*(1), 57–61. https://doi.org/10.1016/j.psychres.2008.07.022

Prigerson, H. G., Vanderwerker, L. C., & Maciejewski, P. K. (2008). A case for inclusion of prolonged grief disorder in DSM-V. *Handbook of Bereavement Research and Practice: Advances in Theory and Intervention,* 165–186. American Psychological Association. https://doi.org/10.1037/14498-008

Rando, T. A. (1993). *Treatment of complicated mourning.* Research Press.

Shear, M. K., Frank, E., Houck, P. R., & Reynolds, C. F. (2005). Treatment of complicated grief: A randomized controlled trial. *JAMA, 293*(21), 2601–2608. https://doi.org/10.1001/jama.293.21.2601

Shear, M. K., & Shair, H. (2005). Attachment, loss, and complicated grief. *Developmental Psychobiology, 47*(3), 253–267. https://doi.org/10.1002/dev.20091

Shear, M. K. (2015). Complicated grief. *New England Journal of Medicine, 372*(2), 153–160. https://doi.org/10.1056/NEJMcp1315618

Stroebe, M., Schut, H., & Stroebe, W. (2007). Health outcomes of bereavement. *The Lancet, 370*(9603), 1960–1973. https://doi.org/10.1016/S0140-6736(07)61816-9

Stroebe, M., & Schut, H. (1999). The dual process model of coping with bereavement: Rationale and description. *Death Studies, 23*(3), 197–224. https://doi.org/10.1080/074811899201046

Stroebe, M., Schut, H., & Boerner, K. (2010). Continuing bonds in adaptation to bereavement: Toward theoretical integration. *Clinical Psychology Review, 30*(2), 259–268. https://doi.org/10.1016/j.cpr.2009.11.007

Thompson, N. (2002). *Loss and grief: A guide for human services practitioners.* Palgrave Macmillan.

Walter, C. A., & McCoyd, J. L. M. (2009). *Grief and loss across the lifespan: A biopsychosocial perspective.* Springer Publishing Company.

Worden, J. W. (2009). *Grief counseling and grief therapy: A handbook for the mental health practitioner* (4th ed.). Springer.

Yalom, I. D., & Lieberman, M. A. (1991). Bereavement and heightened existential awareness. *Psychiatry: Interpersonal and Biological Processes, 54*(3), 334–345. https://doi.org/10.1080/00332747.1991.11024559

Zisook, S., & Shear, K. (2009). Grief and bereavement: What psychiatrists need to know. *World Psychiatry, 8*(2), 67–74. https://doi.org/10.1002/j.2051-5545.2009.tb00217.x

Zisook, S., Simon, N. M., Reynolds, C. F., & Pies, R. (2010). Bereavement, complicated grief, and DSM, part 2: Complicated grief. *Journal of Clinical Psychiatry, 71*(8), 1097–1098. https://doi.org/10.4088/JCP.10ac06272

Chapter 26

Guided Imagery and Guided Meditation

Senona Kalappa School of Liberal Studies (SLS), CMR University, Bangalore

Introduction

We all experience some level of stress in our daily life. This could be triggered by many situations. Stress is a normal body response. When the body fails to control the stressful stimuli, it is known as anxiety. To control the same, one of the techniques used by psychotherapists is Guided imagery. The constant stress in one's life can take a huge toll or his health, both mental and physical. This in turn, makes it very difficult to feel relaxed or calm. During these cases, Guided imagery comes for the rescue.

Meditation is a very powerful tool used to reduce the level of stress in the individual. This also improves focus and attention and promotes overall well-being in the client. Both physical and mental well-being. Guided meditation involves focusing on the client's breathing, concentrating on the thoughts without any kind of judgement. This involves a step-by-step instruction given by the guide that one needs to follow. Guided meditation helps in these aspects.

Guided imagery, known by other names like 'katathym-imaginative psychotherapy' or even 'guided affective imagery' is a mind-body intervention that a therapist uses to help the client overcome obstacles of life with ease. A psychotherapist or a trained practitioner helps the individual generate images in the mind that stimulate all the sensory perceptions like sight, smell, taste, movement, sound.

Guided imagery has many names attached to it namely visualization or even guided meditation. Guided imagery can be helpful in many ways, it helps reduce the stress levels in a person, promotes a sense of positive well-being etc. The technique is done consciously, meaning the individual visualizes a positive, reliable, peaceful scenario or image.

Relaxation techniques like this one are generally very safe to use without any repercussions. The main aim of Guided imagery is to promote the body's natural relaxation response time. This could be measured by certain physiological changes like, number of breaths per minute is lowered, the blood pressure is decreased, the heart rate is reduced etc.

Applications of Guided Imagery and Guided Meditation

Post-Traumatic Stress Disorder (PTSD)

PTSD starts from when the individual witnesses a traumatic event firsthand. This includes events like death of a loved one, significant threat to others or to the self, or the experience of any serious injury. These images are intrusive and is described by the patient as flashbacks from the event. This is common across all demographics. This mental image provokes memory of the original event. This is accompanied by heightened emotions and the subject experiences of threat to the individual in the present.

Social Anxiety

These individuals experience higher than normal tendency of fear, especially situations that involve public attention. This could be when the individual has to speak in front of a audience, meeting and talking to new people, attending events that could be unpredictable or when the limelight is on the individual. In this case, the negative memory that the individual has experienced could be shame, awkwardness, or embarrassment. Mental images contribute widely to the persistence and maintenance of social anxiety too. The mental imageries are described as the 'observer perspective' by the cognitive psychologists. These kinds of images are also common among those having anxiety. These individuals usually have a very depleting ability to produce positive, pleasant, or neutral imageries.

Depression

The ability to evoke positive affirmations either through voluntary or involuntary practices is difficult. Sustained positive mood and optimistic mindset is often found impaired especially with those who have depression. This includes cognitive impairment and emotional distress which may include feeling hopeless and pessimism, pervasive sadness, reduced motivation, social isolation and withdrawal, difficulty to concentrate on physical and mental tasks, decreased sleep etc. when we hear depression, we associate it with recurrence of negative verbal thoughts but almost more than 90% of individuals with depression, report mental imageries that often simulate the previously the previously experienced negative experiences. These negative emotions are usually hyped or intensified by the depressed individuals which leads to the hopelessness and despair. The mental images created by these individuals are usually images related to suicide which are referred to as flash-forwards by some psychiatrists or psychologists.

Bipolar disorder

The bipolar disorder is characterized by periods of mania and depression. In this case, almost 90% of people experience some sort of comorbid anxiety disorder at any stage of the bipolar disorder. Because of the same, the suicide rate is very prevalent among this population. Mental images that are indicative of mania or hyperactivity and hopelessness significantly contribute to the depressive or manic episodes in bipolar disorder.

Principles of Guided Imagery Techniques

The guided imagery technique uses other methods too, such as receptive music therapy, guided meditation, and many other relaxation techniques as well. It also uses physical medication, psychotherapy, and rehabilitation in extreme cases. All these methods aim to psycho-educate the individual about modifying the mental images, altering the images that give pain give more flashbacks of the events that were more distressing and those that intensify the emotions of hopelessness or and not induce emotions of optimism and positivity.

The guided imagery whether provided by a facilitator or given in-person, or through the audio-visual medium, through verbal instructions, that are intended to direct the attention to the tactile, auditory, gustatory, or olfactory sensation that induce positive emotions or responses, all these enhance physical and mental relaxation and reduce the amount of physical and mental stress in the individual.

All the above outcomes are desired by the individual himself and the therapist and practitioners as well, these results are achieved by the use of guided imagery technique. These also involve encouraging and motivating the client to imagine an altered thought, perspective or image that is more towards the positive side. For the client too, all these mechanisms will increase the chances of them developing some more positive copying mechanisms.

Stages or Steps

Image generation:

This involves generating or producing new mental images. This could be done through any sensory receptors and/or perceptual experiences, through fantasies experienced by the individual on a day-to-day basis or even extracted from the short-term memory or the long-term memory.

Image maintenance

As the name suggests, this involves the maintaining of the imagery. Without this there would be a rapid decline in the mental image formed in the mind of the individal. This could be at a whooping speed of less than 250 milliseconds. There are many reasons for the same to occur. It usually happens to avoid any kind of disruption in the process of sensory perception of anything.

This stage is very important for the other preceding stages like the image inspection stage and the image transformation stage to follow up which requires a lot of attention and concentration to process.

Image inspection

Once the above-mentioned steps are taken, there is room for the process of image inspection and image transformation now. This process is usually done to scan the image. By doing so, the individual focusses around and across the image which helps in the perceptual process. The image inspection process helps with both, the images created in response to verbal description given by the practitioner and the spontaneous image generated.

Image transformation

With the assistance given by the practitioner of guided imagery, the client will often modify and transform the verbal instructions given by them in order to create images in the mind. This is done so that the negative and provoking mental images produce can be substituted to the more positive emotions that are resourceful and helps the individual cope with the negative images produced. This technique is also used during the process of cognitive behavioral therapy (CBT) too. Although may researched have focused more on the visual mental imagery, there is also some amount of evidence that backs up the auditory and haptic imagery as well.

Benefits of Guided Imagery and Guided Meditation

Relieves pain and boosts immunity:

Since stress has this wired ability to worsen the perception of pain, this technique of guided meditation and guided imagery helps the individual 'distract' from the pain he or she is going through. This technique helps in managing the pain causing symptoms as well. For example, if a person with arthritis experiences a lot of discomfort, pain and inflammation in his joints, he might opt for some psychosocial strategies that can help him cope with the same. It can also have other benefits like less fatigue experienced and decreased levels of stress in the individual. Some researchers have also shown that a combination of guided imagery and progressive muscle relaxation technique, helps with the easing of pain among cancer patients. It also improves the immune functioning in the body of the individual hence protecting him against disease and different types of illness.

Alleviates stress and anxiety:

Stress affects the brain and the body too; this technique helps with the relieving of chronic stress in the individual. Some studies have also shown that the technique have helped in the reduction of short and/or long-term stress among pregnant teenagers. It has also been found that there are decreased levels of cortisol (stress hormone) in the saliva.

Helps quit smoking:

Smoking is one of the leading causes of death in many countries. Research has shown that using the guided imagery and guided meditation technique is very practical for copying with smoking addiction or any other addiction for that matter.

Decreases depressive symptoms, promotes well-being:

The appearance of negative images is very important for the individual to go to this state. One study on people having hemodialysis suggested that these individuals commonly have anxiety and depression. The study found that those individuals who underwent guided imagery had lower levels of anxiety in depression. It also suggested the same for patients having cancer as well. It helps promote happiness and positive and well-being which harness the inner peace in the individual. It also promotes positive emotions like love, gratitude, compassion etc.

Improves sleep quality:

A lot of people who undergo surgery for example have trouble falling asleep or to stay asleep, guided imagery has proven to help in these aspects as well. With some people, this technique has also helped solve their insomnia. It is also clear that mindfulness meditation helps improve and harness the body's response to stress as well. It helps you with the quality of sleep that u have and reduce the trouble of falling asleep. Increased sleep quality helps promote cognitive functions, boosts mood, reduced the risk of getting a chronic disease etc.

Increases self-awareness, focus and concentration:

Guided imagery and guided meditation help the individual with focus and concentration which would one complete his deadlines and achieve his goals better and faster. This also improves self-awareness which helps gain a better and deeper understanding of the thoughts, behaviors, and emotions that one is going through. This helps with having a greater sense of compassion towards self and have a positive impact on the individual's life.

Case Studies

Case Study 1: Reducing trauma symptoms in refugee Adolescents with Guided Imagery and Trauma-Focused Cognitive Behavioral Therapy (TF-CBT)

Client Details

Name: 10 refugee adolescents

Age: between 14 – 18 years

Educational background: college

Socio-economic background:

- war refugees
- low-income background
- diverse ethnicity (middle eastern and African refugees)

Chief complaints:

- Classic symptoms of PTSD
- Flashbacks
- Hyperarousal
- Avoidance
- Social isolation
- Having guilt and fear
- Traumatic experiences from war, violence, displacement

Duration of treatment:

12-week group therapy (TF-CBT plus guided imagery)

Treatment goals:

- Reduce trauma symptoms
- Increase emotional stability
- Participant should feel safe and empowered
- Cognitive reconstruction
- Emotional regulation
- Increase optimism
- Enhance resilience
- Regulate positive visualizations

Therapeutic Approach:

1. **Trauma-focused cognitive behavioral therapy (TF-CBT)**

   The refugee adolescents participated in the Trauma-focused cognitive behavioral therapy (TF-CBT). This technique helps them learn about the trauma that they are undergoing. The therapy also helped them with certain types of coping skills for the same. Different methods of coping were addressed to regulate the emotional responses and the intrusive memories that bothered them. This technique also helped them with their Cognitive reconstruction. This cognitive reconstruction helped the adolescent refugees to work the thought of guilt and fear that was associated with the whole displacement, violence, killing and war experience.

   - Group Setting: Adolescents engaged in group sessions, where they learned about the effects of trauma, developing a shared understanding that reduced feelings of isolation.
   - Psychoeducation and Coping Skills: Participants were taught to recognize the physiological and psychological impact of trauma, building awareness of their symptoms and triggers. The therapist introduced coping skills to manage stress responses, which included grounding techniques, breathing exercises, and muscle relaxation.
   - Cognitive Restructuring: Through cognitive restructuring exercises, participants worked on identifying and challenging negative or distorted thoughts related to their experiences, such as self-blame or fear. The group explored healthier ways to view their trauma, reducing feelings of guilt and increasing self-compassion.

2. **Guided imagery**

   During the guided imagery sessions, each refugee participant visualized a "safe place" that they could mentally whenever they feel stressed, at any time. For some of the participants, this mental safe space was the memory of their home or a peaceful scenery that they visited, or their village, or a shopping mall scene with their loved on or a birthday celebration they had with the family just before the war displacement. Some of them visualized their childhood, when they played with the toys with their siblings that they had lost during the war or displacement period. For each individual it was different.

   The later sessions focused on the visualizations of the future, that they anticipated to be more positive and far from war like situations. They felt a lot safer and more empowered which helped them overcome the challenges faster. This also built a more positive outlook towards life and bought resilience in them. The combination of Trauma-Focused Cognitive Behavioral Therapy (TF-CBT) and guided imagery in treating refugee adolescents can be highly effective, particularly given the complex trauma and instability many of these youths have experienced. These approaches target multiple facets of trauma like physiological responses (hyperarousal), cognitive restructuring (working through guilt and fear), and emotional regulation through grounding techniques like guided imagery.

   - Creating a "Safe Place": Guided imagery was used as a mental anchor, where each adolescent visualized a place where they felt safe and calm. This "safe place" was tailored to each participant's preferences, often drawing on comforting memories of home, peaceful natural scenes, or imagined sanctuaries. This practice helped them access a sense of peace and grounding during moments of distress.

   - Future-Oriented Visualization: In later sessions, the therapist guided participants through exercises in which they visualized themselves overcoming challenges and thriving in their new environment. These visualizations helped participants imagine a positive future, one in which they could see themselves feeling safe, empowered, and capable of achieving their goals.

Observed Outcomes

- Reduction in Trauma Symptoms: TF-CBT's structured approach enables adolescents to process their trauma in a safe, supportive group setting. By combining psychoeducation and skill-building, TF-CBT helps participants understand their trauma responses and reduce intrusive symptoms like flashbacks. Guided imagery, particularly the mental creation of a "safe place," serves as an effective grounding technique, giving them a tool to use during moments of distress.
- Emotional Stability: Building a personal "safe place" through guided imagery allows participants to cultivate a sense of control over their emotional states. This technique empowers them to self-regulate and reduce anxiety when facing triggering situations, fostering a sense of resilience and autonomy.
- Increased Optimism and Resilience: Visualizing a positive future helps these adolescents move beyond survival mode, encouraging them to think about their goals and potential. This mindset shift is essential for fostering resilience and motivation, particularly as they adapt to life in a new environment with different cultural and societal expectations.

Qualitative Feedback and Reflections

- Participants described their mental "safe place" as a valuable personal refuge. Many noted that this visualization technique became an important part of their emotional toolkit, enabling them to cope independently outside of therapy sessions. Several adolescents expressed that, for the first time since their traumatic experiences, they felt a renewed sense of hope and a vision for their future.
- Additionally, the group therapy format allowed for shared experiences, reducing feelings of isolation, and fostering a supportive community among the adolescents. Knowing that they were not alone in their experiences was a powerful aspect of healing and resilience-building.

Conclusion

This 12-week intervention shows promising outcomes by integrating trauma processing with emotional regulation and positive visualization, providing a comprehensive framework to help refugee adolescents manage symptoms and envision a brighter future. Future considerations could involve individual follow-ups and integration with community resources to reinforce the skills learned during therapy.

This case study underscores the potential of combining TF-CBT and guided imagery in a group setting to support refugee adolescents in coping with trauma. The intervention's success suggests that similar programs could be implemented in other refugee support settings to improve mental health outcomes for young individuals dealing with complex trauma. Future programs might consider extending follow-up sessions to reinforce learned skills and ensure the continued support of participants as they face ongoing adaptation challenges. Integration with additional community resources, such as school support systems and mentorship programs, could further support these adolescents' paths to stability and empowerment.

These two techniques also helped reduce the symptoms of trauma of many participants. Many of the adolescents, reported that post-therapy, they had fewer flashbacks and decreased the hyperarousal symptoms. They felt that guided imagery and trauma-focused cognitive behavioral therapy helped them combat the situation better and in turn helped cope with the separate from their traumatic moments. This also helped to increase the levels of optimism amongst the refugees. The combination of these two techniques namely the trauma-focused cognitive behavioral therapy and guided imagery, helped participants visualize and more positive outlook towards their future which also fostered hope in them, which was especially impactful given their challenging experiences.

Case Study 2: Chronic pain management among older adults

Client Details

Name: 40 older adults

Age: 60 to 75 years old

Socio-economic background:

- mostly low-income families
- racial background – 50% African American, 30% Caucasian, 20% Hispanic

Treatment setting: pain clinic in a urban hospital in the United States

Chief complaints:

- Chronic musculoskeletal pain
- Arthritis
- Back pain
- Fibromyalgia
- Sleep disturbances

Duration of treatment: 3 months; each session 60 mins of guided imagery

Treatment goals:

- reduce pain intensity
- improved sleep quality
- reduce pain perception
- empower to manage pain

Therapeutic Approach:

1. **Guided imagery technique**

   Each session of the whole 3 months period began with the relaxation techniques which included deep breathing. This helped the client enter a state of calm. Each session was 60 minutes long. They were then guided to visualize that their pain is moving away, they visualized soothing. They also visualized pain-relieving scenes like lying down on the beach with the warm sunlight kissing their muscles that relieved their pain, or them floating on the gentle waves of the beach which supported and soothed their pain. As the participants focused on the pain-relieving scenes, they were motivated to focus on the sensation of warmth, relaxation and lightness which helped create a physical sense of relief from their pain symptoms. This was designed to evoke feelings of warmth and relaxation, helping to alleviate pain.

2. **At-home practices**

   Participants were provided with a recording of the guided imagery sessions, that were easy to use which they could play at home and practice them when they felt the pain and couldn't come to the clinic. This allowed them to practice the technique daily which gave them better and quicker results. This at-home practice was essential, especially for those who experienced pain flare-ups between sessions. This reinforced the technique's benefits between sessions.

Outcomes

- Pain reduction: post 3 months of the guided imagery sessions, the participants reported an average of 25 % reduction of the pain intensity and not the pain perception. This was measured using the Numerical Pain Raring Scale (NPRS). This is a standardized test to measure pain severity. The scale also indicated that there was a substantial improvement by the technique used to manage the same.
- Improved sleep quality: many of the participants reported that they have better sleep after they have engaged themselves in the guided imagery sessions. This also gave fewer interruptions during sleep because of the pain. Meaning, it reduced the night-time interruptions that they experienced which allowed them to have a restful sleep as through the night.
- Empowerment and coping: qualitative feedback given by the participants revealed that they had regained a sense of control over their pain, that they experienced. Because of the limited access to different types of medical interventions, the participants appreciated and preferred the non-pharmaceutical approach, as this technique provided a new method to get some relief from pain. It was also useful as it gave access to independent use of the method even without any assistance whenever they perceived pain.

Case Study 3: Managing Emotional Dysregulation in Adolescents with Guided Imagery and Dialectical Behavior Therapy (DBT)

Client Details

Name: MIA

Age: 17 years old

Sex: female

Educational background: high school student

Socio-economic background:

- lower-middle class
- lives with her mother
- mother also has history of depression

Chief complaints:

- Emotional dysfunction
- Intense mood swings
- Impulsive behavior exhibited
- Has trouble at school and home

Duration of treatment: 16-weeks of DBT with guided imagery integrated over the last 8 - weeks

Treatment goals:

- Emotion regulation
- Reduce impulsivity
- Develop distress tolerance

Therapeutic Approach:

1. **Dialectical Behavior Therapy (DBT)**

   MIA was taught techniques used in DBT which included emotion regulation and distress tolerance skills. This helped her manage and understand her own intense emotional reactions which reduced her likelihood of impulsive reactions. This included therapy technique like stop, take a break, observe and proceed mindfully. This was employed while the client experienced moments of strong emotional arousal. With a lot of practice, MIA could apply the Dialectical Behavior Therapy (DBT) strategies more effectively in real-life situations which improved her self-awareness and control over her emotional responses.

2. **Guided imagery**

   During the final 8-weeks of MIA's therapy, her therapist introduced her to the technique of guided imagery exercises in which MIA could visualize a safe and calming place which she visited mentally whenever she felt and seemed overwhelmed. This could be anything like a cozy room or a natural scene.

During the guided imagery sessions MIA practiced the techniques all by herself which helped her cope with her emotional challenges which increased her confidence in using the DBT technique all by herself, independently. This technique was used as a supplementary tool that helped regulate her emotions. Through this technique, MIA practiced imagining herself able to handle the emotional challenges that she encountered successfully. This boosted her confidence and reinforced her ability to use the DBT skills under pressure.

Outcomes

- Improved Emotional Regulation: MIA reported that she could identify her emotions earlier and reduce their intensity before they escalated to impulsive actions like lasing out verbally or physically.
- Enhanced Distress Tolerance: Guided imagery provided Mia with an internal "safe space," a mental anchor that she perceived which helped her endure moments of distress without immediately reacting.
- Better Relationships: As MIA's emotional regulation improved, so did her relationship with her mother. She learned to respond to conflicts with calmness and understanding, reducing tensions and fostering a more positive home environment. MIA's relationship with her mother improved, as she began responding with more calmness and understanding during conflicts.

References

Guided Imagery vs. Guided Meditation: Unravelling the Differences. (2023, June 19). The Healing Mind.https://thehealingmind.org/blogs/the-healing-mind-audio-and-video-sessions/guided-imagery-vs-guided-meditation

Harden, R. N., Oaklander, A. L., Burton, A. W., & Perez, R. S. G. M (2013). Complex Regional Pain Syndrome: Practical Diagnostic and Treatment Guidelines, 4th edition. *Pain Medicine, 14*(2), 180–229. https://doi.org/10.1111/pme.12033

LeBoff, M. S., Greenspan, S. L., Insogna, K. L., Lewiecki, E. M., Saag, K. G., Singer, A. J., & Siris, E. S. (2022). The clinician's guide to prevention and treatment of osteoporosis. *Osteoporosis International, 33*(10), 2049–2102. https://doi.org/10.1007/s00198-021-05900-y

Meierhenrich, J. (2007). The trauma of genocide. *Journal of Genocide Research, 9*(4), 549–573. https://doi.org/10.1080/14623520701643327

Nunez, K. (2020, September 10). *The benefits of guided imagery and how to do it.* Healthline. https://www.healthline.com/health/guided-imagery#tips-for-beginners

Steward, M. (2024, September 27). *What is Guided Meditation?* THE MINDFUL STEWARD. https://themindfulsteward.com/meditation/what-is-guided-meditation/

Verduijn, N., & Vincken, M. (2014). Judith Cohen, Anthony Mannarino & Esther Deblinger (red.) (2012). Trauma-Focused CBT for children and adolescents: treatment applications. New York: Guilford Press. 308 p., € 38,95. *Tijdschrift Voor Psychotherapie*, *40*(3), 236–238. https://doi.org/10.1007/s12485-014-0031-2

West, M. (2022, April 21). *What to know about guided imagery.* https://www.medicalnewstoday.com/articles/guided-imagery#tips

Wikipedia contributors. (2023, December 27). Guided imagery. Wikipedia. https://en.wikipedia.org/wiki/Guided_imagery

Chapter 27

Hellenistic Therapy - Greek Philosophical Approaches

Surashree Dey School of Liberal Studies (SLS), CMR University, Bangalore

Introduction

Hellenistic therapy represents a therapeutic approach that seamlessly integrates ancient Greek philosophical thought with contemporary psychotherapeutic techniques. Drawing primarily from the intellectual traditions of the Hellenistic period (circa 323–31 BCE), this form of therapy utilizes the wisdom of prominent Greek philosophers such as Socrates, Plato, and Aristotle. Hellenistic therapy stands at the intersection of philosophical exploration and modern psychological treatment, offering a holistic model of mental well-being.

By incorporating cognitive restructuring, mindfulness practices, and emotional resilience, it presents an opportunity to heal not just the symptoms of psychological distress but also to cultivate a deeper understanding of one's emotional and cognitive landscape.

Historical Context and Background

The foundation of Hellenistic therapy is built upon the rich intellectual legacy of Greek philosophy, especially during the period following the death of Alexander the Great in 323 BCE, known as the Hellenistic era. This era marked a time of cultural and intellectual expansion, as Greek influence spread across the Mediterranean, blending with local philosophies and religions. In this environment, philosophical schools emerged that would lay the groundwork for modern therapeutic practices.

Philosophical Foundations of Hellenistic Therapy

Socratic Philosophy

Socrates, one of the earliest Greek philosophers, introduced a method of philosophical inquiry now known as the "Socratic method," which is central to the development of modern psychotherapy. This method involved dialectical questioning to uncover assumptions and challenge prevailing beliefs. Socrates emphasized the importance of self-knowledge and personal responsibility in achieving inner peace. His approach laid the groundwork for what would later be known as cognitive restructuring, a cornerstone of cognitive behavioral therapy (CBT).

Platonism and the Theory of the Soul Plato

Socrates' student introduced the idea of the soul's tripartite nature—reason, spirit, and appetite—concepts that align with modern psychological theories of the mind. Plato's emphasis on the harmony of the soul suggests that mental well-being arises when reason governs the emotions and desires. This idea resonates with contemporary psychotherapeutic practices that aim to restore balance and alignment between the conscious and unconscious mind.

Aristotle's Nicomachean Ethics

Aristotle's virtue ethics, particularly his notion of achieving eudaimonia (flourishing or well-being), is highly influential in Hellenistic therapy. Aristotle argued that happiness is the result of living a life in accordance with virtue—rational activity and self-control. This philosophy strongly parallels modern psychotherapeutic goals of helping individuals live a meaningful, purpose-driven life by promoting emotional regulation and rational thinking.

Stoicism

The Stoics, including Zeno of Citium, Epictetus, and Marcus Aurelius, profoundly shaped Hellenistic therapy. The Stoic emphasis on controlling one's reactions, accepting what is beyond control, and cultivating virtues such as courage, wisdom, and temperance directly aligns with the principles of modern psychotherapy. Stoic practices are foundational to contemporary therapeutic techniques like mindfulness, acceptance, and commitment therapy (ACT), as well as cognitive behavioural strategies.

Epicureanism

Epicurus, a philosopher who espoused the pursuit of pleasure and the avoidance of pain, emphasized the importance of seeking tranquility through self-reflection and moderation. His views echo the modern therapeutic principles of self-care, stress management, and emotional resilience, emphasizing balance and personal contentment.

The Rise of Psychotherapy in the Western Traditions

The philosophical insights of the Hellenistic period began to influence Western thought and practice centuries later, especially during the development of modern psychology and psychotherapy in the 19th and 20th centuries. The emergence of psychoanalysis, cognitive-behavioural therapy (CBT), humanistic psychology, and existential psychotherapy drew from ancient philosophical practices but adapted them into structured therapeutic frameworks.

Psychoanalysis

Sigmund Freud's psychoanalytic theory emphasised the importance of unconscious processes and early childhood experiences in shaping the human psyche. While distinct from Hellenistic therapy in its focus on the unconscious, some aspects of psychoanalysis, such as the exploration of unconscious beliefs and emotional conflicts, echo Socratic self-exploration and the pursuit of self-knowledge.

Cognitive Behavioural Therapy (CBT)

Aaron T. Beck and Albert Ellis, shares significant overlap with Stoicism, particularly in its focus on identifying irrational beliefs and replacing them with more rational thoughts. The use of Socratic questioning in CBT mirrors the dialectical approach of Socrates, emphasising the importance of self-examination and logical reasoning in overcoming emotional distress.

Humanistic and Existential Therapy

These therapeutic approaches, associated with figures such as Carl Rogers and Viktor Frankl, share a focus on the individual's search for meaning and personal growth, aligning with Aristotle's notion of flourishing (eudaimonia) and the Stoic emphasis on virtue and personal responsibility.

Hellenistic therapy draws from these rich historical traditions, synthesizing philosophical principles with psychotherapeutic methods to offer a contemporary approach to mental health. The therapy's dual focus on emotional regulation and self-reflection provides a comprehensive and adaptive framework for addressing psychological challenges.

Principles of Hellenistic Therapy

Cognitive Restructuring Influenced by Socratic questioning and Stoic thought, cognitive restructuring is a central element of Hellenistic therapy. It involves identifying and challenging irrational beliefs that contribute to emotional distress. The therapist guides the client in examining their thoughts and replacing dysfunctional patterns with more rational and adaptive ones.

Emotional Regulation Drawing heavily from Stoicism, Hellenistic therapy emphasises emotional resilience. Clients are encouraged to accept what is outside their control while focusing on cultivating virtues like patience, self-control, and emotional detachment. By practising mindfulness and reflection, individuals learn to regulate their emotional responses to external events.

Virtue and Flourishing Like Aristotle's concept of eudaimonia, Hellenistic therapy aims at promoting well-being through the cultivation of virtues such as wisdom, courage, and temperance. The therapy encourages individuals to lead lives in alignment with their values, promoting long-term fulfilment and happiness.

Mindfulness and Reflection inspired by both Stoic practices and modern mindfulness techniques, Hellenistic therapy encourages clients to develop a present-centred awareness. Through regular self-reflection and mindfulness practices, individuals gain greater insight into their thoughts and emotions, fostering greater self-awareness and psychological flexibility.

Therapeutic Techniques

Socratic Questioning

This technique is central to both Hellenistic therapy and cognitive-behavioural therapy (CBT). Therapists using Socratic questioning help clients identify and challenge irrational beliefs by prompting them to reflect on their thought processes critically. While Socrates is credited with the original method, Albert Ellis, founder of Rational Emotive Behaviour Therapy (REBT), and Aaron T. Beck, creator of Cognitive Therapy (later CBT), adapted Socratic questioning techniques in the 20th century. Ellis, influenced by Stoicism, developed REBT to challenge irrational beliefs actively, and Beck used Socratic questioning to guide clients toward cognitive restructuring.

Cognitive Restructuring

Derived from the Stoic principle that "it is not things that upset us, but our judgments about them" (Epictetus), cognitive restructuring involves identifying and modifying irrational thoughts. By recognizing that their responses to situations are influenced by their own interpretations, clients learn to reframe distressing thoughts into more constructive perspectives.

Aaron Beck's work in developing Cognitive Therapy emphasised the importance of re-evaluating maladaptive thoughts. His cognitive restructuring method has become a foundational practice in CBT, widely used to treat anxiety, depression, and various mood disorders.

Mindfulness and Negative Visualisation

Inspired by Stoic techniques, mindfulness in Hellenistic therapy involves practising present-moment awareness to foster resilience and acceptance. Negative visualisation, a Stoic exercise, asks individuals to imagine adverse events to prepare for potential challenges and better appreciate positive experiences.

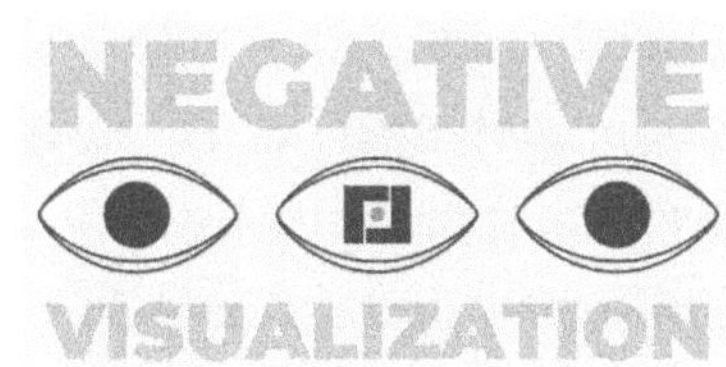

Values-Based Living

Emphasising Aristotle's idea of 'eudaimonia', or living according to one's values, Hellenistic therapy incorporates values clarification exercises to help clients identify and act according to their core principles. Therapists assist clients in recognizing what truly matters to them, guiding them toward purposeful and fulfilling lives.

Viktor Frankl, the founder of logotherapy, was influenced by Greek philosophy and believed that meaning and purpose are central to human well-being. Frankl's approach aligns with the Aristotelian view of a meaningful life, integrating purpose-oriented therapy that encourages individuals to align their actions with their values.

Dichotomy of Control

The Stoic practice of distinguishing between what is within one's control and what is not helps clients focus on factors they can influence, reducing anxiety about external circumstances. This exercise is fundamental in Hellenistic therapy for helping clients accept things outside their control, ultimately fostering a sense of peace and resilience.

Modern psychologists like William James and Carl Rogers contributed indirectly to this idea through their emphasis on self-acceptance and personal agency.

Modern Practitioners and Influences

Albert Ellis, inspired by Stoic philosophy, developed Rational Emotive Behaviors Therapy (REBT) to address irrational beliefs. He incorporated the Stoic approach of examining one's judgments to foster emotional resilience and cognitive restructuring. Ellis's techniques are foundational to many therapeutic practices today, especially those focusing on reducing irrational thought patterns. *Aaron T. Beck*, often regarded as the father of cognitive therapy, Beck used Socratic questioning and cognitive restructuring to address depression, anxiety, and other psychological challenges. His therapy model emphasizes examining core beliefs, challenging irrational thoughts, and replacing them with healthier interpretations. Beck's work, deeply rooted in the principles of Hellenistic philosophy, remains one of the most widely applied methods in contemporary psychotherapy. *Donald Robertson* is a modern therapist and writer who integrates Stoicism directly with cognitive-behavioural techniques, particularly in his work with anxiety and emotional resilience. His book, '*How to Think Like a Roman Emperor*', draws connections between Stoic practices and therapeutic techniques, demonstrating how ancient philosophy can enhance mental well-being.

Therapeutic Process

Initial Assessment and Value Exploration

The first step in Hellenistic Therapy involves an in-depth assessment of the client's background, challenges, and personal values. The therapist works with the client to identify the specific issues they are facing and any underlying beliefs, values, and goals. This value exploration draws from Aristotle's notion of eudaimonia (flourishing or well-being) and focuses on the concept of virtuous living, guiding clients to clarify what matters most to them. In practice, this phase may involve reflective questioning and values clarification exercises that encourage clients to examine their priorities and identify potential discrepancies between their beliefs and actions.

Identifying Cognitive Distortions

Once core values have been identified, the therapist and client explore any cognitive distortions or maladaptive beliefs that may be contributing to emotional distress. This stage is deeply influenced by Stoic philosophy, particularly Epictetus's teaching that "it is not things themselves that disturb people, but their judgments about those things." By helping clients recognize how their thoughts influence their emotional responses, therapists guide them toward more rational interpretations of challenging situations. Techniques like Socratic questioning are used in this stage to challenge and reframe irrational beliefs.

Cognitive Restructuring and Reframing

Building on the identification of cognitive distortions, cognitive restructuring focuses on actively changing irrational thoughts and beliefs. The therapist works with the client to replace self-defeating or distressing thoughts with more constructive, reality-based alternatives. In doing so, clients learn to adjust their emotional reactions and cultivate a more resilient mindset. This stage resonates strongly with Stoicism's dichotomy of control, which distinguishes between what individuals can control and what they cannot. By focusing on factors within their control—such as their reactions, beliefs, and choices—clients can let go of unrealistic expectations or anxieties about uncontrollable events. The cognitive restructuring process is a cornerstone of Hellenistic Therapy and aligns with cognitive-behavioural approaches in modern psychotherapy.

Practising Mindfulness and Negative Visualisation

Mindfulness practices are introduced to help clients manage stress and focus on the present moment, a technique rooted in both Hellenistic and contemporary therapeutic practices. Inspired by Stoic practices of acceptance and present-mindedness, clients are encouraged to engage in mindfulness exercises, paying close attention to their thoughts, emotions, and physical sensations without judgement. Negative visualisation, a Stoic exercise, involves imagining potential negative outcomes in a controlled and intentional way. This practice helps individuals mentally prepare for adversity, building resilience and gratitude.

Values-Based Living and Setting Purposeful Goals

Hellenistic Therapy encourages clients to translate their values into concrete, meaningful goals that align with their broader life purpose. This stage, influenced by Aristotle's focus on eudaimonia, aims to help clients pursue virtuous living, emphasising actions that align with their values.

Application of Hellenistic Therapy

Anxiety and Depression:

Hellenistic Therapy helps individuals with anxiety and depression by identifying irrational beliefs and reframing negative thoughts. Through techniques like Socratic questioning and cognitive restructuring, clients learn to view their situations more realistically, reducing distress.

Stress Management:

The Stoic practices of mindfulness and the dichotomy of control are particularly effective in stress management. By focusing on aspects within their control, clients can develop healthy coping strategies and let go of unrealistic expectations or fears about uncontrollable events.

Life Transitions and Grief:

Hellenistic Therapy aids individuals during major life transitions, such as divorce, loss, or career change. Stoic principles encourage acceptance and resilience in the face of change, helping clients build coping skills that can alleviate stress and improve emotional well-being.

Building Self-Esteem and Purpose:

By emphasising values-based living, Hellenistic Therapy enables clients to identify their core values and develop self-worth independent of external validation. Clients learn to pursue meaningful goals aligned with their values, enhancing their sense of purpose and fulfilment.

Strengths and Challenges of Hellenistic Therapy

Strengths

- ***Holistic Approach***: Hellenistic Therapy integrates ancient wisdom with evidence-based psychotherapy, offering a comprehensive approach that emphasises both emotional and philosophical resilience.
- ***Focus on Values and Purpose***: By encouraging clients to pursue values-based goals, Hellenistic Therapy promotes long-term fulfilment and personal growth, offering more than symptom reduction.
- ***Versatility***: Techniques from Hellenistic Therapy can be applied across a range of psychological issues, from anxiety and depression to stress and grief, making it adaptable and accessible.
- ***Practicality***: Many of the techniques, such as cognitive restructuring and mindfulness, are practical and actionable, equipping clients with skills to handle life's challenges outside of therapy.

Weaknesses

- ***Complexity in Integrating Philosophy***: Some clients may find it challenging to connect with ancient Greek concepts, requiring therapists to adapt these ideas to modern contexts and diverse cultural backgrounds.
- ***Potential Overemphasis on Rationality***: Hellenistic Therapy's focus on rationality may inadvertently neglect emotional expression, potentially limiting its effectiveness for clients who need more affective-based approaches.
- ***Dependence on Self-Reflection Skills***: Techniques like Socratic questioning and values clarification require a certain level of self-reflection and cognitive engagement, which may be challenging for clients unfamiliar with introspection.
- ***Adaptation Challenges for Therapists***: Therapists need a deep understanding of both philosophy and psychology to integrate Hellenistic Therapy effectively, requiring specialised training and commitment to philosophical principles.

Hellenistic Therapy: Case Studies

Case Study 1: Overcoming Anxiety and Regaining Control

Background

Maria, a 32-year-old elementary school teacher from a middle-class urban background, experienced increasing anxiety, particularly around professional responsibilities and personal relationships. A high-achiever, Maria was often overwhelmed by perfectionism and self-doubt, feeling pressure to maintain high standards. These anxieties stemmed partly from her upbringing in a family that emphasized hard work and success, with limited tolerance for failure.

Therapeutic Process

Through Socratic questioning, Maria explored the origins of her beliefs about success and self-worth. She discovered that she often tied her sense of value to her achievements and approval from others.

Inspired by Stoic principles, Maria began practising the "dichotomy of control," focusing on actions within her control (such as her effort and attitude) and letting go of external validation.

Discussion

By distinguishing between factors within and beyond her control, Maria gradually reduced her stress and gained a sense of agency. Socratic questioning helped her identify irrational beliefs about perfection, and cognitive restructuring allowed her to replace self-critical thoughts with self-compassionate ones.

Conclusion

Maria's progress highlights the effectiveness of Hellenistic Therapy in managing anxiety by reframing self-perceptions and focusing on controllable factors. With continuous practice, she developed confidence and embraced self-worth beyond her achievements.

Case Study 2: Coping with Loss and Finding Purpose

Background

Alex, a 55-year-old construction worker from a lower socio-economic background, sought therapy following the loss of his spouse. As a father of three adult children, he felt a significant void and struggled with grief and feelings of purposelessness. Alex's childhood involved financial struggles, and his marriage had been a primary source of support and companionship.

Therapeutic Process

In therapy, Alex was introduced to the Stoic practice of mindfulness and negative visualisation, which helped him reflect on and accept life's uncertainties. Through discussions about values and purpose, Alex connected with the idea of eudaimonia (flourishing) from Aristotle, focusing on living in alignment with his values and responsibilities to his family. The therapist also encouraged Alex to explore new goals that gave him purpose, such as volunteering and participating in his local community.

Discussion

Alex's focus on values-based living helped him find meaning in his everyday actions. By engaging in activities that aligned with his values, he discovered purpose in nurturing his relationships with his children and contributing to his community. Practicing mindfulness also helped him cope with his grief by focusing on present experiences and accepting the reality of loss.

Conclusion

Alex's case illustrates how Hellenistic Therapy can help clients find purpose after loss by reconnecting them with their values and fostering acceptance. Through values-based goals, he was able to transform his grief into meaningful action, emphasising resilience and community support.

Case Study 3: Navigating Career Transition and Self-Worth

Background

Priya, a 40-year-old first-generation immigrant from a lower-middle-class family, worked in a corporate role for over a decade before her company downsized, resulting in her unexpected layoff. Priya's parents had sacrificed a great deal to support her education, and she held herself to high standards, believing that professional success was a testament to her family's hard work. The layoff left her feeling a sense of failure and uncertainty about her future.

Therapeutic Process

Hellenistic Therapy helped Priya confront her beliefs about success and self-worth through cognitive restructuring and Socratic questioning. By examining her beliefs, Priya recognized that she had internalized societal expectations about success and self-worth, and that these beliefs were not aligned with her personal values. The therapist guided her to identify her core values beyond work and explore potential goals that resonated with her sense of purpose.

Discussion

Priya engaged in the practice of values clarification, which allowed her to redefine success on her terms. She started exploring goals that aligned with her passions, such as volunteering in community education and mentoring youth, which offered her a renewed sense of purpose. Through mindfulness and reframing techniques, she learned to handle uncertainty without internalising it as a personal failure.

Conclusion

Priya's case illustrates the importance of values clarification in navigating career transitions. By disentangling her self-worth from external achievements, Priya embraced a broader perspective on personal fulfilment, empowering her to pursue meaningful, values-based goals.

Conclusion

Hellenistic Therapy offers a distinctive and comprehensive approach to mental health care by integrating ancient Western philosophy with modern psychotherapy. By guiding clients to cultivate inner resilience, identify core values, and set purposeful goals, Hellenistic Therapy fosters emotional stability and personal growth. Despite some limitations—such as the complexity of its philosophical foundations and the need for self-reflection skills—the therapeutic model remains highly effective for clients seeking a values-driven approach to well-being.

References

Aristotle. (1999). Nicomachean ethics (W. D. Ross, Trans.). The Internet Classics Archive. http://classics.mit.edu/Aristotle/nicomachaen.html

Beck, A. T. (1976). Cognitive therapy and the emotional disorders. International Universities Press.

Ellis, A. (2004). Rational emotive behaviour therapy: A therapist's guide. Springer.

Epictetus. (1995). The discourses of Epictetus. The Modern Library.

Frankl, V. E. (1985). Man's search for meaning. Beacon Press.

Hadot, P. (2002). The inner citadel: The meditations of Marcus Aurelius. Harvard University Press.

Robertson, D. (2019). How to think like a Roman emperor: The stoic philosophy of Marcus Aurelius. St. Martin's Press.

Seneca, L. A. (2004). Letters from a stoic (R. Campbell, Trans.). Penguin Classics.

Chapter 28

Hypnotherapy

Dr Monalisa Nayak, Sunanda Chowdhury School of Liberal Studies (SLS), CMR University, Bangalore

Therapeutic Hypnosis is a therapeutic technique that uses guided relaxation, focused attention, and suggestion to help individuals achieve a state of heightened awareness, known as hypnosis, in which they may become more open to addressing underlying psychological or behavioral issues (American Psychological Association [APA], 2013). This approach is often used to manage pain, reduce stress, improve focus, and treat various mental health conditions, like anxiety and phobias, by promoting positive behavioral changes (APA, 2013).

Therapeutic Hypnosis, also known as clinical hypnosis, is a form of therapy that employs hypnosis to create a state of focused attention and heightened suggestibility in patients. This altered state of consciousness can facilitate changes in perception, memory, and behavior (American Psychological Association [APA], 2013). Therapeutic Hypnosis often involves using verbal cues, guided imagery, and relaxation techniques to help individuals access their subconscious mind, enabling them to address various psychological issues, such as phobias, anxiety, depression, and habits like smoking or overeating (Elkins, 2017).

Benefits

Pain Management

Therapeutic Hypnosis has been widely recognized as an effective intervention for managing chronic pain, particularly in conditions like fibromyalgia, arthritis, and cancer. Studies show that hypnosis can alter pain perception by redirecting focus away from pain and reducing pain-related anxiety (Elkins, 2017; Jensen et al., 2015). Research indicates that hypnotherapy helps lower the intensity and frequency of pain, offering patients a non-pharmacological option to supplement medical treatments (Jensen, Patterson, & Gertz, 2015).

Anxiety and Stress Reduction

Therapeutic Hypnosis is effective in reducing symptoms of anxiety and stress by promoting a deep state of relaxation and increasing one's ability to cope with stressors (American Psychological Association [APA], 2013). During hypnosis, individuals can reframe negative thought patterns, which can significantly reduce stress levels and help manage conditions like generalized anxiety disorder and social anxiety disorder (Hammond, 2010).

Improvement in Sleep Quality

Therapeutic Hypnosis has shown promise in treating insomnia and other sleep disorders by helping individuals relax and overcome sleep disturbances. Hypnosis can help regulate sleep patterns and increase total sleep time, making it useful for both chronic and short-term insomnia (Elkins, 2017). According to studies, hypnotherapy aids in addressing underlying psychological issues that contribute to sleep disturbances, such as anxiety and depression (APA, 2013).

Behavioral Change and Habit Control

Therapeutic Hypnosis can support positive behavioral changes by influencing the subconscious mind, making it a helpful tool for modifying habits such as smoking, overeating, or excessive alcohol consumption. Hypnosis can enhance self-control and motivation by making individuals more receptive to behavioral suggestions (Green & Lynn, 2010). Studies show that it has been effective in smoking cessation programs, with some reporting higher success rates when combined with other therapeutic approaches (APA, 2013).

Support in Managing Gastrointestinal Disorders

Therapeutic Hypnosis has been found to be beneficial for managing symptoms of gastrointestinal disorders, particularly irritable bowel syndrome (IBS). Research has shown that hypnotherapy reduces IBS symptoms by modulating the brain-gut connection, reducing pain and discomfort, and helping patients manage stress-induced symptoms (Tan et al., 2015). Hypnosis has also been associated with long-term symptom relief for many patients with IBS (Gonsalkorale, 2006).

Enhanced Emotional Well-being

Therapeutic Hypnosis can improve emotional resilience and help people process trauma by creating a safe space for revisiting and reframing traumatic memories (Hammond, 2010). This therapeutic approach is often used in conjunction with other therapies to address post-traumatic stress disorder (PTSD) and other mood disorders, enhancing recovery and helping patients build coping mechanisms for emotional distress (APA, 2013).

History

The history of hypnotherapy spans centuries and has evolved significantly from its early origins to its status as a scientifically recognized therapeutic practice. Here is a detailed overview of its development:

Ancient Roots

Hypnotic-like practices can be traced back thousands of years to ancient civilizations. Ancient Egyptians and Greeks used forms of trance and meditation for healing, often invlving rituals that promoted deep relaxation and altered states of consciousness (American Psychological Association [APA], 2013).

18th Century: Mesmerism and the Foundations of Hypnosis

Modern hypnotherapy's roots are often credited to Franz Anton Mesmer, an 18th-century Austrian physician who developed "mesmerism." Mesmer theorized that an invisible fluid or "animal magnetism" existed within individuals, and he believed he could manipulate this fluid to cure ailments through the power of suggestion (Ellenberger, 1970).

19th Century: Scientific Exploration and Medical Recognition

In the 19th century, Scottish surgeon James Braid pioneered the scientific understanding of hypnosis by recognizing it as a psychological state rather than a mystical one. Braid introduced the term "hypnosis" (from the Greek word hypnos, meaning "sleep") and rejected Mesmer's theories, instead identifying hypnosis as a state of focused attention and heightened suggestibility (Braid, 1843). Braid's work marked a shift from spiritual interpretations to scientific inquiry, helping establish hypnosis as a credible field.

Later in the century, physicians like Jean-Martin Charcot and Hippolyte Bernheim further advanced hypnosis in medical contexts. Charcot used hypnosis in treating hysteria, while Bernheim argued that hypnosis was a normal psychological phenomenon with therapeutic applications, emphasizing suggestion as a powerful tool for treatment (Gauld, 1992).

20th Century: Therapeutic Hypnosis as a Recognized Practice

In the 20th century, hypnosis became more widely accepted in psychology and medicine. Milton H. Erickson, a pioneering psychiatrist, introduced new therapeutic techniques, viewing hypnosis as a flexible and individualized approach. Erickson's methods emphasized indirect suggestions and the use of storytelling to guide patients into trance states, influencing modern hypnotherapy and making it more accessible for various clinical applications (Erickson, 1980).

Hypnosis gained formal recognition from medical and psychological associations. In 1958, both the American Medical Association (AMA) and the American Psychological Association (APA) endorsed hypnotherapy as a valid treatment, helping to further its acceptance and integration into medical and psychological practice (APA, 2013).

Contemporary Therapeutic Hypnosis

Today, hypnotherapy is used to address a range of conditions, including pain management, anxiety, phobias, and behavioral issues. Modern research continues to explore its effectiveness and mechanisms, focusing on how hypnosis affects brain activity and emotional regulation (Elkins, 2017). Advances in neuroimaging technology have allowed researchers to observe changes in brain function during hypnosis, reinforcing its efficacy and contributing to a more comprehensive understanding of its therapeutic potential (Oakley & Halligan, 2013).

Theoretical background

The theoretical background of hypnotherapy involves understanding the psychological and physiological processes that allow hypnosis to facilitate therapeutic change. Several theories attempt to explain how hypnotherapy works.

Dissociation Theory

Dissociation theory suggests that hypnosis involves a splitting of consciousness, allowing individuals to separate certain cognitive processes from their conscious awareness. First proposed by Pierre Janet in the late 19th century, this theory argues that hypnosis enables individuals to access parts of the mind typically outside of conscious control (Janet, 1889). Modern interpretations, like those of Ernest

Hilgard's "neodissociation" theory, propose that hypnosis creates a "hidden observer," where one part of the mind remains aware while the hypnotized part of the mind follows suggestions. This theory helps explain phenomena like pain reduction under hypnosis, as individuals can dissociate from physical sensations (Hilgard, 1977).

Social-Cognitive Theory

Social-cognitive theory, developed by researchers such as Nicholas Spanos, posits that hypnosis is not an altered state of consciousness but rather a form of social influence in which individuals behave according to their expectations of hypnosis (Spanos, 1986).

According to this view, hypnotized individuals are highly motivated to follow suggestions, acting in ways they believe they are supposed to under hypnosis. This perspective explains hypnosis as a learned, voluntary behavior influenced by social cues, rather than a unique psychological state.

State vs. Non-State Debate

The "state vs. non-state" debate addresses whether hypnosis is a unique, altered state of consciousness or simply a heightened state of suggestibility without an altered state.

State theorists argue that hypnosis involves specific changes in brain activity and consciousness, evidenced by neuroimaging studies showing differences in brain regions associated with perception and self-regulation during hypnosis (Oakley & Halligan, 2013). Non-state theorists, however, argue that hypnosis relies on psychological factors like expectancy, attention, and role-playing, without any fundamental shift in consciousness (Lynn & Kirsch, 2006).

Cognitive-Behavioral Perspective

Some psychologists view hypnotherapies as a tool that works within a cognitive- behavioral framework, using suggestion and imagination to influence thought patterns, emotions, and behaviors. Hypnosis is believed to alter automatic thoughts and emotional responses by leveraging cognitive mechanisms, making it effective for treating anxiety, phobias, and habit disorders (Kirsch, 1996). From this perspective, hypnotherapy serves as a catalyst for change by altering underlying cognitive structures, facilitating responses that support therapeutic goals.

Neurobiological Theories

Advances in neuroimaging have led to neurobiological theories of hypnosis, which explore how hypnosis affects brain function. Studies using fMRI and EEG show that hypnosis can alter brain activity in regions associated with attention, perception, and pain processing, supporting the idea that hypnosis involves unique brain changes (Oakley & Halligan, 2013). Hypnosis may engage specific neural circuits to modify sensory processing, as seen in reduced activity in pain-related brain regions during hypnotic analgesia (Derbyshire et al., 2009). Neurobiological theories provide a scientific basis for the physical and psychological effects of hypnotherapy.

Integrative Approaches

Many modern hypnotherapists take an integrative approach, combining elements from multiple theories to inform clinical practice. For example, they might use cognitive- behavioral techniques within a dissociative framework, recognizing that hypnosis can modify thought patterns, facilitate dissociation from discomfort, and enhance suggestibility to promote therapeutic change (Yapko, 2012). Integrative approaches consider hypnotherapy as a multi-faceted tool that can adapt to individual client needs and various psychological frameworks.

Applications

Pain Management

Therapeutic Hypnosis is extensively used to manage acute and chronic pain, particularly in cases of cancer pain, fibromyalgia, arthritis, and post-surgical recovery. Hypnotic suggestions can alter pain perception and reduce the intensity of pain signals by helping individuals mentally "detach" from their pain (Elkins et al., 2013).

Anxiety and Stress Reduction

Therapeutic Hypnosis has shown efficacy in managing anxiety, generalized anxiety disorder (GAD), and stress-related disorders. By guiding patients into a deeply relaxed state, hypnotherapy helps to reduce the body's stress response, such as the release of cortisol, and promotes feelings of calm (Hammond, 2010). Hypnosis allows individuals to replace negative thought patterns with more constructive ones, which can reduce anxiety symptoms and enhance coping strategies (Alladin, 2016).

Treatment of Insomnia and Sleep Disorders

Therapeutic Hypnosis is a viable option for treating sleep disorders, particularly insomnia, by helping patients relax and overcome psychological barriers to restful sleep. Through suggestions for relaxation and sleep induction, hypnosis can improve sleep onset and duration (Elkins et al., 2013).

Behavioral Change and Habit Control

Therapeutic Hypnosis is commonly used for modifying problematic behaviors, such as smoking, overeating, and excessive alcohol consumption. By enhancing suggestibility, hypnosis helps patients reframe their cravings and build motivation for healthy behaviors (Green & Lynn, 2010).

Irritable Bowel Syndrome (IBS) and Gastrointestinal Disorders

Therapeutic Hypnosis has been shown to reduce symptoms of IBS, including abdominal pain, bloating, and irregular bowel movements. Known as "gut-directed hypnotherapy," this application involves using hypnosis to influence the brain-gut connection, thereby alleviating the stress that can trigger or worsen IBS symptoms (Whorwell, 2006).

Post-Traumatic Stress Disorder (PTSD) and Trauma Recovery

Therapeutic Hypnosis can be an effective treatment for PTSD by creating a safe environment for patients to process traumatic memories. Through guided relaxation and controlled visualization, hypnosis helps patients reduce the emotional intensity of traumatic experiences, allowing them to approach these memories with less distress (Cardena, 2000).

Improvement in Sports Performance and Motivation

Therapeutic Hypnosis has applications in sports psychology, where it is used to improve focus, enhance motivation, and reduce performance-related anxiety. Hypnotic suggestions can help athletes visualize success and reinforce positive self-beliefs, boosting confidence and concentration during competition (Barker & Jones, 2008).

Childbirth and Labor Pain Management

Therapeutic Hypnosis, commonly referred to as "hypnobirthing" in the context of childbirth, is used to reduce pain and anxiety during labor. Hypnotic techniques help expectant mothers relax and focus, reducing fear and creating a sense of control over the labor process (Madden et al., 2012).

Steps or Process

Preparation and Pre-Talk

The first step in hypnotherapy involves building rapport and discussing the client's expectations, goals, and any concerns they may have. The hypnotherapist explains the nature of hypnosis, addressing any misconceptions or anxieties, and ensures the client understands the process (Yapko, 2012). This stage is essential for establishing trust, which is critical for the effectiveness of hypnotherapy, as clients who feel comfortable and informed are more receptive to hypnosis (Hammond, 2010).

Induction

The induction stage involves guiding the client into a hypnotic state, which typically involves deep relaxation and focused attention. Common induction techniques include progressive muscle relaxation, deep breathing, and imagery, where the client visualizes a peaceful scene to encourage mental and physical relaxation (Heap & Aravind, 2002).

Some hypnotherapists may also use eye fixation or a soothing voice to facilitate this relaxed state. The goal of induction is to help clients reach a heightened state of suggestibility, where they can focus more fully on the therapist's guidance (Spiegel & Spiegel, 2004).

Deepening

Following induction, the hypnotherapist may use deepening techniques to deepen the hypnotic state, making the client even more receptive to therapeutic suggestions.

Techniques such as countdowns, visual imagery, and suggestions for "sinking deeper" help clients reach a state of deeper relaxation and concentration (Lynn & Kirsch, 2006). Deepening allows the client to become more focused and detached from their surroundings, which enhances their responsiveness to the upcoming therapeutic interventions (Elkins et al., 2013).

Therapeutic Intervention (Suggestion Phase)

The therapeutic intervention phase is where the hypnotherapist introduces specific suggestions or therapeutic content tailored to the client's issues. Depending on the client's goals, these suggestions might focus on changing habits, managing pain, reducing anxiety, or improving self-esteem. Techniques used during this phase include direct suggestions (e.g., "You will feel calm in stressful situations") and indirect suggestions or metaphors, which are intended to influence the subconscious mind (Hammond, 2010). For issues like phobias, hypnotherapists might use systematic desensitization or guided imagery to help clients confront and reduce their fears (Heap & Aravind, 2002).

Ego Strengthening and Positive Reinforcement

Many hypnotherapists incorporate ego-strengthening techniques to boost the client's confidence, self-worth, and resilience. Positive affirmations and suggestions that reinforce the client's ability to handle challenges are commonly used. This process helps build a foundation of positive beliefs, which can improve the client's general well-being and response to treatment (Yapko, 2012). Ego-strengthening can be particularly useful for clients with self-esteem issues or depression, helping them internalize empowering messages (Spiegel & Spiegel, 2004).

Re-orientation and Emergence

Once the therapeutic work is complete, the hypnotherapist gradually brings the client out of the hypnotic state. This process, called re-orientation or emergence, involves gently guiding the client back to full awareness. Techniques for re-orientation often include counting from one to five or suggesting that the client is gradually becoming more awake and alert (Heap & Aravind, 2002). The hypnotherapist may also provide suggestions for the client to feel refreshed and alert upon waking.

Debriefing and Post-Hypnotic Discussion

After the session, the hypnotherapist discusses the experience with the client, exploring their feelings, perceptions, and any insights they may have gained. This debriefing helps consolidate the therapeutic gains and allows the client to express any residual emotions or questions. The therapist may also reinforce post-hypnotic suggestions, intended to influence behavior outside of hypnosis, such as feeling calm in stressful situations or avoiding certain behaviors (Hammond, 2010). Debriefing is essential for integrating the hypnotic experience into the client's daily life and supporting ongoing therapeutic change.

Case study

Therapeutic Hypnosis for Anxiety and Phobia Treatment

Background: Maria, a 35-year-old marketing professional, sought hypnotherapy to manage her severe public speaking anxiety, which had started to impact her job performance. Maria experienced physical symptoms like sweating, shaking, and a racing heart whenever she was required to speak in front of an audience. These symptoms worsened to the point where she began avoiding meetings and presentations, risking her career progression.

Intervention: Maria's therapist, trained in clinical hypnotherapy, suggested a treatment plan that combined cognitive behavioral strategies with hypnotherapy to target the anxiety. The plan included six hypnotherapy sessions, each focusing on different aspects of her phobia and anxiety.

Initial Consultation and Preparation:

In the first session, the therapist explained the process of hypnotherapy and worked with Maria to understand her specific triggers and goals. This helped establish trust and gave Maria a sense of control, which is essential for effective hypnotherapy.

Induction and Deepening Techniques:

In the second session, Maria was guided into a relaxed state through progressive muscle relaxation and breathing exercises. The therapist used deepening techniques to enhance her receptivity to therapeutic suggestions, helping Maria achieve a calm, focused state.

Direct and Indirect Suggestions:

The therapist introduced a combination of direct and indirect suggestions to help Maria view public speaking situations in a positive light. For instance, the therapist suggested, "You are calm and confident when speaking in front of others," while also using metaphors of resilience and strength. These suggestions aimed to reinforce Maria's self -confidence and reduce her fear response.

Ego-Strengthening Techniques:

To further enhance her self-esteem, Maria received ego-strengthening suggestions, such as affirmations that she could handle any situation with ease. This stage was essential in building her inner resilience and reducing negative self-talk, making her feel more capable and in control.

Post-Hypnotic and Future-Directed Suggestions:

The therapist provided post-hypnotic suggestions that Maria could draw upon in daily life. For example, "When you take a deep breath before speaking, you will feel calm and in control." Additionally, future-directed suggestions helped Maria visualize herself handling future public speaking situations confidently, preparing her mentally for upcoming challenges.

Desensitization through Imagery:

In later sessions, the therapist used guided imagery to gradually expose Maria to situations that resembled her real-life speaking engagements. By visualizing these scenarios while in a deeply relaxed state, Maria was able to desensitize her fear response, reducing her anticipatory anxiety around public speaking.

Outcome: Over the course of six sessions, Maria reported a significant reduction in her public speaking anxiety. By her final session, she no longer experienced intense physical symptoms and felt more comfortable speaking in small group meetings. Follow-up sessions confirmed that the positive effects had continued, and Maria's self-reported anxiety levels were substantially lower than when she began therapy. Therapeutic Hypnosis helped her regain confidence in her professional environment and contributed positively to her career growth.

Discussion: This case study highlights the effectiveness of hypnotherapy in addressing specific anxiety-related issues by combining relaxation techniques with positive suggestion and guided imagery. The tailored approach, focusing on Maria's specific needs, reinforced her confidence and alleviated her physical anxiety symptoms.

References

American Psychological Association. (2013). Hypnosis. In APA Dictionary of Psychology.

Alladin, A. (2016). Cognitive hypnotherapy: An integrated approach to the treatment of emotional disorders. Journal of Cognitive Psychotherapy, 30(4), 220-232.

Barker, J. B., & Jones, M. V. (2008). The effects of hypnosis on self-efficacy, affect, and sport performance: A case study from professional English soccer. Journal of Clinical Sport Psychology, 2(2), 127-147.

Braid, J. (1843). Neurypnology: The rationale of nervous sleep considered in relation with animal magnetism. John Churchill.

Cardena, E. (2000). Hypnosis in the treatment of trauma: A promising, but potentially risky intervention. Journal of Trauma & Dissociation, 1(3), 95-113.

Derbyshire, S. W. G., Whalley, M. G., Stenger, V. A., & Oakley, D. A. (2009). Cerebral activation during hypnotically induced and imagined pain. NeuroImage, 47(3), 1172-1180.

Elkins, G. (2017). Handbook of Medical and Psychological Hypnosis: Foundations, Applications, and Professional Issues. Springer Publishing Company.

Elkins, G., Jensen, M. P., & Patterson, D. R. (2013). Therapeutic Hypnosis for the management of chronic pain. International Journal of Clinical and Experimental Hypnosis, 61(4), 454-468.

Ellenberger, H. F. (1970). The discovery of the unconscious: The history and evolution of dynamic psychiatry. Basic Books.

Erickson, M. H. (1980). The collected papers of Milton H. Erickson on hypnosis: Volume I. Irvington Publishers.

Gauld, A. (1992). A history of hypnotism. Cambridge University Press.

Gonsalkorale, W. M. (2006). Gut-directed hypnotherapy: The Manchester approach for treatment of irritable bowel syndrome. International Journal of Clinical and Experimental Hypnosis, 54(1), 27-50.

Green, J. P., & Lynn, S. J. (2010). Hypnosis and suggestion-based approaches to smoking cessation: An examination of the evidence. International Journal of Clinical and Experimental Hypnosis, 58(2), 197-209.

Hammond, D. C. (2010). Hypnosis in the treatment of anxiety- and stress-related disorders. Expert Review of Neurotherapeutics, 10(2), 263-273.

Heap, M., & Aravind, K. K. (2002). Hartland's Medical and Dental Hypnosis (4th ed.). Churchill Livingstone.

Hilgard, E. R. (1977). Divided consciousness: Multiple controls in human thought and action. Wiley.

Janet, P. (1889). L'automatisme psychologique: Essai de psychologie expérimentale sur les formes inférieures de l'activité humaine. Félix Alcan.

Jensen, M. P., Patterson, D. R., & Gertz, K. J. (2015). Hypnosis and biofeedback for pain management. In M. P. Jensen (Ed.), Hypnosis for Chronic Pain Management: Therapist Guide (pp. 12-25).

Kirsch, I. (1996). Hypnotic enhancement of cognitive-behavioral weight loss treatments—Another meta-reanalysis. Journal of Consulting and Clinical Psychology, 64(3), 517–519.

Lynn, S. J., & Kirsch, I. (2006). Essentials of clinical hypnosis: An evidence-based approach. In M. Nash & A. J. Barnier (Eds.), The Oxford handbook of hypnosis: Theory, research, and practice. Oxford University Press.

Madden, K., Middleton, P., Cyna, A. M., Matthewson, M., & Jones, L. (2012). Hypnosis for pain management during labor and childbirth. Cochrane Database of Systematic Reviews, 11(7), CD009356.

Oakley, D. A., & Halligan, P. W. (2013). Hypnotic suggestion: Opportunities for cognitive neuroscience. Nature Reviews Neuroscience, 14(8), 565-576.

Spanos, N. P. (1986). Hypnotic behavior: A social-psychological interpretation of amnesia, analgesia, and "trance logic." Behavioral and Brain Sciences, 9(3), 449-502.

Spiegel, H., & Spiegel, D. (2004). Trance and Treatment: Clinical Uses of Hypnosis. American Psychiatric Publishing.

Tan, G., Hammond, D. C., & Joseph, G. (2015). Hypnosis and irritable bowel syndrome: A review of efficacy and mechanism of action. American Journal of Clinical Hypnosis, 58(1), 24-44.

Whorwell, P. J. (2006). Gut-focused hypnotherapy for functional gastrointestinal disorders. Digestive Diseases, 24(3-4), 332-338.

Yapko, M. D. (2012). Trancework: An introduction to the practice of clinical hypnosis (4th ed.). Routledge.

Chapter 29

Interpersonal Therapy

Smriti Narayan School of Liberal Studies (SLS), CMR University, Bangalore

Introduction

Interpersonal therapy (IPT) is a short-term type of psychotherapy that treats mental health conditions, including depression. IPT typically consists of 12–16 hour-long sessions with a trained therapist. Sessions occur in one-on-one or group settings. It focusses on an individual's current social relationships and interactions. It is goal orientated and focused on present. It is highly structured and based on evidence. In the short-term, the goal of IPT is to help patients adjust to their immediate social situation. In the long term, the goal is usually to help patients develop strategies that can apply to a broader scope of relationships and situations. So that the patient can gain skills to better manage relationships.

History

IPT was developed by Psychiatrist Gerald Klerman, Research Dr. Myrna Weissman and colleagues in the 1970s as a part of a research study on depression. The therapy was postulate at Yale University and later refined at Columbia University. It is based on American psychiatrist Harry Stack Sullivan's interpersonal theory—the idea that interpersonal relationships are the primary driving force in human life. Initial Purpose: The therapy was initially created as a manualized form of treatment for depression. Its manualized nature helped ensure that treatments were consistent in clinical trials, allowing researchers to reliably assess its efficacy.

Benefits

- Depression and types such as seasonal affective disorder (SAD), postpartum depression, and dysthymia
- Anxiety disorders such as social anxiety disorder, panic disorder, and generalized anxiety disorder
- Eating disorders such as anorexia nervosa, bulimia nervosa, and binge eating disorder
- Personality disorders such as borderline personality disorder, narcissistic personality disorder, and avoidant personality disorder.
- Bipolar disorder
- Substance abuse disorders
- Post-traumatic stress disorder (PTSD)

IPT also helps us improve areas of life:

- improved mental health symptoms
- improved relationships with family and friends
- better communication skills
- greater self-awareness
- increased ability to manage conflict
- reduced feelings of isolation and loneliness.

Theoretical Background

Psychodynamic Theory:

The therapy encourages patients to become more aware of their emotional responses and how these relate to their interpersonal interactions, borrowing the psychodynamic emphasis on emotional insight.

Cognitive-Behavioral Theory:

IPT incorporates elements of cognitive-behavioral therapy (CBT) by helping patients learn practical communication skills and engage in problem-solving. The emphasis is not on changing distorted thoughts directly (as in CBT) but on understanding how thoughts and emotions are linked to interpersonal situations.

Social Theory:

IPT is based on the notion that social and interpersonal relationships are central to mental health. Problems within these relationships can lead to or exacerbate psychological distress. By improving interpersonal functioning, patients can alleviate psychological symptoms and develop healthier, more supportive relationships. This aligns with social theory's focus on the importance of social roles and communication.

Attachment Theory:

IPT draws on the idea that early attachment patterns influence interpersonal relationships throughout life. Secure or insecure attachments with caregivers impact how individuals perceive and respond to social interactions. IPT therapists use this understanding to help patients recognize how their past relationships may be affecting current interactions and emotional responses.

Grief Theory:

IPT includes a focus on unresolved grief, where mourning is seen as a necessary process for psychological health. The therapy provides a structured way for patients to process loss and move toward emotional recovery This aspect is vital when working with patients who have suffered significant losses that impact their interpersonal functioning.

Applications

Depression

- ***Primary Use:*** IPT was originally developed to treat major depressive disorder and remains widely used for this purpose.

- ***Approach:*** It helps patients identify and resolve specific interpersonal problems related to their depression, such as grief, role disputes, role transitions, and interpersonal deficits.
- ***Goal:*** To reduce depressive symptoms by improving communication, social support, and relationships.

Anxiety Disorders

- ***Adaptations:*** IPT has been adapted for the treatment of social anxiety disorder and generalized anxiety disorder.
- ***Method:*** The therapy helps individuals understand how their anxiety affects their interactions with others and works on reducing symptoms by addressing these interpersonal challenges.

Bipolar Disorder

- ***Maintenance Therapy:*** IPT, often combined with medication, is used to prevent relapse and manage the interpersonal stressors that may trigger mood episodes.
- ***Focus Areas:*** It targets maintaining stable routines and addressing conflicts that could precipitate mood shifts.

Postpartum Depression

- ***Application:*** IPT is particularly beneficial for new mothers experiencing depression related to role transitions and changes in social support.
- ***Outcomes:*** It focuses on managing the changes in roles, expectations, and relationship dynamics after childbirth.

Adolescents

- ***Adapted Use:*** IPT-A (Interpersonal Therapy for Adolescents) addresses issues like peer pressure, family conflict, and the challenges of social development.
- ***Effectiveness:*** It helps teenagers improve their social functioning and coping skills during critical developmental periods.

Grief and Loss

- ***Bereavement:*** IPT can help individuals who struggle with complicated grief by facilitating the expression of emotions and finding new ways to form relationships and gain support after a loss.

References

Klerman, G. L., & Weissman, M. M. (1993). Interpersonal psychotherapy of depression: A guide to the theory and practice. New York: Basic Books.

Weissman, M. M., & Markowitz, J. C. (2004). Interpersonal psychotherapy: A clinician's guide. New York: Guilford Press.

Chapter 30

Light Therapy

Rijo.S.John School of Liberal Studies (SLS), CMR University, Bangalore

Introduction to Light Therapy and its Historical roots.

Light therapy, also known as phototherapy, is a non-invasive treatment that harnesses specific wavelengths of light to promote healing and improve well-being. Developed in the early 20th century, light therapy has evolved significantly, with roots tracing back to ancient practices of using sunlight for health benefits. The modern era of light therapy began in the 1900s, particularly with the work of Danish physician Niels Ryberg Finsen, who is often credited with pioneering its medical use (Finsen, 1903). Finsen's work in the late 1890s and early 1900s, particularly at the Finsen Institute in Copenhagen, focused on treating skin conditions with concentrated sunlight, leading to his recognition with the Nobel Prize in Medicine in 1903 (Sethi et al., 2014).

Seasonal Affective Disorder (SAD) is a subtype of depression characterized by recurrent depressive episodes that occur during specific seasons, most commonly in the fall and winter months, and remit during the spring and summer. Individuals affected by SAD experience a range of symptoms, including low mood, loss of interest in activities, fatigue, increased need for sleep, changes in appetite, difficulty concentrating, and feelings of hopelessness or worthlessness. This condition can significantly impair daily functioning and quality of life for those affected, highlighting the importance of understanding its causes, symptoms, and effective treatments.

One of the key factors believed to contribute to the development of SAD is the reduced exposure to natural sunlight that occurs during the fall and winter months in certain geographic regions. This phenomenon is particularly pronounced in locations with higher latitudes, where daylight hours become significantly shorter during the winter season.

In addition to light exposure, other factors such as genetic predisposition, biochemical imbalances, and psychosocial stressors may also contribute to the development of SAD. Family and twin studies have provided evidence of a genetic component in the susceptibility to seasonal mood changes, suggesting that certain individuals may have a genetic predisposition to develop SAD. Furthermore, disruptions in the balance of neurotransmitters such as serotonin, which is involved in regulating mood, have been implicated in the pathophysiology of SAD.

Psychosocial factors, such as stress, lifestyle changes, and social isolation, can also exacerbate symptoms of SAD. The holiday season, which coincides with the onset of winter in many cultures, can be particularly challenging for individuals with SAD due to increased stress, social obligations, and disruptions in routine.

Light therapy, also known as phototherapy or bright light therapy, is a non-invasive and effective treatment modality used to alleviate symptoms of Seasonal Affective Disorder (SAD). SAD, a subtype of depression characterized by recurrent depressive episodes that occur during specific seasons, most commonly in the fall and winter months, has been associated with reduced exposure to natural sunlight.

Light therapy works by influencing the body's internal biological clock, known as the circadian rhythm, which regulates various physiological processes, including sleep-wake cycles, hormone secretion, and mood. Exposure to bright light, particularly in the morning upon waking, helps synchronize the circadian rhythm and promote alertness and wakefulness.

The implementation of light therapy typically involves sitting or working near a light therapy box, which emits bright, full-spectrum light that is several times brighter than indoor lighting. The recommended duration of daily light exposure varies depending on individual factors such as the intensity of symptoms, the specific type of light therapy device used, and individual response to treatment. Several factors contribute to the effectiveness of light therapy for SAD, including the intensity, duration, and timing of light exposure.

In conclusion, light therapy is a widely recognized and evidence-based treatment for Seasonal Affective Disorder (SAD), offering a non-invasive and effective approach to alleviating symptoms of depression during the fall and winter months.

Applications & Challenges

Applications of Light Therapy

Mental Health:

- **Seasonal Affective Disorder (SAD):** It is highly used in lighting depressive conditions during winter seasons by mimicking natural sunlight illumination.
- **Other Mood Disorders:** It assists individuals affected by non-seasonal depression and those who are diagnosed with the bipolar disorder.
- **Skin Conditions:** *Psoriasis, Eczema, and Acne*: With different wavelengths, UV light finds specific applications in treating inflammatory skin conditions.
- **Wound Healing:** It may assist in promoting tissue repair and decreasing inflammation in wounds.
- **Sleep Disorders:** *Regulation of Circadian Rhythm:* Bright light exposure in the morning will reset the body's circadian rhythm, enhancing sleep quality.
- **Pain Management:** *Chronic Pain:* Some forms of light therapy are used to reduce pain and inflammation. Conditions most associated with these effects are those of arthritis.
- **Dermatologic Uses:** *Photodynamic Therapy (PDT):* In this process, drug substances that are responsive to certain wavelengths of light are used to kill cancerous cells or other problematic tissue. PDT can be used to treat skin cancer.

Limitations of Light Therapy

- ***Inter-Individual Variation:*** It can differ from one individual to another; thus, it has been challenging to have standardized treatment protocols.
- ***Availability:*** Though home devices are becoming increasingly common, there are issues with availability of professional-grade equipment and therapies, especially in very rural and underserved areas.
- ***Treatment Adherence:*** It requires consistency, but with some clients, sticking to recommended daily exposure times has been a challenge.
- ***Side Effects:*** Side effects of exposure to light from a device may include eye strain, headaches, or skin irritation for some users; such effects are significantly more likely to occur at prolonged exposure times.
- ***Legal and Commercial:*** Light therapy devices are heterogeneous in regulations and standards. Therefore, differences in quality and efficacy can be noted between products commercially marketed to consumers.
- ***Limitations in Research:*** Evidence continues to build to support light therapy; however, there is still a lack of considerable, high-quality studies, especially concerning mechanisms, ideal regimens, and long-term outcomes.

In summary, light therapy presents potential applications particularly in mental and dermatological health, but encounters the challenges of individual variability, access, adherence, and research. Overcoming the challenges mentioned above will make light therapy even more effective and acceptable in the clinical setting.

Theoretical Background of Light Therapy

Light therapy, also known as phototherapy, is a form of non-invasive treatment based on the use of specified wavelengths of light in the treatment of various conditions including mood disorders such as SAD, sleep disorders, and certain skin disorders such as psoriasis. Light therapy is based on the theoretical principle of understanding how light reacts to biological functions in a human body, especially in connection with the circadian rhythm and the production of hormones like melatonin and serotonin.

The underlying concept in light therapy is that light, and even bright light, between a range of intensities of 2,500 to 10,000 lux can be responsible for altering the biological clock, particularly the SCN in the hypothalamus, which determines sleep-wake patterns. The SCN has been reputed as having sensitivity to light exposure, especially during the morning hours. Light from the eyes reaches and interacts with the SCN. It consequently causes hormone production modification: melatonin is the hormone regulating sleep, while serotonin is the neurotransmitter in charge of mood regulations.

Action Mechanism

The key way in which light therapy operates is by resetting the circadian rhythm, often referred to as the body's internal clock that governs the sleep-wake cycles. Data dictates how the light resets the body's clock through brightening at certain times in the day-this is very much helpful in disorders like insomnia, jet lag, and seasonal affective disorder (SAD).

Melatonin Suppression: Light suppresses melatonin, especially light in the blue spectrum. This helps sleepers become more awake during the day; and because of this, light therapy is useful for sleepers who have difficulty waking up or getting into a regular pattern of sleep and waking.

Serotonin Production: Another hypothesis is that the bright light exposure increases the neurotransmitter serotonin in the brain. This neurotransmitter is believed to play a part in fighting depression, especially for people who have seasonal affective disorder in which lack of sunlight during the winter months leads to feelings of despair.

There are specific photoreceptors in the retina that are sensitive to light, particularly to the blue spectrum around 480 nm, that are involved in synchronizing the biological clock. These trigger neurochemical cascades that initiate the action in the SCN through the optic nerve to influence mood, sleep, and alertness.

How Does Light Therapy Work?

Light therapy works to replace sunshine in the human body that may bring back the human body's natural rhythms and thus cure all symptoms associated with various diseases.

Important aspects of how light therapy works:

Intensity: Light therapy devices provide light at an intensity of 2,500 to 10,000 lux, or significantly brighter than standard indoor lighting (about 100-300 lux).

Timing: The timing of light exposure is particularly crucial and relates to individual circadian rhythm, and ideally this is during the morning time, as it has a most profound impact on resetting the body's inner clock.

Duration: The length of the therapy in terms of the duration that is usually recommended varies between 20 minutes up to an hour daily. Longer treatment periods are usually necessary for more severe cases.

Ideally, sit at a specified distance from the light source, preferably between 16 to 24 inches. Direct the light towards your face, but there is no need to stare directly into the light source.

Steps to Follow for Light Therapy Session

Preparation

Select the Right Lightbox or Device: Select a light therapy device that is particularly designed to target your condition. Ideally, it should produce at least 2,500 lux with no UV rays to avoid photodamage.

Pin Time: Most conditions, like mood disorders, are best treated with light therapy in the morning. In fact, most people see better results if their light therapy starts within the first hour or two of waking.

Evaluate Room Setup: Place the lightbox at about 16-24 inches from your eyes. The light should be focused directly into your eyes. The setting must be considerably distraction-free during the session.

Beginning the Session

Most people can sit comfortably in front of the lightbox at an angle. Do not stare into the light; just keep it somewhere in your peripheral vision.

Set Duration: It should be set according to the advisable time set, usually 20 to 30 minutes for beginners. However, the duration can be increased depending on the subject's tolerance and the recommendations by the doctors.

In Session

Participate in Other Activities: In this session, you can read, work, or any other quiet activity, only that your eyes should keep in the line of this light. You do not need to look at this light itself.

Relax Your Mind: While sitting during this session, you should relax and not take your eyes away because of something that may disturb this light.

Post Session

Monitor Effects: One often finds changes in mood, energy, or sleep patterns after the session. Some may feel it immediately, but others are better in a few days to weeks or several weeks into the cycle of exposure during darker months or according to the health professional's suggestion.

Maintain Regular Schedule: Normally, consistency yields the best effects. Most people experience benefits if they expose themselves daily for several weeks during the darker months or as per the suggestion of a health professional.

Adjustment: The time or the strength of treatment sessions can be adjusted by depending on the patient's adjustment to the treatment, if necessary.

Monitoring Side Effects: Minor side effects may include eye strain, headache, or nausea. Report these immediately. If these continue, you need to adjust the light setting or increase the duration or consult a medical professional.

Light therapy is the safe and effective treatment for many conditions that have causation to circadian rhythm disturbances, such as depression, sleep disorders, and seasonal affective disorders. This is because light affects the biological clock of the body through simulating real sunlight, how it enters the biological avenues, thereby promoting serotonin release at appropriate times and suppressing melatonin levels.

Case Study

Patient History:

Name: Jane Smith

Age: 34 years

Sex: Female

Occupation: Marketing Executive

Marital Status: Single

Residence: Alone in an urban apartment

Chief Complaint:

Jane presents herself with seasonal depressive symptoms, which usually occur during the winters. She feels low in energy, she becomes irritable, cannot concentrate, and has generally lost interest in doing things. They have been present for the last 5 years, and they generally worsen during the fall and winter seasons. It starts around late October and resolves by March or early April. She has had mood improvement in the spring and summer, which she started to question with some suspicion regarding a seasonal pattern of her symptoms.

History of Presenting Illness:

- **Incidence:** Jane has been experiencing the symptoms annually between October to winter seasons for five consecutive years. The symptoms started to appear approximately 4-5 months. The symptoms are at the peak during winter months, that is from between December months to February.
- Presents with complaints of depressed low mood, sadness and irritation. The patient has difficulty in falling asleep and sleeping while experiencing unrefreshing early morning waking.
- **Energy:** Lack of energy and low motivation coupled with an insidious onset of persistent tiredness, especially in the morning
- **Social Withdrawal:** The young woman also has a lack of interest in company, social life, and relationships with friends and family
- **Cognitive Function:** Poor concentration at work, forgetfulness and bad judgment
- **Appetite:** There is no direct change in appetite; however, the patient has a carbohydrate craving
- **Previous Episodes:** Jane was diagnosed with the same symptoms in previous years but was given a pass without formal treatment. She says that this year, she is feeling much better in spring and summer, and all her symptoms will go away without any medical care.

Past Medical History:

- **General Health:** Generally healthy and without any major medical condition
- **Psychiatric History:** Was diagnosed with major depression and other psychiatric conditions but she only had episodes of feeling down and blue during the winter months.
- **Drug History:** Never taken psychiatric medications; no active prescriptions. She takes over-the-counter sleep aids every 2-3 months when sleep disruption is very problematic.
- **Allergies:** None known; drugs

Family History:

No family history for major psychiatric illnesses; mother comments about similar low mood in winters, however never diagnosed with SAD.

Social History:

- **Lifestyle:** Jane is a highly demanding marketing executive who works full-time in a conducive office environment. The work schedule is quite demanding with the late hours of work most evenings. She enjoys her warm months practicing with friends, but confines herself indoors normally abhorring socialization when she goes down during winter periods.

- **Exercise:** Typically inactive during winter, however does walk frequently. Does outdoor exercise, including hiking and biking, spring and summer.
- **Diet:** Eats healthy diet. Indicated that she desires high-carb diets during the winter months.
- **Substance Use:** Social drinker. Never smoked or used illegal drugs.
- **Sleep:** Difficulty sleeping at night, frequent wake-ups, had a feeling of sleepiness in the morning.

Physical Examination:

- **General:** Nothing significant change in weight; experienced a few throbbing head hurts in the morning.
- **Cardiovascular:** No chest pain; no chest aching; no palpitations.
- **Respiratory:** No respiratory distress; no shortness of breath; no cough.
- **Gastrointestinal:** No gastrointestinal complaint.
- **Neurological:** No dizziness; no seizure; no loss of coordination.
- **Endocrine:** No thyroid and metabolic disorders.
- **General Appearance:** Clearly exhausted, otherwise well cared for. No acute distress.
- **Skin:** Healthy, no rashes or lesions.
- **Neurological:** No abnormalities. Reflexes, strength, coordination all within normal limits.

Psychiatric Assessment:

- **Mood:** Depressed, with occasional irritability. Reports being "down" for much of the winter months.
- **Affect:** Blunted to some extent, yet interactive during the interview
- **Thought Process:** Logical and coherent.
- **Cognition:** Moderate dementia with intermittent inability to focus at work and recollection of tasks
- **Sleep:** Insomnia; wakes up early in the morning and does not feel refreshed in the morning.
- **Suicidal Ideation:** Does not report any attempt to harm self nor have suicidal ideas.
- **Social Functioning:** Avoids social settings, especially during winter months. Avoids friends and relatives.

Primary Diagnosis:

Seasonal Affective Disorder ICD-10 F33.1 – Major depressive disorder, recurrent, moderate, with seasonal pattern Differential Diagnoses: Major Depressive Disorder (without seasonal pattern) Hypothyroidism (Screening tests for thyroid function were within normal limits) Generalized Anxiety Disorder (no relevant anxiety symptoms were reported) Treatment Plan: Light Therapy: \\ Device: 10,000 lux lightbox (UV-free), daily application in the morning for 30 minutes, within one hour of waking up.

Diagnosis

After an assessment, including a detailed clinical interview and screening for mood disorders, Jane is diagnosed with Seasonal Affective Disorder (SAD). This type of depression is characterized by a pattern of recurring depressive episodes during the winter months, which improve or remit during the spring and summer. SAD is often linked to circadian rhythm disturbances caused by a lack of natural sunlight, leading to disrupted sleep-wake cycles and an imbalance in mood-regulating hormones, particularly serotonin and melatonin. Given that Jane's symptoms occur seasonally, and no other underlying conditions are present, the diagnosis of SAD is confirmed.

Treatment Plan

After discussing treatment options with her healthcare provider, Jane opts for light therapy as her primary treatment modality. She prefers this non-invasive therapy over pharmaceutical interventions, though she is aware that some patients may combine light therapy with medications or psychotherapy.

Light Therapy Plan:

- Light Source: Jane is prescribed a 10,000 lux lightbox, which is designed to simulate natural sunlight. The device should be UV-free to protect her skin and eyes.
- Treatment Timing: The light therapy is to be administered in the morning, ideally within 1 hour of waking, to help regulate her circadian rhythm and improve her mood.
- Session Duration: Initially, Jane will start with 30-minute daily sessions, increasing the duration to 45 minutes if needed after the first week based on her response.
- Session Environment: Jane is instructed to sit in front of the lightbox at 16-24 inches and at an angle that ensures the light hits her eyes indirectly. She can engage in light activities such as reading, working, or having breakfast during the session.

Results and Outcome

After completing 4 weeks of light therapy, Jane shows significant improvement in both her mood and daily functioning. She reports:

- A marked reduction in depressive symptoms such as irritability, fatigue, and sadness.
- Improved social engagement and energy levels.
- Better sleep quality and more regular sleep-wake cycles.

Her healthcare provider also recommends maintaining a healthy lifestyle with regular exercise, a balanced diet, and good sleep hygiene to complement the light therapy.

Lessons Learned

- Consistency is Key: Jane's response to light therapy is gradual, but she experiences the most significant improvements after 2-3 weeks of consistent daily exposure.
- Morning Exposure: Timely morning exposure to bright light is essential for optimal results. Even on cloudy days, the light therapy device was effective.
- Individual Variability: While Jane responded well to light therapy, other patients may require adjustments in light intensity, session duration, or the addition of other treatments (such as psychotherapy or medication).
- Side Effects: Jane experienced mild side effects (headache and eye strain) early on but did not need to adjust the therapy significantly. Monitoring and proper device setup are crucial for minimizing discomfort.

Conclusion

This case study demonstrates that light therapy can be a highly effective treatment for Seasonal Affective Disorder (SAD), leading to significant improvements in mood, energy, and overall well-being. For Jane, light therapy successfully alleviated her wintertime depressive symptoms and helped restore her circadian rhythm, allowing her to function optimally throughout the day. Regular follow-ups and adjustments ensured the therapy remained effective and well-tolerated.

References

Rosenthal, N. E., Sack, D. A., Gillin, J. C., Lewy, A. J., Goodwin, F. K., Davenport, Y., ... & Wehr, T. A. (1984). Seasonal affective disorder: a description of the syndrome and preliminary findings with light therapy. Archives of general psychiatry, 41(1), 72-80.

Lam, R. W., Levitt, A. J., Levitan, R. D., Enns, M. W., Morehouse, R., Michalak, E. E., & Tam, E. M. (2006). The Can-SAD study: a randomized controlled trial of the effectiveness of light therapy and fluoxetine in patients with winter seasonal affective disorder. American Journal of Psychiatry, 163(5), 805-812.

Magnusson, A., Stefánsson, J. G., & Axelson, D. A. (2000). Genetic and environmental contributions to the seasonal variation of depressive symptoms in the Icelandic population. American Journal of Psychiatry, 157(5), 747-749.

Rosenthal, N. E., Sack, D. A., Gillin, J. C., Lewy, A. J., Goodwin, F. K., Davenport, Y., ... & Wehr, T. A. (1984). Seasonal affective disorder: a description of the syndrome and preliminary findings with light therapy. Archives of general psychiatry, 41(1), 72-80.

Lam, R. W., Levitt, A. J., Levitan, R. D., Enns, M. W., Morehouse, R., Michalak, E. E., & Tam, E. M. (2006). The Can-SAD study: a randomized controlled trial of the effectiveness of light therapy and fluoxetine in patients with winter seasonal affective disorder. American Journal of Psychiatry, 163(5), 805-812.

Terman, M., Terman, J. S., & Ross, D. C. (1998). A controlled trial of timed bright light and negative air ionization for treatment of winter depression. Archives of general psychiatry, 55(10), 875-882.

Rosenthal, N. E., Sack, D. A., Gillin, J. C., Lewy, A. J., Goodwin, F. K., Davenport, Y., ... & Wehr, T. A. (1984). Seasonal affective disorder: a description of the syndrome and preliminary findings with light therapy. Archives of general psychiatry, 41(1), 72-80.

Avery, D. H., & Kripke, D. F. (2009). Bright light treatment of depression for older adults. *Journal of Affective Disorders*, 114(1-3), 195-199. https://doi.org/10.1016/j.jad.2008.07.010

Chellappa, S. L., et al. (2011). Bright light therapy improves sleep and circadian timing in chronic insomnia. *Sleep Medicine*, 12(6), 561-567. https://doi.org/10.1016/j.sleep.2010.10.016

Goetz, C. S., et al. (2014). The impact of light therapy on circadian rhythms in the treatment of depression. *Chronobiology International*, 31(1), 113-125. https://doi.org/10.3109/07420528.2013.831560

Kohler, S., et al. (2007). Light therapy for the treatment of depressive disorders in non-seasonal depression. *Psychiatry Research*, 149(1-3), 147-153. https://doi.org/10.1016/j.psychres.2006.02.007

Lewy, A. J., Sack, D. A., & Singer, C. M. (1987). Light therapy for winter depression: A review of the evidence. *Acta Psychiatrica Scandinavica*, 75(5), 469-476. https://doi.org/10.1111/j.1600-0447.1987.tb02767.x

Minkel, J. R., et al. (2009). Bright light treatment of sleep disturbances and depression in elderly individuals. *American Journal of Geriatric Psychiatry*, 17(4), 314-322. https://doi.org/10.1097/JGP.0b013e31819f1b7a

Pail, G., et al. (2011). Bright light therapy in the treatment of depression: A critical review.*Journal of Affective Disorders*, 121(3), 197-214. https://doi.org/10.1016/j.jad.2009.06.037\

Rohan, K. J., et al. (2004). Cognitive-behavioral therapy and light therapy for seasonal affective disorder. *Journal of Consulting and Clinical Psychology*, 72(3), 507-516. https://doi.org/10.1037/0022-006X.72.3.507

Terman, M., Terman, J. S., & Ross, D. C. (2001). Efficacy of bright light in the treatment of winter depression: A meta-analysis. *American Journal of Psychiatry*, 158(4), 573-580. https://doi.org/10.1176/appi.ajp.158.4.573

Wirz-Justice, A., et al. (2006). Light treatment for seasonal affective disorder: A review of efficacy and mechanisms. *CNS Spectrums*, 11(12), 707-713. https://doi.org/10.1017/S1092852900007451

Chapter 31

Mediterranean Healing Traditions

Sunanda Chowdhury School of Liberal Studies (SLS), CMR University, Bangalore

Mediterranean healing traditions refer to the holistic health practices originating from the countries bordering the Mediterranean Sea, including Greece, Italy, Spain, Turkey, and parts of the Middle East and North Africa. These traditions emphasize a balanced and integrative approach to health, combining diet, physical activity, herbal remedies, social support, and spiritual practices. The core of these traditions lies in the "Mediterranean diet," which is rich in vegetables, fruits, whole grains, olive oil, and fish, while limiting processed foods and red meat. Alongside the diet, Mediterranean healing includes natural remedies, often using locally sourced herbs and oils, and places value on mental and emotional wellness, emphasizing social connection and mindfulness (Bach-Faig et al., 2011; Martínez-González & Sánchez-Villegas, 2016).

Mediterranean healing is rooted in ancient systems like Greek and Arabic medicine, which integrated knowledge from Hippocrates, Galen, and Avicenna. This system highlights preventive health measures, recognizing the role of lifestyle factors, such as diet and stress management, in promoting long-term wellness and reducing risks for chronic illnesses like heart disease and mental health disorders (Psaltopoulou et al., 2013). It also emphasizes the importance of natural treatments and remedies, including olive oil for anti-inflammatory benefits, herbal teas for digestion and relaxation, and various traditional practices aimed at harmonizing the mind, body, and spirit.

The Mediterranean Diet

Nutrient-Dense, Plant-Based Diet: At the heart of Mediterranean healing is the diet, rich in plant-based foods like vegetables, fruits, whole grains, and legumes. Olive oil is the primary fat source, providing monounsaturated fats that are beneficial for heart health (Bach-Faig et al., 2011).

Moderate Consumption of Animal Products: Mediterranean diets include moderate portions of fish, poultry, and dairy, while red meat is consumed sparingly. This dietary pattern has been associated with reduced risks for cardiovascular disease, type 2 diabetes, and certain cancers (Martínez-González & Sánchez-Villegas, 2016).

Moderate Alcohol Consumption: In some Mediterranean traditions, moderate wine intake, especially red wine, is common and thought to provide antioxidant benefits, though it is consumed in moderation and often with meals (Grosso & Galvano, 2016).

Herbal Remedies and Natural Medicine

Local Herbs for Health: Mediterranean cultures use a variety of herbs, such as rosemary, oregano, thyme, and sage, believed to have anti-inflammatory, antimicrobial, and digestive properties. These are used in cooking and as teas to aid digestion and boost immunity (Petropoulos et al., 2017).

Olive Oil and Honey: Olive oil is prized not only for its culinary uses but also for its medicinal properties, such as supporting skin health and reducing inflammation. Honey is another common remedy, used for its antibacterial properties and in soothing ailments like sore throats and coughs (Bach-Faig et al., 2011).

Physical Activity and Daily Movement

Natural Movement and Walking: Physical activity is often incorporated naturally into daily routines, including walking, gardening, and household tasks. This promotes cardiovascular health and reduces stress, which aligns with the Mediterranean philosophy of maintaining a balanced lifestyle (Martínez-González et al., 2016).

Moderate, Social Exercise: Activities are often social, like dancing or playing sports, which not only foster physical health but also contribute to a sense of community and mental well-being (Bach-Faig et al., 2011).

Social Connection and Mental Wellness

Social Support and Community: Mediterranean cultures highly value social relationships and community gatherings. Strong family and social ties contribute to reduced stress levels, mental resilience, and overall happiness, factors that play a role in longevity and lower rates of mental health issues (Psaltopoulou et al., 2013).

Spiritual and Emotional Balance: In many Mediterranean cultures, spiritual practices and rituals are part of the healing process. Practices include prayer, gratitude, and mindfulness, which are believed to maintain emotional and psychological balance (Petropoulos et al., 2017).

Preventive Health and Holistic View

Holistic, Preventive Approach: Rather than focusing only on treating illness, Mediterranean healing traditions emphasize prevention and maintaining wellness through a balanced lifestyle. This includes dietary variety, moderate exercise, social interaction, and natural remedies (Grosso & Galvano, 2016).

Integrative Health Philosophy: Drawing from Greek, Roman, and Arab influences, Mediterranean traditions view health as a balance of physical, mental, and spiritual well-being, encouraging individuals to live in harmony with their environment and community.

Benefits of Mediterranean Healing Traditions:

Cardiovascular Health

Reduced Risk of Heart Disease: The Mediterranean diet, with its emphasis on healthy fats from olive oil, nuts, and fish, as well as a high intake of fruits, vegetables, and whole grains, has been shown to lower the risk of heart disease. Monounsaturated fats in olive oil, along with antioxidants in fruits and vegetables, help reduce inflammation and improve cholesterol levels (Martínez-González & Sánchez-Villegas, 2016).

Lower Blood Pressure and Improved Lipid Profiles: The Mediterranean diet has also been associated with lower blood pressure and improved blood lipid profiles, both of which contribute to heart health and longevity (Estruch et al., 2018).

Reduced Risk of Chronic Diseases

Diabetes Prevention and Management: The Mediterranean diet is effective in preventing and managing type 2 diabetes, largely due to its low glycemic load, fiber-rich foods, and healthy fats. This dietary pattern helps maintain stable blood sugar levels and improves insulin sensitivity (Salas-Salvadó et al., 2014).

Reduced Cancer Risk: High intakes of antioxidants from fruits, vegetables, and whole grains in the Mediterranean diet have been associated with a lower risk of certain cancers, particularly breast and colorectal cancers (Bach-Faig et al., 2011).

Mental Health Benefits

Reduced Risk of Depression and Anxiety: Studies have linked the Mediterranean diet with improved mental health outcomes, including reduced risks of depression and anxiety. Nutrients such as omega-3 fatty acids from fish, antioxidants from fruits and vegetables, and the anti-inflammatory effects of olive oil contribute to better mental health (Psaltopoulou et al., 2013).

Improved Cognitive Function: The Mediterranean diet and lifestyle have been shown to protect against cognitive decline and neurodegenerative diseases like Alzheimer's. Antioxidants, polyphenols, and anti-inflammatory foods are believed to help maintain cognitive health (Scarmeas et al., 2006).

Longevity and Improved Quality of Life

Increased Lifespan: The emphasis on balanced eating, moderate physical activity, and strong social connections in Mediterranean cultures contributes to greater longevity and a lower incidence of age-related diseases (Sofi et al., 2010).

Enhanced Quality of Life: The Mediterranean approach to health, which includes social interaction, relaxation, and mindfulness, enhances overall quality of life and life satisfaction. Regular social interaction and reduced stress levels have been linked to positive mental health outcomes and a stronger immune response (Grosso & Galvano, 2016).

Weight Management and Metabolic Health

Healthy Weight Maintenance: The Mediterranean diet's focus on plant-based foods, healthy fats, and controlled portions of protein sources supports healthy weight management without calorie restriction. This approach can prevent obesity and related conditions, such as metabolic syndrome (Estruch et al., 2018).

Improved Metabolic Health: The diet's low intake of processed foods and sugars helps regulate blood sugar levels and support metabolic health, reducing the risk of obesity-related complications (Salas-Salvadó et al., 2014).

History of Mediterranean Healing Traditions

Mediterranean healing traditions date back thousands of years and have been shaped by the diverse cultural and scientific influences of the Mediterranean region. Influences from ancient Egyptian,

Greek, Roman, and Arabic civilizations, as well as Jewish and Christian thought, helped create a holistic approach to health. This approach emphasizes balance, preventive care, and the integration of mind, body, and spirit.

Ancient Egyptian Influence

Ancient Egyptians were among the earliest to document medical practices, blending spiritual beliefs with empirical treatments. They used a wide variety of plants and herbs, many of which, such as garlic and honey, are still associated with Mediterranean healing (Nunn, 2002). Egyptian healing also integrated spirituality, with priests often acting as healers and employing rituals to support physical treatments (Nunn, 2002).

Greek Contributions

Ancient Greece made significant advancements in medicine, particularly through the works of Hippocrates (460–370 BCE), who is often regarded as the "Father of Medicine." Hippocrates introduced the concept of the four humors (blood, phlegm, black bile, and yellow bile), linking health to a balance among them. He also emphasized the importance of diet, exercise, and lifestyle in maintaining health (Jones, 2005).

Roman Influence

The Romans adopted and expanded Greek medical knowledge. Galen (129–216 CE), a prominent Roman physician, built on Hippocrates' theories and wrote extensively on medicine, anatomy, and pharmacology. Galen's teachings influenced medical practices in the Mediterranean and Europe for centuries (Nutton, 2013).

Romans also emphasized hygiene and public health, building aqueducts, baths, and sewage systems, which helped prevent disease—a principle that aligns with the preventive aspects of Mediterranean healing (Scarborough, 1991).

Arab and Islamic Contributions

During the Islamic Golden Age (8th–13th centuries), scholars in the Mediterranean, especially in centers like Baghdad and Cordoba, preserved, translated, and expanded upon Greek and Roman medical texts. Figures such as Avicenna (Ibn Sina) wrote comprehensive medical texts like The Canon of Medicine, which synthesized Greek, Roman, and Islamic medicine and emphasized the importance of diet, lifestyle, and natural remedies (Dhanani, 2004).

The Islamic influence contributed significantly to herbal medicine, pharmacology, and holistic approaches. The Arabic traditions introduced many herbs and spices into Mediterranean healing practices, some of which are still widely used today (Zargaran et al., 2012).

Jewish and Christian Influences

Jewish and Christian traditions also shaped Mediterranean healing practices, particularly through monastic medicine. Monasteries preserved medical knowledge and often served as centers for herbal medicine and healing (McVaugh, 1974).

Jewish communities, particularly those in Spain and North Africa, contributed to the preservation and expansion of medical knowledge, blending Greco-Roman, Arabic, and local practices to create a unique approach to health that respected spiritual, dietary, and holistic health practices (Taub, 2017).

Modern Integration and Scientific Validation

In the 20th century, the Mediterranean diet and lifestyle practices began receiving scientific validation. Studies by Ancel Keys in the 1950s linked the Mediterranean diet to lower rates of heart disease, bringing international attention to the health benefits of this traditional lifestyle (Keys, 1970). Since then, numerous studies have supported the effectiveness of Mediterranean healing in reducing risks for chronic diseases and promoting longevity (Bach-Faig et al., 2011).

Theoretical Background of Mediterranean Healing Traditions

The Theory of the Four Humors

Concept of Balance: The ancient Greek theory of the four humors, introduced by Hippocrates and expanded by Galen, posits that human health is governed by the balance of four bodily fluids—blood, phlegm, black bile, and yellow bile. Each humor corresponds with different physical and emotional traits, and disease was believed to occur when these humors were out of balance (Jones, 2005).

Dietary and Lifestyle Adjustments: Mediterranean healing practices often aim to restore balance by using foods, herbs, and lifestyle adjustments to correct imbalances. For example, diets that include cooling foods (such as vegetables and fruits) and warming foods (like spices and meat) help maintain internal harmony based on individual needs (Nutton, 2013).

Hippocratic Approach to Diet and Preventive Care

Food as Medicine: Hippocrates famously stated, "Let food be thy medicine," which has become a foundational concept in Mediterranean healing. The diet-centric approach, emphasizing whole foods, minimal processing, and natural ingredients, aligns with the modern Mediterranean diet and its focus on plant-based, nutrient-rich foods (Bach-Faig et al., 2011).

Preventive Health and Lifestyle: Hippocrates and later Greek physicians also believed in the importance of physical activity, adequate rest, and emotional well-being as essential to health. This view of preventive health influences the Mediterranean lifestyle today, with daily movement, community connections, and dietary practices at its core (Jones, 2005).

Islamic Medical Theory and the Integration of Greco-Roman Knowledge

Holistic and Integrated Medicine: During the Islamic Golden Age, scholars like Avicenna synthesized Greco-Roman theories with Islamic knowledge, emphasizing a holistic approach that considers physical, mental, and spiritual health (Dhanani, 2004). Avicenna's Canon of Medicine introduced systematic approaches to diet, exercise, and herbal remedies, influencing Mediterranean healing practices.

Herbal and Natural Remedies: Arabic medical theories introduced a wide array of herbs and spices, as well as theories on their "temperaments" or qualities (such as hot, cold, dry, and moist), which were used to balance the body's internal environment. This temperamental approach to natural remedies persists in Mediterranean herbal practices (Zargaran et al., 2012).

Jewish and Christian Philosophical Contributions

Healing and Compassion in Christian Monastic Medicine: In medieval Europe, Christian monasteries became centers for healing and preservation of medical knowledge. Monks integrated spiritual practices with herbal remedies, fostering a compassionate approach to healing that emphasized caregiving and palliative care, values still associated with Mediterranean healing (Taub, 2017).

Jewish Contributions to Medical Knowledge: Jewish scholars in the Mediterranean often blended Greco-Roman and Arabic theories with local practices, particularly in Spain. Their emphasis on dietary laws, moderation, and the interconnectedness of body and spirit shaped the development of Mediterranean health traditions (Muntner, 1971).

Modern Public Health and Lifestyle Medicine Integration

The Mediterranean Diet as Preventive Medicine: Ancel Keys' research in the 20th century demonstrated the benefits of traditional Mediterranean diets for cardiovascular health. Keys' studies emphasized the low rates of heart disease among Mediterranean populations and helped frame the diet as a preventive health measure (Keys, 1970).

Holistic Health Frameworks in Modern Medicine: Contemporary public health theories draw on Mediterranean principles of lifestyle-based care, supporting balanced nutrition, physical activity, and social well-being as key components of health. This integrative approach aligns with WHO recommendations on lifestyle medicine and preventive care (Bach-Faig et al., 2011).

Applications of Mediterranean Healing Traditions

Dietary Interventions for Cardiovascular Health

Mediterranean Diet for Heart Health: The Mediterranean diet has become widely recognized and adopted as a dietary intervention for reducing cardiovascular disease (CVD) risk. Rich in fruits, vegetables, whole grains, olive oil, and fish, it has been shown to lower blood pressure, reduce LDL cholesterol, and improve vascular function (Estruch et al., 2018).

Dietary Guidelines: Many national and international health organizations have integrated Mediterranean dietary principles into their dietary guidelines. This application in public health policy aims to promote cardiovascular health and prevent related diseases (Bach-Faig et al., 2011).

Mental Health and Cognitive Benefits

Nutritional Psychiatry: The nutrient-dense nature of the Mediterranean diet has been applied in the field of nutritional psychiatry, where it is used to support mental health and reduce depression and anxiety. Omega-3 fatty acids, antioxidants, and polyphenols in the diet have shown positive effects on mood and cognitive function (Psaltopoulou et al., 2013).

Prevention of Cognitive Decline: Regular consumption of Mediterranean foods has been associated with a lower risk of Alzheimer's disease and dementia. This has led to its application as a dietary strategy for cognitive health in aging populations (Scarmeas et al., 2006).

Preventive Healthcare and Chronic Disease Management

Diabetes Prevention and Management: The Mediterranean diet has been shown to be effective in managing and preventing type 2 diabetes. Its low glycemic load, healthy fats, and high fiber content help maintain blood sugar levels and improve insulin sensitivity, leading to its recommendation as a dietary approach for diabetes patients (Salas-Salvadó et al., 2014).

Weight Management and Metabolic Health: The Mediterranean lifestyle, which emphasizes portion control, balanced meals, and regular physical activity, has been applied in weight management programs. This approach helps individuals achieve and maintain a healthy weight, thus reducing the risk of metabolic syndrome and related conditions (Estruch et al., 2018).

Herbal and Natural Medicine

Use of Mediterranean Herbs in Complementary Medicine: Herbal medicines derived from the Mediterranean, such as chamomile, oregano, and rosemary, have therapeutic applications for digestive issues, respiratory ailments, and inflammation. These herbs are used in traditional remedies as well as complementary and integrative medicine settings today (Tapsell et al., 2006).

Natural Remedies for Inflammation and Pain: Many Mediterranean traditions use anti-inflammatory herbs and spices such as turmeric and ginger for managing pain and inflammation. These are often applied as natural remedies in complementary medicine to reduce reliance on pharmaceutical treatments (Zargaran et al., 2012).

Holistic and Lifestyle-Based Health Programs

Integration of Lifestyle Interventions: Mediterranean healing traditions emphasize a balanced lifestyle that includes physical activity, community involvement, and relaxation. Modern health programs apply these principles, promoting regular physical exercise, social engagement, and stress management as part of comprehensive lifestyle-based health interventions (Sofi et al., 2010).

Community and Social Health: Social connections and communal meals are important aspects of the Mediterranean lifestyle, associated with enhanced mental well-being and reduced stress. Many modern wellness programs incorporate these social aspects by encouraging group activities and communal support to improve overall quality of life (Grosso & Galvano, 2016).

Steps or Process of Mediterranean Healing Traditions

Assessment of Individual Needs and Balance

Determining Balance in the Body: Historically, Mediterranean healing involved assessing individual humoral balance, based on the Greek theory of the four humors. Healers would identify any imbalances (excess or deficiency of humors) that could affect physical and emotional well-being. Even though modern medicine does not use humoral theory, the concept of personalized care remains central to Mediterranean health practices (Jones, 2005).

Personalized Dietary and Lifestyle Recommendations: Healers would recommend specific dietary and lifestyle practices tailored to the individual's needs, an approach similar to personalized nutrition in modern Mediterranean diet applications (Nutton, 2013).

Dietary Intervention as a Core Treatment Step

Adoption of the Mediterranean Diet: A cornerstone of Mediterranean healing is the diet, rich in vegetables, fruits, whole grains, olive oil, legumes, and lean protein sources like fish. Individuals are encouraged to follow a diet that emphasizes whole, minimally processed foods and to use herbs and spices instead of salt (Estruch et al., 2018).

Moderation and Balanced Eating Habits: The diet promotes portion control and the balance of macronutrients to foster satiety and prevent overeating. Meal structure, such as having a balanced lunch as the largest meal, is also key, as it aligns with traditional Mediterranean eating patterns (Bach-Faig et al., 2011).

Incorporating Physical Activity and Social Interactions

Daily Physical Activity: Regular movement, whether through walking, gardening, or other forms of moderate exercise, is integral to Mediterranean healing traditions. Physical activity is not only seen as a way to maintain physical health but also to support mental well-being by reducing stress and enhancing mood (Sofi et al., 2010).

Social Engagement and Communal Meals: Sharing meals with family and friends is central to Mediterranean culture, reinforcing social bonds, reducing stress, and enhancing emotional health. Communal meals contribute to a slower, more mindful eating experience, which supports digestion and a healthy relationship with food (Grosso & Galvano, 2016).

Herbal and Natural Remedies for Prevention and Healing

Using Medicinal Herbs and Spices: Mediterranean traditions use various herbs like rosemary, oregano, and sage for their healing properties. These are incorporated into daily meals or used as herbal infusions for their anti-inflammatory, digestive, or immune-boosting effects (Tapsell et al., 2006).

Therapeutic Applications: For specific ailments, herbal remedies are applied based on traditional knowledge. For example, chamomile tea is used to aid digestion and promote relaxation, while olive oil is used topically for its anti-inflammatory properties. Such remedies align with modern integrative medicine practices (Zargaran et al., 2012).

Mental and Emotional Health Practices

Mindfulness and Relaxation: Mediterranean healing promotes mental well-being through practices that encourage relaxation and mindfulness, such as enjoying leisurely meals and time in nature. Such practices align with contemporary techniques to reduce stress and promote psychological resilience (Psaltopoulou et al., 2013).

Community and Spiritual Support: Emotional support from family, friends, and community is an essential part of Mediterranean healing, as social ties are believed to promote mental health and reduce stress. In traditional settings, this support also included spiritual practices, often connected to religious or cultural rituals (Taub, 2017).

Monitoring and Adjustment

Regular Assessment and Adjustment: The Mediterranean approach to healing emphasizes continual monitoring of one's health, particularly in response to lifestyle, dietary, and environmental changes. Adjustments are made as needed to maintain balance and address any emerging health concerns, reflecting a preventive care mindset that allows individuals to stay proactive about their health (Salas-Salvadó et al., 2014).

Case study

Application of Mediterranean Healing Traditions in Preventive Health

Background - Maria, a 52-year-old woman from southern Italy, was recently diagnosed with prediabetes and high cholesterol. Her doctor advised lifestyle changes to prevent progression to type 2 diabetes and manage her cardiovascular risk factors. In addition to medical advice, Maria explored traditional Mediterranean practices as part of her lifestyle adjustments. The following case study details Maria's experience incorporating Mediterranean healing traditions into her life and their effects on her health.

Approach and Steps

Adopting a Mediterranean Diet

Dietary Modifications: Following the advice of her doctor and a local dietitian familiar with Mediterranean traditions, Maria adopted a diet rich in vegetables, fruits, whole grains, legumes, olive oil, and fish. She minimized her intake of red meat, processed foods, and refined sugars. This dietary approach has been linked with reduced risk factors for metabolic syndrome and cardiovascular disease (Estruch et al., 2018).

Emphasis on Fresh, Local Ingredients: Maria sourced locally grown vegetables and fresh fish from nearby markets, an aspect central to traditional Mediterranean diets. Research shows that adherence to a diet with minimally processed, seasonal ingredients aligns with health benefits like improved metabolic function and reduced inflammation (Bach-Faig et al., 2011).

Incorporating Daily Physical Activity

Walking and Outdoor Activities: Maria integrated regular walks into her daily routine, often meeting friends for group walks, which added a social component. She also began swimming at the beach twice a week, activities that are both traditional and consistent with Mediterranean lifestyle practices. Regular physical activity supports cardiovascular health, enhances mental well-being, and reduces the risk of chronic diseases (Sofi et al., 2010).

Natural Physical Activity: Rather than following a strict workout plan, Maria's approach was aligned with Mediterranean practices, which emphasize natural, moderate physical activity. This kind of exercise has shown mental health benefits, such as reduced stress and improved mood (Grosso & Galvano, 2016).

Using Herbal and Natural Remedies

Chamomile and Fennel Teas: Maria incorporated chamomile tea before bed to promote relaxation and better sleep. Chamomile, widely used in Mediterranean folk medicine, has mild sedative effects and may help improve sleep quality (Tapsell et al., 2006). She also used fennel tea after meals to aid digestion, another traditional remedy.

Olive Oil as a Topical and Dietary Aid: In addition to using olive oil in her cooking, Maria applied it to her skin, as it has traditionally been used for its anti-inflammatory and antioxidant properties. Olive oil, both as a dietary and topical treatment, can provide cardiovascular benefits and improve skin health (Zargaran et al., 2012).

Prioritizing Social and Emotional Well-being

Regular Family Meals: Maria regularly ate meals with her family, enhancing her emotional well-being and reducing stress. Shared meals are a significant aspect of Mediterranean culture, promoting social bonding and mindful eating habits that benefit both mental and physical health (Psaltopoulou et al., 2013).

Practicing Mindfulness and Leisure: Maria took time for leisure, often spending evenings reading or in quiet contemplation by the sea. Such practices, common in Mediterranean cultures, allow individuals to recharge and manage stress more effectively. This mindfulness practice aligns with research showing that leisure activities and time spent in nature improve emotional resilience (Scarmeas et al., 2006).

Outcomes - After six months, Maria's blood sugar levels and cholesterol improved significantly. Her doctor noted a reduction in her prediabetes markers, and her cholesterol levels dropped to within the normal range. Additionally, Maria reported enhanced well-being, reduced stress, and better sleep.

Analysis - Maria's case illustrates the effectiveness of Mediterranean healing traditions when integrated into a holistic health plan. Research supports her outcomes, as the Mediterranean diet, regular physical activity, social connection, and herbal remedies contribute to physical and mental health benefits (Estruch et al., 2018; Sofi et al., 2010).

This case study demonstrates how Mediterranean healing traditions can complement modern medical advice, supporting both physical health and emotional well-being.

Conclusion of Mediterranean Healing Traditions

Mediterranean healing traditions offer a holistic approach to health, emphasizing balance through diet, physical activity, social connection, and natural remedies. Rooted in centuries-old practices, this lifestyle has proven to promote not only physical health but also emotional well-being. Studies consistently highlight the benefits of a Mediterranean diet rich in vegetables, fruits, whole grains, legumes, and olive oil, showing its potential to reduce cardiovascular disease, metabolic syndrome, and diabetes risk (Estruch et al., 2018; Sofi et al., 2010). Additionally, incorporating natural forms of physical activity and social engagement supports mental health, reduces stress, and builds resilience (Grosso & Galvano, 2016).

The effectiveness of these practices is rooted in their holistic nature. For example, shared meals and community activities foster social bonds that protect against anxiety and depression, while natural remedies like chamomile and fennel aid in relaxation and digestive health (Psaltopoulou et al., 2013; Tapsell et al., 2006). By focusing on preventive health and integrating these traditions, individuals may achieve improved quality of life, highlighting the value of a Mediterranean lifestyle in modern healthcare.

The resurgence of interest in Mediterranean healing traditions underscores the benefits of integrating cultural health practices into daily life. As scientific research continues to validate these age-old practices, the Mediterranean approach is increasingly recognized as an effective model for achieving sustainable, holistic health (Scarmeas et al., 2006).

References

Bach-Faig, A., Berry, E. M., Lairon, D., Reguant, J., Trichopoulou, A., Dernini, S., ... & Serra-Majem, L. (2011). Mediterranean diet pyramid today. Public Health Nutrition, 14(12A), 2274-2284. https://doi.org/10.1017/S1368980011002515

Dhanani, A. (2004). Islamic medicine and its influence on the medieval west. Science in Context, 14(1-2), 13-24. https://doi.org/10.1017/S0269889701000326

Estruch, R., Ros, E., Salas-Salvadó, J., Covas, M. I., Corella, D., Arós, F., ... & Martínez-González, M. A. (2018). Primary prevention of cardiovascular disease with a Mediterranean diet supplemented with extra-virgin olive oil or nuts. New England Journal of Medicine, 378(25), e34. https://doi.org/10.1056/NEJMoa1800389

Grosso, G., & Galvano, F. (2016). Mediterranean diet adherence in children and adolescents in southern European countries. Nutrition, Metabolism and Cardiovascular Diseases, 26(4), 315-325. https://doi.org/10.1016/j.numecd.2016.01.008

Hankinson, R. J. (2013). The Cambridge companion to Galen. Cambridge University Press.

Jones, W. H. S. (2005). Hippocrates Collected Works I. Harvard University Press.

Keys, A. (1970). Coronary heart disease in seven countries. Circulation, 41(1), I-186-I-195. https://doi.org/10.1161/01.CIR.41.4S1.I-186

Martínez-González, M. A., & Sánchez-Villegas, A. (2016). The emerging role of Mediterranean diets in cardiovascular epidemiology: Monounsaturated fats, olive oil, red wine or the whole pattern? European Journal of Epidemiology, 31(5), 437-446. https://doi.org/10.1007/s10654-016-0151-8

Muntner, S. (1971). The medicinal teachings of Maimonides. Proceedings of the Royal Society of Medicine, 64(4), 371–376.

McVaugh, M. (1974). The rationality of medieval medicine. Princeton University Press.

Mediterranean diet supplemented with extra-virgin olive oil or nuts. New England Journal of Medicine, 378(25), e34. https://doi.org/10.1056/NEJMoa1800389

Nunn, J. F. (2002). Ancient Egyptian medicine. University of Oklahoma Press.

Nutton, V. (2013). Ancient medicine. Routledge.

Petropoulos, S. A., Fernandes, Â., Barros, L., & Ferreira, I. C. (2017). Chemical composition, nutritional value and antioxidant properties of Mediterranean edible wild greens and green sprouts. Food and Research International, 100, 179-187. https://doi.org/10.1016/j.foodres.2017.04.031

Psaltopoulou, T., Sergentanis, T. N., Panagiotakos, D. B., Sergentanis, I. N., Kosti, R., & Scarmeas, N. (2013). Mediterranean diet, stroke, cognitive impairment, and depression: A meta-analysis. Annals of Neurology, 74(4), 580-591. https://doi.org/10.1002/ana.23944

Salas-Salvadó, J., Bulló, M., Babio, N., Martínez-González, M. Á., Ibarrola-Jurado, N., Basora, J., ... & Serra-Majem, L. (2014). Reduction in the incidence of type 2 diabetes with the Mediterranean diet: Results of the PREDIMED-Reus nutrition intervention randomized trial. Diabetes Care, 34(1), 14-19. https://doi.org/10.2337/dc10-1288

Scarborough, J. (1991). Roman medicine. American Journal of Archaeology, 95(4), 743-744. https://doi.org/10.2307/506742

Scarmeas, N., Luchsinger, J. A., Stern, Y., Gu, Y., & He, J. (2006). Mediterranean diet and risk for Alzheimer's disease. Annals of Neurology, 59(6), 912-921. https://doi.org/10.1002/ana.20854

Sofi, F., Cesari, F., Abbate, R., Gensini, G. F., & Casini, A. (2010). Adherence to Mediterranean diet and health status: Meta-analysis. BMJ, 337, a1344. https://doi.org/10.1136/bmj.a1344

Tapsell, L. C., Hemphill, I., Cobiac, L., Patch, C. S., Sullivan, D. R., Fenech, M., ... & Inge, K. E. (2006). Health benefits of herbs and spices: The past, the present, the future. Medical Journal of Australia, 185(4), S4-S24. https://doi.org/10.5694/j.1326-5377.2006.tb00500.x

Taub, L. (2017). A History of Jewish Medicine: The Guide of the Perplexed. Princeton University Press.

Zargaran, A., Zarshenas, M. M., Karimi, A., Yarmohammadi, H., & Borhani-Haghighi, A. (2012). Avicenna (980–1037 AD) and early descriptions of trigeminal neuralgia. Journal of Medical Biography, 20(3), 168-172. https://doi.org/10.1258/jmb.2011.011025

Chapter 32

Native American Healing Practices

Shreelekha Kayal School of Liberal Studies (SLS), CMR University, Bangalore

Introduction

Native American healing practices are deeply rooted in spiritual, communal, and holistic traditions that have been passed down through generations. These practices often emphasize the interconnectedness of mind, body, spirit, and nature, and are guided by values of respect, balance, and harmony. In the context of psychotherapy, these practices can offer therapeutic benefits by addressing mental health concerns through non-Western paradigms, allowing clients to reconnect with their heritage and personal identity.

History and Foundational Practices:

Native American healing traditions predate Western medical systems and are based on the beliefs and practices of various Indigenous tribes across North America. These traditions vary widely among tribes, each having its unique healing rituals, symbols, and deities, yet they share common themes, such as the belief in spiritual healing, the importance of community, and the integration of nature. Early interactions with Western medicine during colonial periods led to suppression and stigmatization of these practices. Over time, however, there has been a resurgence and growing appreciation for these practices in the mental health field, with mental health professionals recognizing their therapeutic potential (Gone, 2013).

Core Practices and Founders

American healing practices often involve ceremonies, such as the sweat lodge, the use of medicinal plants, smudging, drumming, and storytelling, all led by spiritual leaders or healers within the community. Healers, also called medicine men or women, are regarded as both spiritual leaders and healthcare providers who are highly respected in their communities. Unlike Western psychotherapies with identifiable founders, Native American healing practices evolved organically through centuries of cultural wisdom, without a single founder. These healers serve as cultural custodians, carrying forward the wisdom and traditions necessary to restore balance and wellbeing in individuals.

Steps in Native American Healing Practices:

Preparation and Intention Setting:

The process often begins with preparing the client and healer through rituals such as smudging, where smoke from sacred herbs like sage or cedar is used to purify the space and participants.

Ceremonial Practice:

Healing ceremonies may include activities like chanting, drumming, or storytelling to evoke the spirit world, fostering spiritual healing and personal insight.

Connection to Ancestors and Nature:

Many practices include a connection with ancestral spirits or nature, promoting mindfulness and reflection.

Community Involvement:

Healing is often seen as a communal process, with community members providing support to the individual.

Closure and Reflection:

After the ritual, participants often engage in reflective practices or discussions that reinforce the insights gained during the healing process (Duran & Duran, 1995).

Application in Psychotherapy

Native American healing practices are applied in psychotherapy as a means of promoting mental health through spiritual and cultural approaches. These practices are particularly valuable in treating Native American clients, as they allow individuals to connect with their heritage and identity in ways that Western therapeutic models may overlook. For instance, storytelling can serve as a form of *narrative therapy*, helping clients reframe traumatic experiences in the context of cultural identity. *Smudging or drumming* can provide clients with a means of grounding themselves, thus aiding in managing anxiety and stress. Healing ceremonies encourage introspection and personal growth, fostering resilience and empowerment. In settings where these practices are integrated with Western psychotherapy, clients may experience a sense of cultural belonging that can enhance the therapeutic alliance and outcomes (Gone, 2010).

Benefits of Native American Healing Practices in Psychotherapy:

Holistic Approach:

Native American healing practices consider the mind, body, spirit, and emotions as interconnected. This approach aligns well with integrative psychotherapy, which seeks to address multiple facets of a client's life for comprehensive healing (Gone, 2013).

Emphasis on Community and Connection:

Rituals and healing practices often involve family and community, providing a sense of belonging and support that can be therapeutic for individuals dealing with isolation or disconnection (Brave Heart et al., 2011).

Use of Traditional Storytelling:

Storytelling, a core component of Native American healing, fosters self-reflection and resilience, allowing clients to reframe their personal narratives in a healing way (Duran & Duran, 1995).

Mindfulness and Nature-Based Practices:

These practices promote mindfulness and grounding through connection with nature, helping clients reduce stress and improve emotional regulation (Yellow Horse Brave Heart, 2003).

Strengths of Native American Healing Practices in Psychotherapy:

Holistic Approach:

Native American healing practices emphasize the interconnection between mind, body, and spirit, aligning with holistic models of mental health.

Cultural Relevance:

For Native American clients, these practices offer culturally relevant therapy that respects their heritage and identity, which can increase engagement and acceptance.

Community Support:

Healing practices often involve communal participation, fostering a sense of belonging and social support that can be essential for mental health recovery.

Empowerment and Resilience:

These practices can help individuals find strength within themselves and their culture, fostering resilience in the face of adversity.

Challenges in Integrating Native American Healing Practices:

Cultural Sensitivity and Appropriation:

One of the greatest challenges in integrating these practices into psychotherapy is ensuring that they are applied with respect and cultural sensitivity. Misinterpretation or misuse of these practices can lead to cultural appropriation and disrespect for Native American traditions.

Lack of Standardization:

Native American healing practices are diverse and vary widely across tribes, making it challenging to develop standardized protocols that can be applied universally in psychotherapy.

Resistance from Western Medical Professionals:

Some practitioners may be hesitant to integrate these practices due to a lack of scientific evidence or concerns about the efficacy of traditional healing methods.

Access and Availability:

Access to qualified Native healers or cultural consultants may be limited, especially in non-Native communities, creating logistical challenges for implementing these practices in psychotherapy settings (Gone & Calf Looking, 2011).

Case Studies

Case Study 1: Integrating Talking Circles with Group Therapy for Trauma Healing

Background:

A group of Native American adolescents, all from a single community, struggle with trauma stemming from historical oppression and current socioeconomic challenges. Many members of this group have experienced personal loss, substance abuse issues, and a disconnection from their cultural roots.

Healing Approach:

The therapist, who is experienced in cross-cultural psychotherapy, collaborates with a Native American healer from the community. Together, they incorporate "talking circles" into group therapy sessions. Talking circles are a traditional practice that allows each participant to speak freely without interruption, fostering a non-hierarchical environment and supporting cultural expression.

Therapeutic Process:

The healer leads the talking circles with a "talking stick" or "feather," which is passed around to each participant as they share their experiences. In conjunction with the traditional circle, the therapist guides group discussions, emphasizing active listening and cognitive-behavioral techniques. This dual approach allows for both cultural resonance and psychological processing.

Outcome:

Over time, participants report feeling a stronger sense of belonging and less stigma around discussing their feelings. The talking circles reinforce cultural pride and resilience, while modern therapeutic tools help participants develop coping strategies for trauma-related symptoms.

Case Study 2: Incorporating Smudging Rituals in Treatment for Anxiety and Depression

Background:

A Native American man in his mid-thirties is struggling with chronic anxiety and depression, which have been compounded by feelings of cultural disconnection and isolation. He has experienced discrimination, both personally and professionally, and often feels out of place in his environment.

Healing Approach:

The therapist works alongside a Native American elder to integrate smudging, a cleansing ritual using sage, cedar, or sweetgrass, into the client's treatment plan. Smudging is believed to purify energy and release negative emotions, aligning the individual with their environment and promoting spiritual balance.

Therapeutic Process:

Smudging rituals are conducted at the beginning of therapy sessions. The client is encouraged to participate actively, setting intentions for his emotional well-being. Following the ritual, the therapist engages the client in mindfulness-based cognitive therapy, using meditation and grounding exercises to enhance awareness of his emotional state.

Outcome:

The combination of smudging and mindfulness helps the client report a reduction in anxiety symptoms and an improved sense of inner peace. The ritual gives him a culturally meaningful way to connect with his heritage, while mindfulness exercises improve his ability to manage anxious thoughts in daily life.

References

Brave Heart, M. Y. H., Chase, J., Elkins, J., & Altschul, D. B. (2011). Historical trauma among Indigenous peoples of the Americas: Concepts, research, and clinical considerations. Journal of Psychoactive Drugs, 43(4), 282-290.

Duran, E., & Duran, B. (1995). Native American postcolonial psychology. Albany: State University of New York Press.

Duran, E., & Duran, B. (1995). Native American postcolonial psychology. State University of New York Press.

Gone, J. P. (2010). Psychotherapy and traditional healing for American Indians: Exploring the prospects for therapeutic integration. The Counseling Psychologist, 38(2), 166–235. https://doi.org/10.1177/0011000008330831

Gone, J. P. (2013). Redressing First Nations historical trauma: Theorizing mechanisms for indigenous culture as mental health treatment. Transcultural Psychiatry, 50(5), 683–706. https://doi.org/10.1177/1363461513487669

Gone, J. P., & Calf Looking, P. E. (2011). American Indian culture as substance abuse treatment: Pursuing evidence for a local intervention. Journal of Psychoactive Drugs, 43(4), 291- 296. https://doi.org/10.1080/02791072.2011.628915

Yellow Horse Brave Heart, M. (2003). The historical trauma response among natives and its relationship to substance abuse: A Lakota illustration. Journal of Psychoactive Drugs, 35(1), 7-13.

Chapter 33

Paws and Purpose: A Comprehensive Guide to Animal-Assisted Therapy

Taral Kolvekar School of Liberal Studies (SLS), CMR University, Bangalore

Introduction

The use of animals in therapeutic settings, known as Animal-Assisted Therapy (AAT), has become a respected and research-backed approach to promoting mental and emotional well-being. While the formalization of AAT is a relatively recent development, the bond between humans and animals has been recognized for centuries, with early examples of animals providing comfort, companionship, and therapeutic benefits to those in need.

Animal therapy is also known as pet therapy or animal-assisted therapy, involves using animals to support individuals dealing with specific physical or mental health challenges. Animals can offer comfort, alert others in emergency situations, and even perform actions that assist with a person's condition when needed. As a complementary or alternative therapy, animal therapy is intended to supplement, rather than replace, other treatments.

The primary aim of animal-assisted therapy is to help individuals manage or reduce certain symptoms of various health conditions. The specific approach to animal therapy can differ widely, depending on the individual's needs, the type of animal involved, and the form of therapy provided.

Early Uses of Animals in Therapeutic Contexts

Historical accounts suggest that animals have long been associated with healing and spiritual well-being. In ancient Egypt, Greece, and other early civilizations, animals were seen as symbols of protection and healing. By the 9th century, European monks in Gheel, Belgium, encouraged individuals with mental illnesses to care for animals, believing that these interactions promoted responsibility, calmness, and a sense of purpose. This early instance laid a foundational understanding of how animal companionship could support mental health, though it was largely anecdotal and lacked formal structure.

One of the earliest recorded uses of animals in mental health treatment occurred at the York Retreat in England in 1792. Founded by Quaker William Tuke, the retreat offered a humane alternative to the often harsh and isolating treatment of individuals with mental health conditions. Tuke observed that allowing residents to engage with animals helped reduce agitation and fostered a sense of peace, demonstrating the potential for animals to serve a therapeutic role. This early institution provided a framework for incorporating animals into mental health settings, though it would be decades before scientific inquiry began to explore these benefits systematically.

19th-Century Observations: Florence Nightingale's Influence

In the 19th century, Florence Nightingale, a pioneer in nursing and healthcare reform, documented her observations of the therapeutic effects of animals. She noted that pets could alleviate loneliness and despair, particularly among patients suffering from chronic illnesses and mental health conditions. Nightingale recommended the presence of small pets for patients, observing that animals could provide emotional support and improve patients' outlooks (Hines, 2003). Her insights laid the groundwork for considering animals as a source of comfort and companionship in medical settings.

Mid-20th Century: Early Scientific Observations and Studies

In the 20th century, notable figures in psychology began to explore the therapeutic potential of animals. Sigmund Freud, though primarily recognized for his contributions to psychoanalysis, observed how his dog, Jofi, influenced his patients during therapy sessions. Freud noted that Jofi's presence seemed to help patients relax, and he even used the dog's behavior as a barometer for clients' emotional states, highlighting an intuitive recognition of animals' calming influence. Around this same period, animals also played a role in supporting soldiers returning from World War II. Smoky, a dog owned by Corporal William Wynne, was credited with boosting morale among wounded soldiers, providing comfort during a period of intense trauma.

The formalization of AAT, however, is widely attributed to DR. Boris Levinson, a psychologist who inadvertently discovered the therapeutic potential of animals in the 1960s.

Establishing Animal-Assisted Therapy:

The 1970s and 1980s marked a period of growth and professionalization for AAT. In 1977, the Delta Society (now known as Pet Partners) was established in the United States to promote and standardize AAT practices. The organization trained therapy animal teams, set ethical guidelines, and advocated for the use of animals in healthcare, mental health, and education settings. As more therapists began incorporating animals into treatment, research on AAT's psychological and physiological benefits expanded, with studies showing reduced stress, decreased cortisol levels, and improved emotional regulation in those interacting with therapy animals.

One notable area of research has been the use of AAT to assist individuals with post-traumatic stress disorder (PTSD). Studies have shown that veterans and trauma survivors who engage with therapy animals, particularly dogs, experience reductions in anxiety, increased feelings of safety, and greater emotional stability. Additionally, animal-assisted interventions have proven beneficial in pediatric settings, providing comfort to children undergoing medical procedures and helping them manage pain and fear. The therapeutic benefits are not limited to mental health; for example, AAT has been shown to improve physical health markers, such as blood pressure and heart rate, indicating a holistic impact on well-being.

Modern Animal-Assisted Therapy: A Evidence-Based Practice

In recent decades, AAT has become widely recognized and incorporated into diverse healthcare settings, including hospitals, schools, nursing homes, and prisons. The American Psychological Association (APA) and the American Veterinary Medical Association (AVMA) now endorse the integration of therapy animals for specific psychological and medical conditions. Research has supported AAT's effectiveness in treating a range of conditions, from autism spectrum disorder to depression and anxiety. As studies continue to document the physiological and psychological benefits of animal-assisted interventions, AAT has solidified its role as a valuable complement to traditional therapy.

Theoretical Background Supporting Animal-Assisted Therapy

The theoretical underpinnings of AAT incorporate principles from several psychological frameworks, each contributing to an understanding of how and why human-animal interactions promote healing.

Attachment Theory:

AAT aligns closely with attachment theory, which posits that forming secure bonds is crucial for mental health. Developed by John Bowlby, attachment theory suggests that humans need consistent, supportive relationships to feel safe and valued. Therapy animals often fulfill this need, offering a source of nonjudgmental, unconditional support, which can alleviate feelings of loneliness and anxiety. For individuals with trauma or attachment disorders, animals can help create a secure base, fostering a sense of trust that may translate into improved interpersonal relationships.

Biophilia Hypothesis:

Proposed by biologist E.O. Wilson, the biophilia hypothesis suggests that humans have an innate tendency to connect with nature and other living organisms. This theory posits that this connection can lead to reduced stress and an overall sense of well-being. AAT leverages this innate connection, providing a setting where human-animal interactions satisfy a deep-seated psychological and emotional need, promoting relaxation and calm.

Social Support Theory:

Social support theory emphasizes the psychological benefits of supportive relationships, which reduce stress and promote resilience. Animals provide a unique form of social support because they are nonjudgmental, consistent, and emotionally responsive. For people who struggle with social interaction or experience social isolation, such as those with autism or depression, animals can offer companionship and an accessible source of emotional support.

Behavioral and Cognitive-Behavioral Theory:

Behavioural and cognitive-behavioural theories suggest that AAT can help modify maladaptive thoughts and behaviours. In behavioural terms, animals can serve as reinforcement in therapy, motivating clients to engage in positive social behaviours. In cognitive-behavioural therapy (CBT), animals may help reduce anxiety, promoting positive engagement through enjoyable interactions. This experience of safety and non-threatening interaction helps clients develop new, positive ways of thinking.

Applications of Animal-Assisted Therapy

Mental Health Treatment:

AAT is frequently used to manage mental health conditions such as anxiety, depression, PTSD, and trauma-related disorders. Research has shown that interactions with therapy animals can reduce symptoms of anxiety and promote feelings of calm, helping individuals become more receptive to therapeutic intervention.

Developmental Disorders:

Children with autism spectrum disorder (ASD) often struggle with social skills, communication, and emotional regulation. Interactions with therapy animals have been shown to improve social engagement, empathy, and communication among children with ASD. Therapy animals provide nonverbal support, making them ideal for children with communication challenges.

Geriatric Care:

In nursing homes and other eldercare settings, AAT is used to alleviate loneliness and depression among older adults. Studies have shown that therapy animals can help stimulate memory, promote physical activity, and reduce symptoms of dementia. The companionship of therapy animals provides emotional comfort, improving quality of life.

Physical Rehabilitation:

AAT is often integrated into physical rehabilitation programs to motivate patients recovering from injury or surgery. Activities such as walking or playing with a therapy animal encourage movement, coordination, and balance, supporting physical recovery.

Educational and Social Skill Development:

In educational settings, AAT has been shown to benefit children, especially those with learning disabilities or emotional difficulties. The presence of animals has been associated with improved focus, empathy, and social interaction, fostering a supportive learning environment.

Steps in Animal Assisted Therapy

Selection of Animals:

The animals selected for AAT are carefully chosen based on their temperament, behaviour, and ability to adapt to varied environments. Common animals used in therapy include dogs, horses, rabbits, and even dolphins, each chosen for their unique qualities that align with therapeutic goals. For example, dogs and horses are popular in AAT because they are responsive, highly trainable, and possess a natural inclination for social bonding. Dogs, with their loyalty and ability to offer unconditional acceptance, can provide clients with a non-judgmental companion, while horses, used in equine therapy, offer physical and emotional challenges that foster resilience and self-confidence. These animals undergo specific training to ensure they can handle the demands of therapeutic interactions, particularly with individuals experiencing heightened emotional states or physical disabilities.

Therapist and Animal Handler Role:

The role of the therapist and, where necessary, the animal handler is critical in facilitating AAT. These professionals assess each client's needs and develop tailored therapeutic activities involving the animal to address specific goals, such as reducing anxiety, improving social skills, enhancing physical rehabilitation, or promoting trauma recovery. For example, in sessions with children on the autism spectrum, dogs are often used to encourage social interactions. Children may feel more comfortable practicing eye contact, gestures, and basic communication with an animal, whose presence is calming and non-threatening. Similarly, elderly clients in assisted living facilities might benefit from petting or brushing a therapy dog, an activity that can reduce feelings of isolation, decrease blood pressure, and improve mood.

Goals of Therapy

The goals of animal-assisted therapy (AAT) are diverse and adaptable, tailored to meet each client's specific therapeutic needs, whether physical, emotional, or social. AAT can reduce anxiety by providing a calming presence, as animals naturally help people feel more grounded and secure. For individuals recovering from trauma, animals serve as gentle, non-judgmental companions, fostering a safe environment where clients can work through their feelings. In cases of physical rehabilitation, AAT can support motor skill development; activities like petting, brushing, or walking an animal can enhance strength, coordination, and mobility. For children with autism or social challenges, animals encourage social engagement by prompting eye contact, facial expressions, gestures, and interactive communication. These goals collectively highlight AAT's unique ability to connect with individuals across a wide spectrum of therapeutic needs, offering both practical and emotional support that enhances overall well-being.

Therapeutic Activities

Therapeutic activities in AAT vary but are always designed to encourage client engagement and interaction with the animal in a meaningful way. These activities might involve grooming, petting, playing, walking, or simply sitting quietly with the animal. Through such interactions, clients develop empathy, trust, and responsibility, often leading to enhanced self-esteem and emotional resilience. In equine therapy, for instance, clients learn to care for, lead, and ride horses, building confidence and self-control through the challenges of connecting with a larger, sensitive animal. These tasks help clients develop essential life skills, which can extend into their everyday lives, particularly for those working through issues of trust, self-confidence, or behavioural regulation.

Psychological and Physiological Benefits

One of the unique benefits of AAT is its ability to elicit both psychological and physiological responses that contribute to healing. Studies have shown that interacting with animals can reduce levels of cortisol, a stress hormone, while increasing levels of oxytocin, a hormone associated with feelings of relaxation and bonding. These biochemical changes can enhance mood, reduce anxiety, and create a sense of comfort and security, which is particularly beneficial for clients who may feel hesitant or vulnerable in a traditional therapeutic setting. For individuals with post-traumatic stress disorder (PTSD), animals can help reestablish a sense of safety, acting as a grounding presence during moments of anxiety or fear.

How does it work?

Animal therapy serves multiple purposes, which guide its approach. The specific type and focus of therapy are tailored to the individual's condition and needs. Common goals of animal therapy include:

- Offering comfort and helping to reduce pain levels
- Enhancing movement or motor skills
- Building social or behavioural skills
- Boosting motivation for activities like exercise or social interaction

The therapy process usually involves an animal handler—often the animal's owner—who brings the animal to sessions. The handler collaborates with a doctor to help the person meet their therapeutic goals.

Various organizations train handlers and connect them with healthcare providers, with many handlers volunteering. Both the handler and the animal must pass several certifications before being approved for therapy. The handler typically completes a training course on engaging with individuals and performing therapeutic techniques.

The animal also undergoes evaluations, including checking immunization records and physical exams to ensure it is healthy and disease-free. Temperament testing ensures the animal behaves appropriately with both the handler and others. Additionally, the handler-animal pair completes obedience training. These thorough certifications ensure safety and professionalism, providing high-quality therapy sessions for participants.

Who Can Benefit?

Animal therapy may support individuals with a variety of health issues including mental and physical health;

Mental Health

According to the Pet Partners organization, animal therapy may benefit mental health by:

- Reducing anxiety and stress
- Lowering perceptions of pain
- Easing feelings of fear or worry

- Enhancing social support
- Increasing motivation, stimulation, and focus

Animal therapy may be valuable for conditions like:

- Dementia
- Depression
- Anxiety
- Autism spectrum disorder
- Attention deficit hyperactivity disorder (ADHD)
- Schizophrenia

Studies involving therapy horses and dogs also suggest potential benefits for easing symptoms of post-traumatic stress disorder (PTSD). Moreover, animal-assisted therapy may support recovery and promote a sense of well-being among individuals undergoing treatment for substance use disorders.

Physical Health

Animal therapy may also help with physical health markers, benefiting conditions like:

- Epilepsy
- Heart failure
- Pain from cancer treatment
- Post-surgery recovery
- Recovery after strokes or other conditions that impact motor skills

Case Studies

Case Study 1: Animal-Assisted Therapy for PTSD in a Veteran

John, a 45-year-old veteran, sought therapy for symptoms related to post-traumatic stress disorder (PTSD), stemming from his military service. He reported heightened levels of hypervigilance, insomnia, intrusive memories, and social withdrawal. Traditional therapeutic approaches had proven somewhat helpful, but John continued to struggle with feeling safe and connected in social environments.

Therapeutic Approach

A certified therapy dog named Luna, a calm Labrador retriever, was introduced to provide John with companionship and help him establish a sense of security. Luna's gentle and non-threatening demeanor was intended to ease John's anxiety, allowing him to develop trust within a controlled, safe environment.

Intervention and Activities

1. **Grounding Techniques:** During each session, John was encouraged to focus on Luna's breathing, warmth, and physical presence. This grounding exercise helped him manage hypervigilance by anchoring him to the present moment, reducing the intensity of his physical and emotional anxiety responses.
2. **Desensitization Exercises:** John and Luna engaged in short, structured walks in public spaces. These sessions were designed to gradually reintroduce John to social environments, increasing

his comfort in public without triggering his hypervigilance. Luna's presence provided a calming influence, allowing John to feel less exposed and more at ease.

3. **Emotional Regulation:** Luna's nonjudgmental companionship served as an emotional anchor, helping John process difficult emotions in a safe, supportive environment. He reported feeling a sense of safety with Luna, which encouraged him to confront and express emotions associated with his trauma.

Outcome

After three months, John showed marked improvement in his ability to manage PTSD symptoms. He reported a reduction in hypervigilance and experienced fewer flashbacks. John's comfort with public spaces increased, and he began reconnecting with friends and family, indicating a decrease in social isolation. Luna's companionship helped him establish trust and emotional resilience, laying the groundwork for a more socially integrated and less trauma-driven life.

Case Study 2: Animal-Assisted Therapy for a Child with Autism Spectrum Disorder

Lily, an 8-year-old girl diagnosed with autism spectrum disorder (ASD), faced difficulties in sensory processing, communication, and social interactions. Her parents were concerned about her anxiety levels and tendency to engage in repetitive behaviors as coping mechanisms.

Therapeutic Approach

A therapy rabbit named Benny, selected for his gentle and calm disposition, was introduced to Lily. Rabbits are known to have calming effects, making them ideal for children with sensory sensitivities. Benny's small size and soft fur were comforting for Lily, encouraging her to approach him with curiosity and warmth.

Intervention and Activities

1. **Sensory Desensitization:** During sessions, Lily was encouraged to pet Benny gently and observe his movements. This activity helped her become accustomed to physical touch in a soothing manner, gradually desensitizing her to sensory stimuli she might normally find overwhelming.
2. **Social Interaction Skills:** Lily and Benny engaged in structured turn-taking games, such as feeding him treats or gently guiding him back to his enclosure. These interactions encouraged reciprocal communication and served as a foundation for building Lily's social skills, reinforcing positive behaviours like eye contact and turn-taking.
3. **Emotional Regulation:** Observing Benny's calm demeanour helped Lily model similar behaviours, reducing her repetitive actions and anxiety. Benny's steady presence provided a sense of stability, helping Lily learn self-soothing techniques.

Outcome

After four months, Lily showed notable improvements in her ability to manage sensory input and regulate her emotions. Her parents reported increased tolerance for physical touch, reduced repetitive behaviours, and improved communication skills. She initiated more social interactions and expressed excitement about her time with Benny, indicating increased emotional resilience and comfort in social contexts.

Case Study 3: Animal-Assisted Therapy for Grief and Loss

Sarah, a 60-year-old woman, was dealing with intense grief following the recent death of her husband. She experienced overwhelming loneliness, a lack of motivation, and found it difficult to reestablish a routine. Sarah's family encouraged her to seek therapy to help her process her emotions and re engage with life.

Therapeutic Approach

A therapy cat named Felix, known for his affectionate and calm personality, was introduced to Sarah's sessions. Cats are often perceived as gentle companions, offering comfort and affection without demanding extensive engagement, which made Felix an ideal choice for Sarah's needs.

Intervention and Activities

1. **Companionship and Routine Building:** Felix provided a reason for Sarah to create structure in her life. Caring for Felix—by petting, feeding, and engaging with him—gave her a sense of purpose and routine, which helped her reestablish daily habits.
2. **Emotional Expression:** Felix's calming presence encouraged Sarah to express her feelings, often prompting her to share memories and emotions associated with her late husband. Talking to Felix allowed Sarah to process her grief in a safe, accepting environment without fear of judgment.
3. **Mindfulness and Coping:** By observing Felix's quiet and relaxed behaviors, Sarah learned mindfulness techniques that helped her stay present and grounded. Focusing on Felix's calming influence provided respite from intrusive thoughts and gave her an outlet for managing her grief.

Outcome

Over the course of three months, Sarah experienced a reduction in loneliness and gained a greater sense of peace regarding her loss. She reported feeling more emotionally balanced and began reintegrating into social activities. Felix's companionship helped her feel connected to life again, reinforcing her resilience and capacity for healing.

Advancements in Indian Culture

Significant advancements and major work in animal-assisted therapy (AAT) are primarily concentrated in the Western world. In contrast, countries in the East, such as China, Japan, Sri Lanka, and India, are still in the early stages of developing AAT practices.

In India, animals hold a sacred status, with numerous cultural beliefs surrounding them. Animals such as cows, elephants, and dogs are deeply connected to Hindu traditions, valued based on their associations with Hindu deities. Additionally, other major religions in India—including Christianity, Islam, Buddhism,

Jainism, and Sikhism—also attribute significant importance to animals, viewing them as integral to nature and the universe. These religious beliefs, with their unique perspectives, are essential in shaping the practice of animal-assisted therapy within these communities.

History

Records of animal-assisted therapy (AAT) in India date back to 1996, when Blue Cross of India partnered with the Saraswathi Kendra Learning Centre for children with special needs to launch the country's first AAT program in Chennai. In 2001, the Animals Asia Foundation (AAF) introduced the DR. Dog program to support children with special needs and elderly individuals in Chennai also notes the expansion of this program to other cities, including Ludhiana, Tirupati, Bangalore, and Visakhapatnam.

The term "animal-assisted therapy" in India gained recognition largely due to the efforts of the Animal Angels Foundation, an influential organization with branches in Pune and Mumbai. As a member of the International Association of Human-Animal Interaction Organizations (IAHAIO), the Foundation's therapists are certified by the University of North Texas. Minal Kavishwar, founder of Animal Angels Foundation, and her therapy dog Kutty were India's first registered therapy-dog handler team, honoured with the Delta Society's Beyond Limits Award in 2008. The organization has actively participated in prominent conferences, including the Green Chimneys Conference, the IAHAIO International Conference in 2011, and the NIH-Waltham Workshop in 2015, to discuss perspectives on AAT in India.

In 2000, Pushpa Bopaiah, a PATH International-certified equine therapist, established India's first equine therapy center, Healing Horses, in Bengaluru to serve children with disabilities (Nair, 2008). A second equine therapy park followed in Hyderabad in 2012 under her guidance (The Hindu, 2012). The Indian Cancer Society has also recently adopted equine therapy to help cancer patients cope with emotions such as fear and loss of control associated with their diagnosis (Shelar, 2017).

Founded in 2004 in Mumbai, the Manav Foundation, a public charitable trust, includes AAT as part of its rehabilitation services for individuals with mental illness and emotional disorders. In 2005, clinical psychologists and certified AAT professionals Rohini Fernandes and Radhika Nair established the Animal Angels Foundation in Mumbai, focusing on using AAT to enhance skills and aid recovery in both children and adults (Animal Angels Foundation, 2021).

In 2013, Brijesh Dash founded the Hands and Paws Foundation in Bhubaneswar to work with underserved populations, including slum children, children with autism, individuals with substance use issues, and elderly clients, using a therapy dog named Magic (Sahu, 2014). More recently, in 2015, a donkey sanctuary in Ahmedabad introduced donkey therapy, training two donkeys to assist children with special needs through therapeutic riding (Naik, 2015). This brief history highlights the gradual development of animal-assisted therapy in India.

Development of Animal-Assisted Therapy in India

Although animal-assisted therapy (AAT) is still relatively new in India, it has significant potential for positively impacting both physical and mental health. Establishing AAT as a recognized therapeutic approach will require extensive groundwork within society. Addressing the challenges associated with implementing AAT and finding solutions to overcome these barriers will support the field's growth. As awareness of the therapeutic benefits of animals increases among pet owners, interest in AAT is likely to rise. However, to fully integrate AAT into mainstream therapeutic practices in India, several essential steps need to be undertaken.

The most crucial step for advancing animal-assisted therapy (AAT) in India is education. Academia plays a significant role in raising awareness about human-animal interactions and how these can contribute to broader societal benefits. Indian educational institutions should consider incorporating AAT as a primary subject or offering certificate courses that cover AAT fundamentals along with practical training.

Research is another vital component for the development of any healthcare field. Due to limited research on AAT within the Indian context, demonstrating its effectiveness for Indian populations can be challenging. While studies generally show positive effects of therapy animals, varying methodologies, small sample sizes, limited long-term impact assessments, and inconclusive results prevent broad conclusions. Comprehensive research with well-designed studies is necessary. Given the complexity of studying human-animal interactions, both qualitative and quantitative methods are essential for a complete analysis of outcomes. Reducing the research gap in India will require greater curiosity and exploration by researchers, and organizations or practitioners in the field can play a key role in fostering this interest.

A significant role of AAT organizations is to build awareness among the public and healthcare professionals about this unique therapy and its benefits. This can be achieved through various human-animal interaction programs across the country. Social media, too, can be instrumental in promoting agencies involved in AAT.

While animal-assisted therapy (AAT) is still emerging in India, there is significant potential for its development as a valuable therapeutic approach. Key steps include expanding education and research, documenting clinical successes, and establishing standardized guidelines to ensure consistent, ethical practices across disciplines. By fostering awareness through success stories, research, and collaboration with AAT organizations, India can build public and professional confidence in this therapy. Additionally, advocating for policy support based on evidence-based research can secure the resources and recognition needed to integrate AAT into mainstream healthcare. Addressing these foundational areas will not only enhance the quality of AAT but also help India leverage the therapeutic power of human-animal interactions across diverse populations, ultimately contributing to the well-being of both individuals and communities.

Overall, the article supports the idea that animal-assisted therapy fosters a mutually beneficial relationship, making the healing process smoother for individuals while promoting positive outcomes for animals, contributing to the well-being of both parties involved.

References

Narvekar, H. N. (2021). A reflection on the current status of animal-assisted therapy in India. *Springer Nature Switzerland AG.* https://doi.org/10.1007/s12603-021-01400-w Animal Angels Foundation. (2021). Retrieved February 12, 2021 from http://www.animalangelsfoundation.com/

Johnson, J. (2020, July 10). *Animal therapy: Benefits and types.* Medical News Today. https://www.medicalnewstoday.com/articles/animal-therapy

Johnson, J. (2022, July 20). *The healing power of animals: Benefits of animal-assisted therapy.* Medical News Today. https://www.medicalnewstoday.com/articles/animal-therapy

Feldman, S., Fine, A., & Melfi, L. (2019). Research, practice, science and public policy: How they fit together in the context of AAI. In: Fine, A. (Ed.). *Handbook on animal assisted therapy.* (5th ed. pp. 417–424). Elsevier/Academic Press Manav Foundation. (2004). Retrieved February 12, 2020 from https://www.manavfoundation.org.in/

Equestrian Therapy. (n.d.). *[Image of a horse therapy session].* Retrieved December 2, 2024, from https://www.equestriantherapy.com/wp-content/uploads/2014/04/horse-therapy-history-1.jpg

iStock. (n.d.). *Young girl with autism connecting with horses in a special center [Photograph].* Retrieved December 2, 2024, from https://media.istockphoto.com/id/1165138760/photo/young-girl-with-autism-connecting-with-horses-in-a-special-center.jpg?s=612x612&w=0&k=20&c=FCBK8TwU24IngkEo937SWmx_E8VVnXKzqnuopRbWQgo=

Vincent's Place. (n.d.). *[Image of therapy involving animals].* Retrieved December 2, 2024, from https://www.vincentsplace.org/About/therapy/files/stacks-image-5bcced2.jpg

The Times of India. (n.d.). *[Image associated with article ID 70191653].* Retrieved December 2, 2024, from https://static.toiimg.com/thumb/imgsize-23456,msid-70191653,width-600,resizemode-4/70191653.jpg

Neuharth, E. (2018, February 5). *Health benefits of animal-assisted therapy.* Recovery. Retrieved [insert retrieval date if applicable], from https://images.app.goo.gl/a9je1CHAA9BmmKRp8

Chapter 34

Play Therapy Tanishqua Rai School of Liberal Studies (SLS), CMR University, Bangalore

Play therapy is defined as the systematic use of a theoretical model that establishes an interpersonal process in which therapists use the therapeutic power of play to help children prevent or resolve psychosocial difficulties and achieve optimal growth Play therapy is a form of psychotherapeutic approach of the children and a psycho-diagnostic tool. (Association for Play Therapy, 1997)

It is a powerful means of joining with the innate, creative, non-verbal capacities of children. It is a developmentally appropriate, evidence-based approach to counselling youngsters. In play therapy children can play out, literally or metaphorically, their inner and real-life experiences in a way that builds insight and capacity. Play therapy enables children to express, manage, and communicate emotions, as well as practice and refine new skills, including as their emotional responses.

Landreth (2012) defines play therapy as *a dynamic interpersonal relationship between a child (or person of any age) and a therapist...who provides selected play materials and facilitates the development of a safe relationship for the child ... to fully express and explore self (feelings, thoughts, experiences, and behaviours) through play, the child's natural medium of communication, for optimal growth and development. (p. 11)*

Types of Play Therapy

Directive Play Therapy

Directive play therapy is an approach wherein the therapist takes an active role in guiding the child's play. The therapist introduces specific toys, games, or activities with the intention of eliciting responses or addressing identifies problems. In this approach, the therapist may provide directions, ask focused questions, or offer interpretations to help the child explore their thoughts, feelings, and behaviours.

Non-Directive Play Therapy

Non-directive play therapy allows for the child to take the lead in their play, with the therapist adopting a more passive observational role. The therapist fosters a secure and accepting environment, in which the child can freely explore and express themselves via play, without any explicit directives or interpretations. This approach is often grounded in the principles of child- centred therapy, where the therapist focuses on creating a supportive and empathetic relationship with the child, and the child is given the autonomy to direct the course of therapy

Aspect	Directive Play Therapy	Non-Directive Play therapy
Characteristics	Highly structured, therapist guided	Less structured, child-led
Goals	Behavioural change, skill development, symptom reduction	Emotional expression, self-exploration, building trust
Techniques	Role-playing, modeling,	Reflective listening, unstructured play, observational methods
Materials Used	Puppets, board games, art supplies	Dollhouses, sand trays, various sorts of toys
Advantages	Focused and efficient, clear structure, helps in skill building.	Flexible, builds trust and rapport
Limitations	Less flexible, potential resistance from child	Less structured, less focused, takes longer to achieve specific therapeutic goals

Materials and Toys

Play therapists utilize a wide range of materials and toys to facilitate the therapeutic process. Some common materials and toys used in play therapy include

- **Art supplies** (e.g., crayons, paints, sand, etc.) which can help children express their emotions and experiences and allow children to depict their feelings visually.
- **Dress up clothes and props** that allow for pretend play and sociodramatic exploration of different identities and scenarios.
- **Dolls and action figures**, which can represent family members or other important figures, and can be used to act out scenarios and relationships.
- **Vehicles and building materials** that encourage constructive and creative play.
- **Board games**, which can teach social skills, patience, and rule-following while providing a fun, engaging context.
- **Play dough or clay**, which encourage tactile exploration and creative expression.
- **Sensory materials** like water tables, kinetic sand, or textured objects may be included to help children self-regulate and explore their emotions through tactile experiences.

The selection of materials and toys used in play therapy is often influenced by the child's age, developmental age, and the specific goals of the therapy. The use of toys and materials in play therapy can help children develop a sense of autonomy, foster emotional expression and regulation, and facilitate the exploration of interpersonal relationships and problem- solving skills.

Play Therapy Techniques

Play therapy encompasses various techniques designed to facilitate communication, emotional expression, and problem-solving in children through engaging and playful interactions. These techniques create a safe and supportive environment where children can explore their feelings, build resilience, and practice coping strategies.

Role Playing

Role-playing involves children taking on different roles or scenarios using dolls, action figures, or puppets. This technique provides a safe outlet for expressing emotions, confronting fears, and rehearsing solutions to challenges. This includes

- ***Superhero play***: here, children draw their favourite superheroes and their powers. The therapist helps the child connect these superpowers to their own strengths, encouraging them to use their abilities in a positive and empowering way.
- ***Puppet play***: herein, puppets help children communicate, especially those with selective mutism. In the Family Puppet Interview, family members use puppets to share a story, uncovering dynamics and expressing feelings

Sandplay Therapy

Sand play therapy involves using a sandbox and miniature figures to construct scenes that reflect a child's inner world. This non-verbal technique allows therapists to gain insights into the child's emotional state by observing the symbolic representations they create.

Art Therapy

Art therapy uses materials like crayons, paints, and clay to help children visually express complex emotions they may struggle to articulate verbally, offering therapists a deeper understanding of their experiences. it includes, clay play therapy, painting play therapy, draw a family, etc.

Story-telling

Storytelling incorporates books, puppet shows, or narratives that resonate with the child's experiences, making it easier for them to discuss emotions and situations.

Therapeutic Storymaking

Therapeutic story making allows children to create their own narratives, helping them explore personal challenges creatively and develop problem-solving skills.

Games

Games, such as board or interactive activities, provide an opportunity to foster social skills, teamwork, and emotional regulation in a structured and enjoyable setting. These activities also teach children how to manage winning and losing gracefully, promoting resilience and positive social interactions. These games involve:

- ***Communication games***: A popular play therapy activity like a classic board game. Children roll dice to move along a path and draw a talking, feeling, or doing card based on where they land. The game concludes when a player collects the most chips, helping reveal feelings and psychological issues.
- ***Self-control play therapy techniques***: "Simon Says" teaches self-control and attention, promoting children to engage while following commands that begin with "Simon Says."
- ***Strategy games techniques***: Games like checkers and chess enhance problem-solving, teaching patience and emotional regulation through winning and losing scenarios.

Movement and Dance

Movement and dance serve as another powerful tool in play therapy, allowing children to express emotions physically and release pent-up energy. Through engaging in dance or movement-based activities, children can process feelings in a non-verbal and dynamic way.

Imaginary and Fantasy Play

Imaginary play, which involves creating imaginary worlds and situations, encourages experimentation with different roles and scenarios. This technique aids children in processing emotions tied to real-life events and exploring potential solutions in a safe, imaginative space. It includes:

- ***The world technique***: Children build an imaginary world using toys, expressing emotions and creativity. Observing and asking questions reveals their reality while improving problem-solving skills.
- ***Family relations technique***: Provide a makeshift mailbox for each family member and strips of paper with statements like "loves me" or "hates me." Sorting the "mail" reveals family dynamics and encourages communication.
- ***Worry dolls***: Children assign their worries to dolls or stuffed animals, leaving the "worries" behind after the session. Discussing these later helps them process and let go of concerns.

Emotion Identification Activities

Emotion identification activities, such as using emotion cards or recognizing facial expressions, are instrumental in enhancing emotional literacy. By helping children label and understand their feelings, these activities foster self-awareness and improve their ability to articulate emotions effectively.

Benefits of Play Therapy

Play therapy is a highly effective therapeutic approach that has the power of play to promote emotional healing and growth in children. The following are few benefits of play therapy.

1. **Coping Strategies:** play allows children to explore and express their emotions, thoughts, and experiences. This approach allows children to build appropriate coping mechanisms to navigate difficult situations as well as managing their emotions.
2. **Self-Respect:** play therapy promotes self-respect and self-esteem in youngsters. It allows them to make decisions, take chances, and achieve achievement, building a good self-image.

3. **Empathy:** it encourages children to understand and empathize with the emotions and experience of others. Through play- therapy, children learn to consider different viewpoints, and enhance their ability to relate to others and support them.
4. **Social Skills:** play therapy provides a supportive environment for children to develop and practice social skills such as effective communication, negotiation, turns-taking, and conflict resolution within a safe and guided setting.
5. **Emotional Expression:** play therapy allows children to express their emotions freely without fear of judgement. Through this process, they can let go of repressed emotions and acquire a greater understanding of their emotional experiences.
6. **Behavior Management:** play therapy addresses behavioral disorders by helping children identify and understand the underlying causes of their problematic behaviors. They can create healthy forms of self-expression by examining these challenges in play.
7. **Learning Disabilities:** Children with learning difficulties can benefit from play therapy because it offers an interactive and engaging approach for them to learn new things. Their academic performance, problem-solving ability, and cognitive capacities can all be improved through play.
8. **Trauma Recovery:** Children who have experienced trauma might benefit greatly from play therapy. Their traumatic experiences can be safely revisited and processed via play, which helps kids slowly incorporate them into their story and find healing.
9. **Building Relationships:** Building safe and trustworthy interactions between the child and the therapist is facilitated by play therapy. This connection gives the youngstesr a strong basis to build positive relationships with people outside of the therapeutic setting.

Limitations

1. **Dependence on Play Materials**: Some children may become reliant on toys or materials, which could limit their verbal expression. If children are too focused on play materials, it may hinder their ability to articulate their experiences or emotions clearly.
2. **Requires Specific Training**: Therapists need specific training in play therapy, which may not be available in all settings. Not all mental health professionals are trained in these techniques, leading to inconsistencies in therapy quality.
3. **Subjectivity in Interpretation**: Responses and actions during play can be highly subjective, leading to varying interpretations by therapists. Different therapists may understand the same play scenario in contrasting ways, which can impact treatment outcomes.
4. **Limitations with Older Children**: Play therapy may be less effective for older children or adolescents who may prefer traditional talk therapy methods. As children mature, they may have a greater capacity for verbal communication, making conventional therapeutic approaches more suitable.

History and Development of Play Therapy

The pioneers of child psychotherapy were the first ones to elucidate the role of play in therapy, every tradition of psychotherapy has its own theories and practices for addressing play. However, each tradition is connected by the central proposition that play transmits and communicates the child's unconscious experiences, desires, thoughts, and emotions.

Play Therapy draws its foundations from elements of child psychotherapy, with its theoretical basis rooted primarily in Humanistic psychology and Attachment theory.

Hermine Hug-Hellmuth is recognized as the first psychoanalyst to specialize in child therapy, pioneering the use of play as a therapeutic tool. In 1921, she formalized play therapy by providing children with materials to aid in self-expression, advocating for its use to explore their inner worlds. Similarly, **Melanie Klein** utilized play both as an analytic technique and to engage children, believing it offered valuable insights into a child's unconscious mind.

David Levy introduced "release therapy" in 1938, a structured approach designed for traumatized children. This method involved free play, gradually incorporating materials related to the trauma to help children re-experience and process unresolved emotions. **Joseph Soloman** developed "active play" to support children with impulsive or disruptive behaviors. He believed that expressing emotions like fear and anger through play would lead to more socially appropriate behavior.

Anna Freud emphasized the role of play in fostering a positive relationship between the child and therapist, which she saw as essential for accessing the child's thoughts and emotions. **Carl Rogers**, in the 1940s and 1950s, developed person-centered therapy, focusing on authenticity, trust, and acceptance within the therapeutic relationship. **Virginia Axline** later adapted Rogers' approach into nondirective play therapy, specifically tailored for children.

In the early 1980s, **Roger Phillips** proposed combining cognitive therapy with play therapy, creating cognitive-behavioral play therapy. This approach has since been used to treat children as young as two, blending cognitive techniques with play to address developmental and emotional challenges.

Theoretical Background of Play Therapy

Play therapy is typically grounded in three essential theoretical principles. One of the key theoretical frameworks in play-based therapy is the ***child- centred approach***. This approach, developed by Virginia Axline, highlights the importance of fostering a therapeutic relationship built on unconditional positive regard, empathy, and authenticity. The therapist creates a safe space for the child to freely express their thoughts and feelings through play, without judgement or interpretation.

This framework views the child as the expert in their own experiences, with the therapist adopting the role of a supportive facilitator who supports and guides the child's self-exploration.

Another theoretical framework used in play therapy is ***filial approach***, i.e. in this approach the parents or caregiver are trained to become active participants in their children's therapy sessions. They learn techniques and strategies to engage in therapeutic play with their children fostering healing and growth within the parent-child relationship. This approach recognizes the pivotal role of parents in shaping their child's development and emotional well-being.

The ***dyadic approach*** is another theoretical framework that focuses on the specific dynamics between the child and the therapist. It emphasizes the importance of the therapeutic relationship in enabling change and growth. The therapist actively engages with the child in play, building trust and attachment, providing a nurturing, and accepting environment.

Applications

Emotional Expression

Children often lack the vocabulary and verbal skills needed to articulate complex emotions, which can leave them feeling frustrated or misunderstood. Play therapy provides a safe way to express feelings like anger or sadness through toys, art, or storytelling. For example, a child might use figurines to act out conflicts, helping therapists understand and address their emotional needs.

Trauma Resolution

Play therapy offers a structured and secure space for children to process traumatic experiences, allowing them to approach their memories gradually and symbolically, rather than reliving them directly. This indirect approach can make the experience feel more manageable, helping children confront and cope with trauma. For instance, a child involved in a car accident might use toy cars to replay the event, gaining control and emotional resolution in a safe environment.

Behavioral Issues

Children with behavioral challenges, such as aggression, defiance, or social withdrawal, can use play therapy as a space to explore and practice healthier ways of expressing themselves. Through specific activities and therapeutic play, children are encouraged to release emotions safely and learn coping mechanisms that reduce destructive behavior patterns. For instance, a child with a tendency toward aggression might be encouraged to engage in physical play, such as punching a pillow or molding clay, to release frustration safely. Over time, the therapist can guide the child through games and activities that promote patience, empathy, and constructive problem-solving, helping them develop alternative ways to handle strong emotions.

Developmental Delays

Play therapy also supports children with developmental delays or learning disabilities by enhancing social, emotional, and cognitive skills through structured play activities. These activities are often designed to strengthen fine motor skills, improve attention spans, and encourage positive social interactions, all of which are critical for daily functioning and academic success.

Family Dynamics

Family issues, such as divorce, separation, or ongoing conflict, can be incredibly challenging for children to understand and process. Play therapy can be an effective way to support children through these situations by improving family dynamics and fostering communication within the family unit. Family play therapy sessions may involve parents, siblings, or other caregivers, creating a space where all family members can express their feelings and concerns in a structured and supportive setting.

Anxiety and Depression

Play therapy offers a constructive outlet for children who are dealing with anxiety or depression. By engaging in creative activities, children can manage difficult emotions in a way that feels safe and empowering, reducing overall tension and stress. For example, a child with social anxiety might participate in role-playing games that mimic social interactions, allowing them to practice these scenarios in a non-threatening environment.

Medical Procedures

For children undergoing medical treatments or dealing with chronic illnesses, play therapy can be instrumental in helping them understand and cope with medical procedures. By using play materials that mimic medical tools, children can familiarize themselves with what they may encounter, which reduces fear and anxiety. For instance, a child facing surgery might play with toy stethoscopes, syringes, or surgical masks, allowing them to role-play the procedure in a controlled environment. This kind of preparation helps children feel more in control and less frightened, enabling them to approach medical situations with greater resilience and understanding.

Steps or Processes

Initiation Phase

The first stage of play therapy, also known as the initiation phase or exploratory stage, lays the foundation for future therapeutic work. During the initial 4-6 sessions, the therapist builds trust and creates a safe environment for the child to express themselves freely. Children learn what to expect in each session, become familiar with the playroom, and understand their roles. Some children explore eagerly, while others may be hesitant. The therapist empowers the child to take the lead, encouraging them to engage at their own pace. Caregivers are advised to be patient and support their child's comfort, sometimes joining for part of the session to provide additional reassurance.

Resistance Phase

The resistance phase, also known as the negative reaction stage, is when children begin to confront the underlying issues causing their behavioral symptoms. This phase represents a shift from comfort to change and can be challenging for the child. They may show reluctance to attend therapy, experience emotional outbursts, or display temporary regressions. This stage is critical for building emotional intelligence and resilience. Caregivers can support their child by validating their feelings, encouraging them to continue, and reinforcing that they are capable of handling difficult emotions.

Growing Phase

The growing phase or work phase is often the longest stage of play therapy. During this time, children fully engage in the therapeutic process, showing growth in self-esteem, communication skills, and emotional regulation. Setbacks may occasionally occur, as old habits resurface, but these moments are part of reinforcing new behavioral patterns. Caregivers are encouraged to practice empathy and consistency, reminding the child of their progress, and helping them build resilience and self-confidence.

Termination Phase

The termination phase marks the end of play therapy, occurring when the child consistently demonstrates their new skills and stabilized behaviours. Sessions are gradually reduced, allowing the child to adjust to less frequent support. Though it can be difficult for children to part with the therapist, the therapist helps them reflect on their progress, creating a positive sense of closure. Minor regressions may arise, but overall, children adapt well, feeling empowered to handle life independently with the skills they have developed.

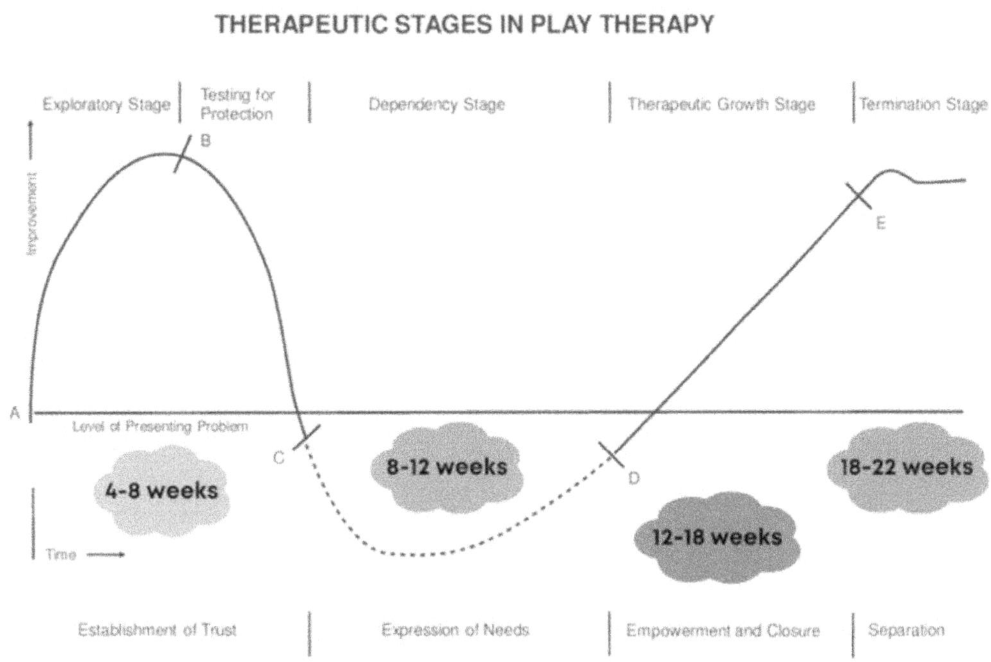

Figure 2. Carmichael, 2006; Landreth, 2002

Case Studies

Case Study 1: Separation Anxiety (Lily, 6 years old)

Presenting Problem:

Lily, a 6-year-old girl, experiencing intense anxiety upon starting first grade. She refuses to go to school, clings to her mother, and exhibits physical symptoms such as stomach aches and headaches on school days. Lily's parents report that she becomes extremely distressed when they try to leave her at school, often crying uncontrollably and pleading to go home. This behaviour has persisted for over a month, causing significant disruption to the family's routine and Lily's education.

Background

Lily is the youngest of three children in a middle class family. She had no previous issues with separation during preschool or kindergarten. Her parents describe her as generally shy but previously able to adapt to new situations when given time. The family recently moved to a new neighbourhood which coincided with lily staring her 1st grade at a new school.

Assessment and Observations:

1. **Clinical interview with parents:** it revealed that lily's anxiety symptoms began shortly after the family's move and increased when school started. Parents report no significant traumatic events or changes in family dynamics except the recent move.
2. **Observation of lily's interaction with her mother:** lily displays excessive clinginess, constantly seeking physical proximity to her mother. She becomes visibly distressed when her mother attempts to create even minor physical distance.
3. Separation anxiety rating scales:
    a. lily scored high on the separation anxiety subscale of screen for child anxiety related disorders (SCARED)
    b. separation anxiety assessment scale-child version (SAAS-C), results indicated significant separation anxiety symptoms, particularly related to school attendance.
4. **Teacher report:** lily's teacher notes that when successfully brought to school, lily remains anxious throughout the day, often asking to call home visit the medical room.
5. **Play therapy observations:** During initial sessions, Lily repeatedly uses dolls to reenact leaving home, expressing sadness and fear through the dolls' voices. She avoids playing with toys representing school or separation scenarios.

Diagnosis:

Based on the assessment results and observations, Lily meets the DSM-5 criteria for Separation Anxiety Disorder (309.21).

Treatment Plan:

- **Non-directive play therapy** (weekly 45-minute sessions for 12 weeks) focused on creating a safe space for Lily to express her anxiety through play. Use dolls and dollhouse to explore separation themes, gradually introducing school-related play. And encourage emotional expression and development of coping skills.
- **Integrate Cognitive Behavioural Therapy (CBT)** elements into play therapy. Teach relaxation techniques (deep breathing, progressive muscle relaxation) through playful activities. Develop a "bravery kit" with comforting items Lily can take to school. And create a visual schedule to increase predictability of separation times.
- **Gradual exposure to separation:** Collaboration with parents to implement a step-by-step plan for increasing separation periods and use role-play in therapy to practice goodbye routines.
- **Parent involvement**: Provide psychoeducation about separation anxiety to parents. Teach parents how to respond supportively to Lily's anxiety while encouraging independence and implementing a reward system for Lily's brave behaviors.
- **Regular progress monitoring:** Weekly check-ins with parents and bi-weekly communication with Lily's teacher

Expected Outcomes:

- Reduction in separation anxiety symptoms as measured by standardized scales.
- Increased ability to separate from parents and attend school regularly.
- Development of coping strategies for managing anxiety.
- Improved overall functioning at home and school.

Case Study 2: Anger Management (Eshan, 8 Years Old)

Presenting Problem:

Eshan, an 8-year-old boy, is displaying frequent anger outbursts both at home and school. His parents report that he often resorts to physical aggression, including hitting siblings and throwing objects when frustrated. At school, Eshan's teacher notes that he has difficulty controlling his temper during group activities and transitions, sometimes pushing or yelling at classmates. These behaviors have led to social isolation and academic difficulties.

Background:

Eshan is the middle child in a family of three children. His parents describe him as bright but easily frustrated. They report that his anger issues began about a year ago, coinciding with increased academic pressure and the birth of his younger sibling. Eshan's father travels frequently for work, and his mother works part-time, often leaving Eshan in the care of his grandmother.

Assessment and Observations:

1. **Clinical interviews with parents and teachers:**
    a. Parents report escalating anger incidents at home, particularly during homework time and when interacting with siblings.
    b. Teacher describes Eshan as quick to anger when faced with challenging tasks or peer conflicts.
2. **Behavioural observations:** In-class observation reveals Eshan clenching fists, face reddening, and verbal outbursts when frustrated with schoolwork. At home, Eshan demonstrates aggressive play with toys and frequent arguments with siblings.
3. **Anger management assessments:**
    a. Children's Inventory of Anger (ChIA): Eshan scores high on frustration-related anger and physical aggression subscales.
    b. STAXI-C (State-Trait Anger Expression Inventory for Children): Results indicate high anger expression-out and low anger control.
4. **Play therapy observations:** Initially, Eshan uses puppets to act out aggressive scenarios, hitting and yelling. He struggles to verbalize his feelings, often responding "I don't know" when asked about emotions.

Diagnosis:

Based on the assessment results and observations, Eshan meets criteria for Intermittent Explosive Disorder (312.34) as per DSM-5.

Treatment Plan:

- **Directive play therapy** (weekly 50-minute sessions for around 16 weeks). Using puppets and role-playing to teach anger management techniques, focusing on identifying anger triggers and physical cues of anger escalation. Practice expressing anger verbally instead of physically.
- **Integrate Cognitive-Behavioral Therapy (CBT) elements.** Teach "Stop and Think" technique using visual cues and role-play. Introduce problem-solving strategies through age-appropriate games and activities. And develop a personalized "Calm Down Kit" with sensory tools and visual reminders.
- **Relaxation and self-regulation skills:** Teach deep breathing exercises using imaginative scenarios (e.g., "balloon breathing"), Practice progressive muscle relaxation through playful activities and Introduce mindfulness exercises adapted for children.
- **Parent training:** Provide psychoeducation on childhood anger and appropriate developmental expectations and teach parents consistent discipline strategies and positive reinforcement techniques.
- **Social skills training:** Use group play therapy sessions to practice peer interactions and conflict resolution and teach assertiveness skills through role-play and puppet scenarios.
- **Regular progress monitoring:** Weekly check-ins with parents and bi-weekly communication with teacher. Re-administration of anger assessments at 8 and 16 weeks. Track frequency and intensity of anger outbursts using a daily log.

Expected Outcomes:

- Reduction in frequency and intensity of anger outbursts at home and school.
- Improved ability to identify and verbalize emotions.
- Development of effective anger management and problem-solving strategies.
- Enhanced social relationships with peers and family members.
- Improved academic performance due to better emotional regulation.

Case Study 3: Trauma (Maya, 9 Years Old)

Presenting Problem:

Maya, a 9-year-old girl, has been referred for psychological evaluation and treatment following a devastating hurricane that struck her coastal hometown three months ago. Her parents report that Maya has been experiencing frequent nightmares, increased anxiety, and a marked change in behavior since the traumatic event. She refuses to sleep alone, becomes visibly distressed during rainstorms, and has shown a decline in academic performance.

Background:

Maya lives with her parents and younger brother in a rebuilt home after their previous residence was severely damaged by the hurricane. The family was evacuated during the storm but returned to find significant destruction in their neighborhood. Maya witnessed uprooted trees, destroyed homes, and was exposed to the distress of community members. Her school was closed for several weeks following the disaster, disrupting her routine and social connections.

Assessment and Observations:

1. **Clinical Interview:**
    a. Parents report Maya's sleep disturbances, including difficulty falling asleep and frequent nightmares about "big waves" and "houses flying away."
    b. Maya expresses fear of being separated from her parents and reluctance to discuss the hurricane.
    c. Teachers note increased startle response to loud noises and difficulty concentrating in class.
2. **Rating Scales:**
    a. Trauma Symptom Checklist for Children (TSCC): Elevated scores on Anxiety, Depression, and Post-traumatic Stress subscales. Particularly high scores on items related to intrusive thoughts and avoidance behaviors.
    b. Child PTSD Symptom Scale (CPSS): Scores indicate clinically significant levels of post-traumatic stress symptoms. High endorsement of re-experiencing and hyperarousal symptoms.
3. **Observation of Play Therapy:** During free play, Maya avoids toys related to weather or buildings. She repeatedly enacts rescue scenarios with dolls, often leaving one doll "trapped" or "lost." When presented with a dollhouse, Maya becomes visibly anxious and refuses to engage.
4. **Art Assessment:** Maya's drawings depict the hurricane using dark, chaotic lines and distorted figures. She draws her family huddled together, surrounded by swirling black and gray shapes. When asked about her artwork, Maya becomes withdrawn and changes the subject.

Diagnosis:

Based on the assessment results and clinical presentation, Maya meets the criteria for Posttraumatic Stress Disorder (309.81) as per DSM-5.

Treatment Plan:

1. **Trauma-Focused Cognitive Behavioural Therapy (TF-CBT)**, around 16 weekly sessions. Psychoeducation about trauma and its effects, tailored for Maya's age. Gradual exposure to trauma-related memories through narrative techniques and titration. Cognitive restructuring to address maladaptive beliefs about safety and control.

2. **Play Therapy:** Incorporate directive and non-directive play techniques to process traumatic experiences. Usage of sand tray therapy to create a safe, symbolic representation of Maya's world. Introduce weather-related toys gradually to desensitize and build resilience.
3. **Art Therapy:** Encourage expression of emotions through various art mediums. Create a "feelings collage" to help Maya identify and articulate her emotions.
4. **Relaxation and Coping Skills:** Teach child-friendly mindfulness exercises using imagery techniques, practice progressive muscle relaxation through "Spaghetti Toes" technique. And develop a personalized "Courage Kit" with comforting items and coping cards.
5. **Family Therapy:** Bi-weekly sessions to address family dynamics and support Maya's recovery. Teach parents how to respond to Maya's anxiety and nightmares effectively and develop a family safety plan to increase sense of security.
6. **Group Therapy:** Enroll Maya in a children's support group for hurricane survivors and focus on shared experiences, coping strategies, and building peer support.

Expected Outcomes:

- Reduction in frequency and intensity of nightmares and anxiety symptoms.
- Development of effective coping strategies for managing stress and fear.
- Enhanced sense of safety and control in daily life.
- Improved ability to discuss and process traumatic memories.
- Improved academic performance and social engagement at school.
- Increased family cohesion and communication around trauma-related issues

References

Boucher S, Downing J, Shemilt R. The role of play in children's palliative care. Children Basel). 2014 Dec; 1(3): 302-317. doi: 10.3390/children1030302

British Association of Play Therapists (BAPT). (n.d.). *History of play therapy*. http://www.bapt.info/play-therapy/history-play-therapy

Homeyer, L. E. & Morrison, M. O. (2008). *Play therapy: Practice, issues, and trends*. Retrieved from http://www.journalofplay.org/sites/www.journalofplay.org/files/pdf-articles/1-2-article-play-therapy.pdf

Kool, R., & Lawver, T. (2010, October 1). *Play Therapy: Considerations and applications for the practitioner*. https://pmc.ncbi.nlm.nih.gov/articles/PMC2989834/

Kottman, T. Play Therapy: Basics and Beyond 2eds. Alexandria, VA: American Counseling Association, 2011

Koukourikos, K., Tsaloglidou, A., Tzeha, L., Iliadis, C., Frantzana, A., Katsimbeli, A., & Kourkouta, L. (2021). An overview of play therapy. *Materia Socio Medica, 33*(4), 293. https://doi.org/10.5455/msm.2021.33.293-297

Lanyado, M., & Horne, A. (Eds.). (1999). The Handbook of Child and Adolescent Psychotherapy: Psychoanalytic Approaches (1st ed.). Routledge. https://doi.org/10.4324/9780203135341

Lee, J., & Jung, H. (2014). User Interface of Interactive Media Art Works using Five senses as Play Therapy. *International Journal of Bio-Science and Bio-Technology*, *6*(1), 137–144. https://doi.org/10.14257/ijbsbt.2014.6.1.15

Main, P. (2023, August 3). *Play therapy*. Structural Learning. https://www.structural-learning.com/post/play-therapy

Play Therapy United Kingdom. (n.d.). *An introduction to play therapy*. Retrieved from http://www.playtherapy.org.uk/Resources/Articles/ArticleMBIntro1.htm

Post, P. B., Ceballos, P. L., & Penn, S. L. (2011). Collaborating with parents to establish behavioral goals in Child-Centered Play therapy. *The Family Journal*, *20*(1), 51–57. https://doi.org/10.1177/1066480711425472

Russ SW. Pretend Play: A resource for children who are coping with stress and managing anxiety. NYS Psychologist. 2007; 19(5): 13-17.

Sepp, J. (2023, October 17). *Stages of play therapy — ensemble therapy*. Ensemble Therapy. https://www.ensembletherapy.com/blog-posts/stages-in-play-therapy

Chapter 35

Queer Affirmative Therapy

Sanjana Desai
School of Liberal Studies (SLS), CMR University, Bangalore

Introduction

The LGBTQIA+ population has historically faced discrimination in several cultures, making it a marginalized group. Since homosexuality was first listed as a mental health illness in the Diagnostic Statistical Manual (DSM)-I, published by the American Psychology Association, there is a complex relationship between the LGBT community and psychology. The DSM's second edition also revealed that homosexuality was still classified as a mental health condition. This led to the introduction of conversion therapy for gay men, lesbians, and transgender people, creating the false belief that sexuality is a choice rather than an unchangeable scientific fact (Farley & Lawrie, 2021).

Lesbian, Gay, Bisexual, Transgender, Queer, Intersexual, Asexual, and more are the acronyms for the LGBTQIA+, which also includes 13 more gender categories that members of the community identify with. Following the DSM-III's 1973 decision to exclude homosexuality as a mental health condition, gay and lesbian activists at the historic and revolutionary Stone Wall rights movement and later in New York City fought for the rights of queer people and supported psychiatric programs and approaches to homosexuality, which clearly helped to de-stigmatize queer identity in society. There have been historical references to homosexuality even before the Stone Wall riots, when eastern legends viewed LGBT people as criminals, sinners, and unnatural. Although marriage was not seen to be acceptable for same-sex partnerships at the time, literature on LGBTQ identities coexisting among heterosexual communities in India depicted high-status individuals engaging in eastern gay culture. The higher prevalence of depression, anxiety, and suicide among LGBTQIA+ people are clearly a result of the oppression they have endured throughout history.

Queer Affirmative Therapy: A Comprehensive Introduction

The relatively new idea of Queer Affirmative Therapy (QAT) was created especially to support and encourage members of the LGBTQIA+ community. Many gender identities and sexual orientations are represented in this group. These frameworks' primary objective is to give LGBT groups a secure, accepting, and powerful environment where they can explore their identities, relationships, and mental health without fear of condemnation or condemnation. The goal of QAT is to challenge the cis-normative and heteronormative assumptions that have long dominated conventional mental health practices. Its foundation is an understanding of the LGBT community's historical, social, and psychological challenges. Queer-Affirmative Therapy (QAT) expresses comprehension of the trauma that members of the queer community have faced over time. This understanding enables the therapists to actively engage in self-reflection aimed at questioning the heteronormative and cis-normative standards that are prevalent in traditional practices of mental health. In that way, it also seeks to address the institutionalized biases and, in some cases, discrimination that actively contributes to the overall mental health crisis that the LGBTQIA+ community finds itself in while also redeeming the humanity of such individuals (Drescher, 2015; Singh & Moss, 2016).

Cleveland's work on what today is known as Queer Affirmative Therapy (QAT) always brings with it the history of other spheres of life including the queer sphere of identity. Many queer individuals began a long battle beginning in the latter part of the 19th century, seeking intersex liberation in the mid-20th century through what we know today as undergraduate and graduate intersectional LGBTQ+ rights, LGBTQ+ pride, and queer identity. The anger and resistance originated from the common practice of psychological persecution targeted against queer identities, such as reparative practices, electroshock, and shock therapy that began with the disaggregation of prejudice.

It should be noted that prior to the year 1973, homosexuality was tagged as a mental disorder. Even with the removal of this label, queer individuals were still subjected to ridicule and discrimination, particularly by the health practitioners (Spitzer, 1981). It is in awareness of this past injury that QAT was created – to redress the biases and assumptions that had operated against LGBTQIA+ in the practice of psychiatry. It simply turns the problem of queerness from something to be addressed to one of a wider appreciation of the different forms of human diversity (Bieschke, Perez, & De Bord, 2007).

As a matter of fact, the understanding and core philosophy of Queer Affirmative Therapy rests on the premise that, a queer person is never 'questioned' but instead celebrated for all their queer identities. Borrowing from QAT perspective, there are no clients who are hetero or cis or whatever, at least there shouldn't be those sorts of clients in a therapy room. Because LGBTQIA+ people experience particular pressures such discrimination, rejection from family, bias at work, and internalized stigma, this is especially important (Meyer, 2003). When taken as a whole, they are known as "minority stress," and research has demonstrated that LGBT people experience higher rates of anxiety, depression, substance misuse, and suicidality than their cisgender, heterosexual peers. By fostering self-acceptance, resilience, and a feeling of community among LGBT people, QAT directly addresses these stressors (Riggle, Rostosky, & Horne,2010).

Among the characteristics of Queer Affirmative Therapy are intersectionality and cultural competence. The unique characteristics of gender and sexual diversity, as well as how these interact with other facets of a client's identity, including race, ethnicity, religion, and socioeconomic status, are taught to QAT practitioners.

This is especially crucial because LGBTQIA+ individuals face unique stressors, such as discrimination, family rejection, workplace bias, and internalized stigma (Meyer, 2003). Collectively, these are referred to as "minority stress," which has been shown to disproportionately affect the mental health and well-being of queer individuals, with higher rates of anxiety, depression, substance abuse, and suicidality than their cisgender, heterosexual counterparts. QAT directly tackles these stressors by enhancing resilience, self-acceptance, and a sense of belonging within the queer community (Riggle, Rostosky, & Horne, 2010).

Cultural competence and intersectionality are some of the hallmarks of Queer Affirmative Therapy. QAT practitioners are taught to appreciate the particularities of gender and sexual diversity, and how these intersect with other aspects of a client's identity, such as race, ethnicity, religion, socioeconomic status, and ability (Crenshaw, 1991). This intersectional perspective ensures that the therapist acknowledges and addresses the full complexity of the client's lived experience, recognizing that queer individuals are not a monolith and that their experiences are shaped by multiple overlapping systems of privilege and oppression. For instance, a black transgender woman might face both transphobia and the intersectional issues of racism and misogyny, rendering therapeutic needs far different than those of a white gay man (Singh & McKleroy, 2011). QAT, in incorporating an intersectional perspective, attempts to provide a more nuanced and specific approach to mental health service provision for queer people.

This forms one of the most important basic elements of QAT; it advocates empowerment. In addition to support within the therapeutic context, QAT challenges clients to think critically about and challenge societal norms and advocate for their rights and well-being outside of the therapeutic context. This can be as simple as helping a client come out in a hostile environment, advocating for gender-affirming care, or working on workplace discrimination (Bieschke et al., 2007).

Practitioners of QAT tend to view themselves as allies and advocates, in addition to the client. In this way, Queer Affirmative Therapy not only supports client change in session but also works toward changing communities and institutions through systemic work. Of course, growth and change, in and between all people, are part of the methodology. QAT also highlights the role of community as a factor that promotes the resilience and psychological strength in queer individuals. For most members of the LGBTQIA+ community, being part of an affirming community might be a transformative experience. It is particularly so when one has experienced rejection or estrangement from their familiar backgrounds.

Queer affirmative therapy encompasses conversations related to developing and sustaining healthy interpersonal relationships within the queer community, negotiating a chosen family, and obtaining affirming environments in which the client can feel a sense of safety and mutuality (Riggle et al., 2010). This is not at all contradictory to expansive humanistic and relational approaches but speaks directly to how these unique challenges and opportunities unfold with queer existence.

In a nutshell, this is a paradigmatic shift in mental health, as Queer Affirmative Therapy leaves behind the deconstruction or stigmatization of old approaches in favour of empowering and affirming and celebrating subjects. It creates an atmosphere for working through their queer clients' specific challenges of their identities, developing resilience in order to thrive in a way that is more authentic than what they have been through. It places its focus on cultural competency, intersectionality, empowerment, and community, being dedicated to something greater than helping individual clients through mere treatment of the systemic inequities within their being. In more progressive societies that further embrace the wide range of gender and sexual diversity, Queer Affirmative Therapy continues to be crucial and transformative in creating positive mental health and wellness among the members.

Applications of Queer Affirmative Therapy

Use of Queer Affirmative Therapy:

Identity Assertion- QAT helps clients explore and affirm their sexual orientation and gender identity without judgment. Therapists actively validate diverse identities, providing a safe space for self-expression and self-acceptance (Singh & Dickey, 2016).

Confronting Minority Stress- QAT acknowledges societal bias and discrimination's psychological ramifications, which include internalized stigma and stress experienced by these minorities. It offers patients resources to deal with these adversaries effectively. (Meyer, 2003)

Develop Resilience - Therapists foster resilience by emphasizing clients' strengths, coping strategies, and supportive relationships within the LGBTQIA+ community (Pachankis & Goldfried, 2013).

Relationship and Family Problems - QAT helps clients cope with problems in relationships, families, and chosen communities, particularly regarding rejection or lack of acceptance (Bieschke et al., 2007)

Intersectionality - This approach also integrates the understanding of how intersecting identities (such as race, ethnicity, or disability) relate to gender and sexuality to ensure that therapy is culturally competent and inclusive. Crenshaw, 1991; Moradi et al., 2010 Therapeutic Alliance QAT establishes the necessity of mutual non-pathologizing therapeutic alliance and reduction of power imbalance that takes into account the client's actual life experiences (Langdridge, 2007).

Obstacles Associated with Queer Affirmative Therapy

- Discrimination in society Social stigma, bias, and institutional impediments hinder the effectiveness of therapeutic therapies for both clients and therapists. Because of internalized stigma or bad experiences in healthcare contacts, clients may fear rejection or stigma even during therapy. Particularly in extremely conservative environments, affirmative therapy practitioners may encounter resistance from their profession or an antagonistic culture.
- Prejudice based on culture These deeply ingrained cultural norms represent a major obstacle for both clients and therapists. Clients from certain cultural identification contexts may experience severe stigma when identifying non-heteronormative identities or outright denial, which prevents them from always having the chance to express their identities openly.

Intervention Methods in Queer Affirmative Therapy

1. Identity Confirmations Exploration

Therapists create a safe setting for the client to explore and understand his or her sexual orientation and gender identity. The process helps clients get clear and confident as they affirm themselves.

2. Addressing Minority Stress

It emphasizes alleviating distress arising due to societal discrimination. Such a therapist guides their client into acknowledgment and management of the anxiety triggered by stigmatizing or rejection-oriented and alienation-oriented events.

3. Empowerment through Psychoeducation

This method educates clients on LGBTQIA + identities and systemic oppression normalizing their experiences and legitimizing their emotions and thus removing feelings of isolation.

4. Intersections in Therapy

The technique addresses the way intersecting factors, like race, religion, and socioeconomic status, shape a client's experiences and that therapy is inclusive of addressing the unique layers of oppression.

5. Strength-Based Approach

Highlights clients' resilience and coping skills, encouraging them to focus on their abilities rather than perceived deficits, fostering empowerment and self-worth.

Techniques Used in Queer Affirmative Therapy

- **Validation and Standardization:** Therapists help clients feel understood and less alone by normalizing their difficulties and validating their feelings.
- **Cognitive Behavioural Therapy (CBT):** CBT is used to address and reframe negative ideas related to internalized stigma in order to promote more positive self-perceptions.
- Narrative therapy encourages clients to rewrite their own narrative, removing societal biases and emphasizing their agency and strengths.
- **Positive role models:** To help clients navigate social norms and interpersonal relationships with confidence, therapists provide examples of supportive language and behaviours.
- **Mindfulness and self-compassion techniques:** Self-compassion helps clients overcome feelings of shame and self-criticism, while mindfulness lowers anxiety and encourages present-moment awareness.

Case Studies

Client Information

Name: Emily Doe (She/They)

Age: 26

Gender: Nonbinary (assigned female at birth, identifies as nonbinary and lesbian)

Sexual Orientation: Lesbian

Ethnicity: Hispanic

Relationship Status: Single

Occupation: Marketing Specialist

Socio-Economic Status: Middle-class, financially stable

Living Situation: Lives alone in an urban apartment; close-knit family with traditional cultural values; struggles with being closeted due to fear of rejection.

Presenting Problem - Emily sought therapy due to intense anxiety and stress related to being closeted about her nonbinary identity and lesbian sexual orientation. She complained of distress in trying to reconcile herself with societal and family expectations toward her gender identity and claimed to be afraid of rejections from her family members. Emily has frequent experiences of sadness, self-hatred, and regret due to her inability to live authentically; her anxiety is particularly expressed in family interactions and when she feels pressure to cope with a "straight" persona in social situations.

Physical Examination

- General Appearance: Well-cared for, somewhat subdued; dresses modestly not to be judged.
- Vital Signs: Blood pressure (118/78), resting pulse (75 bpm), respiration rate (16 breaths/min).
- Physical Health: Reports sporadic insomnia and physical anxiety but no major medical history.
- Screening: No indication of physical abuse, substance abuse, or self-harm.

Mental Status Exam:

- Appearance: Neat, with appropriate attire; somewhat withdrawn.
- Mood/Affect: Anxious, sad, and self-critical, with a flat affect.
- Speech: Slow, soft, and hesitant at times.
- Thought Process: Logical and coherent but marked by guilt and shame related to identity.
- Cognition: Alert and oriented to time, place, and person.
- Insight: Knowledge of emotional conflicts but still fearful of fully expressing a gender identity.
- Judgment: Intact; however, judgmental or evaluative thinking is impacted because the individual fears others might judge or reject them.
- Risk Assessment: There was no active suicidal thought and planning, but there have been passive thoughts of hopelessness with distress.

Diagnosis

Primary Diagnoses (DSM-5):

1. ***Generalized Anxiety Disorder (GAD)***

   Persistent and excessive worry about being discovered and fear of rejection in familial and social settings.

   Associated physical symptoms include tension, restlessness, and difficulty concentrating.

2. ***Adjustment Disorder with Mixed Anxiety and Depressed Mood***

   Emotional symptoms associated with stressors of concealing her identity and fear of societal judgment.

   Characterized by anxiety, depression, and emotional distress caused by her closeted status.

Treatment Plan

Therapeutic Interventions

Discuss options - Build a nurturing and reassuring setting to discuss and then authenticate Emily's gender and sexuality identity.

1. ***Cognitive Behavioural Therapy-*** Acknowledge distorted thoughts related to fearing rejection and a general negative view of oneself in your thoughts. Replace this behaviour with healthier coping ways toward dealing with anxiety.

   Narrative Therapy: Assist Emily in reframing her personal story in relation to resilience and authenticity; this will help her focus on those aspects and fight fears of rejection from the society and family.

   Mindfulness-Based Stress Reduction (MBSR): Incorporate mindfulness practices to reduce physical symptoms of anxiety and promote self-compassion.
2. ***Family Therapy*** - Family therapy can be considered in case Emily decides to open up to her family. This would focus on preparing her family for her disclosure and healthy communication.
3. ***Group Therapy*** - Support Emily to seek LGBTQIA+ support groups to reduce the feeling of isolation and find others with similar experiences.
4. ***Social Support-*** Strengthen Emily's relationships with supportive friends and allies, who can provide emotional validation and support.
5. ***Medication*** - Consider an SSRI if symptoms of anxiety and depression are significantly impairing daily functioning or if insomnia is persistent.
6. ***Follow-Up*** - Begin with weekly therapy sessions to focus on identity exploration, anxiety management, and building self-acceptance. Progress will be monitored closely, with adjustments to the treatment plan as needed.

Socio-Economic Considerations

- Emily has access to healthcare and mental health services through her employment, though financial constraints, such as familial financial obligations, may limit access to additional non-essential services.
- She resides in an openly LGBTQIA+ city community, but her closeted condition prevents her from actively partaking in it.
- Emily feels isolated and apprehensive about being judged within her work life as well as family life; due to this, she controls her gender expression as well as her authentic self.

Progress:

Emily showed more readiness to live more authentically in her personal and professional life. Developed a safety plan for coming out to family, if and when she feels ready.

Over six weeks, Emily progressed significantly in anxiety management and self-acceptance. She gained insight into her identity, developed coping strategies, and established connections with supportive peers. Challenges remain in her relationship with her family, but Emily feels more empowered to navigate them with time and continued support. Regular therapy and participation in LGBTQIA+ groups will reinforce her growth and resilience.

Prognosis

Emily's prognosis is optimistic with consistent therapeutic intervention. She will likely experience reduced anxiety and improved self-acceptance over time, with a focus on identity affirmation, anxiety management, and community support. The main challenges are her fear of family rejection and eventual coming-out process, which will require careful preparation and support. Participation in LGBTQIA+ groups and therapy will help mitigate feelings of isolation and foster resilience.

This case study shows the application of Queer Affirmative Therapy in supporting Emily in addressing anxiety, exploring her identity, and finding a path toward authenticity in the midst of familial and societal challenges.

References

American Psychological Association. (2009). *Report of the Task Force on Appropriate Therapeutic Responses to Sexual Orientation*. APA.

Bieschke, K. J., Perez, R. M., & DeBord, K. A. (Eds.). (2007). *Handbook of counselling and psychotherapy with lesbian, gay, bisexual, and transgender clients*. American Psychological Association. https://doi.org/10.1037/11482-000

Crenshaw, K. (1991). Mapping the margins: Intersectionality, identity politics, and violence against women of colour. *Stanford Law Review, 43*(6), 1241–1299. https://doi.org/10.2307/1229039

Drescher, J. (2015). Out of DSM: De-pathologizing homosexuality. *Behavioural Sciences, 5*(4), 565–75. https://doi.org/10.3390/bs5040565

Meyer, I. H. (2003). Prejudice, social stress, and mental health in lesbian, gay, and bisexual populations: Conceptual issues and research evidence. *Psychological Bulletin, 129*(5), 674–697. https://doi.org/10.1037/0033-2909.129.5.674

Riggle, E. D., Rostosky, S. S., & Horne, S. G. (2010). Psychological distress, well-being, and legal recognition in same-sex couple relationships. *Journal of Family Psychology, 24*(5), 82–90. https://doi.org/10.1037/a0017942

Singh, A. A., & McKleroy, V. S. (2011). "Just getting out of bed is a revolutionary act": The resilience of transgender people of colour who have survived traumatic life events. *Traumatology, 17*(2), 34–44. https://doi.org/10.1177/1534765610369261

Singh, A. A., & Moss, L. (2016). Queer-affirming counselling for trauma survivors. In M. Englar-Carlson, M. P. Evans, & T. Duffey (Eds.), *A counsellor's guide to working with men* (pp. 267–285). Wiley.

Spitzer, R. L. (1981). The diagnostic status of homosexuality in DSM-III: A reformulation of the issues. *American Journal of Psychiatry, 138*(2), 210–215. https://doi.org/10.1176/ajp.138.2.210 American Psychological Association. (2009). *Report of the Task Force on Appropriate Therapeutic Responses to Sexual Orientation*. APA.

Bieschke, K. J., Perez, R. M., & DeBord, K. A. (Eds.). (2007). *Handbook of counselling and psychotherapy with lesbian, gay, bisexual, and transgender clients.* American Psychological Association. https://doi.org/10.1037/11482-000

Crenshaw, K. (1991). Mapping the margins: Intersectionality, identity politics, and violence against women of colour. *Stanford Law Review, 43*(6), 1241–1299. https://doi.org/10.2307/1229039

Drescher, J. (2015). Out of DSM: De-pathologizing homosexuality. *Behavioural Sciences, 5*(4), 565–75. https://doi.org/10.3390/bs5040565

Meyer, I. H. (2003). Prejudice, social stress, and mental health in lesbian, gay, and bisexual populations: Conceptual issues and research evidence. *Psychological Bulletin, 129*(5), 674–697. https://doi.org/10.1037/0033-2909.129.5.674

Riggle, E. D., Rostosky, S. S., & Horne, S. G. (2010). Psychological distress, well-being, and legal recognition in same-sex couple relationships. *Journal of Family Psychology, 24*(5), 82–90. https://doi.org/10.1037/a0017942

Singh, A. A., & McKleroy, V. S. (2011). "Just getting out of bed is a revolutionary act": The resilience of transgender people of colour who have survived traumatic life events. *Traumatology, 17*(2), 34–44. https://doi.org/10.1177/1534765610369261

Singh, A. A., & Moss, L. (2016). Queer-affirming counselling for trauma survivors. In M. Englar-Carlson, M. P. Evans, & T. Duffey (Eds.), *A counsellor's guide to working with men* (pp. 267–285). Wiley.

Spitzer, R. L. (1981). The diagnostic status of homosexuality in DSM-III: A reformulation of the issues. *American Journal of Psychiatry, 138*(2), 210–215. https://doi.org/10.1176/ajp.138.2.210

Farley, T., & Lawrie, M. (2021). *Title of the article or book. Title of the Journal or Publisher*, Volume (Issue), Page numbers. https://doi.org/xxxxx

Chapter 36

Roman Catholic Healing & Confessions

Vaishnavi T.N School of Liberal Studies (SLS), CMR University, Bangalore

Introduction to Roman Catholic Healing and Confession

In Roman Catholicism, the sacraments of healing and confession are fundamental to the spiritual life of believers. These practices are grounded in the Church's understanding of the human person as both physical and spiritual, emphasizing that true well-being involves healing on multiple levels: physical, emotional, and spiritual. Central to this spiritual healing is the Sacrament of Penance, also known as Confession or Reconciliation, a ritual through which Catholics seek forgiveness for their sins, restore their relationship with God, and experience spiritual renewal. Alongside confession, the Catholic Church also offers the Sacrament of the Sick, which addresses physical ailments and provides spiritual comfort for those suffering from serious illness or impending death. Both sacraments underscore the Catholic belief in the transformative power of God's grace, which is believed to heal the soul and guide individuals toward moral and spiritual wholeness.

At the heart of Catholic healing lies the Sacrament of Confession, which is a process of acknowledging one's sins, expressing sorrow and contrition, and receiving absolution from a priest. In this sacrament, Catholics seek not only the forgiveness of sins but also spiritual healing, as it restores the grace lost through sin. The process involves several steps: the penitent's examination of conscience, the confession of sins to a priest, the performance of penance (such as prayers or acts of charity), and the priest's absolution. Catholics believe that through this sacrament, their sins are forgiven, their relationship with God is restored, and they are spiritually healed. This sacrament is considered essential for maintaining spiritual health, as it provides a means for individuals to turn away from sin, receive God's mercy, and grow in holiness (Catechism of the Catholic Church [CCC], 1997).

In addition to confession, the Sacrament of the Sick offers another form of healing. This sacrament is administered to those suffering from serious illness or preparing for surgery. Unlike Confession, which primarily addresses spiritual healing, the Sacrament of the Sick is seen as providing both spiritual and physical healing, although it is not guaranteed that physical healing will occur. The sacrament involves the anointing of the sick person with oil, accompanied by prayers for strength, comfort, and healing. It is a reminder that God's presence is especially near in times of suffering, offering peace and strength to endure trials (CCC, 1997).

1. The Sacrament of Confession (Penance and Reconciliation)

Purpose and Significance

The Sacrament of Confession is the primary means by which Catholics seek forgiveness for their sins and experience spiritual healing. According to Catholic doctrine, sin damages a person's relationship with God, and confession offers a way to restore this relationship. The sacrament involves a personal encounter with God through the priest, who acts as a mediator. The Catechism of the Catholic Church (CCC) explains that through confession, Catholics confess their sins, express genuine remorse (contrition), and receive absolution, which restores their sanctifying grace (CCC, 1997).

Process of Confession

The process of confession includes several key steps:

- **Examination of Conscience:** The penitent reflects on their actions, omissions, and attitudes to recognize sins.
- **Confession of Sins:** The penitent admits sins to a priest, who listens and offers counsel.
- **Penance:** After confession, the priest assigns a penance, usually prayers or acts of charity, as a way of demonstrating repentance and restoring balance.
- **Absolution:** The priest grants absolution, pronouncing the words of forgiveness: "I absolve you from your sins in the name of the Father, and of the Son, and of the Holy Spirit."
- This sacrament is not only about the forgiveness of sins but also about spiritual healing, as it strengthens the individual's relationship with God and the Church (CCC, 1997). It helps the individual turn away from sin and grow in holiness.

2. The Sacrament of the Sick (Anointing of the Sick)

Purpose and Significance

The Sacrament of the Sick, sometimes referred to as the Anointing of the Sick, is another form of healing offered by the Catholic Church. This sacrament is typically administered to those who are seriously ill, elderly, or preparing for surgery. The purpose is both spiritual and physical: to offer God's grace, provide comfort, and strengthen the individual during times of suffering or approaching death. The Catechism of the Catholic Church (1997) highlights that this sacrament is not a "last rites" ritual, but a source of spiritual healing and a reminder of God's mercy in times of difficulty.

Process of the Sacrament of the Sick

The sacrament includes:

- **Anointing with Oil:** A priest anoints the sick person with oil blessed for this purpose, usually on the forehead and hands.
- **Prayer of Healing:** Prayers are offered for the individual's healing, comfort, and strength, whether physical or spiritual.
- **Spiritual Healing:** While the sacrament may lead to physical healing, its primary focus is on providing peace, strength, and the grace to face suffering with faith.

3. The Role of the Priest in Healing

Mediator of God's Grace

In both the Sacrament of Confession and the Sacrament of the Sick, the priest plays a crucial role. Acting as a mediator between God and the individual, the priest is seen as the one who administers God's grace through the sacraments. The priest, however, does not act on his own authority but rather in the person of Christ, a concept known as in persona Christi. In the case of Confession, the priest offers absolution and spiritual guidance; in the case of the Sacrament of the Sick, he administers the anointing and prays for the individual's healing.

Spiritual Counsel and Support

Beyond administering sacraments, the priest often provides spiritual counsel to help individuals navigate their struggles with sin, illness, or suffering. The pastoral care offered by priests in the context of confession and healing services is central to the Church's mission to heal and restore people spiritually (Murray, 2001).

4. Theological Foundation: Healing Through God's Grace

Both sacraments emphasize the central Catholic belief in God's grace as the primary agent of healing. The Church teaches that all healing comes from God, whether it is spiritual healing through forgiveness or physical healing through prayer and the sacramental life. The sacraments serve as channels through which believers receive divine grace, which helps restore them to health and holiness. According to Catholic theology, God's mercy is unbounded, and the healing process, whether in the context of confession or illness, is a manifestation of God's love and care for His people (Cary, 2016).

5. The Importance of Healing in Catholic Spirituality

Healing, in Catholicism, is not limited to the physical realm but extends to the spiritual and emotional dimensions of the human experience. Confession and the Sacrament of the Sick are vital in helping individuals reconcile with God and face suffering with courage and hope. These sacraments remind the faithful that God's mercy is always available, particularly during times of distress or personal failure. By participating in these rites, Catholics believe they are being spiritually transformed, restored, and strengthened to live out their faith with greater commitment (Catechism of the Catholic Church, 1997).

Benefits of Roman Catholic Healing and Confession

Spiritual Healing and Reconciliation with God

One of the primary benefits of the Sacrament of Confession is spiritual healing. In Catholic theology, sin is seen as a rupture in one's relationship with God. When a person sins, they not only harm themselves but also damage their bond with God and the Church. The sacrament of confession provides a means of restoring this broken relationship. By confessing sins, expressing genuine contrition, and performing penance, the individual receives absolution from the priest, who acts in the person of Christ (in persona Christi), and their sins are forgiven. This leads to spiritual renewal and the restoration of sanctifying grace, which Catholics believe is essential for salvation (Catechism of the Catholic Church [CCC], 1997).

Benefits:

- **Forgiveness of sins:** Catholics believe that the Sacrament of Confession restores a person to a state of grace by forgiving mortal and venial sins. This is seen as a cleansing process that frees the soul from guilt and the spiritual weight of sin (CCC, 1997).
- **Reconciliation with God:** Confession is not just about forgiveness but about reconciliation. It brings the individual back into communion with God, restoring their spiritual health. Catholics view this reconciliation as a way of healing their relationship with the divine.
- **Restoration of peace and joy:** By experiencing the healing grace of God, the penitent feels spiritual peace and joy, knowing that their sins have been forgiven and their relationship with God has been restored.

Emotional and Psychological Benefits

The emotional and psychological benefits of the Sacrament of Confession are profound. Sin often brings emotional distress, guilt, anxiety, and shame. Confession provides a cathartic release, helping the individual to confront and acknowledge their failures in a safe, non judgmental environment. The priest, acting as a spiritual guide, listens with compassion and offers counsel, which can provide emotional healing and clarity.

Benefits:

- **Relief from guilt and shame:** The sacrament provides a means to release the emotional burden of guilt and shame that often accompanies sinful actions. Confession allows the penitent to unburden themselves, letting go of the weight of sin and finding emotional relief (Murray, 2001).
- **Healing from emotional wounds:** Catholics believe that sin and unresolved guilt can cause emotional wounds that affect mental health and relationships. Confession helps heal these wounds, offering the penitent the emotional freedom to move forward with peace of mind (Cary, 2016).
- **Increased emotional resilience:** Confession and absolution can lead to greater emotional strength, helping individuals handle life's stresses and challenges with a renewed sense of inner peace and trust in God.

Personal Transformation and Growth in Holiness

Catholics believe that the Sacrament of Confession fosters personal transformation by encouraging the penitent to grow in holiness. By regularly participating in Confession, Catholics are called to examine their conscience and reflect on their moral life. This self examination leads to greater self-awareness and provides opportunities for growth and change. The process of repentance involves not just seeking forgiveness but also a commitment to avoid sin in the future, which helps individuals lead a more virtuous and holy life.

Benefits:

- **Spiritual growth and moral improvement:** Through Confession, Catholics receive grace that helps them grow in virtue and make moral progress. The sacrament
  - encourages self-reflection and a deeper commitment to living a Christ-like life (CCC, 1997).
- **Strengthened resolve against temptation:** By regularly receiving the grace of Confession, Catholics believe they are empowered to resist future temptations. The grace received helps to fortify them against sin, fostering a life of greater discipline and moral integrity (Cary, 2016).
- **A deeper relationship with God:** Confession is a form of spiritual exercise that draws individuals closer to God. As Catholics repent and receive forgiveness, they cultivate a deeper, more intimate relationship with the Divine, becoming more attuned to God's will in their lives.

Restoring Peace in Relationships

While the Sacrament of Confession primarily focuses on healing the relationship between the individual and God, it also has a significant impact on interpersonal relationships. Confession often involves recognizing the harm one's actions may have caused to others, leading to a spirit of reconciliation in relationships. The process of confession encourages Catholics to seek forgiveness not only from God but also from those they have wronged, promoting healing in broken relationships.

Benefits:

- **Improved relationships:** By recognizing one's faults and taking steps toward reconciliation, Confession helps repair relationships with family, friends, and the broader community (Murray, 2001). The grace received strengthens individuals to seek forgiveness from others and to forgive those who have wronged them.
- **Restoration of peace:** Forgiving others and seeking forgiveness leads to emotional and relational peace. Confession helps remove barriers that sin creates in relationships, allowing individuals to experience harmony and unity in their relationships (CCC, 1997).

Physical and Spiritual Healing in the Sacrament of the Sick

The Sacrament of the Sick (also called Anointing of the Sick) is another sacrament that offers both physical and spiritual healing. Although it is most commonly administered to those who are seriously ill or nearing death, the sacrament provides spiritual strength and comfort, helping the individual face their illness with faith and hope. Catholics believe that while physical healing is not always guaranteed, the sacrament offers profound spiritual benefits, such as the strength to endure suffering and the grace of peace.

Benefits:

- **Spiritual strength during illness:** The anointing and prayers offer the sick person grace to endure their illness with peace and courage. It reminds them of God's presence in their suffering, offering comfort and spiritual healing (CCC, 1997).

- **Potential for physical healing:** While the sacrament's primary focus is spiritual, many Catholics believe that God can also heal the body through this sacrament. The prayer and anointing may result in physical healing, or it may provide the strength needed to accept illness with grace.
- **Preparation for death:** In cases where illness is severe, the Sacrament of the Sick is seen as a way to prepare spiritually for death, ensuring that the person is at peace with God and ready to face the afterlife (Cary, 2016).

Strengthened Community and Church Unity

The sacraments of Confession and the Sick are also beneficial in strengthening the sense of community within the Church. By participating in these sacraments, individuals are not only restored spiritually but are also united with the broader Church. Confession helps to reconcile the individual with the Church community, particularly when sins have affected others. The Sacrament of the Sick encourages solidarity with the sick and suffering members of the Church, fostering a spirit of compassion and care within the faith community.

Benefits:

- **Reconciliation with the Church:** Confession allows Catholics to reconcile not only with God but also with the Church, which is viewed as the body of Christ. This fosters a sense of belonging and unity within the faith community (CCC, 1997).
- **Support for the sick and suffering:** The Sacrament of the Sick encourages the community to care for and support its suffering members. It strengthens the Church's role in offering comfort and compassion to those in need, deepening the bonds of Christian charity (Cary, 2016).

History of Roman Catholic Healing and Confession

The history of Catholic healing and confession is deeply rooted in the early Christian tradition, influenced by both the teachings of Jesus Christ and the practices of the Apostles. The development of these sacraments evolved over centuries, shaped by theological debates, liturgical practices, and the pastoral needs of the Church. The Sacrament of Penance (Confession) and the Sacrament of the Sick (Anointing of the Sick) have both evolved into formal sacraments over time, yet their origins lie in the ministry of healing and reconciliation practiced by Jesus and the Apostles. Below is a detailed historical overview of how these sacraments developed.

1. The Roots in the Ministry of Jesus and the Apostles

The origins of Catholic healing and confession can be traced back to the ministry of Jesus Christ. During His life, Jesus demonstrated a profound concern for healing—both physical and spiritual. The Gospels record numerous instances where Jesus healed the sick, exorcised demons, and forgave sins, demonstrating His authority over both spiritual and physical realms.

Healing Ministry of Jesus:

- Jesus' healing ministry was an essential part of His public mission. He not only performed miracles of physical healing, such as curing the blind and the lame (Matthew 9:27-30), but also offered forgiveness of sins, which was a form of spiritual healing (Mark 2:5-12). The power to forgive sins was considered a prerogative of God alone, and when Jesus forgave sins, it highlighted His divine authority and the intimate connection between physical and spiritual healing.

- Jesus also sent His Apostles to continue His work of healing. In the Gospel of Matthew, He empowers His followers to heal the sick and cast out demons (Matthew 10:1, Luke 9:2), foreshadowing the establishment of sacramental rites for healing within the Church.

2. The Early Christian Church (1st–4th Centuries)

In the early Christian Church, the practice of healing and forgiveness continued, although it was less formalized than it would later become. The first Christians viewed confession and healing as part of a broader ministry of reconciliation, especially in response to sin.

Confession and Reconciliation in the Early Church:

- **Private Confession:** Initially, Christians would confess their sins publicly in front of the Church community, particularly in cases of grave sins, such as apostasy or adultery. Public penance was common, and sinners would undergo a period of exclusion from the Eucharist, followed by a form of reconciliation after the completion of penance. This practice was based on the early Christian emphasis on the public nature of sin and the community's role in reconciliation (Tertullian, 3rd century).
- **Ritual of Penance:** In the 3rd and 4th centuries, the Church began to move toward a more formalized practice of penance. The Church Fathers, such as Cyprian of Carthage (3rd century), taught that the power to forgive sins rested with the Church, which could grant absolution after penance was completed. The Didache, an early Christian manual (c. 100 AD), also shows that the early Church practiced confession, but it was generally public and did not yet involve the private confession to a priest that would later develop.

The Role of Healing in the Early Church:

- **Healing of the Sick:** The early Christians continued to practice the healing ministry of Jesus, and healing was seen as an important part of the Christian mission. The Anointing of the Sick, while not yet fully formalized as a sacrament, was practiced by the Apostles. St. James, in his epistle, writes, "Is anyone among you sick? Let them call the elders of the church to pray over them and anoint them with oil in the name of the Lord" (James 5:14-15). This passage is foundational for the later development of the Sacrament of the Sick.
- Early Christians continued to emphasize the connection between physical healing and the forgiveness of sins, viewing illness and sin as often interrelated. Healing, both spiritual and physical, was seen as part of the Church's mission to continue Christ's work on earth.

3. The Formalization of Confession and the Sacrament of Penance (5th–9th Centuries)

As the Christian Church grew and became more institutionalized, the practice of confession began to take on more structure and formality.

Confession Becomes Private (6th Century):

- The practice of private confession (as opposed to public confession) emerged in Ireland in the 6th century. St. Patrick of Ireland and other early Irish missionaries introduced a private sacramental practice for penance, influenced by the monastic movement. The Irish monks developed the custom of confessing sins privately to a priest, who would then assign a penance, such as fasting or prayer.
- This practice spread to other parts of Europe, and by the 9th century, private confession had largely replaced the public penance system. The Sacrament of Penance became formalized, and the Church began to teach that individuals could confess their sins directly to a priest, who, acting in the person of Christ, would grant absolution.

Theological Developments:

- The 12th-century theologian Peter Lombard and others helped define the theological understanding of confession and absolution, affirming the priest's role in mediating God's grace and forgiveness. The Church officially codified Confession as a sacrament during the Fourth Lateran Council in 1215, which decreed that all Catholics must confess their sins at least once a year (Canon 21).

4. The Development of the Sacrament of the Sick (4th–12th Centuries)

The Sacrament of the Sick, or Anointing of the Sick, also developed gradually over time, with its roots in the early Christian practice described in James 5:14-15.

Early Christian Practice:

Early Christians practiced anointing the sick with oil, but it was not yet a formalized sacrament. The anointing was often performed by bishops or presbyters (priests) for healing purposes, and it was especially associated with spiritual healing.

The Rise of "Extreme Unction" (Middle Ages):

In the Middle Ages, the sacrament of anointing became more associated with death and last rites. This practice, known as Extreme Unction, was often administered to those in danger of death. By the 12th century, it became common for the sick and dying to receive anointing from a priest as a way of preparing for death, and the sacrament began to be linked with the forgiveness of sins and the final preparation for the afterlife.

Theological Clarification:

The Council of Trent (1545–1563) clarified the nature of the Sacrament of the Sick, affirming its status as one of the seven sacraments and defining its purposes as healing, comfort, and preparation for death. The Council also rejected the idea that the sacrament was only for the dying, emphasizing its role in offering spiritual and physical healing to the sick, not just those near death.

5. Modern Developments (Post-Vatican II)

The Second Vatican Council (1962–1965) brought significant reforms to Catholic sacramental practice, including a renewed emphasis on the pastoral role of the sacraments. The Sacrament of Penance was revised to focus more on the healing and reconciliation aspects of confession, emphasizing the penitent's personal encounter with God rather than simply the fulfilment of a legal obligation.

Vatican II also promoted the importance of the Sacrament of the Sick, particularly in the context of modern medicine. The Council emphasized that the sacrament should be administered not only to those near death but also to anyone suffering from serious illness, recognizing the need for both spiritual healing and physical comfort(Lumen Gentium, 1964).

Applications of Roman Catholic Healing and Confession

The Sacrament of Penance (Confession) and the Sacrament of the Sick (Anointing of the Sick) are integral to the Roman Catholic tradition, offering practical benefits in the lives of the faithful. These sacraments are not merely theological concepts but play an active role in

the spiritual, emotional, and physical well-being of individuals and communities. The applications of these sacraments span personal healing, mental health, communal life, and pastoral care. Below are key applications of these sacraments with corresponding theological and practical insights.

1. Spiritual and Emotional Healing

Application: Personal Healing and Reconciliation

The Sacrament of Confession is a primary means of spiritual healing in Catholic life. It allows individuals to confess their sins and seek absolution, which restores their relationship with God and the Church. This sacrament is especially effective in emotional healing, offering peace and closure. By acknowledging sins, Catholics can move past feelings of guilt, shame, and spiritual turmoil, experiencing reconciliation not only with God but also with themselves (Hughes, 2019).

The act of confession has been shown to contribute to improved mental health. Psychologically, confessing sins can provide a sense of relief, reducing anxiety and

fostering inner peace (Pargament, 2013). In the words of Catholic theology, absolution (the forgiveness granted by the priest) acts as a healing balm for the soul, alleviating the burden of sin and restoring the individual to a state of grace.

2. Mental Health and Stress Relief

Application: Reducing Anxiety and Promoting Psychological Well-Being

Confession also serves as a form of psychological therapy by providing Catholics with an outlet for emotional and spiritual burdens. Research shows that religious rituals such as confession have a therapeutic effect, reducing stress, anxiety, and feelings of isolation (Koenig et al., 2001). For many Catholics, the sacrament of reconciliation is a deeply cathartic experience that helps them confront personal struggles, such as fear, resentment, and shame.

The Sacrament of the Sick, similarly, plays a significant role in alleviating stress and anxiety for those who are seriously ill. The anointing with oil and prayers for healing provide comfort and hope to the sick, particularly when faced with terminal illness or serious disease (Hughes, 2017). This sacrament helps individuals to accept suffering and prepares them for death with spiritual peace, knowing that God's grace accompanies them.

Mental Health Applications: Both sacraments can be a powerful tool in coping with mental health challenges, providing individuals with emotional support, comfort, and a sense of divine presence. Regular participation in these sacraments helps individuals find meaning in suffering, reducing despair and increasing resilience.

3. Strengthening Community Bonds

Application: Restoring Relationships Within the Church Community

One of the broader applications of both Confession and Anointing of the Sick is their role in strengthening communal relationships within the Church. Confession is not only a personal experience but also has a communal aspect, as sin is viewed as a break in the communion with the Church. Through absolution, the penitent is restored not only to God but to the community of the faithful (O'Malley, 2015).

The Sacrament of Penance can help heal divisions within the Church community, especially in cases where personal conflicts or misunderstandings have caused division. By reconciling with God, individuals can also reconcile with one another, fostering a spirit of forgiveness and unity. The Anointing of the Sick also reinforces the Church's commitment to the care of the vulnerable, particularly the sick and dying, further strengthening the bonds of compassion and support within the parish (Congar, 1960).

4. Pastoral Care and End-of-Life Support

Application: Care for the Sick and Dying

The Sacrament of the Sick, especially in its role as Extreme Unction, provides essential pastoral care to those facing terminal illness or death. This sacrament offers spiritual preparation for death, ensuring that the individual is spiritually ready to meet God. It provides peace in the final moments of life, aligning the individual's suffering with Christ's Passion (Crombie, 2008).

Catholic theology teaches that death is a transition, not an end, and the Anointing of the Sick helps individuals move through that transition with the grace of God. For family members and loved ones, the sacrament can also be a source of comfort and hope, affirming that God's mercy extends even in moments of physical decline (Sullivan, 2002).

5. Promoting Holistic Well-Being

Application: Holistic Integration of Body, Mind, and Spirit

Both the Sacrament of Penance and the Sacrament of the Sick contribute to a holistic approach to health that integrates physical, emotional, and spiritual well-being. Catholic theology holds that human beings are a unity of body, soul, and spirit, and the sacraments address the whole person. Confession offers spiritual healing, while the Anointing of the Sick provides physical and spiritual comfort. This holistic approach is seen as crucial for individuals who are navigating complex life situations, whether they are dealing with sin, illness, or the challenges of aging and death (Tanner, 2003).

Steps and Process of Roman Catholic Healing and Confession

In Roman Catholicism, the sacraments of Penance (Confession) and Anointing of the Sick are structured rituals that involve specific steps designed to facilitate the process of spiritual healing, reconciliation, and, in the case of the Sick, physical and emotional comfort. Below, we explore the detailed steps and processes for each of these sacraments.

1. The Sacrament of Penance (Confession)

The Sacrament of Penance, also known as Confession, is a central practice in Roman Catholic spirituality, where a person confesses their sins to a priest in order to receive absolution and be reconciled with God and the Church. The process involves several key steps:

Step 1: Examination of Conscience

Before going to Confession, the individual is encouraged to examine their conscience. This is a personal reflection on one's actions, thoughts, and omissions to identify sins (both mortal and venial) committed since the last confession. The Church offers guides to assist with this examination, often focusing on the Ten Commandments, the Beatitudes, and the moral teachings of the Church.

Purpose: The goal is to recall any wrongdoings and the intent to seek forgiveness with a sincere heart.

Step 2: Preparation and Contritions

Once the sins are identified, the penitent must prepare for Confession by cultivating contrition. Contrition is a sincere sorrow for having sinned, coupled with the resolve to amend one's life and avoid sin in the future. The Church recognizes two types of contrition:

> **Perfect Contrition:** Sorrow for sin out of love for God, typically prompted by an awareness of God's goodness and the offense caused by sin.
>
> **Imperfect Contrition:** Sorrow motivated by the fear of punishment or a desire to avoid the consequences of sin.
>
> **Purpose:** Contrition ensures that the person is genuinely seeking forgiveness, not just fulfilling an obligation.

Step 3: The Confession of Sins

The penitent then enters the confessional and begins by greeting the priest. The ritual often begins with the priest saying, "In the name of the Father, and of the Son, and of the Holy Spirit." The penitent then confesses their sins, either in general or in detail, depending on their own conscience and the priest's guidance. Catholics are expected to confess all mortal sins (serious sins) to be forgiven properly, but they may also confess venial sins.

> **Purpose:** This step acknowledges the reality of sin and the need for divine forgiveness. It also emphasizes humility and accountability in the process.

Step 4: The Priest's Counsel and Penance

After the confession, the priest may offer spiritual counsel or guidance to help the penitent grow in faith and avoid sin in the future. The priest may also assign a penance, which often consists of prayer (e.g., saying certain prayers like the Our Father or Hail Mary), acts of charity, or other actions to make amends for the sin.

> **Purpose:** The penance is a form of reparation, a way to restore the harm caused by sin and demonstrate a willingness to amend one's life.

Step 5: Absolution

The priest then grants absolution, declaring that the penitent's sins are forgiven. The priest speaks the words of absolution: "I absolve you from your sins in the name of the Father, and of the Son, and of the Holy Spirit." Absolution is the key to the sacrament, as it is through the priest's words, acting in the person of Christ, that the penitent is reconciled with God.

> **Purpose:** Absolution restores the penitent's relationship with God and the Church, removing the guilt of sin and reestablishing the grace lost through wrongdoing.

Step 6: Completion of the Penance

After the confession, the penitent is expected to complete the assigned penance as soon as possible, often in the form of prayer or acts of kindness. This is part of the process of demonstrating true contrition and seeking to live a life in alignment with God's will.

> **Purpose:** To finalize the act of reconciliation and begin the process of spiritual renewal and healing.

2. The Sacrament of the Sick (Anointing of the Sick)

The Sacrament of the Sick is offered to those who are suffering from serious illness, injury, or old age, as well as to those near death. It involves the anointing of the sick person with holy oil and prayers for healing and comfort. This sacrament is often confused with "Extreme Unction," but it is broader and can be administered at any time during serious illness, not only at the point of death.

Step 1: Call for a Priest

When someone is seriously ill, the family or individual may request the sacrament by calling a priest to administer the sacrament. This is an important step because the sacrament involves both the priest's prayers and the anointing of the sick person with holy oil, which is considered a powerful symbol of God's healing presence.

> **Purpose:** To formally request divine intervention through the Church's sacramental ministry, offering comfort and strength to the sick person.

Step 2: Prayers and Greeting

The priest begins the sacrament by greeting the sick person and their family with words of comfort. He often leads a prayer of penance to help the individual express sorrow for any sins. If the person is conscious and able to participate, they may also express their desire for healing and their faith in God.

> **Purpose:** To prepare the sick person spiritually for the sacrament by fostering a sense of God's presence and peace.

Step 3: Laying of Hands

The priest then lays his hands on the sick person's head, which is a sign of the Holy Spirit's presence and the extension of Christ's healing power. The laying of hands symbolizes the healing touch of Christ, who cured the sick during His earthly ministry.

> **Purpose:** To invoke the Holy Spirit's power and to remind the sick person that healing, whether physical or spiritual, is ultimately in God's hands.

Step 4: Anointing with Oil

Next, the priest anoints the sick person with blessed oil, typically on the forehead and the hands. This oil, known as the Oil of the Sick, is consecrated by the bishop at a special Mass. The anointing is accompanied by a prayer, which asks for God's healing grace, both physical and spiritual.

The prayer includes phrases like:

"Through this holy anointing, may the Lord in His love and mercy help you with the grace of the Holy Spirit. May the Lord who frees you from sin save you and raise you up."

> **Purpose:** The anointing signifies God's healing presence and mercy. It is not necessarily a guarantee of physical recovery, but it is meant to bring spiritual comfort and strength during illness or suffering.

Step 5: Prayers for Healing and Strength

Following the anointing, the priest continues with prayers for spiritual strength, healing, and peace. He may ask God to grant the sick person the strength to endure their illness with courage and the grace to prepare for whatever outcome God has planned.

> **Purpose:** To provide spiritual healing, emotional comfort, and peace. The prayer emphasizes that the person is not alone in their suffering but is supported by the Church's prayer and the presence of the Holy Spirit.

Step 6: Conclusion

The sacrament concludes with a prayer for the sick person's complete well-being—both physical and spiritual—and a blessing. If the individual is near death, the priest may administer the Apostolic Pardon, a special form of absolution given at the time of death, which grants the forgiveness of sins and the remission of temporal punishment.

> **Purpose:** To complete the sacrament, offering a final blessing, comfort, and peace in preparation for the possibility of death.

Incorporating Roman Catholic Healing and Confession in Psychotherapy: A Comparative Approach

Roman Catholic sacraments, particularly Confession (Penance) and Anointing of the Sick, provide spiritual healing through practices like forgiveness, reconciliation, and emotional support. These elements can be integrated into psychotherapy, especially within the context of spirituality and healing, providing a holistic approach to mental health. The similarities

between these sacraments and various therapeutic techniques can be explored, as both aim to address psychological and emotional distress, though through different lenses.

Confession in Psychotherapy: A Tool for Emotional Release and Healing Incorporating *Confession in Psychotherapy*

The process of Confession in the Roman Catholic tradition revolves around acknowledging sins, expressing remorse, and receiving absolution from the priest. Psychologically, this process resembles several therapeutic techniques used in psychotherapy, such as cognitive behavioural therapy (CBT), psychodynamic therapy, and existential therapy. These therapeutic approaches similarly aim to help clients confront internal conflicts, process emotions, and find a path toward emotional release and healing.

Incorporation

In psychotherapy, a clinician could incorporate elements of Confession through therapeutic confession or emotional processing. This would involve clients verbally expressing past wrongdoings, guilt, or unresolved conflicts, followed by acknowledgment and validation from the therapist. This practice would help clients achieve a sense of emotional release, similar to the relief felt after confession in the Catholic sacrament.

Therapists can also encourage self-forgiveness and reconciliation, allowing the client to let go of self-blame or guilt in a healthy way. For instance, incorporating narrative therapy, a therapeutic approach where clients rewrite their life stories, could help them reframe past transgressions as part of their larger life journey and growth.

Comparison to Psychotherapy

In many psychotherapeutic models, acknowledging and processing guilt or shame is an essential step in emotional healing. For example:

- **Cognitive Behavioural Therapy (CBT):** One key aspect of CBT is identifying and challenging negative thought patterns (e.g., "I am a bad person") that often result from guilt or shame. The therapeutic process helps the individual reframe these thoughts and focus on self-compassion and growth rather than self-punishment.
- **Psychodynamic Therapy:** This form of therapy emphasizes uncovering unconscious conflicts, often stemming from childhood experiences or unresolved guilt. Similar to the sacrament of confession, psychodynamic therapy works to bring

unconscious shame and guilt to the conscious level so that the individual can process and heal from it.

2. Anointing of the Sick in Psychotherapy: Providing Comfort and Healing Incorporating *Anointing of the Sick in Psychotherapy*

The Sacrament of the Sick offers spiritual healing through anointing with oil and prayers for strength and comfort. This sacrament is particularly relevant to psychotherapy when working with clients facing terminal illness, chronic pain, or mental health crises. Psychotherapists can integrate the spiritual aspect of healing by offering emotional support, comfort, and validation in situations where the client is suffering or facing end-of-life issues.

Incorporation:

- **Spiritual Counselling:** For clients who are religious, integrating aspects of spirituality—such as offering prayers, spiritual rituals, or ritualistic healing—can provide comfort and a sense of peace in therapy. For instance, therapists could work with clients to reconcile existential fears, such as fear of death or fear of suffering, by incorporating themes of acceptance, faith, and peace similar to the sacrament of Anointing of the Sick.
- **Mindfulness and Healing:** In a therapeutic setting, techniques like mindfulness based therapy or acceptance and commitment therapy (ACT) mirror the peaceful and healing intentions of

the sacrament. These therapies focus on acknowledging suffering and fostering acceptance, which can align with the spiritual

comfort provided in the Anointing of the Sick sacrament.

Comparison to Psychotherapy

The Anointing of the Sick bears similarities to therapeutic techniques that aim to help clients manage physical illness or terminal conditions:

- **Palliative Care and Psychotherapy:** In psychotherapy, the approach to terminal illness often involves palliative care therapy, which seeks to alleviate emotional and psychological suffering in the face of serious illness. Similar to the Sacrament of the Sick, this therapy focuses on comfort, acceptance, and providing a peaceful transition for patients nearing death.
- **Existential Therapy:** This approach focuses on helping individuals confront the inevitability of death and the challenges that arise from life's meaning. Existential therapists may guide clients through spiritual and emotional reconciliation with their mortality, which parallels the intentions of Anointing of the Sick to provide spiritual peace during illness or approaching death.

3. Forgiveness and Reconciliation in Psychotherapy

Both the Sacrament of Penance and psychotherapy place significant emphasis on the role of forgiveness and reconciliation. In Confession, the penitent is not only seeking forgiveness from God but also reconciling with their own sense of morality and the Church community. Psychotherapy similarly emphasizes the importance of self-forgiveness and the healing power of accepting personal flaws.

Incorporation in Psychotherapy:

- **Forgiveness Therapy:** Forgiveness is a common therapeutic technique used to help clients overcome the burden of resentment or guilt that affects their emotional health. Forgiveness therapy helps individuals let go of past grievances, similarly to how Confession helps individuals reconcile with God and others. Forgiveness therapy may involve encouraging clients to reflect on their emotional responses to past events, facilitating a path toward letting go of negative emotions and promoting healing.
- **Reconciliation and Relationship Repair:** For clients who experience relationship conflicts or ruptures due to past behaviours, psychotherapists can encourage practices of emotional honesty, communication, and restoration of trust, which are similar to the reconciliation experienced in the Sacrament of Penance.

4. Rituals and Symbolism in Psychotherapy

Both the Sacraments of Penance and Anointing of the Sick involve symbolic rituals, such as the laying on of hands and the anointing with oil, which are designed to convey spiritual truths and promote healing. Rituals in therapy can also be symbolic, creating a safe space for emotional release and spiritual connection.

Incorporation in Psychotherapy:

- **Therapeutic Rituals:** Therapists can use rituals, such as ceremonies of closure or symbolic acts of letting go, to help clients process grief, loss, or unresolved trauma. For example, rituals of forgiveness, such as writing letters to those we have wronged or who have wronged us, can promote emotional healing and symbolic reconciliation.
- **Symbolic Healing:** Drawing on the symbolic act of anointing with oil in the Sacrament of the Sick, therapists can guide clients to symbolically wash away negative emotions through practices like guided imagery, visualization, or symbolic acts such as burning old, painful memories or creating life-affirming rituals.

Integrating Roman Catholic Healing into Psychotherapy

The integration of Roman Catholic healing practices like Confession and Anointing of the Sick into psychotherapy can offer a holistic approach that combines spiritual, emotional, and psychological healing. While the sacraments focus on sin, forgiveness, and reconciliation in the context of religious belief, psychotherapy aims to address emotional distress, trauma, and interpersonal conflicts. By drawing on the parallels between these two approaches, therapists can integrate spiritual and symbolic rituals, forgiveness practices, and comforting interventions into psychotherapy, thereby enriching the therapeutic process and supporting clients' emotional well-being and spiritual peace.

Both Roman Catholic healing practices and psychotherapy seek to help individuals face inner turmoil, heal emotional wounds, and find peace, whether in their relationship with God, others, or themselves. Through careful integration, psychotherapists can create a space for holistic healing that respects the spiritual beliefs of clients while also promoting psychological well-being.

Case Studies

Case Study 1: Incorporating Confession and Forgiveness Therapy in Treating Guilt and Shame

Background:

Anna, a 32-year-old woman, sought psychotherapy due to persistent feelings of guilt and shame following a difficult breakup with her fiancé. She described her actions during the breakup as "unforgivable" and felt as though her behaviour had severely damaged her relationship with God and others. She expressed that she was unable to move forward

because of these overwhelming emotions. Anna had been raised in a Roman Catholic household and regularly participated in the sacrament of Confession but struggled to accept the forgiveness she received from God and the Church.

Therapeutic Approach:

In therapy, the therapist introduced elements of forgiveness therapy and explored how the process of Confession could be integrated into Anna's healing. The therapist encouraged Anna to revisit the themes of guilt and self-blame in the context of the breakup and helped her explore negative beliefs about herself, such as the idea that she was inherently "bad" or "unworthy." Drawing from Cognitive Behavioural Therapy (CBT) techniques, the therapist guided Anna to challenge these beliefs, helping her to recognize that everyone makes mistakes and that her actions, while painful, did not define her moral worth.

The therapist also integrated spiritual practices into the sessions, aligning with Anna's religious beliefs. They explored how the sacrament of Confession (which Anna had experienced in the past) could be applied to her emotional process. Anna was encouraged to imagine a spiritual dialogue with God, similar to the confessional experience, where she could express her remorse and receive absolution in a way that would provide emotional relief and self-compassion. The therapist also emphasized the importance of self forgiveness and healing from within as the first steps in rebuilding her relationship with others.

Outcome:

Over the course of several sessions, Anna began to report a reduction in her guilt and an increase in her sense of peace. By integrating both psychotherapeutic techniques and the spiritual ritual of forgiveness, Anna was able to process the breakup in a way that felt both emotionally authentic and aligned with her faith. She began to feel that her past mistakes were a part of her personal growth, rather than a source of permanent shame.

This case demonstrates the potential benefits of incorporating elements of Confession and forgiveness therapy to help individuals address deep-rooted guilt and promote emotional healing.

Case Study 2: Integrating Anointing of the Sick and Palliative Psychotherapy for Terminal Illness

Background:

John, a 60-year-old man, was diagnosed with terminal cancer. He was struggling with feelings of hopelessness, fear of death, and deep regret over unresolved conflicts with his family. John had been a practicing Catholic throughout his life, and although he had previously received the Sacrament of Anointing of the Sick when his diagnosis became terminal, he continued to experience emotional distress. He felt disconnected from God and struggled with the existential questions about the meaning of his suffering and impending death.

Therapeutic Approach:

In therapy, the therapist integrated palliative psychotherapy with aspects of spiritual healing akin to the Sacrament of the Sick. The therapist focused on existential therapy, helping John address his fear of death and his emotional pain about unresolved issues. The therapy emphasized themes of life review, legacy, and the search for meaning in the final stages of life.

The therapist also acknowledged the spiritual aspect of John's distress, recognizing his need for both emotional comfort and spiritual peace. John's experience with Anointing of the Sick was brought into the therapeutic process by encouraging him to reflect on the prayers and anointing as a form of spiritual reassurance and healing. The therapist helped John integrate mindfulness and spiritual rituals (e.g., prayer, forgiveness) into his therapy, fostering acceptance of his physical limitations and providing a framework for peaceful acceptance of death.

Outcome:

After several weeks, John reported feeling more at peace with his condition and less fearful of the future. By combining spiritual reflection from the sacrament and

the psychological support from palliative psychotherapy, John was able to make peace with his past, reconcile with estranged family members, and focus on creating meaningful moments in his final days. He expressed a sense of spiritual readiness for death, and his anxiety about the dying process was significantly alleviated.

This case highlights the holistic approach of integrating spiritual care (similar to Anointing of the Sick) into psychotherapy, emphasizing the need for both psychological comfort and spiritual healing in end-of-life care.

Case Study 3: Using Confession to Address Trauma and Forgiveness in a Survivor of Abuse

Background:

Sarah, a 25-year-old woman, presented with symptoms of post-traumatic stress disorder (PTSD) following years of sexual abuse during childhood. Despite having received counselling in the past, she continued to struggle with feelings of guilt and self-blame, particularly regarding her inability to stop the abuse at the time. Sarah was raised in a Catholic household and had been taught the importance of forgiveness in the context of Confession. However, she felt disconnected from her faith because of her trauma, and she experienced difficulty reconciling her sense of guilt with the teachings of her religion.

Therapeutic Approach:

The therapist decided to incorporate forgiveness therapy and spiritual practices into the treatment process. Initially, the therapist helped Sarah process her trauma through trauma focused cognitive behavioural therapy (TF-CBT), addressing the core beliefs of self blame and worthlessness that often stemmed from her experience of abuse. Through this process, Sarah began to understand that the abuse was not her fault and that forgiveness was about releasing herself from the shackles of self-blame rather than condoning the actions of the abuser.

The therapist also integrated elements of the Sacrament of Confession into the therapy process, helping Sarah reframe her sense of guilt. The therapist encouraged Sarah to engage in symbolic confession, where she would express her feelings of shame and guilt in a safe

and non-judgmental environment. This process was designed to allow Sarah to experience a sense of absolution and emotional release without the need for self-punishment.

Outcome:

Over several months, Sarah showed significant progress in healing from the trauma and reducing her feelings of guilt and shame. The integration of spiritual

healing and forgiveness into her therapy allowed her to accept that her worth was not determined by the abuse and that she could forgive herself and reclaim her faith. This process ultimately led to her experiencing a renewed connection with her spiritual beliefs, while also making peace with her past trauma. She reported feeling a sense of emotional relief and spiritual peace as she was able to separate her faith from her trauma and embrace self-compassion.

This case study illustrates the effectiveness of integrating religious practices such as Confession into trauma therapy, helping clients address complex issues of guilt, shame, and forgiveness.

Conclusion

The integration of Roman Catholic healing practices, such as Confession (Penance) and Anointing of the Sick, into psychotherapy offers a powerful, holistic approach to emotional, psychological, and spiritual healing. Both of these sacraments emphasize themes of forgiveness, reconciliation, and spiritual comfort, which align closely with therapeutic principles found in various forms of psychotherapy, including forgiveness therapy, existential therapy, and cognitive behavioural therapy (CBT). By addressing the deep emotional needs of individuals through both psychological and spiritual means, therapists can create a supportive environment where clients can confront internal struggles, heal from trauma, and make peace with their past.

As demonstrated in the case studies, the integration of Catholic rituals such as confession allows clients to express guilt and shame, while spiritual forgiveness offers a path to self-compassion and emotional release. Similarly, Anointing of the Sick aligns with palliative psychotherapy, where spiritual and emotional support are offered to those facing terminal illness or severe suffering, allowing them to find peace, acceptance, and meaning in their circumstances.

Incorporating religious rituals and spiritual healing into therapy offers a more comprehensive treatment model, particularly for clients who identify strongly with religious beliefs. This approach helps to address not only psychological distress but also the spiritual suffering that can accompany life's most difficult challenges, such as guilt, trauma, and mortality. By offering a balanced integration of both faith-based practices and evidence-based therapeutic techniques, therapists can provide holistic care that aligns with the client's values and beliefs, ultimately enhancing their emotional well being and spiritual peace.

In conclusion, the synergy between Roman Catholic healing rituals and psychotherapy holds significant potential for helping individuals heal from emotional wounds, achieve self forgiveness, reconciliation, and find comfort and meaning in their spiritual and emotional journeys. This integrated approach can foster profound personal growth and healing, leading to a healthier, more balanced life where individuals feel connected not only to themselves but also to their faith, their community, and their higher sense of purpose.

References

Aquinas, T. (1947). *Summa Theologica* (Fathers of the English Dominican Province, Trans.). Benziger Brothers.

Catechism of the Catholic Church. (1997). *Sacrament of penance.* Vatican Publishing House.

Catechism of the Catholic Church. (1997). *Sacrament of the sick.* Vatican Publishing House.

Crombie, J. R. (2008). *The pastoral care of the sick: The sacrament of the sick and the theology of healing.* Journal of Catholic Health Care, 43(2), 101– 110. https://doi.org/10.1177/0305735608312323

Cary, P. (2016). *The healing sacraments in the Catholic Church.* Church Publishing. González, J. L. (2007). *A short history of Christian doctrine.* Abingdon Press.

Koenig, H. G., McCullough, M. E., & Larson, D. B. (2001). *Handbook of religion and health.* Oxford University Press.

Lumen Gentium. (1964). *Dogmatic Constitution on the Church.* Vatican II Documents. Murray, J. P. (2001). *The role of the priest in Catholic sacramental healing.* Pastoral Press.

Pargament, K. I. (2013). *Spiritually integrated psychotherapy: Understanding and addressing the sacred.* The Guilford Press.

Rahner, K. (1970). *Theological investigations: Volume 10, The sacrament of the sick and other writings.* Crossroad Publishing.

Schillebeeckx, E. (1979). *The Eucharist: Symbol of the new community.* Sheed & Ward. Sullivan, F. A. (2002). *The final years: The Church's role in end-of-life care.* Paulist Press.

Tanner, N. P. (2003). *The holistic care of the sick: Theology and practice.* Theological Studies, 64(1), 51–70. https://doi.org/10.1177/004056390306400104

Chapter 37

Roman and Medieval Healing Traditions

Wandarihun Iangrai, Dr Monalisa Nayak School of Liberal Studies (Sls), CMR University, Bangalore

Roman and medieval healing traditions reflect two distinct yet connected eras in the history of medicine, shaped by the social, cultural, and scientific landscapes of their times. The Romans built on the medical knowledge of the Greeks, creating a system of healing that emphasised practicality and public health. Greek physicians like Hippocrates, who developed the theory of the four humours, and Galen, whose writings became the cornerstone of Roman medicine, greatly influenced Roman practices. Roman doctors used herbal remedies, performed surgeries, and stressed hygiene as a means of disease prevention. Public health infrastructure, such as aqueducts, public baths, and sewage systems, demonstrated their focus on cleanliness and community health. At the same time, healing often had a religious dimension, with temples dedicated to Asclepius, the god of medicine, acting as sanctuaries where people sought cures through rituals and dreams.

Medieval healing traditions, emerging after the fall of the Roman Empire, were more fragmented and diverse, reflecting the challenges of a decentralised society. With the rise of Christianity, monasteries became centres for medical knowledge and care. Monks preserved Greek and Roman texts, often translating them into Latin, ensuring their survival for future generations. Healing in the medieval period was deeply intertwined with faith, relying on prayers, blessings, and relics to treat illness. For many, sickness was seen as a test or punishment from God, which meant spiritual remedies were as important as physical treatments. Folk medicine, passed down orally, played a significant role, relying on local herbs and traditional practices.

Meanwhile, the medieval world benefited from the transmission of medical knowledge from the Islamic Golden Age. Physicians like Avicenna and Al-Razi expanded upon Greek theories, blending them with new discoveries in anatomy, pharmacology, and diagnostics. Texts such as Avicenna's "Canon of Medicine" influenced European medicine during the later Middle Ages, introducing more systematic and observational approaches to healing.

Despite their differences, both Roman and medieval healing traditions reflect a common effort to balance empirical knowledge with spiritual understanding. They highlight how cultural and religious beliefs shaped the approach to health and laid the groundwork for modern medical advancements.

Each period contributed uniquely to the development of medical practices, with important continuities and significant changes influenced by religion, science, and cultural exchange.

Roman Healing Traditions

Roman medicine was pragmatic, blending Greek theory with Roman organizational skills and engineering. It focused on preventing illness through public health and hygiene. Some key aspects include:

- **Public Health Infrastructure:** Romans believed that environmental factors contributed to disease. They built aqueducts to provide clean water, sewer systems to remove waste, and public baths to promote hygiene. Their understanding of sanitation was advanced for the time and significantly improved life expectancy in urban areas.
- **Military Medicine:** The Roman military needed healthy soldiers, leading to the development of mobile field hospitals "valetudinarian" and surgical tools. Roman surgeons performed amputations, treated wounds, and even conducted rudimentary eye surgeries.
- **Pharmacology and Herbal Remedies:** Romans used plants like garlic, willow (a precursor to aspirin), and honey for their medicinal properties. *Dioscorides' De Materia Medica*, a pharmacological text from the Roman era, remained a reference for centuries.
- **Religious Healing:** Beyond practical methods, Romans turned to divine intervention. The *Asclepieia* (healing temples) were places of pilgrimage where priests performed rituals and interpreted dreams for cures.

Medieval Healing Traditions

The medieval period, spanning roughly from the 5th to the 15th century, saw the fragmentation of Roman medical systems but also the preservation and expansion of ancient knowledge through new cultural lenses.

- **Faith and Healing:** The medieval worldview was deeply rooted in Christianity, and illness was often seen as a spiritual matter. Healing involved prayer, sacraments, and relics, which were believed to have miraculous powers. Saints like St. Roch and St. Blaise became associated with specific ailments.
- **Monastic Medicine:** Monasteries were central to medical care and learning. Monks copied ancient texts, maintained herb gardens, and provided care to the sick. The *Benedictine Rule* encouraged the treatment of the sick as a core part of Christian service.
- **The Four Humours:** Medieval medicine relied heavily on the ancient Greek theory of the four humours—blood, phlegm, black bile, and yellow bile. Physicians aimed to balance these humours through diet, bloodletting, and purging.
- **Folk Medicine:** In rural areas, knowledge of healing was passed down orally. Wise women and herbalists provided remedies using local plants, such as comfrey for broken bones or chamomile for digestive issues. These practices often blended with superstition, such as charms and spells.
- **Global Exchange:** The Islamic Golden Age brought significant advancements to medieval medicine. Arabic texts introduced surgical techniques, detailed anatomical knowledge, and

a systematic approach to pharmacology. The translation of works like Avicenna's *Canon of Medicine* into Latin revitalized European medicine in the High Middle Ages.

History

Roman Healing Traditions:

The Roman Empire (27 BCE–476 CE) inherited much of its medical knowledge from the Greeks, particularly Hippocrates and his humoral theory. Roman medicine blended Greek practices with practical approaches suited to their expansive empire.

1. ***Public Health and Sanitation:*** Romans established advanced public health systems to prevent disease. They constructed aqueducts for clean water, sewers for waste removal, and public baths to promote hygiene. These innovations significantly reduced disease spread in urban areas.
2. ***Military Medicine:*** The Roman military developed efficient healthcare systems, including field hospitals to treat soldiers. Standardized tools and techniques for cleaning wounds, amputations, and managing trauma were implemented to ensure rapid recovery.
3. ***Medical Practitioners:*** Roman physicians often served in urban clinics or households. The elite had access to Greek-trained doctors, while rural populations relied on herbalists and healers. Galen of Pergamon, a Greek physician serving in Rome, became a dominant figure. His extensive writings on anatomy, pharmacology, and the humors influenced Western medicine for over a millennium.
4. ***Herbal and Holistic Medicine:*** Roman texts like Dioscorides' *De Materia Medica* cataloged hundreds of medicinal plants. Roman medicine emphasized balancing lifestyle factors such as diet, exercise, and mental health alongside treatments.

Medieval Healing Traditions

After the fall of the Roman Empire, Western Europe entered the medieval period (500–1500 CE), during which medical knowledge was preserved and expanded, blending classical, Islamic, and Christian influences.

1. ***Monastic Medicine:*** In early medieval Europe, monasteries became centers of medical knowledge. Monks copied ancient texts, grew medicinal herbs, and offered care to the sick. The Benedictine Rule encouraged hospitality, leading to the establishment of hospital-like facilities.
2. ***Islamic Influence:*** During the Islamic Golden Age (8th–13th centuries), scholars translated and expanded on Greek and Roman medical texts. Physicians like Avicenna (Ibn Sina) and Al-Razi (Rhazes) made significant contributions. Their works, including Avicenna's *Canon of Medicine*, were later adopted in Europe.
3. ***University Medicine:*** By the 12th century, medical schools like those in Salerno, Bologna, and Montpellier emerged, formalizing medical training. These institutions relied heavily on classical texts but also introduced new surgical techniques and pharmacological studies.

4. ***Spiritual and Folk Healing:*** Medicine in the medieval period often intertwined with religion. Illness was sometimes seen as a punishment or test from God, and spiritual healing through prayer, relics, and pilgrimages was common. Folk medicine thrived among rural populations, with remedies based on local plants and traditions. Midwives and local healers played crucial roles, especially for childbirth and minor illnesses.
5. ***Black Death and Medical Shifts:*** The Black Death (1347–1351) highlighted the limitations of medieval medicine and led to increased scrutiny of traditional practices. This period saw a growing emphasis on empirical observation and public health measures.

Theoretical Background of Roman and Medieval Healing Traditions:

The Roman and medieval healing traditions were deeply rooted in the prevailing philosophical, cultural, and religious frameworks of their respective times. Their theoretical foundations blended empirical observations, spiritual beliefs, and inherited knowledge from earlier civilizations, shaping a distinctive approach to health and medicine.

Roman Healing Traditions

The Roman medical system was largely influenced by Greek medicine, particularly the humoral theory established by Hippocrates and expanded by Galen. This theoretical framework, alongside Roman pragmatism, formed the backbone of their healing traditions.

1. ***Humoral Theory:*** The body was believed to consist of four humors: blood, phlegm, yellow bile, and black bile. Health was maintained by keeping these humors in balance, while imbalances were thought to cause illness. Treatments like bloodletting, purgation, and dietary adjustments aimed to restore this balance.
2. ***Empiricism and Practicality:*** Roman medicine emphasized observation and practicality. Physicians were trained to recognize symptoms and prescribe treatments based on past successes. Public health measures like sanitation systems were grounded in the belief that a clean environment prevented diseases.
3. ***Philosophical Influences:*** Stoicism and natural philosophy shaped Roman attitudes toward health. The belief in living in harmony with nature influenced medical practices, such as the use of natural remedies and physical fitness.
4. ***Military Necessity:*** The Roman Empire's military campaigns necessitated advancements in trauma care and surgical techniques, reinforcing the empirical approach to medicine.
5. ***Spirituality and Religion:*** Although Romans generally relied on empirical methods, they also invoked divine intervention in healing, worshiping gods like Aesculapius, the god of medicine.

Medieval Healing Traditions

Medieval medicine drew heavily on Roman, Greek, and Islamic influences, synthesizing ancient theories with the Christian worldview. It was characterized by a blend of humoral theory, religious practices, and evolving empirical methods.

1. ***Humoral and Galenic Medicine:*** The humoral theory persisted during the medieval period, primarily through the works of Galen, whose writings were preserved and studied in both Europe and the Islamic world. Balancing humors remained central, with treatments like bloodletting, herbal remedies, and dietary control.
2. ***Christian Influence:*** Christianity played a pivotal role in shaping medieval healing traditions. Illness was often viewed as a test of faith or punishment for sin, and spiritual healing through prayer, confession, and relics was common. Monastic medicine emerged as a key institution, combining spiritual care with practical treatment. Monasteries preserved classical texts and cultivated medicinal herbs.
3. ***Islamic Medicine and Its Transmission:*** During the Islamic Golden Age, scholars translated Greek and Roman medical texts into Arabic, enriching them with their own observations. Prominent figures like Avicenna and Al-Razi provided theoretical foundations that later influenced European medicine. These texts reintroduced empirical methods and systematic approaches to medical education in medieval Europe.
4. ***Philosophical and Theological Underpinnings:*** Medieval medical theory often intertwined with Scholasticism, which sought to reconcile classical knowledge with Christian theology. This framework encouraged rigorous study but also constrained innovation within theological boundaries.
5. ***Folk and Community-Based Healing:*** Beyond formal theory, folk traditions played a critical role, rooted in local customs, herbal knowledge, and practical wisdom passed through generations. This represented a decentralized, accessible approach to healing.

Roman Healing Traditions and Their Application in Psychotherapy

While Roman medicine was primarily concerned with physical health, it did recognize the interconnectedness of the body and mind, laying the groundwork for concepts used in modern psychotherapy. Roman physicians often applied a holistic approach to healing, acknowledging that emotional and psychological well-being could influence physical health. Although they did not have a sophisticated understanding of mental health as we do today, Roman medical practices included principles that resonate with current psychotherapeutic methods.

The Humoral Theory and Emotional Balance

The Roman approach to health, heavily influenced by Greek medicine, revolved around the theory of the four humors: blood, phlegm, yellow bile, and black bile. Each humor was associated with different personality traits and emotional states. For example, an excess of blood (associated with the sanguine temperament) was thought to result in cheerfulness and a healthy disposition, while an excess of black bile was believed to lead to melancholia, or what we might now recognize as depression. The understanding that emotional states could have physiological consequences is similar to modern psychotherapy's recognition of the mind-body connection.

In contemporary psychotherapy, emotional imbalance is often seen as a central factor in mental health issues. For example, cognitive-behavioral therapy (CBT) and psychodynamic therapies both recognize that unbalanced or maladaptive emotional states can lead to mental health issues. Just as the Romans focused on balancing the humors, modern therapy focuses on achieving emotional equilibrium, often through techniques like emotional regulation and cognitive restructuring. Both traditions seek to understand how emotional disturbances manifest in both psychological and physical symptoms.

Therapeutic Use of Conversation and Counseling

Although the Romans didn't practice psychotherapy in the way we understand it today, the concept of engaging with the patient through conversation was an important part of their medical approach. Roman physicians, such as Galen, believed that understanding a patient's personal background, emotional state, and even their environment was crucial to diagnosing and treating their condition. Physicians like Galen promoted the idea of "listening" to patients and forming a strong doctor-patient relationship, which parallels modern psychotherapeutic practices.

In modern psychotherapy, conversation is the primary tool for understanding the client's emotional and psychological state. Techniques such as talk therapy, where clients are encouraged to express their emotions, concerns, and thoughts, are deeply rooted in the Roman tradition of dialogue-based treatment. By providing a space where patients can openly discuss their feelings, psychotherapists aim to help clients gain insight into their mental health challenges and explore solutions, much as Roman physicians attempted to address both physical and mental health through conversation.

Mind-Body Connection and Stress Management

Roman healing traditions also emphasized the importance of maintaining both physical and mental health, which is highly relevant to modern psychotherapy, especially within the frameworks that emphasize somatic therapies or mind-body integration. Romans believed that exercise, diet, and proper hygiene contributed to a balanced life, and these practices could influence not just physical health but also mental clarity. Roman healers often recommended activities like walking, bathing, and relaxation as remedies to ease both physical ailments and emotional distress.

In contemporary psychotherapy, this holistic approach is reflected in therapies such as mindfulness-based stress reduction (MBSR) and somatic experiencing, which aim to address the connection between the body and mind. Therapists might encourage clients to engage in physical activities like yoga, exercise, or mindfulness meditation to help regulate their emotions and reduce stress. These practices are grounded in the same idea that the body's health impacts mental health, and vice versa.

Medieval Healing Traditions and Their Application in Psychotherapy

Medieval healing traditions, though strongly influenced by religious beliefs, also had elements that align with modern psychotherapy, especially in their focus on emotional support, community care, and the idea of a holistic approach to health. Medieval healing was largely about treating both the body and the soul, with a strong focus on spirituality, but many of the principles from this period continue to resonate with psychotherapeutic practices today.

Holistic Healing and Mental Health

Medieval healing practices often integrated physical, emotional, and spiritual care. Monastic hospitals, for example, were places where patients received not just medical care but also emotional and spiritual comfort. In many cases, illness was seen as a spiritual imbalance or a form of divine punishment. Therefore, medieval healers would use a combination of herbal remedies, religious prayers, and spiritual rituals to restore balance to both the body and the soul.

This holistic view of health, where emotional and spiritual healing were equally important as physical treatment, is echoed in modern psychotherapies like integrative or transpersonal therapy. These approaches aim to treat the whole person, recognizing the interconnectedness of the mind, body, and spirit. Modern therapists may focus on how spiritual concerns, life purpose, or existential anxiety impact mental well-being, just as medieval healers did by addressing both physical and spiritual health. Today, therapies like mindfulness-based cognitive therapy (MBCT) incorporate spiritual principles to help clients develop a deeper understanding of themselves, which reflects the medieval understanding that true healing comes from an integration of mind, body, and spirit.

The Role of Prayer, Rituals, and Emotional Support

In medieval healing, prayer and religious rituals were central to the treatment process. People often turned to religious figures, such as monks or priests, to seek healing, believing that divine intervention was necessary for recovery. Prayer, pilgrimages to sacred sites, and the use of relics were considered effective treatments for both physical and mental ailments. Even though modern psychotherapy does not include prayer or religious rituals, the principle of providing emotional support remains central to therapeutic practice.

In psychotherapy today, the therapist's role is often one of emotional and psychological support, helping clients explore their feelings, fears, and anxieties in a safe, nonjudgmental space. Much like medieval healers who provided comfort and hope through religious practices, therapists today aim to provide emotional support that fosters a sense of trust and safety for clients. By helping clients feel heard and understood, therapists can guide them through their struggles and promote healing, whether that is emotional, psychological, or existential in nature.

Isolation and Reflection

During the medieval period, practices like quarantine were introduced as measures to control the spread of disease, especially during pandemics like the Black Death. While these measures were designed to isolate individuals to protect public health, they can also be seen as an early form of creating space for reflection. In psychotherapy, particularly in approaches such as cognitive-behavioral therapy (CBT), there is a similar practice of "isolation" in the form of helping clients focus on their internal emotional experiences and thoughts, away from external distractions. This type of introspective work helps clients process emotional pain and stress, which can lead to healing.

Moreover, modern therapies like dialectical behavior therapy (DBT) or acceptance and commitment therapy (ACT) encourage clients to step back from their usual environment, reflecting on their emotions, thought patterns, and behaviors. The medieval practice of quarantine thus shares similarities with modern techniques that create a deliberate space for individuals to confront and process their mental health issues in a focused, reflective way.

Community Support in Healing

Medieval healers often worked within communities, providing care for the sick in monasteries and religious institutions. These communities were an essential part of the healing process, where individuals could find both physical care and emotional support. In modern psychotherapy, this idea of community support is reflected in group therapy, where individuals come together to share their struggles and provide mutual support.

Group therapy, especially in modalities like support groups or family therapy, allows individuals to connect with others who may share similar experiences, providing them with a sense of belonging and validation. Just as medieval patients found solace in the communal care provided by religious institutions, modern clients benefit from the shared experiences and emotional support that group therapy offers.

Roman and medieval healing traditions, while rooted in their respective historical and cultural contexts, contain principles that are strikingly relevant to modern psychotherapy. Both traditions understood the importance of emotional balance, spiritual well-being, and the interconnectedness of mind, body, and spirit. The holistic and community-focused approaches of medieval healers and the empirical, observational methods of Roman physicians continue to resonate in contemporary therapeutic practices. By examining these ancient practices, we can see how they laid the groundwork for many of the principles that are central to psychotherapy today—principles that emphasize emotional support, self-reflection, and the interconnectedness of mental and physical health.

Steps and Processes of Roman Healing Traditions

Roman healing practices combined empirical observation, preventative measures, and practical treatments, relying heavily on natural remedies and surgical techniques. The following steps outline the typical healing process in ancient Roman medicine.

Diagnosis and Observation:

The healing process in Roman medicine often began with a thorough examination of the patient. Roman physicians, influenced by Greek practices, would assess the patient's symptoms, physical condition, and humoral balance (the theory that the body's health depended on the balance of four bodily fluids: blood, phlegm, yellow bile, and black bile). Physicians like Galen used methods like pulse-taking and urine analysis to diagnose ailments. In addition to physical observations, Roman medicine also considered the environmental factors that might contribute to illness, such as climate and diet.

Preventative Care and Public Health

Romans placed a strong emphasis on prevention, particularly in urban settings. Public health measures like clean water, sanitation, and the construction of bathhouses were central to Roman medicine. Cities such as Pompeii had extensive aqueduct systems and sewage disposal to prevent disease outbreaks.

Romans understood the importance of hygiene, and bathing was not only a social activity but also a method of maintaining health. Furthermore, physicians advised on diet and exercise as preventive measures against illnesses, highlighting the importance of maintaining balance in life.

Treatment with Herbal Remedies

The Romans utilized a variety of herbal treatments, many of which were based on earlier Greek knowledge. These remedies were used for everything from digestive issues to infections. Roman texts, such as Pliny the Elder's *Natural History*, contain extensive information on medicinal plants like garlic, mint, and willow bark (which contained salicylic acid, an early precursor to aspirin). Medicinal herbs were often prepared as infusions, poultices, or oils and were considered a primary treatment method alongside dietary adjustments.

Surgical Interventions

Roman surgeons, especially those treating gladiators and soldiers, developed significant expertise in trauma care and surgery. Techniques for setting bones, suturing wounds, and performing amputations were common. Roman tools included scalpels, forceps, and other instruments that allowed for relatively advanced surgical procedures. Surgical treatments were generally reserved for serious injuries, especially in military settings, but Roman medicine also included some minor surgeries for less severe conditions. Despite a lack of anesthesia, Roman surgeons used wine and opium to dull pain.

Spiritual and Religious Healing

Roman healing traditions also involved religious rituals. Temples dedicated to healing gods, such as Asclepius, were common, and prayers or offerings to these gods were often included as part of the treatment process. Healing sanctuaries, called *valetudinaria*, were established, where priests and physicians worked together to provide care for the sick, blending medicine with divine intervention.

Steps and Processes of Medieval Healing Traditions

Medieval healing traditions integrated Roman medical knowledge with religious beliefs, cultural practices, and folk remedies. Healing in the medieval period was often a communal and spiritual process, focusing on both the body and the soul. Here is an overview of the typical steps in medieval healing traditions.

Diagnosis and Humoral Theory

In medieval medicine, diagnosis typically began with an assessment of the patient's symptoms in relation to the four humors (blood, phlegm, yellow bile, and black bile), a theory inherited from Roman and Greek medicine. Medieval physicians, influenced by scholars like Hippocrates and Galen, would diagnose based on an imbalance of these humors. A physician would also consider the patient's lifestyle, diet, and environment when making a diagnosis, as medieval practitioners believed that the body's health was influenced by both physical and spiritual factors.

Use of Herbal Remedies

Medieval healers relied heavily on herbal remedies, which were often drawn from ancient texts such as *De Materia Medica* by Dioscorides. These remedies were used for a wide range of ailments, including digestive problems, infections, and wounds. The *Leechbook of Bald*, a medieval manuscript, contains numerous herbal prescriptions for ailments like fever and cough, including garlic and onion mixtures, both of which were recognized for their antimicrobial properties. These remedies were prepared in various forms, including teas, poultices, and ointments.

Spiritual and Religious Interventions

Spiritual healing played a central role in medieval medical practices. Religion and medicine were closely intertwined, and many diseases were considered to be the result of sin, divine punishment, or spiritual imbalance. Healing often involved prayers, the use of holy water, pilgrimages to shrines, or the invocation of saints. Relics from saints were believed to have miraculous healing powers, and monasteries were centers of both medical and spiritual care. Physicians in monastic settings often provided herbal treatments in conjunction with religious rituals to restore both the body and the soul.

Surgery and Bloodletting

Surgical practices in medieval times were rudimentary compared to modern standards, but they made significant advancements from the Roman period. Surgeons often performed bloodletting, a practice rooted in the theory of humoral imbalance, to "correct" excess blood or to treat various ailments. Other common procedures included trepanation (the drilling of holes in the skull), setting broken bones, and treating wounds, particularly those resulting from battle or accidents. Surgical practices were often carried out by barber-surgeons, who were not fully trained physicians but performed basic medical procedures.

Quarantine and Disease Control

The Black Death in the 14th century marked a turning point in medieval medicine, as it prompted early forms of public health interventions. Cities like Venice implemented quarantine measures, isolating the sick from the healthy in an effort to curb the spread of the plague. While the medieval understanding of disease transmission was limited, these early quarantines were a critical step in the development of modern epidemiology. The implementation of such measures, along with the establishment of pesthouses (isolated areas for plague victims), laid the groundwork for the later development of public health practices.

Care in Monastic Hospitals

Monastic hospitals became central to medieval healing, where monks and nuns provided holistic care that included both physical treatments and spiritual comfort. These hospitals were places of refuge where patients received herbal remedies, nutritious food, and prayer. Many monasteries maintained extensive gardens of medicinal plants, and their healers were knowledgeable in the use of herbs, as well as offering emotional and spiritual support through prayer and meditation. This combination of physical care and spiritual healing was essential in medieval medical practices, emphasizing the belief that health depended on the harmony between the body and soul.

Both Roman and medieval healing traditions reflect the societies they emerged from: Roman medicine with its practical, preventative, and empirical foundations, and medieval healing practices, which combined physical treatments with strong spiritual and religious elements. Though each was shaped by its time, the processes from both periods contributed to the development of modern medical systems and continue to influence healthcare today.

Case Studies in Roman Healing Traditions

Treatment of Gladiators:

Roman gladiators, subjected to brutal combat in arenas, relied on skilled physicians for their survival and recovery. These physicians were often stationed in gladiatorial schools and specialized in trauma care. The first step in treating a gladiator's injury involved cleaning wounds with vinegar or wine, substances known for their antiseptic properties. Sutures made from catgut were used to stitch deep cuts. For bone fractures, doctors employed splints or wooden braces to stabilize and promote proper healing. Beyond immediate care, gladiators were given nutrient-dense diets, rich in barley, beans, and meat, to expedite recovery and build muscle. Rehabilitation often included light physical activity and massages to restore mobility. This structured and advanced medical care significantly increased survival rates among gladiators, showcasing the Romans' advanced understanding of trauma medicine and recovery.

Pliny the Elder's Herbal Medicine Practices:

Pliny the Elder's "Natural History" serves as a key example of Roman reliance on botanical remedies. His documentation of over 1,000 medicinal plants reflects the Romans' extensive use of herbs for healing. Remedies included willow bark for pain relief (a precursor to aspirin), garlic for infections and digestion, and mint for soothing stomach ailments. Pliny advocated for observing plants in their natural habitats and experimenting with their uses to treat specific ailments. These practices highlight the Romans' empirical approach to herbal medicine, which continued to influence European healing traditions for centuries.

Case Studies in Medieval Healing Traditions

Responses to the Black Death

The Black Death devastated Europe in the mid-14th century, killing millions and overwhelming medical knowledge of the time. Physicians attempted to treat the disease by aligning with the humoral theory, using bloodletting and purgatives to restore balance. Herbal sachets containing aromatic plants like rosemary, lavender, and sage were carried to "purify" the air from miasmas believed to cause the plague. Cities like Venice pioneered quarantine measures, isolating ships and individuals for 40 days before allowing them to enter the city. Religious interpretations of the plague led to acts of penitence, such as public flagellation and mass prayers, aimed at appeasing divine wrath. While many treatments failed to stop the spread of the plague, quarantine practices proved effective, marking a pivotal moment in public health management.

Monastic Care at St. John's Hospital in Bruges

St. John's Hospital in Bruges, one of Europe's oldest hospitals, exemplified the fusion of spiritual and medical care. Monastic caregivers employed herbal remedies grown in their gardens, such as chamomile for relaxation, sage for infections, and comfrey for healing wounds. Treatments were often complemented with prayers and the administration of sacraments, reflecting the belief that illness had both physical and spiritual dimensions. Patients were given simple, nutritious meals like broths and bread, and encouraged to rest in clean, quiet environments. This holistic care model prioritized compassion and comfort, setting the stage for later developments in institutional healthcare.

Conclusion

The exploration of Roman and medieval healing traditions offers a comprehensive understanding of the evolution of medical practices, shaped by both the limitations and the ingenuity of their time. Despite their differences in methodology, both Roman and medieval medicine made crucial contributions to the foundations of modern healthcare, blending empirical practices, cultural influences, and early scientific inquiry. By studying these historical periods, we can better appreciate the long trajectory of medical advancements that continue to influence contemporary health systems.

Roman medicine was marked by its systematic approach to health, grounded in practical solutions and an early understanding of anatomy, public health, and surgery. Roman physicians, such as Galen, contributed to the knowledge of the human body and surgical techniques that remained influential for centuries. Roman trauma care, particularly the treatments provided to gladiators, demonstrated a sophisticated level of care, using methods like antiseptic washes, suturing, and rehabilitation strategies that are still relevant in modern surgical practices. Their innovations in public health, such as the creation of aqueducts, sewer systems, and bathhouses, helped prevent the spread of disease and established the Romans as pioneers in environmental health. However, despite these advancements, Roman medicine was not without its limitations. Treatments often relied on trial and error, and access to healthcare was largely reserved for the wealthy and elite, with limited provisions for the lower classes and rural populations.

Medieval healing traditions, while continuing to draw on Roman knowledge, took a more holistic and spiritual approach to medicine, reflecting the social and religious context of the time. The medieval period saw the rise of monastic hospitals, which offered a unique combination of physical care, spiritual healing, and community support. In places like St. John's Hospital in Bruges, patients were treated with a combination of herbal remedies, diet, and prayer, illustrating the medieval belief that physical healing was intertwined with the soul's well-being. Although many medical treatments during the Middle Ages, such as bloodletting or the use of harmful substances like mercury, were ineffective and based on outdated theories, this period also saw the development of important health practices. For example, the implementation of quarantine measures during the Black Death reflected an early understanding of contagion and disease prevention, foreshadowing modern epidemiological practices. Additionally, physicians like Guy de Chauliac made significant strides in surgery by emphasizing hygiene and detailed observation, improving surgical practices during a time when healthcare was still rudimentary by modern standards.

Despite the influence of superstition and religious doctrine in medieval medicine, both Roman and medieval traditions were marked by their adaptability and resourcefulness. Roman physicians were among the first to document and categorize illnesses, using herbal remedies and surgical tools that would later become commonplace in Western medicine. In medieval Europe, the focus on natural remedies, many of which were derived from plants known to have antimicrobial properties (like garlic and honey), demonstrated a practical knowledge of healing that modern research has validated. Yet, the integration of religious rituals into the healing process sometimes hindered the development of a purely empirical, scientific approach to medicine. The persistence of beliefs in humoral imbalances, the influence of astrology, and the reliance on religious healing (such as the use of saints' relics or prayers) reflect the difficulty of separating science from spirituality in these times.

Looking at both Roman and medieval healing traditions through a modern lens, we can see that their greatest contributions to healthcare were not just in specific treatments but in their holistic understanding of health. Roman medicine set the stage for advancements in surgery, public health, and pharmacology, while medieval traditions built upon this knowledge and introduced important innovations in disease prevention, patient care, and the integration of health and spirituality. These periods emphasized observation, patient care, and the importance of medical knowledge being passed down through generations. The foundations laid by these ancient and medieval practices allowed for the eventual rise of Renaissance medicine, which would refine and expand many of the methods and theories introduced during these earlier times.

To conclude, Roman and medieval healing traditions remind us that medicine has always been shaped by the cultural, social, and scientific contexts in which it developed. While modern medicine has surpassed these ancient practices in terms of technology and knowledge, the spirit of observation, empirical study, and holistic care pioneered by Roman and medieval healers continues to influence contemporary healthcare. As we face today's global health challenges, the lessons from these early traditions—such as the importance of public health systems, the integration of mental and physical health, and the necessity of adaptability in times of crisis—remain just as relevant now as they were centuries ago. Ultimately, the enduring legacy of Roman and medieval healing practices lies not just in their successes but also in their capacity to evolve, adapt, and inform the ongoing development of healthcare for future generations.

References

Parker, S. (1996). *The Roman World*. Routledge.

Wilson, A. (2000). Drainage and sanitation in the Roman world. *World Archaeology, 32*(3), 349–363.

Hodge, A. T. (2002). *The Roman aqueducts of the world*. University of North Carolina Press.

Nutton, V. (2012). *Ancient medicine*. Routledge.

Baker, P. A. (2004). *Medical care for the Roman army on the Rhine, Danube, and British frontiers in the first, second, and early third centuries AD*. British Archaeological Reports.

Scarborough, J. (1969). Roman medicine: A review of the literature. *Classical World, 62*(5), 153–161.

Dioscorides, P. (c. 50 AD). *De materia medica* (L. Y. Beck, Trans.). IBIDIS Press (2011).

McGuffin, M., et al. (2013). *Herbal medicine: Biomolecular and clinical aspects*. CRC Press/Taylor & Francis.

Mattingly, D. (2011). *The archaeology of medicine in the Roman world*. Cambridge University Press.

Smith, R. (2007). Roman medical writers. In *The Cambridge companion to the Roman Republic* (pp. 257–280). Cambridge University Press.

Lonie, I. M. (2001). *Galen: On the natural faculties*. University of Toronto Press.

Irby-Massie, S. (2003). Religion and medicine in ancient Rome. *Journal of Roman Archaeology, 16*(2), 214–228.

McVaugh, M. R. (1993). *Medicine before the plague: Practitioners and their patients in the Crown of Aragon, 1285–1345*. Cambridge University Press.

Rawcliffe, C. (1999). *Medicine and society in later medieval England*. Sutton Publishing.

Thrupp, S. (1950). Monastic medicine and care in the Middle Ages. *The University of Chicago Press.*

Voigts, L. E. (1979). Anglo-Saxon plant remedies and the Anglo-Saxons. *Speculum, 54*(2), 259–277.

Bennett, A. (2007). Healing practices in medieval Europe: Local healers and folk medicine.

Medieval Health and Healing, 15(3), 37–52.

Cantor, N. F. (2001). *In the wake of the plague: The Black Death and the world it made*. Free Press.

Kohn, M. H. (2010). Epidemics and medicine in the medieval period. *Journal of Medieval Studies, 42*(1), 11–45.

Jordan, W. C. (1996). *The Black Death: A turning point in history*. HarperCollins.

Guy de Chauliac. (1363). *Chirurgia magna* (T. W. Hunt, Trans.). *A history of surgery* (2006). Royal College of Surgeons.

Bickerman, E. (2000). *Medieval surgery: Techniques and instruments*. Cambridge University Press.

Biller, P. (2001). The healing power of prayer in the Middle Ages. *History Compass, 2*(3), 1–15.

Head, R. (2008). *Pilgrimage and healing in the Middle Ages*. Oxford University Press.

Siraisi, N. G. (1997). *Medieval and early Renaissance medicine: An introduction to knowledge and practice*. University of Chicago Press.

Weiner, M. (2006). *Medieval medicine and its application in European universities*. Springer.

Nutton, V. (2004). *Ancient medicine*. Routledge.

Rawcliffe, C. (1999). *Medicine and society in later medieval England*. Sutton Publishing.

Conrad, L. I., et al. (1995). *The western medical tradition: 800 BC to AD 1800*. Cambridge

University Press.

Smith, P. (1997). Medical knowledge in the Roman and medieval worlds: Bridging the gap. *Medical History Journal, 41*(2), 28–46.

Macfarlane, I. (2008). *The therapeutic use of herbs in ancient Rome and the Middle Ages*. Routledge.

Lopez, L. R. (2009). Medieval herbal remedies and their influence on modern medicine. *Journal of Medicinal Plants, 31*(4), 315–322.

Jordan, W. C. (1996). *The Black Death: A turning point in history*. HarperCollins.

Hodge, A. T. (2002). *The Roman aqueducts of the world*. University of North Carolina Press.

Chapter 38

Rangoa Moari

Vaishnavi Magal School of Liberal Studies (SLS), CMR University, Bangalore

Rongoā Māori is a traditional Māori healing system deeply rooted in the cultural and spiritual practices of the Māori people of New Zealand. It encompasses a holistic view of health, emphasizing the interconnection between physical, spiritual, mental, and environmental well-being. This approach combines plant-based medicine (rongoā rākau), physical therapies such as massage (mirimiri), and spiritual healing through prayer (karakia).

Introduction and Historical Background

Rongoā Māori has origins that predate European colonization and has been passed down orally across generations. The arrival of European settlers in the 1800s disrupted the practice, particularly after the Tohunga Suppression Act of 1907, which sought to suppress Māori healing in favor of Western medicine. Despite these challenges, Rongoā Māori persisted, and in recent years, there has been a resurgence of interest in traditional healing as part of a broader movement to revitalize Māori culture and integrate Indigenous knowledge into mainstream healthcare practices.

Cultural Context of Rongoā Māori

The cultural foundations of Rongoā Māori revolve around principles such as whakapapa (genealogy), tapu (sacredness), and mana (dignity or spiritual power). Health is perceived as an integrated experience, involving the physical, spiritual, emotional, and social dimensions, consistent with the Māori worldview, *Te Ao* Māori.

- **Whakapapa (Genealogy)** is central in Rongoā Māori, as it acknowledges individuals› connections with their ancestors and the natural world. Whakapapa promotes a sense of identity, belonging, and continuity, elements critical to holistic well-being in Māori culture (Durie, 1994; McGowan & Palmer, 2017).
- **Tapu and Mana** recognize the sacredness and inherent dignity of all individuals. In Rongoā Māori, these concepts create respect and integrity in therapeutic relationships, aligning with principles that honor clients› identity and experiences (Durie, 2001).
- **Te Ao** Māori (Māori Worldview) provides a framework that perceives health as interconnected with environment, spirituality, and family. Psychotherapy that respects this perspective attends to multiple dimensions of well-being beyond symptom relief, involving mind, body, and spirit (Mark & Lyons, 2010; Waitoki & Levy, 2016).

Traditional New Zealand Medicinal Plants in Rongoā Māori: Mental Health and Psychological Benefits

In Rongoā Māori, the traditional Māori healing system, native plants play a crucial role in addressing physical, mental, and spiritual well-being. Each plant is valued not only for its physiological effects but also for its therapeutic impact on mental health. By supporting both physical and psychological recovery, these plants promote holistic healing that aligns with Māori cultural perspectives on health. Below are some of the key plants in Rongoā Māori, their uses, and their specific mental health benefits:

Mānuka (Leptospermum scoparium)

Description: Known as tea-tree, mānuka has a rich, earthy aroma and is used throughout New Zealand. Its bark and leaves have been traditionally infused, burned, and applied for various therapeutic purposes.

Mental Health Benefits:

Stress Reduction: Mānuka infusions provide a calming effect, reducing anxiety and helping people relax. The sedative properties of the bark infusion can ease mental strain and promote restful sleep, essential for individuals facing high levels of stress or burnout.

Grounding and Spiritual Cleansing: When inhaled, the steam from boiled mānuka leaves serves as a grounding ritual, which can clear the mind and restore emotional balance, especially during times of grief or heightened emotions.

Koromiko (Hebe stricta)

Description: Koromiko is abundant throughout New Zealand, with leaves traditionally used for digestive health and healing.

Mental Health Benefits:

Anxiety and Digestive Connection: Koromiko supports gut health, which is closely linked to mental well-being. By calming digestive upset, koromiko reduces anxiety-related symptoms such as stomach discomfort, fostering a sense of ease.

Emotional Resilience: As a tonic, koromiko strengthens the body and spirit, helping individuals feel more resilient and grounded. This support can be especially helpful for those struggling with ongoing stress or trauma.

Harakeke (Phormium tenax)

Description: Harakeke, or New Zealand flax, is recognized for its versatility and is commonly used in Rongoā Māori for its therapeutic and practical properties.

Mental Health Benefits:

Soothing and Relaxation: The flax sap is applied to skin abrasions and burns, and its gentle, soothing effect extends to mental well-being. Using harakeke in self-care rituals, such as massages or poultices, can create a calming experience that supports emotional release and reduces tension.

Kawakawa (Macropiper excelsum)

Description: A common forest plant with heart-shaped leaves, kawakawa is used widely for both its physical and mental health benefits.

Mental Health Benefits:

Calming Nervous System: Kawakawa is known for its ability to calm the nervous system. Its leaves are made into teas or infusions that can reduce symptoms of anxiety, promote relaxation, and help regulate mood, making it a valuable plant for individuals facing stress, anxiety, or emotional instability.

Symbol of Resilience and Healing: The visual resilience of kawakawa, often showing insect holes in its leaves, represents endurance and strength, making it a powerful symbol in mental health recovery. Using kawakawa in healing rituals can boost mental resilience, inspiring individuals to overcome challenges and build inner strength.

Pain and Anxiety Relief: Kawakawa poultices applied to aching joints or wounds help alleviate physical pain, which in turn can improve mental well-being by reducing the emotional toll of chronic pain and discomfort.

Tutu (Coriaria species)

Description: Though poisonous if improperly used, tutu has long been used in Rongoā Māori for its healing properties when applied correctly.

Mental Health Benefits:

Alleviating Pain and Promoting Relaxation: Tutu's applications for physical pain, such as in cases of arthritis and muscle strains, help reduce physical discomfort, which can significantly impact psychological well-being. Alleviating pain promotes relaxation and can ease the mental burden associated with chronic physical ailments.

Support for Emotional Healing: In carefully managed applications, tutu has been used to treat conditions that have both physical and emotional components, such as gout and arthritis. By reducing physical symptoms, it indirectly supports mental health, helping patients feel physically and mentally lighter.

Cultural Resilience and Empowerment: Tutu's careful, deliberate preparation encourages mindfulness and respect, reinforcing values of patience and empowerment that can support emotional resilience and provide a sense of mastery in one's healing journey.

Use of Rongoā Māori in Psychotherapy

In psychotherapy, Rongoā Māori offers a culturally affirming approach, particularly beneficial for Māori clients, by incorporating traditional values and practices. This approach allows therapy to be more responsive to Māori worldviews and holistic healing principles.

- **Culturally Affirming Practice**: Integrating Rongoā Māori principles, such as whakapapa, karakia, and whānau support, offers Māori clients a therapeutic space that reflects their cultural values. This can empower clients to reconnect with their identity, which is particularly valuable for individuals experiencing cultural dislocation or identity-related issues (Durie, 2001; Pitama et al., 2014).
- **Blending with Western Techniques**: Therapists often combine Rongoā Māori techniques with Western therapeutic approaches. For example, integrating mindfulness with karakia or using whakapapa discussions alongside cognitive-behavioral strategies to strengthen clients' self-identity and resilience (Mark & Lyons, 2010).
- **Supporting Mana and Whakapapa**: Rongoā Māori promotes an individual›s mana and connection to whakapapa, aiding in self-awareness and identity development. Recognizing the spiritual aspects of health, therapists can support Māori clients in enhancing their self-worth and fostering a connection to their ancestry (Durie, 1994; Waitoki & Levy, 2016).

Incorporating Rongoā Māori into psychotherapy supports culturally responsive care and can foster a more profound, meaningful therapeutic experience for Māori clients, ensuring therapy aligns with their unique cultural values and worldviews.

Integrative Mental Health Benefits in Rongoā Māori

These plants, when used in combination, foster mental health benefits that go beyond physical healing. Rongoā Māori healing practices often incorporate:

- **Grounding and Centering**: Through rituals involving plants like mānuka and kawakawa, individuals feel more connected to themselves and their environment.
- **Support for Trauma Recovery**: The hands-on preparation and application of these plants, especially through massage and infusion rituals, offer a nurturing, hands-on approach that can help individuals process trauma and reclaim agency over their well-being.
- **Building Resilience and Inner Strength**: The symbolism of these plants, particularly kawakawa with its "healed scars," reminds individuals of resilience, encouraging strength and healing in their mental health journey.

Incorporating Rongoā Māori practices in mental health care allows Māori patients, and increasingly others, to experience culturally resonant healing that aligns with holistic well-being. Through these plants and practices, mental health recovery becomes a connected, grounded process that respects tradition and fosters resilience.

Therapeutic Techniques in Rongoā Māori

Rongoā Māori involves a range of therapeutic methods, each deeply rooted in Māori traditions and values. These include:

- **Mirimiri (Bodywork or Massage Therapy)**: Mirimiri involves massage and bodywork to release tension and unblock emotional and spiritual energies. This technique aligns with somatic therapy approaches, focusing on the body as a pathway to emotional and psychological healing (McGowan & Palmer, 2017). Mirimiri is a therapeutic massage technique aimed at relieving physical and emotional pain, often performed by tohunga (healers). This practice can also include elements of spirituality and energy work, which reflect the Māori belief in the interconnectedness of the physical and spiritual realms.
- **Rākau Rongoā (Herbal Medicine)**: Traditional herbal remedies made from native plants are used to promote healing and health. While not directly applied in psychotherapy, understanding Rākau Rongoā offers therapists a holistic view of health practices that may complement mental health interventions for Māori clients (Durie, 1994). A variety of native plants are used in Rongoā Māori for their medicinal properties, including kawakawa (Māori pepper tree), mānuka (tea tree), and harakeke (flax). These plants are prepared into poultices, teas, and infusions to treat ailments ranging from infections to digestive issues. Each plant is carefully selected and used following tikanga, or Māori customs, to ensure safety and efficacy.
- **Karakia (Prayers and Incantations)**: Karakia are prayers or chants used to invoke spiritual support and protection. When integrated respectfully into therapy, karakia can serve as a grounding or mindfulness practice, providing clients with spiritual comfort and enhancing the therapeutic process (Waitoki & Levy, 2016; McGowan & Palmer, 2017). Karakia, or prayer, is a critical component of healing, often used to seek guidance, protection, or intervention from spiritual forces. This method reflects the belief that some illnesses may have supernatural causes and require spiritual treatment.
- **Whānau (Family and Community Support)**: Rongoā Māori values whānau (family) and collective support. Therapy sessions may include family members or focus on strengthening family connections, enabling a supportive environment for clients. This community-centered approach is critical in building resilience and well-being (Durie, 2001; Pitama, Huria, & Lacey, 2014).

Strengths of Rongoā Māori in Mental Health and Psychotherapy

Rongoā Māori offers a holistic approach to health, treating not only the physical but also emotional, spiritual, and social dimensions of well-being. This aligns with the Māori framework of *te whare tapa whā* (the four pillars of health), which views health as a balance across *wairua* (spirit), *hinengaro* (mind), *tinana* (body), and *whānau* (family). Such a comprehensive approach complements mental health care by addressing underlying emotional and social factors, which are often overlooked in Western treatments.

Cultural relevance is another strength of Rongoā Māori. The practice fosters a strong sense of identity, cultural pride, and connection, which is particularly empowering for Māori patients. Familiar, culturally-rooted practices give patients a sense of agency and control over their healing process, a crucial aspect for individuals who may feel alienated by mainstream mental health services. Additionally, the use of plant-based remedies, such as *harakeke* (flax) and *kawakawa*, offers a natural, non-invasive alternative to pharmaceutical interventions. These remedies are accessible, sustainable, and align with Māori environmental values, avoiding many of the side effects associated with conventional medications.

Rongoā Māori emphasizes person-centered care, tailoring treatments like *mirimiri* (traditional massage) and *romiromi* (deep tissue bodywork) to each individual's needs, which fosters a therapeutic connection and enhances trust. By attending to unique physical and spiritual needs, Rongoā offers a deep, individualized approach. Additionally, the spiritual components of Rongoā, such as *karakia* (prayers or blessings), are effective in promoting emotional well-being, helping patients feel grounded and resilient. This strength-based approach to spiritual and mental health care reinforces the support systems provided by family and community, an integral part of mental health recovery. Social connections are strengthened as family members often participate in the healing process, reducing stigma around mental health and normalizing the practice of seeking help.

Finally, Rongoā Māori aligns with the growing interest in integrative healthcare, appealing to those who seek a more holistic alternative to conventional methods. By offering an inclusive model that respects and values diverse healing traditions, Rongoā could potentially bridge traditional and modern practices, creating a culturally inclusive and rich addition to mental health care.

Limitations of Rongoā Māori in Mental Health and Psychotherapy

Despite its strengths, Rongoā Māori faces limitations, particularly in terms of scientific validation. Many practices lack rigorous scientific research, making it difficult for Rongoā to gain acceptance within evidence-based healthcare frameworks. Limited funding and resources further exacerbate this gap, often leaving Rongoā out of mainstream medical validation processes and research studies.

The integration of Rongoā into New Zealand's predominantly Western healthcare system poses another significant challenge. Differences in understanding and belief about health, healing, and outcome measurement can lead to misunderstandings or dismissal of Rongoā methods by non-Māori healthcare providers. Regulatory and funding constraints can also impede Rongoā's incorporation into official healthcare settings.

Another limitation is inconsistent availability. Access to qualified Rongoā practitioners may be restricted to certain areas, limiting its reach, especially in urban centers with predominantly non-Māori populations. Rongoā's effectiveness also depends on the quality and training of practitioners, but without a standardized accreditation system, there can be wide variation in practice quality, leading to potential issues of trust and consistency in care.

There are also challenges related to combining Rongoā with conventional treatments, especially with pharmaceuticals. Although Rongoā is primarily natural, certain plant-based remedies may interact with prescribed medications, leading to complications if treatments are not coordinated properly. The lack of clear guidelines on integrating Rongoā with pharmaceutical treatments can create risks for patients who rely on both types of care.

Cultural sensitivity is essential when considering Rongoā, as there is a risk of cultural appropriation or misrepresentation, especially as interest in holistic treatments grows. If Rongoā practices are adopted by non-Māori practitioners without a deep understanding of Māori cultural values, there is a risk that they will be diluted or misused, reducing their effectiveness and potentially causing cultural harm.

Furthermore, certain aspects of Rongoā, like *karakia* (prayers), may be viewed skeptically by those with a Western clinical background, leading to a perception that some Rongoā practices are merely placebo. This perspective can limit acceptance within mental health care and reduce funding opportunities for further research. Finally, documentation and evaluation are essential in Western medicine, but Rongoā's holistic and spiritual approach does not always align with standard methods of measurement. Attempts to document or quantify Rongoā practices may oversimplify or misrepresent its complexities, potentially altering its effectiveness.

Future Directions

Interest in Rongoā Māori continues to grow, with increasing efforts to integrate traditional healing into mainstream healthcare settings in New Zealand. The Ministry of Health has established standards to ensure that Rongoā Māori practitioners can work alongside conventional medical practitioners, enhancing healthcare options for Māori and non-Māori alike. Future research aims to deepen the scientific understanding of Māori plant remedies and further incorporate Rongoā into therapeutic and community health settings.

In-Depth Case Studies of Rongoā Māori in Mental Health Care

Case Study 1: Reducing Anxiety and Depression in a Clinical Setting

Background:

In a mental health clinic primarily serving Māori clients, practitioners observed that standard approaches to anxiety and depression did not fully resonate with patients. Many clients felt disconnected from these methods, resulting in low engagement and motivation. To address this, the clinic introduced Rongoā Māori practices alongside conventional therapy to offer a culturally familiar therapeutic experience.

Therapeutic Techniques Used:

- **Mirimiri (Therapeutic Massage)**: Mirimiri was incorporated as a means to help patients physically release tension and relax. For clients experiencing anxiety, this practice provided a comforting, non-verbal way to connect with their emotions.

- **Kawakawa Tea**: Known for its calming and soothing properties, kawakawa tea was served to patients before therapy sessions to reduce anxiety, foster relaxation, and prepare them for emotional work.
- **Whakapapa Discussions**: Therapists encouraged clients to discuss their whakapapa (ancestral lineage) to deepen self-understanding and connection to family and heritage, promoting self-worth and resilience.

What Worked:

The combination of mirimiri and kawakawa tea created a calming, welcoming environment, helping clients feel more grounded and open to therapy. The inclusion of whakapapa discussions allowed clients to explore their cultural identity and heritage, which significantly improved self-awareness and emotional resilience.

Outcome:

Patients showed greater engagement in therapy, feeling more connected and respected. Anxiety and depression symptoms decreased as clients felt validated in their experiences and rooted in their culture. This approach also helped reduce stigma around mental health by integrating therapy into a framework familiar to Māori clients. Overall, the clinic saw improved mental health outcomes and a stronger therapeutic alliance.

Case Study 2: Healing from Trauma in Abuse Survivors

Background:

A support program for survivors of abuse found that traditional Western therapeutic techniques alone did not fully address the complex needs of Māori clients. Many survivors experienced cultural disconnection and unresolved spiritual distress following their trauma. To offer a culturally attuned approach, the program integrated Rongoā Māori practices focused on emotional release and spiritual healing.

Therapeutic Techniques Used:

- **Mirimiri (Therapeutic Massage)**: Mirimiri was provided to help clients release physical manifestations of trauma, such as muscle tension and stress. This approach gave clients a culturally aligned way to reconnect with their bodies and begin healing in a safe space.
- **Karakia (Prayers and Chants)**: Karakia were performed with clients to address their spiritual needs, create a sense of safety, and encourage emotional resilience.
- **Harakeke and Kawakawa Infusions**: Infusions made from harakeke (New Zealand flax) and kawakawa were given to support emotional balance and calm the nervous system, helping to stabilize clients emotionally.

What Worked:

Mirimiri helped survivors release emotional trauma stored in the body, which was especially valuable for those with a history of abuse. Karakia provided spiritual support, fostering a sense of protection and grounding. The harakeke and kawakawa infusions proved helpful for managing stress and stabilizing emotional responses, aiding clients in processing their trauma.

Outcome:

Clients reported reduced symptoms of stress and anxiety, with an increased sense of emotional release and empowerment. By connecting with their cultural heritage, survivors were able to navigate their trauma in a supportive environment. This culturally aligned approach fostered resilience and contributed positively to their healing journey.

Case Study 3: Supporting Young Māori with PTSD Symptoms

Background:

A youth support organization noticed that young Māori clients with post-traumatic stress disorder (PTSD) struggled to engage with conventional talk therapy, often finding it difficult to articulate their experiences. To provide more accessible mental health support, the organization introduced Rongoā Māori techniques aimed at emotional release and self-identity reinforcement.

Therapeutic Techniques Used:

- **Whakawhanaungatanga (Building Relationships)**: Therapists focused on building relationships and trust, aligning with the Māori concept of whakawhanaungatanga, which emphasizes establishing strong connections.
- **Mirimiri and Deep Breathing Exercises**: Mirimiri sessions helped these youth relax and connect with their bodies, while deep breathing exercises, taught as part of the sessions, allowed them to manage PTSD symptoms such as hyperarousal.
- **Whakapapa Exploration**: Discussions on whakapapa were used to help youth understand their place within their families and ancestry, offering a culturally affirming perspective that contributed to a stronger sense of self.

What Worked:

Whakawhanaungatanga helped build trust, enabling young clients to open up more gradually. Mirimiri and breathing exercises were effective in reducing physical tension and aiding emotional regulation. Exploring whakapapa gave clients a sense of stability, identity, and pride, which was essential for recovery.

Outcome:

Youth reported a stronger sense of identity and reduced PTSD symptoms, such as anxiety and hypervigilance. These practices helped clients feel more connected to their cultural identity, providing a powerful foundation for healing. The organization noted that these clients showed improved engagement and better coping strategies, reducing the likelihood of symptom recurrence.

References

Jones, R. (2007, September 24). *Rongoā – Medicinal use of plants*. Te Ara - The Encyclopedia of New Zealand. Retrieved November 9, 2024, from http://www.TeAra.govt.nz/en/rongoa-medicinal-use-of-plants

Kiniec, A., Spychalski, M., Miziniak, W., Palacz, M., & Kukawka, R. (2024). The use of thyme (Thymus vulgaris) essential oil for controlling Cercospora leaf spot (Cercospora beticola) on sugar beets (Beta vulgaris). *Agriculture, 14*(11), 2017. https://doi.org/10.3390/agriculture14112017

Durie, M. (1994). *Whaiora: Maori Health Development*. Oxford University Press.

Durie, M. (2001). *Nga Kahui Pou: Launching Māori Futures*. Huia Publishers.

Mark, G., & Lyons, A. C. (2010). Māori healers' views on wellbeing: The importance of mind, body, spirit, family, and land. *Social Science & Medicine*, 70(11), 1756-1764.

McGowan, R., & Palmer, S. (2017). *Rongoā* Māori: Traditional Māori Healing. Auckland University Press.

Pitama, S., Huria, T., & Lacey, C. (2014). Improving Māori health through clinical assessment: Waikare o te Waka o Meihana. *The New Zealand Medical Journal*, 127(1393).

Waitoki, W., & Levy, M. P. (2016). *Te Manu Kai i Te Mātauranga: Indigenous Psychology in Aotearoa/New Zealand*. New Zealand Psychological Society.

Durie, M. (1994). *Whaiora: Māori health development*. Auckland University Press.

Jones, R., & Rameka, M. (2017). The Rongoā Māori framework: Towards an Indigenous evaluation framework for Māori healing. *Evaluation Matters—He Take Tō Te Aromatawai, 3*, 31-61.

Waitangi Tribunal. (2019). *Hauora: Report on Stage One of the Health Services and Outcomes Kaupapa Inquiry* (Wai 2575). Wellington, NZ: Legislation Direct.

New Zealand Ministry of Health. (2020). *Ngā Rautaki Hauora Māori (Māori Health Strategies)*. Retrieved from https://www.health.govt.nz

McGough, S., & Wynne-Jones, J. (2021). Rongoā Māori and mental health: Reconnecting culture and wellbeing. *Journal of Indigenous Wellbeing, 6*(1), 22-37.

Ahuriri-Driscoll, A., Boulton, A., Stewart, A., Hudson, M., & Mika, C. (2008). Māori healing practices and indicators of health: A systematic review of literature. *Journal of Alternative and Complementary Medicine, 14*(7), 819-824.

Chapter 39

Schema Therapy

Swathi Shajil School of Liberal studies, CMR University, Bangalore

Definition

Jeffrey Young introduced schema therapy, an integrative therapeutic method, in 1990 to treat clients with personality disorders, chronic characterological problems, and other difficult issues that affect both individuals and couples. Schema therapy, which developed from Beck's cognitive therapy, incorporates aspects of behavioral, object relations, Gestalt, constructivist, cognitive-behavioral, attachment, and psychoanalytic therapies. Instead of only treating acute symptoms, it concentrates on the long-lasting, underlying patterns or "schemas" that shape chronic and characterological features of illnesses.

Details

Schema therapy is a treatment method that combines cognitive-behavioral therapy (CBT), attachment theory, gestalt, and psychoanalytic techniques to address deeply rooted emotional patterns. It was created by Jeffrey Young and is especially beneficial for individuals with personality disorders, persistent emotional concerns, and complicated mental health challenges such as chronic anxiety, depression, and relationship problems.

Maladaptive schemas are deeply embedded negative beliefs acquired early in life, frequently as a result of unmet desires or unfavorable experiences. These schemas might contain themes like as abandonment, distrust, or defectiveness, which influence clients' emotions, ideas, and actions. Schema therapy detects these schemas and categorizes them into modes (emotionally driven states), such as the "vulnerable child" or "punitive parent," helping individuals understand and modify their emotional reactions and behaviors associated with each mode.

1. **Schema Assessment:** Tools such as the Young Schema Questionnaire (YSQ) and the Schema Mode Inventory (SMI) are used to assess clients' maladaptive schemas and modes.
2. **Cognitive Restructuring:** The therapist works to reframe or challenge harmful attitudes and thoughts.
3. **Experiential Techniques:** Techniques like as imagery rescripting enable clients to re-experience and alter negative experiences in order to reduce schema level of severity.

4. **Behavioural Pattern Breaking:** Therapists urge clients to engage in new actions that contradict their schemas, allowing them to replace old habits with better responses.

Schema therapy is often a longer-term therapy due to the deep-rooted nature of the issues it addresses, and it aims to promote resilience, improve relationships, and help clients develop adaptive, fulfilling ways of meeting emotional needs. It offers a versatile approach tailored to each client's needs, targeting schemas, coping styles, and modes. The primary goal is schema healing, achieved through cognitive, behavioral, experiential, and relational techniques. By reducing the strength of memories, emotions, and beliefs linked to maladaptive schemas, clients learn healthier behaviors and less reactive responses, enhancing resilience. Central to schema therapy is the therapeutic relationship, where therapists model the "Healthy Adult" mode and use "empathic confrontation" and "limited reparenting" to address clients' early unmet needs within safe boundaries.

Advantages of Schema Therapy

Most comprehensive:

It is a combination of cognitive, behavioural, experiential, and interpersonal techniques that enable the chosen treatment approach to be holistic and specific to the problem and needs of the individual.

Revealing the root:

Addressing the deeply entrenched schemas formed in childhood allows clients to start seeing and understanding the origins of their emotion and behaviour patterns.

Increased self-awareness:

Clients learn to identify maladaptive schemas and how they affect thoughts and behaviour, thereby gaining more insight into their experiences.

Increased emotional regulation:

Clients acquire a better emotional coping scheme through experiential techniques. Negative feelings thus cause less distress to them.

Improved relationships in interpersonal life:

Schema therapy will train people to nurture a better environment of relationships with others by helping them identify and modify self-destructive patterns of behaviour in interactions.

Disorders Addressed with Schema Therapy

Personality Disorders

- Essentially borderline personality disorder and narcissistic personality disorder.
- Chronic Anxiety Disorders: Such as generalized anxiety disorder and social anxiety.
- Depressive Disorders: Encompassing major depressive disorder and dysthymia.
- Eating Disorders: Like binge eating disorder and anorexia.
- PTSD: Mostly in cases with a complex trauma history.

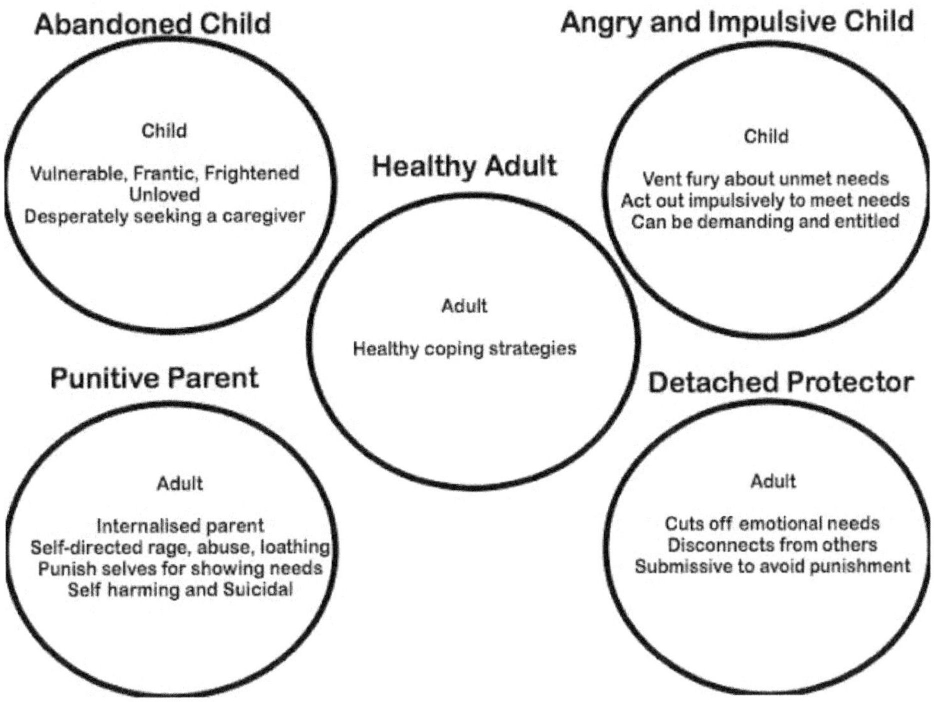

History

The concept of the "schema," within psychology, was influenced by Carl Jung's usage of the term to describe mental structures that help in organizing and interpretation of information by individuals. Jung's theories served to shape the concept of schemas as the learning frameworks of experiences which affected perception and behavior. The notion was then developed mainly by schema therapy instituted by Jeffrey Young, which focuses on the maladaptive schemas formed during early life and their effects on emotional health and interpersonal relationships.

Young developed and formulated schema therapy because of his clinical experiences and cognitive-behavioral approaches that identified the necessity for flexible treatment approaches for treating deeply rooted emotional problems and chronic behavior patterns (Young, Klosko, & Weishaar, 2003). Traditional cognitive-behavioral therapy (CBT) had been quite successful in the treatment of many Axis I illnesses such as anxiety and depression (Barlow, 2001). Young, however, saw that CBT interventions sometimes failed to provide lasting gains for clients who were laboring under ingrained characterological features and persistent underlying personality disturbances that complicated the therapy and made it more time-consuming and difficult.

Although cognitive-behavioral therapy (CBT) is typically short-term and aimed at addressing current issues, some clients experience chronic dysfunction or deeper-rooted problems that may not be effectively treated within the conventional CBT framework. For instance, research indicates that up to 40% of clients with depression do not respond to initial therapy, and about 30% of those who do show improvement relapse within a year (Young, Weinberger, & Beck, 2001). Clients with personality disorders, such as borderline or avoidant personality disorders, often struggle with the traditional

CBT structure due to their rigid and inflexible thinking patterns, a tendency to avoid emotions and conflicts, and deep-seated attachment issues that hinder the formation of a productive therapeutic alliance (Beck, Freeman, & Associates, 1990).

Young's approach expanded the cognitive-behavioral framework by integrating ideas from object relations, Gestalt therapy, constructivist models, attachment theories, and psychoanalytic philosophy. This combination led to the creation of schema therapy, which offers a more flexible and long-term treatment option for individuals facing both Axis I disorders and complex characterological challenges. By shifting the focus from short-term symptom relief to identifying and addressing deeply ingrained "schemas"—the persistent patterns of thought, emotion, and behavior—schema therapy may be more effective in engaging individuals with personality disorders who find standard CBT unhelpful.

Schema therapy was initially developed to tackle personality issues, but it quickly demonstrated its effectiveness for a variety of chronic conditions. It has shown potential in treating chronic anxiety and depression, long-standing relationship difficulties, eating disorders, and preventing drug relapse. This approach has been particularly helpful for those grappling with complex and pervasive issues, such as ongoing dissatisfaction with relationships, work, and personal well-being—challenges that are often vague and hard to define within the traditional CBT framework. Schema therapy is now recommended for clients facing chronic, long-term difficulties, especially those with enduring relationship problems or persistent Axis I disorders that do not respond to conventional treatments. It is also beneficial for individuals exhibiting rigid thinking, avoidance behaviors, or excessive emotional dependence and entitlement. Nowadays, schema therapy is utilized for a broad spectrum of persistent and intricate psychological challenges, frequently offering clients a solid framework to address their deeply ingrained maladaptive patterns and foster lasting improvements in their emotional and relational well-being.

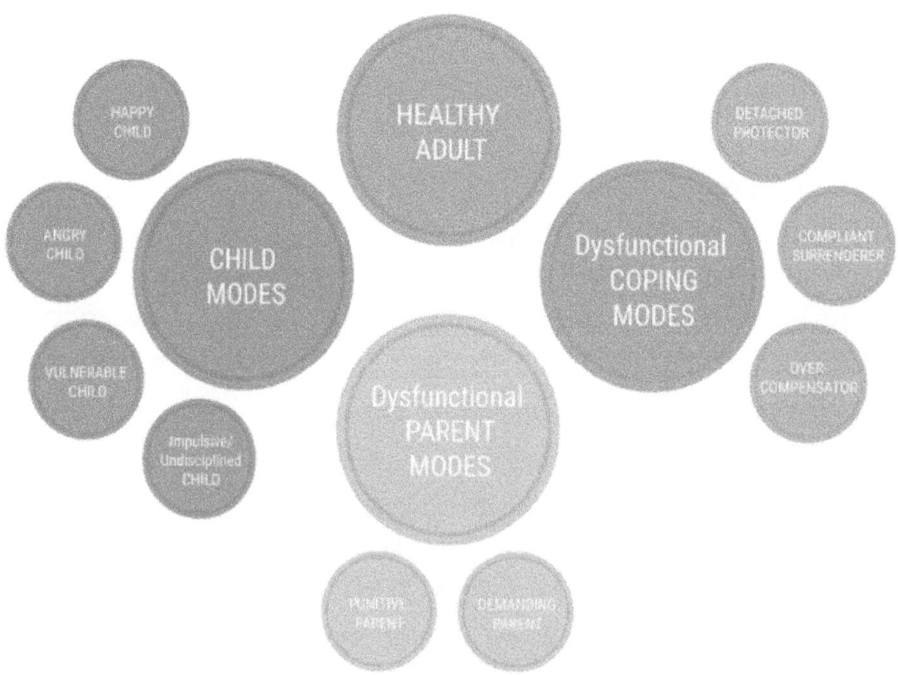

mindviewpsychology.com.au

Theoretical background

Schemas are a fundamental concept in psychology, serving as cognitive frameworks or mental structures that assist individuals in organizing and interpreting information. The notion of schemas has developed over time, influenced by various psychological theories and disciplines.

Historical Foundations

The idea of schemas can be traced back to early psychological theories:

Jean Piaget's Cognitive Development Theory (1936)

Piaget characterized schemas as mental structures that children utilize to make sense of the world. He proposed that schemas evolve through processes of assimilation (where new information is integrated into existing schemas) and accommodation (where schemas are adjusted when new information does not fit).

Bartlett's Memory Research (1932)

Frederic Bartlett introduced the concept of schemas in his memory studies, demonstrating that individuals rely on pre-existing knowledge structures to interpret and recall information. He contended that schemas shape how we perceive, store, and reconstruct our experiences.

Cognitive Psychology (1960s)

With the rise of cognitive psychology, schemas became linked to information processing. Psychologists such as Ulric Neisser and David Rumelhart highlighted schemas as templates that direct attention, perception, and memory.=

Schema Theory in Clinical Psychology

In clinical settings, schemas have become significant through the contributions of Aaron Beck and Jeffrey Young:

Aaron Beck's Cognitive Therapy

Beck's cognitive model highlighted the impact of maladaptive schemas on automatic thoughts, emotions, and behaviors. He concentrated on negative core beliefs, such as "I'm unlovable" or "The world is unsafe," which play a role in conditions like depression and anxiety.

Jeffrey Young's Schema Therapy

Young built upon Beck's foundation, incorporating elements from attachment theory, psychodynamic approaches, and cognitive-behavioral therapy (CBT). He introduced the idea of ***Early Maladaptive Schemas (EMS):***

EMS are deeply ingrained, widespread patterns of thought and feeling that arise in childhood due to unmet emotional needs.

Young identified 18 maladaptive schemas (e.g., Abandonment, Defectiveness/Shame, Emotional Deprivation) and connected them to five essential emotional needs: safety, autonomy, connection, self-esteem, and play.

Key Components of Schema Theory

Development of Schemas

Schemas develop through early life experiences, especially during interactions with caregivers. Positive experiences help create healthy schemas, while unmet needs or negative experiences can result in maladaptive schemas.

For instance: A child who faces consistent emotional neglect might form an Emotional Deprivation schema, leading them to believe their needs will never be fulfilled.

Similarly, a child who is frequently criticized may adopt a Defectiveness/Shame schema, perceiving themselves as fundamentally flawed.

Maintenance of Schemas

Schemas endure because individuals often unconsciously seek to validate them, even if they are harmful. There are three coping styles that help maintain schemas:

1. ***Surrender:*** Accepting the schema as reality and acting in accordance with it.
2. ***Avoidance:*** Steering clear of situations that could trigger the schema.
3. ***Overcompensation:*** Reacting in extreme ways to counter the schema, which can create additional problems.

Schema Modes

Schema therapy introduces the idea of schema modes, which are emotional states or coping responses triggered by schemas. Common modes include:

1. ***Vulnerable Child:*** Reflects unmet emotional needs and feelings of sadness, fear, or isolation.
2. ***Punitive Parent:*** Involves harsh self-criticism or blaming thoughts.
3. ***Healthy Adult:*** The aim of therapy is to strengthen this mode, allowing individuals to meet their own emotional needs in a healthy way.

Application of Schema Theory

Application of Schema Theory in Therapy

- Schema therapy integrates cognitive, behavioral, and experiential methods to assist clients in:
- Recognizing and comprehending their schemas.
- Reworking distressing childhood memories linked to these schemas (for instance, through imagery rescripting).
- Creating healthier coping mechanisms to substitute maladaptive ones.
- Enhancing the healthy adult mode to effectively meet unmet emotional needs.

Strengths of Schema Theory

- **Holistic Approach:** It brings together cognitive, emotional, and interpersonal aspects.
- **Focus on Emotional Needs:** It highlights how unmet needs play a crucial role in the development of psychopathology.

- **Effective for Chronic Issues:** It is especially beneficial for addressing personality disorders, chronic depression, and complex trauma.

Criticisms of Schema Theory

- **Complexity:** The intricate classification of schemas and modes can be quite daunting.
- **Limited Empirical Support:** Although schema therapy has shown potential, it doesn't have the extensive research backing that traditional CBT enjoys.
- **Time-Intensive:** Working through deeply rooted schemas often necessitates long-term therapy.

Steps or processes

Assessment and Education Phase

The Empathic Exploration: The therapist creates a safe and trusting environment in which the client feels safe to share their inner life with their deep personal experiences.

Schema Identification: By means such as the Young Schema Questionnaire, the therapist helps the client to identify and name maladaptive schemas and modes.

Psychoeducation: The therapist educates clients about how schemas are formed, often resulting from some unmet emotional needs in early life, thus facilitating their understanding of schema functioning in their present.

Change Phase

Corrective Responses: The therapist helps the client challenge unproductive thinking by reframing the process in an empathetic yet realistic manner.

Experiential Techniques: Imagery Rescripting allows clients to re-experience traumatic memories with new supportive narratives.

Chair Work facilitates dialogues between conflicting parts of themselves, like the "Vulnerable Child" and "Healthy Adult."

Breaking Through Behavioral Patterns: The client is encouraged to engage in new, healthier behaviors that stand in direct contrast with maladaptive patterns of behavior under the supportive guidance of the therapist.

The Therapeutic Alliance: Very core to that process is that the therapist in modeling the "Healthy Adult" role provides the client with some empathy regarding confrontation and "limited reparenting" to meet the client's unmet emotional needs, provided that appropriate boundaries are respected.

Long-Term Integration

Support and Reflection for Life: The therapist will help clients to develop self-compassion, which will nurture resiliency and adaptive emotional responses over time.

Relational Healing: The therapy works to improve interpersonal relations by addressing self-destructive patterns while nurturing healthier connections.

Case Study

Case Study 1: Schema Therapy Journey

Background

Jane, a 30-year-old marketing executive, sought therapy to address her ongoing struggles with low self-esteem, conflicts in her relationships, and stress at work. She often felt intense emotions of abandonment and rejection, which caused her to react defensively in her relationships. Additionally, her deep-seated fear of failure held her back from pursuing career advancements.

Initial Assessment

Through interviews and the Young Schema Questionnaire (YSQ), the therapist identified several key maladaptive schemas in Jane's life. The most prominent schemas included "Abandonment," "Defectiveness/Shame," and "Failure." These schemas were deeply rooted in Jane's past experiences, including parental neglect and early academic difficulties. As a result, Jane developed patterns of anticipating rejection and avoiding situations where she feared criticism.

Treatment Plan and Phases

The integrative approach of schema therapy was customized to address Jane's cognitive, behavioral, and emotional challenges through the following phases:

1. **Awareness and Identification**

   The therapist helped Jane understand her schema "modes," which are distinct emotional states associated with her schemas. Jane learned to identify her "Vulnerable Child" and "Punitive Parent" modes, reflecting her feelings of inadequacy and self-criticism. Through imagery exercises, she explored memories that triggered these modes, gaining a clearer understanding of the origins of her schemas.

2. **Cognitive Restructuring**

   Together, Jane and her therapist focused on reframing her schemas. For example, she challenged her "Defectiveness" schema by recalling instances when she received positive feedback. The therapist employed "Socratic questioning" to encourage Jane to critically evaluate the validity of her self-assessments, helping her build evidence against her belief in her inadequacy.

3. **Experiential Techniques**

   Through imagery rescripting, Jane revisited her painful memories to change her emotional reactions. In one session, she envisioned a supportive figure standing up to her inner critic, providing her with the emotional validation she needed. Over time, this practice allowed Jane to replace her past fears with compassion and a stronger sense of self-worth.

4. **Behavioural Pattern-Breaking**

   Jane was encouraged to take part in "corrective experiences," such as assertively expressing her needs both at work and in her personal life. These behavioral experiments helped her face her fears of rejection, leading her to discover that people often responded positively when she communicated her needs.

5. **Building a Strong Therapeutic Alliance**

   Throughout her therapy, Jane's therapist consistently offered validation and modeled healthy relationship dynamics. This strong alliance enabled Jane to build trust and address her relational fears in a safe space.

By the end of her treatment, Jane reported a notable decrease in feelings of inadequacy and fear of abandonment. She enhanced her communication skills, established healthier boundaries, and even pursued a managerial position at work. Schema therapy empowered her to replace harmful patterns with adaptive strategies, nurturing a stronger sense of self-worth and stability in her relationships.

Case Study 2

Age: 28

Occupation: Graphic Designer

Presenting Problem: The client sought therapy due to ongoing feelings of abandonment, low self-worth, and challenges in maintaining relationships. She described experiencing intense emotional reactions, engaging in self-sabotaging behaviors, and feeling chronically lonely.

Initial Assessment

Using assessment tools such as the Young Schema Questionnaire and through discussions, the therapist identified Sarah's core schemas:

- Abandonment/Instability: A fear that significant others would leave her.
- Defectiveness/Shame: A deep-rooted belief that she was unlovable.
- Emotional Deprivation: A sense that her emotional needs would never be fulfilled.

Therapeutic Goals

- Decrease the intensity of maladaptive schemas.
- Replace unhealthy coping mechanisms with healthier alternatives.
- Foster a more stable and positive self-image.

Schema Therapy Interventions

Psychoeducation - She learned about schemas and their impact on her thoughts, feelings, and behaviors. Gaining insight into her schemas helped her understand that her reactions stemmed from childhood experiences rather than her present circumstances.

Experiential Techniques

Imagery Rescripting: She visualized a painful memory of being ignored by her parents when she expressed her feelings. During this exercise, her therapist guided her to imagine stepping in as a protective figure to comfort her younger self.

Chair Work: She engaged in dialogues between her "healthy adult" self and her "vulnerable child" self, which helped her cultivate a nurturing inner voice.

Cognitive Restructuring - Together, the client and her therapist focused on challenging and reframing negative thoughts such as, "People will leave me if they see my flaws." They reinforced new, healthier beliefs like, "I am deserving of love, even with my imperfections."

She worked on tolerating discomfort when she felt insecure in her relationships, choosing to face those feelings rather than withdrawing or trying too hard to please others. She established boundaries in her relationships, moving away from her previous habit of over-pleasing.

Over the course of six months in therapy, the client noticed significant improvements:

- She began to build healthier relationships and her fear of abandonment lessened considerably.
- She expressed feeling more self-compassionate and started recognizing and addressing her own emotional needs.
- While the old schemas still triggered her from time to time, Sarah was now able to handle them without reverting to her previous behaviors.

Case Study 3: Overcoming Fear of Failure

A middle-aged professional struggled with self-doubt and procrastination, even though they seemed successful in their career. They were reluctant to take on new challenges due to a deep-rooted belief that failure was inevitable. This fear originated from childhood experiences, where they were often compared to a high-achieving sibling, which led to feelings of inadequacy when they didn't measure up.

Therapeutic Journey

- **Assessment** - The primary schema identified was Failure, which involved the belief that they were fundamentally incapable of achieving success. This schema was reinforced through avoidance behaviors and negative self-talk.
- **Imagery Rescripting** - In therapy, they revisited a painful memory of being criticized for not achieving perfect grades. During the rescripting exercise, they imagined a supportive adult comforting their younger self and confronting the critical parent figure, introducing a more balanced perspective.
- **Cognitive Restructuring** - The therapist and client worked together to examine and challenge thoughts like, "If I fail, I'll lose everything," replacing them with, "Failure is part of growth, and I've succeeded many times before."
- **Behavioral Experiments** - To break the cycle of avoidance, they began taking small, manageable risks at work, such as leading a project presentation. Over time, these experiences boosted their confidence and provided evidence against the validity of the schema.

Reflection

This case demonstrated how schemas can persist into adulthood, often shaping behaviors and emotions. By reprocessing formative memories and challenging unhelpful beliefs, the client developed a healthier relationship with failure, seeing it as an opportunity for learning rather than a sign of inadequacy. They became more resilient and willing to face challenges, illustrating how experiential and cognitive techniques in schema therapy can lead to meaningful transformation.

Overall Reflections on Schema Therapy

1. Healing Childhood Wounds: Each case highlighted how schemas often originate in childhood and persist into adulthood, influencing beliefs and behaviors. Techniques such as imagery rescripting played a key role in reprocessing these formative memories, allowing clients to address emotional needs that had been overlooked or invalidated.

2. Behavioral Change as a Catalyst: Although cognitive and emotional strategies were important, significant transformation happened when clients altered the behaviors that reinforced their maladaptive schemas. Engaging socially or embracing imperfection, for instance, provided clients with tangible evidence to question their longstanding beliefs.

3. Empathy and Self-Compassion: It was crucial to encourage clients to cultivate a nurturing internal dialogue, which helped them reframe their fundamental beliefs. By fostering a connection between their healthy adult self and their vulnerable child self, clients learned to fulfill their emotional needs in a compassionate and sustainable manner.

4. Long-Term Impact: While schemas were not completely eradicated, the therapy equipped clients with the skills to manage them effectively. By enhancing resilience and self-awareness, clients acquired the tools necessary for ongoing personal development beyond the therapy sessions.

The integrative nature of schema therapy, which combines cognitive, experiential, and behavioral techniques, demonstrated its effectiveness in tackling deep-seated issues and promoting enduring change in these cases.

References

Beck, A. T., Freeman, A., & Associates. (1990). Cognitive therapy of personality disorders. Guilford Press.

Barlow, D. H. (2001). Anxiety and its disorders: The nature and treatment of anxiety and panic (2nd ed.). Guilford Press.

Bartlett, F. C. (1932). Remembering: A study in experimental and social psychology. Cambridge University Press.

Martin, R., & Young, J. E. (2010). Schema therapy. In K. Dobson (Ed.), Handbook of cognitive-behavioral therapies (3rd ed., pp. 317–346). Guilford Press.

Piaget, J. (1936). The origins of intelligence in children. International Universities Press.

Young, J. E., Klosko, J. S., & Weishaar, M. E. (2003). Schema therapy: A practitioner's guide. Guilford Press.

Young, J. E., Weinberger, A. D., & Beck, A. T. (2001). Cognitive therapy for depression. In D. H. Barlow (Ed.), Clinical handbook of psychological disorders (3rd ed., pp. 264–308). Guilford Press.

Neisser, U. (1967). Cognitive psychology. Prentice-Hall.

Chapter 40

Shamanism

Tanyaa Taj School of Liberal Studies (SLS), CMR University, Bengaluru

A ritual that involves a person communicating with the spirits to heal people of their illness or carry a soul to the outer world seems weird. The very thought of communicating with the spirits sounds eerie. But believe it or not, some people known as Shamans practice this art.

Shamanism represents one of humanity's earliest systematic approaches to healing and consciousness exploration, with archaeological evidence suggesting practices dating back at least 30,000 years (Whitley, 2009). As a healing tradition, shamanism has garnered significant attention from anthropologists, psychologists, and mental health practitioners for its potential insights into human consciousness and therapeutic processes (Krippner, 2000).

Origins and Etymology

The term "shaman" originates from the Tungusic word "šaman" of the Evenki people in Siberia, though similar practices have been documented across all inhabited continents under various cultural designations (Eliade, 1964). Anthropological research suggests that shamanic practices developed independently in multiple cultures, indicating a universal human tendency to seek healing through altered states of consciousness and spiritual intermediaries (Winkelman, 2010).

Traditional Foundations and Worldview

Shamanic traditions are rooted in an animistic worldview, where all aspects of nature are considered alive and imbued with spirit (Harner, 1990). Within this paradigm, shamans function as intermediaries between the physical and spirit worlds, utilizing altered states of consciousness to diagnose and treat various ailments (Walsh, 2007). The shamanic worldview conceptualizes illness as a manifestation of spiritual disharmony, requiring intervention at both physical and metaphysical levels (Ripinsky-Naxon, 1993).

Historical Development Through Ages

Ancient Period (Pre-history - 3000 BCE)

Archaeological evidence, including cave paintings in France and Spain dating to 30,000-40,000 BCE, suggests sophisticated shamanic practices involving altered states of consciousness and healing rituals (Clottes & Lewis-Williams, 1998). These early shamanic traditions laid the groundwork for organized healing practices and later religious systems.

Classical and Medieval Period (3000 BCE - 1500 CE)

During this period, shamanic practices became increasingly systematized while adapting to emerging religious frameworks. In many regions, shamanic healers faced persecution, particularly during the European witch hunts, leading to the suppression of traditional healing knowledge (Ginzburg, 1991).

Modern Era (1500 CE - Present)

Academic interest in shamanism emerged in the late 19th century through anthropological studies, notably with Mircea Eliade's seminal work "Shamanism: Archaic Techniques of Ecstasy" (1964). The counterculture movement of the 1960s sparked renewed Western interest in shamanic practices, leading to various attempts to integrate traditional healing methods with modern psychological approaches.

Psychological Perspectives and Contemporary Applications

Modern psychological perspectives on shamanism have evolved significantly since Carl Jung's initial observations of parallels between shamanic practices and his concept of the collective unconscious (Jung, 1969). Contemporary researchers have identified potential therapeutic applications of shamanic techniques in treating various psychological conditions, including:

- Depression and anxiety disorders (Krippner, 2012)
- Post-traumatic stress disorder (PTSD) (Winkelman, 2003)
- Addiction recovery (Mabit et al., 1996)

Founders and Key figures in Shamanic tradition

Unlike many spiritual and healing traditions, shamanism does not have a single founder or point of origin. Instead, it emerged independently across various cultures and regions, developed by numerous indigenous societies throughout human history (Vitebsky, 1995). However, several key historical figures have been instrumental in documenting, preserving, and developing shamanic practices, both in traditional societies and in modern contexts.

Early Documentation and Academic Pioneers

Sergei Mikhailovich Shirokogoroff (1887-1939) - As one of the first anthropologists to conduct extensive research on shamanic practices, Shirokogoroff's work among the Tungus people of Siberia provided the foundational understanding of classical shamanism. His seminal work, "Psychomental Complex of the Tungus" (1935), established the first comprehensive academic framework for understanding shamanic practices and their social-psychological functions (Znamenski, 2007).

Mircea Eliade (1907-1986) - Eliade's groundbreaking work "Shamanism: Archaic Techniques of Ecstasy" (1964) represented the first major academic synthesis of shamanic practices worldwide. His research established shamanism as a legitimate field of study within religious studies and anthropology, identifying common elements across different cultural contexts (Morris, 2006).

Indigenous Knowledge Keepers

Black Elk (1863-1950)- Nicholas Black Elk, a Lakota holy man, played a crucial role in preserving and transmitting Native American shamanic traditions. Through his collaboration with John G. Neihardt, documented in "Black Elk Speaks" (1932), he provided detailed insights into traditional healing practices and spiritual ceremonies of the Lakota people (DeMallie, 1984).

Maria Sabina (1894-1985) - A Mazatec curandera from Mexico, Maria Sabina was instrumental in preserving traditional Mexican shamanic healing practices. Her work with sacred mushrooms and healing ceremonies brought international attention to indigenous healing practices, though she later expressed regret about sharing sacred knowledge with outsiders (Estrada, 1981).

Modern Integration and Development

Michael Harner (1929-2018) - Harner significantly influenced the modern understanding and practice of shamanism. After extensive fieldwork with various indigenous groups, he developed "core shamanism," a system designed to make shamanic practices accessible to Western practitioners while respecting indigenous traditions. His 1980 work "The Way of the Shaman" served as a textbook for contemporary shamanic practice (Harner, 1990).

Carlos Castaneda (1925-1998) - Though controversial, Castaneda's works, beginning with "The Teachings of Don Juan" (1968), brought shamanic concepts to mainstream attention. While the authenticity of his accounts has been questioned, his impact on popular understanding of shamanic practices is undeniable (De Mille, 1976).

Regional Traditions and Their Keepers

Siberian Tradition- Siberian shamanism, considered by many scholars to be the most "classical" form, was preserved through lineages of traditional healers. Notable figures include Ksenofont Khankharov, who documented Buryat shamanic practices in the early 20th century (Humphrey, 1996).

South American Traditions - Various indigenous leaders have been crucial in maintaining Amazonian shamanic traditions:

- Don José Campos, a Peruvian curandero known for preserving traditional Amazonian healing practices
- Don Miguel Chuspe, who worked to protect and transmit Shipibo-Conibo healing traditions (Luna, 1986)

Contemporary Contributors

Sandra Ingerman (1956-present) - Building on Harner's work, Ingerman has been influential in developing modern applications of shamanic healing, particularly through her work on soul retrieval techniques. Her contributions have helped bridge traditional shamanic practices with contemporary psychological healing methods (Ingerman, 1991).

Malidoma Patrice Somé (1956-2021) - A West African elder and scholar, Somé worked to translate traditional Dagara shamanic practices for Western audiences while maintaining their cultural integrity. His work provided valuable insights into African spiritual healing traditions (Somé, 1994).

Theoretical frameworks

Shamanism's theoretical foundation spans multiple disciplines, including anthropology, psychology, neuroscience, and religious studies. The theoretical understanding of shamanic practices has evolved significantly from early anthropological observations to contemporary neuroscientific investigations (Winkelman, 2010). This comprehensive analysis explores the various theoretical frameworks that have been used to understand and explain shamanic practices and their effects.

Anthropological Theoretical Framework

Structural-Functional Theory

Anthropologists initially approached shamanism through a structural-functional lens, examining how shamanic practices contributed to social cohesion and community wellbeing. Lévi-Strauss (1963) proposed that shamanic healing worked through a process of "symbolic efficacy," where cultural symbols and mythological narratives created meaningful frameworks for understanding and treating illness. This theoretical perspective suggests that shamanic healing operates through socially constructed meaning systems that mediate between individual experience and collective understanding (Turner, 1969).

Cultural-Ecological Theory

Researchers have examined shamanism within its ecological context, suggesting that shamanic practices evolved as adaptive responses to environmental challenges. Reichel-Dolmatoff's (1976) work demonstrated how shamanic knowledge often incorporated sophisticated understanding of local ecosystems, suggesting that shamanic practices served as mechanisms for environmental adaptation and resource management.

Psychological Theoretical Perspectives

Depth Psychology - Jung's analytical psychology provided one of the first psychological frameworks for understanding shamanic practices. Jung (1972) interpreted shamanic journeys as expressions of the collective unconscious, suggesting that shamanic symbols and experiences represented universal archetypal patterns. He viewed shamanic healing as a process of psychological integration and transformation (von Franz, 1975).

Transpersonal Psychology - Transpersonal theorists have developed frameworks for understanding shamanic states of consciousness and their therapeutic potential. Grof (1988) proposed that shamanic experiences accessed "holotropic" states of consciousness that could facilitate psychological healing and personal transformation. Walsh (1990) developed a comprehensive theoretical framework comparing shamanic states with other altered states of consciousness, suggesting specific mechanisms for their therapeutic effects.

Neuroscientific Theoretical Models

Neurobiological Framework - Modern neuroscience has provided new theoretical perspectives on shamanic practices. Winkelman (2000) proposed a "neuroecological" theory of shamanism, suggesting that shamanic practices evolved to utilize specific brain mechanisms and neural networks. This theory posits that shamanic techniques activate integrative brain functions, particularly the limbic system and temporal lobe structures.

Psychoneuroimmunology - Research in psychoneuroimmunology has provided theoretical frameworks for understanding the physical effects of shamanic healing. Koen (2018) suggests that shamanic practices influence the interaction between psychological processes and immune system function through mechanisms involving stress reduction and altered states of consciousness.

Consciousness Studies Theory

Altered States Theory - Studies of altered states of consciousness provide a significant theoretical framework for understanding shamanism. Krippner (2002) developed a theoretical model suggesting that shamanic techniques induce specific patterns of brain activity that facilitate healing and information processing. This theory proposes that shamanic states represent distinct modes of consciousness with specific functional properties.

Information Processing Theory - Theorists have proposed that shamanic states involve altered modes of information processing. Peters and Price-Williams (1980) suggested that shamanic consciousness represents a specific mode of processing that integrates multiple levels of perception and cognition.

Social-Cognitive Theory

Meaning-Making Framework - Recent theoretical approaches emphasise the role of meaning-making in shamanic healing. Dow (1986) proposed a "symbolic healing" theory, suggesting that shamanic practices work by manipulating universal symbolic processes within culturally specific frameworks. This theory emphasises how shamanic healing creates transformative experiences by manipulating symbolic meanings and social relationships.

Embodiment Theory - Contemporary theoretical frameworks emphasize the embodied nature of shamanic practices. Csordas (1993) developed a theoretical perspective suggesting that shamanic healing works through processes of somatic attention and bodily experience, creating transformative experiences through embodied practice.

Western Perspectives on Shamanism in Psychology

Historical Divide

In the Western scientific and psychological tradition, healing has been largely viewed through the lens of **materialism** and **empiricism**, emphasizing the physical and cognitive aspects of mental health. Practices like psychotherapy, cognitive-behavioural techniques, and medications have been dominant in the West. Shamanism, by contrast, operates within a framework that emphasizes the **spiritual** and **energetic** aspects of healing, which can conflict with Western science's focus on measurable, evidence-based methods.

Integration into Western Practices

Despite these differences, some Western psychologists, therapists, and holistic healers have integrated elements of shamanism into their work. For example, **transpersonal psychology** and **eco-psychology** are branches of psychology that are more open to spiritual and mystical experiences, and some practitioners in these fields incorporate shamanic techniques like visualization, drumming, or ritual into therapy. In this context, shamanism is viewed as a complementary tool rather than a standalone treatment.

New Age Influence

The resurgence of interest in shamanism in the West is often connected to the **New Age movement**, which blends various spiritual traditions, including Eastern and Indigenous healing practices. In this sense, shamanism has been adopted and adapted to fit into the alternative healing landscape in the West, but it is still rooted in non-Western traditions.

Modern Western Psychology's Approach to Shamanism:

Carl Jung and other depth psychologists

Explored shamanic-like processes, such as the use of symbols, myths, and archetypes in healing. Jung was particularly interested in the **spiritual journey** and the role of the unconscious, which has some conceptual overlap with shamanism.

Transpersonal psychology

Developed by figures like Abraham Maslow and Stanislav Grof, also incorporates spiritual aspects of healing and consciousness, aligning more with shamanic ideas than with traditional Western medical models.

The practice:

The practice of shamanism is done to assist a person through three passages, namely birth, marriage, and death.

While performing this ritual, a shaman wears a crown fashioned out of iron with horns on the top. These horns are believed to guide the spirits into the shaman's body. During the ritual, it is thought that an ordinary man should not look into the eyes of a shaman as it can harm them.

The shaman beats a drum which, when it starts to slow down, leads to the fall of the shaman on the floor. After this, the shaman starts spinning on the ground. This marks the entry of the spirit into the body of the shaman. It is said that when the spirit enters the shaman's body, their soul leaves to create space for the spirit to take over. This leads to several changes in the minds of the Shaman.

Some shamans say that these changes affect them spiritually, and hence to get out of this trance zone, they take the help of music. They practice throat singing which allows them to keep the evil spirits at bay which try to take over people.

Before the ritual, the birch tree is cut and kept near the shaman. After the end of the ceremony, the birch tree is prayed to with the hope that the spirits will accept the people's gifts.

As part of their offerings to the spirits, they give them the so-called white food like bread, cheese, etc. Milk and vodka are also considered peace offerings to spirits.

The blue scarfs tried near the holy place are believed to carry the wishes and prayers to the sky.

The belief behind the practice:

Shaman's worship Ober which is a sanctuary for spirits. They are regarded as their local masters.

In the past, it was also believed that shamans, by combing with spirits, had the power to control the weather, travel long distances, or levitate by hovering over the birch trees.

The place where the bonfire is lit, the holy place, is cleaned before every ritual, and then rice and beans are spread out to show forgiveness for causing inconvenience to the earth and local spirits.

The holy place is guarded by the pine truck carved image of the tiger's ruler. Its work is to keep the Glade safe from any intruders.

Spirits harm the people by causing illness and hence need to be appeased. The Shamans of Siberia believe in the sacrifice of renderers to offer as peace offerings. This illness is also thought to be caused by losing a soul. This means what it says. The soul is said to leave the body and go to the spirits who play with it by torturing it. Lastly, the entering of spirits into a person's body can also cause illness, and hence it is on Shamans to shoo them away.

The lit bonfire also decides which illness will be cured in the ritual. This means that the number of branches or the level chooses what world is being contacted. For example, if there are some seven layers, then a lower world is contacted to relieve the souls of the sick. People ask for spirits to help them get rid of their ailments or wish them good luck for their journey by offering milk to them using a spoon.

Kinds of conditions treated

Shamanism is practiced making a person feel whole again by focusing on healing their souls or retrieving parts of their souls. It can also help in ailments like nagging back pain or infectious disease. They can also help with physical handicaps, mental disorders, family problems, etc.

A study done by Kho Nishimura in Tokyo showed how people in that area heavily relied on shamans to cure their mental illnesses. This dependency ranges from schizophrenia, atypical psychosis, depression, nervous conditions, alcoholism, epilepsy, and other organic mental disorders.

Success rate

The range of treating shamanism diseases, whether material or mental problems, gives shamans the title of being beta versions of modern healers. They do not discriminate between different illnesses or concerns. Using natural healers like trees and herbs gives shamanism added benefit. The ability to interact with spirits and neutralize their effects has been claimed to be effective by several anthropologists. Shamanism works because of its ability to play with the minds of people. It targets the already-built associations to give meaning to life. In other words, having a story to tell that seems huge makes one find meaning in their life and get out of their mental trance.

Case Studies

Case Study 1: Integrating Shamanism and Eye Movement Desensitization and Reprocessing (EMDR) to Treat Trauma-Induced Depression

Background: A 42-year-old woman, referred to as "Maria," was suffering from trauma-induced depression and anxiety after experiencing childhood abuse. For years, she had struggled with low self-esteem, persistent sadness, dissociation, and chronic anxiety. Traditional therapy methods provided minimal relief, leading her to seek alternative approaches.

Maria's treatment involved the integration of **Shamanic healing** and **Eye Movement Desensitization and Reprocessing (EMDR)**, a well-established psychological treatment for trauma. The shamanic elements were introduced to help her reconnect spiritually and heal at a deeper level, while EMDR helped her process and desensitize the traumatic memories.

Shamanic healing was introduced to Maria to help her deal with the spiritual and energetic aspects of her trauma. Shamanism, as practised by her healer, involved connecting to the spirit world to gain insight and retrieve lost aspects of Maria's spiritual self.

In conjunction with shamanic healing, Maria underwent EMDR sessions with a licensed trauma therapist. EMDR is a structured therapy that helps people process traumatic memories through bilateral stimulation (such as eye movements, tapping, or sounds).

The shamanic practitioner and the EMDR therapist worked together to ensure that both treatments complemented each other rather than conflicting. Maria's sessions were structured so that she alternated between the two modalities.

Key Integration Points:

- **Spiritual and emotional healing:** Shamanic healing focused on Maria's spiritual recovery, helping her integrate lost parts of herself, while EMDR helped her process the trauma cognitively and emotionally.
- **Balancing mind and body:** Shamanism allowed Maria to access altered states of consciousness in a safe environment, where she could symbolically address her trauma. EMDR, on the other hand, focused on grounding her in the present and reducing her hyperarousal and anxiety responses.
- **Restoring a sense of wholeness:** While EMDR helped desensitize the pain of past memories, shamanic practices helped Maria rebuild a sense of meaning and wholeness. The integration of these two approaches allowed Maria to not only process the traumatic content but to spiritually and emotionally reclaim her sense of self.

Over the course of nine months, Maria showed significant improvements in her emotional well-being. Her depressive symptoms lessened, and she experienced fewer bouts of dissociation and anxiety. She felt more connected to her inner self and reported a deep sense of emotional healing that traditional talk therapy had not achieved.

Maria mentioned that the combination of shamanic soul retrieval and EMDR helped her feel as if she had regained parts of herself that had been "frozen in time" since her abuse. She also noted that shamanic rituals gave her a renewed sense of purpose and connection to her spiritual life.

Case Study 2: Integrating Shamanism with Cognitive Behavioral Therapy (CBT) to Treat PTSD

Background: A 35-year-old man, referred to as "John," suffered from chronic Post-Traumatic Stress Disorder (PTSD) following a traumatic car accident. Despite traditional therapeutic interventions, including Cognitive Behavioral Therapy (CBT), John's symptoms persisted. He experienced flashbacks, hyperarousal, sleep disturbances, and emotional numbness.

To explore alternative approaches, John sought help from a shamanic practitioner alongside his ongoing sessions with a licensed psychologist. This case study highlights how shamanism and CBT were used in tandem to address his PTSD.

Shamanism was introduced to help John access non-ordinary states of consciousness. The shamanic practitioner used traditional methods like drumming and guided visualizations to facilitate John's connection with his inner self and help him confront the trauma on a spiritual and symbolic level.

Simultaneously, John continued regular CBT sessions with his psychologist. The therapist focused on helping John:

- Recognize and challenge distorted thinking patterns related to the trauma.
- Develop coping mechanisms for anxiety and stress management.
- Use exposure techniques to gradually reduce the emotional charge of his traumatic memories.

Treatment Integration: The psychologist and the shamanic practitioner collaborated, respecting each other's fields of expertise. The integration of shamanism with CBT allowed for a holistic approach that treated both the psychological and spiritual dimensions of John's trauma.

Key Integration Points:

- **Processing trauma holistically:** While CBT addressed John's cognitive distortions and maladaptive behavior patterns, shamanic practices facilitated emotional and spiritual healing that helped John reconnect with aspects of himself that had been "lost" or disowned.
- **Emotional regulation through ritual:** The symbolic and ritualistic nature of shamanic practices helped John express emotions that were difficult to verbalize in CBT. The rituals provided a sacred space where John could safely express grief and fear.
- **Empowerment and meaning-making:** Shamanism helped John construct a new narrative around his trauma, seeing it as a journey of personal growth and transformation rather than purely a source of suffering. The efforts of CBT were complemented by reframing the negative thought patterns.

Outcome: After six months of integrated treatment, John reported significant improvements. His PTSD symptoms decreased dramatically, with fewer flashbacks, reduced anxiety, and better sleep quality. He also experienced a sense of spiritual renewal, reporting that he felt "whole" and more connected to his inner self. His sense of empowerment increased, and he could cope better with triggers related to his trauma.

Case Study 3: Integrating Shamanism and Dialectical Behavior Therapy (DBT) for Borderline Personality Disorder (BPD)

Background: A 28-year-old woman, "Sarah," was diagnosed with Borderline Personality Disorder (BPD), a complex mental health condition characterized by emotional instability, intense interpersonal relationships, impulsivity, and chronic feelings of emptiness. Despite undergoing Dialectical Behavior Therapy (DBT) for several months, Sarah struggled to connect with the therapy at a deeper emotional level and reported persistent feelings of disconnection and spiritual emptiness.

After expressing a desire to explore her spirituality as part of her healing, Sarah's therapist recommended combining **shamanic practices** with her ongoing DBT treatment. This integration aimed to address Sarah's spiritual and emotional needs while continuing to work on her DBT skills.

Sarah's core treatment for BPD was DBT, a structured therapeutic approach that emphasizes emotional regulation, distress tolerance, interpersonal effectiveness, and mindfulness.

To address Sarah's underlying feelings of emptiness and disconnection, a shamanic practitioner was introduced to her treatment plan. Shamanic healing sessions were scheduled between her DBT sessions, where she participated in various spiritual and symbolic practices

Treatment Integration: The combination of DBT and shamanism required careful coordination. The DBT therapist and shamanic practitioner maintained open communication and respect for each other's expertise to ensure the integration was seamless and effective.

Key integration strategies included:

- **Reinforcing mindfulness with shamanic journeying:** The shamanic practices complemented DBT's mindfulness by giving Sarah an alternative way to explore her internal landscape, making mindfulness more meaningful and personal for her.
- **Addressing "soul loss" with distress tolerance:** The soul retrieval work helped Sarah experience a sense of "wholeness," which reduced feelings of emptiness, while DBT's distress tolerance skills allowed her to manage the emotional processing that emerged during these shamanic sessions.
- **Combining grounding rituals with emotional regulation:** The nature-based rituals helped reinforce DBT's emotional regulation by giving Sarah practical ways to center herself and cope with overwhelming feelings in a symbolic, meaningful way.

Outcome: Over six months, Sarah showed significant progress in managing her BPD symptoms. There was a marked reduction in her chronic feelings of emptiness and social disconnection. She reported a deeper connection to herself, greater control over her impulsive behaviors, and an increased sense of purpose. Her relationships improved, and she developed a healthier approach to her emotions.

Sarah's spiritual growth through shamanism also deepened her commitment to DBT, as she felt more connected to her healing process. Her emotional episodes became less frequent and intense, and she was able to use her DBT skills more effectively, having found a sense of wholeness and personal meaning through the shamanic practices.

References

Amann, T. (2017). Integrating traditional healing practices with contemporary psychotherapy. *Journal of Psychotherapy Integration, 27*(1), 14–22.

Clottes, J., & Lewis-Williams, D. (1998). *The shamans of prehistory: Trance and magic in the painted caves.* Harry N. Abrams.

Csordas, T. J. (1993). Somatic modes of attention. *Cultural Anthropology, 8*(2), 135–156.

De Mille, R. (1976). *Castaneda's journey: The power and the allegory*. Capra Press.

DeMallie, R. J. (1984). *The sixth grandfather: Black Elk's teachings given to John G. Neihardt.* University of Nebraska Press.

Dow, J. (1986). Universal aspects of symbolic healing: A theoretical synthesis. *American Anthropologist, 88*(1), 56–69.

Eliade, M. (1964). *Shamanism: Archaic techniques of ecstasy*. Princeton University Press.

Estrada, A. (1981). *Maria Sabina: Her life and chants*. Ross-Erikson Publishers.

Ginzburg, C. (1991). *Ecstasies: Deciphering the witches' sabbath*. University of Chicago Press.

Grof, S. (1988). *The adventure of self-discovery*. SUNY Press.

Harner, M. (1990). *The way of the shaman*. HarperOne.

Harris, D. A., Crawford, J., Reigle, R., Haeny, A., & Franta, K. (2018). Creative arts therapy and traditional healing for complex trauma. *The Arts in Psychotherapy, 58*, 27–35.

Humphrey, C. (1996). *Shamans and elders: Experience, knowledge, and power among the Daur Mongols*. Oxford University Press.

Ingerman, S. (1991). *Soul retrieval: Mending the fragmented self*. HarperOne.

Jung, C. G. (1969). *The archetypes and the collective unconscious*. Princeton University Press.

Jung, C. G. (1972). *Psychology and religion: West and east*. Princeton University Press.

Kirmayer, L. J., Lemelson, R., & Cummings, C. A. (Eds.). (2015). *Re-visioning psychiatry: Cultural phenomenology, critical neuroscience, and global mental health*. Cambridge University Press.

Koen, B. D. (2018). *Beyond the roof of the world: Music, prayer, and healing in the Pamir Mountains*. Oxford University Press.

Krippner, S. (2000). The epistemology and technologies of shamanic states of consciousness. *Journal of Consciousness Studies, 7*(11–12), 93–118.

Krippner, S. (2002). Conflicting perspectives on shamans and shamanism: Points and counterpoints. *American Psychologist, 57*(11), 962–977.

Lévi-Strauss, C. (1963). *Structural anthropology*. Basic Books.

Luna, L. E. (1986). *Vegetalismo: Shamanism among the mestizo population of the Peruvian Amazon*. Stockholm Studies in Comparative Religion.

Morris, B. (2006). *Religion and anthropology: A critical introduction*. Cambridge University Press.

Peters, L. G., & Price-Williams, D. (1980). Towards an experiential analysis of shamanism. *American Ethnologist, 7*(3), 397–418.

Reichel-Dolmatoff, G. (1976). Cosmology as ecological analysis: A view from the rain forest. *Man, 11*(3), 307–318.

Shirokogoroff, S. M. (1935). *Psychomental complex of the Tungus*. Kegan Paul, Trench, Trubner & Co.

Somé, M. P. (1994). *Of water and the spirit: Ritual, magic, and initiation in the life of an African shaman*. Penguin Books.

Turner, R. P., & Turner, T. L. (2019). Traditional healing and modern psychotherapy: An integrative approach to treatment. *International Journal of Psychology and Counselling, 11*(3), 45–58.

Turner, V. (1969). *The ritual process: Structure and anti-structure*. Aldine Publishing.

Vitebsky, P. (1995). *The shaman: Voyages of the soul trance, ecstasy and healing from Siberia to the Amazon.* Duncan Baird Publishers.

von Franz, M. L. (1975). *C. G. Jung: His myth in our time.* Putnam.

Walsh, R. (1990). *The spirit of shamanism.* Jeremy P. Tarcher.

Winkelman, M. (2000). *Shamanism: The neural ecology of consciousness and healing.* Bergin & Garvey.

Winkelman, M. (2010). *Shamanism: A biopsychosocial paradigm of consciousness and healing* (2nd ed.). Praeger.

Znamenski, A. A. (2007). *The beauty of the primitive: Shamanism and Western imagination.* Oxford University Press.

Chapter 41

Talking Circles

Shahma Kunhi Mohamed School of Liberal Studies (SLS), CMR University, Bangalore

Introduction

Talking Circles are a meaningful and inclusive way to bring people together, encouraging open and respectful communication. This method, inspired by Indigenous traditions, is about more than just talking—it's about listening deeply and connecting with others on a human level. In a Talking Circle, participants sit together, often in a circular arrangement to symbolize equality and unity. Each person has a chance to speak, guided using a "talking piece"—an object that is passed around to indicate whose turn it is to share. This practice ensures that everyone can express themselves while others listen attentively without interruption (Pranis, 2005).

Unlike many modern conversations, which can feel rushed or competitive, Talking Circles create a space where people feel safe to share their thoughts and experiences. It's not just about what is being said but how it is said, with an emphasis on honesty, empathy, and mutual respect. Historically, this approach was integral to Indigenous communities, where it was used for decision-making, conflict resolution, storytelling, and building relationships. Today, its value extends far beyond these roots, as Talking Circles are used in schools, therapy, workplaces, and community gatherings to foster understanding and connection.

The power of Talking Circles lies in their simplicity and humanity. They remind us of the importance of slowing down, listening to others, and reflecting before responding. In a world where conversations often feel like debates, Talking Circles offer a refreshing alternative—a chance to communicate in a way that brings people closer and builds trust.

Benefits

1. Encourages Active Listening

One of the most important aspects of Talking Circles is the emphasis on listening. In these circles, participants are encouraged to listen without interruption, fostering an environment where each individual's words are given full attention. This form of active listening promotes empathy and deeper understanding, helping participants engage meaningfully with each other's perspectives (Pranis, 2005).

2. Ensures Equal Participation

Talking Circles are designed to give everyone an equal opportunity to speak. The circular structure symbolizes equality, ensuring no one person dominates the conversation. This balanced approach is particularly important in diverse groups where some individuals might otherwise feel their voices are overlooked or undervalued (Blackstock, 2009).

3. Fosters a Sense of Belonging

By encouraging everyone to share their thoughts and experiences, Talking Circles help create a sense of community and interconnectedness. This environment of mutual respect and inclusion can build stronger relationships, promote trust, and foster a greater sense of belonging among participants (Ross, 2006).

4. Supports Conflict Resolution

In conflict resolution, Talking Circles are especially effective because they provide a safe space for individuals to express their concerns without fear of being interrupted or judged. The structure of the circle promotes calm, reflective dialogue, making it easier to understand differing viewpoints and work toward a resolution in a non-confrontational way (Pranis, 2005).

5. Encourages Emotional Healing

Talking Circles are often used in therapeutic contexts, offering a space where individuals can share their emotions and experiences in a supportive environment. This practice allows for emotional release and personal healing, helping participants process difficult feelings and gain perspective on their challenges (Blackstock, 2009).

6. Builds Empathy and Understanding

One of the most powerful aspects of Talking Circles is their ability to build empathy. As participants listen to each other's stories, they gain insight into different life experiences and perspectives. This often leads to greater compassion and a deeper appreciation for the challenges others face (Ross, 2006).

7. Facilitates Collaborative Decision-Making

In group settings, Talking Circles can be a valuable tool for decision-making. The inclusive nature of the circle ensures that all voices are heard, allowing for decisions that reflect the diverse perspectives of the group. This collaborative approach helps create more thoughtful, balanced, and widely supported outcomes (Pranis, 2005).

History

Talking Circles have been an essential practice in many Indigenous cultures, providing a meaningful way for communities to communicate, share wisdom, and resolve conflicts. These circles were historically used for decision-making, storytelling, and conflict resolution, with the structure emphasizing unity and equality. The circle itself was seen as a symbol of interconnectedness, where all voices were considered equal, and no one person held more importance than another (Ross, 2006).

Indigenous peoples used Talking Circles to foster a sense of belonging and to nurture a deep respect for each individual's perspective. The practice encouraged thoughtful, reflective communication, where participants were given space to listen and speak in turn, promoting understanding and empathy. This approach helped strengthen bonds within the community and ensured that decisions were made with collective input and mutual respect (Pranis, 2005).

Despite the disruptive impacts of colonization, which sought to diminish Indigenous traditions, Talking Circles have persisted. Indigenous communities maintained and protected these practices, passing them down through generations. In more recent years, Talking Circles have been embraced in various modern contexts such as education, restorative justice, and community-building, where they continue to promote healing, understanding, and collaboration (Blackstock, 2009).

While the practice originates from specific cultural traditions, the values that underpin Talking Circles—such as equality, respect, and connectedness—are universally relevant. They offer valuable lessons in how to communicate more thoughtfully and inclusively, creating spaces where everyone is heard and valued.

Theoretical Background

Talking Circles are deeply rooted in Indigenous knowledge systems and carry rich cultural significance. These circles are more than just a way to communicate—they represent an approach to life that emphasizes connection, respect, and shared understanding. The theoretical foundations of Talking Circles reflect these values, focusing on equality, healing, and community.

A central idea behind Talking Circles is relationality, which stresses the importance of relationships and interconnectedness in all aspects of life (Ross, 2006). In a Talking Circle, the focus is on building and maintaining strong, respectful relationships within the community. The circle itself is a powerful symbol of equality and unity, where no one person's voice is considered more important than another's. This setup creates a space where everyone has the chance to speak and be heard, fostering a sense of belonging and collective ownership in the conversation.

Another key theory behind Talking Circles comes from restorative justice, which centers on healing, reconciliation, and the restoration of relationships rather than punishment (Pranis, 2005). Talking Circles, particularly in restorative justice contexts, provide a safe space for individuals to discuss harm, express feelings, and work through conflicts. The goal is not to assign blame, but to understand the impact of actions, rebuild trust, and promote mutual healing. This process helps individuals grow emotionally and socially, moving past their differences with empathy and understanding.

Talking Circles also align with constructivist learning theories, which emphasize how people learn and create meaning together (Blackstock, 2009). In a Talking Circle, each person brings their own perspective, contributing to a collective understanding that's shaped by the group. The process is collaborative—each participant not only listens but actively shapes the conversation. This collaborative approach encourages empathy, critical thinking, and deeper connection, as people are able to share their thoughts and hear others' experiences in a supportive setting.

Finally, the symbolic meaning of the circle plays a significant role in the effectiveness of Talking Circles. Symbolic interactionism suggests that objects and structures have meaning that influences how we behave and interact (Pranis, 2005). The circle, in this case, is more than just a seating arrangement—it's a symbol of balance, unity, and wholeness. It encourages openness and equality, reminding participants that every voice matters, and that the space is shared by all.

Ultimately, the theoretical background of Talking Circles draws from a blend of relational, restorative, and constructivist ideas, creating a framework that encourages healing, learning, and community-building. This holistic approach makes Talking Circles an invaluable tool for fostering understanding and positive change, whether in conflict resolution, education, or group communication.

Applications

Restorative Justice

In restorative justice, Talking Circles help individuals affected by harm—whether victims, offenders, or community members—come together to discuss their feelings and experiences. Rather than focusing on punishment, the goal is to understand the impact of the harm, promote accountability, and work toward healing. This method fosters empathy and provides a way for people to restore relationships and move forward in a positive direction (Pranis, 2005).

Therapy and Support Groups

Talking Circles are often used in therapy to help people feel heard and supported. In group settings, participants take turns speaking about their challenges, emotions, and experiences. This method helps people feel more connected and less isolated. It's particularly effective in substance abuse recovery, trauma counseling, and mental health support, where sharing personal stories in a safe and supportive environment can aid in emotional healing and growth (Blackstock, 2009).

Education and Schools

In classrooms, Talking Circles are a way to promote open dialogue, build trust, and address conflicts. Teachers use them to foster a sense of community and ensure that every student's voice is heard. Circles encourage students to talk about their experiences, solve problems together, and develop important skills like empathy and active listening (Ross, 2006). They are also effective in addressing bullying and helping students work through challenging topics in a supportive environment.

Workplace Communication

Talking Circles are increasingly used in workplaces to improve communication and resolve conflicts. In a circle, all employees, regardless of rank or position, have an equal opportunity to speak. This approach builds trust, transparency, and stronger teamwork. It encourages employees to share their thoughts and ideas, which can lead to more creative solutions and better collaboration (Pranis, 2005).

Community Building

Talking Circles are valuable tools for building stronger communities. In neighborhoods, organizations, and social groups, they provide a space for people to talk about issues they care about, resolve conflicts, and find common ground. The circle format helps everyone feel equally involved and promotes cooperation. It creates an opportunity for people to listen to one another and work together toward solutions, strengthening community bonds (Ross, 2006).

Steps or Processes in Talking Circles

Setting up the Circle

The process starts with arranging the space. Participants sit in a circle to symbolize equality—there's no "head of the table" or hierarchy here. The circle itself represents unity and shared purpose, making everyone feel they are on equal footing. Creating a welcoming and calm environment is key, as it helps participants feel comfortable and ready to share (Pranis, 2005).

Starting with Intention

The facilitator, or "circle keeper," opens the session by explaining the purpose of the circle. This could be to resolve a conflict, share personal experiences, or simply build understanding within a group. They might start with a moment of silence, a reflection, or even a meaningful story to set a positive and focused tone. This opening helps everyone feel grounded and connected to the process (Ross, 2006).

Agreeing on Guidelines

Before the discussion begins, the group agrees on some basic ground rules. These might include listening without interrupting, speaking honestly, and respecting confidentiality. The guidelines are simple but crucial, as they create an environment where everyone feels safe and respected. When people know they won't be judged or interrupted, it's much easier to open up (Pranis, 2005).

Sharing in the Circle

Once the circle starts, each person has the chance to speak in turn. Participants can share their thoughts, feelings, or experiences, while others listen quietly and respectfully. There's no pressure to speak if someone isn't ready, but having the opportunity to share in a non-judgmental space can be incredibly powerful. This process encourages deep listening and understanding, helping participants connect on a meaningful level (Ross, 2006).

Reflecting Together

After everyone has spoken, there's usually a chance for reflection. Participants might respond to what they've heard, share additional thoughts, or express how the discussion impacted them. The focus remains on respectful dialogue, with the goal of building understanding rather than debating or convincing others (Blackstock, 2009).

Closing the Circle

The session ends with a closing activity or ritual. This could be a final round where participants share something they're grateful for or a reflection on what they've learned. The facilitator might also lead a moment of silence or offer closing remarks to bring the circle to a peaceful conclusion. This step helps participants leave the circle feeling connected, valued, and supported (Pranis, 2005).

Through these steps, Talking Circles create a space where every voice matters, and people can build trust and understanding. The process is flexible and can be adapted to fit the needs of any group, making it a powerful tool for communication, healing, and community building.

Case Studies

Case Study 1 - Addressing Substance Use and Mental Health in Canadian Communities

In Saskatchewan, Canada, a community-based initiative incorporated Talking Circles into primary care settings as a method of supporting individuals dealing with substance use and mental health challenges. The program aimed to provide a culturally appropriate, supportive environment for individuals who might otherwise feel disconnected from more traditional healthcare approaches.

Methodology: Over a span of three years, 1,211 participants joined the program, with 415 completing follow-up assessments. The Talking Circles provided structured sessions where participants could share experiences and listen to others in a respectful, non-judgmental environment.

Results: Participants reported significant improvements in their perceived mental health and overall quality of life. The program demonstrated the effectiveness of culturally grounded approaches in addressing mental health challenges in Indigenous and non-Indigenous populations.

Case Study 2 - Restorative Justice in Schools

A U.S. middle school adopted Talking Circles as a restorative justice tool to address bullying and promote empathy and accountability among students.

Methodology: Facilitated by trained educators, students involved in conflicts participated in circles, taking turns to express their emotions and perspectives. This approach emphasized accountability and understanding, rather than punitive measures.

Results: The use of Talking Circles reduced repeated incidents of bullying and fostered a stronger sense of community within the school. Students reported feeling more connected and empathetic toward their peers.

Case Study 3 - Support for Grieving Families in Australia

In an Indigenous Australian community, Talking Circles were implemented to support families dealing with grief and loss. The initiative sought to combine traditional healing practices with modern therapeutic approaches.

Methodology: Circles were facilitated by community elders and therapists, allowing participants to share stories of loss in a culturally safe space. Emphasis was placed on collective storytelling and mutual support.

Results: Families reported reduced feelings of isolation and increased emotional connection within their community. The culturally integrated approach highlighted the value of combining traditional practices with therapeutic interventions.

Conclusion

Talking Circles remind us of the strength found in coming together as equals to share and listen with care. Their power lies in creating a space where everyone feels seen and heard, free from judgment or interruption. Rooted in Indigenous traditions, these circles offer much more than a method of communication—they provide a way to connect deeply with others and ourselves.

Across various settings—whether in schools, workplaces, or communities—Talking Circles have proven their value. They help build trust, foster empathy, and resolve conflicts in a way that is both respectful and transformative. The simplicity of the process, combined with its ability to address complex human emotions and relationships, makes it a timeless tool for healing and growth.

In a world that often feels rushed and disconnected, Talking Circles offer an antidote. They encourage us to slow down, listen with intention, and appreciate the shared humanity in those around us. More than anything, they remind us that meaningful change begins with a willingness to hear and be heard.

References

Blackstock, C. (2009). *The occasional evil of angels: Learning from the experiences of Aboriginal peoples and social work. First Peoples Child & Family Review*, 4(1), 28–37.

Happiest Health. (2024). Talking circles: The power of hearing out. Retrieved from https://www.happiesthealth.com

Pranis, K. (2005). *The little book of circle processes: A new/old approach to peacemaking*. Good Books.

Pranis, K., Stuart, B., & Wedge, M. (2015). Peacemaking circles: From conflict to community. Living Justice Press.

Ross, R. (2006). *Returning to the teachings: Exploring Aboriginal justice*. Penguin Canada.

The Permanente Journal. (2014). Implementation of culturally responsive care: Addressing substance use and mental health in Saskatchewan. *The Permanente Journal, 18*(4), 60-68.

Zion, S., & Kozleski, E. B. (2005). Understanding culture through the process of storytelling. *Urban Education*, 40(4), 364–384. https://doi.org/10.1177/0042085905278177

Chapter 42

The Western Perspective on Sufi Healing and Ruqyah: Understanding Traditional Islamic Therapy through a Modern Lens

Shashirekha P School of Liberal Studies (SLS), CMR University, Bangalore

Introduction to Sufism

Sufism, or Islamic mysticism, underscores the experiential, inner features of Islam instead of the outer, legalistic ones. It is a spiritual discipline that takes one to the knowledge of divine love and brings the human soul near to God (Chittick, 2007). "Sufi" comes from the Arabic word "suf," wool, since early Sufis wore simple woolen clothes that symbolized their life of austerity and detachment from worldly lust (Schimmel, 2011). The central purpose of Sufism is the attainment of direct, personal communion with the Divine, often via the forms of meditation known as muraqaba, chanting known as dhikr, and poems that vent the rapturous pleasure of love for God, such as those written by Rumi and Hafiz (Helminski,1999).

Traditionally, Sufi healing is not just the cure for the body but ensures that health at both emotions and spirit are essentially connected together.

Cultural Background of Sufism

Although belonging deep in the traditions of Islam, Sufism has found ways to transcend cultural and geographical boundaries. It originated in the Middle East and was spread from Persia through North Africa, Turkey, and the Indian subcontinent. Over time, this merged with indigenous customs to become a beautiful tapestry of various Sufi practices (Nasr, 2007). Indeed, every region features its own specificities: Persian Sufis are characterized with passionate poetry, Turkish Sufis with whirling meditation practices, and Indian Sufis with their syncretic approach to spirituality (Ernst 2003).

Despite its Islamic foundations, Sufism has been embraced by spiritual seekers worldwide, particularly in Western countries, where its messages of divine love and unity resonate across various religious backgrounds (Schimmel, 2011). Movements such as the Whirling Dervishes of Turkey or the widespread popularity of Rumi's poetry are examples of how Sufism has permeated Western spiritual consciousness (Chittick, 1989).

Sufi healing practices, though deeply anchored in the Islamic tradition, have also found resonance in global movements focusing on holistic healing. The Sufi approach to wellness—prioritizing the alignment of the soul, heart, and body with the Divine—finds parallels in various Western alternative healing practices, such as energy healing and mindfulness (Ernst, 1997).

The term "Sufi" is derived from the Arabic word "suf", meaning wool, and it refers to the woolen garments worn by early Sufi mystics. These simple woolen robes represented the Sufis' ascetic lifestyle and their rejection of material wealth and worldly pleasures. According to Annemarie Schimmel (2011), Sufis viewed material attachments as distractions that pulled them away from the spiritual path. Their focus was on the inner life—attaining purity of heart and spirit through humility, simplicity, and devotion to God.

Definition of Sufi Healing (Ruqyah)

One basic approach of Sufi healing is called Ruqyah, a form of mystical cure in which one would employ verses from the Quran and invocations with prayer with an intention to cleanse persons of negative energies, emotions and even physical diseases. Basic is in that belief that spiritual energy can be either good or bad, and such powers could attract one to anything concerning illness (Rahman, 2009). Negative energies "within", through personal vices or emotional trauma and "without", through evil spiritual forces associated with evil eye or black magic-feel to have pushed blocks in such places. Many of them manifest as emotional uprootedness or physical illness (Haleem, 2010). Ruqyah is based highly on the prophetic traditions of Islam. The Prophet Muhammad (PBUH) both acted and promoted Ruqyah as healing, something which has been mentioned in various Hadiths concerning the sayings and actions of the Prophet. The most frequently quoted quotes have to do with the occasions when he used to read Surah Al-Fatiha, which is one of the chapters of the Quran, for the healing of an ill person (Haleem, 2010). The present practice of Ruqyah involves recitation of words of verses over water or oil, whereby they can be taken inside or applied on the body or may be spoken directly to one who needs it (Rahman, 2009). However, in reality, Ruqyah cannot be reduced merely to that of repeating words of a book-it is as much an affair of the intention and the belief of one seeking God's mercy and intervention.

History of Sufi Healing

The roots of Sufi healing date back to the foundational years of Islam, which saw early ascetic practitioners known as zuhhad focus on spiritual purification and the development of the soul (Schimmel, 1998). They tried to lead profoundly ascetic lives without letting worldly distractions capture their attention, thus focusing their attention on God alone. Healing, therefore, was not only with respect to the body but about making the heart pure by eliminating jealousies, anger, and more evil from it (Nasr, 2007).

The Prophet Muhammad (PBUH) himself underlined the need for spiritual balance and emotional equilibrium in actual physical health. His teachings, known as Hadith, frequently record spiritual remedies for physical sufferings, such as saying specific verses from the Book of Qur'an or kinds of prayers for healing (Chittick, 1989). The Prophet also believed that some foods, honey, and black seed, for instance, have healing properties with both physical and spiritual medicine (Rahman, 2009).

As Sufism grew into being standardized into orders like Qadiriyya, Naqshbandiyya, Mevlevi, etc., the healing practices were formalized so that they would be closer to God. All the Sufi orders would inherently hold the principles of Ruqyah, Dhikr, and meditation that inspired thousands of generations of healers to follow their way (Ernst, 1997).

Theoretical Background: The Philosophy Behind Sufi Healing

The theoretical underpinning of Sufi healing lies in the concept that any type of malady, whether it is intellectual, spiritual, or corporal, is formed from a conflict continued within the self-spirit of a person. Sufism teaches that human pain, either psychological or physical, finds its origin when the soul becomes disordered from harmony with the Divine order (Chittick, 2007). It is based upon many core Sufi principles:

1. Tawhid (Oneness of God)

Tawhid, the doctrine in Islamic theology and Sufi mysticism that holds meaning to oneness with God, is the center of every teaching of Islam. Sufis believe that the universe reveals God's unity through all souls that exist, but amid the concealing distractions and worldly desires and attachments of life, the person is separated from God (Schimmel, 2011). So, healing becomes a journey unto the original unity-the throwing off of the veils of ego and worldly concerns to return to balance and harmony.

Such healing, however goes further than the general removal of symptoms of illness peculiar to the person. Such healing should lead one back into a state of Tawhidan harmonious integrity with God's will (Nasr, 2007). Here, the Sufi healer becomes a channel through which divine grace could find its way to the person and bridge them back to the source of life and healing.

2. Nafs (The Ego/Self)

In Sufism philosophy, the nafs, which can be translated as ego or self, forms a great obstacle to the progress of the spiritual life. It is almost consubstantial with the lowest, animalistic impulses found in human psychology and draws man toward materialism, selfishness, and hedonism, away from God (Helminski, 1999). It is for many, therefore, of the healing practices applied by Sufism used to subdue and purify the nafs so that the soul may rise to higher plains of spirituality. Healing in Sufism primarily begins with nafs analysis, the considered root of most psychic and spiritual torments, including anxiety, anger, and depression. Through strict spiritual purification of nafs using processes like Ruqyah, meditation, and Dhikr, one becomes capable of overcoming psychic turmoil and achieving inner balance (Chittick, 1989).

3. Dhikr (Remembrance of God)

One of the most invaluable concepts within Sufi healing is Dhikr —the continuous remembrance of God. However, Dhikr is more than simply repeating the names of God and verses from the Qur'an; rather, it encompasses a practice which purifies the heart, dissolves the ego, and guides one toward a state of divine presence (Helminski, 1999).

4. Barakah (Spiritual Blessing)

Another main principle in Sufi healing is Barakah, or divine blessing, which is believed to emanate from God through select persons, prayers, or sacred objects. Sufi healers often ask the invoked blessings of Barakah for healing, believing that the blessings of God are powerful enough to enhance the effectiveness of the treatment (Schimmel, 2011).

Barakah is also not only a source of healing but also something of an armour that prevents damage. More and more Sufi healers believe that there are prayers, verses, or objects filled with a certain kind of Barakah, which can protect their clients from dangerous spiritual forces, evil eye, or black magic (Ernst, 1997).

5. Love as Restorative Energy

In Sufi thought, love is found at the very center of spiritual growth and healing. The Sufi journey is often described as an affair full of love, moving initiates toward the discovery of divine love a power to change and heal the soul (Helminski, 1999). Sufi greats such as Rumi and Hafiz beautifully take love as potent liquor which heals the wounds of the soul and ultimately includes union with God (Schimmel, 2011). What Sufi healers also emphasize in their healing work is to evoke love and sympathy. The heart full of divine love is stronger against the opposing negative energies, emotional turmoil, and illness, they postulate (Chittick, 1989).

Applications and Therapeutic Techniques of Sufi Healing

Sufi healing is an intricate system that applies spiritual practices to address a wide range of emotional, physical, and spiritual ailments. Ruqyah is one such technique, but it is part of a broader set of therapeutic tools designed to restore balance to the individual. These practices are grounded in the belief that emotional ailments like grief, anxiety, and depression are deeply connected to the state of one's soul.

1. Ruqyah (Qur'anic Recitation)

The central therapeutic technique in Sufi healing is Ruqyah, which involves the recitation of specific Qur'anic verses, prayers, and invocations over the person seeking healing. These recitations are believed to bring divine intervention and protection, removing spiritual impurities and restoring harmony (Haleem, 2010).

Ruqyah may be used to address a wide range of issues, including:

- Spiritual Afflictions: Individuals suffering from spiritual attacks, such as sihr (black magic), jinn possession, or the evil eye, are often treated with Ruqyah. The recitation of the Qur'an is believed to cleanse the person of these negative influences.
- Emotional Distress: Ruqyah is also employed to heal emotional ailments such as anxiety, depression, and grief, which are seen as manifestations of spiritual imbalances (Rahman, 2009).
- Physical Ailments: Although it is primarily a spiritual tool, Ruqyah has been used to treat physical illnesses, especially those thought to have a spiritual component (Haleem, 2010). For

example, chronic headaches, unexplained pain, or insomnia may be addressed through the recitation of Qur'anic verses.

2. Dhikr (Chanting and Recitation)

In addition to Ruqyah, Sufi healers frequently recommend Dhikr as a therapeutic practice. Dhikr involves the repetition of divine names, prayers, or Qur'anic verses in a meditative state (Helminski, 1999). The continuous remembrance of God purifies the heart and mind, helping the individual transcend emotional suffering and spiritual blockages.

There are various forms of Dhikr, including:

- Silent Dhikr: The repetition of sacred phrases internally, without vocalization. This form of Dhikr is often practiced in a meditative state, fostering deep introspection and spiritual renewal (Chittick, 1989).
- Loud Dhikr: Chanting or singing sacred phrases aloud, often in a group setting. This form of Dhikr is commonly practiced by Sufi orders during communal gatherings and is considered a powerful way to invoke divine presence and healing (Helminski, 1999).

3. Meditation (Muraqaba)

Meditation, or Muraqaba, is another key practice in Sufi healing. Muraqaba involves sitting in quiet contemplation, often focusing on the heart or on a specific attribute of God (Chittick, 2007). The goal of Muraqaba is to achieve a state of inner stillness and receptivity to divine guidance.

In the context of healing, Muraqaba helps individuals connect with their innermost selves and release emotional trauma or spiritual confusion. By meditating on God's presence, the individual can dissolve the barriers between the self and the Divine, leading to profound healing (Helminski, 1999).

4. Use of Sacred Objects and Water

In some healing practices, sacred objects such as prayer beads (tasbih) or blessed water (zamzam) are used in conjunction with Qur'anic recitations. For instance, a healer may blow upon water after reciting Qur'anic verses, which the patient then drinks to absorb the spiritual energy (Schimmel, 1998). Similarly, olive oil infused with prayers may be applied to the body as part of the healing process (Rahman, 2009).

Steps or Process of Sufi Healing (Ruqyah)

The process of Ruqyah is both systematic and deeply spiritual. It involves several key steps that a healer must follow to ensure the effectiveness of the treatment. The healer must maintain a clear and pure intention to serve as a conduit for divine intervention.

1. Setting the Intention (Niyyah)

The first step in the healing process is to set the intention (niyyah). Both the healer and the individual seeking healing must approach the session with a pure intention, asking for God's intervention, protection, and healing. In Sufi healing, the power of intention is central, as it aligns the individual's will with divine will (Chittick, 1989).

The healer often begins by making a silent prayer or invocation, seeking God's assistance in facilitating the healing process. They may also instruct the patient to do the same, fostering a state of receptivity and surrender to divine grace (Rahman, 2009).

2. Purification (Taharah)

Before beginning Ruqyah, both the healer and the person receiving the treatment must be in a state of physical and spiritual purity. This includes performing ritual ablution (wudu) or even a full-body purification (ghusl) to cleanse the body and soul (Nasr, 2007). Purification is important because it prepares the individual to receive divine blessings without interference from spiritual impurities.

3. Recitation of Qur'anic Verses

The core of the Ruqyah process involves the recitation of specific Qur'anic verses and prayers. Some of the most commonly used verses include:

- Surah Al-Fatiha: Known as the "Opening" of the Qur'an, this chapter is recited for healing and protection.
- Ayat-ul-Kursi (2:255): This verse, known as the "Throne Verse," is recited for protection from spiritual harm.
- Surah Al-Ikhlas (112): This chapter emphasizes the oneness of God and is often recited for spiritual purification and healing (Haleem, 2010).

The healer may recite these verses directly over the patient or over water or oil, which can then be applied to the body or consumed by the individual. The healer may also blow gently over the affected area following the recitation (Rahman, 2009).

4. Invocation of Prayers (Dua)

In addition to Qur'anic verses, specific supplications (dua) are made to invoke God's healing power. The healer may place their hands on the affected area while reciting the prayers, asking for God's mercy in removing the affliction (Schimmel, 2011).

Healers often stress the importance of sincerity and presence during the prayer. It is not just the words of the prayer that matter, but the heartfelt intention behind them (Chittick, 1989).

5. Use of Dhikr (Remembrance of God)

Following the recitation of Qur'anic verses and prayers, the healer may engage in Dhikr. The repetitive invocation of God's names or attributes helps realign the individual's spiritual state with the Divine. Dhikr is often considered a continuous practice in Sufism, as it helps maintain spiritual protection and emotional balance over time (Helminski, 1999).

6. Blowing and Anointing

After the recitation, the healer may blow gently over the patient or anoint specific parts of the body with blessed water or oil. This is believed to transfer the healing energy invoked during the recitations, sealing the process with God's blessings (Rahman, 2009).

Benefits of Sufi Healing

1. Emotional Balance

One of the most significant benefits of Sufi healing is its ability to alleviate emotional distress. By addressing the spiritual roots of anxiety, depression, and grief, Sufi healing helps individuals achieve emotional stability and inner peace. Practices like Ruqyah and Dhikr realign the heart with God, dissolving negative emotions and fostering a sense of divine protection and comfort (Chittick, 2007).

2. Spiritual Protection

Sufi healing is also renowned for its ability to provide spiritual protection. Whether dealing with malevolent forces such as the evil eye or black magic, or simply trying to ward off negative influences, Ruqyah and related practices offer a shield of protection by invoking God's mercy and grace (Schimmel, 2011).

3. Physical Recovery

Though primarily focused on spiritual and emotional healing, Sufi practices can also have positive effects on physical health. Ruqyah is frequently used to cure ailments believed to stem from spiritual causes, such as chronic pain, fatigue, or insomnia. Many believers have reported experiencing physical relief after undergoing Ruqyah sessions (Haleem, 2010).

4. Closer Connection to God

One of the most profound benefits of Sufi healing is the deepening of the individual's relationship with God. Through the practices of Ruqyah, Dhikr, and Muraqaba, individuals are drawn closer to the Divine, experiencing a more intimate connection with their Creator. This connection fosters spiritual growth, contentment, and resilience when dealing with life's challenges (Nasr, 2007).

Case Studies

Case Study 1: Ali's Healing from Anxiety with Sufi Practices

I. Identifying Data

- Name: Ali
- Age: 29
- Nationality: Pakistani
- Gender: Male
- Marital Status: Married
- Occupation: IT Consultant
- Chief Complaint: "I feel constant anxiety, as if something bad is going to happen. I can't control my thoughts, and it's draining me."

II. Chief Complaint

- A. Interview from the Patient: Ali reported experiencing persistent anxiety, difficulty sleeping, and racing thoughts. He also mentioned feeling spiritually disconnected, which exacerbated his anxiety.
- B. Interview from Family Members: His wife noted that Ali has been more withdrawn recently and often wakes up during the night, restless and worrying about things he cannot control.
- C. Interview from Community: Friends described Ali as a dependable and calm person but mentioned he recently seemed more agitated and anxious.

III. Client's History

- A. Past Illness: Ali had no history of mental illness but experienced panic attacks after a stressful work project.
- B. Family History:
    - Father: Retired banker, age 65.
    - Mother: Homemaker, age 58.
    - Siblings: Two younger sisters, both married.
- C. Personal History / Anamnesis
    - Childhood: Ali was spiritual and regularly engaged in prayers but stopped after starting his demanding job.
    - Adulthood:
        - Occupational: Works in a highly stressful environment, contributing to his anxiety.
        - Marital & Relationship: Happily married but struggles to communicate his stress to his wife.
    - Current Living Situation: Lives with his wife in a small apartment.
    - Fantasies & Dreams: Dreams of peace and feeling spiritually grounded.
    - Values: Values faith, family, and hard work.

IV. Mental Status Examination

- Appearance: Ali appeared tired, with dark circles under his eyes. He was neatly dressed and well-groomed.
- Speech: Fast-paced and anxious, with frequent pauses.
- Mood: Anxious; often expressed worry about his future.
- Affect: Restrained; Ali showed limited emotional expression.
- Insights and Judgment: Good insight into his anxiety but struggles to manage it.
- Sensorium: Oriented, no cognitive impairment.

V. Behavioral Observation

- Mood/Feelings: Restless, constantly tapping his fingers.
- Interaction Style: Cautious and hesitant but willing to discuss his issues.

VI. Healing Process

Ali's healing journey involved Sufi practices, specifically Ruqyah and Dhikr (remembrance of God). The Sufi healer recited Surah Al-Falaq and Surah An-Nas to protect Ali from negative energy and alleviate his anxiety. Ali was also encouraged to engage in daily Dhikr, repeating "Hasbiyallahu la ilaha illa Huwa" ("God is sufficient for me; there is no god but He"). This practice focused his mind on the Divine presence and provided a sense of spiritual calm.

VII. Outcome

After several weeks, Ali reported a significant decrease in anxiety. The Ruqyah sessions helped him sleep better, and daily Dhikr brought him a sense of peace and spiritual reconnection. He continues to use these spiritual tools as part of his holistic self-care.

Case Study 2: Fatima's Struggle with Depression and Spiritual Disconnection

I. Identifying Data

- Name: Fatima
- Age: 35
- Nationality: Moroccan
- Gender: Female
- Marital Status: Divorced
- Occupation: Teacher
- Chief Complaint: "I feel lost and empty. I don't feel God's presence in my life anymore, and nothing seems to matter."

II. Chief Complaint

- A. Interview from the Patient: Fatima described overwhelming sadness, a lack of interest in daily life, and a deep sense of spiritual disconnection after her divorce. She felt abandoned by God and questioned her faith.
- B. Interview from Family Members: Her mother noted Fatima had become more withdrawn and seemed uninterested in spiritual practices, which was out of character for her.
- C. Interview from Community: Friends observed that Fatima stopped attending gatherings and frequently spoke about feeling disconnected from her religious faith.

III. Client's History

- A. Past Illness: Fatima had a history of depression during her adolescent years, which was treated with counseling.
- B. Family History:
    - Father: Deceased.
    - Mother: Homemaker, age 60.
    - Siblings: Two older brothers, both married.

- C. Personal History / Anamnesis
  - Childhood: Raised in a religious family, Fatima was deeply spiritual but struggled with depression during adolescence.
  - Adulthood:
    - Occupational: Works as a high school teacher but finds it difficult to engage with her students since her divorce.
    - Marital & Relationship: Divorced; she felt her marriage failed because she wasn't "good enough."
  - Current Living Situation: Lives alone in a small house.
  - Fantasies & Dreams: Dreams of feeling God's love and reconnecting with her faith.
  - Values: Faith, family, and community.

IV. Mental Status Examination

- Appearance: Fatima appeared fatigued, with little effort in her appearance.
- Speech: Slow, soft, and hopeless.
- Mood: Depressed, with a heavy focus on feelings of worthlessness.
- Affect: Flat, showing little emotional expression.
- Insights and Judgment: Good insight into her depression but struggles to cope.
- Sensorium: Oriented, no cognitive issues.

V. Behavioral Observation

- Mood/Feelings: Deep sadness, tearful at times.
- Interaction Style: Reflective but emotionally distant.

VI. Healing Process

Fatima's healing involved Ruqyah with the recitation of Surah Al-Fatiha and Ayat al-Kursi for spiritual protection and relief from the emotional darkness she was experiencing. The healer also guided her in Muraqaba (Sufi meditation), where Fatima focused on feeling the presence of God. She was encouraged to meditate daily and engage in Dhikr by repeating "Ya Latif" (The Gentle One) to reconnect with the compassionate aspect of the Divine.

VII. Outcome

Over time, Fatima reported a gradual shift in her emotional state. The Ruqyah provided her with a sense of spiritual purification, while the Muraqaba and Dhikr practices helped her reconnect with her faith. She began to feel God›s presence again, which lifted some of her emotional burden. Continued practice helped her regain a sense of purpose and inner peace.

Case Study 3: Ahmed's Recovery from Nightmares and Fear

I. Identifying Data

- Name: Ahmed
- Age: 40

- Nationality: Egyptian
- Gender: Male
- Marital Status: Married
- Occupation: Construction Worker
- Chief Complaint: "I keep having vivid nightmares that something is after me. I wake up terrified and can't go back to sleep."

II. Chief Complaint

- A. Interview from the Patient: Ahmed described frequent nightmares where he felt chased or threatened by an unknown force. These dreams left him feeling fearful and anxious, disrupting his sleep.
- B. Interview from Family Members: His wife mentioned that Ahmed often woke up in the middle of the night, shouting or sweating, and had trouble falling back asleep.
- C. Interview from Community: Friends noted that Ahmed recently became more withdrawn and anxious, avoiding evening gatherings because of his fear of the nightmares.

III. Client's History

- A. Past Illness: Ahmed had no history of major illness or psychological issues.
- B. Family History:
    - Father: Deceased.
    - Mother: Homemaker, age 70.
    - Siblings: One younger brother, age 35.
- C. Personal History / Anamnesis
    - Childhood: Ahmed grew up in a rural area where spiritual beliefs were deeply ingrained.
    - Adulthood:
        - Occupational: Works in construction and enjoys his job but has been more anxious due to nightmares.
        - Marital & Relationship: Married with two children; his family life is supportive.
    - Current Living Situation: Lives with his family in a house.
    - Fantasies & Dreams: Dreams of living without fear and sleeping peacefully.
    - Values: Family, faith, and hard work.

IV. Mental Status Examination

- Appearance: Ahmed appeared tired and anxious, with visible signs of stress.
- Speech: Fast-paced and jittery when discussing his nightmares.
- Mood: Fearful and anxious.
- Affect: Fearful, with visible signs of distress.
- Insights and Judgment: Good insight into his fear but unsure how to address it.
- Sensorium: Oriented, no cognitive impairment.

V. Behavioral Observation

- Mood/Feelings: Fearful and restless.
- Interaction Style: Nervous and fidgety.

VI. Healing Process

Ahmed's healing involved Ruqyah with the recitation of Surah Al-Ikhlas, Surah Al-Falaq, and Surah An-Nas before bedtime to protect him from spiritual harm or evil influences. The healer also gave him blessed water (Zamzam) to drink before sleep. Additionally, he was instructed to engage in Dhikr by repeating "Hasbunallahu wa ni'mal wakeel" ("God is sufficient for us, and He is the best disposer of affairs") to calm his mind and shield him from fear.

VII. Outcome

After several weeks of Ruqyah and Dhikr, Ahmed's nightmares became less frequent, and he reported feeling calmer before bed. The blessed water and spiritual recitations helped him feel protected, and his fear significantly diminished. He now sleeps more peacefully and is less anxious during the day.

Conclusion

Sufi healing, particularly through Ruqyah, offers a profound and holistic approach to wellness. By integrating emotional, spiritual, and physical healing, it aligns the soul with the Divine, providing protection, restoration, and peace. Sufi healing practices, such as Dhikr, Ruqyah, and Muraqaba, offer a deeply spiritual way to navigate life's challenges, helping individuals achieve inner harmony and closeness to God. Through centuries of practice, Sufi healing has proven its timeless relevance, offering individuals an effective means for addressing emotional distress, spiritual afflictions, and physical ailments. It is not just a method of healing but a path toward spiritual growth and divine love, reminding us of the delicate balance between body, mind, and soul.

References

Abu-Rabi', I. M. (2008). Sufism and its influence on Islamic healing practices. Islamic Studies Review, 7(3), 58-74.Chishti, H. M. (n.d.). Sufi healing and herbal medicine. Sufi Healing. http://www.sufihealing.com/herbalmedicine.htm.

Chittick, W. (1989). The Sufi Path of Knowledge: Ibn al-Arabi's Metaphysics of Imagination. SUNY Press.

Chittick, W. (2007). Sufism: A Beginner's Guide. Oneworld Publications.

Dagli, C. (2008). The Sufi tradition and the healing arts. Journal of Islamic Studies, 19(2), 130-150. https://doi.org/10.1093/jis/etm032. Encyclopaedia Britannica. (2020). Sufism | Islamic Mysticism. https://www.britannica.com/topic/Sufism.

Ernst, C. (1997). The Shambhala Guide to Sufism. Shambhala Publications.

Ernst, C. (2003). Following Muhammad: Rethinking Islam in the Contemporary World. University of North Carolina Press.

Ernst, C. W. (2005). Situating sufism and yoga. Journal of the Royal Asiatic Society of Great Britain & Ireland, 15(1), 15–43. https://doi.org/10.1017/s1356186304004675.

Haleem, M. A. (2010). Understanding the Qur'an: Themes and Style. Bloomsbury Publishing.

Helminski, K. (1999). The Knowing Heart: A Sufi Path of Transformation. Shambhala Publications. Islamic Texts Society. (n.d.). Sufism and Islamic Mysticism. https://www.islamictextssociety.org/.

Karamustafa, A. (1994). Origins of Sufism. In P. M. Holt, A. K. S. Lambton, & B. Lewis (Eds.), The Cambridge history of Islam (pp. 661-680). Cambridge University Press.

Knysh, A. (2019). Sufism (Fall 2019 ed.). Stanford Encyclopedia of Philosophy. https://plato.stanford.edu/entries/sufism/.

Muskokayogafestival. (2024, April 25). Muraqaba (Sufi Meditation Technique) - Definition & Detailed Explanation - Meditation & Mindfulness. muskokayogafestival.com. https://muskokayogafestival.com/meditation-mindfulness-glossary/muraqaba-sufi-meditation-technique.

Nasr, S. H. (2007). Islamic Spirituality: Foundations. Routledge. Nimatullahi Sufi Order. (n.d.). Sufi healing practices: Traditional and spiritual healing methods. https://www.nimatullahi.org/sufi-healing/.

Rahman, F. (2009). Major Themes of the Qur'an. University of Chicago Press.

Schimmel, A. (1998). Islamic Calligraphy. Brill.

Schimmel, A. (2011). Mystical Dimensions of Islam. University of North Carolina Press.The Muhyiddin Ibn Arabi Society. (n.d.). The Muhyiddin Ibn Arabi Society. https://ibnarabisociety.org/.

The Sufi Journal. (n.d.). Sufi Journal: A Journal of Mystical Philosophy and Practice. https://sufijournal.org/.

Trottmann, B. (2000). Ritual healing and the Sufi tradition. Journal of Ritual Studies, 14(2), 36-51.

www.ingramcontent.com/pod-product-compliance
Lightning Source LLC
LaVergne TN
LVHW070906210926
848482LV00017B/1003
9798896996514